PRINCIPLES OF
PASSIVE SUPPLEMENTAL DAMPING AND
SEISMIC ISOLATION

CONSTANTIN CHRISTOPOULOS
University of Toronto

ANDRÉ FILIATRAULT
University at Buffalo

IUSS PRESS, Pavia - Italy

prodotto da:
Multimedia Cardano
Via Cardano 14 - 27100 Pavia, Italy
Tel.: (+39) 0382.539776 - fax: (+39) 0382.22558 - e-mail: info@multimediacardano.it

distribuito da:
IUSS Press
IUSS, Collegio Giasone del Maino, Via Luino 4 - 27100 Pavia, Italy
Tel.: (+39) 0382.516911 - fax: (+39) 0382.529131 - email: info@iusspress.it - web: www.iusspress.it

To Malama and to our Parents,

To Louise, Lou-Anne and Sydney

PREFACE

The basic principle of conventional earthquake-resistant design is to ensure an acceptable safety level while avoiding catastrophic failures and loss of life. When a structure does not collapse during a major earthquake, and the occupants can evacuate safely, it is considered that this structure has fulfilled its function even though it may never be functional again. Generally, designing for the so-called "life-safety" performance level is considered adequate for ordinary structures and has been the basis for modern seismic provisions up to this day.

For mission-critical structures, however, higher performance levels can be expected, while keeping economic factors in mind. For example, avoiding collapse is not sufficient for facilities such as hospitals, police stations, communication centers and many other structures that must remain functional immediately after an earthquake. Over the last 30 years, a large amount of research has been devoted into developing innovative earthquake-resistant systems in order to raise the seismic performance level of structures, while keeping construction costs reasonable. Most of these systems are intended to dissipate the seismic energy introduced into the structure during an earthquake by supplemental damping mechanisms and/or to isolate the main structural elements from receiving this energy through isolation systems.

This book targets practicing structural engineers, graduate students, and graduate university educators with an interest in the seismic response of structures equipped with supplemental damping and seismic isolation systems. The main objective of the book is to familiarize structural engineers with the various innovative systems that have demonstrated considerable potential through analytical studies, experimental testing and actual structural implementation. The discussion focuses on passive energy dissipation systems and seismic isolation systems. Readers of this book should have a strong background on linear and nonlinear dynamic analyses and conventional seismic design to fully appreciate its content. This book can be used as the textbook for the last of a series of graduate courses on the general topic of structural dynamics and earthquake engineering.

After assimilating the material contained in this book, readers should have the necessary background to provide critical comparisons of various supplemental damping and seismic isolation systems, model and design various systems with general structural analysis software and recommend optimum systems for particular seismic design or retrofit projects.

Each chapter of the book deals with a particular supplemental damping or seismic isolation system and is divided into discussions related to its physical behaviour, analytical modelling, experimental investigations and practical implementations. Chapters 1 and 2 provide background materials on the basic principles of supplemental damping and seismic isolation systems and review the current seismic design philosophies. It is argued that properly designed supplemental damping and/or seismic isolation systems can result in an "immediate occupancy" performance level for a structure after a seismic event. Chapter 3 discusses the use of energy concepts in earthquake engineering. Since the main purpose of supplemental damping and seismic isolation systems is either to dissipate or filter the input seismic energy, this chapter lays out the foundation for the rest of the material covered in the book. Chapter 4 presents the basic concept of passive energy dissipation systems, as opposed to active or semi-active systems. Chapters 5 to 8 present in details the behaviour, analytical modelling, supporting experimental studies, design methods and practical applications of various supplemental damping systems, namely: hysteretic dampers, viscous and viscoelastic dampers, self-centering systems and tuned-mass dampers. Chapter 9 presents the basic concept of seismic isolation systems. Chapter 10 presents in details the behaviour, analytical modelling, supporting experimental studies, design methods and practical applications of various seismic isolation systems, namely elastomeric, lead-rubber, metallic and sliding bearings. Finally, Chapter 11 presents two sample retrofit projects incorporating supplemental damping and seismic isolation systems. Each sample project contains several self-contained phases and can be used as a term project for a graduate course. The first sample project deals with the seismic retrofit of a steel building, while the second one deals with the seismic retrofit of a steel bridge.

The material covered in this book originates from class notes for a graduate advanced seismic design course taught by the second author at the University of California at San Diego during the 1998-2003 period. The authors gratefully acknowledges many graduate students at the University of California at San Diego, the University of Toronto and the University at Buffalo for their useful comments to improve the content of this book. A special thank you is expressed to students Karen Woo and Jeffrey Erochko at the University of Toronto for their help in creating some of the figures in the book and to Antonis Tsitos from the University at Buffalo for creating the index of this book.

The authors would like to gratefully acknowledge the I.U.S.S. press and the Rose School for publishing this book, particularly Professors G. Michele Calvi and Nigel Priestley, Directors of the Rose School, for their encouragements during the course of this project.

The authors would like to thank Professor Nigel Priestley, and Professor Avigtor Rutenberg from the Israel Technical University for their thorough reviews of the draft manuscript that have lead to substantial improvements to the book. Finally the authors would like to thank Professor Stefano Pampanin from the University of Canterbury in New Zealand for his contributions and review of Chapter 7 on Self-Centering Systems, Professor Athol J. Carr from the same Institution for providing a student version of the computer program Ruaumoko contained in the CD-ROM accompanying this book and finally to Professor Emeritus Vitelmo V. Bertero from the University of California at Berkeley for authoring the foreword to this book.

Constantin Christopoulos, Ph.D.
University of Toronto
Toronto, Canada

André Filiatrault, Ph.D., Eng.
University at Buffalo
State University of New York
Buffalo, USA

FOREWORD

I became interested in the study of the Engineering Problems originated by Earthquakes (EQs) in 1944 as a consequence of the M7.8 San Juan (Argentina) EQ. At that time, the term Earthquake Engineering (EE) was not known. Apparently in the U.S. the first time that the term EE was officially used was in 1949 with the establishment of the Earthquake Engineering Research Institute (EERI). Internationally the term EE started to be known and used as a consequence of the following two historical conferences that were organized by EERI: The first one entitled "Symposium on Earthquake and Blast Effects on Structures", held in 1952 at the University of California at Los Angeles; and the second one entitled "World Conference on EE (WCEE)(later called the First WCEE) held in 1956 at Berkeley, California which was sponsored by both the EERI and the University of California at Berkeley (UCB). The second WCEE was held in Japan in 1960 and since then WCEEs, which were held on average every four years, have successfully brought together many EE researchers, practitioners and public officials. One can follow the traces of growth, advances and developments of EE by following the milestones of the WCEEs, as it has been pointed out by Professor Hudson in his keynote lecture at the 9th WCEE in 1988. Undoubtedly there has been an impressive increase in knowledge on the nature and effects of earthquakes and perhaps even in EE, if the goal of EE is assumed to be achieving life safety. Thus the question is what is the definition of EE?

It has to be noted that according to the analyses that I have conducted regarding specific definitions of EE, the first definition was offered by professor Okamoto in a Japanese book, that was translated into English in 1973, who stated: "In earthquake engineering a wide range of knowledge that includes geophysics, geology, seismology, vibration theory, structural dynamics, material dynamics, structural engineering and construction techniques are necessary. More specifically, earthquake engineering is the application of this knowledge to the single objective of building structures that are safe against earthquakes". From this definition, it is evident that in Japan, at least until the early 1970s, the main objective and goal of EE was to design and construct structures that should withstand earthquake ground motions without loss of lives.

Regarding the practice of EE in the U.S. in the 1970s, and, in general, up to the present, the above was also the main objective and goal of EE, despite the fact that some experts (researchers as well as practitioners) had already started in the 1960s to point out the need for considering different hazard levels (design earthquakes) and the cost of repair, rehabilitation of existing structures and nonstructural components and utility or service lines. Furthermore, in 1975, in the commentary for the fourth edition of the SEAOC Blue Book on Recommended Lateral Force Requirements it was stated: The SEAOC recommendations are intended to provide criteria to fulfill the life safety concept. More specifically with regards to earthquakes, structures designed in conformance with the provisions and principles set forth therein should in general, be able to:

- Resist minor earthquakes without damage;

- Resist moderate earthquakes without structural damage;

- Resist major earthquakes, of the intensity or severity of the strongest ones experienced in California, without collapse, but with some structural as well as nonstructural damage.

In spite of the above Blue Book statements, which seem to indicate that in the design of earthquake-resistant structures it should be necessary to consider the above multi-tiered performance capabilities (which was in accordance with the world wide accepted philosophy), most practicing engineers interpreted that the intent of the code was just to provide life safety and not prevent damage or preserve capital investment in real-estate property. As the primary function of a building code is to provide minimum standards to ensure public safety, it is not surprising that the basic philosophy and primary goal of the seismic codes have been to protect the public, in and around the facilities to be designed and constructed, from loss of life and serious injuries during major earthquakes. However being familiar with the probabilistic approach to the design of buildings that was proposed by Professor Sawyer in 1963 under the name of "Comprehensive Design" that allowed to consider the above multi-tiered performance capabilities, I insisted in my teaching in a need for a change in the code design methodologies, which were based on just one level of design earthquake.

After my retirement from teaching, I devoted most of my research efforts on conducting studies regarding: i) what should be understood by the term "modern EE"; and ii) what was needed for its reliable implementation in practice. Regarding what should be understood by modern earthquake engineering, from the search conducted in 1991 and 1992, I found that since 1984 the following authors have proposed definitions of EE that could be considered as definitions of modern EE: Housner (1984); Hudson (1984 and 1988); Clough (1992); and Davidovici (1992). Based on an analysis of these definitions, I proposed the following definition: "Earthquake Engineering is the branch of engineering that encompasses the practical efforts to reduce, and ideally to avoid earthquake hazards". However, in 2004, based on a new analysis of all the definitions available and the considerable evolution of EE since 1960, Bozorgnia and I offered the following definition: "Earthquake Engineering encompasses multidisciplinary efforts from various branches of science and engineering with the goal of controlling the seismic risks to socio-economically acceptable levels."

In early 2005, after reviewing the progress made in the implementation of Performance-Based Seismic Design (P-B SE), I reached the conclusion that there have been significant misinterpretations of the meaning of this term that have led to its misuse not only in the literature discussing it, but in its actual implementation in practice. As I considered that this misinterpretation was perhaps a consequence of the misinterpretation of the definition of modern EE (or the consideration of its earlier traditional definition) as well as a lack of consideration of the lessons learned from the 1985 Mexico Earthquakes, I decided to propose not only a change in the definition of modern EE, but also a change of the term P-B SE (or P-B EE).

The proposed definition of modern EE was: "Earthquake Engineering encompasses multidisciplinary efforts from various branches of science, practical technical activities of architecture and engineering, as well as non technical issues with the goal of reducing the potential seismic hazards and so controlling the seismic risks of not only the individual facilities, but of the environment in which these individual facilities are constructed (i.e. of the urban area), to socio-economically acceptable levels." It should be noted that according to this definition, depending on their social and economical significance, not only life-safety risks but other risks (including financial and health) should also be controlled. I also proposed a change of the term P-B EE to Performance-Based Seismic Hazard Reduction (P-B SHR) or Performance-Based Seismic Risk Reduction (P-B SRR). This proposed change was triggered by my observation that while the reports, papers and books on P-B E, P-B EE (or P-B SE) had caught the interest of engineers (particularly structural engineers), they had not sparked the interest of most of the other players that are involved in developing a safe seismic environment (i.e. architects, urban planners, public policy makers, contractors, public officials, inspectors, community leaders, owners, etc.). It appears to me that perhaps the word "engineering" in the terms P-BE, P-B SE and P-B EE instead of attracting these other players, has deterred them or resulted in their misconception that this new approach should be the concern of just engineers.

Turning now to the subject of this book "Principles of Passive Supplemental Damping and Seismic Isolation", after reviewing a draft of it, I felt not only that I would like to go back to my function as a teacher at the University offering a graduate course on the subject of "Performance-Based Seismic Hazard Reduction Using Innovative Strategies and Techniques", but also that I would be able to do so because I now have the ideal textbook. As it has been clearly pointed out in the introduction of this new book by Professors C. Christopoulos and A. Filiatrault [as well as later in each of the chapters devoted to the discussion of the different types of energy dissipation devices (or mechanical dampers), self-centering systems, tuned-mass dampers, and seismic isolation systems], although the concepts involved in the development of some of these devices and/or systems are old (more than a century in the case of base isolation and about fifty years for the energy dissipation devices) the modern application of these concepts into the development of what is at present denominated innovative strategies and techniques (or innovative earthquake-resistant systems) in order to raise (or improve) seismic performance (or response) while keeping construction cost, started to be investigated since the 1960s and some were applied already in the late 1960s.

Furthermore, most of the above devices and/or systems were already developed in 1995 when the "SEAOC Vision 2000 Performance-Based Seismic Engineering of Buildings and Recommendations" report was published. Thus, as it is indicated by the authors of the book, at the end of the 1990s, there was already a lot of information about the results of the large amount of research conducted on these innovative devices and systems as well as on their implementation in practice. However, their application in the practice of earthquake-resistant design was limited to very few special civil engineering facilities, and this continues to be so at present not only in the US but world-wide (with perhaps the exception of Japan in the case of seismic isolation systems) as it is well illustrated by the list of implementations offered by the authors of the book in the Appendices A, B, C and D. Then the questions that can be raised are: Why have these innovative strategies and techniques not been used more in practice particularly immediately after the formulations of the recommendations for P-B SE? Was this a consequence of a shortage of the needed information? I have believed that the answer to the above question is no, and that the lack of wide-scale implementation was due to the lack of a book that could be considered as a textbook for teaching the principles of these innovative (or modern) strategies and techniques, as well as how they can be implemented in the practice of modern earthquake engineering. Not only were these principles not taught widely enough to students interested in earthquake-resistant design, but also the lack of a proper textbook made it very difficult to practicing engineers to come to grips with such innovative strategies and techniques.

Although since the early 2000's several books and handbooks on Earthquake Engineering have been published, which have offered at least one up to four chapters to the discussion of the principles and implementation of innovative strategies and techniques for controlling the seismic risks of buildings and bridges, and even an excellent EERI monograph on "Seismic Design with Supplemental Energy Dissipation Devices" by R.D. Hanson and T.T. Soong was published in 2001, unfortunately none could be considered as a textbook on the above subject and thus compete with the book by Professors Christopoulos and Filiatrault.

This book provides the most comprehensive collection of information on the advances that have been achieved since the early 1960s on the mitigation of the effects of significant earthquake ground motions on different civil engineering facilities (with particular emphasis on buildings and bridges) through the technological development of what can be called "innovative strategies and techniques". Although all the chapters present and discuss valuable information on recent advances on the innovative strategies and techniques for reducing the seismic risks in our urban areas, the chapter that I believe deserves very special attention is chapter 7 i.e. the one that discusses the so called Self-Centering Systems. Why? Because it deals with the solution to some problems that have been of concern to me for a long time regarding the seismic performance of facilities whose structures could be subjected to significant plastic deformations, which in the case of Earthquake Ground Motions (EQGM) of long duration can result in cumulative damage leading to failure of the structure due to low cyclic fatigue or unacceptable incremental deformations. My concerns that these types of failure could occur increased in the 1960s, when it became clear to me that moderate and severe earthquakes are not just a single event (as it has been assumed in the building codes and continued to be assumed even in the present building codes since they require the design of our structures against the seismic hazards induced by EQGMs which are represented by just the response spectra of the expected main-shocks), but they usually are multi-events (i.e. fore-shocks, main-shock and after-shocks) and even the main-shock can be a consequence of multi-events.

In chapter 7 the authors not only present, discuss and illustrate very clearly the problems that can be created when the hysteretic dissipation of energy is based on just the use of yielding inducing large physical ductility, which can result in unacceptable large residual deformations, but also results describing the dynamics of self-centering hysteretic systems are thoroughly examined. This is followed by a description of systems exhibiting self-centering hysteretic behaviour either through specialized devices, smart materials or structural systems making use of traditional materials and post-tensioned techniques.

Furthermore, already in Chapter 2 the authors proposed a framework for explicit consideration of residual deformations in Performance-Based Earthquake Engineering. This is done through a Residual Deformation Damage Index (RDDI) that could be used as an additional indicator of performance. There is no doubt that this is an important contribution because, as pointed out by the authors, a combination of maximum drift and residual drift (RD) in the format of a RD-Based Performance Matrix will be a more comprehensive tool to evaluate the actual performance of structures.

Summarizing, this book provides the most comprehensive treatment on the principles of modern passive supplemental damping and seismic isolation that is available at present. The technical information is presented and clearly discussed in a format that makes it the ideal textbook for the education of all graduate students in structural engineering that are interested in the implementation of modern earthquake engineering, either through a graduate course or by just self-learning. Furthermore, the excellent collected information that is presented will be of great value to practicing engineers that are interested in self-learning about the above subject. It will also be of great value for those that are already engaged in seismic design using some of the available innovative strategies and techniques but want to improve their understanding of the reliable implementation of these innovative devices and systems for achieving a much needed reduction in the seismic risk facing the built environment in our cities.

Thus, this book should be considered as a major contribution to modern earthquake engineering and the authors are to be congratulated for their efforts in conceiving and producing it.

Professor Emeritus Vitelmo V. Bertero, April 2006

University of California, Berkeley, USA

TABLE OF CONTENTS

CHAPTER 1: INTRODUCTION TO PASSIVE SUPPLEMENTAL DAMPING AND SEISMIC ISOLATION

1.1 FUNDAMENTAL CONCEPTS

The basic principle of conventional earthquake-resistant design that has been applied for the last 75 years is intended to ensure an acceptable safety level while avoiding catastrophic failures and loss of life. When a structure does not collapse when subjected to a design-level seismic ground motion, and the occupants can evacuate it safely, it is considered that this structure has fulfilled its function even though it may never be functional again. Until recently, the aim of the earthquake engineering community, also reflected in design codes up to the 1990s, was mainly to achieve this life safety performance objective under a rare level of ground shaking intensity. Although this still remains an implicit basic performance level of any structure engineered in an earthquake prone area, the socio-economic reality in developed countries throughout the world has pushed the barrier considerably higher. Important structures such as hospitals, police stations, communication centers and major highway bridges must be designed to achieve significantly higher performance levels under severe earthquake shaking because of their importance in the immediate emergency response and recovery activities following a catastrophic event. Furthermore, building owners are increasingly considering the impact of a major earthquake on their structures as an economic decision variable. The cost of a new structure designed to meet higher performance levels or the cost of an upgrade to an existing structure are weighed against the estimated losses associated with damage, loss of property and downtime in the event of a major earthquake. This is reflected in the recently published International Building Code (ICC 2003) which favors performance-based assessment approaches, and leads to the seismic design of structures to meet several specific performance levels under increasing levels of seismic intensity. For structures of common importance, the basic safety objective translates into a life safety performance level under the design-level earthquake and to a collapse prevention performance level under the maximum credible earthquake.

Over the last half century, a large amount of research has been conducted into developing innovative earthquake-resistant systems in order to raise seismic performance levels while keeping construction costs reasonable. Most of these systems are (i) designed to dissipate the seismic energy introduced into a structure by *supplemental damping mechanisms* and/or (ii) designed to limit the transmission of seismic energy to the main structure by *isolation of the main structural elements.*

Supplemental damping systems use special devices that are often referred to as "mechanical dampers". This supplemental mechanical energy dissipation, activated through movements of the main structural system, reduces the overall dynamic response of the structure during a major earthquake. Furthermore, the main elements of the structure are protected by diverting the seismic energy to these mechanical devices that can be inspected and even replaced following an earthquake. Ideally, if all the seismic energy is absorbed by the mechanical dampers, the main structure will not sustain any damage.

Seismic isolation systems involve the installation of isolators beneath the supporting points of a structure. For buildings, the isolators are usually located between the superstructure and the foundations while for bridges they are introduced between the deck and the piers. The isolators, designed to have a much lower lateral stiffness than the superstructure they protect, separate the main structure from structural elements connected to the ground. From an energy point of view, a seismic isolation system limits the transfer of seismic energy to the superstructure. Ideally, if no seismic energy is transmitted to the superstructure, it remains literally unaffected by a seismic attack. Conversely, the isolators must be capable of undergoing the movements imposed by the ground shaking, while maintaining their ability to carry gravity loads from the superstructure to the ground. To reduce the deformations of the isolators, supplemental damping systems can also be provided. Seismic isolation systems are therefore comprised of two main components:

- An isolator, such as a sliding surface or pads, with lateral stiffness significantly lower than the lateral stiffness of the superstructure, installed between the foundation and the supports of the structure.

- A supplemental damping mechanism (damper) that dissipates the seismic input energy, reducing both the forces transmitted to the superstructure and the deformations of the isolator.

Maximum elastic seismic forces are usually felt by structures with natural periods in the range of 0.1 to 1s, with most severe responses in the range of 0.2 to 0.6s. The most important characteristic of seismic isolation is the lengthening of the vibrational period of the system associated with the increased flexibility of the isolation system. This period shift controls the amount of forces induced into the structure, while excessive displacements are controlled by providing supplemental damping to the seismic isolation system. These displacements occur at the seismic isolator level and must be accommodated.

When a structure is equipped with either supplemental damping devices or seismic isolation systems, its seismic response is greatly altered. Although the intention of any seismic protection system is to improve the performance of a structure, because of the complexity of the dynamic response of structures to earthquake ground motions and the uncertainty associated with ground motion characteristics, this is not guaranteed. A thorough understanding of the impact of adding supplemental damping to, or isolating, a structure, is therefore necessary to ensure the effectiveness of the system.

The portal frame illustrated in Figure 1.1a has a natural period of 1s with a damping ratio ξ =5% of critical. The same portal frame is shown in Figure 1.1b equipped with a supplemental damping device and on a base isolation system in Figure 1.1c.

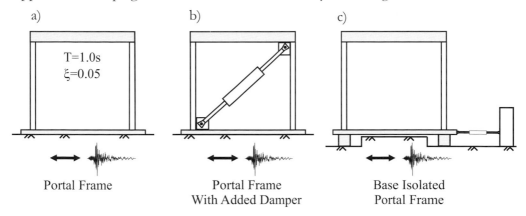

Figure 1.1 Portal Frame with Supplemental Damping and Base Isolation

In Figure 1.2, the elastic absolute acceleration and relative displacement response spectra are plotted for the S00W component of the 1940 Imperial Valley, California (El Centro) earthquake and for different values of structural damping. Point A denotes the maximum acceleration and displacement response of the bare portal frame (Figure 1.1a). If enough supplemental damping is provided to this structure by the added damper (Figure 1.1b) such that its damping is increased to ξ =20% of critical without altering its natural period, the response of this upgraded system is indicated by point B in Figure 1.2. Both the maximum absolute acceleration and maximum relative displacement are reduced. However, if the addition of the supplemental damping device increases the stiffness of the system such that the natural period of the system is reduced to 0.55s while increasing the damping to ξ = 20% of critical, the maximum absolute acceleration of the structure increases (compare point C to point A) because the reduction of natural period is associated with a larger spectral acceleration for this earthquake. Point D corresponds to the response of the portal frame with the added damper if the damper does not dissipate any energy but simply acts like an added bracing element, which reduces the natural period of the bare portal frame to 0.55s. If a base isolation system is introduced (Figure 1.1c), such that the fundamental period of the two degrees-of-freedom system is increased to a value of 2s, the spectral acceleration is significantly reduced while the spectral displacement is increased (point E). If the isolation system is paired with a supplemental damper such that its damping value is increased to $\xi = 20\%$ of critical, the response of the structure, denoted by point F, is further reduced. The reduction of the maximum acceleration is small (point E vs. point F), whereas a significant reduction in the isolator displacement is observed.

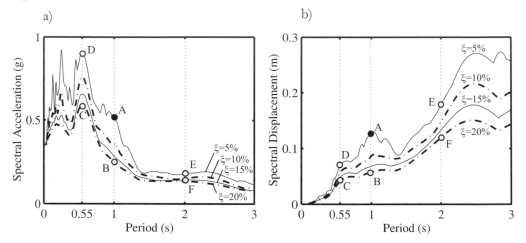

**Figure 1.2 Elastic Response Spectra for 1940, El Centro (S00W Component):
a) Absolute Acceleration, b) Relative Displacement**

It is therefore a combination of period shift and added energy dissipation that must be considered jointly in order to fully understand the effectiveness of added supplemental damping devices and/or base isolation systems on the seismic response of a structure.

In this illustration, the response of the main structural elements is considered linear elastic, whereas in reality they may undergo inelastic deformations. The extension of the problem to cases where the main structure does undergo inelastic deformations is significantly more complex and cannot easily or effectively be captured by examining only elastic response spectra. As will be presented in Chapter 3, energy methods are the most suitable for assessing the effectiveness of supplemental damping and/or base isolation systems on the seismic response of a structure.

1.2 BRIEF HISTORY OF SUPPLEMENTAL DAMPING AND SEISMIC ISOLATION SYSTEMS

The development of supplemental damping and seismic isolation systems is intimately linked to the development of earthquake engineering for which foundations were laid in the nineteenth century by British scientists (Housner 1984). The founding of the modern seismic isolation concept is usually attributed to John Milne, a British scientist, who was a Professor of Mining Engineering at the Imperial College of Engineering in Tokyo from 1875 to 1895.

In 1885, Milne built a base-isolated wood house (Naeim and Kelly 1999). The structure was founded on piles. The heads of the piles incorporated balls made of cast-iron plates with saucer-like edges. After the construction was completed, it was found that significant movement of the foundation occurred during wind loading. Milne modified his design several times. The final design incorporated 6-mm diameter cast-iron shots at the top of the piles. The final design was successful and subsequently the structure performed well under real earthquake ground motions.

In 1909, J.A. Calantarients, an English medical doctor, filed a patent application for a new construction method in which buildings could be built on lubricated "free joints" on a layer of fine material. This construction method would allow the building to freely slide during an earthquake, thereby reducing the forces transmitted to the structural elements.

Although the concept is more than a century old, the modern application of seismic isolation came only in the late sixties, with the development of modern materials, such as rubber vulcanized to thin steel sheets. These multi-layer elastomeric bearings are very stiff and strong in the vertical direction, but are very flexible in the horizontal direction, thereby ideal for isolating structures under horizontal ground motions.

The first application of rubber isolation system was realized in Skopje, Yugoslavia, in 1969. A three-storey concrete elementary school structure was isolated by rubber bearings (Staudacher et al. 1970). Since this first application, seismic isolation technology has spread to many active seismic regions of the world. A wide variety of isolation systems is now available including: elastomeric bearings, high damping rubber bearings, lead-rubber bearings, metallic bearings, lead-extrusion bearings and friction pendulum bearings.

The early development of supplemental damping systems is more recent than that of seismic isolation systems and can be attributed to the pioneering work of Housner (1956) who laid out the foundations for the seismic design of structures based on energy concepts. The concept of using separate elements to increase the damping in a structure was first postulated in the late sixties in Japan (Muto 1969) and the early seventies in New Zealand (Kelly at al. 1972, Skinner et al. 1975). These original studies have led to the development of a variety of metallic dampers, in which increased damping is achieved through the energy dissipation of hysteretic yielding elements.

One of the first applications of metallic dampers in structural systems took place on the South Rangitikei viaduct in New Zealand in 1981. This railroad bridge is 70 m tall, with six spans of prestressed concrete hollow-box girders and overall length of 315 m (Cormack 1988). The structure is base isolated to allow for the sideways rocking of the pairs of slender reinforced concrete piers. Torsional metallic dampers are used to increase damping and limit the amount of rocking.

Similarly, the concept of introducing friction damping systems in seismic design originated in New Zealand in the early seventies (Tyler 1977). Further pioneering work on friction dampers took place in Canada in the early eighties (Pall et al. 1980). Friction dampers were introduced for the first time in a building at the Library of Concordia University in Montreal (Pall et al. 1987).

The development of fluid-type viscous dampers for seismic design primarily took place at the University at Buffalo in the early nineties (Constantinou and Symans 1992). Fluid viscous dampers were first used in a building in 1995 for the new three-storey Pacific Bell North Area Operations Center in Sacramento, California (Aiken 1997).

In the last two decades, supplemental damping systems have gained acceptance and have been implemented in hundreds of buildings around the world. A wide variety of supplemental damping systems is now available for various applications, including: metallic dampers, friction dampers, viscoelastic dampers, fluid viscous dampers and semi-active and active control systems.

The application of supplemental damping and seismic isolation systems has been heavily influenced by the occurrence of major earthquakes near densely populated areas and also by the economic development. The case of Japan is particularly interesting from this point of view. During the period of its largest economic growth (1985 to 1994), Japan became the leading country in terms of the number of buildings incorporating seismic isolation technology, as illustrated in Figure 1.3. Also shown in this figure is the rapid increase in base isolated buildings in Japan after the 1995 Kobe earthquake. On a yearly basis, the number of buildings incorporating seismic isolation technology rose from ten buildings per year before the occurrence of the Kobe earthquake to 150 buildings per year thereafter (Pan et al. 2004). Based on a survey conducted among Japanese construction companies and design engineers (Clark et al. 2000), it was concluded that proliferation of base isolated buildings in Japan following the Kobe earthquake was the result of the catastrophic human and economic loss caused by the earthquake on pre-1980 conventionally designed buildings coupled with the fact that at the time of the earthquake, seismic isolation techniques had matured to the point that wide spread application was feasible.

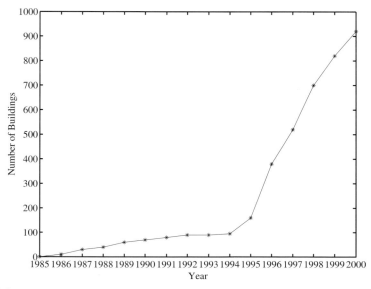

Figure 1.3 Total Base Isolated Buildings in Japan, 1985-2000 (after Pan et al. 2004)

1.3 CATEGORIES OF SUPPLEMENTAL DAMPING AND SEISMIC ISOLATION SYSTEMS

Supplemental damping and seismic isolation systems can be classified in different categories of seismic protection systems, as shown in Table 1-1. Each group incorporates a different approach to mitigate the effects of earthquakes on structures. Conventional systems are based on the traditional seismic design philosophy that leads to energy dissipation through stable inelastic mechanisms. These mechanisms can be achieved through flexural hinging of beams, columns and walls, through axial tension-yielding compression-buckling of brace elements and through shear hinging of steel elements. These energy dissipation mechanisms can lead to a good seismic performance, if proper capacity design principles are enforced. However, the hysteretic energy used to dissipate the seismic input energy in these systems corresponds directly to structural damage, and is tolerated as long as the gravity load-carrying capacity of the structure is not jeopardized.

Table 1-1: Seismic Protection Systems

Conventional Systems	Supplemental Damping Systems		Isolation Systems
	Passive Dampers	Semi-Active/ Active Dampers	
Flexural Plastic Hinges	Metallic	Braces	Elastomeric
Shear Plastic Hinges	Friction	Tuned-Mass	Lead-Rubber
Yielding Braces	Viscoelastic	Variable Stiffness	High-Damping Rubber
	Viscous	Variable Damping	Metallic
	Tuned-Mass	Piezoelectric	Lead-Extrusion
	Self-centering	Rheological	Friction Pendulum

Supplemental damping systems can be divided in two categories: passive systems and semi-active/active systems. Passive energy dissipation systems are intended to dissipate a portion of the seismic energy input to a structure without external power sources, such as actuators, power supplies, computers, etc., necessary for active control technology, and are activated by the movements of the main structural system.

As discussed earlier, a seismic isolation system is typically placed between the foundation and the supporting points for buildings and between the deck and the piers for bridges, and is designed to provide a lateral stiffness much lower than the lateral stiffness of the superstructure, such that the fundamental period of the isolated structure lengthens substantially. Coupled with these soft bearings, a supplemental damping system controls the amplitudes of the displacement at the structure-isolation interface.

1.4 OBJECTIVES OF THE BOOK

The main objective of this book is to familiarize structural engineers with the various supplemental damping and seismic isolation systems that have demonstrated considerable potential through analytical studies, experimental testing and actual structural implementations.

The theoretical background in energy formulations is provided as a basis for the development of the tools that are necessary to properly assess the effectiveness of each system presented in this book. Parameters influencing the mechanical performance of each system are also presented. Practical application issues are discussed and real implementations are presented. It is assumed that the reader is familiar with standard linear and nonlinear dynamic analysis methods.

After reading the book, the reader should be able to:

- Provide a critical comparison of various supplemental damping and seismic isolation systems.

- Model and design various supplemental damping and seismic isolation systems with general structural engineering software.

- Recommend optimum supplemental damping and seismic isolation systems for particular seismic design or retrofit projects.

- Assess the practical implications of various supplemental damping and seismic isolation systems.

- Provide a complete assessment, including advantages and limitations, of the performance of structures equipped with various supplemental damping and seismic isolation systems.

Finally, another objective of this book is to provide some practical experience on the retrofit of real structures with supplemental damping and seismic isolation systems. For this purpose, the last chapter of the book includes two sample projects on the seismic retrofit of a building and of a bridge incorporating various supplemental damping devices and seismic isolation systems. These sample projects are laid out in several logical phases that can be used for projects in a classroom environment or for self-learning purposes. A student version of the computer program RUAUMOKO (Carr 2004) required to execute the sample projects along with data files of the building and bridge structures are also included in the CD-ROM accompanying this book. A commercial version of RUAUMOKO can be obtained through Professor A.J. Carr from the University of Canterbury in New Zealand (*a.carr@civil.canterbury.ac.nz*).

CHAPTER 2: REVIEW OF SEISMIC DESIGN PHILOSOPHIES AND ANALYSIS METHODS

2.1 INTRODUCTION

Before discussing supplemental damping and seismic isolation systems, this chapter provides a brief review of current seismic design philosophies and analysis methods. The discussion in this chapter focuses first on the force-based seismic design method which is the basis of most modern design codes. A brief description of the fundamental concepts behind force-based seismic design is given. These concepts are then extended to the static linear and dynamic linear analysis methods. After a discussion on the limitations of current force-based seismic design methods, performance-based seismic design concepts are introduced. The nonlinear static and nonlinear dynamic analysis methods are also discussed. Finally, the direct displacement-based seismic design method is presented.

Since supplemental damping and seismic isolation systems can be implemented using either of these seismic design philosophies and analysis methods, this chapter can be viewed as a basic framework for the rest of the material covered in this book.

2.2 FORCE-BASED SEISMIC DESIGN PROCEDURE

2.2.1 Principles and Objectives

Seismic design provisions included in current design codes in North America and Europe (ICBO 1997, ICC 2003, NRC 2005, CEN 2004) use a force-based seismic design approach. This approach uses elastic spectral accelerations to determine the required lateral strength that the structure must resist if it were to remain elastic. The design lateral strength of the structure is then obtained by dividing the elastic strength by a force reduction factor R representing the inherent overstrength and global ductility capacity of the lateral load-resisting system selected.

The seismic provisions based on the force-based seismic design procedure must be considered as minimum requirements, providing the degree of seismic safety that has been considered reasonable up to now. Structures, mostly buildings, designed according to these requirements, should have a certain level of lateral stiffness, strength and ductility. In low-intensity earthquakes, sufficient lateral stiffness allows for protection against damage to architectural and nonstructural components. In moderate-intensity earthquakes, sufficient lateral strength limits important damage to the main structure. In major earthquakes, adequate lateral ductility of the structure is needed to allow for large inelastic displacements but without collapse of the vertical load-carrying system. In this context, a structure is said to have reached collapse when evacuation of its occupants is obstructed by the final state of the structure.

2.2.2 Concept of Ductility

The concept of ductility is the key element of the force-based seismic design procedure. To illustrate this concept, consider the simple portal frame shown in Figure 2.1a. It is assumed that the period of this structure is 1.04s. The other properties of the structure are given in Table 2-1. As shown in Figure 2.1b, the base shear coefficient, defined as the lateral load-resisting capacity divided by the weight of the structure, is equal to 0.13. The corresponding lateral drift at yield is 1.2% of the height of the structure. For simplicity, it is assumed that the structure is able to develop an elastic-perfectly plastic response.

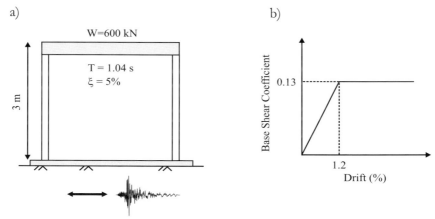

Figure 2.1 Yielding Portal Frame: a) Properties, b) Force-Displacement Relation

The portal frame shown in Figure 2.1a is subjected to the S00W component of the Imperial Valley earthquake, recorded at El Centro on May 18, 1940. The characteristics of this strong motion record are well known and can be found in several references (e.g. Bolt 1988, Chopra 2001, see also Figure 1.2).

A nonlinear time-history dynamic analysis (Filiatrault 2002), which takes into account yielding of the structural elements, is performed to obtain the response of the structure under the El Centro record. For the purpose of this analysis, a damping ratio of 5% of critical is assumed, and the integration of the equation of motion is performed at increments of 0.01s.

Table 2-1: Properties of Portal Frame

Property	Value
Weight, W	600 kN
Lateral Stiffness, k	2.22 MN/m
Fundamental Period, T	1.04 s
Base Shear Coefficient	0.13
Drift at Yield	1.2%

The analysis is then repeated for various values of base shear coefficient in order to observe the effect of lateral strength on the seismic response of the structure. Note that the period of the structure is not varied in these analyses.

Figure 2.2 presents the main results of these analyses by showing the peak transient drift reached by the structure for base shear coefficient values varying from 0.06 to 0.48. For base shear coefficients higher than 0.48, the peak transient drift does not vary anymore as the structure remains in the elastic range.

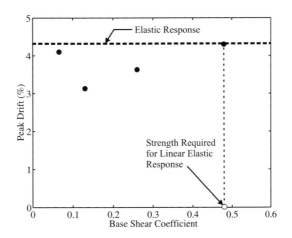

Figure 2.2 Relation Between Peak Transient Drift and Base Shear Coefficient for Portal Frame under the El Centro Record

The results shown in Figure 2.2 indicate that the peak transient drift is not greatly influenced by changes in the lateral load-resisting capacity of the structure. This empirical observation, first made by Veletsos and Newmark (1960), is referred to as the *equal displacement approximation*. It forms the basis for the seismic provisions included in most modern design codes. Figure 2.3 illustrates the equal displacement approximation for the one-sided envelope of the lateral force-displacement relationship of a structure.

The length of the yield plateau relative to the yield displacement in Figure 2.3 is defined as the displacement ductility ratio μ_Δ:

$$\mu_\Delta = \frac{\delta_{max}}{\delta_y} = \frac{V_E}{V_y} \approx R \geq 1 \tag{2.1}$$

where δ_{max} is the maximum inelastic lateral displacement reached by the structure, δ_y is the lateral displacement of the structure at first yield, V_E is the maximum lateral load or base shear capacity required for the structure to remain elastic, and V_y is the actual or yield lateral load capacity of the structure. It is clear that $\mu_\Delta = 1$ for a structure that remains elastic and $\mu_\Delta > 1$ for a structure that deforms in the inelastic range of its structural elements. Figure 2.3 illustrates that seismic design provisions in modern design codes are not based on the actual lateral loads that a structure needs to resist in order to remain elastic, but are rather based on the lateral displacement level that it can withstand without collapsing. Mainly because of socio-economic factors, inelastic deformations and damage of certain structural members are tolerated, as long as the inelastic behaviour is ductile and the structure's global integrity is not jeopardized during and immediately after an earthquake. The desired level of overall ductility is achieved through special seismic detailing procedures specified in design codes for each lateral load-resisting system.

2.2.3 Linear Static Analysis Method

In most current design codes, the forced-based seismic design procedure is applied to regular structures through the so-called *Linear Static Analysis Method*. Regular structures are defined based on several criteria that aim at ensuring that the dynamic behaviour is dominated by the fundamental mode of vibration without significant torsional effects. This analysis method is consistent with a single seismic performance level (usually life safety), and is based on the re-writing of Equation (2.1):

$$V_y = \frac{V_E}{\mu_\Delta} \approx \frac{V_E}{R} \tag{2.2}$$

The static linear analysis procedure consists of first calculating a base shear corresponding to the lateral load-carrying capacity if the structure were to remain elastic. This elastic base shear is then divided by a force reduction factor to reflect the ductility capacity of the lateral load-resisting system selected for the design. In most modern building codes (e.g. CEN 2004, NRC 2005, ICBO 1997, ICC 2003), Equation (2.2) is expressed in terms of a design base shear V as:

$$V = \frac{C_S \, S(T) \, I}{R} \, W \tag{2.3}$$

The factors C_S, $S(T)$, I, R and W are described as follows:

- Seismic coefficient, C_S

The seismic coefficient C_S depends mainly on the design seismic hazard level, seismic activity and on the soil profile at the construction site. In some design codes (e.g. ICBO

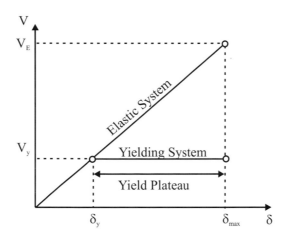

Figure 2.3 Idealized Lateral Force-Displacement Behaviour of a Structure According to the Equal Displacement Approximation

1997, ICC 2003), the seismic coefficient is also increased for sites located near active seismic faults.

- Seismic response factor, $S(T)$

The seismic response factor $S(T)$ represents a normalized elastic response spectrum shape, and is a function of the fundamental period of vibration of the structure T. Empirical formulas are usually employed to estimate this fundamental period. These formulas also serve as upper bounds in cases where more sophisticated structural analyses are used to estimate the fundamental period.

- Importance factor, I

The importance factor I is usually greater than unity for buildings that must remain operational immediately after an earthquake (hospitals, police stations, fire stations, radio stations and towers, power stations, water pumping stations, etc.) and for schools. For other types of buildings, the importance factor is usually set to unity.

- Force reduction factor, R

An empirical force reduction factor R is assigned to each type of structural system, and arises from the experience acquired in terms of seismic design and construction as well as from the study of the performance of each structural system during real earthquakes. The force modification factor attempts to take into account the following effects:

- The seismic energy absorption capability of the structure (ductility).

- The redundancy of the lateral load-resisting system. It is preferable to have a statically indeterminate system in order to reduce the risk of collapse.

– The stiffness of the lateral load-resisting system. Rigid systems tend to attract higher forces.

• Seismic weight, W

The seismic weight of a structure is usually defined as the total dead load plus a portion of the live load for storage areas and tanks, and a portion of the roof snow load if applicable. The seismic weight attempts to represent the permanent and applied weight that would actually contribute to the lateral inertia forces during the design earthquake.

The design base shear V given by Equation (2.3) is the algebraic sum of the inertia (or seismic) forces reacting on the masses of the structure as a result of a horizontal movement at the base. If the structure reacts mostly in its first mode of vibration, these inertial forces are distributed over the height in a triangular shape with its base at the top of the structure. Furthermore, most design codes recommend that a portion F_t of the total lateral force be applied at the top level of the structure to take into account the possible influence of higher modes of vibration. Therefore, the remaining total lateral force is distributed proportionally to the weights of each level i W_i according to:

$$F_i = \frac{W_i h_i}{\sum_{j=1}^{N_f} W_j h_j} (V - F_t)$$
(2.4)

where h_i is the height of level i above the base and N_f is the number of floor levels above the base.

The design of the lateral load-resisting elements of the structure then proceeds by combining the design lateral forces with the design gravity loads. The design is then completed by estimating the inelastic lateral drifts at each level of the structure. For this purpose, the drifts at first yield are first obtained by performing a linear static analysis under the design lateral forces given by Equation (2.4). The inelastic drifts are then estimated by multiplying these drifts at first yield by empirical coefficients.

2.2.4 Linear Dynamic Analysis Method

For tall and/or irregular structures for which higher modes and torsional effects are important, the forced-based seismic design procedure is applied through the so-called *Linear Dynamic Analysis Method*. This method is based on a dynamic analysis procedure using linear modal superposition (e.g. Filiatrault 2002, Chopra 2001) and design absolute acceleration response spectra to define the ground excitation. The peak transient linear response in each mode of vibration of the structure is first computed. These peak modal responses are then combined statistically to obtain an estimate of the multi-modal peak transient response of the structure.

The elastic base shear obtained from the modal superposition V_E is then scaled to the value of the design base shear V computed in Equation (2.3) using the *Linear Static Analysis Method*. Therefore, the main purpose of the *Linear Dynamic Analysis Method* is to obtain an improved distribution of the design lateral forces on the structure that includes the effects of higher modes and/or torsional effects.

2.2.5 Advantages and Limitations of Force-Based Seismic Design Procedures

The force-based seismic design approach described above is simple to apply to a single performance level and is economically viable since the design base shear V is lower than the strength that would be required if the structure were to remain elastic during the design seismic event. It is of paramount importance, however, that this strength reduction be associated with an adequate ductility capacity of the lateral load-resisting system. Inelastic deformations are tolerated during the design seismic event, provided that failure is avoided.

Although the force-based seismic design approach has been used extensively in the last half century and remains the cornerstone of seismic design requirements included in current editions of design codes, it has several shortcomings:

- The force-based seismic design process is initiated with an estimate of the elastic fundamental period of the structure, which is not representative of the vibrational characteristics of the structure in the inelastic range. In fact, the whole notion of elastic period can be considered unrepresentative of the true seismic response of a structure since most structures exhibit inelastic response over practically the entire range of their lateral deformations.

- The force reduction factors R are difficult to justify since they are based primarily on judgment. Without knowledge of the global system response, R factors are difficult to determine rationally. They are also currently specified independently of the natural period of the system despite the fact that structures with shorter natural periods are expected to undergo significantly more inelastic deformations than structures with similar structural configurations but of longer natural periods.

- The reduction of the elastic base shear by an R factor implies that the maximum displacement that the structure would undergo if remained elastic is equal to the maximum displacement of the actual inelastic structure. This equal displacement approximation is not always adequate, particularly for short period structures.

- Deformation limit-states are not directly addressed by the force-based seismic design procedure. Limiting deformations is paramount since a large portion of the structural and nonstructural damage to structures resulting from recent earthquakes has been associated with excessive lateral displacements.

- R factors are associated with the global ductility capacity of the structure. This displacement ductility is defined as the ratio of ultimate displacement to first-yield displacement. A great variability exists among the research and engineering community on the definitions of yield and ultimate displacements.

These limitations of the force-based seismic design procedure, coupled with the fact that it is currently applied to a single performance level (usually life safety), do not allow for an adequate assessment of the seismic safety when considering the various limit-states that modern structures may have to confront during their service life. A more rational seismic design approach should be based on several performance levels, and should consider displacement parameters as the main focus of the design process.

2.3 PERFORMANCE-BASED EARTHQUAKE ENGINEERING

2.3.1 Background and Need for Performance-Based Earthquake Engineering

Performance-based earthquake engineering, in a general sense, was already implicitly part of early modern earthquake engineering codes. The definition of "limit states" in the design process is in fact a form of performance-based design. However, only a single performance level, consisting of assuring life safety under the design level earthquake, has been considered to date in design codes.

Following major recent earthquakes, especially those of Northridge, California in 1994 and Kobe, Japan in 1995, the earthquake engineering community overwhelmingly acknowledged that single performance-based seismic design presented serious limitations since it did not allow building designers and owners to rationally consider seismic risk as a design and decision tool, nor did it account for the progressive nature of seismic damage and the real costs related to it. An illustration of these limitations is the 1994 Northridge, California earthquake in which, although a significant number of unexpected fractures in steel moment-resisting frames were observed (SAC 1994), the life safety performance level required by the code was achieved in all cases. Only a single steel building was demolished following this earthquake. The reality, though, is that most building owners expected significantly higher performance levels. This was especially true considering that the cost of the structure represented only a small fraction of the cost of disrupted operations or lost equipment and materials.

2.3.2 Current Performance-Based Seismic Design Framework

The concept of performance-based earthquake engineering relies primarily on the definition of multiple performance objectives that are obtained by coupling both structural and nonstructural performance levels to different intensity levels of seismic input. Defining realistic characteristics of seismic input for given probabilities of exceedence, as well as quantifying structural systems reliably enough to assess their performance level under these inputs, are the two key parameters to performance-based earthquake engineering.

This performance-based design philosophy was first generally formulated in the Vision 2000 document (SEAOC 1995), then further developed in the NEHRP Guidelines for the Seismic Rehabilitation of Buildings, FEMA-273 (BSSC 1997). Recently it has been extended to a Prestandard and Commentary for the Seismic Rehabilitation of Buildings in the FEMA 356 document (ASCE 2000), and to the FEMA-450 NEHRP Recommended Provisions for Seismic Regulations for New Buildings and Other Structures (BSSC 2003). It is of interest to note that both FEMA-356 and FEMA-450 documents are extended to the design of structures equipped with seismic isolation systems and supplemental damping devices. These guidelines for supplemental damping and seismic isolation systems will be discussed in Chapter 4 and in Chapter 9, respectively.

Figure 2.4 illustrates the performance-based seismic design framework as presented in the above mentioned documents. The performance-based seismic design framework starts

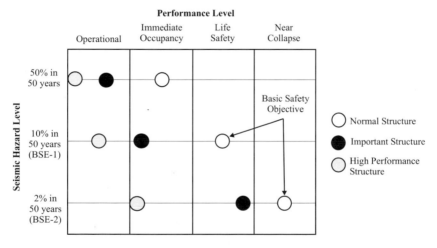

Figure 2.4 Performance-Based Seismic Design Framework (adapted from SEAOC 1996, BSSC 1997, ASCE 2000)

with the definition of ground shaking characteristics at a given site corresponding to different values of probability of exceedence (or seismic hazard level). The Maximum Credible Earthquake (MCE) corresponds to a probability of exceedence of 2% in 50 while its response spectrum, scaled down to two thirds, has been used to represent a probability of exceedence of 10% in 50 years (or a return period of 475 years) for California earthquakes. These levels correspond to the BSE-2 (Basic Safety Earthquake) and BSE-1 respectively (ASCE 2000). The basic safety objective (BSO) is attained when a structure achieves both the Life Safety Performance level under the BSE-1 level earthquake and the

Collapse Prevention Performance level under the BSE-2 level earthquake. Such a structure is represented in Figure 2.4 by the white dots. For more important structures, as illustrated by the black dots, the performance levels corresponding to the BSE-1 and BSE-2 levels of ground shaking are higher. Also illustrated in Figure 2.4 by grey filled dots is a high performance structure, where no damage is tolerated under the lowest intensity earthquakes (50% in 50 years) and only limited damage is tolerated even under the BSE-2 level shaking. This latter group is of special interest for this book, since in most applications, supplemental damping devices or seismic isolation systems are required to achieve high performance levels even under severe ground shaking.

This framework is not currently explicitly part of the latest design codes (ICBO 1997, ICC 2003, NBCC 2005 and CEN 2004), although the rationale behind performance-based seismic design is widely accepted. It is likely, however, that this philosophy will be incorporated into future editions of building codes. In an effort to bridge the gap between this philosophy and practice, an extensive research program on performance-based earthquake engineering is under way in the United States under the auspices of the Pacific Earthquake Engineering Research Center (PEER 2003).

2.3.3 Explicit Consideration of Residual Deformations in Performance-Based Earthquake Engineering

Most systems undergoing inelastic deformations are expected to sustain residual deformations. These permanent deformations depend primarily on the maximum ductility reached during the seismic loading. Nonetheless, because of the variable nature of seismic ground motions and because of the different hysteretic characteristics of structural systems, residual deformations vary appreciably. Residual deformations can result in the partial or total loss of a building if static incipient collapse is reached, if the structure appears unsafe to occupants, or if the response of the system to a subsequent earthquake is impaired by the new at-rest position of the structure. Furthermore, they can also result in increased cost of repair or replacement of nonstructural elements as the new at-rest position of the building is altered.

These aspects are not reflected in current performance assessment approaches, where the performance assessment is primarily made by determining the peak transient response or the cumulative damage sustained by the structure.

Furthermore, as will be discussed in Chapter 7, recent developments in precast concrete and steel constructions have provided a conceptual and technological tool to control residual deformations. The enhanced characteristics of the performance of these structures that undergo similar maximum drifts as conventional systems but do not sustain any residual deformations, cannot be captured by means of current damage indices.

In light of these observations, a Residual Deformation Damage Index (RDDI) to be used as an additional indicator of performance has recently been proposed by Christopoulos et al. (2003) and Pampanin et al. (2003). A combination of maximum drift and residual drift (RD), in the format of a RD-Based Performance Matrix, is suggested as a more comprehensive tool to evaluate the actual performance of framed structures. The independent RDDI scale can thus be adequately combined with commonly used existing performance levels based on maximum response or cumulative damage, to form a more general performance domain. For different seismic intensity levels this results in a full three-dimensional performance domain, as shown in Figure 2.5. This three-dimensional performance domain should be evaluated for both the structural and nonstructural elements in order to obtain a full evaluation of a structure's performance.

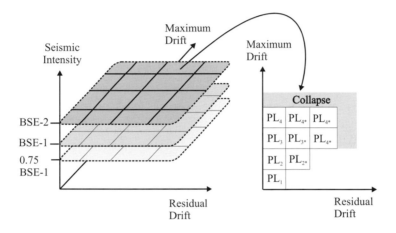

Figure 2.5 Performance Matrix Including Residual Deformations

For a given seismic intensity, the performance matrix consists of a template of pre-defined performance domains (Figure 2.5) that can then be compared to plots of maximum and residual indices from seismic response. For a given maximum response index, the resultant performance limits would result in a poorer combined performance level for higher level of residual deformations: the main performance levels PL_i based on maximum limits are extended in sub-domains PL_i^* depending on the associated residual drift values. When, for example, a maximum drift level corresponding to PL_2 is combined with a large residual drift, the actual performance level is shifted to level PL_2^*. Note that the performance level PL_1 is limited to a single square, as the elastic response of any structural system should not result in any residual drift. Thus, although being subjected to similar interstorey drift demands, structures can be assigned substantially different levels of performance, depending on the value of their residual response indices.

2.4 STATIC NONLINEAR (PUSHOVER AND PUSH-PULL) ANALYSIS METHODS

2.4.1 Need for Improved Seismic Design and Assessment Techniques

Performance-based seismic design philosophies have triggered an important research effort aimed at better characterizing structural performance levels, both at the local member and at the global system levels. This aspect of the performance-based methodology is in fact the most challenging one, since rational decisions on what constitutes damage in a complex structure must be made. Current design procedures do not explicitly capture the nonlinear response of earthquake-resisting systems, but simply attempt to limit damage by imposing a check on maximum interstorey drifts. As discussed in Section 2.2.3, these estimates of maximum deflections are achieved by empirical formulas. In an attempt to improve the understanding of the response of structures in the nonlinear range, and considering the importance of this step in the performance-based seismic design framework, more advanced design and assessment techniques were developed within FEMA-273 (BSSC 1997) and FEMA-356 (ASCE 2000).

2.4.2 Background

Nonlinear static or *pushover analysis* procedures have been used in practice for several decades in the offshore platform industry. The main idea behind this methodology is to investigate the progressive nonlinear deformations of a structure as the applied lateral loads are increased monotonically. This procedure serves a number of purposes: i) it attempts to reveal any undesirable nonlinear mechanisms that result from a poor choice of stiffness and strength distribution that can greatly impair the response of the structure, ii) it allows for an assessment of the maximum deformation capacity of the structure, iii) it allows for continuous monitoring of the damage induced to the structure with increasing deformations and finally iv) it allows for a better estimate of the maximum deformations under a given level of seismic loading.

2.4.3 Fundamentals of Nonlinear Static Analysis Methods

The nonlinear static analysis method consists of first developing a nonlinear model able to capture all local nonlinearity effects of importance to the global response of the structure, and subjecting this model to increasing levels of lateral loads. The lateral loads are increased until a target displacement is reached or until it reaches collapse under combined lateral loads and P-Δ effects. Figure 2.6 shows a typical pushover curve for a multi-degree-of-freedom framed structure. As the lateral load is increased, the structure first undergoes linear elastic deformations until the first structural element yields. As the load is increased, additional elements yield progressively until a full mechanism is formed. Once the mechanism is fully formed, the structure undergoes inelastic deformations until elements progressively fail. The pushover curve terminates when the complete collapse of the structure is reached. Note that the strength of the system at first yield does not coincide with the strength of the system when a full mechanism is formed. The difference between these two strength levels is defined as the overstrength of the system. As illustrated in Figure 2.6, for practical purposes, the initial stiffness and the post-yielding stiffness lines are extended, and the effective yield point is defined as the intersection of the two.

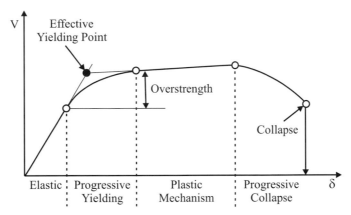

**Figure 2.6 Typical Pushover Curve for a Framed Structure
(adapted from BSSC 2003)**

The pushover analysis procedure does not capture the cyclic behaviour that is expected under seismic loading but relies on an estimate based on the strength envelope of the system. Considering that numerical models capable of adequately reproducing the nonlinear behaviour of a structure under monotonically increasing loads can usually be extended with little additional effort to capture the cyclic response of a structure, valuable information can be obtained by applying cyclic loading to the structure. Information on stiffness degradation as well as energy dissipation, both key parameters in the nonlinear seismic response of structures, can be derived by simply reversing the loading once the target displacement has been reached, and by repeating the pushover analysis in the opposite direction. This can also be done for different values of positive and negative peak displacements, thus yielding a complete relationship between maximum displacement and energy dissipation characteristics. This information is especially useful for the derivation of ductility-damping curves for a direct displacement-based seismic design as discussed in the following paragraph. This procedure was applied recently to study the variation of equivalent viscous damping with building drift for wood light-frame structures that exhibit a highly nonlinear pinched hysteretic behaviour (Filiatrault et al. 2003), as illustrated in Figure 2.7.

In the framework of FEMA-450 (BSSC 2003), the nonlinear static analysis procedure (NSP) is initiated with an initial design of the structure using linear static analysis methods. In this initial design, members are sized and the target maximum deflection of a control

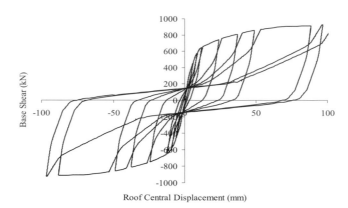

Figure 2.7 Cyclic Pushover Curve for a Wood Light-Frame Building (adapted from Filiatrault et al. 2003)

point, usually identified by the center of mass of the highest level of the structure, is established.

Following this first step, the nonlinear static procedure is carried out by:

- developing a nonlinear model of the structure;

- applying a pre-defined lateral load pattern to the structure with increasing amplitude and recording the evolution of member deformations and forces;

- comparing the member deformations obtained when the structure reaches the target deformation at the control point to the member deformation capacities predicted by analyses or laboratory tests;

- comparing the interstorey drifts obtained from the analysis to drift limitations.

The expected inelastic deformations of a system when subjected to a specific ground motion or to a level of seismic hazard represented by an elastic response spectrum are obtained by approximate equivalent "linearization" techniques. Such techniques, derived from the "equivalent" secant stiffness method, have been originally proposed by Jennings (1968). The capacity spectrum analysis method developed by Freeman et al. (1975, 1998), which will be discussed in the next paragraph, is the basis of the methods for estimating the inelastic deformations of nonlinear systems in the NSP methods.

2.4.4 Capacity Spectrum Analysis Method

The capacity spectrum analysis method, first proposed and gradually developed by Freeman et al. (1975, 1998), is a graphical representation of the "equivalent" secant linearization of a nonlinear system. Seismic demand spectra are plotted in a spectral acceleration-displacement format for different values of equivalent viscous damping and compared, on the same figure, to the pushover capacity curve of the structure. The intersection of the capacity curve with the seismic demand spectra represents possible maximum responses of the system with respect to displacements and accelerations. A priori knowledge of the equivalent viscous damping of the system at each inelastic displacement level is necessary. The method consists of identifying the intersection point between these two curves for which the equivalent viscous damping is consistent between the target displacement and the spectrum. In Figure 2.8, the demand spectra for the 1999 Chi Chi earthquake in Taiwan (TCU065 station) in acceleration-displacement format are shown for three different values of equivalent viscous damping.

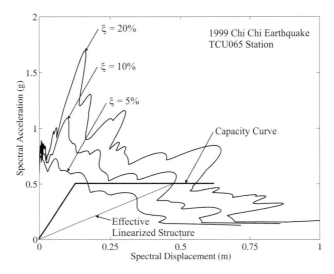

Figure 2.8 Capacity Spectrum Method

Also shown in this figure is the capacity pushover curve of a structure where the base shear has been transformed to a corresponding absolute spectral acceleration. In addition to the plots in Figure 2.8, a third plot representing the relationship between the structural displacement and the equivalent viscous damping of a structural system can be included to expedite the design process. Radial lines anchored at the origin of the figure are directly related to the effective secant periods at the target maximum displacement.

Recognizing the limitations associated with the equivalent linearization of nonlinear systems, Bertero (1995), Reinhorn (1997), Fajfar (1999) among others have recommended the extension of the proposed method to inelastic response spectra.

Limitations associated with pushover analysis methods have been reported in the literature. The two primary sources of discrepancies between the real seismic response of structures as obtained by nonlinear time-history analyses and predictions obtained from pushover analysis methods are the applied load patterns to account for the progressive distribution of nonlinearities along the structure and the effects of higher modes. A study by Krawinkler and Seneviratna (1998) identified a number of these limitations. Kunnath and Gupta (2000) also identified inconsistencies in the different pushover analysis procedures currently used in FEMA-356, while Iwan (1999) demonstrated the limitations of pushover analysis methods to predict demands for pulse-like near fault ground motions. To address these shortcomings, a number of more sophisticated pushover analysis procedures, such as modal pushovers (Sasaki et al. 1998, Chopra and Goel 2002, Antoniou et al. 2002), as well as adaptive pushovers (Carr 1998, Gupta and Kunnath 2000) have been proposed.

The more advanced pushover methods do provide a better estimate of the deformation demands on structural members at the cost, however, of significantly increased computational effort. In assessing the usefulness of such techniques, a comparison with the computational cost of full nonlinear time-history analyses must also be made.

2.5 DIRECT DISPLACEMENT-BASED SEISMIC DESIGN PROCEDURE

2.5.1 Fundamentals of Direct Displacement-Based Seismic Design Procedure

Since displacement is a key parameter for the control of seismic damage in structures, it is rational to examine a procedure wherein displacements are considered at the center of the seismic design process. The fundamental components of this procedure, known as the direct-displacement method, are now discussed.

The central concept of the direct-displacement method, as originally proposed by Priestley (1993, 1998, 2000) is that the seismic design of the structure is based on a specified target displacement for a given seismic hazard level.

For this purpose, the structure is modeled as an equivalent single-degree-of-freedom (SDOF) system with equivalent elastic lateral stiffness and total equivalent viscous damping properties representative of the global behaviour of the structure at the target displacement. The total viscous damping of the structure is obtained by summing the assumed inherent viscous damping to the equivalent viscous damping provided by the hysteretic response of the structure at the target displacement. For SDOF structures this step is straightforward, whereas for MDOF structures an assumption on the deflected shape of the system at the target deformation must be made before defining the equivalent SDOF structure.

Figure 2.9 presents a flowchart illustrating the steps of the direct-displacement seismic design process. These steps are briefly described below:

- **Step 1**: Definition of Target Displacement and Seismic Hazard

The first step in the design procedure is the definition of the target displacement Δ_t that the building should not exceed under a given seismic hazard level. Based on a first mode response, the target displacement can be obtained through the following relationship:

$$\Delta_t = \frac{\Delta_r}{\alpha_1 A_r^1} \tag{2.5}$$

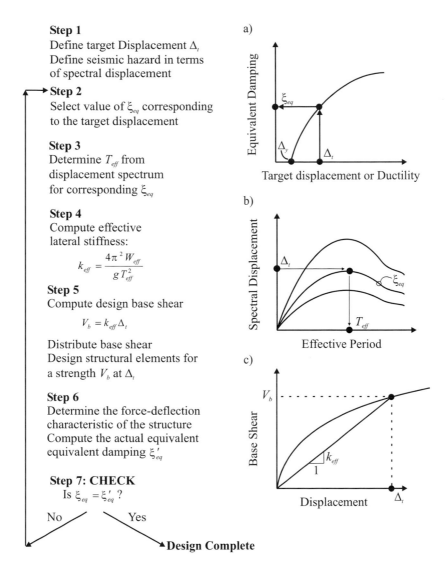

Step 1
Define target Displacement Δ_t
Define seismic hazard in terms
of spectral displacement

Step 2
Select value of ξ_{eq} corresponding
to the target displacement

Step 3
Determine T_{eff} from
displacement spectrum
for corresponding ξ_{eq}

Step 4
Compute effective
lateral stiffness:

$$k_{eff} = \frac{4\pi^2 W_{eff}}{g\, T_{eff}^2}$$

Step 5
Compute design base shear

$$V_b = k_{eff}\Delta_t$$

Distribute base shear
Design structural elements for
a strength V_b at Δ_t

Step 6
Determine the force-deflection
characteristic of the structure
Compute the actual equivalent
equivalent damping ξ'_{eq}

Step 7: CHECK
Is $\xi_{eq} = \xi'_{eq}$?

No   Yes

→ Design Complete

a)

Equivalent Damping

ξ_{eq}

Δ_y Δ_t

Target displacement or Ductility

b)

Spectral Displacement

Δ_t

ξ_{eq}

T_{eff}

Effective Period

c)

V_b

Base Shear

k_{eff}
1

Displacement Δ_t

Figure 2.9 Flowchart of Direct-Displacement Seismic Design

where Δ_r is the maximum roof lateral displacement, α_1 is the first modal participation factor and A_r^1 is the roof component of the fundamental mode shape.

The seismic hazard associated with the target displacement must then be defined in terms of a design relative displacement response spectrum. This can be obtained by transforming the code design spectral accelerations for a given seismic zone S_{ACode} into corresponding spectral displacement values S_{DCode}:

$$S_{DCode} = \frac{T_{eff}^2}{4\pi^2} S_{ACode} \qquad (2.6)$$

where T_{eff} is the effective elastic secant period of the building at the target displacement Δ_t. Considering that Equation (2.6) is less accurate for longer period structures, it is suggested that design displacement spectra such as the ones included in Eurocode 8 (CEN 2004) be used directly.

Code spectral values are typically specified for an equivalent viscous damping level equal to 5% of critical damping ($S_{D\ 0.05}$). The target spectral displacement corresponding to the actual total viscous damping level of the structure $S_{D\xi_{eq}}$ can be obtained through empirical modification factors. Figure 2.10 presents some modification factors that have been proposed.

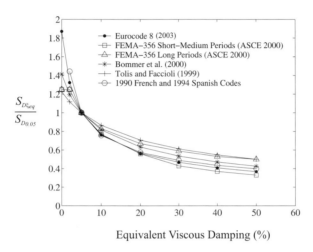

Figure 2.10 Empirical Modification Factors for Damping

If the design is based on a performance level other than achieving the life safety limit state, the corresponding design spectral displacement S_{DT_r} corresponding to a different return period must be obtained. According to the FEMA-356 document (ASCE 2000), for example, this can be approximated by scaling the code spectral values:

$$S_{DT_r} = \left(\frac{T_r}{475}\right)^n S_{DCode} \tag{2.7}$$

where T_r is the mean return period of the ground motion (in years) corresponding to the desired performance level, and n is a power factor less than unity that depends on the seismic zone (ASCE 2000).

- **Step 2:** Determination of Equivalent Viscous Damping

In order to capture the energy dissipation characteristics of the structure at the target displacement Δ_t, an equivalent viscous damping ratio ξ_{eq} is determined:

$$\xi_{eq} = \frac{E_{D\Delta_t}}{2\pi\ k_{eff}\ \Delta_t^2} \tag{2.8}$$

where $E_{D\Delta_t}$ is the energy dissipated per cycle at the target displacement Δ_t and k_{eff} is the effective (secant) lateral stiffness of the structure at the same target displacement. The energy dissipation characteristic of other structural and nonstructural elements in the structure (inherent damping) can be accounted for by adding a small amount of damping to ξ_{eq} in Equation (2.8).

In the first design iteration, an approximate value of damping at the specified target displacement is assigned based on past experience with the structural system considered. In subsequent iterations, when actual structural member sizes are available, the determination of ξ_{eq} is either based on a cyclic push-pull analysis of the structure or on a damping database derived for the selected structural system considered and based on the global hysteretic behaviour of the structure to which the inherent damping is added.

As illustrated schematically in Figure 2.9a, equivalent damping values are related to the nonlinear characteristics of the structure that can be defined by the maximum displacement of systems with continuous nonlinear hysteretic relations or as a ductility measurement when a yield displacement can be clearly defined.

- **Step 3**: Determination of Effective Elastic Period

Knowing the target displacement Δ_t and the equivalent viscous damping ξ_{eq} of the structure at that target displacement, the effective elastic period of the building T_{eff} can be obtained directly from the design displacement response spectrum (see Figure 2.9b).

- **Step 4**: Computation of Effective Lateral Stiffness

Representing the building as an equivalent linear SDOF system (secant to the target displacement), the effective lateral stiffness k_{eff} can be obtained:

$$k_{eff} = \frac{4\pi^2 W_{eff}}{g T_{eff}^2} \tag{2.9}$$

where W_{eff} is the effective seismic weight acting on the structure and g is the acceleration of gravity.

- **Step 5**: Computation of Design Base Shear

The design base shear at the target displacement V_b (see Figure 2.9c) is then computed by:

$$V_b = k_{eff}\,\Delta_t \tag{2.10}$$

This base shear is distributed along the height of the structure, and structural elements are designed such that the strength of the system at the target displacement is equal to the design base shear. For structures with elements with well defined yield displacements, an equivalent base shear at first yield is derived from the design base shear V_b at the target displacement allowing for a conventional load and resistance factor design to be used. After the yielding elements are designed, well known capacity design principles are used to complete the design process for all other elements.

- **Step 6**: Determination of Actual Force-Deflection Characteristic

The actual force-deflection characteristic of the structure is then derived, and the correct value of equivalent viscous damping ξ'_{eq} is computed and compared to the assumed value ξ_{eq}.

- **Step 7**: Verification

If the actual viscous damping of the system is equal to the viscous damping of the system assumed in step 2, the design process is complete. If not, the process is repeated from step 2 by replacing the equivalent damping by the new value.

It must be noted that the need for a complete assessment of the cyclic nonlinear characteristics of the structure at each iteration can be eliminated if considerable information about the relationship between system equivalent damping and system global inelastic deformation is known. For reinforced concrete structures, for example, the relationship suggested by Priestley (1993, 1998) between the equivalent viscous damping and the displacement ductility can be used generically without a case by case evaluation of damping characteristics. As suggested by Priestley, if the yield displacement of reinforced concrete elements is considered as a section property, independent of strength, the design objective can be achieved with only a few iterations.

As discussed by Filiatrault and Folz (2002), for structures with no clear yield point, such as woodframe buildings, a relationship between displacement ductility and equivalent damping is not possible and therefore the maximum deformation is used. Furthermore, the direct displacement-based seismic design can be significantly simplified if a data base of pushover analyses and damping-deformation curves for different structural configurations is developed *a priori*.

A recent study (Priestley and Grant 2005) suggests that the amount of inherent damping, usually assigned relative to the initial elastic stiffness of the structure, must be modified in order to be used with the effective secant stiffness used in direct displacement-based design. It is also highlighted that, when verifying displacement demands predicted by the Direct Displacement-Based Design procedure via nonlinear time-history analyses, a tangent stiffness proportional model for the inherent damping of the structure results in significantly more consistent responses. It is also stipulated that such a model better represents the inherent damping that is present during the nonlinear response and is likely to lead to more realistic results.

2.5.2 Advantages and Disadvantages of Direct Displacement-Based Seismic Design

The performance-based seismic design of structures using the direct displacement-based strategy, as outlined above, has the following advantages over the traditional forced-based design:

- No estimation of the elastic period of the building is required.

- Force reduction factors do not enter the design process.

- Displacements drive the design process.

- The relationship between the elastic and inelastic displacements is not required.

- The yield displacement, if it cannot be readily identified, need not enter the design process.

The direct displacement-based seismic design strategy, on the other hand, requires detailed knowledge of the global nonlinear monotonic load-displacement behaviour (pushover) of the structure, as well as the variation of the global equivalent viscous damping with displacement amplitude. These requirements can be considered a disadvantage of the direct displacement-based seismic design procedure since knowledge of the behaviour of some types of structural systems may not be well established. To obtain this information, system level testing is required in parallel with the development of specialized structural analysis models.

2.6 NONLINEAR DYNAMIC ANALYSES

For very tall and/or highly irregular important structures, *nonlinear time-history dynamic analyses* can be performed. For this purpose, the ground motion input must be represented by an ensemble of acceleration time-histories that are compatible with the seismic hazard level at the construction site, including the possibility of multiple sources capable of producing significant ground shaking at the considered site. Scaled historical ground acceleration time-histories, recorded in the same region or in other regions, exhibiting similar seismo-tectonic mechanisms as that of the construction site must be selected. As an alternative, synthetic records that are compatible with the design response spectrum for the site can be generated.

A nonlinear model of the structure needs also to be generated. This model needs to contain sufficient degrees-of-freedom to represent adequately the spatial distribution of the mass and stiffness of the structure in order to capture its dynamic behaviour. Furthermore, the cyclic behaviour of the structural elements that are deemed to respond in the inelastic range of the material needs to be included, with realistic representation of limit states. Typically, this nonlinear behaviour is taken into account by lumped hysteretic plasticity rules. Finally, nonlinear geometric effects may also need to be included.

Although the emergence of powerful desktop computers has brought the nonlinear time-history dynamic analysis method within the reach of most practicing engineers, the level of difficulty involved is still limiting its wide application. Therefore, nonlinear time-history dynamic analyses are usually performed nowadays at the end of the design process for verification purposes.

2.7 INCREMENTAL DYNAMIC ANALYSES

In order to investigate the seismic capacity of structural systems, incremental dynamic analyses have been proposed (Vamvatsikos and Cornell 2002). In this approach, nonlinear time-history dynamic analyses are performed for an ensemble of earthquake ground motions scaled to a given intensity level. The scaling of the ground motions can take several forms. For example, the median spectral acceleration of the records at a given period (e.g. the fundamental period of the structure under investigation or another arbitrary period) can be considered. From the results of each dynamic analysis, a peak displacement response parameter of the structure is retained. The maximum interstorey drift is often used for this purpose. For each ground motion record, the analyses are repeated for increasing intensities until the displacement parameter grows beyond a prescribed value associated with a given limit state (e.g. collapse). The intensity of the ground motion causing this displacement value can then be associated with the intensity of this particular ground motion causing the limit state to occur in the structure. The process is then repeated for all ground motions and a series of intensity-displacement plots can be obtained, as illustrated in Figure 2.11a. From this plot, a fragility curve giving the relationship between the probability of exceeding the given limit state as a function of the intensity measure can be obtained, as illustrated in Figure 2.11b. The probability of

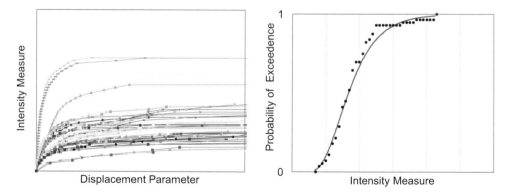

Figure 2.11 Illustrations of Incremental Dynamic Analyses: a)Intensity-Displacement Plot, b) Fragility Curve

exceedence for a given intensity level can be estimated by counting the number of ground motion records causing the displacement parameter to exceed the prescribed limit state level and dividing this value by the total number of records considered in the incremental dynamic analyses.

2.8 NEED FOR SUPPLEMENTAL DAMPING AND SEISMIC ISOLATION SYSTEMS

The main aim of current seismic design philosophies and analysis methods briefly reviewed in this chapter concentrates mainly on ensuring adequate safety by avoiding catastrophic failures and loss of life. When a structure does not collapse during a major earthquake, and the occupants can be evacuated safely, it is considered that this structure has fulfilled its function even though it may never be functional again and would ultimately have to be demolished. Economic parameters, such as the cost of damage to equipment and stored goods, and the cost associated with the loss of operation following a moderate/ strong earthquake, are not currently accounted for in the design process. The continuing development of performance-based seismic design intends to encompass, directly or indirectly, those parameters within a set of performance objectives aimed at ensuring predictable behaviour of the entire building or bridge system.

Although this current seismic design approach still remains an implicit general goal of any structure engineered in an earthquake prone area, socio-economic realities have pushed the barrier considerably higher. Critical facilities and structures such as hospitals, police stations, communication centers and major bridges must be designed to achieve significantly higher performance levels under severe earthquake shaking because of their importance in the immediate emergency response following a catastrophic event. Furthermore, building owners and insurance companies are increasingly considering the impact of a major earthquake on their portfolio as an economic decision tool. The cost of a new structure designed to meet higher performance levels or the cost of an upgrade to an existing structure are weighed against the estimated losses associated with damage, loss of property and downtime in the event of a major earthquake.

Supplemental damping and seismic isolation systems can, therefore, be viewed as the means to achieving higher performance levels at a reasonable cost. This design approach using supplemental damping and/or seismic isolation systems goes beyond the traditional earthquake-resistance philosophy that tolerates damage as long as life safety is guaranteed and aims to minimize damage to structural and nonstructural elements even under severe earthquake ground motions.

CHAPTER 3: ENERGY CONCEPTS IN EARTHQUAKE ENGINEERING

3.1 INTRODUCTION

Since the main purpose of using supplemental damping and seismic isolation systems is to dissipate a significant portion of the seismic input energy and/or to isolate the structure from receiving this energy, it is natural to formulate the seismic problem within an energy framework. The main advantage of the energy formulation is the replacement of vector quantities, such as displacements, velocities and accelerations, by scalar energy quantities. With this approach, the flow of these energy quantities can be tracked during the seismic response of the structure. Furthermore, the impact of introducing supplemental damping and seismic isolation systems on these energy flows can be readily observed.

In this chapter, the energy balance formulation is derived for Multi-Degrees-Of-Freedom (MDOF) systems subjected to earthquake ground motions. First, the energy flow within a structural system under earthquake ground motion is illustrated through a rain flow analogy. Then, the mathematical derivations leading to the general energy balance equation are presented. The relationship between the absolute and relative seismic input energy is established. The chapter ends with numerical examples of energy computations that illustrate the effects of supplemental damping and seismic isolation on energy quantities.

3.2 RAIN FLOW ANALOGY

The migration of energy quantities in a structure during an earthquake can be visualized easily through the rain flow analogy shown in Figure 3.1. This figure illustrates a fictitious hangar with a retractable roof subjected to a rainstorm (Figure 3.1a). The rainstorm symbolizes the earthquake input, while the amount of rain water entering the system represents the total seismic energy input into the structure. This amount of rain water entering the system depends on the extent of the roof opening, symbolizing the dependence of the input energy on the structural properties during an earthquake and emphasizing the fact that the input energy is not the same for every structure subjected to the same ground motion. If the roof is completely open, the structure would absorb all the seismic energy input generated at the site by the earthquake. This case symbolizes quasi-resonance between the ground motion and the dynamic response of the structure. If the

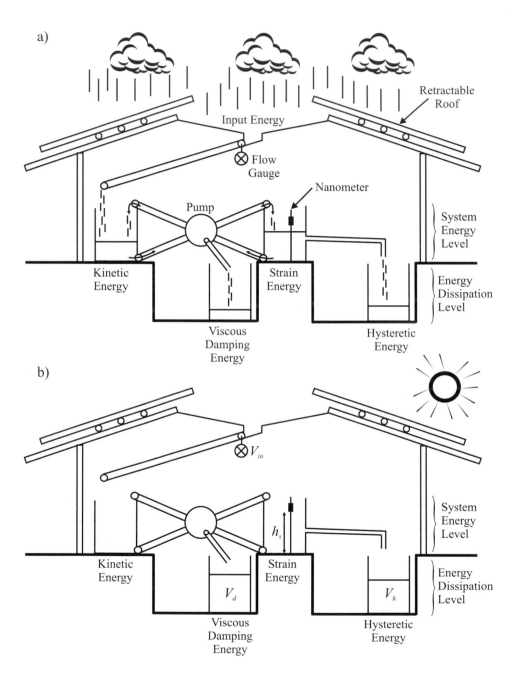

Figure 3.1 Rain Flow Analogy: a)During Seismic Shaking, b) At the End of Seismic Shaking

roof is completely closed, the structure does not receive any seismic input energy. This situation corresponds to a perfectly isolated structure.

The rain water entering the structure, symbolizing the seismic input energy, is collected just below the ceiling line, and is routed towards a kinetic energy pail. The amount of rainwater collected by this pail represents the kinetic energy generated by the masses of the structure as their inertia reacts to the seismic input energy transmitted to the structure. The hosepipe collecting the rainwater entering from the roof is equipped with a flow gauge in order to measure the total amount of seismic input energy transmitted to the structure.

The rain water that slides down on each side of the closed portion of the roof symbolizes the amount of seismic input energy generated by the earthquake that is not transmitted to the structure, but is rather radiated back to the ground. In other words, not all the seismic input energy generated at the site is absorbed by the structure.

As the masses of the structure vibrate, the structural elements deform and absorb strain energy. When the masses stop moving at the end of a cycle of vibration, the kinetic energy is transferred into strain energy. This process is illustrated in Figure 3.1a by a two-way oscillating pump connecting the bottom of the kinetic energy pail to the top of the strain energy pail and the bottom of the strain energy pail to the top of the kinetic energy pail. The flow rate of the pump is associated with the effective periods of vibration of the structure. This pump is activated as long as rain water is still present in either of these two pails. The vibration of the structure can therefore be visualized as a constant transfer of kinetic energy into strain energy and vice-versa. The equivalent viscous damping of the structural system is symbolized by a flow loss in the two-way oscillating pump between the kinetic energy pail and the strain energy pail. This flow loss is proportional to the flow rates transiting through the pump. This is analogous to the velocity dependence of the equivalent viscous damping model. The amount of lost rain water is collected permanently by a viscous damping pail symbolizing the amount of energy absorbed by equivalent viscous damping.

It is of interest to note that the system composed of the kinetic, strain and viscous damping energy pails represents a viscously damped linear elastic system. If only an initial amount of input energy is introduced to the system, resulting in a damped free-vibration response, rain water will be pumped between the kinetic and strain energy pails until all the rain water is transmitted to the viscous damping pail through losses in the pump.

When the level of rain water in the strain energy pail reaches a critical level, some of the water is drained permanently into a hysteretic energy pail. The critical water level in the strain energy pail symbolizes the amount of strain energy that is absorbed by the structure before it starts deforming in the inelastic range. The nanometer in the strain energy pail indicates the maximum total (recoverable + hysteretic) strain energy absorbed by the structural elements at any time during the earthquake. This reading is directly related to the peak transient response of the structure. Therefore, damage in the structure is associated with both the amount of rain water accumulated in the hysteretic energy pail and the final reading of the nanometer.

The energy state of the structure at the end of the shaking is illustrated in Figure 3.1b. Both the kinetic and recoverable strain energy pails are empty as the structure comes to rest. If the structure remains in the elastic range of the material during the earthquake, all the input energy ends up in the equivalent viscous damping pail. If the structural elements experience inelastic deformations during the earthquake, a portion of the seismic input energy is also collected by the hysteretic energy pail. Therefore, the sum of the volumes of rain water collected by the equivalent viscous damping pail V_d and by the hysteretic energy pail V_h must be equal to the equivalent volume of rainwater recorded by the flow gauge V_{in}:

$$V_{in} = V_d + V_h \tag{3.1}$$

From the rain flow analogy discussed above, the strategies for incorporating supplemental damping and seismic isolation systems against earthquake attacks become obvious. Two possible intervention strategies are possible. The first strategy consists of minimizing (or even eliminating) the amount of rain water collected by the hysteretic energy pail that is directly linked to damage. This can be achieved by supplemental damping mechanisms. The other intervention strategy consists of reducing the size of the roof opening in order to minimize the amount of rain flow collected by the seismic input energy pail. This symbolizes the primary function of a seismic isolation system.

3.3 ENERGY BALANCE EQUATION

3.3.1 Derivation

The governing differential equations of motion for a general nonlinear MDOF system excited at the base by a horizontal translation from an earthquake ground motion are given in matrix form by:

$$[M]\{\ddot{x}(t)\} + [C]\{\dot{x}(t)\} + \{F_r(t)\} = -[M]\{r\}\ddot{x}_g(t) + \{F_s\} \tag{3.2}$$

where:

- $[M]$ is the global mass matrix.

- $[C]$ is the global viscous damping matrix which accounts for all inherent velocity dependent energy dissipating mechanisms in the structure other than the inelastic hysteretic energy dissipated by the structural members. Note that these damping mechanisms are usually not velocity dependent, but are expressed in this way for mathematical convenience.

- $\{\ddot{x}(t)\}$, $\{\dot{x}(t)\}$ and $\{x(t)\}$ are respectively the vectors of global accelerations, velocities and displacements relative to the moving base at time t.

- $\{F_r(t)\}$ is the vector of global nonlinear restoring forces at time t generated by the hysteretic characteristics of the structural elements.

- $\{r\}$ is a vector coupling the directions of the ground motion input with the directions of the DOFs of the structure.

- $\ddot{x}_g(t)$ is the horizontal acceleration of the ground at time t.

- $\{F_s\}$ is the vector of global static loads applied to the structure prior to and maintained during the seismic excitation.

The formulation presented in Equation (3.2) is derived for equal excitation at all support points of the structure. For non-synchronous excitation at the different supports of the structure (multiple support excitation), the right hand side of Equation (3.2) is modified as presented in Chopra (2001).

The energy formulation is obtained by integrating the work done by each element in Equation (3.2) over an increment of global structural displacements $\{dx\}$:

$$\int \{dx\}^T [M]\{\ddot{x}(t)\} + \int \{dx\}^T [C]\{\dot{x}(t)\} + \int \{dx\}^T \{F_r(t)\}$$
$$= -\int \{dx\}^T [M]\{r\}\ddot{x}_g(t) + \int \{dx\}^T \{F_s\}$$

$$(3.3)$$

Recalling the differential relationships:

$$\{dx(t)\} = \{\dot{x}(t)\}dt \qquad (3.4)$$

$$\{d\dot{x}(t)\} = \{\ddot{x}(t)\}dt \qquad (3.5)$$

Using Equation (3.4), the first two terms on the left side of Equation (3.3) are first rewritten as:

$$\int \{dx\}^T [M]\{\ddot{x}(t)\} = \int \{\dot{x}\}^T [M]\{\ddot{x}(t)\}dt$$
$$\int \{dx\}^T [C]\{\dot{x}(t)\} = \int \{\dot{x}\}^T [C]\{\dot{x}(t)\}dt$$

$$(3.6)$$

where the integrals on the right hand side are taken over time.

Using Equations (3.4) and (3.5), the expressions obtained in Equation (3.6) are rewritten as:

$$\int \{\dot{x}\}^T [M]\{\ddot{x}(t)\}dt = \int \{\dot{x}\}^T [M]\{d\dot{x}(t)\}$$
$$\int \{\dot{x}\}^T [C]\{\dot{x}(t)\}dt = \int \{\dot{x}\}^T [C]\{dx(t)\}$$

$$(3.7)$$

The energy formulation is finally written as:

$$\int \{\dot{x}(t)\}^T [M]\{d\dot{x}(t)\} + \int \{\dot{x}(t)\}^T [C]\{dx(t)\} + \int \{dx\}^T \{F_r(t)\}$$
$$= -\int \{dx\}^T [M]\{r\}\ddot{x}_g(t) + \int \{dx\}^T \{F_s\}$$

$$(3.8)$$

The first term of Equation (3.8) can be integrated directly and expressed as:

$$\int \{\dot{x}(t)\}^T [M]\{d\dot{x}(t)\} = \frac{1}{2}\{\dot{x}(t)\}^T [M]\{\dot{x}(t)\} \qquad (3.9)$$

Based on Equation (3.8) the energy balance equation is defined as:

$$E_k^r(t) + E_{vd}(t) + E_a(t) = E_{in}^r(t) + E_{st}(t) \qquad (3.10)$$

where:

- $E_k^r(t)$ is defined as the relative kinetic energy at time t:

$$E_k^r(t) = \frac{1}{2}\{\dot{x}(t)\}^T [M]\{\dot{x}(t)\} \qquad (3.11)$$

- $E_{vd}(t)$ is the energy dissipated by viscous damping from the beginning of the record up to time t:

$$E_{vd}(t) = \int \{\dot{x}(t)\}^T [C]\{dx(t)\} \qquad (3.12)$$

- $E_a(t)$ is the absorbed energy from the beginning of the record up to time t:

$$E_a(t) = \int \{dx\}^T \{F_r(t)\} \qquad (3.13)$$

- $E_{in}^r(t)$ is the relative input energy from the beginning of the record up to time t:

$$E_{in}^r(t) = -\int \{dx\}^T [M]\{r\}\ddot{x}_g(t) \qquad (3.14)$$

- $E_{st}(t)$ is the work done by static loads applied before and maintained during the seismic excitation from the moment of application of the forces up to time t:

$$E_{st}(t) = \int \{dx\}^T \{F_s\} \qquad (3.15)$$

The absorbed energy term $E_a(t)$ represents the total amount of energy that the structure has absorbed either through elastic straining or unrecoverable inelastic deformations of its elements. The peak absorbed energy during an earthquake represents the largest demand on structural members and is expressed as the sum of two components:

$$E_a(t) = E_{es}(t) + E_h(t) \qquad (3.16)$$

where $E_{es}(t)$ is the recoverable elastic strain energy at time t and $E_h(t)$ is the energy dissipated through hysteretic damping of the structural elements up to time t, and depends on the hysteretic relation of each structural member. The definition of the elastic strain energy and hysteretic energy terms is further discussed in the following paragraph where the energy formulation is presented in discrete expressions.

Recalling Equation (3.4), it can be seen that the damping energy expressed by Equation (3.12) monotonically increases throughout the time-history, whereas the absorbed energy expressed by Equation (3.13) fluctuates while generally increasing. Referring to Equation (3.16), the fluctuations in the absorbed energy are caused by the elastic strain energy that is absorbed and then restored.

3.3.2 Relative Input Energy and Absolute Input Energy

The energy balance equation derived in the previous paragraph (Equation (3.10)) is based on equivalent lateral seismic forces applied to a rigid base structure. This approach does not consider the rigid body translation of the structure and, for this reason, is called a *relative* formulation. The rigid body translation of the structure can be included explicitly in an *absolute* energy formulation. Although the absolute energy formulation can be derived directly from the equations of motion (Uang and Bertero 1990), it is here derived based on the relative formulation to provide more insight into the differences that exist between these two formulations.

To achieve this, the relative input energy $E_{in}^{r}(t)$ is first rewritten using the differential relations of Equation (3.4) as an integral over time:

$$E_{in}^{r}(t) = -\int \{\dot{x}(t)\}^{T}[M]\{r\}\ddot{x}_{g}(t)dt \tag{3.17}$$

Equation (3.17) is then integrated by parts:

$$E_{in}^{r}(t) = -\{\dot{x}(t)\}^{T}[M]\{r\}\dot{x}_{g}(t) + \int \{\ddot{x}(t)\}^{T}[M]\{r\}\dot{x}_{g}(t)dt \tag{3.18}$$

The relative acceleration vector $\{\ddot{x}(t)\}$ can be expressed in terms of the absolute acceleration vector $\{\ddot{x}_{a}(t)\}$ as:

$$\{\ddot{x}(t)\} = \{\ddot{x}_{a}(t)\}-\{r\}\ddot{x}_{g}(t) \tag{3.19}$$

Substituting Equation (3.19) into Equation (3.18) yields:

$$E_{in}^{r}(t) = -\{\dot{x}(t)\}^{T}[M]\{r\}\dot{x}_{g}(t) + \int \{\ddot{x}_{a}(t)\}^{T}[M]\{r\}\dot{x}_{g}(t)dt$$
$$-\int \ddot{x}_{g}(t)\{r\}^{T}[M]\{r\}\dot{x}_{g}(t)dt \tag{3.20}$$

Using the differential relationships expressed in Equations (3.4) and (3.5) in terms of the ground displacement, velocity and accelerations:

$$E_{in}^{r}(t) = -\{\dot{x}(t)\}^{T}[M]\{r\}\dot{x}_{g}(t) + \int \{\ddot{x}_{a}(t)\}^{T}[M]\{r\}dx_{g}(t)$$
$$-\int \dot{x}_{g}(t)\{r\}^{T}[M]\{r\}d\dot{x}_{g}(t) \tag{3.21}$$

The last term of Equation (3.21) can be directly integrated to yield:

$$E_{in}^{r}(t) = -\{\dot{x}(t)\}^{T}[M]\{r\}\dot{x}_{g}(t) + \int \{\ddot{x}_{a}(t)\}^{T}[M]\{r\}dx_{g}(t)$$
$$-\frac{1}{2}\dot{x}_{g}(t)\{r\}^{T}[M]\{r\}\dot{x}_{g}(t) \tag{3.22}$$

Introducing Equation (3.22) into the energy balance equation (Equation (3.8)) results in:

$$\frac{1}{2}\{\dot{x}(t)\}^T[M]\{\dot{x}(t)\} + \{\dot{x}(t)\}^T[M]\{r\}\dot{x}_g(t) + \frac{1}{2}\dot{x}_g(t)\{r\}^T[M]\{r\}\dot{x}_g(t)$$

$$+ E_{vd}(t) + E_a(t) = \int\{\ddot{x}_a(t)\}^T[M]\{r\}dx_g(t) + E_{st}(t)$$

(3.23)

Recognizing a perfect square in the first three terms of the left hand side, Equation (3.23) becomes:

$$\frac{1}{2}\{\{\dot{x}(t)\} + \{r\}\dot{x}_g(t)\}^T[M]\{\{\dot{x}(t)\} + \{r\}\dot{x}_g(t)\}$$

$$+ E_{vd}(t) + E_a(t) = \int\{\ddot{x}_a(t)\}^T[M]\{r\}dx_g(t) + E_{st}(t)$$

(3.24)

Recalling Equation (3.19) and extending it to the relative velocity vector, we get:

$$\{\dot{x}(t)\} = \{\dot{x}_a(t)\} - \{r\}\dot{x}_g(t)$$

(3.25)

Substituting Equation (3.25) into Equation (3.24), we obtain the absolute energy formulation:

$$E_k^a(t) + E_{vd}(t) + E_a(t) = E_{in}^a(t) + E_{st}(t)$$

(3.26)

where:

- $E_k^a(t)$ is defined as the absolute kinetic energy of the system at time t:

$$E_k^a(t) = \frac{1}{2}\{\dot{x}_a(t)\}^T[M]\{\dot{x}_a(t)\}$$

(3.27)

- $E_{in}^a(t)$ is defined as the absolute input energy of the system from the beginning of the record up to time t:

$$E_{in}^a(t) = \int\{\ddot{x}_a(t)\}^T[M]\{r\}dx_g(t)$$

(3.28)

and where $E_{vd}(t)$, $E_a(t)$ and $E_{st}(t)$ have been previously defined in Equations (3.13) and (3.15) and remain unchanged in both relative and absolute energy formulations.

The absolute input energy of the system has a true physical meaning as it is defined as the total base shear integrated over the ground displacement.

Comparing the absolute formulation (Equation (3.26)) to the relative formulation (Equation (3.10)), the following observations can be made:

- Both formulations are mathematically equivalent.

- The sums of the kinetic and input energies in the relative and absolute formulations are equal.

- In the absolute formulation, the ground displacement time-history (that is usually not measured in the field) is required to compute the input energy.

As observed by Uang and Bertero (1990), the input energy expressed in the absolute energy formulation is the true total energy input to the system. However, the input energy computed with both formulations is very similar for structural natural periods ranging from 0.1s to 5.0s, which covers most practical civil engineering structures.

3.3.3 Discrete Energy Expressions

Considering that most energy computations are carried out within discrete time-integration schemes, discrete formulations of the energy terms presented in Equation (3.10) are derived and can be easily included in a computer code.

The kinetic energy quantities at a given time t can be obtained directly from the instantaneous relative velocity vector $\{\dot{x}(t)\}$ included in Equations (3.11) and (3.27) for the relative and absolute formulations respectively. All the other energy quantities, however, require integration through the time domain. Many schemes are available to carry out these integrations. Using the trapezoidal rule, for example, the continuous energy expressions can be obtained for a discretization of time-step Δt as follows:

$$E_{vd}(t) = E_{vd}(t-\Delta t) + \frac{1}{2}(\{\dot{x}(t-\Delta t)\} + \{\dot{x}(t)\})^{T}[C](\{x(t)\} - \{x(t-\Delta t)\}) \quad (3.29)$$

$$E_{a}(t) = E_{a}(t-\Delta t) + \frac{1}{2}(\{x(t)\} - \{x(t-\Delta t)\})^{T}(\{F_{r}(t-\Delta t)\} + \{F_{r}(t)\}) \quad (3.30)$$

$$E_{in}^{r}(t) = E_{in}^{r}(t-\Delta t)$$
$$-\frac{1}{2}(\{x(t)\} - \{x(t-\Delta t)\})^{T}[M]\{r\}(\{\ddot{x}_{g}(t-\Delta t)\} + \{\ddot{x}_{g}(t)\}) \quad (3.31)$$

$$E_{in}^{a}(t) = E_{in}^{a}(t-\Delta t)$$
$$-\frac{1}{2}(\{\ddot{x}_{a}(t-\Delta t)\} + \{\ddot{x}_{a}(t)\})^{T}[M]\{r\}(\{x_{g}(t)\} - x_{g}\{(t-\Delta t)\}) \quad (3.32)$$

If the force-displacement relation of element i is characterized by the elastic perfectly-plastic hysteresis shown in Figure 3.2, the energy absorbed by this element at time t can be computed in a discrete form following the trapezoidal integration rule by:

$$E_{a}^{i}(t) = E_{a}^{i}(t-\Delta t) + \frac{1}{2}(F_{r}^{i}(t-\Delta t) + F_{r}^{i}(t))(u^{i}(t) - u^{i}(t-\Delta t)) \quad (3.33)$$

where $F_{r}^{i}(t)$ and $u^{i}(t)$ are the nonlinear restoring force and deformation of element i at time t respectively. The recoverable elastic strain energy in element i at time t, $E_{es}^{i}(t)$ is given by:

$$E_{es}^{i}(t) = \frac{1}{2}\frac{(F_{r}^{i}(t))^{2}}{k} \quad (3.34)$$

where k is the elastic stiffness of the system. The hysteretic energy in element i at time t, $E_h^i(t)$ is obtained by subtracting $E_{es}^i(t)$ from $E_a^i(t)$.

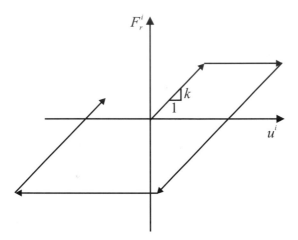

Figure 3.2 Elastoplastic Force-Displacement Hysteretic Relation at DOF *i*

This approach is particularly useful for tracking the energy dissipated by a particular hysteretic element of the structure, either to assess the effectiveness of supplemental damping devices in dissipating energy or to quantify the cumulative damage induced in main structural elements. The system's total energy is obtained by summing these energy quantities over all DOFs. Note that at the end of the earthquake ground motion, and after the structure reaches the at-rest position, the elastic strain energy E_{es} goes to zero and the final amount of the hysteretic energy E_h is equal to the final amount of absorbed energy E_a. Note also that the final amount of absorbed energy is not necessarily the peak value of the absorbed energy since, during the time-history, the sum of the hysteretic energy and elastic strain energy may be higher than the total hysteretic energy. This is especially true for impulsive type loading.

3.3.4 Using Energy Balance as a Criterion for Numerical Accuracy

Since all energy terms in both the relative and absolute formulations (Equations (3.10) and (3.26) respectively) are computed individually based on the vectors of structural displacements, velocities, and accelerations (obtained from the time-marching integration scheme), an Energy Balance Error (EBE) can be calculated at each time-step. The EBE can be used as a criterion for indicating the global accuracy achieved by the time-integration algorithm at each time-step.

The EBE can be normalized in percent as follows:

$$EBE^r(t) = \frac{\left|E^r_{in}(t) + E_{st}(t) - E^r_k(t) - E_{vd}(t) - E_a(t)\right|}{\left|E^r_{in}(t)\right|} \qquad (3.35)$$

for the relative energy formulation, and:

$$EBE^a(t) = \frac{\left|E^a_{in}(t) + E_{st}(t) - E^a_k(t) - E_{vd}(t) - E_a(t)\right|}{\left|E^a_{in}(t)\right|} \qquad (3.36)$$

for the absolute formulation.

In a computer code, a tolerance limit can be set on the EBE, which stops the computations or automatically reduces the time-step, if exceeded. This can save time and computer costs if a time-step, which is deemed too large by the energy balance equation, is used in an initial trial run. A tolerance of 2% to 5% has been suggested for practical analyses (Beshara and Verdi 1991, Belytschoko et al. 1976).

3.3.5 Energy Spectra

Following the concept of elastic response spectra, energy spectra can also be computed for the energy quantities described in the previous paragraph. For a given target displacement ductility factor, energy terms can be plotted as a function of the initial elastic natural period of a nonlinear SDOF oscillator. Most commonly, the seismic input energy, the absorbed energy or the hysteretic energy are plotted in the form of energy spectra.

3.3.6 Energy Based Design Methods

Energy measures can also be used as alternative indices to response quantities such as forces or displacements that form the basis of most current design procedures. Energy measures directly include duration-related seismic damage while most other design procedures are snapshots of the structural response at maximum deformation. In reality, the performance of structural members depend both on the maximum inelastic deformation reached during the seismic loading and on the number of inelastic excursions. If failure of ductile elements is considered as a low-cycle fatigue type phenomenon, then the number of available cycles before failure reduces as the amplitude increases. If an estimate of the hysteretic energy demand can be obtained, it can then be compared to the energy absorption capacity of different structural members as characterized by laboratory experiments. The goal of seismic design is then to provide sufficient energy absorption capacity to all structural members.

Chou and Uang (2000) established attenuation relationships for absorbed energy as a function of earthquake magnitude, source-to-site distance, soil classification and ductility factor based on more than 200 records obtained from 15 earthquakes in Southern California. In a further study, a procedure to evaluate the absorbed energy in low to mid-rise multistorey frames from energy spectra was proposed (Chou and Uang 2003). The main difficulty in developing design procedures fully based on energy criteria is the characterization of the energy absorption capacity of members. Furthermore, it is very difficult to fully characterize performance solely on the basis of absorbed energy since, for well designed ductile elements, the performance level is primarily controlled by the maximum ductility demand.

3.4 EXAMPLES OF ENERGY COMPUTATION

3.4.1 Scope

To appreciate the use of the energy balance concept in seismic analysis, numerical examples are presented in this section for an ensemble of two-storey frame structures idealized as nonlinear two-degrees-of-freedom models. Three of these systems incorporate different supplemental damping and seismic isolation systems. Even for these simple structural models, the energy balance approach reveals the structural responses in a different perspective, which helps understand better the nonlinear behaviour of these structures and the effects of incorporating supplemental damping and seismic isolation systems on the flow of energy. The results presented below were inspired from an initial study by Filiatrault et al. (1994a).

3.4.2 Structural Models

The basic structural models used in the analyses consist of six different two-storey steel plane frames, as shown in Figure 3.3. The structural models considered are:

- A moment-resisting frame (MRF).

- A braced moment-resisting frame (BMRF) obtained by adding bracing members to the MRF.

- A soft storey frame (SSF) obtained by removing the first-floor braces from the BMRF.

- A base isolated frame (BIF) obtained by installing laminated rubber bearings under the BMRF.

- A friction damped braced frame (FDBF) obtained by inserting friction dampers in the bracing elements of the BMRF.

- A viscously damped braced frame (VDBF) obtained by inserting linear viscous dampers in the bracing elements of the BMRF.

The bracing elements are assumed to act elastically in tension and compression (braces are restrained against buckling). Only one degree-of-freedom per floor is considered in the analyses except for the BIF, where one supplemental degree-of-freedom is prescribed just above the isolation bearings. The resulting structural properties of the six frames are

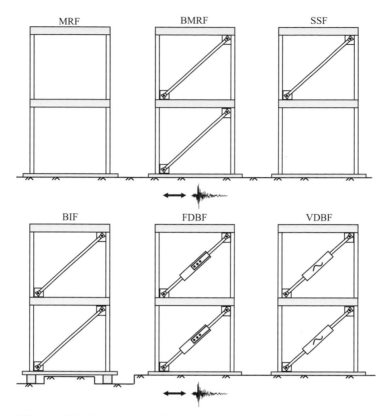

Figure 3.3 Structures Considered in Energy Calculations

presented in Table 3-1. The lateral shear-drift relationship for each element of the structure is modeled as an elastic-perfectly plastic hysteretic behaviour. Rayleigh-type viscous damping with 2% critical damping in each elastic mode of vibration is considered for all structures. The nonlinear time-history dynamic analyses were carried out with the Newmark-Beta average acceleration method at a time-step increment of 0.005 s.

The base isolators of the BIF are modeled as elastic lateral springs. For simplicity, the energy dissipation of the isolators is neglected. This assumption is justified since the hysteresis loops of typical laminated rubber bearings are quite narrow with modest energy dissipation capabilities, as discussed in Chapter 10.

The friction dampers of the FDBF are modeled as simple Coulomb (rigid-plastic) elements attached in series with the same bracing elements of the BMRF. Therefore, the lateral stiffness values of the FDBF before sliding of the friction dampers are identical to those of the BMRF.

The viscous dampers of the VDBF are modeled as simple velocity-dependant linear dashpot elements. The force in each viscous damper F_{VD} is given by:

$$F_{VD} = C_L \dot{x} \tag{3.37}$$

where C_L is the damping constant and $\dot{x}$ is the relative velocity between the ends of the damper. The damping constant can then be converted into a horizontal interstorey damping constant at each floor, C_h, through simple geometrical considerations:

$$C_h = C_L \cos^2\gamma \tag{3.38}$$

where γ is the angle of inclination of the bracing elements with respect to the horizontal.

Table 3-1: Properties of Structures Considered in Energy Calculations

Frame	Mass (kN-s^2/m)		Initial Lateral Stiffness (kN/m)		Yield Shear (kN)		Initial Natural Period (s)	
	Level 1	Level 2	Level 1	Level 2	Level 1	Level 2	Mode 1	Mode 2
MRF	100	100	6850	6850	390	390	1.23	0.47
BMRF	100	100	169000	169000	2630	2630	0.25	0.09
SSF	100	100	6850	169000	390	2630	1.08	0.11
BIF[a]	100	100	169000	169000	2630	2630	2.00	0.13
FDBF	100	100	169000	169000	405[b]	405[b]	0.25	0.09
					780[c]	780[c]		
VDBF[d]	100	100	6850	6850	390	390	1.23	0.47

[a] Isolation bearing lateral stiffness = 1960 kN/m
[b] Interstorey shear corresponding to the sliding of the friction dampers
[c] Interstorey shear corresponding to yielding of the frame structure
[d] Interstorey damping constant for viscous dampers C_h = 640 kN-s/m

For simplicity, the bracing member connected to each viscous damper is assumed rigid and the damping constant assigned to each damper is selected to provide a first modal damping ratio of 23% of critical (the effect of brace flexibility on the performance of viscous dampers is discussed in Chapter 6). The procedure to explicitly obtain the required constants for viscous dampers based on a selected first modal damping ratio will be discussed in Chapter 6. With the 2% structural viscous damping in the first mode of the structure, the total first modal damping ratio of the VDBF is 25% of critical.

3.4.3 Choice of Earthquake Ground Motions

The six structural configurations were subjected to three different ground motions, and their seismic responses were compared from an energy point of view. As shown in Figure 3.4, the earthquake records considered were:

- The 1940 Imperial Valley earthquake recorded at El Centro (S00E)

- The 1988 Saguenay earthquake (Chicoutimi, Quebec, TRAN)

- The 1977 Romania earthquake recorded at Bucharest (North-South)

All the records were scaled to a peak ground acceleration of 0.5 g and only the first 15s of each record were considered. The absolute acceleration response spectra at 2% damping for these three seismic events are shown in Figure 3.5. The initial fundamental periods of the six structural models are also indicated. The El Centro record has its energy distributed over a fairly broad period band, the Saguenay record represents an earthquake with an energy content concentrated at short periods, typical of eastern North America earthquakes, while the Romania record, recorded on soft soil, is an example of a seismic event with an energy content concentrated at the high end of the period spectrum.

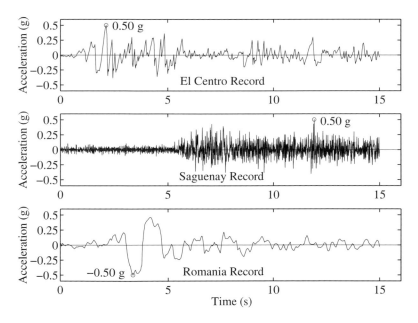

Figure 3.4 Accelerograms of Earthquake Ground Motions Scaled to 0.5g

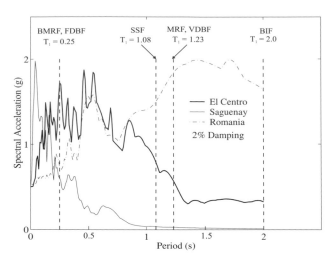

Figure 3.5 Absolute Acceleration Response Spectra of Earthquake Ground Motions

3.4.4 Comparison of Energy Time-Histories

The peak transient displacement ductility ratios, as defined in Section 2.2.2, for both levels of all six structural systems under the three earthquake ground motions considered, are given in Table 3-2. A value of 1 for the ductility ratio at a particular level indicates that the structural elements of that level remained elastic. The largest ductility ratio of 17.6 is experienced by the first level of the SSF under the Romania earthquake, which is only slightly above the ductility ratio of 15.7 experienced by the MRF under the same record. These results indicate that these structural systems would most likely collapse under the Romania record. It is interesting to note that the three other systems (BIF, FDBF and VDBF) reduce substantially the ductility demand under this same record, with the BIF system offering the best performance. For the other two records, the three retrofit schemes prevent the structure from deforming in the inelastic range.

The energy time-histories based on the relative energy formulation (see Equation (3.10)) are presented in Figures 3.6 to 3.11 for the six structural systems subjected to the three earthquake ground motions considered.

Although the energy time-histories generated from a given record vary widely from one structural system to another, each energy component exhibits a particular pattern. The kinetic energy oscillates from zero, when the structure reaches maximum deflections, to positive peaks when the structure passes through its initial underformed position. The energy dissipated by viscous damping, including the energy dissipated by the discrete viscous dampers of the VDBF, always increases with time, as observed above.

Table 3-2: Peak Displacement Ductility Ratios

Ground Motion	Structural System	Displacement Ductility, μ_Δ	
		Level 1	Level 2
El Centro	MRF	2.1	1.6
	BMRF	1.3	1.0
	SSF	2.7	1.0
	BIF	1.0	1.0
	FDBF	1.0	1.0
	VDBF	1.0	1.0
Saguenay	MRF	1.0	1.0
	BMRF	1.0	1.0
	SSF	1.0	1.0
	BIF	1.0	1.0
	FDBF	1.0	1.0
	VDBF	1.0	1.0
Romania	MRF	15.7	1.6
	BMRF	1.0	1.0
	SSF	17.6	1.0
	BIF	1.2	1.0
	FDBF	3.6	1.0
	VDBF	7.1	1.5

As expected, the absorbed energies in the first and second levels present two distinct components: a recoverable elastic component, represented by oscillations out of phase with the kinetic energy, and a non-recoverable component represented by sudden shifts towards positive values as inelastic action occurs in time. The energy absorbed by the friction dampers of the FDBF exhibit the same components, but the energy dissipated by friction is significantly larger than the recoverable strain energy stored in the adjacent bracing members. The relative seismic input energy generally increases with time, but local valleys occur as some of the energy is radiated back into the foundation at the end of vibrations cycles, when the equivalent seismic forces are in the opposite direction of the relative displacements.

The most striking observation that can be made from the results presented in Figures 3.6 to 3.11 is that, although the earthquake records have all the same duration and

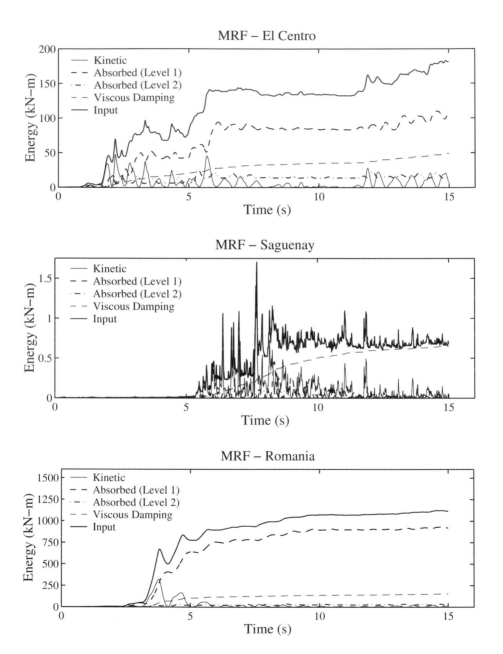

Figure 3.6 Energy Time-Histories for the Moment Resisting Frame (MRF)

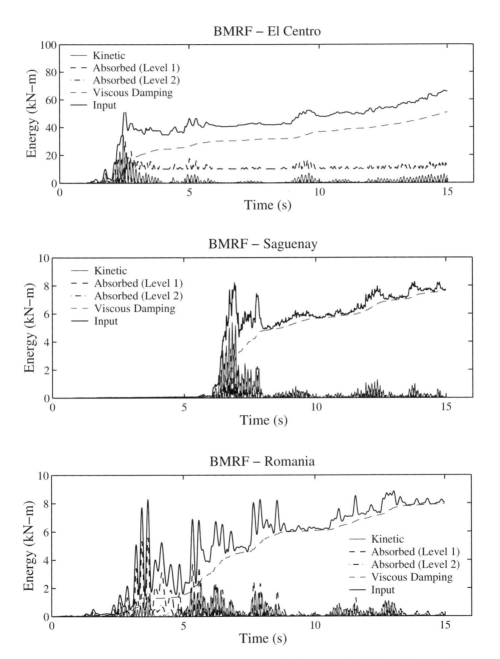

Figure 3.7 Energy Time-Histories for Braced Moment-Resisting Frame (BMRF)

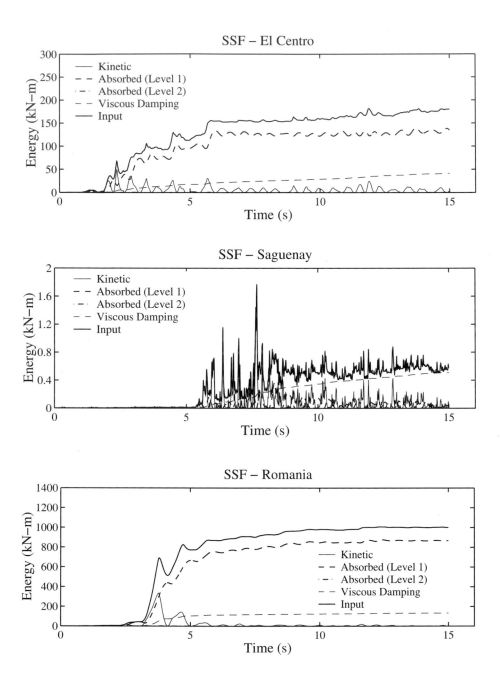

Figure 3.8 Energy Time-Histories for Soft Storey Frame (SSF)

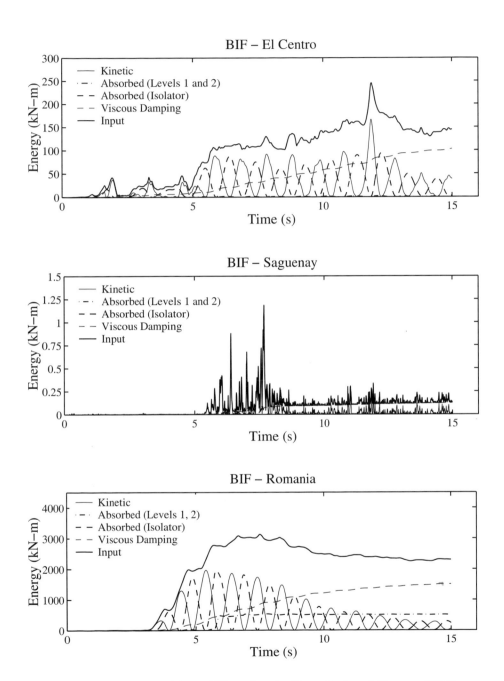

Figure 3.9 Energy Time-Histories for Base Isolated Frame (BIF)

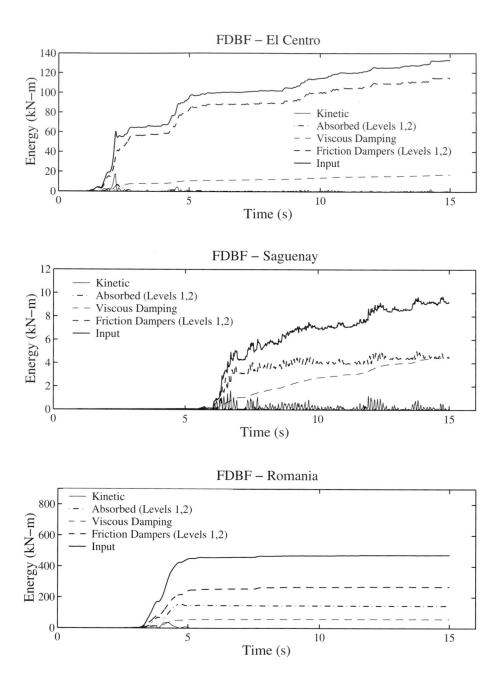

Figure 3.10 Energy Time-Histories for Friction Damped Braced Frame (FDBF)

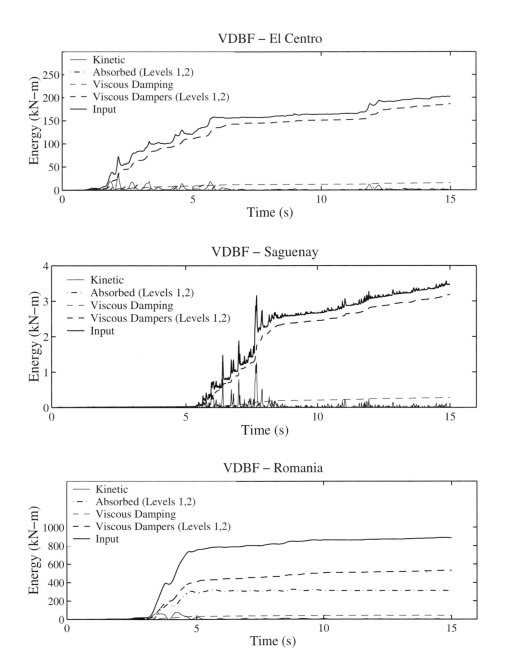

Figure 3.11 Energy Time-Histories for Viscously Damped Braced Frame (VDBF)

peak acceleration, there are very large amplitude differences (up to three orders of magnitude) between the various energy time-histories. To better appreciate this wide difference in the energy quantities, Figure 3.12 compares the relative seismic input energy time-histories generated by the six different models under the three different records. The BIF is very efficient in practically eliminating the seismic input energy for the Saguenay record and induces comparable amount of input energy as the other systems for the El Centro record. For the Romania ground motion, however, the largest values of the seismic input energy are attracted by the BIF. For this earthquake, retrofitting the BMRF with base isolators would be detrimental because of the quasi-resonance occurring due to the close proximity of the fundamental period of the BIF to the predominant period of the ground motion (see Table 3-2 and Figure 3.5). It is also interesting to note that for the Saguenay earthquake, although the seismic input energy values are much lower than for the other two records, the highest input energy values are generated by the FDBF and BMRF, which have both short periods that are close to the predominant period of the Saguenay ground motion. Finally, for the El Centro record, the highest seismic input energy generated at the end of the 15 s of shaking is generated by the VDBF. These results indicate that the structural properties and the characteristics of the design ground motions need to be carefully assessed before selecting a supplemental damping and isolation system for the design or retrofit of a structure. From an energy perspective, the consequences of introducing a soft storey in the first floor of the original BMRF can be seen in Figure 3.13 for the El Centro record. The maximum hysteretic energy demand in the first floor of the SSF is 13.5 times larger than the hysteretic energy in the first floor of the original BMRF.

The efficiency of the added viscous and friction dampers can also by assessed from an energy perspective by computing the fraction of the seismic energy input absorbed by the dampers, as shown in Figure 3.14 for the El Centro and Romania records. At the end of both records, the fraction of the seismic input energy dissipated is similar for both the FDBF and the VDBF systems. Both systems are very efficient for the El Centro record with more than 85% of the seismic input energy dissipated by either system, while they are less efficient for the Romania earthquake with approximately 60% of the input seismic energy dissipated. At the beginning of the records, the fraction of energy dissipated by the FDBF oscillates at much higher frequency than that of the VDBF, reflecting the different fundamental frequencies of the two systems. Between the third and fourth second of the Romania record, corresponding to a strong low frequency pulse (see Figure 3.4), the behaviour of the two systems is quite different. The friction dampers, which are displacement-activated, slip during the impulsive response of the structure and are able to dissipate energy. On the other hand, the viscous dampers that are velocity-activated are not as efficient during the impulsive response since the induced velocities between the damper ends are not very high. Therefore, in the impulsive region, the fraction of absorbed energy drops for the VDBF.

The energy balance formulation for the seismic response of nonlinear structures discussed in this chapter represents a rational procedure to evaluate the effectiveness of

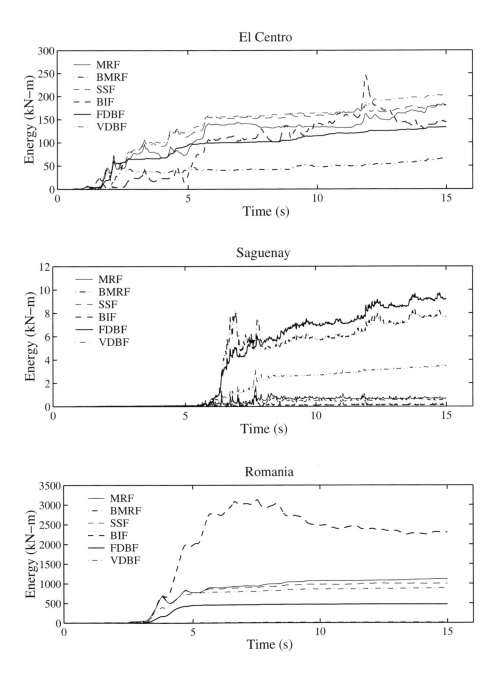

Figure 3.12 Relative Seismic Input Energy Time-Histories

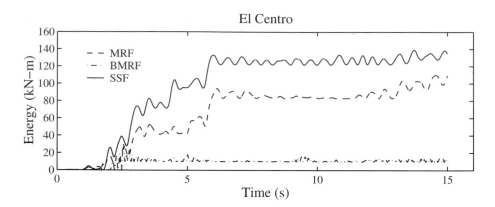

Figure 3.13 First Floor Absorbed (Elastic Strain + Hysteretic) Energy Time-Histories under El Centro Record

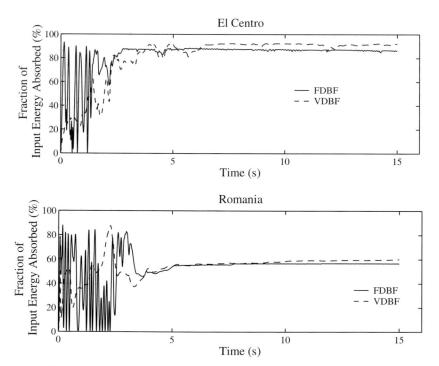

Figure 3.14 Fraction of Input Seismic Energy Absorbed by Friction and Viscous Dampers

supplemental damping and seismic isolation systems. The implementation of this energy balance formulation during the design or retrofit stages requires little extra computational effort, and is available in several structural analysis software packages (e.g. RUAUMOKO). In subsequent chapters, the behaviour and design of the various supplemental damping and seismic isolation systems is discussed in the light of this energy balance formulation. Therefore, the reader is encouraged to refer to the notions covered in this chapter throughout this book.

3.5 PROBLEMS

Problem 3-1

The linear elastic portal frame shown in Figure 3.15 a) is subjected to a short impulsive ground acceleration shown in Figure 3.15 b). The lateral displacement time-history at the girder level of the frame $x(t)$ after the end of the impulse is approximated by:

$$x(t) = \frac{a_g t_1 T}{2\pi} e^{\frac{-\xi T}{2\pi}(t-t_1)} \sin\left(\frac{2\pi}{T}(t-t_1)\right), \quad t \geq t_1$$

where a_g is the peak amplitude of the ground acceleration, t_1 is the duration of the pulse, T is the fundamental period of the frame and ξ is the equivalent viscous damping ratio.

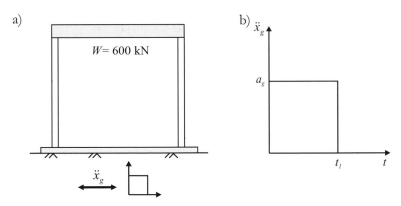

Figure 3.15 Portal Frame Subjected to Short Impulsive Ground Acceleration

Considering the following values: $a_g = 0.1g$, $t_1 = 0.01$s and $T = 1.04$s:

a) Determine closed-form solutions for, and plot, the relative kinetic energy, elastic strain energy and relative input energy time-histories for the first five seconds after the end of the pulse assuming that the system is undamped ($\xi = 0$).

b) Repeat problem a) assuming that the equivalent damping ratio is 5% of critical ($\xi = 0.05$). Add the energy dissipated by viscous damping in the plot. For this damped case, closed-form solutions may be difficult to obtain and discrete energy expressions may be obtained numerically by the trapezoidal rule using a small integration time-step such as 0.01s.

Problem 3-2

The SDOF system consisting of a mass, a nonlinear spring and a linear viscous dashpot shown in Figure 3.16 is subjected to the first 15 seconds of the El Centro (S00E) earthquake. For this record, the CD-ROM accompanying this book includes an ASCII file entitled Problem 3-2.txt containing the following time-histories at intervals of 0.005 s:

- The relative displacement of the mass $x(t)$.

- The relative velocity of the mass $\dot{x}(t)$.

- The force in the nonlinear spring $F_r(t)$.

- The base acceleration $\ddot{x}_g(t)$.

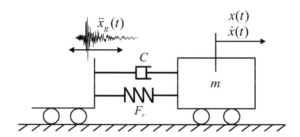

Figure 3.16 SDOF Oscillator with Nonlinear Spring and Linear Dashpot Subjected to El Centro Ground Motion

a) Plot the force-displacement relationship of the nonlinear spring and characterize its behaviour during the seismic response.

b) Plot the force-displacement relationship of the viscous dashpot and comment on its behaviour during the seismic response.

c) Plot all the energy time-histories and show that energy balance is achieved.

CHAPTER 4: BASIC CONCEPTS AND GENERAL DESIGN REQUIREMENTS FOR STRUCTURES WITH PASSIVE ENERGY DISSIPATING SYSTEMS

4.1 INTRODUCTION

Supplemental damping systems are intended to consume a portion of the seismic energy input into a structure. These devices are often referred to as "mechanical dampers". This mechanical energy dissipation reduces the energy dissipation demand on the structural system, thereby reducing its dynamic response during a major earthquake. Research on passive energy dissipation systems started about 30 years ago in New Zealand (Kelly et al. 1972, Skinner et al. 1975).

Supplemental damping systems are often used in conjunction with lateral load-resisting elements, such as bracing members and walls that can also be effective in resisting wind loading. Unless the supplemental damping system is specifically designed to counter wind vibration, a basic design requirement is to ensure that design wind loads are resisted elastically by the adjoining elements of the dampers and/or the main elements of the structure. In other words, for seismic applications, supplemental damping systems are not expected to be active under design wind loads because of the potential residual displacements that can occur at the end of the vibration. Supplemental damping systems are usually distributed throughout a structure to absorb either the kinetic or strain energy transmitted from the ground into the primary structure.

4.2 ACTIVE, SEMI-ACTIVE AND PASSIVE SYSTEMS

Supplemental damping systems can be divided into three wide categories: *active*, *semi-active* and *passive systems*. The main differences among these three classes of systems are discussed briefly in this section.

Active systems are designed to monitor the current state of the structure at a given time, process this information and, in a short time, apply a set of internal forces to modify this state in a more desirable one. Typically, an active control system is composed of three integrated components: i) a *monitoring system* that is able to sense the state of the structure and to record the associated data through an electronic data acquisition system; ii) a *control system* that receives the data from the monitoring system and decides on the countermeasures to be applied and iii) an *actuating system* that physically applies these countermeasures to the structure. Therefore, active systems require a continuous external power source to operate properly.

This dependence on external power sources has been a significant limitation on the seismic application of active systems. During a strong earthquake, the electric transmission and distribution systems can fail. Even backup electrical generating systems can be damaged. Furthermore, the control algorithm may become unstable during strong seismic shaking and/or operating conditions. These concerns have limited the implementation of active and semi-active systems for seismic control of civil engineering structures world wide. Japan is the only exception where active systems have been implemented in several buildings (Connor 2003).

Semi-active systems are in the same category as active systems except that they require a relatively small amount of external energy without the need for a global monitoring system. The control is limited to modifying the local properties of the dampers, such as the geometry of the orifices in a fluid damper, which eliminates the possibility of instability. Because of this low dependence on external power sources and the removal of instability concerns, research on semi-active systems has intensified in recent years. These systems, however, have not yet enjoyed widespread applications in North America and Europe.

Passive systems, on the other hand, are intended to operate without external power supply, actuators, or computers. By definition, passive systems have properties that cannot be modified during the seismic response of the structure. Since seismic input energy is contained in a relatively narrow frequency band, passive systems have been shown to be effective, robust and economical solutions. The implementation of passive systems has outdistanced significantly the implementation of active systems. Active systems will not be discussed further in this book. The reader is referred to other references to learn more about active and semi-active systems (e.g. Connor 2003).

4.3 TYPES OF PASSIVE ENERGY DISSIPATING SYSTEMS

As shown in Table 4-1, passive energy dissipating systems can be divided into three different categories: *displacement-activated* devices, *velocity-activated* devices, and *motion-activated* devices. Note that some systems, such as viscoelastic dampers, can be both displacement- and velocity-activated. Viscoelastic dampers are discussed in Chapter 6.

Displacement-activated devices dissipate energy through the relative displacements that occur between their connected points. These dampers are usually independent of the frequency of the motion. Also, the forces generated by these devices on the structural elements are usually in phase with the internal forces resulting from shaking. Therefore, the maximum forces generated by the dampers occur simultaneously with the maximum internal forces that arise at the end of a vibration cycle corresponding to the peak transient deformations of the structure. Typical dampers falling in this category include metallic dampers, friction dampers and self-centering dampers.

Table 4-1: Categories of Passive Energy Dissipating Systems

Displacement-Activated	Velocity-Activated	Motion-Activated
Metallic Dampers	Viscous Dampers	Tuned-Mass Dampers
Friction Dampers		
Self-Centering Dampers		
Viscoelastic Dampers		

Figure 4.1 shows a metallic damping system consisting of triangular steel plates that deform in flexure. This Added Damping and Added Stiffness (ADAS) system, originally manufactured by Bechtel Corporation, is installed between the apex of chevron bracing elements and the underside of the roof beam. This system dissipates energy through the relative horizontal displacement between the apex of the braces and the roof beam. Metallic dampers are discussed in Chapter 5.

Figure 4.2 shows an example of a friction damping system installed at the intersection of steel cross bracing elements in a reinforced concrete framed structure. This system, manufactured by Pall Dynamics Ltd., dissipates energy through the sliding of superposed slotted plates. Sliding is initiated when the tensile and compressive forces in the adjacent bracing elements exceed the frictional capacity of the damper. The normal forces at the sliding interfaces are provided by high strength steel bolts. Friction dampers are discussed in Chapter 5.

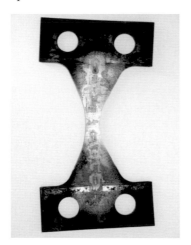

Figure 4.1 Example of Metallic Damping System: ADAS Damper

Figure 4.3 shows an example of the application of a self-centering system to steel moment-resisting framed structures. This Post-Tensioned Energy Dissipating (PTED) steel frame concept, proposed by Christopoulos et al. (2002a, 2002b), is able to return to the zero-force zero-displacement point at every cycle and at the end of the seismic loading. Instead of welding the beam to the column, the moment-resisting connection is provided by a post-tension (PT) force at each floor through high strength bars or tendons located at mid-depth of the beam. Four symmetrically placed energy-dissipating (ED) bars are also included at each connection to provide energy dissipation under flexural cyclic loading. These ED bars are threaded into couplers, which are welded to the inside face of the beam flanges and of the continuity plates in the column for exterior connections and to the inside face of adjacent beam flanges for interior connections. Nonlinear elastic action is introduced when gaps open at each beam-to-column interface. Energy dissipation takes place through yielding of the ED bars once the gap is opened. These two combined actions provide self-centering and energy dissipation at each cycle of vibration. Self-centering systems are discussed in Chapter 7.

Figure 4.2 Example of Friction Damping System: Pall Damper

Velocity-activated devices dissipate energy through the relative velocities that occur between their connected points. The force-displacement response of these dampers usually depends on the frequency of the motion. Also, the forces generated by these devices in the structure are usually out-of-phase with the internal forces resulting from shaking. Therefore, the maximum forces generated by the dampers do not occur simultaneously with the maximum internal forces corresponding to the peak transient deformations of the structure. This results in lower design forces for structural members where the devices are installed as well as in lower design forces for the foundations. Typical dampers falling in this category include purely viscous and visco-elastic dampers. Figure 4.4 shows a viscous fluid-type damper, manufactured by ALGA Corporation, installed between the pier and the deck of a bridge span. The damper, used in conjunction with a seismic isolation system, is designed to reduce the longitudinal vibration of the bridge deck once longitudinal relative velocities are built up between the top of the pier and the underside of the bridge deck. Fluid dampers are discussed in Chapter 6.

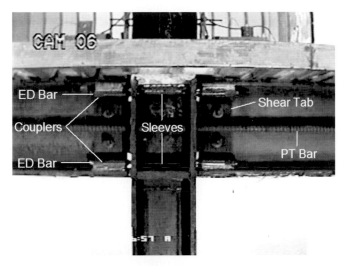

Figure 4.3 Example of Self-Centering System: Post-Tensioned Energy Dissipating Connection (PTED) for Steel Framed Structures

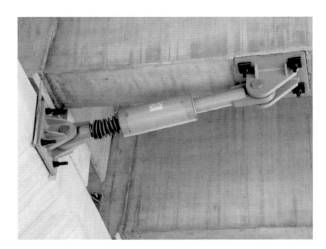

Figure 4.4 Example of Viscous Damping System: ALGA Fluid Damper on a Bridge

A *motion-activated* device disturbs the flow of energy in the structure through the vibration of a secondary system. Tuned-Mass Dampers (TMDs) are examples of motion-activated devices. A TMD is a relatively small secondary mass-spring-dashpot system that is attached to a structure in order to reduce its dynamic response. The secondary system is tuned to be in resonance with the main structure on which it is installed. Under a dynamic excitation, the TMD resonates at the same frequency as the main structure but out-of-phase from it, thereby diverting the input energy from the main structure into itself. The input energy is dissipated by the inertia forces applied by the TMD on the main structure. These systems, usually installed on the roofs of buildings, have been proven effective in reducing wind-induced vibrations in high-rise buildings and floor vibrations induced by occupant activity. Figure 4.5 shows a photograph of the TMD installed in the television antenna of the Canadian National (CN) tower in Toronto, Canada. The TMD, installed during the construction of the tower in 1973, is used to reduce the wind vibration of the antenna that has its tips at 533 m from the ground. Only recently have TMDs been considered for the seismic design of structures. Tuned-mass dampers are discussed in Chapter 8.

Figure 4.5 Tuned-Mass Damper (TMD) in Television Antenna of CN Tower (photo printed with the permission of Canada Lands Company CLC Ltd.)

4.4 INFLUENCE OF PASSIVE ENERGY DISSIPATING SYSTEMS ON ENERGY BALANCE

As discussed in Section 3.4, the introduction of a passive energy dissipating system (displacement-activated, velocity-activated or motion-activated) into a structural system perturbs the energy balance during earthquake shaking. If the passive energy dissipating system is well designed, this perturbation will be beneficial to the structure. From a physical point of view, this energy perturbation can best be visualized using once again the rain flow analogy introduced in Section 3.2.

The energy state during seismic shaking of a structure equipped with a displacement-activated energy dissipating system is illustrated in Figure 4.6a. Referring back to the rain flow analogy presented in Figure 3.1, a second critical rain water level is introduced in the strain energy pail. This second critical level is located below the level where the hysteretic energy pail is connected. This second critical rain water level represents the critical amount of strain energy that is absorbed by the structure when the supplemental dampers are activated. Once this second critical level of rain water in the strain energy pail is reached, some of the rainwater is drained permanently into a supplemental damping energy pail, thereby reducing the total energy flow into the structure.

The energy state of a structure equipped with a velocity-activated energy dissipating system during seismic shaking is illustrated in Figure 4.6b. Referring back to the rain flow analogy presented in Figure 3.1, the presence of the dampers causes an increase of flow loss in the two-way oscillating pump connecting the kinetic energy pail to the strain energy pail. This supplemental energy loss is symbolized by the rain water collected in a supplemental damping pail, thereby reducing once more the total energy flow into the structure.

The energy state of a structure equipped with a motion-activated energy dissipation system such as a TMD is illustrated in Figure 4.7. Referring back to the rain flow analogy presented in Figure 3.1, the introduction of a TMD draws a portion of the kinetic energy from the main system into a TMD kinetic energy pail. This diverted kinetic energy is then pumped from the TMD kinetic energy pail into the TMD strain energy pail, similarly to the main structure (see discussion about Figure 3.1). Through this secondary two-way pump, losses in flow representing the energy dissipated through viscous damping in the TMD accumulate in the TMD viscous damping pail. If the secondary system is perfectly tuned, the opening between the main system's kinetic energy pail and the secondary system's kinetic energy pail is large enough that all the seismic input energy falls directly into the TMD kinetic energy pail, without any energy being pumped into the main structure's strain energy pail. This perfect tuning, which can be achieved only under well defined excitation, is further discussed in Chapter 8.

Mathematically, the absolute energy balance equation derived in Chapter 3, i.e. Equation (3.26), is modified by the introduction of a passive supplemental damping system (energy related to static loads $E_{st}(t)$ is neglected) as follows:

$$E_k^a(t) + E_{vd}(t) + E_a(t) + E_{sd}(t) = E_{in}^a(t) \tag{4.1}$$

where the term $E_{sd}(t)$ represents the energy dissipated by the supplemental damping system from the beginning of the earthquake up to time t.

It is very important to understand that for design purposes, the most desirable response of a structure equipped with a passive energy dissipating system is not necessarily associated with maximum energy dissipation by the dampers. This can be seen by defining the vibrational energy $E_{vb}(t)$, which corresponds to the portion of the input energy at time t that has not been dissipated by viscous damping or by the supplemental damping system and that can potentially cause damage to the structure. The main structure is therefore best protected when $E_{vb}(t)$ is minimized at all times.

From Equation (4.1) and Figure 4.6, it can be seen that the vibrational energy is equal to the sum of the kinetic energy and absorbed energy flowing in the system at time t:

$$E_{vb}(t) = E_k^a(t) + E_a(t) \tag{4.2}$$

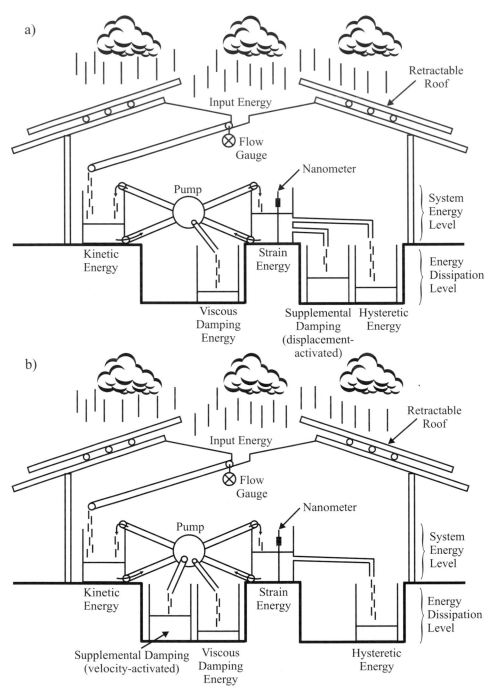

Figure 4.6 Rain Flow Analogy of a Structure with: a)Displacement Activated System and b)Velocity Activated System

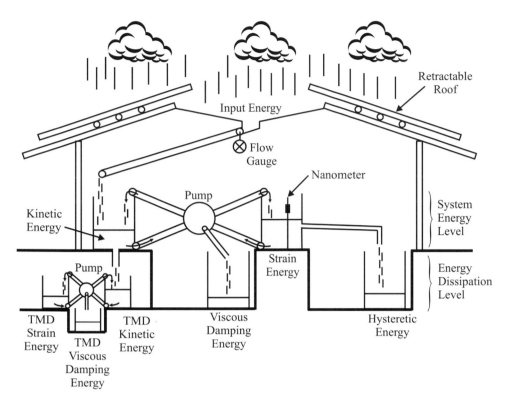

Figure 4.7 Rain Flow Analogy of a Structure with a Tuned-Mass Damper (TMD)

From Equations (4.1) and (4.2), the vibrational energy is also equal to the difference between the seismic input energy and the sum of the energy dissipated by viscous damping in the main structural elements and the supplemental dampers.

$$E_{vb}(t) = E_{in}^{a}(t) - E_{sd}(t) - E_{vd}(t) \qquad (4.3)$$

Equation (4.3) clearly shows that maximizing the energy dissipated by the supplemental dampers does not necessarily lead to a minimum vibrational energy, since the amount of input energy can also increase significantly. Therefore, the design strategy resides in minimizing the difference between the seismic input energy and the energy dissipated by the dampers. This result leads also to the conclusion that for design purposes, the optimum properties of the passive energy dissipating system selected depend on both the properties of the ground motion and of the structural system.

4.5 GENERAL GUIDELINES FOR THE DESIGN AND ANALYSIS OF STRUCTURES WITH PASSIVE SUPPLEMENTAL DAMPING SYSTEMS

The development of guidelines for the design and analysis of structures equipped with passive damping systems has been slow, considering the wide-spread application of this emerging technology during the last decade. In North America and Europe, the only specific guidelines related to passive energy dissipating systems can be found in the FEMA-356 (ASCE 2000) and FEMA-450 (BSSC 2003) documents. These guidelines specify general requirements on the type of analyses and design procedures that should be conducted and on the testing program that should be undertaken on prototype dampers prior to their installation in buildings and other structures. A brief review of the major highlights of these guidelines is presented in the following sections.

4.5.1 FEMA-356 Analysis Procedures

The first general requirements of FEMA-356 pertain to the maximum displacement or velocity that the dampers and their connections should be able to sustain, as shown in Table 4-2, in order to take into account uncertainties in the design ground motions, analysis procedures and effects of other loads. The maximum displacement or velocity is obtained by increasing (1.3 or 2 times) the maximum displacement or velocity computed under the BSE-2 design ground motion (Section 2.3.2), and depends on the level of redundancy provided by the supplemental damping system. Note that it is acknowledged that the amplification factors suggested by FEMA-356 are based on judgment.

Linear or nonlinear procedures can be used to analyze the seismic response of a structure equipped with passive energy dissipating systems. FEMA-356 permits the use of linear analysis procedures provided that the following four criteria are met:

- The main structural elements (excluding the dampers) remain elastic under the design hazard level.

- The effective first mode damping ratio provided by the dampers to the structure does not exceed 30% of critical.

- The secant stiffness of each damper at its calculated maximum displacement is included in the model of the structure equipped with supplemental dampers.

- The dampers are included in the model of the structure when evaluating its regularity.

Two types of linear analysis procedures can be used: the linear static analysis method (Section 2.2.3) and the linear dynamic analysis method (Section 2.2.4). For displacement-activated dampers, FEMA-356 permits the use of the linear static analysis method provided that the following two additional criteria are met:

- The ratio of maximum resistance in each storey, in the direction under consideration, to the storey shear demand computed using the static linear method (Equations (2.3) and (2.4)) shall be between 80% and 120% of the average value of this ratio for all stories of the structure.

- The maximum force induced in all energy dissipation devices in a storey calculated at the displacements expected under the BSE-2, in the considered direction, shall not exceed 50% of the resistance provided by the other structural elements in the storey.

Table 4-2: Design Maximum Displacement or Velocity for Passive Dampers

Conditions	Damper Type	Maximum Design Displacement/Velocity
Four or more dampers in a storey in one principal direction of the building	Displacement-Activated	130% of maximum displacement under BSE-2 earthquake
Minimum of two dampers on each side of the storey center of rigidity	Velocity-Activated	130% of maximum velocity under BSE-2 earthquake
All other cases	Displacement-Activated	200% of maximum displacement under BSE-2 earthquake
	Velocity-Activated	200% of maximum velocity under BSE-2 earthquake

For velocity-activated dampers, FEMA-356 permits the use of the linear static analysis method provided that the maximum force induced in all energy dissipation devices in a storey, in the direction under consideration, shall not exceed 50% of the resistance provided by the other structural elements in the storey at the displacements expected under the BSE-2.

Note that, when evaluating the storey shear demand, the seismic coefficient C_S in Equation (2.3) needs to be reduced to take into account the increased level of damping provided by the energy dissipating system. FEMA-356 provides equations to compute this added damping and the associated reduction factor. Similar equations are derived in Chapters 5, 6 and 9.

FEMA-356 recommends that the design of the structural elements be carried out for three different stages of the seismic response. The first stage corresponds to the time when the structure is at maximum displacement. This design stage will be critical for a structure equipped with displacement-activated dampers. The second stage corresponds to the time when the structure is at maximum velocity and zero displacement. This design stage could be critical for a structure equipped with velocity-activated dampers. The final stage corresponds to the time when the structure experiences maximum acceleration, which corresponds to maximum inertia loads being applied to the structure along with the corresponding damper forces. The magnitude of the damper forces to be applied in conjunction with maximum inertia loads depends on the amount of equivalent viscous damping in the system. This equivalent viscous damping creates a phase between maximum acceleration, zero velocity and maximum displacement under sinusoidal response at the natural period of the structure.

When a linear dynamic analysis method is used, a modified design response spectrum that takes into consideration increased level of damping provided by the energy dissipating system is used to characterize the ground motion input.

For cases where FEMA-356 recommends using nonlinear analysis procedures, either the static nonlinear analysis method (Section 2.4.4) or the nonlinear dynamic analysis method (Section 2.6) should be used.

4.5.2 FEMA-450 Design Procedures

Chapter 15 of the 2003 NEHRP recommended provisions contained in the FEMA-450 document contains guidelines for the design of structures equipped with passive supplemental energy dissipating systems. These design guidelines address all types of passive supplemental damping systems, such as hysteretic, viscous and viscoelastic dampers. The background studies that have led to the development of these design procedures are described in Ramirez et al. (2001, 2002a, 2002b) and Whittaker et al. (2003).

The design philosophy of the NEHRP recommended provisions is centered on the design of a Seismic-Force-Resisting-System (SFRS) that is independent of the supplemental damping system and that is able to provide a complete lateral load path without the supplemental damping system. The presence of the damping devices is accounted for by modifying the characteristics of the SFRS, namely its damping and, in the case of hysteretic or visco-elastic dampers, its lateral stiffness characteristics. In other words, the intent is to raise the performance level of the SFRS by using supplemental damping devices. For this purpose, the NEHRP recommended provisions require that the SFRS be designed for a minimum base shear equal to 75% of the conventional design base shear if no supplemental damping system was implemented.

The modelling approach of the NEHRP recommended procedures for both static and dynamic analyses is similar to the FEMA-356 guidelines discussed in the previous section. The SFRS is modeled as an equivalent linear structure based on the effective secant stiffness at the design displacement with increased equivalent viscous damping because of the effect of the supplemental damping devices. The effective damping ratio β_{eff} in the SFRS is obtained from a combination of three separate components:

a) The inherent damping ratio of the SFRS at or just below yield β_I;

b) The hysteretic damping ratio of hysteretic dampers (if applicable) and of the SFRS β_h;

c) The viscous damping ratio of viscous dampers β_v (if applicable).

The inherent damping ratio β_I would typically be the value used in the design of the SFRS if no supplemental damping system was incorporated. The hysteretic damping ratio β_h at a design displacement D is given by:

$$\beta_h = 0.67\left(\frac{T_s}{T_1}\right)(0.64 - \beta_I)\left(1 - \frac{1}{\mu_D}\right) \qquad (4.4)$$

where μ_D is the effective ductility demand of the SFRS at the design displacement, usually taken as 1.5 to 2.0 for a design displacement associated with the Design-Basis Earthquake (DBE) of the NEHRP provisions (Ramirez et al. 2001), $T_S = S_{D1}/S_{DS}$ where S_{DS} is the short period design spectral acceleration associated with the DBE, and S_{D1} is the 1-second period design spectral acceleration associated with the DBE.

The viscous damping ratio provided by viscous dampers β_v at a design displacement, D is given by:

$$\beta_v = \beta_{Vy}\sqrt{\mu_D} \qquad (4.5)$$

where β_{Vy} is the damping ratio provided by viscous dampers at or just below yield of the SFRS.

Although the NEHRP recommended provisions permit the use of nonlinear (static and dynamic) analysis procedures for all structures and the use of the response spectrum procedure for structures incorporating at least two dampers in each storey of the building and for the effective damping ratio in the fundamental mode vibration less than 35% of critical, it includes also an equivalent lateral force analysis procedure for buildings satisfying the following requirements:

- The building contains at least 2 dampers in each storey;

- The effective damping ratio in the fundamental mode of vibration is less than 35% of critical;

- The SFRS does not have plan irregularity as defined in the NEHRP recommended provisions;

- The SFRS incorporates rigid floor diaphragms per the definition in the recommended provisions;

- The height of the structure does not exceed 30 m.

Only the equivalent lateral force procedure is briefly reviewed in this section. The reader is referred to the FEMA-450 document (BSSC 2003) for details of the other design procedures. In the equivalent lateral force analysis procedure, the response of the SRFS is defined by two modes of vibration: a fundamental mode and a *residual* mode. This residual mode is a new concept, used to approximate the combined effects of higher modes that may be significant to storey velocities in the SFRS.

The seismic design base shear V for the SFRS is given by:

$$V = \sqrt{V_1^2 + V_R^2} \geq V_{min} \qquad (4.6)$$

where V_1 is the first mode design base shear, V_R is the residual mode design base shear and V_{min} is the minimum design base shear given by:

$$V_{min} = \frac{V}{B_{v+I}} \geq 0.75V \qquad (4.7)$$

where B_{v+I} is an effective damping reduction factor corresponding to the sum of viscous damping ratio in the fundamental mode (if viscous dampers are used) plus the inherent damping in the SFRS. The relationship between effective damping ratios β_{eff} and damping reduction factors B is given in Table 4-3 and can also be approximated by:

$$B = \frac{4}{(1 - \ln\beta_{eff})} \qquad (4.8)$$

Table 4-3: Damping Reduction Factors Recommended by the 2003 NEHRP Recommended Provisions (After BSSC 2003)

β_{eff}	B	$\dfrac{4}{(1 - \ln\beta_{eff})}$
< 0.02	0.8	0.81
0.05	1.0	1.00
0.10	1.2	1.21
0.20	1.5	1.53
0.30	1.8	1.81
0.40	2.1	2.09
0.50	2.4	2.40
0.60	2.7	2.65
0.70	3.0	2.95
0.80	3.3	3.27
0.90	3.6	3.62
1.00	4.0	4.00

The design process would usually start by developing a trial design of the SFRS based on a minimum design base shear equal to $0.75\ V$ using the equivalent lateral force procedure of the NEHRP recommended provisions for conventional buildings. Having this trial design, the first mode design base shear V_1 can be computed by:

$$V_1 = C_{s1}\overline{W}_1 \qquad (4.9)$$

The first modal weight $\overline{W}_1$ in Equation (4.9) is obtained by:

$$\overline{W}_1 = \frac{\left(\sum\limits_{i=1}^{n} W_i A_i^1\right)^2}{\sum\limits_{i=1}^{n} W_i (A_i^1)^2} \tag{4.10}$$

where W_i is the seismic weight at level i of the building and A_i^1 is the component of the fundamental mode shape corresponding to the lateral relative displacement of level i. The first mode shape is assumed to be linear such that:

$$A_i^1 = \frac{h_i}{h_r} \tag{4.11}$$

where h_i and h_r are the elevations of the ith and the roof level, respectively.

The first mode seismic response coefficient in Equation (4.9), C_{S1}, is given by:

$$\text{For } T_{1D} < T_S \,, \; C_{S1} = \left(\frac{R}{C_d}\right)\frac{S_{DS}}{\Omega_0 B_{1D}}$$

$$\text{For } T_{1D} \geq T_S \,, \; C_{S1} = \left(\frac{R}{C_d}\right)\frac{S_{D1}}{T_{1D}\Omega_0 B_{1D}} \tag{4.12}$$

where T_{1D} is the effective fundamental period at the design displacement associated with the DBE, R is the force reduction factor associated with the SFRS, Ω_0 is the overstrength factor associated with the SFRS, C_d is the deflection amplification factor associated with the SFRS and B_{1D} is the total effective first mode damping reduction factor at the DBE design displacement.

Equation (4.12) is based on the assumption that for the equivalent lateral force analysis procedure, the pushover curve of the SFRS with supplemental dampers can be idealized by an elastoplastic curve that intersects the real pushover curve of the system at the DBE roof design displacement D_{1D} as shown in Figure 4.8. It is also assumed that the first mode design base shear V_1 is obtained by conservatively reducing the ultimate strength of the equivalent elastoplastic system V_y by the factor $(\Omega_0 C_d)/R$.

Based on the secant stiffness of the SFRS at the DBE design displacement, the effective fundamental period T_{1D} in Equation (4.12) can be obtained by:

$$T_{1D} = T_1\sqrt{\mu_D} \tag{4.13}$$

where T_1 is the elastic fundamental period of the SFRS with supplemental damping and μ_D is the effective ductility demand of the SFRS under DBE.

From Figure 4.8, the ductility demand in Equation (4.13) can be obtained by:

$$\mu_D = \frac{D_{1D}}{D_y} \tag{4.14}$$

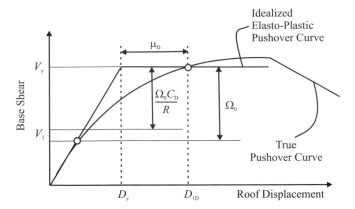

Figure 4.8 Idealized Elastoplastic Pushover Curve for Equivalent Linear Analysis Procedure

where D_{1D} is the first mode design roof displacement under the DBE and D_y is the yield roof displacement of the SFRS with supplemental damping, idealized as an elastoplastic system. From Figure 4.8, D_{1D} is obtained by:

$$\text{For } T_{1D} < T_S \text{ , } D_{1D} = \left(\frac{g}{4\pi^2}\right)\alpha_1\frac{S_{DS}T_{1D}^2}{B_{1D}} \geq \left(\frac{g}{4\pi^2}\right)\alpha_1\frac{S_{DS}T_{1D}^2}{B_{1E}}$$

$$\text{For } T_{1D} \geq T_S \text{ , } D_{1D} = \left(\frac{g}{4\pi^2}\right)\alpha_1\frac{S_{D1}T_{1D}}{B_{1D}} \geq \left(\frac{g}{4\pi^2}\right)\alpha_1\frac{S_{D1}T_{1D}}{B_{1E}}$$

(4.15)

where B_{1D} is the elastic first mode effective damping reduction factor of the SFRS with supplemental damping at the DBE design displacement, B_{1E} is the elastic first mode effective damping coefficient of the SFRS, and D_y (from Figure 4.8) is obtained by:

$$D_y = \left(\frac{g}{4\pi^2}\right)\left(\frac{\Omega_0 C_d}{R}\right)\alpha_1 C_{s1}T_1^2$$

(4.16)

The first modal participation factor α_1 in Equation (4.15) is obtained by:

$$\alpha_1 = \frac{\overline{W}_1}{\sum_{i=1}^{n} W_i A_i^1}$$

(4.17)

The residual mode design base shear V_R is given by:

$$V_R = C_{SR}\overline{W}_R$$

(4.18)

The residual modal weight $\overline{W}_R$ in Equation (4.18) is obtained by:

$$\overline{W}_R = W - \overline{W}_1$$

(4.19)

where W is the total seismic weight of the building.

The residual mode seismic response coefficient in Equation (4.18) C_{SR} is given by:

$$C_{SR} = \left(\frac{R}{C_d}\right)\frac{S_{DS}}{\Omega_0 B_R} \tag{4.20}$$

where B_R is the total effective residual mode damping reduction factor. The design lateral forces at each level i of the SFRS F_i are obtained by:

$$F_i = \sqrt{F_{i1}^2 + F_{iR}^2}$$

$$F_{i1} = W_i A_i^1 \frac{\alpha_1}{\overline{W}_1} V_1 \tag{4.21}$$

$$F_{iR} = W_i A_i^R \frac{\alpha_R}{\overline{W}_R} V_R$$

where F_{i1} is the first mode design lateral force at level i and F_{iR} is the residual mode design lateral force at level i. The residual mode participation factor α_R in Equation (4.21) is given by:

$$\alpha_R = 1 - \alpha_1 \tag{4.22}$$

The component of residual mode at level i in Equation (4.21) A_i^R is given by:

$$A_i^R = \frac{1 - \alpha_1 A_i^1}{1 - \alpha_1} \tag{4.23}$$

Note that the period associated with the residual mode T_R is assumed to be equal to:

$$T_R = 0.4 T_1 \tag{4.24}$$

The design forces in the damping devices and other elements of the supplemental damping system must be determined on the basis of interstorey drifts and velocities at the DBE. The design interstorey drifts at the DBE Δ_D are given by:

$$\Delta_D = \sqrt{\Delta_{1D}^2 + \Delta_{RD}^2} \tag{4.25}$$

where Δ_{1D} and Δ_{RD} are the first and residual mode interstorey drifts at the DBE, respectively. Similarly, the design interstorey velocities at the DBE v_D are given by:

$$v_D = \sqrt{v_{1D}^2 + v_{RD}^2} \tag{4.26}$$

where v_{1D} and v_{RD} are the first and residual mode interstorey velocities at the DBE respectively, and given by:

$$v_{1D} = 2\pi\frac{\Delta_{1D}}{T_{1D}}$$

$$v_{RD} = 2\pi\frac{\Delta_{RD}}{T_{RD}} \tag{4.27}$$

The main steps of the design according to the equivalent lateral force procedure of the 2003 NEHRP recommended provisions are given below:

1) Calculate the minimum base shear V_{min} according to Equation (4.7).

2) Develop a trial design of the SFRS for V_{min}.

3) Establish the first and residual modal properties according to Equations (4.10), (4.11), (4.17), (4.19), (4.22), (4.23) and (4.24).

4) Select a target first mode supplemental damping value β_{v1} to meet the drift limits of the recommended provisions considering elastic response of the SFRS.

5) Assume a trial value of μ_D (in the range of 1.5 to 2.0) and calculate β_{1D} according to Equations (4.4) and (4.5) and T_{1D} according to Equation (4.13).

6) Calculate B_{1D} according to Table 4-3, C_{S1} according to Equation (4.12) and V_1 according to Equation (4.9).

7) If V_1 is approximately equal to V_{min}, proceed to Step 8, otherwise revise the value of μ_D in Step 5.

8) Calculate D_y according to Equation (4.16), D_{1D} according to Equation (4.15) and μ_D according to Equation (4.14).

9) Calculate B_R according to Table 4-3, C_{SR} according to Equation (4.20) and V_R according to Equation (4.18).

10) Calculate the design base shear V according to Equation (4.6) and the design lateral forces F_i according to Equation (4.21).

11) Design the supplemental dampers for the design interstorey drifts and velocities according to Equations (4.25) to (4.27).

12) Verify the components of the SFRS under the maximum forces generated by the supplemental dampers according to the three different stages of the seismic response defined in Section 4.5.1.

4.5.3 Testing Requirements for Supplemental Dampers

One of the most important requirements included in FEMA-356 and FEMA-450 is the testing of actual supplemental damping devices in order to confirm the force-displacement relationship for the dampers assumed in the design, and to demonstrate the robustness of the dampers in case of extreme seismic loading. These testing requirements are particularly important at this stage of development of passive energy dissipating systems considering the recent increase in the number of implementations of these innovative systems. Two types of testing program are required: *prototype testing* and *production testing*.

In the prototype testing program, two full-size devices of each type and size used in the design need to be tested under a rigorous testing sequence comprising two phases:

a) A first cyclic testing phase at an amplitude and number of cycles expected in the design wind storm. The excitation frequency should be equal to the fundamental frequency of the structure incorporating the dampers. It is recommended that each device be tested for at least 2000 fully reversed cycles.

b) A second cyclic testing phase of 20 fully reversed cycles at a displacement corresponding to the DBE and at a frequency corresponding to the fundamental frequency of the structure incorporating the dampers.

FEMA-356 and FEMA-450 incorporate procedures to determine the effective stiffness and equivalent viscous damping ratio of the dampers from test data, and recommend minimal acceptance criteria.

In the production testing phase, a large number of actual devices are tested under only a few cycles in order to confirm their force-displacement relationship. This testing program should also include the testing of installed devices at regular time intervals.

4.6 DESIGN AND ANALYSIS OF ASYMMETRIC STRUTURES INCORPORATING PASSIVE ENERGY DISSIPATING SYSTEMS

The recommended NEHRP provisions presented in the previous section require using nonlinear analysis procedures for irregular structures incorporating passive damping systems. Although this approach is general, for the case of structures exhibiting significant in-plane mass and/or stiffness eccentricities, three-dimensional analyses are often required, which complicate significantly the design process. Various procedures for the design of asymmetric structures have been proposed recently and are briefly reviewed in this section.

One proposed design procedure consists of counter-balancing the eccentricity of the SFRS by the addition of dampers (Goel 2001, Lin and Chopra 2001). According to this approach, the supplemental dampers are deployed around the perimeter of the building and sized such that their center of shear force has an equal but opposite eccentricity with respect to the center of mass of the building as that of the SFRS with respect to its center of rigidity. Wu et al. (1997) proposed a similar approach through the results of a parametric study to evaluate the optimum in-plane distribution of viscoelastic dampers.

Several investigators (Zhang and Soong 1992, Li et al. 1996, Takewaki et al. 1999, Lavan and Levy 2004) evaluated the optimum placements of various types of passive dampers in asymmetric buildings through the minimization of objective functions. Although the optimum distributions obtained varied depending on the objective functions used, most optimum solutions involve the incorporation of supplemental damping along the perimeter of buildings.

CHAPTER 5: METALLIC AND FRICTION (HYSTERETIC) DAMPERS

5.1 INTRODUCTION

Metallic and friction dampers belong to the category of displacement-activated supplemental damping systems. Metallic dampers take advantage of the hysteretic behaviour of metals when deformed into the post-elastic range to dissipate energy. Friction dampers, on the other hand, dissipate the seismic energy by friction that develops at the interface between two solid bodies sliding relative to each other.

Both types of dampers exhibit hysteretic behaviour that can be idealized by an elastic-perfectly plastic load-displacement relationship, as shown in Figure 5.1.

For a metallic damper, the load F_a in Figure 5.1 is the load that activates the damper, which corresponds to the *yield load* of the damper. For a friction damper, F_a corresponds to the *slip load* of the damper. Note also that for most friction dampers, the elastic stiffness $\bar{k}$ is usually very steep and the behaviour is more associated with a rigid-perfectly plastic response. Most friction dampers, however, are used in a bracing configuration, and the elastic stiffness can be associated with the stiffness of the connecting bracing elements. In this chapter, metallic and friction dampers will be referred to as *hysteretic dampers* when discussing common properties or response behaviour.

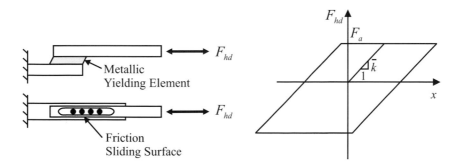

Figure 5.1 Idealized Load-Displacement Relationship for Metallic and Friction Dampers

5.2 BASIC DYNAMIC RESPONSE OF STRUCTURES WITH HYSTERETIC DAMPERS

To begin the study of the effect of hysteretic dampers on the dynamic response of structures, a generic hysteretic device is added to a simple single-degree-of-freedom linear system subjected to ground acceleration $\ddot{x}_g(t)$, as shown in Figure 5.2.

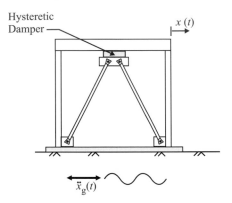

Figure 5.2 Single-Degree-of-Freedom System Incorporating Hysteretic Damper

The equation of motion for the combined system can be written as:

$$m\ddot{x}(t) + c\dot{x}(t) + kx(t) + F_{hd}(t) = -m\ddot{x}_g(t) \tag{5.1}$$

where m, c and k are the mass, the equivalent viscous damping constant and the lateral stiffness of the structure, respectively; $x(t)$, $\dot{x}(t)$ and $\ddot{x}(t)$ are the relative displacement, velocity and acceleration, respectively; $F_{hd}(t)$ is the nonlinear horizontal force provided by the hysteretic damper.

Assume for illustrative purposes that the original structure has no inherent viscous damping. The force-displacement relationship for the hysteretic damper is shown in Figure 5.1.

The structure is subjected to harmonic base excitation given by:

$$\ddot{x}_g = a_g \sin \omega_g t = -\frac{p_0}{m} \sin \omega_g t \tag{5.2}$$

where ω_g is the ground excitation circular frequency, a_g is the peak ground acceleration and p_0 the amplitude of the equivalent applied load.

By nonlinear time-history dynamic analyses, the amplitude of the steady-state response can be obtained. If the amplitude of the response is normalized with respect to the excitation amplitude, the different effects of the added hysteretic damper on the response of the main structure can be seen.

First, the frequency ratio σ is defined as:

$$\sigma = \frac{\omega_g}{\omega_0} \tag{5.3}$$

where:

$$\omega_0 = \sqrt{\frac{k + k_d}{m}} \tag{5.4}$$

and where ω_0 is the natural circular frequency of the structure equipped with the damper before the damper is activated, k is the lateral stiffness of the bare frame and k_d is the lateral stiffness provided by the added damper before it is activated.

The equivalent static lateral displacement of the structure x_{st} is defined as:

$$x_{st} = \frac{p_0}{k} \tag{5.5}$$

Finally, the lateral deflection of the system required to activate the hysteretic damper x_0 can be expressed in terms of the activation load of the damper:

$$x_0 = \frac{F_{lat}}{k_d} \tag{5.6}$$

where F_{lat} is the horizontal lateral load that activates the damper.

In Figure 5.3, the amplitude of the response A normalized by x_{st} is shown for systems with $k_d/k = 0.55$ for different values of x_{st}/x_0. The ratio x_{st}/x_0 can be expressed as:

$$\Lambda_{hd} = \frac{x_{st}}{x_0} = \frac{k_d}{k}\frac{p_0}{F_{lat}} \tag{5.7}$$

The hysteretically damped system's parameter Λ_{hd} is expressed as a function of both the lateral stiffness of the added damper with respect to the stiffness of the original structure (k_d/k) and of the activation load of the damper relative to the amplitude of the applied excitation (p_0/F_{lat}).

As can be seen in Figure 5.3 (for $k_d/k = 0.55$) for values of Λ_{hd} above 0.85, the apparent natural frequency of the system with the hysteretic damper is similar to that of the initial system. The effect of the added damper is similar to an increase in the amount of viscous damping, with lower amplitudes of vibration for lower values of Λ_{hd}. However, for values of Λ_{hd} below 0.85, the apparent natural frequency of the system is affected by the addition of the hysteretic damper. The effect of the added damper is both to increase the amount of damping in the system and to alter its dynamic properties. The amount of damping also increases for decreasing values of Λ_{hd}. When Λ_{hd} is lower than 0.15, the natural period of the system becomes similar to that of the fully braced system. In this range, however, lower values of Λ_{hd} result in higher response amplitudes. In Figure 5.3, the system corresponding to the value of $\Lambda_{hd} \approx 0.45$, which exhibits the lowest response

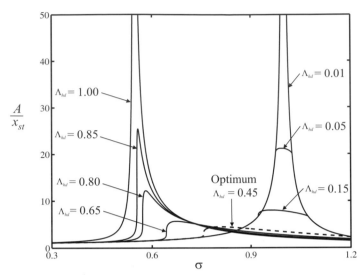

Figure 5.3 Steady-State Response Amplitude of Single-Degree-of-Freedom System with Hysteretic Damper under Harmonic Base Excitation, $k_d/k = 0.55$

amplitude, is shown in dashed lines. The theoretical derivation leading to this optimal value is presented in the following paragraphs.

Based on the above numerical results, the addition of hysteretic dampers to a system can be envisioned as having three possible effects:

- The addition of supplemental damping without significantly modifying the dynamic properties of the system ($\Lambda_{hd} \geq 0.85$ in Figure 5.3).

- The addition of supplemental damping along with a modification of the dynamic properties of the system that optimizes the use of the added damper ($\Lambda_{hd} \approx 0.45$ in Figure 5.3).

- The addition of supplemental damping along with a significant effect on the dynamic properties of the system. This modification is the equivalent of adding a brace to the system ($\Lambda_{hd} \leq 0.15$).

The optimal use of hysteretic dampers will also be further discussed in the following paragraphs.

5.3 APPROXIMATE EQUIVALENT LINEARIZATION

From the results shown in Figure 5.3, it may be tempting to replace a nonlinear structure equipped with hysteretic dampers by a linear system with equivalent viscous damping. This equivalent viscous damping could be calculated from the amplitude of the nonlinear system at resonance (e.g. Filiatrault 2002). Linearization of the nonlinear system greatly simplifies the problem and provides an approximate estimate of the response of a structure equipped with hysteretic dampers for preliminary assessment or design purposes. This approach is reflected in current design and analysis guidelines for structures incorporating passive energy dissipation systems (ASCE 2000, BSSC 2003), as discussed in section 4.5. It must be clearly understood, however, that this equivalent linearization for structures incorporating hysteretic dampers should be used only for preliminary design and for estimating the dynamic response. The addition of this equivalent viscous damping will always cause a reduction of the dynamic response of a single-degree-of-freedom system for any seismic input signal. Because of the nonlinear nature of actual hysteretic devices, the results obtained with the linear system with equivalent viscous damping can be non-conservative.

To illustrate this point, consider the two-storey frame shown in Figure 5.4. The natural period of the structure is 1.35 s, and its equivalent viscous damping is assumed to be 2% of critical in each mode of vibration. The structure is rehabilitated at each level with an elastic-perfectly plastic hysteretic damper with the properties shown in the figure. The lateral stiffness provided by the damper is taken as equal to the lateral stiffness or the original structure, i.e. $k_d/k = 1$. The fundamental period of the rehabilitated structure, before the dampers are activated, shortens to 0.96 s because of the added stiffness of the bracing elements. The lateral force corresponding to the onset of yielding (or slipping) of each damper is equal to 30% of the weight of the structure at each floor level. The original frame and rehabilitated structure are subjected to the S00E component of the 1940 El Centro record.

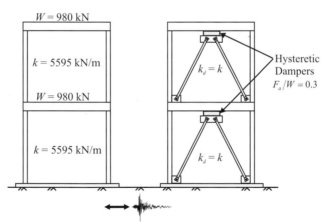

Figure 5.4 Two-Storey Frame Rehabilitated with Elastic-Perfectly Plastic Hysteretic Dampers

Figure 5.5a) shows the relative displacement time-histories for both the original and the rehabilitated structure under the El Centro ground motion. It may be surprising to see that the peak response of the rehabilitated structure is larger than that of the original system. In order words, from a peak response point of view, the introduction of hysteretic devices is detrimental to the original system despite the fact that the first floor damper dissipates a significant amount of energy, as shown in Figure 5.5b), and globally reduces the dynamic response of the structure over a substantial portion of the time-history. To understand why in this case the hysteretic dampers do not reduce the peak seismic response, one can refer to the relative displacement response spectrum shown in Figure 5.6. The fundamental periods associated with three different stages of deformation of the structure are also shown. Initially, the structure is fully braced with a fundamental period of 0.96 s. Once the first level damper is activated, the effective period of vibration lengthens to 1.27s.

a)   b)

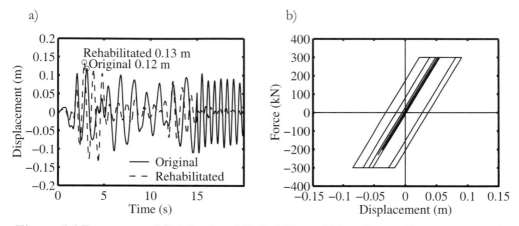

Figure 5.5 Response of Original and Rehabilitated Two-Storey Frame, a)Relative Displacement Time-Histories, b) First Floor Damper Hysteresis

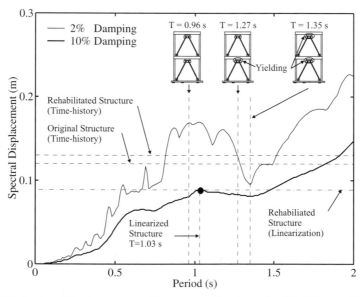

Figure 5.6 Relative Displacement Response Spectra for El Centro Record with Associated Equivalent Periods of Vibration

Finally, when both level dampers are activated, the effective period of vibration reaches its longest possible value (since the structure is assumed to remain elastic) of 1.35s. Note that this period of 1.35s is also equal to the fundamental period of the elastic original structure. By observing the shape of the 2% damped relative displacement response spectrum between periods of 0.96s and 1.35s, it can be seen that the lowest spectral displacement occurs for the period of the elastic structure at 1.35s. Since the second floor damper was not activated under the El Centro record, the rehabilitated structure, as described in Section 2.4.3, can only assume two effective periods that produce spectral displacements which are higher than those of the original structure. Therefore, even if the first level hysteretic damper is activated and increases the effective damping level, the maximum response of the rehabilitated structure may remain higher than that of the original structure. It is interesting to note in Figure 5.6 that the equivalent period corresponding to the peak response of the rehabilitated structure is very close to 1.27s, corresponding to the equivalent period when the first level damper is activated.

A linearization of the structure can be made by computing the effective period of vibration and the equivalent viscous damping for an equivalent single-degree-of-freedom system. For this purpose, a pushover analysis of the rehabilitated structure is carried out under a lateral load distribution consistent with the first mode shape of the structure in its fully braced condition. This lateral load distribution corresponds to 38% of the total lateral load applied on the first floor level and 62% on the second floor level. The relationship between the base shear and the effective lateral displacement, taken at 81% of the height of the structure corresponding to the center of gravity of the applied loading, is shown in Figure 5.7.

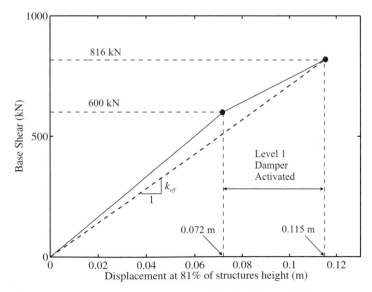

Figure 5.7 Push-Over Analysis of Rehabilitated Structure

From Figure 5.7, the effective lateral stiffness of the structure can be calculated graphically:

$$k_{eff} = \frac{816}{0.115} = 7096 \ kN/m \tag{5.8}$$

From Equation (2.9), the effective period of the structure T_{eff} can be computed using the effective lateral stiffness k_{eff} and the first modal weight of the structure W_1 which is equal to 95% of its total weight:

$$T_{eff} = 2\pi \sqrt{\frac{W_1}{gk_{eff}}} = 1.03s \tag{5.9}$$

The equivalent viscous damping ratio ξ_{eq} provided by the hysteretic damper can be computed by applying Equation (2.8). For a bi-linear system, such as shown in Figure 5.7, this expression can be reduced to:

$$\xi_{eq} = \frac{2(1-\alpha)(\mu_\Delta - 1)}{\pi\mu_\Delta(\alpha\mu_\Delta - \alpha + 1)} \tag{5.10}$$

where α is the ratio of the lateral stiffness once the first level damper is activated to the initial lateral stiffness, and μ_Δ is the global displacement ductility at maximum response. From Figure 5.7, these two quantities are computed as $\alpha = 0.52$ and $\mu_\Delta = 1.55$.

Substituting back in Equation (5.10), the equivalent viscous damping provided by the friction damper is computed as $\xi_{eq} = 8\%$ of critical. The initial equivalent viscous damping of the structure must then be added to obtain the total corrected equivalent viscous damping ratio $\xi_{eq} = 10\%$ of critical.

Figure 5.6 shows the 10% damped relative displacement response spectrum for the El Centro record. At the effective period of 1.03 s, the response of the linearized rehabilitated system is 0.089 m, which is 25% lower than the response obtained from a nonlinear analysis of the rehabilitated structure. This linearized response is even lower than the elastic response of the initial structure.

This example highlights the fact that nonlinear time-history dynamic analyses are required in order to fully assess the effects of hysteretic supplemental damping devices on the dynamic response of civil engineering structures.

5.4 STUDY OF A NONLINEAR MECHANICAL SYSTEM INCORPORATING HYSTERETIC DAMPERS

5.4.1 Scope

An insight into the dynamic characteristics of structures equipped with hysteretic dampers can be gained by studying the steady-state response of an analogous nonlinear single-degree-of-freedom (SDOF) oscillator subjected to harmonic excitation. This approach has been used extensively to characterize the behaviour of nonlinear SDOF systems exhibiting various hysteretic models (Caughey 1960, Jennings 1964, Iwan 1965,

Masri 1975, Iwan and Gates 1979, Capecchi and Vestroni 1985, DebChaudhury 1985, Badrakhan 1988). Although seismic excitation has much broader frequency content than harmonic motion, it can be assumed that when a structure is excited by seismic loading, large portions of its response may be characterized by a quasi-resonant state at its effective fundamental period of vibration.

The study carried out in this section is particularly useful in revealing the non-dimensional parameters governing the response of a simple structure equipped with hysteretic dampers. By extension, these same parameters will be useful in developing a strategy for obtaining the load that activates the damper in order to minimize the seismic response of the structure, as discussed later in this chapter.

5.4.2 Derivation of Closed-Form Frequency Response Function

Consider, as shown in Figure 5.8a), a single storey hysteretically damped structure excited by a harmonic base acceleration:

$$\ddot{x}_g(t) = a_g \cos(\omega_g t) \tag{5.11}$$

where a_g and ω_g are respectively the amplitude and the circular frequency of the base excitation. Provided that the bracing elements connecting the hysteretic damper to the main structural elements remain elastic in tension and compression, the structure can be represented by a nonlinear SDOF oscillator of mass m. The relative displacement of the SDOF oscillator with respect to the base is denoted by $x(t)$. The equation of motion of this system is given by:

$$m\frac{d^2x(t)}{dt^2} + k_b \tilde{f}(x, u, t) = -ma_g \cos\omega_g t \tag{5.12}$$

where $\tilde{f}(x, u, t)$ is the hysteretic restoring force normalized by the initial stiffness k_b as shown in Figure 5.9, and is defined by:

$$\tilde{f}(x, u, t) = \begin{cases} x & \text{if} \quad 0 \le x \le x_0 \\ x_0 + \alpha(x - x_0) & \text{if} \quad x > x_0 \end{cases} \tag{5.13}$$

where x is the displacement of the mass relative to the moving base, x_0 is the lateral deflection required to activate the hysteretic damper, and α is the post-activation stiffness slope ratio, i.e. the ratio of the lateral stiffness of the structure in its unbraced condition k_u (after the damper is activated) to the initial lateral stiffness of the structure in its fully braced condition k_b (before the damper is activated).

Furthermore, a secondary stiffness parameter u is defined in terms of the stiffness values through:

$$u = 1 - \frac{k_u}{k_b} = 1 - \alpha \tag{5.14}$$

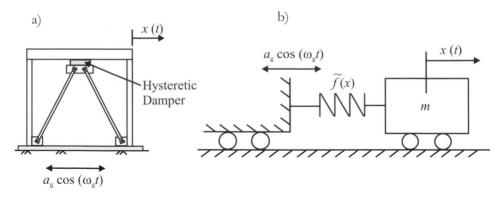

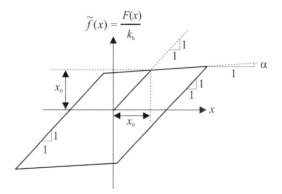

Figure 5.8 a) Single Storey Hysteretically Damped Structure b) Analogous Nonlinear SDOF Oscillator

Figure 5.9 Hysteretic Characteristic of Hysteretically Damped Structure

Finally, the lateral deflection required to activate the hysteretic damper x_0 can be expressed as:

$$x_0 = \frac{F_{lat}}{k_d} \tag{5.15}$$

where F_{lat} is the horizontal lateral load that activates the damper and k_d is the horizontal lateral stiffness provided to the system by the bracing member containing the damper ($k_d = k_b - k_u$).

Note that the inherent damping of the original structure is neglected in order to simplify the analysis and also because it is assumed much smaller than the damping provided by the hysteretic damper.

For the purpose of the derivation, the time variable t is changed to an non-dimensional variable τ using:

$$\tau = \omega_b t \tag{5.16}$$

where ω_b is the natural circular frequency of the fully braced frame (before the damper is activated) given by:

$$\omega_b = \sqrt{\frac{k_b}{m}} \tag{5.17}$$

Carrying out the change of variable and dividing by m, Equation (5.12) becomes:

$$\omega_b^2 \frac{d^2 x(\tau)}{d\tau^2} + \omega_b^2 \tilde{f}(x, u, \tau) = -a_g \cos \sigma \tau \tag{5.18}$$

where σ is the excitation frequency ratio:

$$\sigma = \frac{\omega_g}{\omega_b} \tag{5.19}$$

To simplify the notation, the derivative with respect to τ is denoted by the overdot symbol $\dot{}$ in the following development.

Dividing by ω_b^2, Equation (5.18) becomes:

$$\ddot{x}(\tau) + \tilde{f}(x, u, \tau) = x_{st} \cos \sigma \tau \tag{5.20}$$

where x_{st} is the static deflection defined by:

$$x_{st} = \frac{-m a_g}{k_b} \tag{5.21}$$

Assuming that a steady-state response of the system exists, by analogy to the linear case, the solution to Equation (5.20) is assumed to take the form:

$$x(\tau) = A(\tau) \cos(\sigma \tau - \varphi(\tau)) \tag{5.22}$$

In the case where $\tilde{f}(x, u, \tau)$ is linear and elastic, $A(\tau)$ and $\varphi(\tau)$ are constants and represent respectively the amplitude and phase of the steady-state motion. In the proposed solution, although it is recognized that $A(\tau)$ and $\varphi(\tau)$ are not constant with respect to time, it is assumed that they vary slowly during a cycle of vibration. This method, originally proposed by Krylov and Bogoliubov (Minorski 1947), has been used by many researchers to solve similar frequency response problems for various hysteretic rules. As mentioned earlier, the solution proposed by Caughey (1960) for bilinear elastoplastic systems was the first of such applications and is used here to derive the frequency response of a hysteretically damped SDOF system.

Defining $\theta = \sigma \tau - \varphi(\tau)$ and differentiating Equation (5.22) with respect to τ yields:

$$\dot{x}(\tau) = \dot{A}(\tau) \cos \theta - \sigma A(\tau) \sin \theta + \dot{\varphi}(\tau) A(\tau) \sin \theta \tag{5.23}$$

By analogy to Lagrange's method of variation of a parameter, one may impose the additional restriction:

$$\dot{A}(\tau) \cos \theta + \dot{\varphi}(\tau) A(\tau) \sin \theta = 0 \tag{5.24}$$

Equation (5.24) also assures that the expression of $\dot{x}(\tau)$ has the same form as in the linear case where φ and A are independent of τ:

$$\dot{x}(\tau) = -\sigma A(\tau)\sin\theta \qquad (5.25)$$

Differentiating again Equation (5.25) with respect to τ we obtain:

$$\ddot{x}(\tau) = -\sigma\dot{A}(\tau)\sin\theta - \sigma^2 A(\tau)\cos\theta + \sigma A(\tau)\dot{\varphi}(\tau)\cos\theta \qquad (5.26)$$

Substituting Equation (5.26) into Equation (5.20) we get:

$$-\sigma\dot{A}(\tau)\sin\theta + \sigma A(\tau)\dot{\varphi}(\tau)\cos\theta - \sigma^2 A(\tau)\cos\theta + \tilde{f}\,(A\cos\theta,\,u,\,\tau)$$
$$= x_{st}\cos(\theta + \varphi(\tau)) \qquad (5.27)$$

Equations (5.24) and (5.27) are used to define a system of two equations for two unknowns $A(\tau)$ and $\varphi(\tau)$:

First, Equation (5.27) is multiplied by $\sin\theta$ and Equation (5.24) is multiplied by $\sigma\cos\theta$, and the two are subtracted:

$$-\sigma\dot{A}(\tau) - \sigma^2 A(\tau)\sin\theta\cos\theta + \tilde{f}\,(A\cos\theta,\,u,\,\tau)\sin\theta$$
$$= x_{st}\cos(\theta + \varphi(\tau))\sin\theta \qquad (5.28)$$

Then, Equation (5.24) is multiplied by $\sigma\sin\theta$ and added to Equation (5.27) after the latter is multiplied by $\cos\theta$:

$$\sigma A(\tau)\dot{\varphi}(\tau) - \sigma^2 A(\tau)\cos^2\theta + \tilde{f}\,(A\cos\theta,\,u,\,\tau)\cos\theta$$
$$= x_{st}\cos(\theta + \varphi(\tau))\cos\theta \qquad (5.29)$$

Since $A(\tau)$ and $\varphi(\tau)$ are assumed to be slow-varying, they will remain almost constant during one cycle. The time dependence of these two variables can be lifted by taking the averages of Equations (5.28) and (5.29) over one cycle of vibration. In fact, since these two equations are verified for every value of τ, they are also valid for the averages over one cycle. Equations (5.28) and (5.29) averaged over one cycle of θ yield:

$$-2\sigma\dot{A} + \frac{1}{\pi}\int_0^{2\pi}\tilde{f}\,(A\cos\theta,\,u,\,\tau)\sin\theta\,d\theta = x_{st}\sin\varphi \qquad (5.30)$$

and

$$-2\sigma A\dot{\varphi} - \sigma^2 A + \frac{1}{\pi}\int_0^{2\pi}\tilde{f}\,(A\cos\theta,\,u,\,\tau)\cos\theta\,d\theta = x_{st}\cos\varphi \qquad (5.31)$$

where A, φ, $\dot{A}$ and $\dot{\varphi}$ denote the average values of $A(\tau)$, $\varphi(\tau)$, $\dot{A}(\tau)$ and $\dot{\varphi}(\tau)$ over one cycle. Defining:

$$S(A) = \frac{1}{\pi}\int_0^{2\pi}\tilde{f}\,(A\cos\theta,\,u,\,t)\sin\theta\,d\theta \qquad (5.32)$$

and

$$C(A) = \frac{1}{\pi} \int_0^{2\pi} \tilde{f} (A\cos\theta, u, t)\cos\theta d\theta \tag{5.33}$$

Equations (5.30) and (5.31) then become:

$$- 2\sigma\dot{A} + S(A) = x_{st}\sin\varphi$$
$$- \sigma^2 A - 2\sigma A\dot{\varphi} + C(A) = x_{st}\cos\varphi \tag{5.34}$$

The evaluation of $S(A)$ and $C(A)$ is carried out by integrating the force-displacement response (hysteresis) by parts over each linear branch (see Figure 5.9).

Acknowledging that the hysteresis shape is symmetric, the integrals over one full cycle can be carried out over one half cycle only (from $\theta = 0$ to $\theta = \pi$) and multiplied by two.

The amplitude of the steady-state response A is first normalized:

$$\bar{A} = \frac{A}{x_0} \tag{5.35}$$

and $S(A)$ and $C(A)$ are also normalized by A:

$$\bar{C}(A) = \frac{C(A)}{A}$$
$$\bar{S}(A) = \frac{S(A)}{A} \tag{5.36}$$

It has been shown (Caughey 1960) that:

$$\bar{S}(A) = \begin{cases} 0 & \text{for } \bar{A} < 1 \\ \left(-\dfrac{u}{\pi}\sin^2\theta*\right) & \text{for } \bar{A} > 1 \end{cases} \tag{5.37}$$

and

$$\bar{C}(A) = \begin{cases} 1 & \text{for } \bar{A} < 1 \\ \dfrac{1}{\pi}\left(u\,\theta* + (1-u)\pi - \dfrac{u}{2}\sin 2\theta*\right) & \text{for } \bar{A} > 1 \end{cases} \tag{5.38}$$

where

$$\theta* = \cos^{-1}\left(1 - \frac{2(x_0/x_{st})}{(A/x_{st})}\right) \tag{5.39}$$

When the steady-state response is reached, the average values of the derivatives of $A(\tau)$ and $\varphi(\tau)$ over one full cycle $\dot{A}$ and $\dot{\varphi}$ are equal to zero. Recalling Equation (5.34), squaring and adding the two equations eliminates the terms in φ and yields:

$$\sigma^2 = \ \overline{C}(A) \pm \sqrt{(x_{st}/A) - \overline{S}^2(A)} \tag{5.40}$$

Substituting Equations (5.37) and (5.38) into Equation (5.40) leads to the following transcendental steady-state amplitude solution:

$$\sigma^2 = \begin{cases} 1 \pm \dfrac{x_{st}}{A} & \text{for } (\overline{A} \le 1) \\[2em] \dfrac{1}{\pi}\left[u\theta* + (1-u)\pi - \dfrac{u}{2}\sin 2\theta* \right] \pm \sqrt{\left(\dfrac{x_{st}}{A}\right)^2 - \left(\dfrac{u\sin^2\theta*}{\pi}\right)^2} & \text{for } \overline{A} > 1 \end{cases} \tag{5.41}$$

5.4.3 Closed-Form Frequency Response Analysis

For any particular values of u and x_0/x_{st}, σ^2 can be solved for specific values of x_{st}/A using Equation (5.41). The maximum steady-state amplitude, corresponding to a resonance state, occurs where σ has a double root, that is at the point where:

$$\left(\frac{x_{st}}{A}\right)^2 = \left(\frac{u\sin^2\theta*}{\pi}\right)^2 \tag{5.42}$$

Substituting Equation (5.39) into Equation (5.42) yields an explicit expression for the steady-state amplitude of the response at resonance:

$$\frac{A}{x_{st}} = \frac{\dfrac{4u}{\pi}(x_0/x_{st})}{\dfrac{4u}{\pi} - (x_{st}/x_0)} \tag{5.43}$$

Since the steady-state amplitude A is by definition positive, bounded response at resonance occurs provided that:

$$\frac{x_{st}}{x_0} < \frac{4u}{\pi} \tag{5.44}$$

Substituting Equations (5.14), (5.15) and (5.21) into (5.44) yields the following condition on the activation load of the hysteretic damper for bounded response at resonance:

$$\frac{F_{lat}}{W} \ge \frac{\pi}{4}\frac{a_g}{g} \tag{5.45}$$

where W is the seismic weight of the system and g the acceleration of gravity.

From Equation (5.40), the resonant frequency ratio σ_r^2 is given by:

$$\sigma_r^2 = \overline{C}(A) \tag{5.46}$$

The value of the activation load of the hysteretic damper minimizing the amplitude of motion at resonance can be obtained from (see Equation (5.43)):

$$\frac{\partial(A/x_{st})}{\partial(x_0/x_{st})} = 0 \tag{5.47}$$

which leads to:

$$\frac{x_{st}}{x_0} = \frac{2u}{\pi} \tag{5.48}$$

Substituting Equations (5.14), (5.15) and (5.21) into Equation (5.48) provides a closed form expression for the lateral load required to activate the damper F_{lat}^* that minimizes the resonant amplitude:

$$\frac{F_{lat}^*}{W} = \frac{\pi\, a_g}{2g} \tag{5.49}$$

The minimum resonant amplitude A^* can be obtained by substituting Equation (5.48) into Equation (5.43):

$$\frac{A^*}{x_{st}} = \frac{2x_0}{x_{st}} = \frac{\pi}{u} = \frac{\pi k_b}{k_b - k_u} \tag{5.50}$$

Equation (5.50) also reveals that the hysteretic damper will always be activated at resonance regardless of the value of the activation load used, since $A^* > x_0$. The frequency ratio σ_r^*, at which this optimum resonance occurs, can be obtained by substituting Equations (5.48) and (5.50) into Equation (5.46):

$$\sigma_r^* = \sqrt{\frac{1}{2} + \frac{\omega_u}{2\omega_b}} \tag{5.51}$$

where:

$$\omega_u = \sqrt{\frac{k_u}{m}} \text{ and } \omega_b = \sqrt{\frac{k_b}{m}} \tag{5.52}$$

The condition for which the amplitude of the response is at a minimum for a particular excitation frequency ω_g (other than resonance) cannot be found analytically since Equation (5.41) is transcendental, and A/x_{st} cannot be solved for every frequency ratio σ. However, an analysis of the stability of the steady-state solution of a bilinear hysteretic system (Caughey 1960) shows that this system is always stable and that the families of frequency response curves that can be generated from Equation (5.41) are all single valued. Hence a jump phenomenon, which is characteristic of certain nonlinear systems (Nayfeh and Mook 1979), is not expected to occur in this case. Therefore, Equation (5.41) can be symbolically inverted, such as:

$$\frac{A}{x_{st}} = G\!\left(\frac{\omega_g}{\omega_b}, \frac{x_0}{x_{st}}, u\right) \tag{5.53}$$

where G is a single valued function.

The value of the activation load of the hysteretic damper that minimizes the amplitude of the response at any forcing frequency can be obtained by:

$$\frac{\partial G}{\partial(x_0/x_{st})} = 0 \qquad (5.54)$$

which yields a condition such as:

$$\frac{x_0}{x_{st}} = H\left(\frac{\omega_g}{\omega_b}, u\right) \qquad (5.55)$$

where H is also a single valued function.

Substituting Equations (5.14), (5.15) and (5.21) into Equation (5.55) yields a symbolic expression for the optimum value of the activation load of the hysteretic damper F_{lat}^{opt}:

$$\frac{F_{lat}^{opt}}{W} = \frac{a_g}{g}\left(1 - \frac{k_u}{k_b}\right) H\left\{\frac{\omega_g}{\omega_b}, \left(1 - \frac{k_u}{k_b}\right)\right\} \qquad (5.56)$$

or

$$\frac{F_{lat}^{opt}}{W} = \frac{a_g}{g} Q\left(\frac{T_b}{T_g}, \frac{T_b}{T_u}\right) \qquad (5.57)$$

where Q is another single valued function and:

$T_b = 2\pi/\omega_b$ is the natural period of the fully braced frame;
$T_u = 2\pi/\omega_u$ is the natural period of the unbraced frame;
T_g is the period of the ground motion;
a_g is the peak ground acceleration;
g is the acceleration of gravity, and
W is the seismic weight of the structure.

The significance of Equation (5.57) is that it reveals the non-dimensional parameters governing the optimum activation load of the hysteretic damper for a single storey hysteretically damped structure excited by a harmonic ground motion. It can be expected that these same non-dimensional parameters will also play an important role in the optimum response of a structure excited by a general earthquake ground motion. An important conclusion that can be drawn from Equation (5.57) is that the optimum activation load of an hysteretic damper depends on the frequency and amplitude of the ground motion and is not strictly a structural property. Therefore, the anticipated ground motion must be carefully characterized in the design of structures equipped with hysteretic dampers. Finally, Equation (5.57) predicts that the value of the optimum activation load of an hysteretic damper is linearly proportional to the peak ground acceleration.

5.4.4 Numerical Verification of Closed-Form Frequency Response Function

The closed form solutions obtained in the previous section are verified in this section by computing numerically the steady-state response of a single storey hysteretically damped structure. The physical properties of the structure considered are listed in Table 5-1. Based on these properties, the values of $T_b = 1.08$ s, $T_u = 1.99$ s, $u = 0.70$ and $x_{st} = 14.1$ mm can be computed. Table 5-2 presents the different values of the activation load of the hysteretic damper F_{lat} considered in the numerical investigation along with the corresponding values of x_{st}/x_0.

Table 5-1 : Physical Properties of Single Storey Hysteretically Damped Structure

Seismic weight	$W = 445$ kN
Lateral stiffness of fully braced frame	$k_b = 1521$ kN/m
Lateral stiffness of unbraced frame	$k_u = 454$ kN/m
Peak ground acceleration	$a_g = 0.05$ g

Table 5-2 : Lateral Activation Loads of the Hysteretic Damper in the Numerical Verification

F_{lat} (kN)	x_{st}/x_0
17.5 *	0.89
25.7	0.61
35.0 **	0.45
42.9	0.36
51.4	0.30
60.0	0.26

* Minimum activation load for bounded response at resonance (Equation (5.45))

** Activation load minimizing amplitude at resonance (Equation (5.49))

In the numerical study, the hysteretically damped system was excited by a series of harmonic ground acceleration time-histories having constant amplitude a_g and different forcing frequencies ω_g. An integration time-step of 0.01 s was used in all analyses and the amplitude of the steady-state response A was considered to be the motion amplitude after 20 seconds of excitation.

The comparison between the analytical (Equation (5.41)) and numerical solutions is presented in Figure 5.10. The numerical and analytical results are in good agreement. The slight differences between the two results come from the fact that the steady-state condition may not be totally achieved in the numerical analyses after 20 seconds of vibration. From the figure, it is apparent that the resonant frequency increases as the activation load increases. For very low activation loads of the hysteretic damper, the system behaves as an unbraced structure with a resonant frequency ratio given by:

$$\sigma_r = \sqrt{\frac{k_u}{k_b}} = 0.55 \qquad (5.58)$$

For large activation loads of the hysteretic damper, the system behaves as a fully braced frame with $\sigma_r = 1$. Note that the minimum resonant amplitude occurs for an activation load $F_{lat} = 35$ kN, as predicted by Equation (5.49). The frequency ratio σ_r^* at which this optimum resonance occurs is 0.89, as predicted by Equation (5.51). These trends, which are illustrated here on the basis of theoretical calculations, are also reflected in the experimental results reported by Baktash and Marsh (1986).

Figure 5.11 compares the frequency response functions for three values of the lateral activation load of the hysteretic damper $F_{lat} = 17.54, 35$ and 51.4 kN respectively. As the slip load is increased from low values to the optimum value of 35 kN, the response is greatly reduced.

Figure 5.12 presents the values of the activation load of the hysteretic damper minimizing the steady-state amplitude of the response, when the structure is excited by a harmonic ground motion at a frequency ratio of $\sigma = 0.90$. The results are based on a series of numerical analyses. For each value of peak ground acceleration a_g, the activation load to ensure minimum steady-state amplitude is determined by evaluating the amplitude for increments of the lateral activation load of 2 kN. It is apparent that the optimum activation load of the hysteretic damper F_{lat} is linearly proportional to the peak ground acceleration, as predicted by Equation (5.57).

5.4.5 Summary of Study of Analogous Nonlinear Mechanical System

Some valuable insights are obtained from the study of the simple single storey hysteretically damped structure under harmonic excitation:

- A lower bound value of the activation load of the hysteretic damper has been established such that bounded amplitudes occur at resonance (Equation (5.45)).

- The value of the activation load of the hysteretic damper minimizing the amplitude at resonance has been determined along with the frequency at which this optimum resonance occurs (Equations (5.49) and (5.51)). It has also been pointed out that the system is always stable and that a jump phenomenon does not occur.

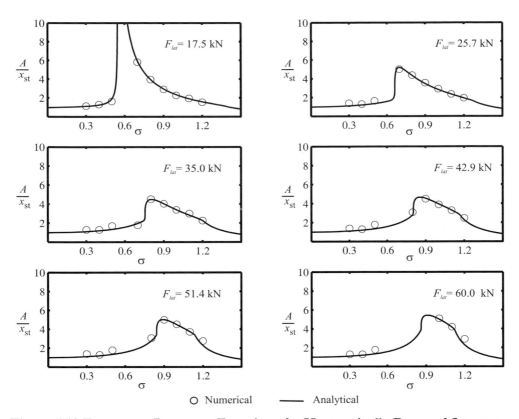

Figure 5.10 Frequency Response Functions for Hysteretically Damped Structures

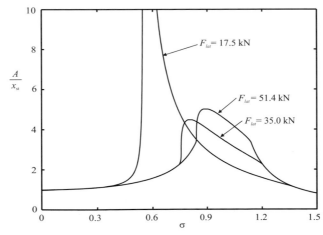

Figure 5.11 Frequency Response Functions for Three Values of Hysteretic
Damper Activation Load

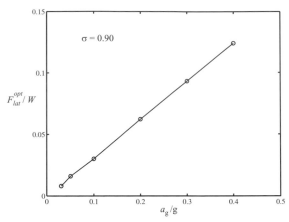

Figure 5.12 Optimum Lateral Activation Load of Hysteretic Damper for Harmonic Ground Motion

- The non-dimensional parameters governing the value of the optimum activation load of the hysteretic damper minimizing the steady-state amplitude for any forcing frequency were determined (Equation (5.57)). It can be expected that similar parameters will also influence the optimum activation load distribution of the array of hysteretic dampers distributed in multi-storey structures under general earthquake loading. These parameters clearly indicate that the optimum activation load of an hysteretic damper is a function of the amplitude and frequency of the ground motion and cannot strictly be defined as a structural property.

5.5 METALLIC DAMPERS

5.5.1 Hysteretic Behaviour of Yielding Steel Elements

When structural steel is stressed beyond its elastic limit σ_y, the material plastifies and exhibits a yielding plateau. If the material is further extended, it enters a strain hardening phase and develops larger stresses than the yield stress. The stress-strain relationship of a steel element subjected to monotonically increasing stress is shown in bold in Figure 5.13. If the material is subjected to cyclic load reversals after it has exceeded the linear elastic range, it exhibits a number of properties. When the material is unloaded, it recovers its elastic modulus E. When the material is loaded in the opposite direction, it starts yielding and softening at a stress lower than the yield stress. This effect is known as the Bauschinger effect (Bannantine et al. 1990). As long as the material is not strained beyond the yield plateau, this cyclic behaviour is repeated with the maximum positive and negative stresses remaining equal to the yield stress $\pm\sigma_y$ and the inelastic straining following the yield plateau (see Figure 5.13). When the material is extended beyond the yield plateau, it still unloads following the initial elastic stiffness E and the Bauschinger effect becomes increasingly pronounced as the maximum strain is increased. In this range of cyclic loading, the yield plateau disappears and the material exhibits a certain post-yield stiffness (see Figure 5.13).

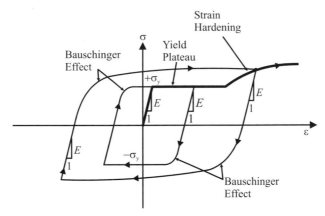

Figure 5.13 Cyclic Stress-Strain Hysteresis of Steel Elements

The actual stress-strain relationship of steel is often approximated by theoretical elastic perfectly plastic or bilinear elastoplastic models. For every cycle in which the material is stressed beyond its elastic limit, the area below the stress-strain curve corresponds to the dissipated hysteretic energy per unit volume that radiates as heat and is unrecoverable. The ability of steel to undergo a large number of inelastic cycles before failing, and therefore to dissipate large amounts of energy, has been used to develop hysteretic dampers that are designed to yield when the structure they are connected to is deformed.

During an earthquake, metallic dampers can be subjected to high strain rates that can affect their mechanical properties and possibly alter the seismic behaviour of the structure. Monjoine (1944) conducted a thorough investigation of the influence of strain rate on the tensile behaviour of mild steel. Test results indicated that the yield stress increases with increasing strain rate, but to a lesser extent in higher strength steels. Within the last few decades, significant research efforts have been devoted to the behaviour of steel members under high strain rate. Most of these investigations reported that the yield strength and tensile (ultimate) strength of steel increase linearly with logarithmically increasing strain rate. It was also recognized that the strain rate had negligible effect on the elastic modulus and the stiffness of steel in the strain-hardening range (Wakabayashi et al. 1984). It was also observed that, as the strain rate increases, the ratio between the ultimate stress and the yield stress decreases, i.e. the ultimate capacity does not increase as much as the yield strength. Higher strength steel was also found to be more susceptible to strain rate effects than lower strength steel (Restrepo-Posada 1993, Restrepo-Posada et al. 1994).

Hysteretic yielding of steel members is a reliable source of energy dissipation that is predictable, repeatable and stable (if buckling of elements is restrained). Furthermore, the hysteretic properties of steel elements are reliable over long periods of time, especially if appropriate measures to protect elements against corrosion are taken.

5.5.2 Geometrical Considerations

Metallic dampers can be used as part of chevron bracing systems as illustrated in Figure 5.14. In this configuration, yielding devices dissipate energy through the relative horizontal displacement between the apex of the chevron and the above floor level. If metallic plates are used, they will act as fixed-fixed beams as shown in Figure 5.14. To maximize the energy dissipation of the device, it is desirable that the plastic moment at any section be reached simultaneously. To achieve this condition, the geometry of the device must be optimized.

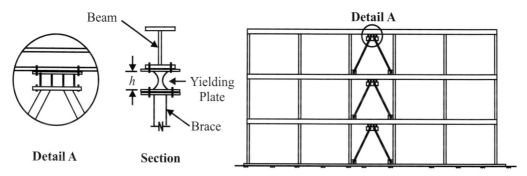

Figure 5.14 Use of Yielding Devices as Part of Chevron Bracing Systems

Consider first a damper made of a single steel plate with a constant width b_0 and a variable depth $d(x)$ as illustrated in Figure 5.15a). When the plastic moment is reached at the ends of the device, the bending moment at any section of the device $M(x)$ is given by:

$$M(x) = \frac{2M_{po}}{h} x = \left(\frac{2}{h}\right)\left(\frac{b_0 d_0^2}{4}\right) F_y\, x\,,\ \text{for } -\frac{h}{2} \leq x \leq \frac{h}{2} \tag{5.59}$$

where M_{po} is the plastic moment at the ends of the device, h is the height of the plate, d_0 is the depth at the ends of the plate, x is the distance taken from the mid-height of the plate, and F_y is the yield strength of the steel.

The plastic moment at any section of the plate $M_p(x)$ is given by:

$$M_p(x) = \frac{b_0\, d(x)^2}{4} F_y \tag{5.60}$$

To ensure simultaneous plastic yielding at all sections, when the plastic moment is reached at the ends of the plate, the moment acting at every section must be equal to the plastic moment of that section. This is achieved by equating Equation (5.59) to

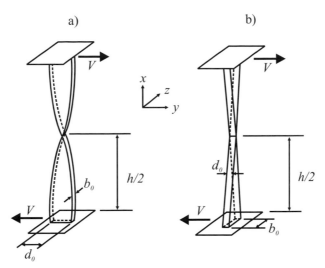

Figure 5.15 Optimum Geometry of Metallic Dampers: a) Constant Width and Variable Depth, b) Constant Depth and Variable Width

Equation (5.60), while neglecting the effect of the axial and shear forces acting on the element. Therefore, the variation of the depth of the metallic damper to maximize energy dissipation is given by:

$$d(x) = d_0 \sqrt{\frac{2x}{h}} \qquad (5.61)$$

This optimum geometry is illustrated in Figure 5.15a). Obviously, from a practical point of view, the depth of the plate can not be zero at mid-height since the plate must also carry the corresponding shear:

$$V = \frac{2M_{po}}{h} \qquad (5.62)$$

Now let's consider a metallic damper made of a single steel plate with a constant depth d_0 and a variable width $b(x)$. The plastic moment at any section of the plate $M_p(x)$ is given by:

$$M_p(x) = \frac{b(x)\, d^2}{4} F_y \qquad (5.63)$$

Again, to ensure plastic yielding simultaneously at all sections, Equation (5.59) is equated to Equation (5.63); the optimum variation of the depth of the plate is then given by:

$$b(x) = \frac{2x}{h}\, b_0 \qquad (5.64)$$

As shown in Figure 5.15b), this optimum geometry results in a linear variation of the width along the height of the plate. Again, from a practical point of view, the width of the device can not be zero at mid-height, as shown in the photograph on the left side of Figure 4.1.

In practice, the second geometry is preferred with d_0 much smaller than b_0 to minimize the possibilities of local buckling and to minimize the thickness of the steel required for uniform yielding along the height of the plate.

5.5.3 Experimental Studies

Since the mid-1970s, significant research effort has been invested on physical testing of yielding devices. In this section, results of experimental studies on the devices that have demonstrated considerable merit are briefly described.

(a) Added Damping - Added Stiffness Systems (ADAS)

The ADAS device originally manufactured by Bechtel Corporation is an evolution of earlier X-plate devices used as damping supports for piping systems (Stiemer et al. 1981). The geometry of the ADAS incorporates several interconnected yielding plates in series. A photograph of an ADAS plate is shown in Figure 4.1.

Extensive investigations on the behaviour of individual ADAS elements and structural systems incorporating ADAS elements have been carried out (Bergman and Goel 1987, Whittaker et al. 1991). As illustrated in Figure 5.16, cyclic tests on a plane frame including gravity loads showed stable hysteretic behaviour for various deformation amplitudes.

The test results indicated that the ADAS elements were capable of sustaining 100 loading cycles at a deformation corresponding to three times the measured yield displacement δ_y without signs of degradation. Based on these tests, it was concluded that ADAS elements can be safely designed for a peak displacement range of up to 10 δ_y.

Note that the apparent stiffening of the hysteresis loops at larger amplitude is due to the coupling between axial and lateral response at large deformations. These geometrical nonlinear effects must be considered at the design stage.

Shake table tests of a three storey, single bay Ductile Moment Resisting Space Frame (DMRSF), having plan dimensions of 3.7 m by 4.9 m and equipped with six ADAS elements made of A36 steel, were also performed by Whittaker et al. (1991). The geometry of the test frame is shown in Figure 5.17.

Table 5-3 presents the measured dynamic characteristics of the test frame with the ADAS system (ADAS) and without the ADAS elements (DMRSF). There is a significant reduction in the fundamental natural period caused by the supplemental stiffness of the chevron bracing and ADAS elements.

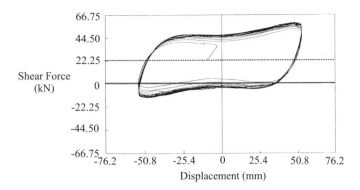

Figure 5.16 Hysteresis Loops of ADAS Elements in a Plane Frame with Gravity Loads (after Whittaker et al. 1991)

Table 5-3 : Dynamic Characteristics of ADAS Test Structure (after Whittaker et al. 1991)

		1st Mode	2nd Mode
DMRSF	Period	0.74	0.22
	Damping ratio (%)	2.10	1.30
ADAS	Period	0.47	0.17
	Damping ratio (%)	3.40	1.70

Several earthquake records were used in the shake table tests. Response comparison with and without the ADAS elements for the 1985 Llolleo, Chile (N10E) earthquake record is shown in Figure 5.18. The beneficial effects of introducing the ADAS elements are evident.

The test structure was also submitted to the 1940 (SOOE) El Centro record. The hysteresis loops obtained from the ADAS elements on all braced bays are shown in Figure 5.19. For the same test, Figure 5.20 presents the global energy time-histories. Again, from these results, the effectiveness of the ADAS elements in dissipating the seismic input energy is evident.

(b) Triangular Added Damping Added Stiffness (TADAS) Systems

Tsai et al. (1993) developed a variation of the ADAS system using triangular metallic plate dampers: Triangular ADAS or TADAS. The TADAS device is similar to the ADAS device, but uses triangular plates, as shown in Figure 5.21. The triangular plates of the TADAS device are rigidly welded to a top plate but are simply connected to a slotted base

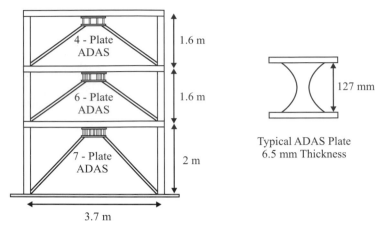

Figure 5.17 Geometry of ADAS Test Structure (from Whittaker et al. 1991, reproduced with the permission of the Earthquake Engineering Research Institute)

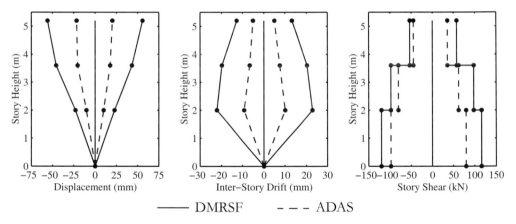

Figure 5.18 Response Comparison for ADAS Test Structure, 1985 Llolleo, Chile (N10E) Earthquake (after Whittaker et al. 1991, reproduced with the permission of the Earthquake Engineering Research Institute)

plate. The main advantage of the TADAS device is that it is not affected by gravity loads because of the slotted holes in the base plate. Also, no rotational restraint is required at the top of the brace connection assemblage. The construction of the TADAS device is however more complicated than that of the ADAS device. Experimental studies have shown that the hysteretic response of TADAS elements is very stable and repeatable without strength degradation (Tsai et al. 1993). Special care must be given to the welding details to avoid premature fractures especially at the areas around the apex of the triangular plates. Large-scale pseudo-dynamic tests also demonstrated the ability of the TADAS elements to significantly improve the seismic response of a steel frame (Tsai 1995).

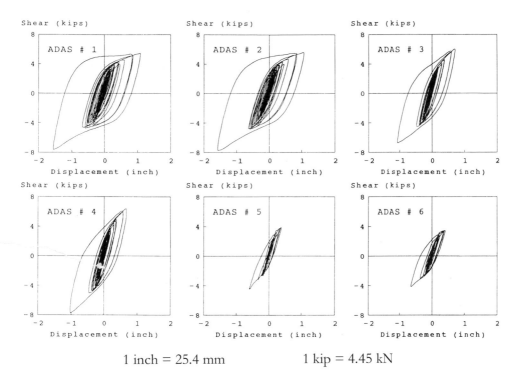

1 inch = 25.4 mm   1 kip = 4.45 kN

Figure 5.19 Hysteresis Loops of ADAS Elements, ADAS-3 Frame, 1940 El Centro S00E (from Whittaker et al. 1991)

1 inch = 25.4 mm

1 kip = 4.45 kN

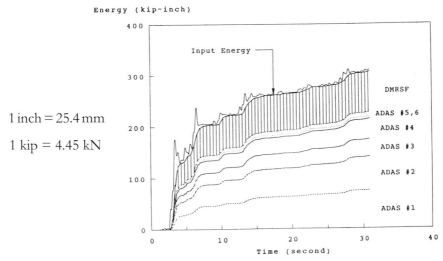

Figure 5.20 Energy Time-Histories, ADAS-3 Frame, 1940 El Centro S00E (from Whittaker et al. 1991)

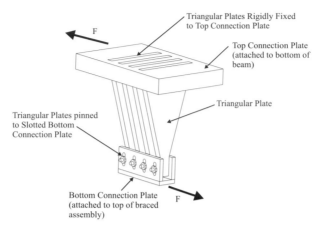

Figure 5.21 TADAS Elements

The concept of triangular yielding plates has also been adapted to diaphragms for slab-on-girder steel bridges (Zahrai and Bruneau 1998).

(c) Lead Extrusion Devices (LED)

In the mid-1970s, metallic dampers that take advantage of the extrusion of lead through orifices have been proposed in New Zealand (Robinson and Greenbank 1976). Figure 5.22 illustrates two different types of LED devices. The first device forces the extrusion of lead through a constricted tube, while the second device uses a bulged shaft that is driven through a lead cylinder. As shown in Figure 5.23, the hysteretic behaviour of LED dampers is essentially rectangular and similar to the hysteresis of yielding steel elements, which maximize energy dissipation for a given applied force and displacement amplitude. In fact, LED dampers have a number of desirable characteristics:

- The hysteretic behaviour is stable and repeatable and is unaffected by the number of load cycles.

- Environmental factors have no significant influence on their behaviour.

- Fatigue is not a major concern since lead is hot worked at room temperature.

- Strain rate has only a minor effect on the hysteretic response.

- Tests have demonstrated insignificant aging effects, as shown in Figure 5.24.

Another shear-type lead damper has been developed in Japan (Sakurai et al. 1992) to prevent pounding of adjacent buildings. As shown in Figure 5.25, the damper is made of a short lead tube that deforms in shear inside an annular steel ring. Nearly perfect rectangular load-deflection response was obtained experimentally for such a device, as shown in Figure 5.26.

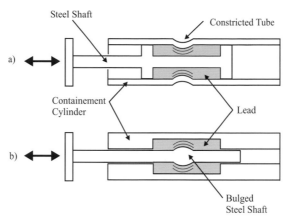

Figure 5.22 Lead-Extrusion Devices: a) Constricted Tube, b) Bulged Shaft (after Robinson and Greenback 1976)

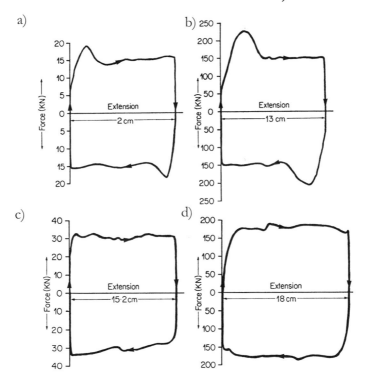

Figure 5.23 Typical Hysteretic Behaviour of LED Dampers at 1 cm/min: a) Constricted Tube: 15 kN, b) Constricted Tube: 150 kN, c) Bulged Shaft: 30 kN, d) Bulged Shaft: 170 kN (from Robinson and Greenback 1976, copyright John Wiley & Sons Ltd., reproduced with permission)

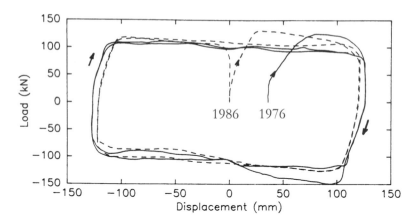

Figure 5.24 Insignificant Aging Effect on LED Dampers (after Robinson and Cousins 1987)

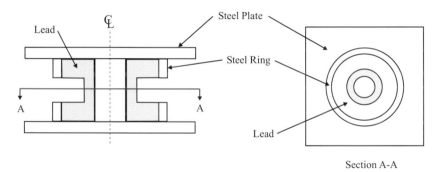

Section A-A

Figure 5.25 Shear-Type Lead Damper to Avoid Pounding of Adjacent Buildings (after Sakurai et al. 1992)

(d) Buckling Restrained Braces (BRBs)

A structural steel element that offers strength and energy dissipation while at the same time exhibiting well-distributed yielding is the buckling-restrained brace (BRB). One such buckling-restrained brace is the unbonded brace, manufactured by Nippon Steel Corporation in Japan. As illustrated in Figure 5.27, the unbonded brace consists of a steel core member, often referred to as the core plate, encased in a steel tube filled with concrete. The steel core carries the axial load while the outer tube, via the concrete, provides lateral support to the core and prevents global buckling. A thin layer of lubricating material along the steel core at the concrete interface eliminates shear transfer and localized strain concentrations during the elongation, while accommodating the longitudinal contraction and expansion of the steel core when it yields in tension and in compression.

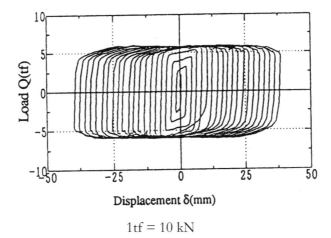

Displacement δ(mm)

1tf = 10 kN

Figure 5.26 Force-Deflection Relationship for Shear-Type Lead Damper (from Sakurai et al. 1992, reproduced with permission from Taylor & Francis)

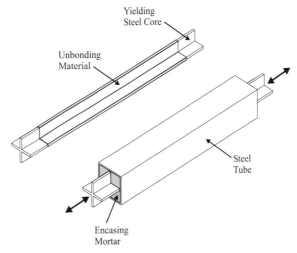

Figure 5.27 Components of an Unbonded Brace

The advantage of buckling-restrained braces over conventional braces is in their ability to carry load, yield, and thus dissipate energy when loaded in both tension and compression. In contrast, conventional braces achieve their full capacity through inelastic yielding when they are loaded in tension, while they buckle without dissipating a substantial amount of energy when loaded in compression. As shown in Figure 5.28, the stable energy dissipation capacity of buckling-restrained braces makes them very attractive for seismic protection applications.

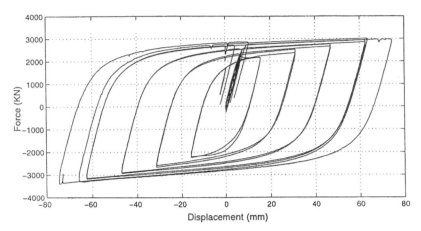

Figure 5.28 Hysteretic Response of Unbonded Brace (from Black et al. 2004, reproduced with permission from the American Society of Civil Engineers)

Cyclic qualification tests have been developed for buckling-restrained braces and are included in the latest *Seismic Provisions for Structural Steel Buildings* (AISC 2005). They include specifications on testing of individual bracing elements as well as on sub-assemblages incorporating buckling-restrained braces. The primary goal of the testing program is to demonstrate the strength and inelastic deformation capacity of systems incorporating buckling restrained braces. Testing on sub-assemblages incorporating buckling restrained braces is necessary because of the rotation demands that are imposed at the bracing ends in typical braced frames. When the inelastic axial deformations are combined with the rotations that are imposed at the extremities of the bracing element by the deformation of the connections in the braced frame, local buckling or premature fracture of the steel core can occur and significantly compromise the strength and ductility capacity of the member. For each deformation level in the testing protocol, full excursions at the prescribed deformation level are carried out in both compression and tension. If a test is carried out on a single brace element, the combination of axial deformations and connection rotations can be applied by eccentric loading setups or by bidirectional loading at each extremity of the brace element. The proposed testing protocol can either be applied by increments of axial and rotational deformations or by applying and maintaining the maximum rotational deformation before applying the entire axial deformation loading protocol (Shuhaibar et al. 2002, Sabelli 2001). If a test is carried out on a sub-assemblage containing a buckling-restrained brace, connection details similar to the ones used in the real application are required to adequately reproduce the rotation demand at the ends of the bracing element. The proposed testing protocol consists of:

- 2 cycles of loading at a deformation corresponding to the axial deformation at first significant yielding of the buckling-restrained brace.

- 2 cycles of loading at 50% of the deformation in the brace corresponding to the design drift level.

- 2 cycles of loading at a deformation in the brace corresponding to the design drift level.

- 2 cycles of loading at 150% of the deformation in the brace corresponding to the design drift level.

- 2 cycles of loading at 200% of the deformation in the brace corresponding to the design drift level.

- Finally, for tests on buckling-restrained braces alone (no sub-assemblage), the protocol suggests additional cycles of loading at 150% of the deformation in the brace corresponding to the design drift level until a cumulative inelastic axial deformation of at least 200 times the yield deformation has been applied. This is not required for sub-assemblage tests.

A joint task group of the American Institute of Steel Construction (AISC) and the Structural Engineers Association of California (SEAOC) have developed design provisions for buckling-restrained braces (AISC/SEAOC 2001).

5.5.4 Structural Implementations

The development of metallic dampers, based mainly on experimental investigations, has led to the implementation of these devices in a number of full-scale structures. Appendix A presents a partial list of buildings around the world equipped with metallic dampers.

5.6 FRICTION DAMPERS

Friction dampers dissipate the seismic energy by friction that develops between two solid bodies sliding relative to one another. Again, a wide variety of devices have been developed that utilize solid friction as the source of energy dissipation. In many ways, the macroscopic modelling of friction dampers is similar to the modelling of metallic devices if the slip load is considered as an equivalent yield force.

5.6.1 Basic Principles of Solid Coulomb Friction

Solid friction has been studied by illustrious scientists such as Leonardo daVinci, Newton, Amontons, and Coulomb. The basic dry friction theory between two sliding solids is based on three assumptions that have been validated experimentally under specific conditions:

- The total frictional force that can be developed is independent of the apparent surface area of contact.

- The total frictional force that can be developed is proportional to the total normal force acting across the sliding interface.

- For the case of sliding with low relative velocities, the total frictional force is independent of that sliding velocity.

Therefore during slipping, the relation between the frictional force F_f acting tangentially within the interfacial plane in the direction opposing the motion and the normal force N can be expressed as:

$$F_f = \mu N \qquad (5.65)$$

where μ is the coefficient of friction.

Although frictional forces are simple to measure or to calculate based on Equation (5.65), the phenomena that relate to what we macroscopically define as friction and the actual processes of the frictional phenomena in sliding interfaces are multiple and complex. A summary of the main phenomena affecting the frictional properties of typical friction type damping devices, presented in Kim et al. (2004), are summarized in the following paragraphs.

Many researchers have tried to explain the frictional phenomena by focusing on the true contact area since it is evident that friction arises from the interaction of solids in this area. The main factors influencing the true contact area are the shape and contour of faying surfaces, the way asperities on the faying surfaces deform when a normal pressure is applied, how they adhere, the role of surface films, and how energy is lost when the surfaces are deformed during sliding. These factors are briefly discussed to better characterize phenomena affecting friction.

Friction is induced by normal pressure applied on faying surfaces. This applied normal pressure causes the deformation of asperities and therefore the true contact area on a sliding interface is dependent on the applied normal pressure. The friction coefficient μ is also influenced by the normal pressure as will be discussed later. Therefore, μ and N in Equation (5.65) are not independent, but closely interrelated.

Before the basic mechanism of friction is described, a distinction must made between two kinds of frictional forces: the static frictional force and the sliding (kinetic) frictional force. Figure 5.29 illustrates a typical relation between the frictional force and the displacement on a sliding interface that consists of a stainless steel in contact with Non-Asbestos Organic (NAO) material under a normal pressure of 45 MPa and low velocity loading conditions (Kim et al. 2004). The static frictional force usually occurs immediately before the initiation or at the reversal of sliding motion and is higher than the sliding frictional force measured at low velocity of sliding after the initiation of motion.

There are three general components that contribute to the work done at the interface between two sliding surfaces: i) the adhesion component along the interface, ii) the ploughing component in the bulk zone and iii) the presence of third bodies such as contaminants or wearing debris (Bowden et al. 1973). These components were first suggested to explain friction between metallic surfaces and further extended to polymers

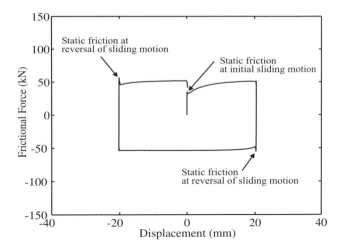

Figure 5.29 Typical Frictional Force-Sliding Displacement Relation (after Kim et al. 2004)

(Briscoe et al. 1988). The interface zone corresponds to a region with high rates of energy dissipation that occurs by converting kinetic energy to heat. On the other hand, the bulk zone involves deformation within a larger volume of material and hence corresponds to lower rates of energy dissipation.

(a) Adhesion Component

Before a normal load is applied, two bodies (Body I and Body II in Figure 5.30(a)) are in contact at asperities. Upon application of the normal load, asperities deform plastically and junctions are formed as illustrated in Figure 5.30(b). Plastic deformations increase until equilibrium is reached, at which point the applied normal pressure and the deformations are compatible. Subsequently, the true contact area is affected by these additional junctions.

The tangential load applied to the faying surfaces increases the area at the junctions, which in turn causes an increase of shear stresses and a reduction of normal stresses. The frictional force is therefore mainly dependent on the properties of the faying surfaces such as the true contact area and the strength of the sliding bodies. This explanation is the main idea behind the adhesion component of friction. The frictional force due to adhesion F_{fa} can be rewritten in terms of the real contact area and the shear strength of the frictional material as (Bowden et al. 1973, Constantinou et al. 1999):

$$F_{fa} = sA_r \tag{5.66}$$

where s is the shear strength of the junctions and A_r is the true contact area. It can be seen from Equation (5.66) that the frictional force increases with an increase of the true contact area and the strength of the frictional materials. Physically, the highest frictional

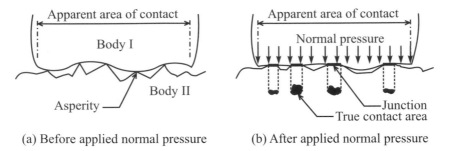

(a) Before applied normal pressure   (b) After applied normal pressure

Figure 5.30 Asperities and Junctions in Sliding Interface

force that can be exhibited occurs when the true contact area becomes the apparent contact area.

It is important to realize that the true contact area and the shear strength are also closely related to each other. A strong frictional material under normal pressure produces a small true contact area because the deformations of the frictional material at the asperities are small whereas a material with a higher shear strength requires a higher frictional force to shear the faying surface.

Larger attraction forces are generated between the same or similar frictional materials than between dissimilar frictional materials.

The origin of the difference between static and sliding frictional force can also be explained by the adhesion component. Immediately after sliding, the true contact area is rapidly reduced and the shear strength of the junctions is lost as well. The sliding frictional force then remains constant within a certain range until reversal of the motion.

(b) Ploughing Component

The ploughing component is explained in terms of surface roughness and plowing. Surface roughness affects frictional properties between two bodies since, during sliding, one body must lift over the roughness of the other. In the apparent area, both positive and negative slopes between frictional bodies coexist as shown in Figure 5.31. Summing up this effect for all contact points, it can be postulated that most of the frictional force relating to the roughness tends to cancel out. Generally, only about 5% of the coefficient of friction of a clean faying surface is provided from the roughness. The fluctuating force due to surface roughness is superimposed to the main adhesive component of the frictional force (Rabinowicz 1966).

The other consideration on the ploughing component is plowing. As mentioned before, surfaces are characterized by asperities. When a normal force is applied to asperities on the sliding interface, some asperities located on the harder frictional material dig into the surface of the softer one while junctions are formed in other asperities. Sharp edges on the surface of the harder frictional material make scores or grooves on the surface of the softer one. The debris from scores or grooves accumulate at the ploughing

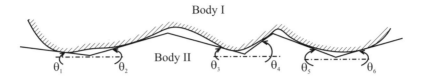

Figure 5.31 Slopes at Contact Points

edge. A larger force is therefore required to overcome the accumulated debris on the sliding path, and this is more prominent as the total slip travel length becomes longer. Usually, $\tan\theta$ (see Figure 5.32) is about 0.05 or less, and the plowing term is generally small (Rabinowicz 1966).

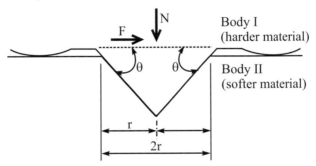

Figure 5.32 Schematic Illustration of Plowing Component

(c) Third Bodies Component

Third bodies, such as contaminants or wearing debris, and cold welding also affect frictional properties. It is difficult to predict the contribution of third bodies on the friction properties because it is dependent on the shape and strength of third bodies as well as the roughness of faying surfaces. For example, third bodies can remain between asperities in high roughness faying surfaces. In this case, third bodies reduce the degree of roughness of the faying surface and increase the true contact area.

If the contaminants are round in shape and made of a strong material, they facilitate sliding by the so called *rolling friction phenomenon*, and the static frictional force would abruptly reduce because the true contact area of the rolling interfaces is significantly smaller than that of the flat interfaces. On the other hand, sharp contaminants would cause plowing such that the static frictional force would be increased. Generally, it is observed that contaminants usually increase the static frictional force.

Furthermore, wearing debris increases during sliding, and the sliding frictional force is influenced by the amount of wearing debris. For this reason, it is very complicated to define the contribution of the wearing debris on the sliding frictional force. The wearing phenomenon will be further discussed in a following paragraph.

For softer materials, when the strength of the junctions exceeds the elastic yielding strength, cold welding occurs at the sliding interface. Cold welding significantly increases frictional forces and can also be interpreted as high adhesion in the true contact area.

5.6.2 Stick-Slip Motion

Stick-Slip (or jerky) motion is a common occurrence at a sliding interface and may be an intrinsic property of the sliding interface. Regular stick-slip motion arises whenever the static coefficient of friction is markedly greater than the kinetic coefficient of friction. Upon reversal of motion, the frictional interface undergoes a momentary stop (movement changes direction). Upon initiation of motion in the reverse direction, the static frictional force, which is usually larger than the sliding friction, is mobilized. Subsequently, irregular stick-slip motion takes place when the frictional force drops with increasing displacement, then increases due to the increase in sliding velocity.

5.6.3 Wear Phenomenon

Wear may be defined as the removal of material from a solid surface as a result of a mechanical action. Thus, wear is characterized by the amount of material removed during sliding. It can be generally classified in four categories: i) adhesive wear, ii) abrasive wear, iii) corrosive wear and iv) surface fatigue wear.

(a) Adhesive Wear

During sliding, fragments are disassembled from their sliding surface and adhere to the other surface. Under continued sliding action, these fragments may come off the surface on which they adhere and be transferred back to the original surface or be completely removed from the sliding interface. The particles which adhere to the other surface due to adhesive wear can change the characteristics of friction of the sliding interface since the surfaces tend to become rougher.

(b) Abrasive Wear

Abrasive wear occurs when a rough harder surface, or a softer surface containing hard particles, slides on a softer surface. The hard particles plow the soft surface. Therefore, abrasive wear is closely related to the plowing phenomenon that was discussed above.

(c) Corrosive Wear and Surface Fatigue Wear

Corrosive wear and surface fatigue wear occur in a corrosive environment and in sliding interfaces subjected to repeated sliding, respectively. Sliding action wears a corroded or fatigued surface film away.

Abrasive wear, corrosive wear and surface fatigue wear can be eliminated by good preparation of faying surfaces such as clean smooth surfaces without hard particles or the use of surfaces with higher corrosion resistance. On the other hand, adhesive wear is universal in nearly all mechanical sliding systems and can not be eliminated, but only reduced. Therefore it is worth further reviewing the mechanism of adhesive wear.

The cause of adhesive wear is the attractive forces which exist between the surface atoms of two materials in a sliding interface. These attractive forces are introduced under conditions similar to cold welding. If the attractive forces are larger than the forces required to maintain the shape of a softer body when a tangential displacement is imposed on the sliding interface, particles may be taken off from the softer body and a trade-off of particles between the two bodies occurs endlessly during sliding.

Based on this mechanism, it is reasonable to infer that the amount of wear is generally proportional to the normal pressure and to the travel length and inversely proportional to the hardness of the surface.

5.6.4 Normal Load in Sliding Interfaces

A number of experimental studies on the friction properties of sliding interfaces, applied to seismic isolation sliding bearing systems, have been performed. Considering that in such applications the sliding devices carry a well distributed normal load, these experiments have been carried out in special testing machines using actuators for applying the normal load (e.g. Bondonet and Filiatrault 1997, Constantinou et al. 1999, Wolff 1999). It can therefore be assumed that the normal load is uniformly distributed on the sliding interface and is constant during the tests. This assumption is usually not true for sliding surfaces where the normal force is applied through bolt preload. The fluctuation of bolt preload can lead to unstable hysteresis loops, and the amount of dissipated energy by friction can be somewhat unpredictable. In the following paragraphs, important aspects of bolt prestressing that influence the frictional response of such systems are discussed. Under the assumption that frictional characteristics in the sliding interfaces are maintained during the lifetime of the frictional system, the variation of the bolt preload causes a change of slip resistance.

(a) Bolt Behaviour under Preload

In practice, bolt preload is usually introduced by torquing the nut against the resistance of the connected material. Since the behaviour of bolts subjected to the preload is governed by the performance of their threaded part, load versus elongation characteristics of a bolt are more significant than the stress versus strain relationship of the fastener metal itself (Kulak et al. 2001, 2002). Consequently, in the following paragraphs, the behaviour of bolts under preload is considered based on their elongation and not their strain.

Bolts can be tightened by using calibrated wrenches, by the turn-of-nut method, or by use of direct tension indicators. Specifically, the turn-of-the-nut method is the common method to obtain a given bolt preload. The bolt preload is obtained by tightening the bolt from snug-tight conditions that can be attained by the full manual effort using an ordinary spud wrench. The required nut rotation, per specifications, from the snug-tight condition, depends on the bolt length and slope between the face normal to the bolt axis and the other face. Figure 5.33 illustrates the relation between bolt preload and the nut rotations of one A325 and one A490 bolt of 22 mm diameter. The nut rotation specified to obtain the minimum tension of the bolt is also shown in the figure.

The length of the thread unengaged below the nut is important to bolt preload because most of the bolt elongation occurs in the threaded portion below the nut. In general, the required rotations can be taken as 1/2 turn for bolt lengths 8 times the bolt diameter or less and 2/3 turn for bolt lengths greater than 8 times the bolt diameter. Large diameter high-strength bolts, especially A490 bolts with short grip lengths, may not reach the specified minimum tension due to the shorter length of the unengaged thread below the nut and the higher strength of the bolts. Bolt manufacturers' specifications should be examined closely before determining the level of tightening that will produce the required pre-load.

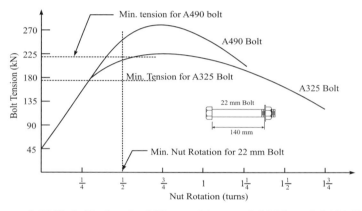

Figure 5.33 Bolt Preload of 22-mm Torqued A325 and A490 Bolts

The long-term effects of bolt preload must be considered, since it is difficult to predict, especially for seismic applications, when the sliding surface will be activated. Relaxation of bolt preload is the most important long-term effect and depends mainly on the stress level of the bolt, since relaxation is more pronounced at high stress levels. The grip length as well as the number of plies are also believed to be among the factors that influence the amount of bolt relaxation. Most of the elongation concentrates on the threaded part and subsequently relaxation also takes place at the same location. Therefore, the relaxation of bolt preload increases as the grip length is decreased. On the other hand, increasing the number of plies for a constant grip length leads to an increase in bolt relaxation. Relatively large losses in bolt preload have been reported for very short grip galvanized bolts (Kulak et al. 2001).

Kulak et al. (2001) reported that, immediately upon completion of the torquing, there is only a 2 to 11% drop in load and the average loss is 5% of the maximum bolt tension. Relaxation tests on A325 bolts showed an additional 4% loss in bolt tension after 21 days as compared with the bolt tension measured 1 minute after torquing. Most of this loss

(90%) occurred during the first day. During the remaining 20 days, the rate of change in bolt load decreased in an exponential manner.

(b) Bolt Preload in Sliding Interfaces

As mentioned above, bolt preload is closely related to the elongation of the bolt. The main components influencing the elongation of a bolt and consequently the bolt preload in sliding interfaces are: wear, temperature rise and accumulation of debris or contaminants on the sliding interfaces.

Wear decreases the elongated bolt length, which leads to a reduction of the bolt preload while the temperature rise of the friction phenomena leads to an expansion of the connected steel plates which in turn causes an increase of the bolt length and the bolt preload if the bolt is in the elastic range. If any debris produced by wearing phenomena or contaminants exists in the sliding interfaces, the length of the bolt is also increased and the effect on the bolt preload is the same as a temperature rise. Poisson's effect and initial non-uniformity in the thickness of the connected plates can also represent sources of variation of bolt preload (Tremblay and Stiemer 1993). In order to explain the variation of the length of a bolt and its preload, the hysteretic behaviour of a bolt is assumed to behave elastic-perfectly plastic as shown in Figure 5.34(a). Figure 5.34(b) illustrates the different stages of the behaviour of a bolt during sliding. In Figure 5.34(b), Δ_{bi} is the initial elongation of the bolt when it is tightened, and the bolt preload at this point is P_u. When only the wearing effect governs the elongation of the bolt, the elongation becomes Δ_{bw} which is smaller than the initial elongation of the bolt Δ_{bi}, and the corresponding bolt preload is P_w which is smaller than the initial bolt preload. However, temperature rise does not influence the bolt preload even if the elongation of the bolt increases to Δ_{bt}. If there is an accumulation of debris instead of wear with temperature rise, the elongation of the bolt further increases to Δ_{btd}, but the bolt preload is still P_u. On the other hand, if the wear exceeds the accumulation of debris and the wearing effect is larger than the temperature rise effect, the elongation of the bolt decreases to Δ_{bwt}, and the bolt preload also decreases to P_{wt}. It is therefore inferred that the variation of bolt preload can be minimized by reducing the effect of wear.

Based on the relation between the bolt preload and several effects stated above, the use of high strength bolts is recommended because of the relative small loss of bolt preload due to wearing and temperature drop, easy fabrication and the use of fewer bolts to obtain the expected slip load. In addition, wearing can be reduced by using smaller bolts since the high wear rate occurs at higher normal pressures. In addition, thicker frictional materials are better for wearing and can also reduce the effect of temperature.

(c) Normal Pressure on Sliding Interfaces with Bolt Pre-Loading

The distribution of the normal pressure applied by prestressed bolts is not uniform but rather variable. The variable distribution of the normal pressure is important for sliding interfaces since wearing may concentrate on the contact area where the highest normal

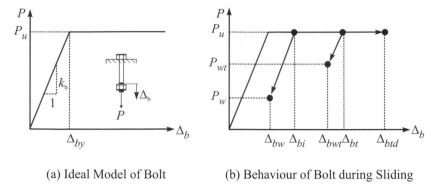

(a) Ideal Model of Bolt   (b) Behaviour of Bolt during Sliding

Figure 5.34 Model of the Assembly of Bolted Connection (after Tremblay and Stiemer 1993)

pressure is applied, and this trend becomes more pronounced as the number of cycles increases.

The variable distribution of the normal pressure can be calculated by a modified semi-infinite wedge model that is derived from the theory of elasticity (Ugural et al. 1995). Figure 5.35 illustrates the modified semi-infinite wedge model as applied to a bolted connection.

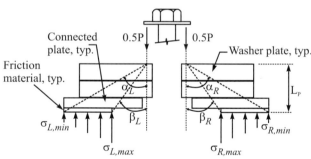

Figure 5.35 Variable Distribution of Normal Pressure on Sliding Interfaces

The normal stress distribution at the sliding interface is defined by $\sigma_{L,min}$, $\sigma_{L,max}$, $\sigma_{R,min}$ and $\sigma_{R,max}$; these stress values correspond to the minimum and maximum values of the normal pressure on the left and right hand side of the bolt, respectively:

$$\sigma_{L,min} = -\frac{2P}{L_P}\frac{\cos^4\alpha_L}{(\sin 2\alpha_L - \sin 2\beta_L) + 2(\alpha_L - \beta_L)} \tag{5.67}$$

$$\sigma_{L,max} = -\frac{2P}{L_P}\frac{\cos^4\beta_L}{(\sin 2\alpha_L - \sin 2\beta_L) + 2(\alpha_L - \beta_L)} \tag{5.68}$$

$$\sigma_{R,min} = -\frac{2P}{L_P} \frac{\cos^4\alpha_R}{(\sin 2\alpha_R - \sin 2\beta_R) + 2(\alpha_R - \beta_R)} \qquad (5.69)$$

$$\sigma_{R,max} = -\frac{2P}{L_P} \frac{\cos^4\beta_R}{(\sin 2\alpha_R - \sin 2\beta_R) + 2(\alpha_R - \beta_R)} \qquad (5.70)$$

The angles α_L, α_R, β_L and β_R in Figure 5.35 are dependent on the geometry of the bolted connection and the width of the frictional material. The thickness of all plates including the thickness of the frictional material is defined as L_P.

As expected, normal pressure increases with proximity to the loading point. From Equations (5.67) to (5.70), L_P is the main parameter for the determination of the variation of the normal pressure, and it can be observed that the variation of normal pressures will be reduced with an increase of L_P.

5.6.5 Effects Influencing Frictional Behaviour

Equation (5.65) simply expresses frictional forces dependent on the coefficient of friction and normal load. But, as previously discussed, the determination of the coefficient of friction is dependent on apparent pressure, sliding velocity, temperature, load dwell, corrosion of the frictional materials, contamination and travel length. This section is devoted to a discussion of the effect of each of these factors on the frictional characteristics, especially on the coefficient of friction. It is assumed that undesirable movements of the sliding bodies from their original position are avoided by special treatment such as the introduction of recesses or welding to the base steel. Another important assumption is that deformations due to normal pressure concentrate on the soft material in the faying surface.

(a) Effect of Apparent Pressure

It has been shown (Bowden et al. 1973) that the coefficient of friction μ is essentially proportional to the inverse of the normal pressure. The sliding coefficient of friction decreases with the increase of normal pressure. When the asperities are overloaded such that they deform plastically, the sliding coefficient of friction remains constant. It should be noted that the sliding coefficient of friction is obtained within the first cycle. As the number of cycles increases, the frictional characteristics change and, thereby, the sliding coefficient of friction is expected to vary as well.

(b) Effect of Sliding Velocity

Before sliding, faying surfaces are covered with a thin film made by a chemical action between the frictional material and oxygen in the air. In fact, the film of the harder frictional material is in contact with the film of the softer frictional material. After the static frictional resistance is overcome, the thin film is sheared as sliding motion occurs. The thin film is easier to shear than the frictional material itself. At very low sliding velocities, a small tangential force is enough to shear this thin film and initiate sliding. This justifies the lower sliding coefficient of friction at very low velocities.

The sliding coefficient of friction, however, increases as the sliding velocity is further increased. This phenomenon can be explained by the fact that the true contact occurs between the frictional materials, not the thin films, and that the debris from the softer material starts to deposit on the surface of the harder material. This leads to an increase of the frictional force at moderate sliding velocities. However, at very high sliding velocities, local melting of the softer frictional material occurs at the sliding interface, which in turn causes the reduction of the strength of the softer frictional material. Therefore, the force required to slide decreases and the sliding coefficient of friction is decreased at very high sliding velocities.

Figure 5.36 illustrates the dependence of the coefficient of friction on the sliding velocity and on the apparent pressure. In this figure, μ_B represents the static coefficient of friction at the instant in which sliding starts in the interface. After initial slip, the coefficient of friction decreases until it reaches the minimum sliding coefficient of friction μ_{min}. The sliding coefficient of friction increases as the sliding velocity increases, and eventually the maximum sliding coefficient of friction μ_{max} is reached. Increase in normal load results in reduction of the sliding coefficient of friction; this reduction eventually diminishes at some limiting value of the normal load. However, as the number of cycles increases, the sliding coefficient of friction will either increase due to the deposit of debris from the softer frictional material or decrease due to the effect of temperature rise

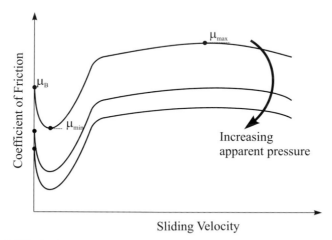

Figure 5.36 Relation Between Sliding Velocity, Pressure and Frictional Coefficient (adapted from Constantinou et al. 1999)

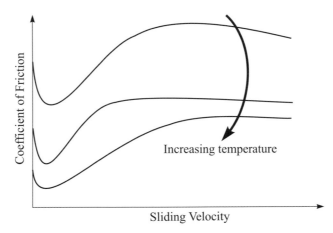

Figure 5.37 Influence of Temperature to Coefficient of Friction (adapted from Constantinou et al. 1999)

(c) Effect of Temperature

Figure 5.37 illustrates the variation of the coefficient of friction as a function of the sliding velocity for various temperatures. After sliding is initiated, the temperature at the interfaces increases due to heat flux caused by friction. The heat flux increases with the increase of sliding velocity, apparent pressure and coefficient of friction. Whereas the heat flux is small at low sliding velocities, it becomes very large at very high sliding velocities that are generally expected under seismic forces. This large heat flux decreases the sliding coefficient of friction. At low sliding velocity ranges, however, the heat flux is small and the sliding coefficient of friction increases with the increase of sliding velocity as mentioned in the previous section.

(d) Effect of Time of Loading (Load Dwell)

It is known from several experiments that the static friction increases rapidly up to about 24 hours of load dwell due to the changes in the cystalline structure of the softer friction material. Time-dependent deformations, such as creep of the soft friction material, can be expected to occur in a very short time and thereby the true contact area quickly becomes approximately equal to the apparent contact area, thus minimizing load dwell effects during the life of systems incorporating such friction interfaces. The combination of soft and hard materials, even if the friction of the sliding interfaces is low, can therefore lead to stable and predictable long term frictional behaviour (Constantinou et al. 1999).

(e) Effect of Corrosion and Contaminants

The roughness of faying surfaces is closely related to corrosion which controls the durability of sliding interfaces. Rust by corrosion or contaminants can be considered as a source of increased surface roughness. Therefore, corrosion and contamination of faying surfaces translates into an equivalent increase in surface roughness.

5.6.6 Studies on the Variation of Coefficient of Friction for Teflon-Steel Interfaces

In order to qualify the frictional characteristics of bridge bearings, Bondonet and Filiatrault (1997) performed more than 100 sinusoidal tests on sheet-type PTFE-steel interfaces. These tests were done at bearing pressures of 5, 15, 30 and 45 MPa, at frequencies of 0.02, 0.2, 1.0, 2.0 and 5.0 Hz, and at displacement amplitudes of ± 10 mm and ± 70 mm. A maximum sliding velocity of 82 cm/s was reached during the tests. The corresponding measured maximum acceleration was 1.03 g.

The steel portion of the interface was made of stainless steel plates, 1.6 mm thick, which were welded on 10-mm mild steel plates. A grade-eight mirror finish was used for the stainless steel. The direction of the predominant surface pattern (surface lays) was parallel to the excitation direction in all tests.

The PTFE portion of the interface was made of Teflon disks having a diameter of 128 mm and a thickness of 5 mm. Three different types of Teflon material were considered: unfilled Teflon, glass-filled Teflon at a composition of 15% per weight and carbon-filled Teflon at a composition of 25% per weight. Both surfaces of each disk were smooth (without recesses). One surface was chemically cleaned so that it could be glued with epoxy to the steel in the recess of a pot-bearing casing. A shake table was used as a loading device. The Teflon-steel interface was inserted horizontally between the shake table and a horizontal reaction frame anchored to the strong floor of the laboratory. The central stainless-steel plate, 13.2 mm thick, was sandwiched between two Teflon disks. Each Teflon disk was glued with epoxy into the 2-mm recess of a standard pot-bearing casing. A 1000-kN hydraulic actuator provided the normal pressure across the interface. The vertical reaction was carried by a vertical reaction frame anchored to the strong floor of the laboratory. The horizontal loading was provided by the hydraulic system of the earthquake simulator.

The frictional response of the unfilled Teflon-steel interface is presented in Figure 5.38 for the complete frequency range at displacement amplitudes of ± 70 mm, and under a confining pressure of 30 MPa. The results are presented in terms of coefficient of friction – sliding displacement (μ - S) hysteresis loops.

For each loop in Figure 5.38, the initial coefficient of friction μ_i and the steady-state coefficient of friction μ_{ss} can be determined. At low excitation frequencies, the difference between μ_i and μ_{ss} is very small. This difference increases with the excitation frequency. Furthermore, as the excitation frequency increases, a significant transient response is observed. Several response cycles are required for the coefficient of friction to migrate from μ_i to μ_{ss}. At an excitation frequency of 2.0 Hz, for example, 17 cycles are required

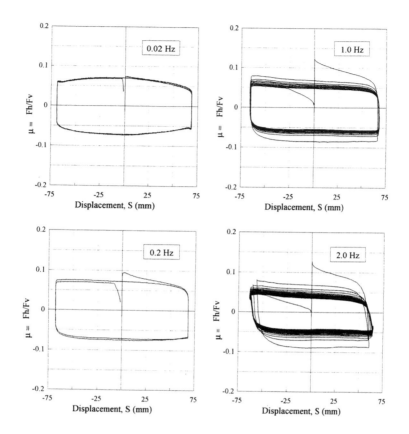

Figure 5.38 Frictional Response of Unfilled Teflon-Steel Interface Under a Confining Pressure of 30 MPa (from Bondonet and Filiatrault 1997, reproduced with permission from the American Society of Civil Engineers)

for the coefficient of friction to decrease from $\mu_i = 0.12$ to $\mu_{ss} = 0.04$. This transient response at high frequencies was observed in all three interfaces considered. Figure 5.39 presents the variations of the initial coefficient of friction μ_i and the steady-state coefficient of friction μ_{ss} with the maximum velocity $\dot{S}_{max}$ developed during each test on the unfilled Teflon. The results are presented for the entire range of confining pressures. As the velocity increases, μ_i increases from a minimum initial coefficient of friction to a maximum initial coefficient of friction. This behaviour was observed for all three interfaces tested.

The behaviour of the steady-state coefficient of friction is different, however, than the initial coefficient of friction. Initially, at low velocities, μ_{ss} exhibits a growth similar to the initial coefficient of friction. For greater velocities, however, μ_{ss} decreases to a final coefficient of friction that can be smaller than the minimum steady-state coefficient of friction. This behaviour was observed for all three interfaces tested.

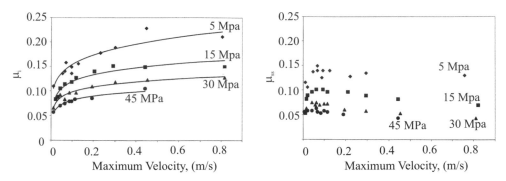

Figure 5.39 Variations of Initial and Steady-State Coefficients of Friction with Absolute Maximum Velocity (after Bondonet and Filiatrault 1997)

Finally, as can be observed in Figure 5.39, both the initial and steady-state coefficients of friction decrease when the confining pressure increases. This observation is presented graphically in Figure 5.40 for the unfilled Teflon-steel interface. These experimental results therefore illustrate the effects influencing the friction behaviour between faying surfaces, as described in section 5.6.5.

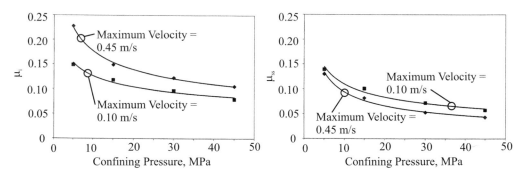

Figure 5.40 Influence of Confining Pressure on (a) Initial Coefficient of Friction; (b) Steady-State Coefficient of Friction (after Bondonet and Filiatrault 1997)

5.6.7 Studies on the Variation of Coefficient of Friction for Metal-Metal Interfaces

Many early seismic applications of friction dampers involved sliding metallic surfaces. Pall et al. (1980) conducted static and dynamic tests on a variety of simple sliding elements having different surface treatments. In these tests, the normal force was applied by pretensioning 12.7 mm diameter high strength bolts. The resulting load-displacement response under monotonic loading is shown in Figure 5.41. Figure 5.42 presents the hysteretic behaviour under constant amplitude displacement-controlled cyclic loading.

Tremblay and Stiemer (1993) performed a series of 42 tests on friction-type bolted brace connections for braced steel frames. Some results of these tests are shown in Figure 5.43. The results show that sliding connections can exhibit a very high energy

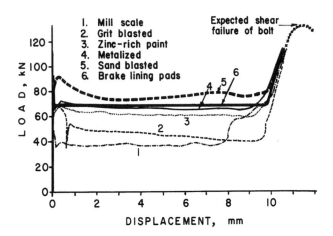

Figure 5.41 Monotonic Response of Limited Slip Bolted Joints (from Pall et al. 1980, reproduced with the permission of the Prestressed Concrete Institute)

dissipation capability under extreme loading conditions, provided that appropriate material and bolt clamping force are used. Employing different materials at the contact surface, such as different steels or plate inserts made from a different alloys (e.g. cobalt or brass), could result in a desirable response. Similar conclusions were also obtained by Grigorian et al. (1993) for steel-brass interfaces as shown in Figure 5.44.

5.6.8 Viscoplastic Model of Friction Process

A continuous viscoplastic friction law proposed, used and extended by several authors (Bouc 1971, Wen 1976, Ozdemir 1976, Constantinou et al. 1987, Graesser and Cozzarelli 1991, Nagarajaiah et al. 1993), can be used to model more accurately the friction process. This formulation has been extended by Bondonet and Filiatrault (1997) to incorporate the initial transient frictional response exhibited by the Teflon-steel interfaces at high frequencies (Figure 5.39). A brief description of this model is presented herein. The kinematic dynamic coefficient of friction μ_k is expressed by:

$$\mu_k = \mu_{mss} I_f Z \tag{5.71}$$

The hysteretic parameter Z in Equation (5.71) is dimensionless and varies between +1 and −1. When the interface is sliding, $Z = +1$ or -1. When the interface is sticking, the absolute value of Z is less than one and represents the elastic behaviour of the interface in static shear conditions. The parameter Z is obtained by solving the following differential equation at every time increment:

$$Y\frac{dZ}{dt} = \{1 - Z^2[\beta + (1-\beta)sign(Z\dot{S})]\}\frac{dS}{dt} \tag{5.72}$$

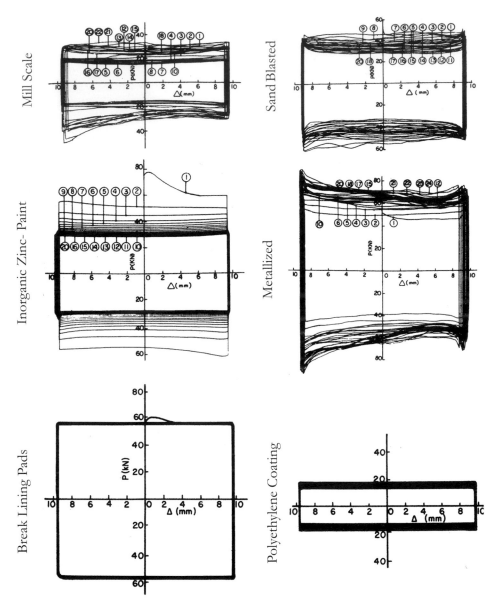

Figure 5.42 Hysteretic Behaviour of Slip Bolted Joints (from Pall et al. 1980, reproduced with the permission of the Prestressed Concrete Institute)

where β is a dimensionless constant and Y is an equivalent yield displacement. The modified steady-state coefficient of friction in Equation (5.71) μ_{mss} is introduced to account for the fact that the steady-state coefficient of friction starts to decrease past a critical velocity $\dot{S}_{crit}$ as shown in Figure 5.39. The impulse factor I_f in Equation (5.71) is initially equal to 1.0 until the interface is on the verge of sliding for the first time. At that time, the impulse factor is made equal to an initial impulse factor $I_{fi} \geq 1$. After this initial sliding has occurred, the impulse factor decreases from I_{fi} to unity. A time function that describes well the experimental data must be constructed to evaluate this transient response (Bondonet and Filiatrault 1997).

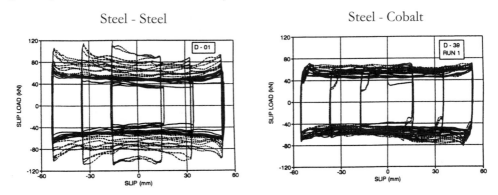

Steel - Steel   Steel - Cobalt

Figure 5.43 Hysteretic behaviour of Friction-Type Bolted Brace Connections (from Tremblay and Stiemer 1993, reproduced with the permission of the authors)

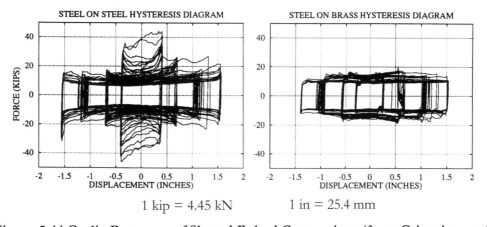

1 kip = 4.45 kN   1 in = 25.4 mm

Figure 5.44 Cyclic Response of Slotted Bolted Connections (from Grigorian et al. 1993, reproduced with the permission of the Earthquake Engineering Research Institute)

5.6.9 Existing Friction Damping Systems

There are a variety of friction devices that have been proposed for seismic energy dissipation. Typically these devices have very good performance characteristics and their behaviour is not significantly affected by load amplitude, frequency, or number of applied cycles. The devices differ in their mechanical complexity and in the materials used for the sliding surfaces. In this section, some of the friction devices that have been developed and implemented in real structures are discussed. Only devices that generate rectangular hysteresis loops, characteristic of Coulomb friction, are considered. Other friction devices exhibiting non-rectangular hysteresis loops will be introduced in Chapter 7 when describing dampers with self-centering capabilities.

(a) Slotted-Bolted Connections

The simplest form of friction dampers consists of introducing simple slotted-bolted connections at the ends of conventional bracing members. The connection must be designed to slip before yielding or buckling of the bracing member occurs. As illustrated in Figure 5.45, each connection incorporates a symmetric shear splice (two shear planes) with slotted holes in the gusset plate and standard circular holes in the connecting plates extending from the bracing member. The length of the slot must be sufficient to

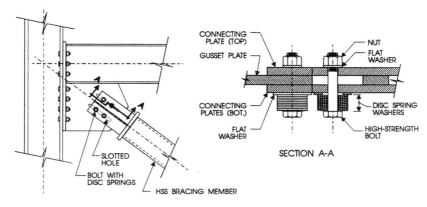

Figure 5.45 Slotted-Bolted Connection for Steel Framed Building (from Tremblay and Stiemer 1993, reproduced with the permission of the authors)

accommodate the maximum slip anticipated from the design earthquake. To maintain a constant slip load, disc spring washers can be used in the bolting assembly. These washers are intended to provide a constant normal force even if the plate thickness varies during the dynamic response of the connection. As discussed in Section 5.6.5, this variation in plate thickness is the result of two major factors:

- The thickness can be reduced due to wear at the contact surfaces.

- The thickness can increase due to temperature rise resulting from the heat generated by the friction process.

Tremblay and Stiemer (1993) tested the slotted-bolted connection illustrated in Figure 5.45 in a full-scale single storey diagonally braced frame mounted horizontally on a rigid floor. As shown in Figure 5.46, the frame was pinned in its four corners and only the slotted-bolted diagonal member provided lateral stiffness and strength.

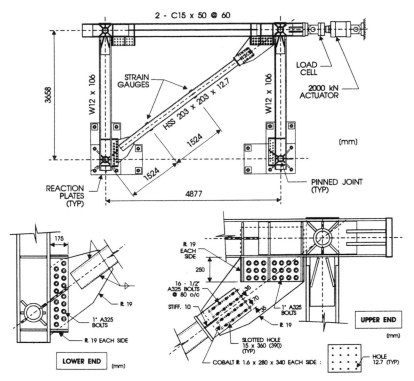

Figure 5.46 Full Scale Testing of Slotted-Bolted Friction Damped Braced Frame (from Tremblay and Stiemer 1993, reproduced with the permission of the authors)

The slotted-bolted connection was introduced at the beam-column corner while, in the lower end of the bracing member, a typical connection was incorporated. The sliding connection included 16-A325 13 mm diameter bolts torqued to their ultimate capacity (no spring washers) with two cobalt plates 1.6mm thick. The overall quasi-static response of the frame is given in Figure 5.47. The connection behaved very smoothly in all tests, and no sign of severe bearing of the bolts against the sides of the slotted holes as slip and lateral displacement were taking place could be noticed. The stable response of the frame within each cycle indicates that the relative rotation of the connected parts did not impair the slip resistance of the connection. Earthquake simulator tests of a three-storey steel building model incorporating slotted-bolted connections have also demonstrated their stable behaviour (Grigorian and Popov 1994).

(b) Sumitomo Friction Device

Figure 5.48 illustrates a more sophisticated friction device manufactured by Sumitomo Metal Industries Ltd. in Japan. The device incorporates a pre-compressed internal spring that induces a force that is converted through the action of inner and outer wedges into a normal force on the friction pads. These copper alloy friction pads contain graphite plug

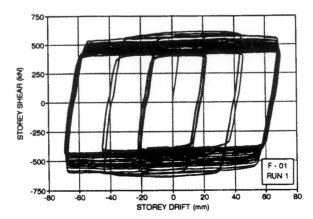

Figure 5.47 Quasi-Static Response of Slotted-Bolted Friction Braced Frame (from Tremblay and Stiemer 1993, reproduced with the permission of the authors)

inserts, which provide dry lubrication. This helps to maintain a consistent coefficient of friction between the pads and the inner surface of the steel casing.

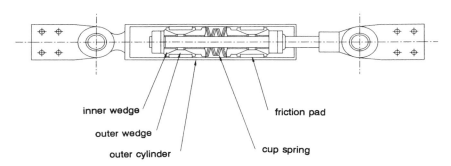

Figure 5.48 Sumitomo Friction Device (after Aiken and Kelly 1993)

As shown in Figure 5.49, the cyclic response of the Sumitomo Device is very regular and repeatable with rectangular hysteresis loops.

Furthermore, the effect of loading frequency and amplitude, number of cycles, or ambient temperature on damper response was reported to be insignificant.

(c) Pall Friction Device

The Pall system (Pall and Marsh 1981) is a friction damping system designed to be mounted in a moment-resisting framed structure. The system consists of a mechanism containing slotted slip joints introduced at the intersection of the frame cross-braces. Figure 5.50 shows the location and general arrangement of the friction device in a typical moment-resisting frame. The device is designed not to slip under normal service loads and moderate earthquakes. During severe seismic excitation, the device slips at a

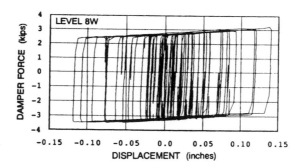

Figure 5.49 Cyclic Behaviour of Sumitomo Friction Device (from Aiken et al. 1993, reproduced with permission from the Earthquake Engineering Research Institute)

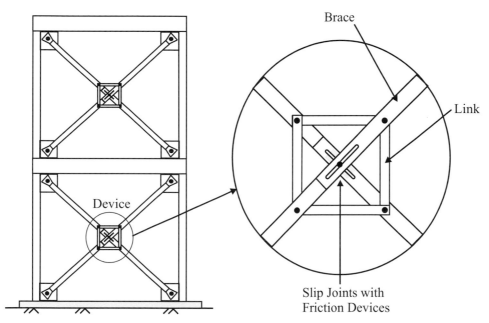

Figure 5.50 General Arrangement of Pall Friction Device

predetermined load, before any yielding of the main structural members has occurred. Slipping of a device changes the natural period of the structure and allows the structure to alter its fundamental mode shape during a severe ground motion. The phenomenon of quasi-resonance between the structure and the earthquake excitation is prevented because of this de-tuning capability of the friction damped structure.

The main characteristic of the Pall system is its ability to dissipate energy in the two slip joints independently of the buckling capacity of the bracing members. As illustrated in Figure 5.51, five different steps can be identified during a cycle of a moment-resisting frame equipped with the Pall friction device:

- **Step 1:** In the early stages of loading, both braces are active and behave elastically in tension and compression.

- **Step 2:** At a given lateral load, the compression brace buckles while the tension brace still stretches elastically in tension.

- **Step 3:** The tension brace starts slipping before its yielding load is reached. As a result, the four links of the mechanism are activated and deform into the rhomboid form shown, which eliminates the buckled shape of the compression brace under the same buckling load. When maximum lateral deformation is reached, the compression brace is essentially straight.

- **Step 4:** When the load is reversed, this straightened braced can immediately absorb energy in tension.

- **Step 5:** After the completion of one cycle, the resulting areas of the hysteresis loops are identical for both braces. In this way, the energy dissipation is comparable with that of a simple friction joint when used in braces which are designed not to buckle in compression. In other words, the energy dissipation of the system is independent of the slenderness ratio of the bracing elements.

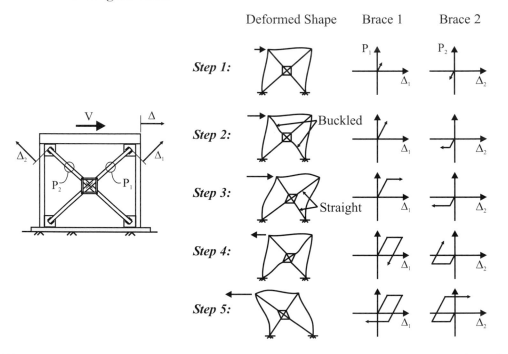

Figure 5.51 Hysteretic Behaviour of Simple Moment-Resisting Frame Equipped with Pall Friction Damping System

To be effective, the slip joints must present very stable, non-deteriorating hysteresis loops. The first generation of Pall devices included asbestos brake lining pads inserted between sliding steel surfaces. Figure 5.52 shows a typical load-displacement curve obtained from cyclic testing of Pall devices incorporating brake lining pads. The performance of the brake lining pads is reliable and repeatable. The hysteresis loops are nearly perfectly rectangular and exhibit negligible deterioration after 50 cycles. The imperfections at the two opposite corners of the hysteresis loops are the result of fabrication tolerances in the friction devices. Current generation of Pall devices use specially treated friction surfaces.

Shake table tests of a three storey, single bay steel Moment Resisting Frame (MRF), having plan dimensions of 2.1m by 1.4m and equipped with six Pall friction devices were also performed by Filiatrault and Cherry (1987). The beam-column connections of the structure were designed such that the Friction Damped Braced Frame (FDBF) could be transformed easily into a Moment Resisting Frame (MRF) and a Braced Moment Resisting Frame (BMRF). The natural frequencies and damping characteristics at low amplitudes of the three different types of construction are summarized in Table 5-4.

Table 5-4 : Dynamic Characteristics of Friction Damped Test Structure (after Filiatrault and Cherry 1987)

		1st Mode
MRF	Fundamental Period (s)	0.35
	Damping Ratio (%)	0.28
BMRF	Fundamental Period (s)	0.20
	Damping Ratio (%)	1.27
FDBF	Fundamental Period (s)	0.14
	Damping Ratio (%)	0.60

The MRF and BMRF did not perform well during the shake table tests corresponding to major earthquakes. Large inelastic strains occurred in the base column and in the first and second floor beams of the BMRF. Several bracing elements of the BMRF yielded in tension. The elongation of the braces was very large and they buckled significantly in compression. The FDBF, on the other hand, performed very well. No damage occurred in any member, and the deflections and accelerations were less than the values measured in the other two systems.

Figure 5.53 shows typical response characteristics of the three structural configurations expressed in terms of the measured top horizontal accelerations when subjected to the most severe test ground motion: the 1952 Taft California earthquake recorded in the Lincoln School Tunnel and scaled to a peak ground acceleration of 0.9 g. A peak

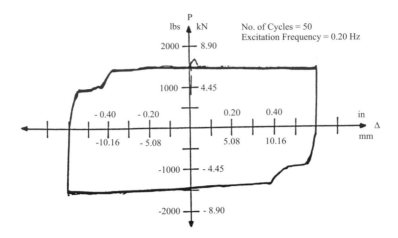

Figure 5.52 Hysteretic Response of Pall Friction Device Incorporating Asbestos Brake Lining Pads (from Filiatrault and Cherry 1987, reproduced with the permission of the Earthquake Engineering Research Institute)

acceleration of 1.42 g was measured at the top of the FDBF compared to peak accelerations of 2.24 g and 2.67 g for the BMRF and MRF, respectively.

5.6.10   Structural Implementations

The development of friction dampers, based mainly on experimental investigations, has led to the implementation of these devices in a number of full-scale structures. Appendix B presents a partial list of buildings equipped with friction dampers.

5.7 DESIGN OF STRUCTURES EQUIPPED WITH HYSTERETIC DAMPERS

In this section, various design procedures proposed for structures equipped with hysteretic dampers are reviewed. As noted earlier, the design of structures equipped with metallic or friction dampers is similar. Only the yield loads of the metallic dampers need to be substituted for the slip loads of the friction dampers. Since the FEMA-356 and FEMA-450 general design guidelines for the rehabilitation of buildings by means of passive energy dissipation systems have been reviewed in Chapters 2 and 4, emphasis is placed here on the determination of optimum parameters for the hysteretic dampers in order for the structure to achieve a given performance level. A number of proposed design procedures are discussed in Mansour and Christopoulos (2005) and are summarized in the following paragraphs.

5.7.1 Design Steps

The design of structures equipped with hysteretic dampers can be divided into four distinct steps:

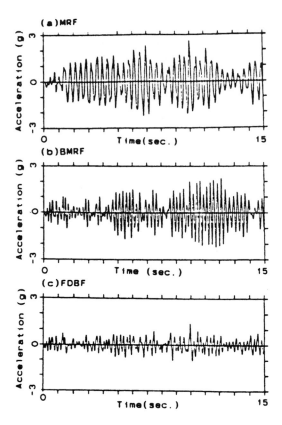

Figure 5.53 Measured Top Accelerations of MRF, BMRF and FDBF under Taft Earthquake Scaled to PGA = 0.9g (from Filiatrault and Cherry 1987, reproduced with the permission of the Earthquake Engineering Research Institute)

- The estimation of the optimum parameters for the hysteretic dampers and adjacent elements (e.g. bracing members) by using simplified methods.

- The design of the hysteretic dampers and adjacent elements to meet the optimum parameters determined above.

- The application of capacity design checks for all members of the structure under the expected ultimate force generated by the hysteretic dampers. This ultimate force represents the yield load for metallic dampers or the slip load for friction dampers and is assumed independent of velocity or frequency.

- The verification of design performance, preferably through nonlinear time-history dynamic analysis of the complete hysteretically damped structure under an ensemble of representative design earthquake ground motions.

5.7.2 Review of Different Design Procedures

The first procedure aimed at selecting adequate slip loads for moment-resisting steel structures equipped with friction dampers was proposed by Baktash and Marsh (1987). In this procedure, a slip force is chosen such that the maximum amount of energy is dissipated when the yield moment is reached at some locations in the frame.

These authors considered a single storey of moment-resisting frame structure with one or several friction-damped braced bays. Neglecting the elastic deformation prior to slipping, the shear deformation of the frame after slipping occurs is taken equal to the slip travel distance. The shear deflection of the storey Δ_s is thus:

$$\Delta_s = \frac{V_t - V_{br}}{k_u} \tag{5.73}$$

where V_t is the total lateral force exerted by the frame and bracing system, V_{br} is the lateral force exerted by the bracing system alone and k_u is the lateral stiffness of the unbraced frame alone.

The energy dissipated by friction E_f can then be written as:

$$E_f = V_{br}\Delta_s = V_{br}\frac{V_t - V_{br}}{k_u} \tag{5.74}$$

The maximum energy dissipated by friction is obtained by differentiating Equation (5.74) with respect to V_{br} and setting it equal to zero:

$$\frac{\partial E_f}{\partial V_{br}} = \frac{V_t}{k_u} - 2\frac{V_{br}}{k_u} = 0 \tag{5.75}$$

which results in the following condition:

$$V_{br} = \frac{V_t}{2} \tag{5.76}$$

This result indicates that, in order to maximize the energy dissipated by friction at the elastic limit of the frame, the total lateral force must be shared equally between the bracing system and the frame.

For a simple single bay frame, using the simplifying assumption of a point of contra-flexure at mid-height of the columns in each storey, and based on a weak-beam strong-column design, the shear force resisted by the frame action is related to the limiting moment in the beams by:

$$M_p = V_s\frac{h}{2} \tag{5.77}$$

where h is the storey height and M_p is the plastic moment capacity of the beam end. Thus, the lateral shear force V_s causing the braces to slip must be equal to the shear force causing the rigid frame to yield:

$$V_s = \frac{2M_p}{h} \tag{5.78}$$

Based on Equation (5.78), Baktash and Marsh (1987) deduced that the optimum slip force of a structure equipped with friction dampers is a property of the structure, unrelated to the type or intensity of seismic activity. This conclusion, however, is based on the assumption that the optimum seismic response of a friction damped structure is associated with maximum energy dissipation by friction at first yield of the structural frame. As outlined previously in Section 4.4, optimum performance from an energy point of view is not necessarily associated with maximum energy dissipation by the hysteretic dampers but rather with the minimization of the difference between the seismic input energy and the energy dissipated by the dampers. As will be seen in the next section, this approach leads to optimum activation loads of the hysteretic dampers that are dependent on both the structural and ground motion characteristics. Furthermore, it has been shown in Section 5.4, that the optimum activation load of a single-storey hysteretically damped structure excited by a harmonic ground motion is linearly dependent on the amplitude of the ground motion.

Ciampi et al. (1990, 1991, 1992, 1995) considered the design of hysteretic bracing systems using an approach based on inelastic response spectra. The design is defined by the choice of two characteristic parameters: the bracing stiffness k_b and the activation load of the bracing members F_a. After normalizing the equation of motion of the system to simplify the expressions, Ciampi et al. introduced the following set of four independent parameters governing the design:

- T_u, the elastic period of the unbraced frame;

- $\eta_u = V_{uy}/(ma_g)$, the ratio of the yield strength of the frame V_{uy} to the product of the mass of the system m times the peak ground acceleration a_g of the design ground motion

- $\lambda = k_b/k_u$, the ratio of bracing system stiffness k_b to the stiffness of the unbraced frame k_u;

- $\beta_\delta = \delta_{by}/\delta_{uy}$, the ratio of the displacement which causes yielding (or slipping) in the brace δ_{by} to the displacement which induces yielding of the frame δ_{uy}.

The authors recognized that the hysteretic bracing system needs to be activated much before yielding of the frame takes place. Consequently, β_δ is always equal to or less than one. Two ductility indices were considered to characterize the response of the frame damage:

- the maximum displacement ductility of the unbraced frame μ_u

- the cumulative ductility of the unbraced frame μ_{Hu} (also known as hysteretic ductility, since it is representative of the energy dissipated through plastic hysteresis).

Inelastic response spectra in terms of μ_u and μ_{Hu} were obtained by averaging the results of nonlinear dynamic time-history analyses over an ensemble of five artificial accelerograms. The spectra were plotted in terms of the four normalized parameters defined above. The design of the hysteretic bracing system can be made, for fixed values of β_δ and for known values T_u and η_u, by choosing a value of λ corresponding to a predefined level of ductility of the unbraced frame. It was noted that the use of the hysteretic ductility measure seems to give better results, since it takes into account the entire response history rather than only a maximum value that seems to systematically overestimate damage.

Ciampi et al. noted also that choosing larger values of β_δ resulted in a more substantial damage reduction. However, larger values of β_δ are also associated with larger values of V_{uy}, with stiffer braces and, consequently, with a larger total base shear. In general, it is suggested that β_δ be taken close to 0.5.

The application of this methodology to MDOF systems requires the selection of proper distributions of stiffness and yield force along the height of the building, aiming at uniform engagement of the bracing system in the energy dissipation process, and to avoid concentrations of damage at specific locations in the frame.

Dowdell and Cherry (1996) proposed a design method for SDOF structures equipped with friction dampers based on the concept of transfer functions. This method is based on minimizing the steady-state Root-Mean-Square (RMS) interstorey drift response of a structure excited by a stationary random process. Earthquake ground motions are neither stationary nor of infinite duration. However, they are random processes, and design events such as large subduction earthquakes are expected to have long enough duration so that many ordinary structures can potentially reach a steady-state response. The proposed method is primarily suited for these conditions.

The RMS interstorey drift is chosen as a matter of convenience since the RMS drift response of a linear viscous damped structure to a stationary random process can be described easily in the frequency domain (Dowdell and Cherry 1996).

Based on this approach, the design of a SDOF friction-damped system requires the following steps:

- Determine the power spectral density function of the input ground motion together with the characteristic RMS base acceleration. This data should be determined for the strong motion duration of the earthquake, which is defined in this study as the time interval required to accumulate between 5% and 95% of the accelerogram's total energy (Trifunac and Brady 1975, Dobry et al. 1978).

- Using the transfer function for the SDOF structure, generate a plot of the RMS interstorey drift as a function of the slip load of the friction damper.

- From the interstorey drift vs. slip load plot, select the slip load that yields the minimum RMS interstorey drift.

This proposed design methodology for SDOF is not easily extrapolated to MDOF systems. However, assuming that the structure responds primarily in its fundamental mode, these authors suggested the following approach:

- Assume an appropriate slip load distribution for the structure.

- Consider the design of an equivalent SDOF structure, using an equivalent mass equal to the total mass of the MDOF structure, and an equivalent frequency equal to that of the fundamental mode of the MDOF structure.

- Follow the above steps to select the optimal slip load of the SDOF structure.

- Equate the first storey slip load in the MDOF system to the slip load determined for the equivalent SDOF structure.

- Proportion the slip loads of the remaining stories based on the assumed slip load distribution.

Fu and Cherry (1999, 2000) proposed a simplified design procedure for SDOF friction damped steel frames based on the determination of an equivalent force reduction factor R. They adopted a tri-linear model to represent the hysteretic properties of the friction-damped structure to account for a situation where the friction damper is slipping and the frame members are yielding. For a system exhibiting nonlinear properties, the maximum displacement response resulting from ground motion excitations can be reasonably approximated from the analysis of an equivalent linear system whose stiffness and damping values are expressed in terms of the characteristic parameters of the nonlinear system. Fu and Cherry adopted the average stiffness and energy method (Iwan and Gates 1979) for the linearization of the tri-linear hysteresis system. The closed-form solutions obtained for the SDOF system study can then be used to evaluate the force modification factor R for the friction-damped system, as a function of the system parameters, to use in its seismic base shear calculations. Assuming that the deformed shape is essentially confined to the first mode, a MDOF friction-damped system can be condensed to a SDOF system by using a displacement transformation matrix. Hence, the response and damper parameters for the SDOF system are converted and applied to the solution of MDOF friction-damped systems. This leads to a code compatible design procedure for friction-damped systems.

To design a friction-damped frame, the design base shear is first calculated by dividing the code specified elastic base shear by the R factor, which is evaluated based on the selected system parameter. The design base shear is then distributed over the height of the frame in the form of lateral force acting at each storey level. The frame strength requirements are then determined and the frame members are sized correspondingly. Relative to the conventional frame design process, an additional design step is introduced at this point. The brace stiffness and the slip force of the friction damper at each storey level are determined in order to implement the target system parameters, and to facilitate the assumed linear deformed shape under the design earthquake.

Levy et al. (2000, 2001) proposed a two-phase iterative procedure for the design of steel frames incorporating friction-damped slotted-bolted connections. The design procedure is based on constraining the interstorey drifts of the friction-damped structure to be equal and incorporate two main phases. In the first phase, the initial unbraced multi-storey frame is condensed to an equivalent SDOF model. It is assumed that all friction dampers are activated simultaneously and that the slipping of each damper is the same. Therefore, the sum of the slip elongations for all dampers can be condensed into a single value in the equivalent SDOF model. The stiffness of the braced equivalent SDOF model is obtained by iterations using a structural optimization procedure to insure equal interstorey drifts in the associated multi-storey friction damped frame. In the second phase of the design process, a two stage iterative scheme is used to produce a distribution of brace stiffness and slip loads so that interstorey drifts are maintained constant after the dampers are activated. The procedure is based on the assumption that the distribution of slip loads in the dampers is proportional to the first modal interstorey shear force.

The optimum planar positioning of friction dampers in asymmetric elastic single-storey structures has been investigated by De LaLlera et al. (2005). It was found that friction dampers can control effectively the lateral-torsional coupling by positioning the dampers such that the so-called empirical center of balance (ECB) of the structure is at equal distance form all edges of the building. A simple equation determining the optimum location of the dampers was derived and can be extended to multi-storey structures.

5.7.3 Optimum Hysteretic Design Spectra

Earlier numerical studies (Filiatrault and Cherry 1988) have indicated the feasibility of using an optimum distribution of shear forces required to activate all hysteretic dampers in a structure that is proportional to the interstorey drift arising from a first mode vibration of the structure. For a building structure equipped with a *pair* of tension-compression bracing members at every level, the activation shear at a given storey i, V_{ai}, is related to the activation load of each damper F_{ai} by:

$$V_{ai} = 2F_{ai}\cos\gamma_i \tag{5.79}$$

where γ_i is the angle of inclination from the horizontal of the braces in storey i.

It has also been shown (Filiatrault and Cherry 1988), however, that little benefit is achieved from the use of this optimum distribution as compared with the use of the simpler uniform activation shear distribution $V_{ai} = V_a$ for $i = 1, 2, ..., N_f$ where N_f is the total number of floor levels. Based on this assumption, an optimum activation shear distribution was determined based on a numerical parametric study that takes into account the frequency content of the ground motion and the dynamic properties of the structure with and without the added bracing system (Filiatrault and Cherry 1990). For a given ground motion, the optimum activation shear distribution is determined by minimizing a Relative Performance Index RPI derived from energy concepts:

$$RPI = \frac{1}{2}\left[\frac{SEA}{SEA_0} + \frac{U_{max}}{U_{max0}}\right] \qquad (5.80)$$

where SEA is the strain energy area, i.e., the area under the strain energy time-history for all structural members of an hysteretically damped structure, SEA_0 is the strain energy area for a zero activation load, U_{max} is the maximum strain energy stored in all structural members of an hysteretically damped structure and U_{max0} is the maximum strain energy for a zero slip load. Values of the RPI are such that:

- $RPI = 1$, the response corresponds to the behaviour of an unbraced structure (activation load = 0).

- $RPI < 1$, the response of the hysteretically damped structure is "smaller" than the response of the unbraced structure.

- $RPI > 1$, the response of the hysteretically damped structure is "larger" than the response of the unbraced structure.

These authors recommended the selection of diagonal cross braces such that:

$$\frac{T_b}{T_u} < 0.40 \qquad (5.81)$$

where T_u is the fundamental period of the unbraced structure and T_b is the fundamental period of the braced structure. It was found that the most desirable response (minimum RPI) of hysteretically damped structures occurs for small values of T_b/T_u, which corresponds to large diagonal cross-braces. Therefore the diagonal cross-braces should be chosen with the largest possible cross-sectional area within the limits of cost and availability of material. Other researchers (e.g. Vulcano and Mazza 2000) have also recognized the effectiveness of friction damped braces with increasing values of bracing stiffness.

The procedure then requires the estimation of the design peak ground acceleration a_g and the predominant period of the design ground motion T_g for the site.

Recalling Equation (5.56), an equation can be written for the total shear force V_0 required to activate all hysteretic dampers in a structure (Filiatrault and Cherry 1990):

$$\frac{V_0}{W} = \frac{a_g}{g}\, Q\!\left(\frac{T_b}{T_g}, \frac{T_b}{T_u}, N_f\right) \qquad (5.82)$$

where Q is an unknown single valued function and N_f is the number of floors. A comprehensive parametric numerical study was conducted by Filiatrault and Cherry (1990) in order to provide an estimate of the function Q that minimizes the RPI value given by Equation (5.80):

$$Q = \begin{cases} \dfrac{T_g}{T_u}\left[(-1.24N_f - 0.31)\dfrac{T_b}{T_u} + 1.04N_f + 0.43\right] & \text{for } 0 \le T_g/T_u \le 1 \\[2ex] \dfrac{T_b}{T_u}\left[(0.01N_f + 0.02)\dfrac{T_g}{T_u} - 1.25N_f - 0.32\right] + \dfrac{T_g}{T_u}(0.002 - 0.002N_f) + 1.04N_f + 0.42 \\[1ex] \qquad\qquad\qquad\qquad\qquad\qquad \text{for } T_g/T_u > 1 \end{cases} \tag{5.83}$$

Equations (5.82) and (5.83) can be used directly to estimate the total optimum activation shear V_0. However, a graphical representation of these equations in the form of optimum hysteretic design spectra provides a more convenient and simplified method for establishing V_0.

If a plot of $V_0/(ma_g)$ (where m is the total seismic mass of the system), versus T_g/T_u is made for particular values of T_b/T_u and N_f, using Equations (5.82) and (5.83), a bilinear curve is obtained as illustrated in Figure 5.54. This curve represents a general hysteretic design spectrum for multi-storey hysteretically damped structures. This spectrum is completely described by specifying the ordinate O_1, corresponding to $T_g/T_u = 1$, and any other ordinate O_2 taken here as the ordinate values at $T_g/T_u = 5$. The ordinates O_1 and O_2 of these points can be obtained through Equation (5.83):

$$O_1 = (-1.24N_f - 0.31)\frac{T_b}{T_u} + 1.04N_f + 0.43$$

$$O_2 = (-1.07N_f - 0.10)\frac{T_b}{T_u} + 1.01N_f + 0.45 \tag{5.84}$$

Figure 5.55 shows optimum hysteretic design spectra for 1 to 10-storey hysteretically damped structures.

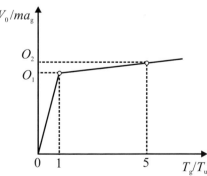

Figure 5.54 Construction of Optimum Hysteretic Design Spectrum

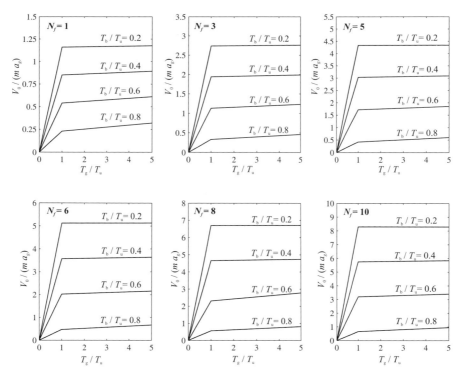

Figure 5.55 Optimum Hysteretic Damping Design Spectra for Structures Ranging from 1 to 10 Stories

Note that several assumptions were made in developing the optimum hysteretic design spectra:

- The study was conducted within the following range of parameters:
  $0.2 \leq T_b/T_u \leq 0.8$, $0.2 \leq T_b/T_g \leq 0.8$, $0.05 \leq a_g/T_g \leq 0.4$ and $N_f \leq 10$.

- The response of the main structural elements was assumed to remain elastic.

- The ground motions that were used to develop the hysteretic design spectra did not contain the damageable severe acceleration pulses that are expected in the near-field of major earthquake events.

- The choice of the two parameters (SEA and U_{max}) may not be appropriate to minimize structural and nonstructural damage in actual buildings. Other parameters such as peak interstorey drifts or floor absolute accelerations are now commonly used to evaluate the seismic performance of a structure.

5.7.4 Design Example

A design example utilizing the optimum hysteretic damping design spectrum is presented by considering the six-storey steel building structure shown in Figure 5.56. This building was originally studied by Popov and Tsai (1989), and was later modified by Hall (1995).

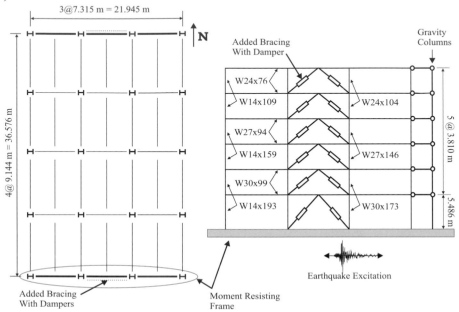

Figure 5.56 Steel Structure Used in Hysteretic Damper Design Example

The building is rectangular in plan and is braced in the East-West direction by two exterior moment-resisting frames. The design complies with the 1994 UBC code requirements (ICBO 1994) for a building located in Zone 4 on soil type S2. Design gravity loads included the roof dead load (3.8 kPa), the floor dead load (4.5 kPa), the roof live load (1.0 kPa), the floor live load (3.8 kPa) and the weight of the exterior cladding (1.7 kPa). A basic wind speed of 113 km/h and an exposure type B were assumed. The steel grade is assumed to be A36 (nominal F_y = 290 MPa) for all members.

The retrofit strategy considered for the structure consisted of introducing a tubular chevron braced frame (each bracing member: HSS 300 x 300 x 13 mm) in the middle bay of each moment-resisting frame, and installing hysteretic dampers at one end of the bracing members, as shown in Figure 5.56. This retrofit scheme with the bracing added only in the middle bay of the frames would likely be the one adopted in practice as it minimizes the level of intervention (i.e., less dampers and braces used and less connections to design, fabricate and install). Brace forces induced by dead loads were ignored in the design of the bracing and friction energy dissipating systems, as it was assumed that the braces would be installed after the building would be completed.

For the structure considered, T_u = 1.304 s and T_b = 0.648 s. Therefore: T_b/T_u = 0.497 in this case, which is close to the recommended value of 0.40 (see Equation (5.81)).

The design procedure outlined above then requires the estimation of the design peak ground acceleration a_g and the predominant ground period T_g for the site. A value of a_g = 0.40 g, corresponding to the Z factor for a zone 4 in the UBC code (ICBO 1994), was retained. Also, a value of T_g = 0.4 s was assumed as it corresponds to the predominant period of simulated ground motions for the Los Angeles region (Graves and Saikia 1995).

From these parameters, an optimum hysteretic design spectrum can be constructed to estimate the total activation shear V_0 of the structure. For this six-storey structure, applying Equation (5.83) yields Q = 0.863 or:

$$\frac{V_0}{W} = 0.863\frac{a_g}{g} = (0.863)(0.4) = 0.345 \tag{5.85}$$

which leads to the following value of the optimum activation shear:

$$V_0 = 0.345W = (0.345)(28950) = 9994 \text{ kN} \tag{5.86}$$

The total activation shear is distributed uniformly among the bracing at each floor of the two exterior frames:

$$V_{si} = \left(\frac{1}{2}\right)\left(\frac{9994}{6}\right) = 830 \text{ kN} \tag{5.87}$$

Using Equation (5.79), the optimum activation load for each of the two dampers located in the first storey F_{a1} is given by:

$$F_{a1} = \frac{830}{2\cos(56.3°)} = 750 \text{ kN} \tag{5.88}$$

The optimum activation load for each damper in all other stories F_{ai} is given by:

$$F_{ai} = \frac{830}{2\cos(46.2°)} = 600 \text{ kN} \quad \text{for } i = 2 \text{ to } 6 \tag{5.89}$$

The structure considered was subjected to a suite of five historical (LA) ground motion recordings from earthquakes with local magnitudes ranging from 6 to 7.3, which were scaled to match the 10% probability of exceedence in 50 years uniform hazard spectrum for Los Angeles (SAC Joint Venture 1997). The unscaled S00E El Centro record from the 1940 Imperial Valley Earthquake and the S69E Taft Lincoln Tunnel record from the 1952 Kern County Earthquake were also included in the analyses. These two ground motions have been used extensively in past studies, and are considered herein as a reference for comparison purposes.

Figure 5.57 presents the variation of peak interstorey drift with total slip shear ratio V_0/W, computed at the first, third and sixth floors of the building studied under each ground motion considered (Filiatrault et al. 2001). The values of V_0/W shown in the figures are within the nominal capacity in compression of the bracing members $(V_0/W) \le 1.80$.

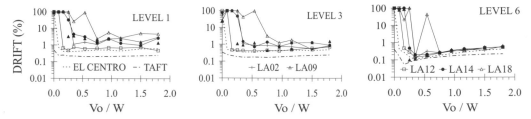

Figure 5.57 Peak Interstorey Drifts for Example Steel Structure (after Filiatrault et al. 2001)

For small values of activation shear, the performance of the building is similar to the behaviour of the unbraced structure ($V_0 = 0$). The LA ground motions, as well as the El Centro record, induce fracture of all beam-to-column welded connections leading to the total collapse of the structure (as indicated by interstorey drift values of 100% at each floor level). Past a threshold value of total activation shear, the building equipped with the hysteretic dampers experiences smaller deformations than the unbraced frame, but the response varies at each level. For the three upper floors, we note that:

- past the threshold value of the activation shear, the reduction in interstorey drift is significant for all ground motions, and

- there is an optimum activation shear that minimizes the interstorey drift. The optimum activation shear predicted by Equation (5.86), $(V_0/W) = 0.345$, nearly corresponds to that obtained from the analyses for the LA ground motions.

For the El Centro and the Taft records, the optimum activation shear is approximately half the predicted value. This is expected since these two records exhibit peak accelerations lower than the LA ground motions, and the computed optimum activation shear in Equation (5.86) is linearly proportional to the peak ground acceleration.

In the lower three floors of the building, the interstorey drifts increase and the performance of the hysteretic dampers becomes less effective. Also, the optimum activation shear is less defined. Under the El Centro and Taft records, the proposed $(V_0/W) = 0.345$ remains an effective solution as the associated interstorey drift is kept below 0.7% at every floor, and does not decrease significantly at higher slip shears. Overall, $(V_0/W) = 0.345$ also gives satisfactory results at level 3 under the LA motions, with peak interstorey drifts remaining within 2.5% of the storey height except for the LA09 record. However, a higher activation load would have further reduced the deformations at levels 2 and 3. Furthermore, the hysteretic dampers were not successful in reducing the interstorey drifts substantially at the bottom floor under the LA02, LA09 and LA14 records.

5.7.5 Significance of Optimal Design

Another reason for selecting the optimal response was put forward by Filiatrault and Cherry (1988) and Pall and Pall (1993). It was suggested that the seismic response of FDBFs is the least sensitive to variations in the slip load (as large as ±20%) when they are tuned to the optimal slip load value. This is schematically shown in Figure 5.58. Variations in the slip load in the friction device may occur due to environmental and constructional factors such as temperature change, adjustment variability and other uncertainties. Therefore, design procedures which target the optimal (minimum) response are likely to yield structures with a reduced sensitivity to variations in their actual slip load.

5.7.6 Performance-Based Design of Hysteretically Damped Structures

Simplified analysis techniques included in design standards (see Chapter 4) offer the means for assessing the response of structures equipped with hysteretic dampers but do not explicitly allow the designer to chose among a number of possible design options. The design procedure therefore consists of iterations until an acceptable solution is found. Approximate optimal design procedures presented in the above paragraphs give the designer additional insight towards a more efficient design by minimizing or optimizing response parameters which describe the performance of the hysteretically damped structure. In general, the optimized performance indices used are either the maximum displacement response or the maximum acceleration response, or factored combinations of both to suggest a single optimized solution. However, both these families of design methods offer limited information about the possible range of different seismic performance that can be achieved by changing the added brace stiffness and/or the damper activation load, and do not allow the designer to explicitly target a desired performance level. In a recent study by Mansour and Christopoulos (2005), an explicit

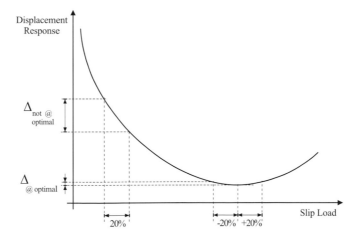

Figure 5.58 Effect of Variation in Slip Load on Displacement Response

performance-based design procedure for structures equipped with hysteretic dampers was suggested. Using a simplified nonlinear time-history dynamic analysis program EUGENIA (Lopez Garcia 2003), inelastic displacements and their corresponding acceleration response spectra for hysteretically damped SDOFs were derived for a range of damper activation loads and of values of T_b/T_u for a suite of twenty historical records. For a given record, the full suite of these response spectra are used to chose one or more solution that meets the desired performance levels for both displacement and accelerations.

In Figure 5.59 typical displacement and acceleration responses of a SDOF system equipped with hysteretic dampers subjected to the 1994 Northridge, California earthquake ground motion are presented in a three-dimensional spectrum format. All response quantities shown in this figure are for one SDOF structure with a value of T_u = 2.0s. The two axes forming the horizontal plane define the stiffness (T_b/T_u) and activation load (SL) properties of the added hysteretic damper. The activation load SL is defined as a fraction of the elastic load SL_e which corresponds to the load developed in the bracing system containing the hysteretic damper, if activation of the damper is impeded, and the structure responds elastically. When SL is set equal to SL_e, the structure responds elastically as a braced frame (with the added stiffness of the braces containing the dampers). Both SL and SL_e are normalized with respect to the weight of the structure. It can be seen that, depending on the desired combination of displacement and acceleration response criteria, a number of substantially different solutions are possible. In this representation, feasible and economical values of T_b/T_u can also be set by establishing the values of T_b corresponding to the largest brace that can reasonably be used for the hysteretic damper. From this matrix of calculations, the optimal design spectra are created for: i) the optimal displacement response, the corresponding acceleration response and the optimizing activation load for displacement; ii) the optimal acceleration response, the corresponding displacement response and the optimizing activation load for acceleration; and iii) the displacement and acceleration responses for varying activation loads in increments of the elastic brace load. Using these design spectra, the designer can choose the brace stiffness and activation load that will achieve the target performance both in terms of acceleration and displacement.

In Figure 5.60 the inelastic response displacements and accelerations for 10 increments of the activation load are shown for a structure with an unbraced period T_u = 2.0s for the 1994 Northridge, California earthquake ground motion record. The horizontal axis represents the period of the braced frame equipped with the hysteretic damper. It can be seen that generally, lower activation loads result in lower accelerations while the displacement response is variable for different values of the braced period. It can also be seen that for braced periods lower than 0.5s, the elastic response is the one which optimizes the displacement so that if the acceleration levels are acceptable, the retrofit strategy can simply consist of adding bracing members without the additional cost of adding the dampers.

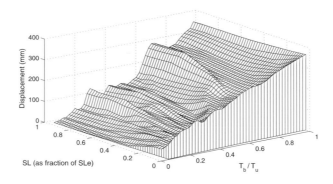

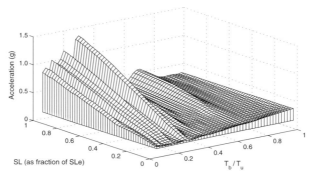

**Figure 5.59 Three-Dimensional Displacement and Acceleration Response
Spectra for Hysteretically Damped SDOFs, T_u = 2.0 s**

The best possible acceleration response of a structure equipped with hysteretic dampers is very close to the spectral acceleration of the unbraced structure and can be reached by using a low stiffness of the added bracing or by using a low activation load of the added damper such that the structure's effective stiffness is similar to that of the unbraced frame during most of the response. In the former case, the displacement response will remain large because of the longer period of the braced frame, whereas in the latter case, when a higher brace stiffness is used in conjunction with a low slip load, not only are the accelerations reduced but the maximum displacement response is also controlled.

As discussed in the previous paragraph, sizing hysteretic dampers for an optimal displacement response is highly desirable. However, the designer must be able to immediately assess the effect of the optimal displacement sized dampers on the acceleration response. Optimal displacement spectra were derived for different values of T_u and the corresponding acceleration response for the optimized systems are also computed. In Figure 5.61, an example of such optimal displacement spectra for structures with T_u ranging from 2.5s to 0.75s for the 1994 Northridge, California earthquake ground

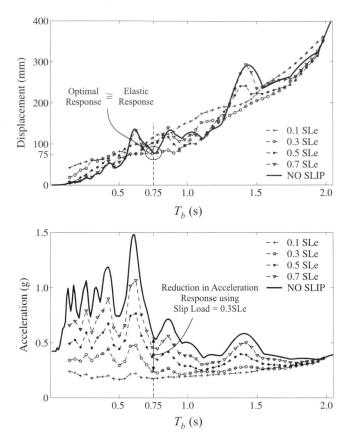

Figure 5.60 Displacement and Acceleration Response Spectra for Hysteretically Damped SDOFs with Various Damper Activation Loads, $T_u = 2.0$ **s**

motion record is shown. The elastic displacement and acceleration response spectra are also shown in dashed lines in the figure.

As it can be seen in this figure, all optimal displacement curves merge onto the optimal curve obtained for $T_u = 2.5$s, indicating that a common back bone curve of optimal displacement systems can be generated for all systems with smaller T_u values. For a given value of T_u, a target displacement is chosen and the value of T_b that achieves this target displacement for an optimal tuning is determined graphically. The corresponding acceleration is read on the acceleration spectrum. If this solution is acceptable to the designer, the activation load leading to this solution is also determined on the acceleration spectrum by solving for the displacement at which the optimal damper is activated Δ_{act}:

$$\Delta_{act}k_b + (\Delta_{opt} - \Delta_{act})k_u = ma_{opt} \qquad (5.90)$$

where the force provided by the assumed inherent viscous damping is neglected and where Δ_{opt} and a_{opt} are the maximum displacement and acceleration values of the

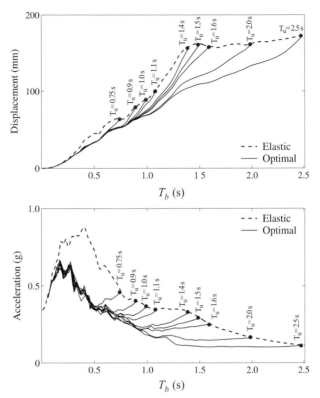

Figure 5.61 Typical Optimal Displacement and Corresponding Acceleration Response Spectra for Hysteretically Damped SDOFs

optimal solution respectively. The activation load is obtained by multiplying Δ_{act} by the initial stiffness of the braced frame.

Such spectra were derived for all twenty individual records and averaged to derive general optimal design spectra and corresponding acceleration spectra. A procedure to extend this approach to MDOF structures was also suggested using a transformation based on the fundamental mode of vibration of the structure. The effect of the distribution of the activation load along the height of the building was also investigated by considering both a uniform activation load and an activation load distribution aimed at achieving simultaneous activation of the hysteretic dampers under the first mode of vibration of the structure. The distributed activation loads were found to improve the response of the structure and to better correspond with the expected response of the structure once it was designed with the method described above. Further work to establish optimum design curves for smooth code spectra is also currently under way. From the results obtained from this study, and as can be seen in Figure 5.61, for the design of new structures, systems with large values of T_u, low values of T_b and optimal activation load lead to systems with controlled displacement and acceleration response.

5.8 PROBLEMS

Problem 5.1

A simple one-storey steel portal frame is to be retrofitted with a friction damper installed in a tension-compression bracing system as shown in Figure 5.62.

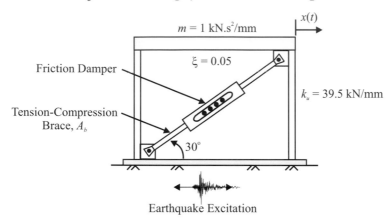

Figure 5.62 Simple One-Storey Steel Portal Frame Retrofitted with a Friction Damper

The design earthquake for the structure is the S00E component of the accelerogram recorded at El Centro on May 18, 1940 (a_g = 0.34 g, T_g = 0.5 s). Assuming that the unbraced frame remains elastic, and using the optimum hysteretic design spectrum discussed in Section 5.7.3:

a)   Estimate the optimum cross-sectional area A_b of the cross brace;

b)   Estimate the optimum slip load of the friction damper;

c)   For the estimated values obtained in a) and b), plot the base shear-displacement hysteresis of the retrofitted structure;

d)   Using the computer program RUAUMOKO contained in the CD-ROM accompanying this book, develop a model of the frame and compute the maximum displacement at the floor level of the retrofitted structure. Compare your answer with the maximum displacement of the original structure (the El Centro record is contained in the file "EL40NSC.EQB" on the CD-ROM).

Problem 5.2

You are asked to perform an equivalent linear dynamic analysis of a structure equipped with a metallic damping system. The force-displacement behaviour of the yielding devices used can be approximated by rigid-plastic rectangular hysteresis loops, as shown in Figure 5.63. The yield load is F_y, while the displacement amplitude is X_0.

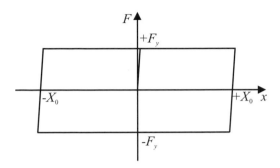

Figure 5.63 Force-Displacement Behaviour of Yielding Device

a)   Determine, as a function of F_y and X_0, the effective stiffness of the devices to be used in the linear model;

b)   Determine the equivalent viscous damping ratio of the devices to be used in the linear model;

c)   Comment on the practice of replacing a nonlinear structure equipped with yielding devices by a linear system with equivalent viscous damping.

CHAPTER 6: VISCOUS AND VISCOELASTIC DAMPERS

6.1 INTRODUCTION

The control of vibrations by viscous and/or viscoelastic materials has been used for several decades on aircrafts and aerospace structures. In Civil Engineering structures, however, the first use of viscoelastic dampers dates back to 1969 when over 10 000 viscoelastic dampers were installed in each of the twin towers of the late World Trade Center in New York (Mahmoodi et al. 1987). These dampers were designed to reduce the vibrations caused by wind.

Only in the last decade have dampers incorporating viscous and/or viscoelastic materials been used in seismic applications. This chapter discusses the behaviour of structures equipped with viscous or viscoelastic dampers under earthquake ground motions.

6.2 HYSTERETIC BEHAVIOUR OF LINEAR AND NONLINEAR VISCOUS DAMPERS

6.2.1 Linear Viscous Dampers

Consider first a pure viscous element subjected to a time-varying relative axial displacement history $x(t)$ given by:

$$x(t) = X_0 \sin \omega t \tag{6.1}$$

where X_0 is the displacement amplitude between the two ends of the element and ω is the circular forcing frequency. The axial force $F(t)$ induced in the element is linearly proportional to the relative velocity between its two ends:

$$F(t) = C_L \dot{x}(t) \tag{6.2}$$

where C_L is the linear viscous damping constant.

Substituting Equation (6.1) into Equation (6.2) yields:

$$F(t) = C_L \omega X_0 \cos \omega t \tag{6.3}$$

From basic trigonometry:

$$\cos \omega t = \pm \sqrt{1 - \sin^2 \omega t} \tag{6.4}$$

Substituting Equation (6.4) into Equation (6.3) yields the force-displacement relationship for the linear viscous damper:

$$F(t) = \pm C_L \omega \sqrt{X_0^2 - x^2(t)} \tag{6.5}$$

or:

$$\frac{F(t)}{X_0 C_L \omega} = \pm \sqrt{1 - \left(\frac{x(t)}{X_0}\right)^2} \tag{6.6}$$

The hysteresis loop described by Equation (6.6) is in the shape of an ellipse as illustrated in Figure 6.1. The amplitude of the maximum induced force in a linear viscous

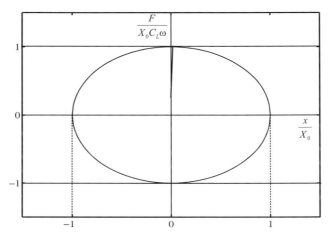

Figure 6.1 Hysteretic Behaviour of a Linear Viscous Damper

damper is linearly proportional to the excitation frequency, to the displacement amplitude and to the damping constant. Also, the maximum force in the linear viscous damper occurs at zero displacement. At maximum displacement, on the other hand, the force in the linear viscous damper is zero. In other words, the forces generated by linear viscous dampers in a structure are "out-of-phase" with the forces generated by the structural system. This is a significant advantage that viscous damping systems have over hysteretic damping systems that generate their maximum forces when the structural system is at its maximum displacements (see Chapter 5).

The energy dissipated by the linear viscous damper in each cycle E_{vd} is the area under the force-displacement relationship:

$$E_{vd} = \int_0^{2\pi/\omega} F(t)\dot{x}(t)dt = C_L \omega^2 X_0^2 \int_0^{2\pi/\omega} \cos^2\omega t \; dt \tag{6.7}$$

which yields:

$$E_{vd} = C_L \omega^2 X_0^2 \left[\frac{t}{2} + \frac{1}{4\omega}\sin 2\omega t\right]\Bigg|_0^{2\pi/\omega} = C_L \pi \, \omega X_0^2 \qquad (6.8)$$

The energy dissipated per cycle is linearly proportional to the linear damping constant and to the excitation frequency, and is proportional to the square of the displacement amplitude.

6.2.2 Nonlinear Viscous Dampers

Fluid type dampers can be designed to behave as nonlinear viscous elements by adjusting their silicone oil and orificing characteristics (see Section 6.6). The main advantage of nonlinear viscous dampers is that, in the event of a velocity spike, the force in the viscous damper is controlled to avoid overloading the damper or the bracing system to which it is connected.

The axial force developed by a nonlinear viscous damper $F(t)$ is expressed by:

$$F(t) = C_{NL}\operatorname{sgn}(\dot{x}(t))|\dot{x}(t)|^{\alpha_{vd}} \qquad (6.9)$$

where C_{NL} is the nonlinear viscous damping constant and α_{vd} is a predetermined velocity coefficient in the range of 0.2 to 1. When $\alpha_{vd} = 1$, the device acts as a linear viscous damper and Equation (6.9) is equivalent to Equation (6.2). When $\alpha_{vd} > 1$, on the other hand, the device acts as a shock transmitting or lock-up unit, by developing large forces at high velocities. Lock-up units can be used to engage multiple lateral load-resisting elements of a structure, such as adjacent spans in a bridge, together during transient wind or seismic excitation.

As illustrated in Figure 6.2, the advantage of using nonlinear viscous dampers with $\alpha_{vd} < 1$ is the reduction of damper forces at high velocities.

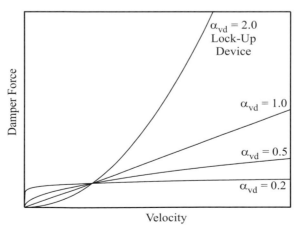

Figure 6.2 Force Velocity Properties of Different Nonlinear Viscous Dampers

Consider a nonlinear viscous damper subjected to a harmonic relative displacement time-history between its ends $x(t)$ given by:

$$x(t) = X_0 \sin \omega t \qquad (6.10)$$

Substituting Equation (6.10) into Equation (6.9) yields:

$$F(t) = C_{NL} \operatorname{sgn}(\cos \omega t)|\omega X_0 \cos \omega t|^{\alpha_{vd}} \qquad (6.11)$$

Substituting Equation (6.4) into Equation (6.11) yields the force-displacement relationship for the nonlinear viscous damper:

$$\frac{F}{C_{NL}(X_0\omega)^{\alpha_{vd}}} = \pm\left(1 - \left(\frac{x(t)}{X_0}\right)^2\right)^{\frac{\alpha_{vd}}{2}} \qquad (6.12)$$

The hysteresis loop described by Equation (6.12) is illustrated in Figure 6.3 for three different values of α_{vd}. Although the forces in nonlinear viscous dampers remain out-of-phase with the forces developed by the structural system, the cyclic response of nonlinear viscous dampers approaches the rectangular load-displacement relationship of hysteretic dampers as the value of α_{vd} decreases. However, the amplitude of the maximum induced force in a nonlinear viscous damper remains linearly proportional to the nonlinear damping constant and proportional to the power of α_{vd}, the excitation frequency and displacement amplitude.

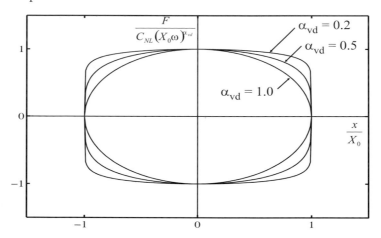

Figure 6.3 Hysteretic Behaviour of Nonlinear Viscous Dampers

The energy dissipated by a nonlinear viscous damper in each cycle E_{vd} is the area under the force-displacement relationship:

$$E_{vd} = \int_0^{2\pi/\omega} F(t)\dot{x}(t)dt = 4C_L(X_0\omega)^{\alpha_{vd}+1} \int_0^{\pi/2\omega} \cos^{\alpha_{vd}+1}\omega t \quad dt \qquad (6.13)$$

Evaluating the integral on the right-hand-side of Equation (6.13), we get:

$$E_{vd} = 4C_{NL}(X_0\omega)^{\alpha_{vd}+1} \frac{\sqrt{\pi}}{2\omega} \frac{\Gamma(1+\alpha_{vd}/2)}{\Gamma(3/2+\alpha_{vd}/2)} \tag{6.14}$$

which can be rearranged to yield:

$$E_{vd} = 2\sqrt{\pi}C_{NL}(X_0)^{\alpha_{vd}+1}\omega^{\alpha_{vd}} \frac{\Gamma(1+\alpha_{vd}/2)}{\Gamma(3/2+\alpha_{vd}/2)} \tag{6.15}$$

where Γ is the gamma function.

6.3 HYSTERETIC BEHAVIOUR OF VISCOELASTIC DAMPERS

Viscous dampers provide only a velocity-dependent force and must therefore be combined with a structure that provides a restoring force to the system. Viscoelastic dampers provide both a velocity dependent force which provides supplemental viscous damping to the system (similarly to viscous dampers), and a displacement-dependent elastic restoring force. Typical viscoelastic dampers used in practice are made of copolymers or glassy substances. Often these dampers are incorporated in bracing members and dissipate the seismic energy through shear deformations of the viscoelastic material, as illustrated in Figure 6.4.

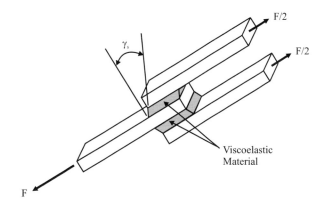

Figure 6.4 Typical Viscoelastic Damper Acting in Shear in a Bracing Member

As their name suggests, viscoelastic materials are not purely viscous but exhibit also an elastic response. A model that can be used to represent this behaviour is the simple Kelvin solid illustrated in Figure 6.5.

The elastic shear modulus is represented by the symbol G_E while the shear viscous damping constant is represented by the symbol G_C.

To derive the shear stress-strain $(\tau_s(t) - \gamma_s(t))$ constitutive relationship for the Kelvin solid, it is assumed that the element in Figure 6.5 is of unit height and unit area. In other words, displacements can be expressed as strains, and forces can be expressed as stresses.

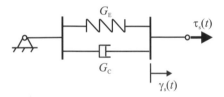

Figure 6.5 Kelvin Solid Model

By equilibrium:

$$\tau_E(t) + \tau_c(t) = \tau_s(t) \tag{6.16}$$

where $\tau_E(t)$ is the shear stress carried by the elastic component of the material at time t and $\tau_c(t)$ is the shear stress carried by the viscous component of the material at time t.

By shear strain compatibility:

$$\gamma_E(t) = \gamma_c(t) = \gamma_s(t) \tag{6.17}$$

where $\gamma_E(t)$ is the elastic shear strain at time t and $\gamma_c(t)$ is the viscous shear strain at time t. The shear strain rate across the element can be obtained by differentiating Equation (6.17) with respect to time:

$$\dot{\gamma}_E(t) = \dot{\gamma}_c(t) = \dot{\gamma}_s(t) \tag{6.18}$$

Replacing the constitutive relations for the elastic and viscous components in Equation (6.18) yields:

$$\frac{\dot{\tau}_E(t)}{G_E} = \frac{\tau_C(t)}{G_C} = \dot{\gamma}_s(t) \tag{6.19}$$

or

$$\tau_E(t) = G_E \gamma_s(t)$$
$$\tau_c(t) = G_C \dot{\gamma}_s(t) \tag{6.20}$$

Substituting Equation (6.20) into Equation (6.16) leads to the shear constitutive relationship for the Kelvin solid:

$$\tau_s(t) = G_E \gamma_s(t) + G_C \dot{\gamma}_s(t) \tag{6.21}$$

If the viscoelastic material has a shear thickness h_s and a shear area A_s, Equation (6.21) can be transformed into a force-displacement relationship $(F(t) - x(t))$:

$$F(t) = \bar{k}\, x(t) + \bar{c}\, \dot{x}(t) \tag{6.22}$$

where:

$$\bar{k} = \frac{G_E A_s}{h} \quad \text{and} \quad \bar{c} = \frac{G_c A_s}{h} \tag{6.23}$$

Now assume that the Kelvin element is subjected to the time-varying relative axial displacement history $x(t)$:

$$x(t) = X_0 \sin \omega t \qquad (6.24)$$

where X_0 is the displacement amplitude between the two ends of the element and ω is the circular forcing frequency. The axial force induced in the viscoelastic damper $F(t)$ is obtained by substituting Equation (6.24) into Equation (6.22):

$$F(t) = \bar{k} X_0 \sin \omega t + \bar{c} X_0 \omega \cos \omega t \qquad (6.25)$$

Substituting Equation (6.4) into Equation (6.25) yields:

$$F(t) = \bar{k} X_0 \sin \omega t \pm \bar{c} X_0 \omega \sqrt{1 - \sin^2 \omega t} \qquad (6.26)$$

or:

$$F(t) = \bar{k}\, x(t) \pm \bar{c} \omega \sqrt{X_0 - x^2(t)} \qquad (6.27)$$

Rearranging Equation (6.27):

$$\frac{F(t)}{X_0 \bar{c} \omega} = \frac{\bar{k}}{\bar{c}\omega} \left(\frac{x(t)}{X_0} \right) \pm \sqrt{1 - \left(\frac{x(t)}{X_0} \right)^2} \qquad (6.28)$$

Equation (6.28) describes an inclined ellipse as shown in Figure 6.6. As was the case for the purely viscous damper (see Figure 6.1), the maximum force in the viscoelastic damper does not occur at the maximum displacement. This out-of-phase behaviour of viscoelastic dampers is not as pronounced as it is for purely viscous dampers. However, for viscoelastic dampers, this phasing can be adjusted for a particular situation by adjusting the viscoelastic material properties $\bar{k}$ and $\bar{c}$.

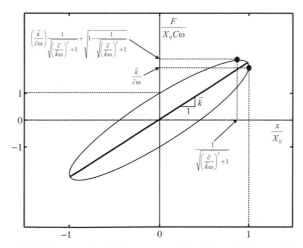

Figure 6.6 Hysteretic Behaviour of a Visco-Elastic Damper

Again, the energy dissipated by the Kelvin solid element in each cycle E_{ved} is the area under the force-displacement relationship.

$$E_{ved} = \int_0^{2\pi/\omega} F(t)\dot{x}(t)dt = \bar{k} X_0^2 \omega \int_0^{2\pi/\omega} \sin\omega t \cos\omega t dt + \bar{c} X_0^2 \omega^2 \int_0^{2\pi/\omega} \cos^2\omega t \, dt \quad (6.29)$$

which yields:

$$E_{ved} = \bar{k} X_0^2 \omega \left[\frac{1}{2\omega}\sin^2\omega t \right]\Big|_0^{2\pi/\omega} + \bar{c} X_0^2 \omega^2 \left[\frac{t}{2} + \frac{1}{4\omega}\sin 2\omega t \right]\Big|_0^{2\pi/\omega} \quad (6.30)$$

and finally:

$$E_{ved} = \bar{c}\pi\omega X_0^2 \quad (6.31)$$

which is the same result as Equation (6.8) for linear viscous dampers. As expected, the elastic stiffness portion of the Kelvin element does not contribute to the energy dissipation as the first term in Equation (6.30) vanishes. Also, the material properties of the Kelvin element, $\bar{k}$ and $\bar{c}$, can easily be obtained from displacement-controlled sinusoidal tests at various excitation frequencies. The elastic stiffness $\bar{k}$ represents the effective stiffness of the hysteresis loops, as shown in Figure 6.6, and the viscous damping coefficient $\bar{c}$ can be obtained from Equation (6.31) once the area under the hysteretic response curve is computed for a given excitation frequency and displacement amplitude.

The equivalent viscous damping ratio of a viscoelastic damper represented by a Kelvin element $\bar{\xi}$ can be obtained from first principles:

$$\bar{\xi} = \frac{\bar{c}}{2\bar{\omega}m} \quad (6.32)$$

where $\bar{\omega}$ is the oscillating circular frequency of the element and m is the mass connected to its ends. Equation (6.32) can be re-written as:

$$\bar{\xi} = \frac{\bar{c}\bar{\omega}^2}{2\bar{\omega}\bar{k}} = \frac{\bar{c}\bar{\omega}}{2\bar{k}} = \frac{G_c\bar{\omega}}{2G_E} \quad (6.33)$$

In the theory of viscoelasticity, G_E is defined as the *shear storage modulus* of the viscoelastic material, which is a measure of the energy stored and recovered per cycle; $G_C\,\bar{\omega}$ is defined as the *shear loss modulus*, which gives a measure of the energy dissipated per cycle. Another measure of the energy dissipation capacity of the viscoelastic material is given by the *loss factor* η defined as:

$$\eta = \frac{G_C\,\bar{\omega}}{G_E} = 2\bar{\xi} \quad (6.34)$$

Note that by combining Equations (6.33) and (6.34), the damping constant of the viscoelastic damper $\bar{c}$ can also be expressed in terms of the loss factor, η:

$$\bar{c} = \frac{\eta \bar{k}}{\bar{\omega}} \qquad (6.35)$$

6.4 VARIATION OF SHEAR STORAGE AND SHEAR LOSS MODULI OF VISCOELASTIC MATERIALS

From the previous discussion, it becomes clear that the shear storage modulus and the shear loss modulus, or the shear storage modulus and the loss factor determine the dynamic response in shear of the viscoelastic material, modeled as a Kelvin solid, under displacement-controlled harmonic excitation. These moduli depend on several parameters: i) the excitation frequency, ii) the ambient temperature, iii) the shear strain level and iv) the variation of the internal temperature within the material during operation.

A number of experimental investigations have been carried out over the last fifteen years to determine the dependence of the shear storage modulus G_E and of the shear loss modulus $G_C \bar{\omega}$ on the excitation frequency, the ambient temperature and the shear strain level γ_s.

In one series of tests, Chang et al. (1993a, b) evaluated the dynamic cyclic shear response of three different types of viscoelastic materials. The configuration of the dampers tested was similar to that of Figure 6.4. The three types of viscoelastic materials are designated herein by A, B, and C. Types A and B are made of the same viscoelastic material but are different in the damper dimensions. Type C is made of a different viscoelastic material. Table 6-1 presents the geometrical properties of the three types of dampers tested.

Table 6-1: Geometry of Viscoelastic Dampers Tested (after Chang et al. 1993a, b)

Material Type	Shear Area (mm^2)	Thickness (mm)	Volume (mm^3)
A	968	5.08	4917
B	1936	7.62	14752
C	11613	3.81	44246

Figure 6.7 presents the hysteretic behaviour of the three types of dampers subjected to displacement-controlled sinusoidal excitations at a frequency of 3.5 Hz and at a peak shear strain level of 5% and for two different ambient temperatures. All hysteresis loops are well rounded, indicating a good energy dissipation capacity of the dampers. The shear storage modulus (effective stiffness) and the energy dissipated per cycle decrease with increasing ambient temperature. Table 6-2 presents the calculated values of the shear storage and shear loss moduli of the three types of viscoelastic dampers for different temperatures. Again, these results were obtained for displacement-controlled sinusoidal excitations at a frequency of 3.5 Hz and a shear strain level of 5%. Although both moduli decrease with

increasing ambient temperature, the loss factor η remains fairly constant for all temperatures. Also, damper type C is less sensitive to the change in ambient temperature.

Table 6-3 presents the moduli values obtained from test results for type B dampers under excitation frequencies of 1 Hz and 3 Hz, ambient temperatures of 24°C and 36°C and shear strain levels of 5% and 20%. The properties of the viscoelastic damper remain fairly independent of shear strain for strain levels below 20% for every temperature and frequency.

Table 6-2: Variations of Viscoelastic Damper Moduli, 5% Shear Strain, 3.5Hz
(after Chang et al. 1993b)

Material Type	Temperature (°C)	G_E (MPa)	$G_C \bar{\omega}$ (MPa)	$\eta = \dfrac{G_C \bar{\omega}}{G_E}$
A	21	2.78	3.01	1.08
	24	2.10	2.38	1.13
	28	1.57	1.90	1.21
	32	1.17	1.37	1.17
	36	0.83	0.90	1.08
	40	0.63	0.63	1.00
B	25	1.73	2.08	1.20
	30	1.29	1.54	1.19
	34	0.94	1.11	1.18
	38	0.76	0.84	1.10
	42	0.62	0.65	1.05
C	25	0.19	0.17	0.90
	30	0.16	0.12	0.75
	34	0.14	0.10	0.71
	38	0.12	0.08	0.67
	42	0.11	0.07	0.64

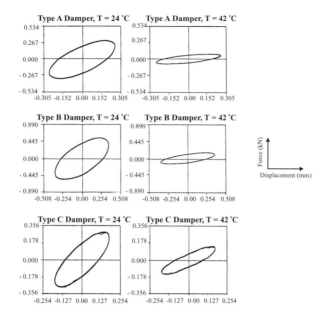

Figure 6.7 Hysteretic Responses of Viscoelastic Dampers, 5% Shear Strain, 3.5 Hz Frequency (after Chang et al. 1993b)

Table 6-3: Variations of Moduli for Viscoelastic Damper Type B (after Chang et al. 1993b)

Temperature (°C)	Excitation Frequency (Hz)	Shear Strain Level (%)	G_E (MPa)	$G_C\,\bar{\omega}$ (MPa)	$\eta = \dfrac{G_C\,\bar{\omega}}{G_E}$
24	1.0	5	0.98	1.17	1.19
		20	0.96	1.15	1.20
	3.0	5	1.88	2.23	1.19
		20	1.77	2.11	1.19
36	1.0	5	0.41	0.46	1.12
		20	0.40	0.45	1.13
	3.0	5	0.74	0.82	1.11
		20	0.71	0.77	1.09

6.5 DYNAMIC ANALYSIS OF STRUCTURES INCORPORATING VISCOUS AND VISCOELASTIC DAMPERS

Consider a one storey frame equipped with a viscoelastic damper incorporated in a diagonal bracing member inclined at an angle γ with the horizontal, and subjected to a ground acceleration, as illustrated in Figure 6.8. As a first approximation, we can assume the bracing member infinitely rigid.

The equation of motion can be written as:

$$m\ddot{x}(t) + c\dot{x}(t) + kx(t) + F_{Ved}(t) = -m\ddot{x}_g(t) \tag{6.36}$$

where F_{Ved} is the lateral force provided by the viscoelastic damper and c is the equivalent viscous damping constant of the unbraced structure. The axial force in the bracing element $F(t)$ corresponding to the shear force across the damping material is given by Equation (6.22):

$$F(t) = \bar{k}\,\Delta(t) + \bar{c}\,\dot{\Delta}(t) \tag{6.37}$$

where $\Delta(t)$ is the displacement between the two ends of (and parallel to) the bracing member.

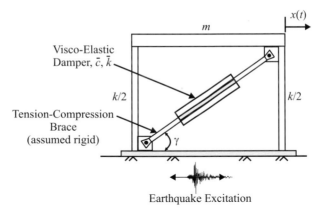

Figure 6.8 Single Storey Structure Equipped with Viscoelastic Dampers

By equilibrium:

$$F_{Ved}(t) = F(t)\cos\gamma \tag{6.38}$$

By compatibility:

$$\Delta(t) = x(t)\cos\gamma \tag{6.39}$$

Substituting Equations (6.38) and (6.39) into Equation (6.37) and the resulting expression into Equation (6.36) yields:

$$m\ddot{x}(t) + c\dot{x}(t) + kx(t) + (\bar{k}x(t) + \bar{c}\dot{x}(t))\cos^2\gamma = -m\ddot{x}_g(t) \tag{6.40}$$

or:

$$m\ddot{x}(t) + (c + \bar{c}\cos^2\gamma)\dot{x}(t) + (k + \bar{k}\cos^2\gamma)x(t) = -m\ddot{x}_g(t) \tag{6.41}$$

Equation (6.41) reveals that the dynamic analysis of a linear single storey frame incorporating a viscoelastic damper can be performed with standard analysis techniques using equivalent stiffness and damping coefficients. Note that Equation (6.41) strictly applies under harmonic motion at a frequency ω. However, it represents a reasonable approximation for more general ground motions within a narrow frequency band, provided that $\bar{k}$ and $\bar{c}$ are nearly constant throughout that frequency band.

The extension of the dynamic analysis to MDOF structures is straightforward. Assuming that the structure remains elastic when equipped with viscoelastic dampers, the equations of motion can be written as:

$$[[M] + [\bar{m}]]\{\ddot{x}(t)\} + [[C] + [\bar{c}]]\{\dot{x}(t)\} + [[K] + [\bar{k}]]\{x(t)\} = -[M]\{r\}\ddot{x}_g(t) \quad (6.42)$$

where $[\bar{m}]$ is the mass matrix corresponding to the added dampers, $[\bar{c}]$ is the added viscous damping matrix attributed to the viscoelastic dampers and $[\bar{k}]$ is the global stiffness matrix attributed to the added viscoelastic dampers.

If the damping matrix corresponding to the added dampers $[\bar{c}]$ is assumed to have the same orthogonality properties as the original mass and stiffness matrices of the structure, standard modal analysis can be used to uncouple Equation (6.42). The equation of motion for the ith mode can be written as:

$$\tilde{M}_i\ddot{u}_i(t) + \tilde{C}_i\dot{u}_i(t) + \tilde{K}_i u_i(t) = \tilde{P}_i(t) \quad (6.43)$$

where:

$\tilde{M}_i = \{A^{(i)}\}^T[[M] + [\bar{m}]]\{A^{(i)}\}$ is the generalized mass in mode i

$\tilde{C}_i = \{A^{(i)}\}^T[[C] + [\bar{c}]]\{A^{(i)}\}$ is the generalized damping coefficient in mode i

$\tilde{K}_i = \{A^{(i)}\}^T[[K] + [\bar{k}]]\{A^{(i)}\}$ is the generalized stiffness coefficient in mode i

$\tilde{P}_i(t) = -\{A^{(i)}\}^T[M]\{r\}\ddot{x}_g(t)$ is the generalized dynamic loading in mode i

The analysis can be simplified by assuming, conservatively, that the inherent damping of the structure is negligible compared to the supplemental damping provided by the added dampers. The mass of the dampers can also be omitted since it is usually negligible compared to the mass of the structure.

The modal response in the ith mode of vibration $u_i(t)$ can be obtained by Duhamel's integral:

$$u_i(t) = \frac{1}{\tilde{M}_i\,\tilde{\omega}_{di}} \int_0^t \tilde{P}_i(\tau)e^{\tilde{\xi}_i\tilde{\omega}_i(t-\tau)}\sin\tilde{\omega}_{di}(t-\tau)d\tau \quad (6.44)$$

where $\tilde{\omega}_i$ is the ith undamped modal frequency of the structure with added viscoelastic dampers, $\tilde{\omega}_{di}$ is the ith damped modal frequency and $\tilde{\xi}_i$ is the ith modal damping ratio due to the added viscoelastic dampers. These quantities are given by:

$$\tilde{\omega}_i^2 = \frac{\tilde{\overline{K}}_i}{\tilde{\overline{M}}_i}$$

$$\tilde{\omega}_{di}^2 = \tilde{\omega}_i^2 \sqrt{1 - \tilde{\xi}_i^2} \tag{6.45}$$

$$\tilde{\xi}_i = \frac{\tilde{\overline{C}}_i}{2\tilde{\omega}_i \tilde{\overline{M}}_i}$$

The ith modal damping ratio $\tilde{\xi}_i$ can be expressed in terms of the properties of the viscoelastic material. For this purpose, one realizes that the elements of $[\bar{c}]$ are a linear combination of the damping constants of the individual viscoelastic dampers in the structure. Assuming that only one viscoelastic material is used, these elements of the $[\bar{c}]$ matrix $\bar{c}_{jk}$ can be related to the elements of the $[\bar{k}]$ matrix $\bar{k}_{jk}$ using Equation (6.35):

$$\bar{c}_{jk} = \frac{2\tilde{\xi}_i \bar{k}_{jk}}{\tilde{\omega}_i} = \frac{\eta_i \bar{k}_{jk}}{\tilde{\omega}_i} \tag{6.46}$$

where η_i is the loss factor of the viscoelastic material at a frequency $\tilde{\omega}_i$.

From Equation (6.46), the $[\bar{c}]$ matrix can be expressed in terms of the $[\bar{k}]$ matrix:

$$[\bar{c}] = \frac{\eta_i}{\tilde{\omega}_i}[\bar{k}] \tag{6.47}$$

Furthermore, the generalized damping coefficient in the ith mode can be expressed in terms of the basic properties of the viscoelastic material (Equations (6.33) and (6.34)):

$$\tilde{\overline{C}}_i = \frac{2\tilde{\xi}_i \tilde{\omega}_i^2 \tilde{\overline{M}}_i}{\tilde{\omega}_i} = \frac{2\tilde{\xi}_i \overline{K}_i}{\tilde{\omega}_i} = \frac{\eta_i \overline{K}_i}{\tilde{\omega}_i} \tag{6.48}$$

where $\overline{K}_i = \{A^{(i)}\}^T [\bar{k}]\{A^{(i)}\}$ is the generalized stiffness coefficient in mode i corresponding only to the added viscoelastic dampers.

From Equation (6.45), the ith modal damping ratio can be obtained by:

$$\tilde{\xi}_i = \frac{\eta_i \overline{K}_i}{2\tilde{\omega}_i^2 \tilde{\overline{M}}_i} = \frac{\eta_i \overline{K}_i}{2\tilde{\overline{K}}_i} = \frac{\eta_i}{2}\left(1 - \frac{\{A^{(i)}\}^T[K]\{A^{(i)}\}}{\{A^{(i)}\}^T[[K]+[\bar{k}]]\{A^{(i)}\}}\right) = \frac{\eta_i}{2}\left(1 - \frac{\omega_i^2}{\tilde{\omega}_i^2}\right) \tag{6.49}$$

where ω_i is the ith modal frequency of the original structure before the viscoelastic dampers are added.

Note that as an alternative to modal analysis, time-history analysis can also be performed. In this case, each individual damper is inserted into the structure with its own mechanical properties $\bar{k}$ and $\bar{c}$. In this case, the properties are assumed constant for all modal frequencies.

6.6 EXISTING VISCOUS AND VISCOELASTIC DAMPERS

A large number of analytical and experimental laboratory studies on the seismic behaviour of steel frames (Ashour and Hanson 1987, Su and Hanson 1990, Lin et al. 1991, Fujita et al. 1992, Kirekawa et al. 1992, Aiken et al. 1993, Bergman and Hanson 1993, Chang et al. 1993a, Chang et al. 1995) and reinforced concrete frames (Foutch et al. 1993, Lobo et al. 1993, Chang et al. 1994, Shen et al. 1995, Lai et al. 1995) incorporating viscoelastic dampers have been carried out over the last 20 years. Furthermore, in-situ studies of steel structures equipped with viscoelastic dampers (Chang et al. 1993b, Lai et al. 1995) have also been conducted.

Despite this significant research effort on viscoelastic dampers, these systems have not seen a wide application in North America and Europe. Purely viscous fluid systems, on the other hand, are now widely used and are the focus of this section.

Typically a fluid damper incorporates a stainless steel piston with a bronze orifice head as shown in Figure 6.9. The device is filled with silicone oil. The piston head utilizes specially shaped orifices that alter the flow characteristics with fluid relative velocity. The force produced by the damper is generated by the pressure differential across the piston head.

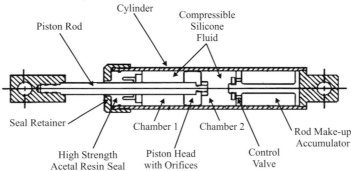

Figure 6.9 Viscous Fluid Device (after Lee 2003)

Consider that the fluid damper shown in Figure 6.9 is subjected to a compression force that causes the piston to move from left to right (compression force). Fluid flows from chamber 2 towards chamber 1. Accordingly, the damping force is proportional to the pressure differential in these two chambers. However, the fluid volume is reduced by the product of travel and piston area. Since the fluid is compressible, this reduction in fluid volume is accompanied by the development of a restoring (spring like) force. This spring effect can be prevented by the use of an accumulator. Test results have indicated that fluid dampers produce no measurable stiffness for piston motions with frequency less than 4Hz. This cut-off frequency depends on the design of the accumulator and can be modified.

Various structural models, with and without fluid dampers manufactured by Taylor Devices Inc., were tested on the shake table at the University at Buffalo in the 1991-1995 period. The experimental results on a three-storey steel structure are briefly described herein (Constantinou et al. 1993). A general view of the 1/4 scale three-storey test structure is shown in Figure 6.10. The model had weights of 28.5 kN distributed equally on the three floors.

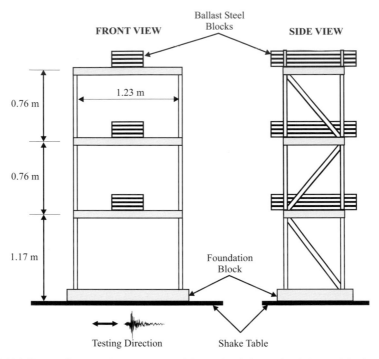

Figure 6.10 Three-Storey Steel Frame Tested with and without Taylor Devices (after Constantinou et al. 1993)

The structure was tested without dampers and with dampers as part of a tension-compression bracing system installed at an angle of approximately 35° between each floor. Tests were conducted for two different damper configurations: i) four dampers installed in the first storey only and ii) six dampers installed in pairs at every storey. Table 6-4 presents the dynamic characteristics of the original structure and the structure with the two different damper configurations.

The fundamental period of the test structure is essentially not affected by the insertion of the fluid dampers. The addition of fluid dampers increased the damping ratio of the structure, but also stiffened the higher modes because of the restoring spring force generated by the dampers above the cutoff frequency of 4 Hz. Table 6-5 presents typical recorded peak response values of the tested three-storey structure. Each earthquake record was compressed by a time-factor of 2 and scaled in peak ground acceleration by the percentage shown in the Table.

Table 6-4: Dynamic Characteristics of Three-Storey Steel Frame (after Constantinou et al. 1993)

Mode		No Dampers	4 Dampers	6 Dampers
1	Frequency (Hz)	2.00	2.11	2.03
	Damping Ratio (%)	1.8	17.7	19.4
2	Frequency (Hz)	6.60	7.52	7.64
	Damping Ratio (%)	0.8	31.9	44.7
3	Frequency (Hz)	12.20	12.16	16.99
	Damping Ratio (%)	0.3	11.3	38.0

The addition of fluid dampers reduced dramatically the peak response of the frame. The storey shear forces including the damper forces were also reduced substantially. Figure 6.11 presents the interstorey shear-drift hysteresis loops of the bare frame under the El Centro record scaled to 50% of its amplitude and also the loops obtained with the frame incorporating six dampers under the same El Centro record scaled to 150% of its amplitude. Although the earthquake record was amplified by a factor of 3 for the structure with the six dampers, the generated shear force levels were similar to the ones for the bare frame. Also, the addition of the fluid dampers did not cause an increase in the lateral stiffness of the frame. Only the energy dissipation capacity was increased.

The experimental results for the structure with six dampers were compared with the prediction of an analytical model of the tested structure. Each damper was simply modeled as a linear viscous element, as described by Equation (6.2). The damping constant was obtained from displacement-controlled tests on the dampers. Figure 6.12 presents experimental force-displacement hysteresis loops of one particular damper for three different excitation frequencies (1, 2 and 4 Hz) at an ambient temperature of 23°C. The purely viscous nature is evident when comparing these experimental results to the theoretical hysteresis loop of a linear viscous element, as shown in Figure 6.1.

Figure 6.13 presents the recorded peak output forces for different peak input velocities for three different ambient temperatures: 0°C, 25°C and 50°C. The damping constant represented by the slope of these relationships is not appreciably affected for ambient temperatures of 24°C and 50°C.

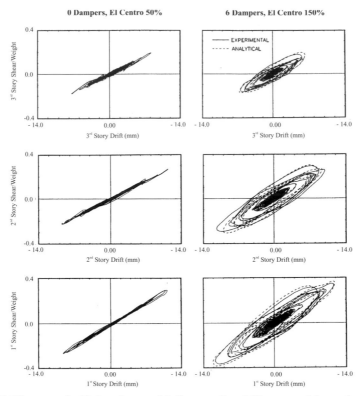

Figure 6.11 Hysteretic Behaviour of 3-Storey Steel Frame with and without Fluid Dampers (after Constantinou et al. 1993)

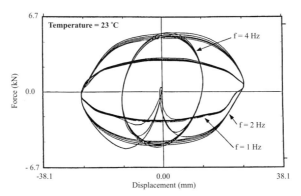

Figure 6.12 Experimental Force-Displacement Hysteresis Loops of Fluid Damper (after Constantinou et al. 1993)

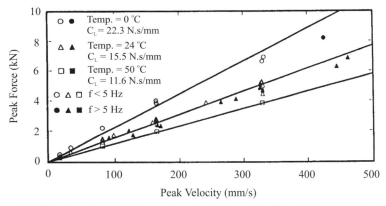

Figure 6.13 Evaluation of Damping Constant for Fluid Damper (after
Constantinou et al. 1993)

Table 6-5: Typical Peak Response of Tested Three-Storey Steel Frame, the floor
at which the peak response was recorded is indicated in ( ), (after Constantinou et
al. 1993)

Excitation	Number of Dampers	Peak Floor Acceleration (g)	Base Shear Total Weight	Storey Drift Height (%)
El Centro 33%	0	0.417 (3)	0.220	1.069 (2)
El Centro 50%	0	0.585 (3)	0.295	1.498 (2)
Taft 100%	0	0.555 (3)	0.255	1.161 (1)
El Centro 50%	4	0.282 (3)	0.159	0.660 (2)
El Centro 100%	4	0.591 (3)	0.314	1.279 (2)
Taft 100%	4	0.246 (3)	0.130	0.638 (2)
El Centro 50%	6	0.205 (3)	0.138	0.510 (2)
El Centro 100%	6	0.368 (3)	0.261	0.998 (2)
El Centro 150%	6	0.534 (3)	0.368	1.492 (2)
Taft 100%	6	0.178 (3)	0.120	0.463 (2)
Taft 200%	6	0.348 (3)	0.235	0.921 (2)
Pacoima Dam 50%	6	0.376 (3)	0.275	1.003 (1)
Hachinohe 100%	6	0.334 (3)	0.256	0.963 (2)
Miyagiken 200%	6	0.342 (3)	0.254	0.963 (2)

6.7 DESIGN OF STRUCTURES EQUIPPED WITH VISCOELASTIC DAMPERS

In the design process of structures equipped with viscoelastic dampers, the primary parameters to be evaluated are the required viscous damping ratio and stiffness of the damping system. The structural properties of the initial building without dampers must be evaluated and a dynamic analysis, linear or nonlinear, must be performed to evaluate the seismic response in its existing conditions. Since it is usually expected that structures equipped with viscoelastic dampers will respond with minimal yielding of the main structural elements under design level earthquakes, most design methods are based on elastic modelling of the main structure. Once the dampers are designed, to further assess the effect of the added dampers on the structural response for more severe ground motions and to investigate the collapse prevention performance level, nonlinear models, capable of capturing the inelastic response of structural members, are used.

The desired damping ratio in the fundamental mode of vibration of the structure ξ_1 must be set. In general, this is done by examining response spectra at various damping ratios and choosing the ratio that corresponds to the desired response level. Once this parameter is established, the desirable and available damper locations in the building must be selected.

The stiffness $\bar{k}$ and loss factor η of each viscoelastic damper must be selected based on the available viscoelastic material and the geometry of the damper. This could be a trial-and-error procedure. These parameters can also be determined based on the assumption that the added stiffness due to the viscoelastic dampers at a storey i, $\bar{k}_i$, be proportional to the ith storey stiffness of the initial structure k_i. This is obtained by applying Equation (6.49) to each storey:

$$\xi_1 = \frac{\eta \bar{k}_i}{2(k_i + \bar{k}_i)} \tag{6.50}$$

or:

$$\bar{k}_i = \frac{2\xi_1 k_i}{\eta - 2\xi_1} \tag{6.51}$$

For a viscoelastic material with known properties G_E and G_C at the design frequency (usually assumed to be the fundamental natural frequency of the structure) and design temperature, the shear area of the damper A_s can be determined by Equation (6.23):

$$A_s = \frac{\bar{k} h_s}{G_E} \tag{6.52}$$

The thickness of the viscoelastic material h_s must be such that the maximum shear strain in the viscoelastic material is lower than the ultimate value.

The modal damping ratio in each mode of vibration $\bar{\xi}_i$ can then be estimated by Equation (6.49). Alternatively, the damping constant for each damper $\bar{c}$ can be determined by Equation (6.23).

Finally, a dynamic analysis (linear or nonlinear) needs to be performed on the structure with added viscoelastic dampers to evaluate if its seismic response is satisfactory.

6.8 DESIGN OF STRUCTURES EQUIPPED WITH VISCOUS DAMPERS

6.8.1 Conceptual Design with Linear Viscous Dampers

Conceptually, the design of structures incorporating linear viscous dampers ($\alpha_{vd} = 1$ in Equation (6.9)) is simple, since the well established method of modal superposition can be used to analyze the damped structure, as shown in Section 6.5. Since viscous dampers are usually inserted in bracing members between diaphragms of the structures (e.g. building floors or bridge decks), the global damping matrix generated by the linear viscous dampers $[\overline{C}_L]$ is proportional to the global stiffness matrix of the structure $[K]$ (Chopra 2001):

$$[C_L] = \alpha_0[K] \tag{6.53}$$

where α_0 is a proportionality constant.

From modal analysis, the generalized damping coefficient in the ith mode of vibration $\overline{C}_i$ is given by:

$$\overline{C}_i = \{A^{(i)}\}^T[\overline{C}_L]\{A^{(i)}\} = \{A^{(i)}\}^T \alpha_0[K]\{A^{(i)}\} = \alpha_0 K_i = 2\xi_i\omega_i M_i \tag{6.54}$$

where $\{A^{(i)}\}$ is the ith mode of vibration, ξ_i is the damping ratio in the ith mode, K_i is the generalized stiffness in the ith mode of the original structure without damper, ω_i is the circular frequency associated with the ith mode of vibration, and M_i is the generalized mass in the ith mode of vibration.

From Equation (6.54), the proportionality constant α_0 can be easily obtained as:

$$\alpha_0 = \frac{2\xi_i}{\omega_i} \tag{6.55}$$

Conceptually, the design process is simple. Once a desired viscous damping ratio in a particular mode is established (usually in the first mode), the proportionality constant α_0 can be computed by Equation (6.55). The resulting global damping matrix $[C_L]$ can then be obtained by Equation (6.53). Each element of this global damping matrix is expressed as a linear combination of the damping constants of all the linear viscous dampers incorporated in the structure. Knowing these linear combinations, the constant for each damper can be extracted.

This conceptually simple approach is, however, difficult to apply for large structural systems for which the explicit form of the global damping matrix may not be obtained easily. Therefore, in most practical design situations, the damping constant for each damper is obtained by trial-and-error. The simple approach described in the next section simplifies this trial-and-error procedure in practical design situations.

6.8.2 Practical Design with Linear Viscous Dampers

Considering that the introduction of linear viscous damping in typical structures yields a stiffness proportional damping matrix, a practical design procedure for estimating the damping constants of individual dampers can be derived. For this purpose, the damping constant C_L^n of the linear viscous damper that is introduced at storey n, is chosen to be proportional to the interstorey lateral stiffness k_n of storey n, in the initial structure:

$$C_L^n = \varepsilon \frac{T_1}{2\pi} k_n \qquad (6.56)$$

where T_1 is the fundamental period of the original (unbraced) structure and ε is a constant. The approach described in the following paragraphs is a simple procedure for determining the value of ε (and ultimately the values of all C_L^n) that will yield the required amount of damping in the desired mode of vibration (usually the damping in the fundamental mode of vibration). For simplicity, the inherent damping of the original structure without dampers is neglected.

A fictitious undamped braced structure is first defined by adding fictitious springs $\hat{k}_0$ at the proposed locations of the linear viscous dampers, and then by distributing them according to the interstorey lateral stiffness of the original structure:

$$\hat{k}_0 = \frac{2\pi}{T_1} C_L \qquad (6.57)$$

With this distribution, the fundamental mode shape of this fictitiously braced structure will be the same as that of the unbraced structure, which ensures the existence of classical normal modes.

The generalized stiffness coefficient in the first mode of the fictitiously braced structure $\hat{K}_1$ can be written as:

$$\hat{K}_1 = \{A^{(1)}\}^T [\hat{K}]\{A^{(1)}\} = \{A^{(1)}\}^T [K]\{A^{(1)}\} + \{A^{(1)}\}^T [\hat{k}]\{A^{(1)}\} = K_1 + \hat{k}_1 \qquad (6.58)$$

where $[\hat{K}]$ is the global stiffness matrix of the braced structure, $[K]$ is the global stiffness matrix of the original (unbraced) structure, $[\hat{k}]$ is the global stiffness matrix corresponding to the fictitious springs alone ($\hat{k}_0$ defined in Equation (6.57)), $\{A^{(1)}\}$ is the first mode shape, K_1 is the generalized stiffness coefficient in the first mode of the original (unbraced) structure, and $\hat{k}_1$ is the generalized stiffness coefficient in the first mode of a structure composed of only fictitious springs.

Equation (6.58) can be re-written as:

$$\hat{k}_1 = \hat{K}_1 - K_1 \qquad (6.59)$$

and using Equation (6.57):

$$\hat{k}_1 = \frac{2\pi}{T_1}\{A^{(1)}\}^T [C_L]\{A^{(1)}\} = \frac{2\pi}{T_1}\overline{C}_1 = \frac{2\pi}{T_1}\left(2\xi_1 \frac{2\pi}{T_1} M_1\right) \qquad (6.60)$$

where $[\overline{C}_L]$ is the global damping matrix arising from all the added viscous dampers with damping constant C_L, $\overline{C}_1$ is the generalized damping coefficient in the first mode of the original (unbraced) structure provided by the added viscous dampers, ξ_1 is the first mode viscous damping ratio resulting from the addition of the viscous dampers, and M_1 is the generalized mass in the first mode of the original structure.

Substituting Equation (6.60) into Equation (6.59) yields:

$$2\xi_1\left(\frac{2\pi}{T_1}\right)^2 = \frac{\hat{K}_1}{M_1} - \frac{K_1}{M_1} = \left(\frac{2\pi}{\hat{T}_1}\right)^2 - \left(\frac{2\pi}{T_1}\right)^2 \tag{6.61}$$

which indicates that the desired first modal damping ratio can be related to the fundamental period of the original (unbraced) structure T_1 and to the fundamental period of the structure braced with the fictitious springs $\hat{T}_1$ defined by Equation (6.57).

Equation (6.61) can be simplified as:

$$\xi_1 = \frac{1}{2}\left[\left(\frac{T_1}{\hat{T}_1}\right)^2 - 1\right] \tag{6.62}$$

A simple design procedure for the required viscous damping constant of each damper C_L can then be established from Equations (6.57) and (6.62):

- Step 1

The properties of the initial unbraced structure are computed including its fundamental period T_1.

- Step 2

The desired first mode viscous damping ratio to be supplied by the viscous dampers, ξ_1, must be selected. In practice, a maximum damping ratio of about 35% of critical can be achieved economically with currently available viscous dampers.

- Step 3

From Equation (6.62), the required fundamental period of the fictitiously braced structure $\hat{T}_1$ is computed.

$$\hat{T}_1 = \frac{T_1}{\sqrt{2\xi_1 + 1}} \tag{6.63}$$

- Step 4

A set of fictitious springs is then introduced at the proposed locations of the linear viscous dampers and distributed according to the lateral stiffness of the unbraced structure. The stiffness constants of these springs must yield a fundamental period of the fictitious braced structure equal to $\hat{T}_1$. Only one iteration is required since the variation of stiffness is linearly proportional to the square of the period. Therefore, the final constant $\hat{k}_0^n$ for the n th fictitious spring in the structure can be obtained from:

$$\hat{k}_0^n = \frac{\bar{k}_{0tr}^n}{1 - \left(\dfrac{\hat{T}_1^2 - \hat{T}_{1tr}^2}{\hat{T}_1^2 - T_1^2}\right)} \tag{6.64}$$

where $\hat{k}_{0tr}^n$ is an initial trial value of the stiffness coefficient of the fictitious spring n and $\hat{T}_{1tr}$ is the corresponding trial value of the fundamental period of the fictitious braced structure obtained with these first trial spring constants.

- Step 5

Once the stiffness constants for the fictitious springs $\hat{k}_0^n$ are obtained, the required viscous damping coefficient of each viscous damper C_L can be computed using Equation (6.57). The initial structure is then fitted with dampers with the corresponding values of C_L^n.

- Step 6

The final bracing member sections are then selected based on the anticipated maximum force in each viscous damper (see Section 4.5).

- Step 7

The final design of each linear viscous damper is performed based on the required damping constant, anticipated maximum force and stroke. Nonlinear dynamic analyses using a representative set of design ground motion ensembles are typically used for estimating these anticipated values. Also, the final design of the dampers is usually left to manufacturers.

6.8.3 Design Example for Linear Viscous Dampers

A design example utilizing the practical design procedure for linear viscous dampers presented above is given for the same six-storey steel building structure discussed in Section 5.7.4 (see Figure 5.60). Recall that the fundamental period of this initial unbraced structure is $T_1 = 1.304$ s.

Similar to the retrofit solution for friction dampers in Section 5.7.4, the retrofit strategy consists of introducing a tubular chevron braced frame in the middle bay of every moment-resisting frame and installing linear viscous dampers at one end of the bracing members.

Assuming that a damping ratio of 35% of critical is required in the first mode of vibration, Equation (6.63) is used to obtain the required fundamental period of the structure braced with the fictitious springs $\tilde{T}_1$:

$$\hat{T}_1 = \frac{T_1}{\sqrt{2\xi_1 + 1}} = \frac{1.304}{\sqrt{2(0.35) + 1}} = 1.000 \text{ s} \tag{6.65}$$

In order to reduce the period of the original structure from 1.304 s to 1.000 s, fictitious springs distributed according to the stiffness of each storey are introduced at the locations of the bracing members. The lateral stiffness of each storey can be estimated by applying unit lateral forces in opposite directions at adjacent floors and evaluating the resulting interstorey drift.

Table 6-6 presents the required constants of these fictitious springs as well as the damping constant for each viscous damper C_L, given by Equation (6.57).

In order to evaluate the adequacy of the practical design procedure described above for linear viscous dampers, two elastic dynamic analyses of the six-storey frame were conducted under the well-known S00E component of the 1940 El Centro earthquake. The first analysis involved the original unbraced structure with Rayleigh damping of 35% of critical based on the first and fifth elastic modes of vibration. In the second analysis, Rayleigh damping was removed and replaced by discrete diagonal dashpot elements having the damping constants C_L shown in Table 6-6.

Table 6-6: Fictitious Spring Constants and Viscous Damping Constants for Six-Storey Steel Building Structure

Level	Fictitious Spring Constants (kN/mm)	Linear Viscous Dampers Constants (kN.s/mm)
6	70	15
5	68	14
4	89	19
3	98	20
2	110	23
1	80	17

Figure 6.14 compares the first ten seconds of the top floor relative displacement time-histories for both analyses. It can be seen that the two results are practically identical, thereby validating that the distribution of linear viscous damping provides the targeted amount of viscous damping in the structure.

6.8.4 Additional Design Considerations for Nonlinear Viscous Dampers

The advantage of using nonlinear viscous dampers is the reduction of damper forces at high velocity. Although a certain amount of trial-and-error is required for selecting appropriate values of damping constant and velocity coefficient, an approximate design procedure can be established based on energy considerations.

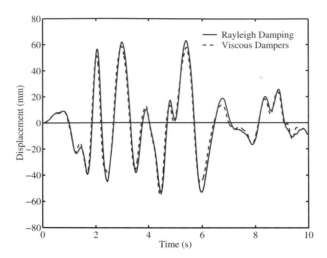

Figure 6.14 Top Floor Displacement Time-Histories of Elastic Six-Storey Steel Building Structure, S00E Component of 1940 El Centro Earthquake: Comparison Between Rayleigh Damping of 35% of Critical in First and Fifth Mode of Vibration and Viscous Dampers of Table 6-6

The energy dissipated per cycle for a linear damper ($\alpha_{vd} = 1$) and for a nonlinear viscous damper ($\alpha_{vd} < 1$) have already been evaluated by Equations (6.8) and (6.15). The value of the damping constant for a nonlinear viscous damper C_{NL} that dissipates the same amount of energy per cycle as a linear viscous damper can be obtained as a function of the velocity coefficient α_{vd}, the displacement amplitude X_0 and the excitation frequency ω by equating these two equations:

$$\frac{C_{NL}}{C_L} = \frac{\sqrt{\pi}}{2}(\omega X_0)^{1-\alpha_{vd}} \frac{\Gamma(3/2 + \alpha_{vd}/2)}{\Gamma(1 + \alpha_{vd}/2)} \tag{6.66}$$

For the typical range of values of the velocity coefficient $0.2 \le \alpha_{vd} \le 1$, the ratio of gamma functions in Equation (6.66) is close to unity and the damping constant can be approximated as:

$$\frac{C_{NL}}{C_L} \approx \frac{\sqrt{\pi}}{2}(\omega X_0)^{1-\alpha_{vd}} \tag{6.67}$$

Note that consistent units must be used since Equations (6.66) and (6.67) are not dimensionally homogeneous.

Equation (6.67) can be used in a design situation to provide initial estimates of nonlinear damping constants once linear damping constants have been established. For this purpose, the excitation frequency can be taken as the fundamental frequency of the original structure without dampers and X_0 can be taken as the displacement in the dampers corresponding to a desired performance drift level. Since the objective of using nonlinear viscous dampers is to limit forces, the value of X_0 cannot be too high in order to limit the value of C_{NL}.

6.8.5 Optimal Distribution of Viscous Dampers

The simple design procedure for linear viscous dampers discussed in Section 6.8.2 is based on achieving a specified first modal damping ratio while preserving the existence of classical normal modes. This design approach leads to a distribution of damping constants proportional to the lateral stiffness of the original structure, which may lead to several different dampers in the structure. Although this approach is very simple, it may not be optimum from an economical point of view where same size dampers should be used as much as possible. Furthermore, the constraint on maintaining classical normal modes is not required particularly if nonlinear time-history dynamic analysis is used in the design process.

The optimum distribution of dampers in a structure can be cast in the context of optimal control theory. Although several design methods for obtaining the optimum distribution of dampers in a structure have been proposed (e.g. De Silva 1981, Gurgoze and Muller 1992, Spencer et al. 1994, Gluck et al. 1996, Tsuji and Nakamura 1996, Takewaki 1997, Ribakov and Gluck 1999, Shukla and Datta 1999, Singh and Moreschi 2001), they are quite evolved and require advanced programming capabilities in order to be implemented.

The sequential search algorithm developed by Zhang and Soong (1992) and simplified by Lopez-Garcia (2001) is simple to implement and is briefly discussed in this paragraph. Although this approach is general and can be used for obtaining the optimum distribution of any type of dampers based on maximizing a given set of optimum location indices, it is derived in this section for linear viscous dampers.

For the case of linear viscous dampers, the optimum location index is simply given by the maximum interstorey velocity, which indicates that the optimum location is between two adjacent stories of the structure. For illustration purposes, a multi-storey structure in which N_d identical linear viscous dampers with constant C_L are to be introduced, is considered. From Equation (6.8) and assuming that the structure responds in its fundamental mode of vibration T_1, the energy dissipated per cycle for all dampers in the structure E_{vd} is given by:

$$E_{vd} = \sum_{i=1}^{N_d} \frac{2\pi^2 C_L \delta_i^2 \cos^2\gamma_i}{T_1} = \frac{2\pi^2 C_L}{T_1} \sum_{i=1}^{N_d} \delta_i^2 \cos^2\gamma_i \tag{6.68}$$

where δ_i is the interstorey drift at the storey where the ith damper is located and γ_i is the inclination angle of the ith damper.

Assuming that the viscous dampers add no supplemental stiffness to the structure, the total recoverable elastic strain energy of the system E_{es} can be written as:

$$E_{es} = \frac{1}{2} \sum_{i=1}^{N_f} k_i \delta_i^2 \tag{6.69}$$

where k_i is the lateral stiffness of the ith storey and N_f is the number of floors (or stories) in the structure.

The first modal damping ratio ξ_1 provided by the viscous dampers can be obtained by:

$$\xi_1 = \frac{E_{vd}}{4\pi E_{es}} = \frac{\pi C_L \sum_{i=1}^{N_d} \delta_i^2 \cos^2 \gamma_i}{T_1 \sum_{i=1}^{N_f} k_i \delta_i^2} \tag{6.70}$$

Re-arranging Equation (6.70), the required damping constant C_L, required for all N_d dampers in order to achieve a given first modal damping ratio ξ_1, can be obtained from:

$$C_L = \frac{\xi_1 T_1 \sum_{i=1}^{N_f} k_i \delta_i^2}{\pi \sum_{i=1}^{N_d} \delta_i^2 \cos^2 \gamma_i} \tag{6.71}$$

For the particular case where all stories have the same height and the fundamental mode shape is approximated by a straight line, the interstorey drifts are all given by:

$$\delta_i = \frac{1}{N_f} \tag{6.72}$$

thereby further simplifying Equation (6.71):

$$C_L = \frac{\xi_1 T_1 \sum_{i=1}^{N_f} k_i}{\pi N_d \cos^2 \gamma} \tag{6.73}$$

6.9 GEOMETRICAL AMPLIFICATION OF DAMPING

So far, the geometrical configuration of all the supplemental damping systems discussed in this book has been either in-line with bracing elements or horizontally located at the apex of chevron bracing. Although it has been shown that supplemental dampers installed in these two configurations can be designed to significantly improve the seismic response of structures, it can be argued that their geometrical configuration is not optimum. A close review of Equation (6.39), for example, indicates that a damper installed in-line with a bracing element experiences a displacement between its two ends less than the interstorey drift induced by the ground motions. At best, if the damper is installed horizontally at the apex of a chevron bracing system, the displacement between the two ends of the damper equals the interstorey drift ($\gamma = 0$) in Equation (6.39).

The efficiency of supplemental damping systems can be improved by providing a geometrical configuration of the bracing system in order to amplify the damper displacement for a specified interstorey drift. Two geometrical configurations have been proposed so far to achieve this goal: the *toggle-brace* configuration (Constantinou et al. 2001) and the *scissor-jack* configuration (Sigaher and Constantinou 2003). Although these geometrical configurations can be used with any type of supplemental damping system, they are presented in this chapter since all of their applications so far have involved fluid viscous dampers.

The general geometrical arrangement of a toggle-brace system incorporating a supplemental damper in a typical building bay is illustrated in Figure 6.15. Instead of using a single diagonal bracing member, the toggle brace system is made of two separate toggle brace assemblies connected by a mounting pin. The damper is then connected between the mounting pin and the opposite lower corner of the bay. Depending on the geometry of the bay and toggle-brace system, the displacement between the ends of the damper can be larger than that of the horizontal interstorey drift.

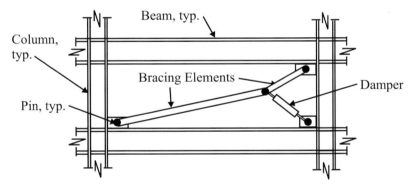

Figure 6.15 Geometrical Arrangement of Toggle-Brace Damping System (after Constantinou 2001)

In a scissor-jack system, the supplemental damper is inserted between assemblies of shallow truss taking the geometrical arrangement of the familiar scissor-jack used in the automobile industry, as illustrated in Figure 6.16. To amplify the damper displacement for a given interstorey drift, the scissor-jack assembly is inserted between the lower corner of the bay and a mounting pin to the top beam.

The damping amplification provided by the toggle-brace and the scissor jack systems can be established by re-writing general forms of the equilibrium and compatibility relationships given by Equations (6.38) and (6.39) for a single-storey structure equipped with a linear viscous damper (see Figure 6.8).

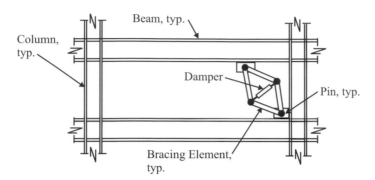

Figure 6.16 Geometrical Arrangement of Scissor-Jack Damping System (after Sigaher and Constantinou 2003)

$$F_{vd}(t) = f\,F(t) \tag{6.74}$$

and

$$\Delta(t) = f\,x(t) \tag{6.75}$$

where f is a geometrical amplification factor equal to $\cos\gamma$ for a diagonal in-line configuration and 1.0 for a horizontal-chevron bracing configuration. Re-calling the constitutive equation for the fluid viscous damper:

$$F(t) = C_L\dot{\Delta}(t) \tag{6.76}$$

Substituting Equations (6.75) and (6.76) into Equation (6.74) leads to a final expression for the horizontal force provided by the damper assembly on the structure:

$$F_{vd}(t) = C_L f^2 \dot{x}(t) \tag{6.77}$$

Therefore, the equivalent viscous damping ratio provided by the damper assembly can be written as (Sigaher and Constantinou 2003):

$$\xi = \frac{C_L f^2 g T}{4\pi W} \tag{6.78}$$

where T is the natural period of the structure and W is the seismic weight. Equation (6.78) indicates that the damping ratio is amplified by the square of the geometrical amplification factor.

Figure 6.17 provides expressions for the geometrical amplification factor f for a single-storey structure equipped with various linear viscous damping system configurations.

In Table 6-7 the damping values produced in a structure for the different configurations shown in Figure 6.17 are given. It is assumed that the linear viscous damper that is used in all configurations provides a damping ratio of 5% of critical when installed horizontally in a chevron bracing system. The examples clearly indicate that the equivalent damping ratios provided by the same damper inserted in toggle-brace and scissor-jack configurations are much higher than those of the in-line diagonal and horizontal-chevron

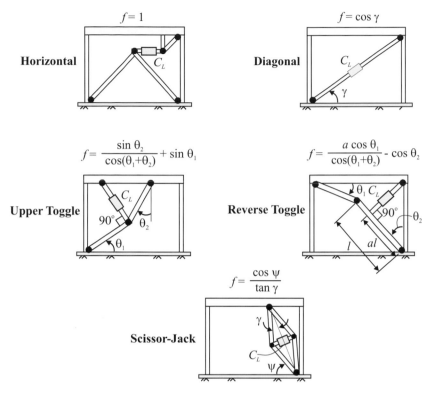

Figure 6.17 Geometrical Amplification Factors and Damping Ratios for Linear Viscous Damping Systems in Single-Storey Structure (after Sigaher and Constantinou 2003)

configurations. Shake table testing of a half-scale steel model confirmed these results (Sigaher and Constantinou 2003).

Table 6-7: Numerical Examples of Damping Provided by Same Viscous Damper in Different Configurations (see Figure 6.17)

Configuration	Geometric Parameters	f	ξ
Horizontal	-	1.00	0.05
Diagonal	$\gamma = 37°$	0.80	0.03
Upper Toggle	$\theta_1 = 31.9°$, $\theta_2 = 43.2°$	3.19	0.51
Reverse Toggle	$\theta_1 = 30°$, $\theta_2 = 49°$, $a = 0.7$	2.52	0.32
Scissor-Jack	$\gamma = 9°$, $\psi = 70°$	2.16	0.23

6.10 STRUCTURAL IMPLEMENTATIONS

The development of viscoelastic and viscous dampers, based mainly on experimental investigations, has led to the implementation of these devices in a number of full-scale structures. *Appendix C* presents a partial list of buildings equipped with viscous and viscoelastic dampers. It is obvious from this list that most of the applications to date involved fluid viscous dampers.

6.11 PROBLEMS

Problem 6.1

A new shear-type viscoelastic damper is subjected to cyclic testing in the laboratory. The damper is subjected to a time-varying axial displacement history $x(t)$ given by:

$x(t) = X_0 \sin \omega t$

where $X_0 = 25$ mm and $\omega = 2\pi$ rad/s.

Results indicate that the energy dissipated per cycle is equal to 12.3 kN-m and the force at peak displacement is 100 kN. Assuming that the damper can be well represented by a Kelvin solid model, determine:

a)   the damping constant $\bar{c}$ of the damper;

b)   the stiffness constant $\bar{k}$ of the damper;

c)   the shear storage modulus G_E and the shear loss factor η of the viscoelastic material if the thickness of the material $h_s = 12$ mm and the shear area is $A_s = 20000$ mm^2.

Problem 6.2

A simple one-storey portal frame with the properties shown in Figure 6.18 is to be retrofitted with a shear-type viscoelastic bracing member. The damping of the original frame can be neglected. The loss factor of the viscous elastic material can be considered a constant equal to 1.2 for the frequency range of expected earthquake ground motions.

a)   Determine the natural period of the braced structure such that the damping ratio of the braced structure is 30% of critical.

b)   Determine the corresponding stiffness coefficient $\bar{k}$ for the viscoelastic bracing.

c)   Determine the corresponding damping coefficient $\bar{c}$ for the viscoelastic bracing.

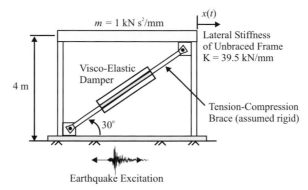

Figure 6.18 Single Storey Frame Fitted with Viscoelastic Damper

Problem 6.3

A two-storey building is modeled as a two-degree-of-freedom system as shown below. The equations of motion of this system in free vibration (ignoring damping) are written as:

$$\begin{bmatrix} 0.0385 & 0 \\ 0 & 0.0245 \end{bmatrix} \left(\frac{\text{kN s}^2}{\text{mm}}\right) \begin{Bmatrix} \ddot{x}_1 \\ \ddot{x}_2 \end{Bmatrix} + \begin{bmatrix} 6.0 & -4.0 \\ -4.0 & 4.0 \end{bmatrix} \left(\frac{\text{kN}}{\text{mm}}\right) \begin{Bmatrix} x_1 \\ x_2 \end{Bmatrix} = \begin{Bmatrix} 0 \\ 0 \end{Bmatrix}$$

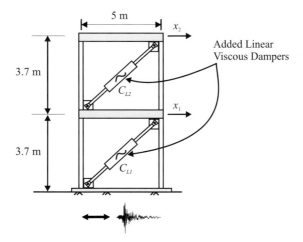

Figure 6.19 Frame Fitted with Viscous Dampers

For the seismic retrofit of the structure, fluid-type linear viscous dampers are to be inserted at the end of diagonal cross braces (assumed rigid) as shown Figure 6.19. The viscous damping constants are C_{L1} and C_{L2} for the viscous damper installed in the first and second floor respectively.

a) Assuming that the bracing members connected to the viscous dampers are rigid and neglecting the damping in the frame itself, determine the required viscous damping constants C_{L1} and C_{L2} for the dampers in order to introduce an equivalent viscous damping ratio 30% of critical in the first vibration mode of the structure.

b) With the damping constants C_{L1} and C_{L2} selected in a), what would the equivalent viscous damping ratio be in the second mode of vibration of the structure?

Problem 6.4

A two-storey building is modeled as a two-degree-of-freedom system as shown in Figure 6.20. The equations of motion of this system in free vibration (ignoring damping) are written as:

$$\begin{bmatrix} 0.0385 & 0 \\ 0 & 0.0245 \end{bmatrix} \left(\frac{\text{kN s}^2}{\text{mm}} \right) \begin{Bmatrix} \ddot{x}_1 \\ \ddot{x}_2 \end{Bmatrix} + \begin{bmatrix} 6.3 & -4.38 \\ -4.38 & 4.38 \end{bmatrix} \left(\frac{\text{kN}}{\text{mm}} \right) \begin{Bmatrix} x_1 \\ x_2 \end{Bmatrix} = \begin{Bmatrix} 0 \\ 0 \end{Bmatrix}$$

The fundamental period of the building is $T_1 = 1.18$ s. For the seismic retrofit of the structure, a single fluid-type viscous damper exhibiting a damping coefficient $C_L = 0.3$ kN s / mm is to be inserted at the end of a diagonal cross brace. The fluid damper could be inserted either in the first or in the second storey as shown in the figure. It can be assumed that the mode shapes of the original structure are not affected by either retrofit scheme. Assuming that the bracing member connected to the viscous damper is

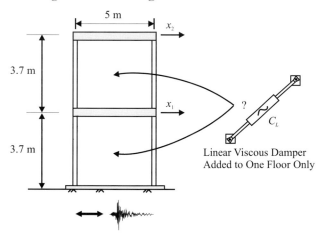

Figure 6.20 Two-Storey Frame Fitted with One Viscous Damper

rigid and neglecting the damping in the frame itself, determine which retrofit scheme would be more beneficial in improving the seismic response of the structure. Justify your answer based on the first modal damping ratio resulting from each retrofit scheme.

CHAPTER 7: SELF-CENTERING SYSTEMS

7.1 INTRODUCTION

The cost associated with the loss of business operation, damage to structural and nonstructural components following a moderately strong earthquake can be significant to modern society. Such cost is often comparable to, if not greater than, the cost of the structure itself. With current design approaches, most structural systems are designed to respond beyond the elastic limit and eventually to develop a mechanism involving ductile inelastic response in specific regions of the structural system while maintaining a stable global response and avoiding loss of life. However, while the principle of mitigating loss of life in a strong earthquake still prevails, resilient communities expect buildings to survive a moderately strong earthquake with no disturbance to business operation. This implies that repairs requiring downtime may no longer be tolerated in small and moderately strong events.

Figure 7.1 shows the idealized force-displacement response of a linear elastic system and of a system representing a yielding structure of equal initial stiffness and mass. The maximum seismic force induced in the yielding system is significantly lower than that of the linear elastic system. The maximum displacement of the yielding system can be smaller, similar, or larger than that of the elastic system, depending on the characteristics of the ground motion, the natural period and the strength of the yielding system. The shaded area in Figure 7.1 represents the energy dissipated per cycle through hysteretic yielding. Although the hysteretic damping systems discussed in Chapter 5 are designed to delay the inelastic response of the main structural elements, the force-displacement response of an hysteretically damped system will be similar to that of Figure 7.1.

Designs aiming for an inelastic response of the structure are very appealing, particularly from the initial cost stand point, but they have two major drawbacks. First, elements of the principal lateral force resisting system (either sacrificial damping elements or structural members) will be sacrificed in moderately strong earthquakes and in need of repair, or they will be damaged beyond repair in strong earthquakes. Second, current design approaches are based on the premise that large energy dissipation capacity is necessary to mitigate the effects induced by earthquakes. This premise has very often led to the notion that a good structural system should be characterized by "fat" hysteresis loops. As a large fraction of the seismic input energy is expected to be dissipated by hysteresis, significant residual displacements can be expected in a building after an earthquake, as illustrated in Figure 7.1.

Excessive residual deformations can even result in the total loss of a structure if second order (P-Δ) effects induced by gravity loads bring the system near collapse (Christopoulos et al. 2003).

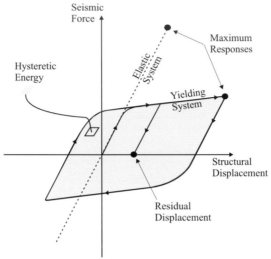

Figure 7.1 Idealized Seismic Response of Yielding Structure (from Christopoulos 2002)

As discussed in Chapter 2, current seismic design philosophies emphasize the importance of designing ductile structural systems to undergo inelastic cycles during earthquake events while sustaining their integrity, recognizing the economic disadvantages of designing buildings to withstand earthquakes elastically. The performance of a structure is typically assessed based on the maximum deformation and/or cumulative inelastic energy absorbed during the earthquake. Most structures designed according to current codes will sustain residual deformations in the event of a design-basis earthquake (DBE), even if they perform exactly as expected. Residual deformations can result in the partial or total loss of a building if static incipient collapse is reached, if the structure appears unsafe to occupants or if the response of the system to a subsequent earthquake or aftershock is impaired by the new at rest position of the structure. Furthermore, residual deformations can also result in increased cost of repair or replacement of nonstructural elements as the new at rest position of the building is altered. These aspects are not explicitly reflected in current performance assessment approaches (see Chapter 2).

As presented in Chapter 2 (see Figure 2.5), a framework for including residual deformations in performance-based seismic design and assessment (Christopoulos et al. 2003, Pampanin et al. 2003) and a procedure for explicitly considering residual deformations at the design stage (Christopoulos and Pampanin 2004) have been proposed recently.

In this chapter, structural *self-centering* systems possessing characteristics that minimize residual deformations and that are economically viable alternatives to current lateral force resisting systems are presented and discussed. After a discussion on the importance of residual deformations in performance-based seismic design, results describing the dynamics of *self-centering* hysteretic systems are examined. A description of systems exhibiting *self-centering* hysteretic behaviour either through specialized devices, smart materials or structural systems making use of traditional materials are then presented. Finally, design approaches for such systems are discussed.

7.2 BEHAVIOUR OF SELF-CENTERING SYSTEMS

The discussion brought forth in the previous paragraphs suggests that an optimal earthquake-resistant system should:

- Incorporate the nonlinear characteristics of yielding or hysteretically damped structures and, thereby, limit the induced seismic forces and provide additional damping characteristics.

- Encompass self-centering properties, allowing the structural system to return to, or near to, its original position after an earthquake.

- Reduce or eliminate cumulative damage to the main structural elements.

Figure 7.2 shows the characteristic *flag-shaped* seismic response of such a self-centering system. The amount of energy dissipation is reduced compared to that of the yielding system shown in Figure 7.1, but, more importantly, the system returns to the zero-force, zero-displacement point at every cycle, and more importantly, at the end of the seismic loading.

Considering the fundamental differences between the self-centering hysteresis and the more traditional full hystereses (such as the elastoplastic one), it is of interest to discuss the nonlinear dynamic response of such systems. From a qualitative point of view, the following main differences between these two types of systems affecting the nonlinear dynamic response can be observed:

- The flag-shaped hysteresis inherently has less energy dissipation, half at most, per cycle than the elasto-plastic hysteresis.

- The flag-shaped hysteresis has more frequent stiffness changes within one nonlinear cycle than the elastoplastic hysteresis.

- The flag-shaped hysteresis returns to the zero-force, zero-displacement point at every cycle whereas yielding of the elastoplastic system at every cycle may lead to cumulative "crawling" of the response in one direction.

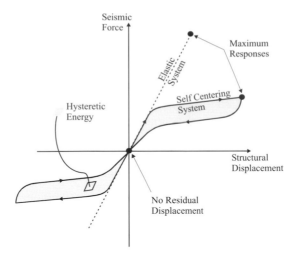

Figure 7.2 Idealized Seismic Response of Self-Centering Structure (from Christopoulos 2002)

To date, there is limited information on the nonlinear dynamic response of hysteretic self-centering systems under seismic loading. In the following paragraphs, results from recent studies on the dynamic characteristics of self-centering systems are presented.

7.3 DYNAMIC CHARACTERISTICS OF SELF-CENTERING SYSTEMS

A study by Priestley and Tao (1993) compared the seismic response of SDOF systems exhibiting a bilinear elastic hysteresis to that of bilinear elastoplastic systems. It was concluded by the authors that "despite the total lack of hysteretic energy absorption in the bilinear elastic model, displacement for medium to long period structures with such force-displacement response would be less than 35 percent larger than that of elastoplastic systems of the same period". Another study investigated through numerical time-history dynamic analyses the response of 5 and 15-storey frame systems exhibiting three different kinds of hysteretic behaviours at the beam-to-column connections (Brewer 1993). The three hysteretic models considered were the bilinear elastic, bilinear degrading and bilinear elastoplastic. In the 15-storey building, similar maximum roof drifts were reached regardless of the connection hysteretic model. For the 5-storey building, significantly larger roof drifts were observed for the bilinear elastic system. These studies give a first insight into the fact that, despite the total lack of energy dissipation of bilinear elastic systems, the increase in maximum displacements (when compared to elastoplastic systems) under seismic loading varies greatly depending on the natural period of the system. The bilinear elastic hysteresis considered in these studies represents the extreme case of the flag-shaped hysteresis with no energy dissipation. As previously discussed, self-centering systems exhibit a predetermined amount of energy dissipation and are therefore expected to have a reduced response when compared to bilinear elastic systems.

7.3.1 Frequency Response of Analogous SDOF Flag-Shaped Hysteretic Systems

The steady-state frequency response of SDOF flag-shaped hysteretic systems under harmonic base excitation was investigated by Christopoulos (2004). This study is summarized in the following paragraphs to provide some fundamental understanding of the dynamics of structures equipped with self-centering systems.

(a) Definition of Hysteretic Models

Two hysteretic behaviours are examined. The first behaviour is an idealized bilinear elastoplastic hysteretic model, representative of the behaviour of yielding or friction systems. This idealization is an upper bound of the actual response, since most traditional earthquake resisting systems exhibit variations of this full hysteretic behaviour with various strength and stiffness degradations. Associated with this hysteretic model is the post-yielding stiffness coefficient α expressed as a fraction of the initial stiffness. The idealized hysteretic force-displacement relationship of such a system is shown in Figure 7.3a). The yield displacement of this hysteretic model is x_y and the force $F(x)$ is normalized by the initial stiffness k_0. The second behaviour is the flag-shaped hysteretic model that is representative of the response of innovative systems such as rocking walls, post-tensioned concrete and steel moment-resisting frames, shape memory alloys as well as specialized viscous dampers that exhibit a self-centering hysteretic behaviour as discussed later in this Chapter. Figure 7.3b) shows the idealized hysteretic force-displacement relationship of such a system. Associated with this hysteretic model are two independent response parameters α and β. The coefficient β reflects the energy dissipation capacity of the system. A lower bound of $\beta = 0.0$ produces a bilinear elastic system. An upper bound of $\beta = 1.0$ results in a system that is at the limit of maintaining the self-centering capability of the hysteretic model. The yield displacement of this hysteretic model is also denoted by x_y and the force $F(x)$ is also normalized by the initial stiffness k_0.

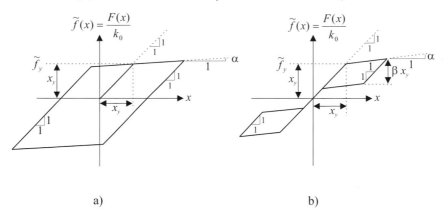

a)   b)

Figure 7.3 Idealized Force-Displacement Relationships: a) Elastoplastic Hysteresis and b) Flag-Shaped Hysteresis

(b) Harmonic Frequency Response of Flag-Shaped Hysteretic SDOF Systems

A first insight into the dynamic characteristics of a system can be achieved by studying the steady-state response of a flag-shaped hysteretic SDOF oscillator subjected to harmonic excitation. For this purpose, the same approach used in section 5.4.1 for an hysteretically damped SDOF system is used here.

Studying the frequency response allows for some insight into the nonlinear dynamic behaviour of oscillators. Although seismic excitation is of much broader frequency content, it can be assumed that when a system is excited by seismic loading, portions of its response may be characterized by a quasi-resonant state.

Furthermore, the frequency response analysis allows for a direct comparison among different hysteretic models. The frequency response of the flag-shaped hysteretic SDOF system yields multiple possible amplitude solutions for certain ranges of excitation frequency. The stability of each of these solutions is examined and the concepts of theoretical and *likely* responses are discussed.

(c) Derivation of Closed-Form Frequency Response Solution

Figure 7.4 shows an equivalent oscillator of mass m exhibiting a nonlinear flag-shaped force-deflection relationship such as the one illustrated in Figure 7.3b) and excited at the base by a harmonic base acceleration defined by:

$$a(t) = a_g \cos(\omega_g t) \tag{7.1}$$

where a_g and ω_g are respectively the amplitude and the circular frequency of the base acceleration.

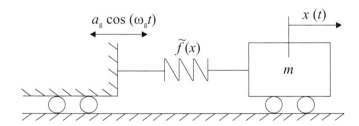

Figure 7.4 Base Excited Nonlinear SDOF Oscillator

The frequency response of any general nonlinear SDOF system subjected to a harmonic base acceleration was derived in Chapter 5 (section 5.4.1) for the elastoplastic hysteresis.

It was shown that the frequency response of any general nonlinear SDOF system can be written as:

$$\sigma^2 = \begin{bmatrix} 1 \pm \dfrac{A_{exc}}{\bar{A}} & \text{for } \bar{A} \leq 1 \\[2ex] \bar{C}(A) \pm \sqrt{\left(\dfrac{A_{exc}}{\bar{A}}\right)^2 - \bar{S}^2(A)} & \text{for } \bar{A} > 1 \end{bmatrix} \tag{7.2}$$

where A_{exc} is the normalized excitation amplitude:

$$A_{exc} = \frac{ma_g}{F_y} \tag{7.3}$$

and

$$\bar{C}(A) = \frac{C(A)}{A}$$

$$\bar{S}(A) = \frac{S(A)}{A} \tag{7.4}$$

where A is the steady-state amplitude of the response, and where $S(A)$ and $C(A)$ are defined by:

$$S(A) = \frac{1}{\pi} \int_0^{2\pi} \tilde{f}(A\cos\theta, \alpha, \beta)\sin\theta\, d\theta \tag{7.5}$$

$$C(A) = \frac{1}{\pi} \int_0^{2\pi} \tilde{f}(A\cos\theta, \alpha, \beta)\cos\theta\, d\theta \tag{7.6}$$

and where:

$$\bar{A} = \frac{A}{x_y} \tag{7.7}$$

Also defined in section 5.4.1 were:

τ a non-dimensional time variable defined as:

$$\tau = \omega_b t \tag{7.8}$$

x_{st} the static deflection:

$$x_{st} = \frac{-ma_g}{k_0} \tag{7.9}$$

σ the excitation frequency ratio:

$$\sigma = \frac{\omega_g}{\omega_0} \tag{7.10}$$

θ defined as:

$$\theta = \sigma\tau - \phi(\tau) \tag{7.11}$$

As previously discussed in section 5.4.1, $S(A)$ and $C(A)$ are evaluated by integrating the hysteresis by parts over each linear branch (see Figure 7.3b).

Recalling that the flag-shaped hysteresis is symmetric, the integrals over one full cycle can be carried out over only one half cycle (from $\theta = 0$ to $\theta = \pi$) and multiplied by two.

It can be shown that:

$$\overline{C}(A) = \Omega_1 + \Omega_2 + \Omega_3 + \Omega_4 \tag{7.12}$$

where Ω_1 through Ω_4 are given by:

$$\Omega_1 = \left(\frac{1}{A} - 1\right)(1 - \alpha)\sin\theta_1 + \frac{\theta_1}{2} + \frac{\sin(2\theta_1)}{4}$$

$$\Omega_2 = \frac{1}{A}(1 - \alpha - \beta + \alpha\beta)(\sin\theta_2 - \sin\theta_1) + \alpha\left(\frac{(\theta_2 - \theta_1)}{2} + \frac{\sin(2\theta_2) - \sin(2\theta_1)}{4}\right)$$

$$\Omega_3 = \frac{\theta_3 - \theta_2}{2} + \frac{\sin(2\theta_3) - \sin(2\theta_2)}{4} \tag{7.13}$$

$$\Omega_4 = \frac{1}{A}(1 - \alpha)\sin\theta_3 + \alpha\left(\frac{\pi - \theta_3}{2} - \frac{\sin(2\theta_3)}{4}\right)$$

and where:

$$\theta_1 = \text{acos}\left(1 - \frac{\beta}{A}\right)$$

$$\theta_2 = \text{acos}\left(\frac{1 - \beta}{A}\right) \tag{7.14}$$

$$\theta_3 = \text{acos}\left(-\frac{1}{A}\right)$$

and:

$$\overline{S}(A) = \frac{\Lambda}{A}\left(1 - \frac{1}{A}\right) \tag{7.15}$$

where

$$\Lambda = \frac{-2}{\pi}\beta(1 - \alpha) \tag{7.16}$$

When the steady-state is reached in the system, the average of the derivatives of $A(\tau)$ and $\varphi(\tau)$ over one full cycle $\dot{A}$ and $\dot{\varphi}$ are equal to zero.

The first expression of Equation (7.2) represents the case where the steady-state response is at an amplitude lower than the yielding displacement of the system. It represents the frequency response of a linear elastic system. The second expression represents the case where the steady-state amplitude exceeds this yield displacement, and the response of the system follows the flag-shaped hysteresis.

Resonance occurs in this system when σ^2 has a double root in the second expression of Equation (7.2), which in turn occurs when:

$$\bar{S}^2(A) = (A_{exc}/\bar{A})^2 = (x_{st}/A)^2 \tag{7.17}$$

and:

$$|\bar{S}(A)| = |x_{st}/A| \tag{7.18}$$

From Equation (7.17) it can be deduced that for an excitation amplitude of x_{st} the normalized steady-state amplitude at resonance $\bar{A}^*$ is:

$$\bar{A}^* = \frac{|\Lambda|}{|\Lambda| - A_{exc}} \tag{7.19}$$

Since in this derivation A has been implicitly defined as positive, unbounded resonance occurs for $A_{exc} \geq |\Lambda|$, which results in the following condition on the system yield force F_y in order to avoid unbounded response at resonance:

$$F_y > \frac{\pi m a_g}{2\beta(1-\alpha)} \tag{7.20}$$

where, as defined earlier, a_g is the amplitude of the base acceleration.

It can be seen in Equation (7.20) that increasing α or reducing β requires a higher system strength to assure a bounded response at resonance.

The solution given by Equation (7.20) is a generalization of the work by Caughey (1960) and Iwan (1965), and collapses into the particular solutions proposed by these authors for fixed values of β. For example, if $\beta = 2$, the system exhibits a bilinear elastoplastic hysteresis, and Equation (7.20) yields a condition on stability which is identical to the solution proposed by Caughey (1960) and derived earlier in Chapter 5 for a single-storey frame equipped with an hysteretic damper (see Equation 5.45). If $\beta = 1$, the hysteresis becomes "double bilinear" (as termed by Iwan, 1965) and the condition on stability is identical to the one proposed by Iwan (1965). Although it is not demonstrated here, it has been verified that the system described by Equation (7.2) also generalizes the solutions proposed by Caughey (1960) and Iwan (1965) for all values of β.

After determining $\bar{A}^*$, the resonant frequency ratio σ_r is given by:

$$\sigma_r = \sqrt{\bar{C}(A)\left(\frac{1}{\bar{A}^*}\right)} \tag{7.21}$$

The solution derived above was validated through numerical time integration analyses. In Figure 7.5 the frequency response curve of a flag-shaped system with $\alpha = 0.05$, $\beta = 0.5$ and $A_{exc} = 0.25$ is compared to the results obtained from numerical time integration analyses. The numerical analyses were carried out by using a constant acceleration Newmark-beta integration scheme. Each of the numerical simulation results was obtained by immediately applying the harmonic loading at the target amplitude and frequency. A very small value of viscous damping was assigned to the system to damp out

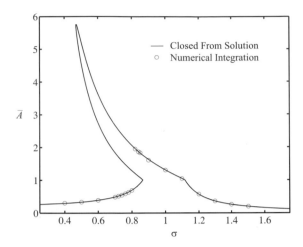

Figure 7.5 Comparison between Theoretical Flag-Shaped Frequency Response Curve and Numerical Integration for A_{exc} = 0.25, α = 0.05 and β = 0.5

the transient component of the response and to reach a steady-state. It was assumed that the numerical solution had reached steady-state when the variation in vibration amplitude between cycle i and cycle $i+1$ was less than 0.1%. The closed form solution is validated by the good agreement with the numerical results.

As can be seen in Figures 7.5 and 7.6, the frequency response curves exhibit a peculiar behaviour that differs significantly from traditional frequency response curves such as those obtained for the elastoplastic hysteresis. The curves lean towards the left (lower values of excitation frequency ratio σ) and the resonant frequency ratio also decreases for increasing amplitude of the excitation. This has been identified as a "soft" system behaviour (Den Hartog 1985). Also peculiar is the fact that, for a certain range of frequencies, unlike the elastoplastic hysteresis (Caughey 1960), three different steady-state amplitudes are possible: one in the linear range ($\bar{A} < 1$) and two in the nonlinear range ($\bar{A} > 1$). An analysis of the stability of each branch, presented in the following paragraph, is therefore necessary to assess which of these solutions is likely to occur.

Figure 7.6 also shows the effect of increasing excitation amplitude on the frequency response. As the base excitation level is increased, the range of frequencies defined by the intersection of the nonlinear branches ($\bar{A} > 1$) and the linear branches ($\bar{A} < 1$) increases. The range of frequencies where multiple solutions are present also increases with increasing excitation amplitude. It can also be noted in Figure 7.6 that the slope of the nonlinear frequency response branches gradually increases for increasing excitation amplitude.

Figure 7.7 shows the frequency response curves for different values of post-yielding stiffness α, an energy dissipation coefficient $\beta = 0.6$ and an amplitude of excitation $A_{exc} = 0.25$. It can be seen that increasing α results in higher amplitudes of steady-state

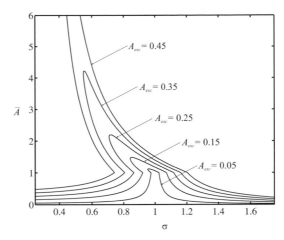

Figure 7.6 Effect of Increasing Amplitude of Excitation on Flag-Shaped Frequency Response Curve for α = 0.10 and β = 0.8

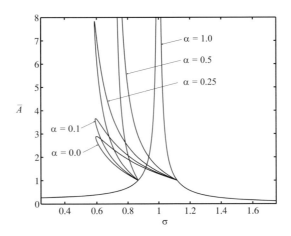

Figure 7.7 Effect of Post-Yielding Stiffness Coefficient α on Flag-Shaped Frequency Response Curve for A_{exc} = 0.25 and β = 0.6

vibration and in a reduced inclination of the frequency response curves. It can also be seen that as α approaches 1, the system approaches the linear elastic case.

Figure 7.8 shows the frequency response curves for different values of the energy dissipation coefficient β, post-yielding stiffness coefficient α = 0.05 and an amplitude of excitation A_{exc} = 0.20. The frequency response amplitudes decrease for increasing values of β. Increasing β is much more efficient in decreasing the frequency response amplitude for small values of β than for larger values of β. In fact, it can be seen that the effect on the frequency response curve is much more significant when β is increased from

0.5 to 0.7 than when it is increased from 0.7 to 1. Note that, as previously observed, for $\beta = 2.0$ the response corresponds to that of an elastoplastic system.

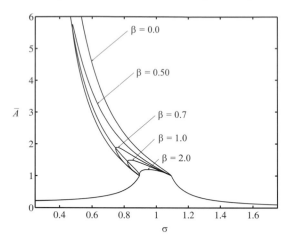

Figure 7.8 Effect of Energy Dissipation Coefficient β on Flag-Shaped Frequency Response Curve for $A_{exc} = 0.20$ and $\alpha = 0.05$

In Figure 7.9, the frequency responses of a flag-shaped ($\alpha = 0.10$ and $\beta = 0.8$) and elastoplastic ($\alpha = 0.10$) systems are compared for two levels of excitation amplitude. It appears that the elastoplastic system results in significantly lower vibration amplitudes. Nonetheless, considering the three possible solutions in the high amplitude range of the flag-shaped system, a comparison can only be made when it is assessed which one of these possible solutions is more likely to occur.

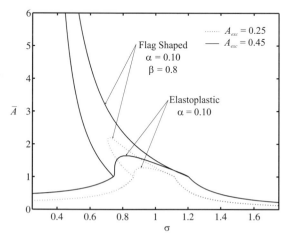

Figure 7.9 Comparison Between Elastoplastic and Flag-Shaped Hysteresis Frequency Response Curves

(d) Stability Analysis of Frequency Response

A number of researchers have studied the stability of SDOF systems exhibiting a softening frequency response with multiple solution branches. The following development is inspired by the work of Caughey (1960) and Iwan (1965).

The stability study is only carried out for the portion of the frequency response curve corresponding to the nonlinear range of the system $(\bar{A} > 1)$. The stability of the linear elastic branches $(\bar{A} < 1)$ is well understood. The excitation frequency ratio σ corresponding to the vertical tangency of the response curve σ_v satisfies the following equation:

$$\frac{d(\sigma^2)}{d\bar{A}} = 0 \tag{7.22}$$

Recalling the expression of σ^2 (Equation (7.2)) for $\bar{A} > 1$, Equation (7.22) becomes:

$$(\sigma_v^2 - \bar{C}(A))\left(\sigma_v^2 - \frac{dC(A)}{dA}\right) + \bar{S}(A)\frac{dS(A)}{dA} = 0 \tag{7.23}$$

since:

$$\frac{dC(A)}{dA} = A\frac{d\bar{C}(A)}{dA} + \bar{C}(A) \tag{7.24}$$

Noting that $\bar{C}(A)$ is equal to $(\sigma_r)^2$ if $\bar{A}$ is taken as $\overline{A^*}$, Equation (7.23) can be rewritten as:

$$(\sigma_v^2 - \sigma_r^2)^2 - (\sigma_v^2 - \sigma_r^2)A\frac{d}{dA}\bar{C}(A) + \bar{S}(A)\frac{dS(A)}{dA} = 0 \tag{7.25}$$

Recognizing that Equation (7.25) is a quadratic in $(\sigma_v^2 - \sigma_r^2)$, the frequencies at vertical tangency are defined by:

$$\sigma_v^2 = \sigma_r^2 + A\frac{d}{dA}\bar{C}(A) \pm \sqrt{\left(A\frac{d}{dA}\bar{C}(A)\right)^2 - 4\left(\bar{S}(A)\frac{dS(A)}{dA}\right)} \tag{7.26}$$

The stability study is carried out by introducing small perturbations χ and ζ to the steady-state amplitude and phase of the system and by determining whether these perturbations decay or grow in time:

$$A = A + \chi$$
$$\varphi = \varphi + \zeta \tag{7.27}$$

where:

$$\chi = \bar{\chi}e^{\rho t}$$
$$\zeta = \bar{\zeta}e^{\rho t} \tag{7.28}$$

The perturbed expressions of A and φ are introduced in the system:

$$2A\sigma\zeta' - S(A)\zeta + (C'(A) - \sigma^2)\chi = 0$$
$$2\sigma\chi' + (\sigma^2 A - C(A))\zeta - S'(A)\chi = 0$$

(7.29)

where the symbol ' denotes the derivative. The expression then yields:

$$(2A\sigma\rho - S(A))\bar{\zeta} + (C'(A) - \sigma^2)\bar{\chi} = 0$$
$$(\sigma^2 A - C(A))\bar{\zeta} + (2\sigma\rho - S'(A))\bar{\chi} = 0$$

(7.30)

Stability is checked by determining the roots of the system. Setting the determinant of the system described in Equation (7.30) equal to 0 we get:

$$(2\sigma\rho)^2 + (2\sigma\rho)\Phi + \Psi = 0$$

(7.31)

where:

$$\Phi = -\bar{S}(A) - S'(A)$$

(7.32)

and:

$$\Psi = (\sigma^2 - \bar{C}(A))\left(\sigma^2 - \frac{dC(A)}{dA}\right) + \bar{S}(A)\frac{dS(A)}{dA}$$

(7.33)

Note that Equation (7.33) is identical to Equation (7.23), which indicates that the values of σ where Ψ is equal to 0 correspond to σ_{v1} and σ_{v2}.

It can be shown that:

$$\Phi = \frac{-\Lambda}{\bar{A}}$$

(7.34)

Since Λ is always negative and $\bar{A}$ is defined as positive, it can be seen that $\Phi > 0$. Recalling Equation (7.25), it can also be shown that:

$$\Psi = (\sigma_v^2 - \sigma_r^2)^2 - (\sigma_v^2 - \sigma_r^2)A\frac{d}{dA}\bar{C}(A) + \bar{S}(A)\frac{dS(A)}{dA}$$

(7.35)

where:

$$\bar{S}(A)\frac{dS(A)}{dA} = \Lambda^2\left(\frac{1}{\bar{A}^3} - \frac{1}{\bar{A}^4}\right)$$

(7.36)

and:

$$A\frac{d}{dA}\bar{C}(A) = \frac{2}{\pi\bar{A}}[K_1(\alpha\beta - \beta) + K_2(-1 + \alpha + \beta - \alpha\beta) + K_3(\alpha - 1)]$$

(7.37)

where K_1, K_2 and K_3 are given by:

$$K_1 = \sqrt{2\beta\bar{B} - \beta^2\bar{B}^2}$$
$$K_2 = \sqrt{1 - \bar{B}^2 + 2\bar{B}^2\beta - \beta^2\bar{B}^2}$$
$$K_3 = \sqrt{1 - \bar{B}^2}$$

(7.38)

with $\bar{B} = \dfrac{1}{\bar{A}}$.

Considering the case where $\bar{A}$ is greater than 1 (i.e. the post-elastic range), with α and β varying between 0 and 1, and with K_1 and K_2 positive by definition, it can be seen that $A\dfrac{d}{dA}\bar{C}(A)$ is negative.

Considering that $A\dfrac{d}{dA}\bar{C}(A)$ is negative and $\bar{S}(A)\dfrac{dS(A)}{dA}$ is positive and recalling Equation (7.36) then:

$$\Psi = (\sigma_v^2 - \sigma_r^2)^2 + (\sigma_v^2 - \sigma_r^2)\left(-A\frac{d}{dA}\bar{C}(A)\right) + \bar{S}(A)\frac{dS(A)}{dA} \qquad (7.39)$$

$$\underset{>0}{\uparrow} \qquad \underset{>0}{\uparrow}$$

It can therefore be inferred that Ψ is quadratic in $(\sigma_v - \sigma_r)$, concave upwards with two real roots σ_{v1} and σ_{v2}. This further implies that $\Psi < 0$ for $\sigma_{v1} < \sigma < \sigma_{v2}$ and that $\Psi > 0$ for $\sigma < \sigma_{v1}$ or $\sigma > \sigma_{v2}$.

When $\Psi > 0$ ($\sigma < \sigma_{v1}$ or $\sigma > \sigma_{v2}$), the real part of both roots of Equation (7.31) will be negative and the system is stable. For $\Psi < 0$, the real part of at least one root of Equation (7.31) will be positive and the system will be unstable.

Figure 7.10 shows the frequency response curves for $\alpha = 0.10$, $\beta = 0.8$ and $A_{exc} = 0.05, 0.25, 1.00$ respectively. The two dotted lines represent the values of σ_{v1} and σ_{v2} for values of $\bar{A}$ greater than 1. In fact, there exist no locations of vertical tangency for $\bar{A}$ smaller than 1. In this figure, the area delimited by σ_{v1} and σ_{v2}, where the previous development predicts unstable solutions, is shaded. It can be seen graphically in this figure that for values of σ where triple amplitude solutions exist, the intermediate one will always be unstable. Note that the intersection of the dashed lines (σ_{v1} and σ_{v2}) and any frequency response curve define the points of vertical tangency of the frequency response curve. Note also that the stable region is fully defined by the parameters α and β and is independent of the amplitude of excitation A_{exc}. The results obtained from this stability study are also identical to the stability analysis results presented by Iwan (1965) for the particular case of $\beta = 1$.

Figure 7.11 shows the effect of the energy dissipation coefficient β on the unstable region of the solution. For increasing values of β, the stable region is slightly skewed towards lower values of σ but, as can be seen on the figure, this effect is small on the total area of the unstable region. Figure 7.12 shows the effect of the post-yielding stiffness coefficient α on the unstable region of the solution. For decreasing values of α, the region is increasingly skewed towards lower values of σ, but in such a way that the unstable area is significantly increased. An interesting physical interpretation of the stability of softening systems is given by Den Hartog (1985). Referring to Figure 7.6, it can be seen that when the amplitude of excitation is increased and the steady-state response

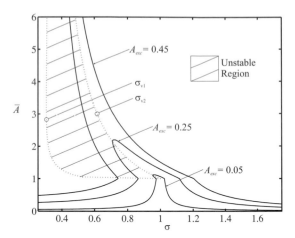

Figure 7.10 Stability of Frequency Response Branches for $\alpha = 0.10$ **and** $\beta = 0.8$

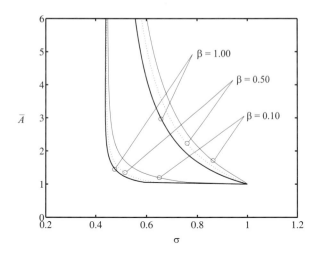

Figure 7.11 Effect of Energy Dissipation Coefficient β **on Unstable Region for** α
= 0.20, $A_{exc} = 0.45$

lies on the unstable branch, the amplitude of the steady-state response is reduced, whereas if it lies on the stable upper or lower branches, the amplitude is increased. This is an indication that the solutions described by the unstable branches are not physically possible.

As a result of the previous findings, it is expected that the system will exhibit a "jump phenomenon". As illustrated in Figure 7.13, the system will follow different response paths depending on how the excitation frequency is approached. When the excitation frequency is decreased from higher to lower frequencies, the frequency response curve will

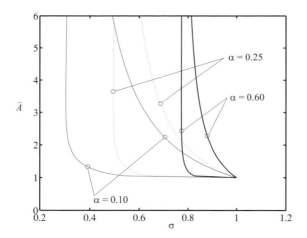

Figure 7.12 Effect of Post-Yielding Coefficient α on Unstable Region for
$$\beta = 0.7, \, A_{exc} = 0.45$$

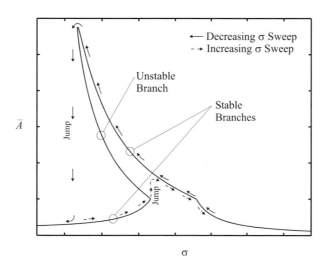

Figure 7.13 Jump Phenomenon in Flag-Shaped Frequency Response Curves

follow the upper stable branch and then jump to the lower branch from the peak of the response curve. If the excitation frequency is increased from lower to higher frequencies, the frequency response will follow the lower stable branch and then jump to the higher stable branch at the point of discontinuity.

Figure 7.14 shows the frequency response curve for $A_{exc} = 0.50$, $\alpha = 0.10$ and $\beta = 0.80$. Also shown are results obtained from sinusoidal sweep time-history dynamic analyses. The system is first excited at $\sigma = 1.3$, and each time the steady-state solution is reached, the frequency is decreased to a new value. This is indicated in the figure by

"Decreasing σ Sweep". A second series of analyses was carried out by starting with an excitation frequency of σ = 0.4 and increasing the frequency to a new value every time a steady-state response was reached. This second run is designated by "Increasing σ Sweep". As can be seen in Figure 7.14, the time-history results illustrate the *jump phenomenon*. Nonetheless, for the "Decreasing σ Sweep" run, the lowest frequency that could be attained on the top stable branch was 0.45. For frequency values smaller than that, the solution follows the lower stable branch.

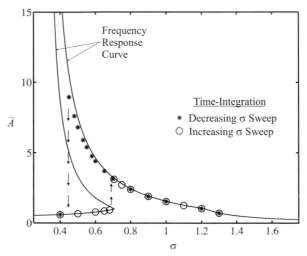

Figure 7.14 Comparison of Results of Time Integration for Increasing and Decreasing Harmonic Sweeps with Flag-shaped Frequency Response Curve,
$$\alpha = 0.10, \ \beta = 0.8, \ A_{exc} = 0.50$$

(e) Theoretical versus "Likely" Frequency Response

Although the results shown in the previous section indicate that the two stable branches of the frequency response curve of a flag-shaped SDOF system can be attained by slowly sweeping the excitation frequency, results from numerical analyses show that the stable branch of higher amplitude can only be achieved if the decrease of frequency is done very slowly with small increments. In fact, small perturbations in the excitation signal cause the system to jump to the lower stable branch. Hence, perturbations can be defined as large jumps in exciting frequency, as a short interruption of the exciting frequency or as the addition of a small amplitude excitation of different frequency to the main excitation. In Figure 7.15a), the frequency is decreased form σ = 0.80 to σ = 0.55. Although the system should follow the predicted amplitude on the top stable branch, the perturbation induced by this large jump causes the system to stabilize at the amplitude predicted by the lower stable branch. Also of interest is the state-space representation ($\dot{A}$ vs. A) shown in Figure 7.15b) in which the cycles corresponding to the steady-state response under an excitation σ = 0.80 are shown. When the frequency is reduced to σ = 0.55, the amplitude of vibration increases but does not stabilize at the predicted amplitude on the higher stable branch: it decreases at every cycle until it stabilizes at the amplitude predicted by the lower branch.

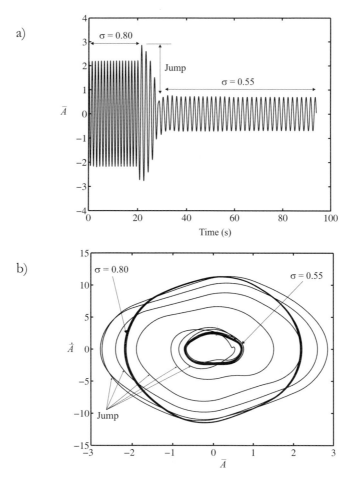

Figure 7.15 Jump Phenomenon for Large Decrease of Excitation Frequency: a) Time-Trace of Amplitude and b) State-Space Representation $\alpha = 0.10$, $\beta = 0.8$, $A_{exc} = 0.50$

For the general case of a seismic excitation composed of a broader range of vibration frequencies, it is very unlikely that the loading conditions will be stationary, with slowly decreasing frequency harmonic loading. It can therefore be inferred that the *likely* frequency response curve of a flag-shape system may actually better be represented by a curve which is single valued at all excitation frequencies and defined by the lowest stable amplitude of the theoretical frequency response curve for any given excitation frequency. This is illustrated in Figure 7.16 where the theoretical frequency response curves of a flag-shaped ($\alpha = 0.10$, $\beta = 0.80$) and elastoplastic ($\alpha = 0.10$) systems are plotted along with the likely frequency response of the flag-shaped system. The *likely* resonance frequency is moved to higher frequencies, and the system exhibits a behaviour more similar to the elastoplastic case. This is one indication that, despite the significantly reduced energy dissipation capacity of the flag-shaped system when compared to the elastoplastic one, the two systems display qualitatively similar *likely* frequency response curves. It must also be noted that for very large excitation amplitudes, the frequency response becomes independent of the value of β.

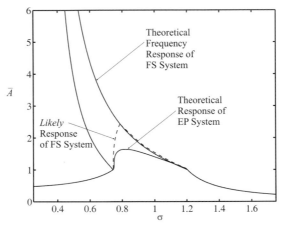

Figure 7.16 Theoretical Frequency Response Curves of Flag-Shaped and Elastoplastic Systems and Likely Response of Flag-Shaped System

(f) Summary on Frequency Response of Self-Centering SDOF systems

The frequency response analysis conducted in the previous sections showed that the flag-shaped hysteresis exhibits a "softening" behaviour with triple solutions in some frequency ranges. A relationship between the system strength F_y and the parameters α and β required to ensure bounded response at resonance was also derived (Equation (7.20)). The stability analysis of the system revealed that the intermediate solution in these triple solution regions is unstable and cannot therefore be physically achieved. It was also shown that the system exhibits a "jump phenomenon" between the two stable branches of the response. The direction of the jump depends on whether the excitation frequency is increasing or decreasing. It was also noted that, although the solutions predicted by the stable branch of higher amplitude could be achieved when the excitation frequency was slowly decreased, small perturbations of the excitation caused the system to stabilize itself at the amplitude predicted by the stable branch of lower amplitudes. Considering that the nature of seismic excitation is of broader frequency range, a "likely" frequency response curve was defined for the flag-shaped system. This likely curve is single valued for all excitation frequencies and is similar in shape to the one exhibited by elastoplastic systems. Results from this study further suggest that systems designed to exhibit a self-centering hysteretic behaviour with sufficient amount of energy dissipation capacity will sustain maximum deformation demands under seismic loading similar to those sustained by equivalent elastoplastic systems, despite the fact that per cycle they dissipate at most half of the energy dissipated by elastoplastic systems. A word of caution is also added here about flag-shaped hysteretic systems, since under loading conditions similar to a sine sweep of slowly decreasing excitation frequency, large resonant vibration amplitudes can be reached.

7.4 SEISMIC RESPONSE OF SELF-CENTERING SDOF SYSTEMS

The response of SDOF oscillators exhibiting flag-shaped hysteretic rule to an ensemble of 20 historical records representative of ordinary ground motions having a probability of exceedence of 10% in 50 years in California was investigated by Christopoulos et al. (2002b). In this section, the dynamic response of these systems is also compared to the response of bilinear elastoplastic SDOF systems.

7.4.1 Normalized Equations of Motion

The equation of motion of a nonlinear SDOF system under seismic excitation is given by:

$$m\ddot{x} + c\dot{x} + F(x) = -m\ddot{x}_g \tag{7.40}$$

where m is the mass of the system, c is the viscous damping coefficient and $F(x)$ is the nonlinear restoring force defined by the hysteretic model of the system. The displacement, velocity and acceleration of the system relative to the ground are denoted by x, $\dot{x}$ and $\ddot{x}$, respectively. The ground acceleration is designated by $\ddot{x}_g$.

For small inherent damping, two key parameters can be used to define the dynamic response of a nonlinear SDOF system: the initial period T_0 and the strength ratio η:

$$T_0 = 2\pi\sqrt{\frac{m}{k_0}} \tag{7.41}$$

$$\eta = \frac{F_y}{mg} \tag{7.42}$$

where k_0 is the initial stiffness of the system, F_y is the yield force and g is the acceleration of gravity.

Using Equation (7.41), Equation (7.42) can be rewritten as:

$$\ddot{x} + 2\xi_0\left(\frac{2\pi}{T_0}\right)\dot{x} + \left(\frac{2\pi}{T_0}\right)^2 \tilde{f}(x) = -\ddot{x}_g \tag{7.43}$$

with ξ_0 denoting the initial fraction of critical damping of the system,

$$\xi_0 = \frac{c}{2\sqrt{k_0 m}} \tag{7.44}$$

and $\tilde{f}(x)$ representing the nonlinear pseudo-restoring force (normalized by the stiffness) of the system (see Figure 7.3):

$$\tilde{f}(x) = \frac{F(x)}{k_0} \tag{7.45}$$

The yield displacement x_y of the system is given by:

$$x_y = \frac{F_y}{k_0} = \tilde{f}_y \tag{7.46}$$

as shown in Figure 7.3.

Using Equations (7.41) and (7.42), the yield displacement can be expressed in terms of the key parameters of the system:

$$x_y = \frac{T_0^2 \eta g}{4\pi^2} \tag{7.47}$$

With this formulation, for a given critical damping ratio ξ_0, initial period T_0 and strength level η, the SDOF system is completely defined for the case when the restoring force-displacement relationship is bilinear elastoplastic (Figure 7.3a) and requires only the additional parameters α and β to be assigned, if the restoring force-displacement relationship exhibits a flag-shaped hysteresis (Figure 7.3b).

The normalized nonlinear equation of motion given by Equation (7.43) is integrated using the Newmark constant average acceleration scheme. The analyses were continued for 20 seconds of zero ground acceleration at the end of each record to allow the system to return to rest.

(a) Energy Balance

As derived in Chapter 3, the energy balance at time t for the normalized equation of motion can be written as:

$$E_k^r(t) + E_{vd}(t) + E_a(t) = E_{in}^r \tag{7.48}$$

where $E_k^r(t)$, $E_{vd}(t)$, $E_a(t)$ and E_{in}^r are the relative kinetic energy at time t, the energy dissipated by viscous damping up to time t, the absorbed energy at time t (recoverable elastic and dissipated hysteretic) and the relative seismic input energy, respectively. For the SDOF system described by Equation (7.43), these energy quantities can be defined as follows:

$$E_k^r(t) = \frac{1}{2}\dot{x}(t)^2 \qquad E_{vd}(t) = 2\xi_0\left(\frac{2\pi}{T_0}\right)\int_0^{x(t)}\dot{x}(t)dx$$

$$\tag{7.49}$$

$$E_a(t) = \left(\frac{2\pi}{T_0}\right)^2 \int_0^{x(t)}\tilde{f}(t)dx \qquad E_{in}^r = -\int_0^{x(t)}\ddot{x}_g(t)dx$$

Equations (7.48) and (7.49) determine how the seismic input energy is distributed in the system over time, and allow for a check on the accuracy of the time integration scheme.

(b) System Response Indices

The inelastic response of SDOF systems under seismic input can be characterized in part by the following normalized non-dimensional response indices:

- The maximum displacement ductility μ_Δ:

$$\mu_\Delta = \frac{max|x(t)|}{x_y}, \; 0 \leq t \leq t_D \tag{7.50}$$

where t_D is the total duration of the seismic input.

In performance-based earthquake engineering, the maximum inelastic displacement, which is an indirect measure of the maximum strains developed at critical sections in the structure, is an important response index to determine damage to structures under seismic loading.

- The normalized maximum absolute acceleration:

$$a_{max} = \frac{max|\ddot{x}(t) + \ddot{x}_g(t)|}{g}, \; 0 \leq t \leq t_D \tag{7.51}$$

This index is a measure of the damage potential to acceleration-sensitive nonstructural components, as well as an indicator of potential injury to occupants during an earthquake event. In addition, this response index is a direct indicator of the force level induced into the system by the seismic input.

- The normalized maximum absorbed energy:

$$E_{abs} = \frac{max|E_a(t)|}{x_y mg}, \; 0 \leq t \leq t_D \tag{7.52}$$

This index is a measure of potential structural damage including duration effects.

- The normalized residual displacement:

$$x_{res} = \frac{|x(t_D)|}{x_y} \tag{7.53}$$

This index is an indicator of the structural damage sustained after an earthquake and of the extent of repair costs. Residual displacements are only computed for the bilinear elastoplastic hysteretic model (see Figure 7.3a). The flag-shaped hysteretic model (see Figure 7.3b), by virtue of its self-centering characteristics, does not sustain any residual displacements.

(c) Ground Motions Considered in Parametric Study

An ensemble of twenty historical strong ground motion records from California, representative of ordinary earthquakes having a probability of exceeding of 10% in fifty years, are used in this study (Krawinkler et al. 2000). These records are free of any forward directivity effects (near-fault effects). Following the method proposed in NEHRP provisions for the seismic rehabilitation of buildings (ASCE, 2000), a 5% damped design elastic acceleration response spectrum for a seismic zone 4 and a soil type C or D was constructed and used as the target spectrum. Soil types C and D corresponding to stiff soil and rock are classified as A and B in the Eurocode 8 (2003). Each of the twenty earthquake records was then scaled to minimize the square of the error between its 5% damped response spectrum and the target NEHRP spectrum at five period values: T = 0.1, 0.25, 0.5, 1.0 and 2.0 seconds. The resulting amplitude scaling factors are listed in Table 7-1. The mean and the envelopes of the maximum and minimum spectral acceleration values of the 20 scaled records along with the NEHRP target spectrum are shown in Figure 7.17. A good match is obtained between the mean spectral values and the target spectrum in the range of periods of interest (0.1s to 2.0s). However, the envelopes of maximum and minimum spectral values indicate the large variability that exists between the records. Table 7-1 also lists the scaled peak ground accelerations (PGA). The mean value of the PGA of the 20 scaled records is 0.43 g, which is very close to the effective design peak acceleration C_a = 0.40 g specified in the NEHRP provisions for a seismic zone 4 and soil types C and D.

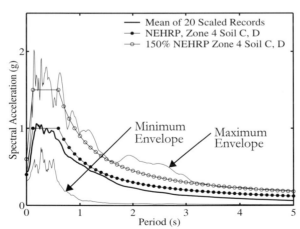

Figure 7.17 Elastic Acceleration Response Spectra of Twenty Scaled Records

(d) Range of Key System and Hysteretic Parameters

The parametric study presented herein focuses on the seismic response of steel MRFs ranging in number of stories from one to twenty. From the seismic provisions of the 1997

Table 7-1 Characteristics of Ground Motions Considered for Seismic Analyses (after Krawinkler et al. 2000)

Earthquake	Year	Moment Magnitude	Station	Epicentral Distance (km)	Soil Type	Duration (s)	Scaling Amplitude Factor	Scaled PGA (g)
Superstition Hills	1987	6.7	Brawley	18.2	D	22.0	2.7	0.31
Superstition Hills	1987	6.7	El Centro	13.9	D	40.0	1.9	0.49
Superstition Hills	1987	6.7	Plaster City	21.0	D	22.2	2.2	0.41
Northridge	1994	6.7	Beverley Hills - 14145 Mulhol.	19.6	C	30.0	0.9	0.37
Northridge	1994	6.7	Canoga Park - Topanga Can	15.8	D	25.0	1.2	0.43
Northridge	1994	6.7	Glendale - Las Palmas	25.4	D	30.0	1.1	0.39
Northridge	1994	6.7	L.A. - Hollywood Stor. F.F.	25.5	D	40.0	1.9	0.44
Northridge	1994	6.7	L.A. N. Faring Rd.	23.9	D	30.0	2.2	0.60
Northridge	1994	6.7	N. Hollywood - Coldwater Can	14.6	C	21.9	1.7	0.46
Northridge	1994	6.7	Sunland - Mt. Gleason Ave.	17.7	C	30.0	2.2	0.35
Loma Prieta	1989	6.9	Capitola	14.5	D	40.0	0.9	0.48
Loma Prieta	1989	6.9	Gilroy Array # 3	14.4	D	39.9	0.7	0.39
Loma Prieta	1989	6.9	Gilroy Array # 4	16.1	D	40.0	1.3	0.54
Loma Prieta	1989	6.9	Gilroy Array # 7	24.2	D	40.0	2.0	0.45
Loma Prieta	1989	6.9	Hollister Diff. Array	25.8	D	39.6	1.3	0.36
Loma Prieta	1989	6.9	Saratoga - W Valley Coll.	13.7	C	40.0	1.4	0.46
Cape Mendocino	1992	7.1	Fortuna Blvd.	23.6	C	44.0	3.8	0.44
Cape Mendocino	1992	7.1	Rio Dell Overpass - F.F.	18.5	C	36.0	1.2	0.46
Landers	1992	7.3	Desert Hot Springs	23.3	C	50.0	2.7	0.42
Landers	1992	7.3	Yermo Fire Station	24.9	D	44.0	2.2	0.33

edition of the Uniform Building Code (ICBO 1997), the natural period range of these structures can be estimated by the equation:

$$T_0 = C_t h_r^{3/4} \tag{7.54}$$

where $C_t = 0.0853$ for steel MRFs, and where h_r is the height of the building in meters. Using Equation (7.54) and assuming a storey height of 3.4 m, the range of periods T_0 for a single storey and for a twenty-storey building respectively is:

$$0.2s \le T_0 \le 2.0s \tag{7.55}$$

The strength ratio corresponding to the ratio η in the UBC (ICBO 1997) is defined as:

$$\eta = \frac{V}{W} = \frac{C_v I}{R T_0} \tag{7.56}$$

where V is the design base shear, W is the weight of the structure, I, taken as 1, is the importance factor, C_v is taken as 0.64 for a zone 4 with soil type D, and R is the force reduction factor taken as 4.5 and 8.5 for an ordinary steel MRF and a special steel MRF, respectively. A lower bound for Equation (7.56) for seismic zone 4 is:

$$\eta = \frac{V}{W} \ge 0.11 C_a I \tag{7.57}$$

where $C_a = 0.44$ for seismic zone 4 and soil type D.

Substituting the lower and upper period bounds (Equation (7.55)) into Equation (7.56) and verifying Equation (7.57), the range of strength factors is found to be:

$$0.05 \le \eta \le 0.71 \tag{7.58}$$

In addition, the flag-shaped hysteretic model requires specifying the parameters α and β to completely define the system. Table 7-2 lists the complete set of parameters T_0, η, α and β considered in this parametric study. These values result in 576 different flag-shaped hysteretic systems.

Table 7-2: SDOF System Values Used in Study

T_0 (s)	η	α	β
0.01	0.05	0.02	0.00
0.25	0.10	0.10	0.30
0.50	0.20	0.20	0.60
1.00	0.30	0.35	1.00
1.50	0.50		
2.00	1.00		

The resulting force-deflection relationships of the flag-shaped hysteretic systems are illustrated qualitatively in Table 7-3 for the specified range of values of α and β. The actual values of the post-yielding stiffness and energy dissipation capacity that are achieved with different self-centering systems are discussed when each of these systems is presented in the following paragraphs. Throughout this study, the fraction of critical damping is taken as 0.05 for all SDOF systems.

Table 7-3: Qualitative Force-Deflection Relationships of Flag-Shaped Hysteretic Systems Considered

Post-Yielding Stiffness Coefficient, α	Energy Dissipation Coefficient, β			
	0.0	0.30	0.60	1.0
0.02	[diagram]	[diagram]	[diagram]	[diagram]
0.10	[diagram]	[diagram]	[diagram]	[diagram]
0.20	[diagram]	[diagram]	[diagram]	[diagram]
0.35	[diagram]	[diagram]	[diagram]	[diagram]

7.4.2 Response of Flag-Shaped SDOF Hysteretic Systems

Mean values over the ensemble of earthquakes of the displacement ductility demand $\bar{\mu}_\Delta$ are shown in Figure 7.18 for all the flag-shaped hysteretic systems considered. For all values of α and β the mean displacement ductility generally increases for decreasing values of initial period T_0 and decreasing values of strength ratio η. The mean displacement ductility is reduced in all cases for increasing values of α and β. This reduction of $\bar{\mu}_\Delta$ with increasing values of α and β is more significant for low period structures ($T_0 \leq 1.0s$) and for structures with lower strength ratios ($\eta \leq 0.3$) where the values of $\bar{\mu}_\Delta$ are also the largest.

Figure 7.19 shows contour maps of the mean displacement ductility $\bar{\mu}_\Delta$ in the $\alpha - \beta$ plane for nine systems with natural periods T_0 of 0.5s, 1.0s and 1.5s, and for strength ratios η of 0.1, 0.2 and 0.3. For structures with short initial periods and lower strength ratios, increasing α is more effective in reducing $\bar{\mu}_\Delta$ than increasing β. This can be seen

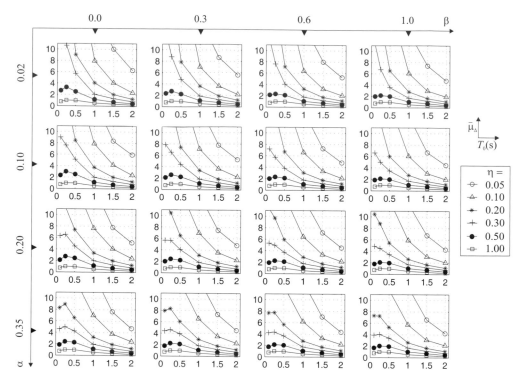

Figure 7.18 Mean Displacement Ductility for Flag-Shaped Hysteretic Systems

in Figure 7.19 for the structure with $\eta = 0.1$ and $T_0 = 0.5$ s where the equal displacement ductility curves are nearly horizontal. As both the strength ratio and initial period of the system increase, the curves rotate clockwise indicating that increasing β is progressively more effective in reducing $\bar{\mu}_\Delta$ than increasing α. For structures with longer initial periods and higher strength ratios, the equal displacement ductility lines are nearly vertical, as shown in Figure 7.19. Note that combining intermediate values of α and β results in mean displacement ductility values that can only be achieved for large values of α when β is zero, or for large values of β when α is taken as its lower bound value of 0.02. For example, for the system with $\eta = 0.20$ and $T_0 = 0.5$ s (see Figure 7.19), the displacement ductility can be reduced from a value of 9.1 for $\alpha = 0.02$ and $\beta = 0.0$, (intersection point of the horizontal and vertical axes), to a value of 6.35 for $\alpha = 0.20$ and $\beta = 0.5$. To achieve this same displacement ductility demand of 6.35, a value of α larger than 0.35 is needed when β is set to 0.0 for a purely bilinear elastic system, and a value of β larger than 1 is needed when α is set to 0.02 which corresponds to the value assigned to the bilinear elastoplastic hysteretic systems.

Mean values over the ensemble of earthquakes of the maximum absolute acceleration $\bar{a}_{max}$ are shown in Figure 7.20. Note that when $\eta = 1.0$, the SDOF oscillator responds in the elastic range for most of the earthquake records considered and for all values of α

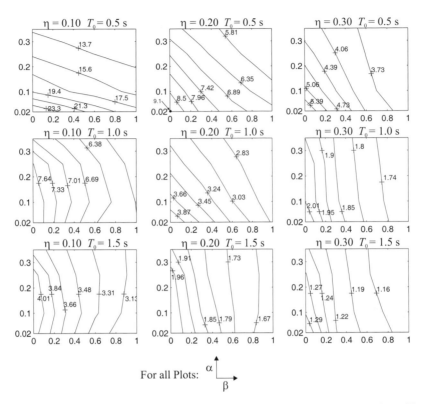

Figure 7.19 Contour Maps of Mean Displacement Ductility for Flag-Shaped Systems

and β. For this case, the plot of the mean maximum absolute acceleration vs. period tends towards the elastic response spectrum. The mean maximum absolute acceleration is insensitive to the value of β as seen in Figure 7.20. When α is increased, the accelerations of systems with lower values of η are increased. For increasing values of α, $\bar{a}_{max}$ for all values of η tends towards the elastic response spectrum. For small values of initial period ($T_0 \leq 0.5$ s), $\bar{a}_{max}$ remains high even when the strength ratio η is reduced. This is due to the combination of non-zero post-yielding stiffness α with large values of displacement ductility demand.

Mean values over the ensemble of earthquakes of the normalized absorbed energy $\bar{E}_{abs}$ are shown in Figure 7.21. In general, the energy absorbed increases for decreasing initial period and for decreasing strength ratios. This trend is similar to that observed for the displacement ductility demand (see Figure 7.18). However for smaller values of η, the absorbed energy (see Figure 7.21) does not increase as much as the displacement ductility demand (Figure 7.18).

The mean absorbed energy is insensitive to increasing values of α, but highly dependent on the value of β. In general, the mean absorbed energy doubles when the

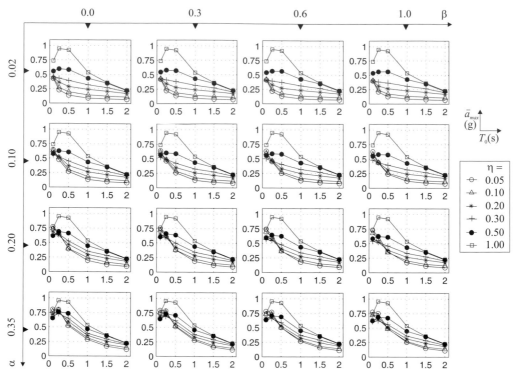

Figure 7.20 Mean Maximum Acceleration for Flag-Shaped Hysteretic Systems

value of β changes from 0 to 1. This increased absorbed energy indicates a higher amount of hysteretic damping but also larger cumulative inelastic excursions of the system.

7.4.3 Response of Bilinear Elastoplastic Hysteretic Systems

For comparison, Figure 7.22 collectively shows mean values, over the ensemble of earthquakes, of displacement ductility $\bar{\mu}_\Delta$, normalized maximum absolute acceleration $\bar{a}_{max}$, normalized absorbed energy $\bar{E}_{abs}$, and normalized residual displacement $\bar{x}_{res}$ for the bilinear elastoplastic hysteretic systems.

Similar to the flag-shaped hysteretic systems, the mean displacement ductility $\bar{\mu}_\Delta$ increases for decreasing values of initial period T_0 and decreasing values of the strength ratio η, as shown in Figure 7.22a.

Mean maximum absolute accelerations $\bar{a}_{max}$ for the case where the strength ratio η = 1.0, as shown in Figure 7.22b, are similar to those of the elastic response spectrum. The maximum accelerations decrease for decreasing values of the strength ratio. Similar to the flag-shaped hysteretic systems, the accelerations for systems with short initial periods (T_0 = 0.1 s) do not decrease when the strength ratio is decreased ($\eta \le 0.3$). This is also due to the combination of the post-yielding stiffness of the bilinear elastoplastic hysteretic systems, α = 0.02, and large displacement ductility values for these systems.

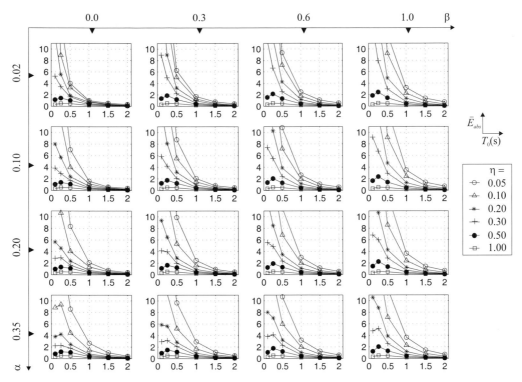

Figure 7.21 Mean Normalized Absorbed Energy for Flag-Shaped Hysteretic Systems

The mean normalized absorbed energy $\bar{E}_{abs}$, as shown in Figure 7.22c, increases for decreasing values of initial period and decreasing values of strength ratio similarly to the displacement ductility. As noted for the flag-shaped hysteretic systems, lowering the strength ratio for lower strength systems, causes a larger increase in the displacement ductility demand than in the absorbed energy. The mean residual displacements $\bar{x}_{res}$ shown in Figure 7.22d increase for decreasing values of initial period and decreasing values of strength ratio. For the highest strength ratio ($\eta = 1.0$) considered where the structures respond in the linear elastic range for most cases, there are no residual displacements at the end of the earthquake. For lower strength values ($\eta \leq 0.3$), residual displacements are more pronounced and more dependent upon the initial period.

7.4.4 Comparative Response of the Flag-Shaped and Elastoplastic Hysteretic Systems

The response of flag-shaped (FS) and bilinear elastoplastic (EP) hysteretic systems is qualitatively very similar as seen by comparing Figures 7.18, 7.20, 7.21 and 7.22. The following three observations can be made on the comparative response of these two types of hysteretic systems:

- For each EP hysteretic system, there is at least one FS hysteretic system of similar initial period and strength ratio that can achieve equal or smaller displacement ductility. In general, the intermediate values of α and β are sufficient to achieve this performance level.

- The maximum absolute accelerations are similar in these two hysteretic models for low values of α. For larger values of α, maximum accelerations are larger for the FS hysteretic systems, especially for systems with lower strength ratios.

- The energy absorbed is in general significantly larger for the EP hysteretic systems than for the FS hysteretic systems, especially for low values of β.

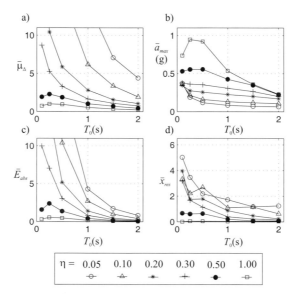

Figure 7.22 Response of Elastoplastic Systems: a) Mean Displacement Ductility, b) Mean Maximum Accelerations, c) Mean Normalized Absorbed Energy, and d) Normalized Residual Displacements

The ratio of the mean displacement ductility of the FS systems to that of the bilinear EP systems with equal initial period T_0 and strength ratio η is plotted in Figure 7.23. This ratio illustrates the same trends previously identified in the discussion of Figure 7.18, since the displacement ductility ratio of the elastoplastic systems is a constant for a given strength ratio and initial period. Nonetheless, this ratio allows for a more direct comparison between the demand on FS and EP systems. It can be seen that this ratio does not follow a clear trend with respect to the strength ratio η. The first row of plots in Figure 7.23, where $\alpha = 0.02$ for all systems, illustrates the effect of increasing β on the mean displacement ductility. For periods larger than 0.5s, the FS and EP systems reach similar values of peak ductility demands. Larger peak ductility demands are observed for

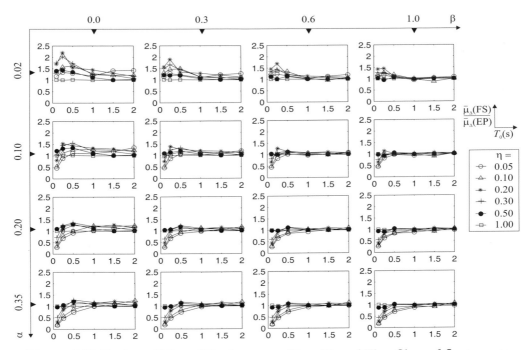

Figure 7.23 Ratios of Mean Displacement Ductility of Flag-Shaped Systems to Mean Displacement Ductility of Elastoplastic Systems

the FS systems for shorter periods (< 0.5 s). Inelastic displacement demands in short period structures are more strongly related to energy dissipation capacity. The differences in displacement ductility demands for these shorter period systems can be explained by the greater energy dissipation capacity of elastoplastic systems. For shorter period structures, a slightly higher strength ratio can be used for the FS systems to reduce the ductility demand to levels similar to the EP systems.

To further compare the response of these two hysteretic models, three particular systems are considered. The first system is characterized by an initial natural period $T_0 = 0.25$ s and a strength ratio $\eta = 0.5$, representing a one-storey steel MRF structure. The second system is characterized by an initial natural period $T_0 = 1.0$ s and a strength ratio $\eta = 0.1$, representing a 7-storey steel MRF structure. The last system considered is characterized by an initial natural period $T_0 = 2.0$ s and a strength ratio $\eta = 0.05$, representing a 20-storey steel MRF structure. For each of these structural configurations, an elastoplastic hysteretic system (EP) and three flag-shaped hysteretic systems (FS) are defined and considered for comparative purposes. The FS systems have the same initial period and strength ratio as the corresponding EP system. As listed in Table 7-4, each FS system has a different combination of post-yielding stiffness coefficient α and energy dissipating coefficient β. Unlike most structural systems and devices exhibiting the EP hysteresis, systems exhibiting the FS hysteresis can be designed to exhibit different values of α and β. The mean response values over the ensemble of earthquakes for these systems are also presented in Table 7-4.

Table 7-4: Response of Three Systems Exhibiting Elastoplastic (EP) Hysteresis and Flag-Shaped (FS) Hysteresis

System 1 $T_0 = 0.25$ s and $\eta = 0.50$	$\bar{\mu}_\Delta$	$\bar{a}_{max}$	$\bar{E}_{abs}$	$\bar{x}_{res}$
EP ($\alpha = 0.02$)	2.28	0.55	2.39	0.61
FS ($\alpha = 0.10$, $\beta = 1.0$)	2.10	0.56	2.46	0.00
FS ($\alpha = 0.20$, $\beta = 0.6$)	2.26	0.64	1.92	0.00
FS ($\alpha = 0.35$, $\beta = 0.3$)	2.27	0.73	1.48	0.00
System 2 $T_0 = 1.0$ s and $\eta = 0.10$	$\bar{\mu}_\Delta$	$\bar{a}_{max}$	$\bar{E}_{abs}$	$\bar{x}_{res}$
EP ($\alpha = 0.02$)	6.19	0.13	2.71	1.10
FS ($\alpha = 0.10$, $\beta = 1.0$)	6.07	0.13	2.27	0.00
FS ($\alpha = 0.20$, $\beta = 0.6$)	6.45	0.22	2.00	0.00
FS ($\alpha = 0.35$, $\beta = 0.3$)	6.19	0.29	1.98	0.00
System 3 $T_0 = 2.0$ s and $\eta = 0.05$	$\bar{\mu}_\Delta$	$\bar{a}_{max}$	$\bar{E}_{abs}$	$\bar{x}_{res}$
EP ($\alpha = 0.02$)	4.41	0.06	0.83	1.25
FS ($\alpha = 0.10$, $\beta = 1.0$)	4.78	0.06	0.70	0.00
FS ($\alpha = 0.20$, $\beta = 0.6$)	4.40	0.09	0.55	0.00
FS ($\alpha = 0.35$, $\beta = 0.3$)	4.21	0.11	0.69	0.00

The mean displacement ductility is similar for the EP and FS hysteresis for all three systems considered. Furthermore, for every EP system there is at least one of the three FS systems considered that has lower mean displacement ductility. The mean maximum absolute accelerations are increased for increasing values of α. The energy absorbed, also as discussed earlier, is larger for the EP systems and is also increased for the FS systems for larger values of β. Finally, unlike the EP systems that sustain significant mean residual deformations, the FS systems sustain no residual displacements.

7.4.5 Examples of Time-History Analyses

To this point, results have been given in terms of non-dimensional mean response quantities over the ensemble of the 20 earthquake records considered. To further compare the two hysteretic models and to provide some insight in their response over time, a series of five structural systems were subjected to the 1989 Loma Prieta earthquake recorded at the Hollister Differential Array and scaled-up to 130% of its amplitude (see Table 7-1). The scaled accelerogram for this record is presented in Figure 7.24a). As shown in Figure 7.24b), the 5% damped elastic response spectrum of the scaled record is in satisfactory agreement with the mean spectrum for the ensemble of the 20 records.

All the systems considered have an initial period of $T_0 = 1.0$ s. and a mass of 4.0 kN.s^2/mm. The resulting initial stiffness is $k_0 = 157.9$ kN/mm. The system so defined

a)   b)

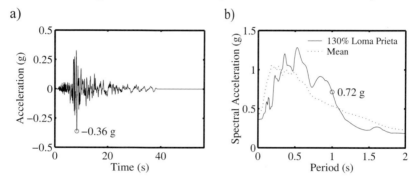

Figure 7.24 Loma Prieta Record Scaled at 130%: a) Accelerogram and b) Elastic Response Spectrum for 5% Damping for Accelerogram and for Ensemble of Earthquake Records

represents a 7-storey steel MRF. As shown in Figure 7.24, the peak ground acceleration is 0.36g while the spectral acceleration at a period of 1.0s is 0.72g. The first system in Table 7-5 designated by EP incorporates the elastoplastic hysteretic model. The four other systems designated by FS1 through FS4 utilize the flag-shaped hysteretic model. The yield force for systems EP, FS1 and FS3 was set equal to 3924 kN corresponding to a strength ratio $\eta = 0.1$. The yield force of systems FS2 and FS4 was set equal to 2747 kN which is equal to 70% of the yield force of systems EP, FS1 and FS3, and corresponds to a strength ratio $\eta = 0.07$. As noted earlier, intermediate values of α and β result in displacement ductility values for the flag-shaped hysteretic model that are similar to systems with large values of α combined with low values of β and vice-versa. For systems FS1 and FS2, α and β were set to 0.25 and 0.30 respectively. For systems FS3 and FS4, α and β were set equal to 0.15 and 0.50 respectively. The defining parameters for these five systems are summarized in Table 7-5. Response values of maximum relative displacement Δ_{max}, maximum absolute acceleration A_{max}, absorbed energy E_a as well as residual displacement Δ_{res} are presented in Table 7-5.

Table 7-5: Response of SDOF Systems with $T_0 = 1.0$ s, $m = 4$ kN.s^2/mm and k_0 = 157.9 kN/mm under 130% of the Loma Prieta Record

System	α	β	η	Δ_y (mm)	F_y (kN)	Δ_{max} (mm)	A_{max} (g)	E_{abs} (kN.mm) x 10^6	Δ_{res} (mm)
EP	0.02	–	0.10	24.9	3924	124.7	0.13	2.00	22.9
FS1	0.25	0.30	0.10	24.9	3924	110.7	0.20	0.74	0.00
FS2	0.25	0.30	0.07	17.5	2747	117.9	0.17	0.83	0.00
FS3	0.15	0.50	0.10	24.9	3924	110.0	0.16	1.10	0.00
FS4	0.15	0.50	0.07	17.5	2747	115.3	0.14	1.11	0.00

It is noted that these response values obtained for the 130% Loma Prieta earthquake record are in close agreement with the mean values obtained over the ensemble of earthquakes (see Table 7-4) and follow similar trends as observed earlier. In all cases, all four flag-shaped hysteretic systems achieve slightly smaller maximum displacements than the elastoplastic system. Systems FS1 and FS2 have greater maximum accelerations and lower absorbed energy than systems FS3 and FS4.

7.5 DYNAMIC RESPONSE OF MDOF SELF-CENTERING SYSTEMS

A limited number of studies are currently available on the seismic response of MDOF structures exhibiting the flag-shaped hysteresis. In one such study (Christopoulos et al. 2002a), the seismic response of 3, 6 and 10 storey self-centering steel frames was investigated numerically and compared to that of traditional Welded Moment Resisting Frames (WMRF) through time-history dynamic analyses. In the self-centering frames, all beam-to-column moment connections were designed to display the flag-shaped hysteresis while the columns were fixed at the base. The self-centering response was obtained through the Post Tensioned Energy Dissipative (PTED) connections that are discussed in more detail later in this chapter (see section 7.11.9). The main results are presented below to illustrate the dynamic response of MDOF self-centering frame structures.

7.5.1 Structures Analyzed

Three frames, designed as Special Moment Resisting Frames (SMRF) by Shen and Akbas (1999) in compliance with the 1994 edition of the Uniform Building Code (ICBO 1994) and using A36 grade steel sections were considered in this study. It was then verified that, if A992 grade steel is used, along with the Reduced Beam Section (RBS) technique (Gross et al. 1999), these same beam and column sections comply with the 1997 edition of the UBC (ICBO 1997) and respect the weak-beam strong-column requirement of the 1997 Seismic Provisions for Structural Steel Buildings (AISC 1997). Details on the design and numerical modelling of the WMRF and PTED frames can be found in Christopoulos (2002).

7.5.2 Ground Motions Used in Analyses

These frames were subjected to an ensemble of six historical strong ground motion records from California, chosen from the records presented in Table 7-1. The characteristics of the scaled records are given in Table 7-6.

Table 7-6: Properties of Scaled Earthquake Records

Name	Earthquake	Year	Station	Scaled PGA (g)
CM2	Cape Mendocino	1992	Rio Dell Overpass	0.46
LAN2	Landers	1992	Yermo Fire Station	0.33
LP3	Loma Prieta	1989	Gilroy Array 4	0.54
NOR3	Northridge	1994	N. Hollywood	0.43
NOR9	Northridge	1994	Canoga Park	0.46
SUP3	Superstition Hills	1987	Plaster City	0.41

The absolute acceleration response spectra for each of these scaled records, for 5% damping, are shown in Figure 7.25.

7.5.3 Results from Numerical Investigation

The natural periods of the 3, 6 and 10 storey WMRFs were respectively 1.11 s, 1.51 s and 2.22 s. The initial natural periods of the 3, 6 and 10 storey PTED frames were 1.05, 1.49 s and 2.30 s respectively. All frames responded within the expected range, i.e. interstorey drifts were limited to a maximum of 2.5% under these design level earthquakes. Furthermore, it was verified that, with the exception of the base columns, no other columns yielded during the time-history analyses, indicating that the desired strong-column week-beam behaviour was achieved. The following indices were used to characterize the seismic response of these frames.

- The maximum interstorey drift ID at storey i is defined as:

$$ID_i = \frac{max\left|D_{(i)}(t) - D_{(i-1)}(t)\right|}{H_{ci}}, \, 0 \leq t \leq t_D \tag{7.59}$$

where $D_i(t)$ is the displacement of storey i relative to the ground at time t, H_{ci} is the height of storey i and t_D is the total duration of the earthquake.

- The residual drift RID_i at storey i is defined as:

$$RID_i = \frac{D_i(t_D) - D_{i-1}(t_D)}{H_{ci}} \qquad (7.60)$$

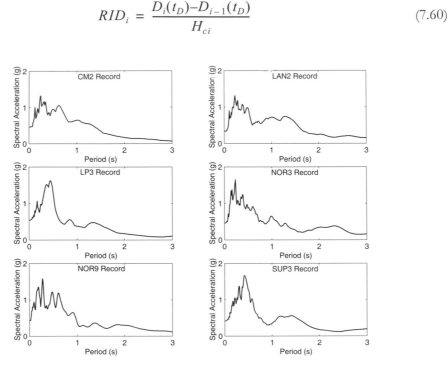

Figure 7.25 Acceleration Response Spectra of Scaled Earthquake Records Used in Analyses

While both the WMRFs and the PTED frames sustain residual drifts at the first storey because of the assumed fixed columns at the base, only the WMRFs are expected to sustain residual drifts for stories above the first one. The maximum absolute acceleration $A_{max\ i}$ at floor i is a direct indicator of the force level induced into the system by the seismic input. In addition to these maximum response indices, the total seismic input energy E_{in} and the total hysteretic energy E_h are computed. The hysteretic energy E_h is the residual value of the absorbed energy at the end of the time-history and is a measure of potential structural damage including duration effects for yielding structures. The input energy is an indicator of the way structures *attract* seismic energy. The input energy is usually used as an indicator of the effect of a change in a structure's properties. For example, if a structure is retrofitted with the addition of passive energy dissipating devices, the added stiffness and energy dissipation may result in a structure which in fact dissipates more energy per vibration cycle, but also attracts more seismic energy, thus making the retrofit inefficient. The reader is referred to chapter 3 for a detailed presentation of energy concepts.

(a) Response of 3-Storey Frames to LP3 Record

The responses of 3-storey WMRF and PTED frames under the LP3 record, which has the highest peak ground acceleration (Table 7-6), are first discussed. Figure 7.26 shows the distribution of maximum interstorey drift ID, residual interstorey drift RID and maximum floor accelerations A_{max} along the height of the WMRF and PTED frames. The

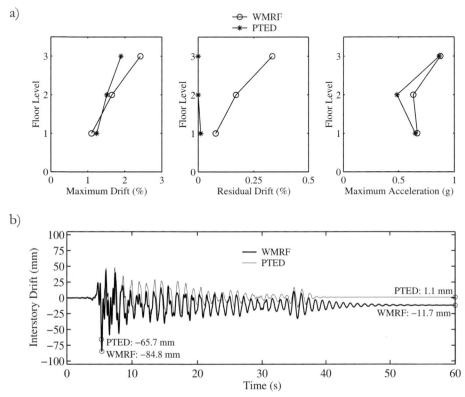

Figure 7.26 Response of 3-Storey Frames under the LP3 Record: a) Distribution of Response Indices along the Height of the Building and b) Time-Histories of 3rd Storey Interstorey Drift

values of ID are similar for the two frames for the two first stories, but the maximum ID of the third storey is significantly larger for the WMRF (2.4%) than for the PTED frame (1.9%). The RID is larger for the WMRF for all floors, reaching a maximum of 0.33% at the third storey. The PTED frame has zero values of RID for all stories except for the first one where an RID of 0.01 is sustained because of yielding of the base columns. The maximum accelerations are slightly larger for the WMRF, while the maximum value occurring at the third storey is nearly the same for the two frames (0.88 g for the WMRF and 0.87 g for the PTED frame). Figure 7.26 shows also the time-histories of the third storey ID, where the maximum ID is measured for both the WMRF and PTED frames.

It can be seen that, although the maximum values occur almost simultaneously, the response of the WMRF is shifted over after this maximum response is reached, while the PTED frame remains symmetric about the zero deformation line. As indicated in the figure, the maximum and residual interstorey drifts are 84.8 mm and 11.7 mm respectively for the WMRF and 65.7 mm and 1.1 mm respectively for the PTED frame.

(b) Response of 3, 6 and 10 Storey Frames to All Records

The maximum values of ID, RID, A_{max} as well as the relative input energy E_{in}^r and hysteretic energy E_h for all the 6 records are summarized in Tables 7-7, 7-8 and 7-9 for the 3, 6 and 10-storey frames, respectively. The maximum ID was greater for the PTED frame than that of the corresponding WMRF under the CM2 and LAN2 records for the 3-storey frames, under the NOR3 record for the 6-storey frames and under the CM2 record for the 10-storey frames. For all other records and for all frames (except for the CM2 record), the maximum ID was higher for the WMRF than that of the corresponding PTED frames. Furthermore, the mean values of the maximum ID are smaller for the PTED frames than the corresponding WMRFs by 10%, 10.6% and 12.6% for the 3, 6 and 10 storey frames respectively.

The highest values of the RID were respectively 0.70%, 0.52% and 0.32% for the 3, 6 and 10-storey WMRFs, respectively. The mean values were 0.37%, 0.25% and 0.18% for the 3, 6 and 10 storey WMRFs, respectively. The PTED frames sustained very low residual drifts with average values of 0.05%, 0.04% and 0.06% for the 3, 6 and 10 storey frames respectively.

The maximum accelerations A_{max} were in general lower for the PTED frames than for the WMRFs. The mean values were 6.5%, 15% and 9.3% lower for the PTED frames than those of the corresponding WMRFs for the 3, 6 and 10 storey frames respectively.

The relative input energy was surprisingly greater for the PTED frames than for the WMRFs for many of the analyses. For the 3-storey frames, the mean value of E_{in}^r was 7.5% greater for the PTED frame than for the WMRF. However, for the 6-storey frames, E_{in}^r was 30% greater for the WMRF than for the PTED frame, and approximately equal for the 10-storey WMRFs and PTED frames. It is of interest to note that in many cases where the PTED frame had a higher value of E_{in}^r, it sustained smaller maximum ID and smaller A_{max}. One such example is the response of the 3-storey frame under the NOR9 record, where the value of E_{in}^r is 0.73 x10^6 kN.mm for both the PTED and WMRF frames, but the maximum ID is 1.72% and 2.00% for the PTED frame and WMRF respectively. The values of A_{max} are 0.62 g and 0.75 g for the PTED frame and WMRF respectively.

Table 7-7: Maximum Values of Response Indices for 3-Storey Frames

Response Index		CM2	LAN2	LP3	NOR3	NOR9	SUP3	MEAN
Maximum Drift	MRF	2.59	2.60	2.43	1.58	2.00	2.36	2.26
(%)	PTED	2.60	2.77	1.89	1.31	1.72	1.86	2.03
Residual Drift	MRF	0.70	0.16	0.33	0.07	0.34	0.65	0.38
(%)	PTED	0.17	0.06	0.01	0.01	0.02	0.15	0.05
Maximum	MRF	0.69	0.85	0.88	0.63	0.75	0.80	0.77
Acceleration (g)	PTED	0.84	0.74	0.87	0.55	0.62	0.70	0.72
E_{in}^{r}	MRF	0.78	1.05	0.46	0.42	0.73	0.67	0.68
(kN.mm) x 10^{6}	PTED	0.84	1.18	0.58	0.38	0.78	0.63	0.73
E_{h}	MRF	0.54	0.70	0.15	0.11	0.37	0.38	0.37
(kN.mm) x 10^{6}	PTED	0.19	0.33	0.04	0.02	0.07	0.13	0.13

Table 7-8: Maximum Values of Response Indices for 6-Storey Frames

Response Index		CM2	LAN2	LP3	NOR3	NOR9	SUP3	MEAN
Maximum Drift	MRF	1.62	2.32	1.91	1.24	1.50	2.01	1.77
(%)	PTED	1.52	1.77	1.70	1.29	1.45	1.83	1.59
Residual Drift	MRF	0.07	0.18	0.37	0.05	0.18	0.52	0.23
(%)	PTED	0.00	0.13	0.02	0.00	0.02	0.05	0.04
Maximum	MRF	0.85	0.86	0.89	0.79	0.77	0.97	0.86
Acceleration (g)	PTED	0.79	0.80	0.75	0.65	0.60	0.79	0.73
E_{in}^{r}	MRF	1.69	3.13	1.26	1.03	0.96	1.41	1.58
(kN.mm) x 10^{6}	PTED	0.74	2.09	0.95	0.67	0.72	1.24	1.07
E_{h}	MRF	0.82	2.00	0.62	0.24	0.31	0.86	0.81
(kN.mm) x 10^{6}	PTED	0.07	0.33	0.19	0.03	0.04	0.21	0.13

Table 7-9: Maximum Values of Response Indices for 10-Storey Frames

Response Index		CM2	LAN2	LP3	NOR3	NOR9	SUP3	MEAN
Maximum Drift	MRF	1.34	1.72	1.47	1.53	2.77	1.23	1.68
(%)	PTED	1.43	1.57	1.37	1.41	1.79	1.21	1.46
Residual Drift	MRF	0.08	0.15	0.10	0.29	0.32	0.10	0.17
(%)	PTED	0.03	0.04	0.00	0.00	0.14	0.12	0.05
Maximum	MRF	0.69	0.66	0.94	0.67	0.81	0.72	0.75
Acceleration (g)	PTED	0.67	0.65	0.76	0.70	0.66	0.61	0.68
E_{in}^{r}	MRF	0.65	1.67	1.05	2.06	3.52	0.64	1.59
(kN.mm) x 10^6	PTED	0.99	2.22	0.70	2.15	2.71	0.80	1.60
E_h	MRF	0.06	0.51	0.08	0.94	2.03	0.05	0.61
(kN.mm) x 10^6	PTED	0.02	0.16	0.00	0.10	0.29	0.02	0.10

The hysteretic energy E_h was significantly lower for the PTED frames for all analyses. This result is expected since only the sacrificial energy dissipating bars yield in the PTED frames (see section 7.11.9) whereas the full beam sections yield in the WMRFs. The mean values of E_h are smaller for the PTED frames than for the WMRFs by 65%, 83% and 84% respectively for the 3, 6 and 10 storey frames.

Results for the 6 records demonstrate that the performance of the PTED frames is equal if not better than that of corresponding WMRFs for the following reasons:

- From a maximum drift point of view, the PTED frames sustained on average lower maximum drifts than those of the WMRFs. In practice, this is the main performance indicator.

- From a maximum floor acceleration point of view, the PTED frames sustained on average lower maximum accelerations than those of the WMRFs.

- The hysteretic energy, which is an indicator of damage to yielding elements of the structure, is significantly lower in all analyses considered for the PTED frames.

- The residual drifts were considerable in some cases for the WMRFs and were nearly zero for the PTED frames.

7.6 ANCIENT APPLICATIONS OF SELF-CENTERING SYSTEMS

Many of the earliest structural systems going as far back as the Antiquity were constructed of structural elements such as stones, blocks or segments that were stacked together. The size of these elements was determined by each civilization's ability to transport and to lift them into position. Because such systems relied on their self-weight to resist lateral loads and on the friction along the interfaces of the segments to transfer shear and torsion, many of them displayed a *rocking* behaviour when subjected to lateral loading.

As discussed by Pampanin (2006), one such example can be found in ancient Greek and Roman temples. The columns of these temples were comprised of carved cylindrical marble segments of approximately 0.6 m to 1 m in height that were interconnected by a poured lead shear and torsion key. Beam and roof elements (also made of marble) completed the structures as illustrated in Figure 7.27. The self-weight of the columns, beams and roof elements provides an appreciable amount of pre-compression to the segmental columns and generates moment resistance at the segment junctions and at the base. Under lateral loading, such as produced by a major earthquake, the segments separate at the junctions and deform relative to each other through a combination of rocking and sliding motions. In addition, the lead shear keys are likely to deform beyond their elastic limit and dissipate energy when rocking and sliding motions are initiated. It is unknown whether such structural systems were designed to resist earthquakes, but a large number of such temples have survived multiple major earthquakes in the Mediterranean region.

a)   b)

Figure 7.27 Ancient Greek Temple: a) General View and b) Segmental Column

7.7 EARLY MODERN APPLICATIONS OF SELF-CENTERING SYSTEMS

The rocking concept combined with added energy dissipation devices used in the design of the "stepping" railway bridge over the south Rangitikei River in New Zealand is conceptually similar to the ancient rocking systems. This bridge, shown in Figure 7.28, has been in operation since 1981. It is 70 m tall, with six spans of prestressed concrete hollow-box girders, and an overall length of 315 m (Cormack 1988). The base isolation is mainly designed to allow the sideways rocking of pairs of slender reinforced concrete piers. Torsional-beam dampers (Skinner et al. 1993) limit the amount of rocking. Note that the weight of the bridge, which allows its re-centering, is not carried by the dampers, but is transmitted to the foundation through thin laminated-rubber bearings.

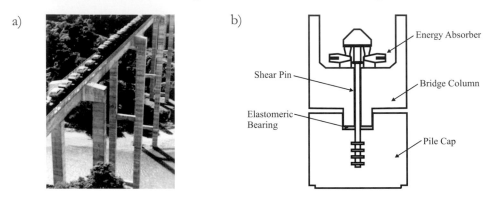

Figure 7.28 Early Applications of Self-Centering Systems on the Rangitikei Railway Bridge in New Zealand: a) Overview of Bridge, b) Detail of Pier Base (Photograph from Restrepo 2002, with permission from the Japan Concrete Institute)

In the past 20 years, a number of systems exhibiting the self-centering response have been developed either in brace configurations using shape memory alloys or mechanical devices, or with the combination of unbonded post-tensioning with more traditional structural elements such as concrete or steel beams, column and walls. These systems are discussed in the following paragraphs.

7.8 SHAPE MEMORY ALLOYS

7.8.1 Superelasticity of Shape Memory Alloys

Shape memory alloys (SMAs) (Funakubo 1984, Patoor et al. 1990, DesRoches et al. 2004) are a class of materials able to develop the so-called superelastic behaviour (or pseudo-elastic behaviour). SMAs are made of two or three different metals. Nitinol, for example, incorporates 49% of Nickel and 51% of Titanium. Copper and zinc can also be alloyed to produce superelastic properties. Depending on the manufacturing process and the temperature range of alloying, several molecular rearrangements of the crystalline structure of the alloy are possible. Chemical phases change when the temperature of alloying is increased. Low alloying temperatures involve a fully martensitic microstructure, whereas high alloying temperatures involve a fully austenitic microstructure. If a cyclic loading is applied to an alloy containing a fully martensitic microstructure, the viscoplastic behaviour illustrated in Figure 7.29a is obtained. If a cyclic loading is applied to an alloy containing a fully austenitic microstructure, a linear-elastic behaviour is obtained as shown in Figure 7.29b. Finally, for intermediate alloying temperatures, both martensitic and austenitic phases can co-exist. Loading of an alloy containing both phases results in the transformation from one phase to the other. Furthermore, unloading of the same alloy implies a re-transformation from the latter phase back into the original phase.

This transformation process results from elastic loading of the stable austenitic parent phase up to a threshold stress. Larger stresses induce a transformation from austenite to martensite. This transformation process occurs at a significantly reduced tangent modulus in a manner analogous to plastic yielding. As deformations take place, the volume of martensite within the microstructure increases and the path of the stress-strain curve follows a stress plateau. As the microstructure becomes fully martensitic, further straining causes the martensite to be loaded elastically. A re-transformation from martensite to austenite takes place during unloading. This re-transformation, however, occurs at a lower stress level than the original transformation. This remarkable process, called superelastic behaviour, produces an hysteretic effect with near zero residual strain as shown in Figure 7.30.

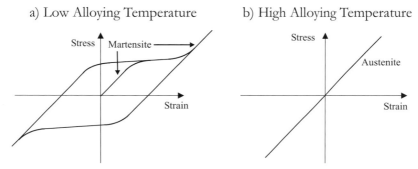

Figure 7.29 SMAs Hysteretic Behaviour: a) for Low Alloying Temperatures and b) for High Alloying Temperatures

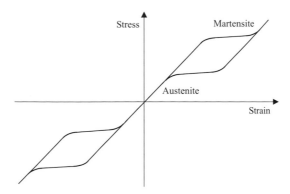

Figure 7.30 SMAs Superelastic Behaviour for Intermediate Alloying Temperatures

The superelastic behaviour has several advantages for supplemental damping purposes. It exhibits high stiffness and strength for small strains. It becomes more flexible for larger strains. It has practically no residual strain and, finally, it is able to dissipate a large amount of energy. The superelastic behaviour, however, is sensitive to fatigue. After a large number of loading cycles, SMAs tend to deteriorate into a classical plastic behaviour with residual strains. Review of the state-of-the-art in the use of shape memory alloys in seismic design has been provided by Desroches and Smith (2004) and Wilson and Wesolowski (2005).

7.8.2 Experimental Studies Involving Shape Memory Alloys

Aiken et al. (1992) studied experimentally the use of Nickel-Titanium SMA (Nitinol) as an energy dissipating element. Shake table tests were performed on a small-scale three-storey steel frame. As shown in Figure 7.31, the model was a three-storey steel moment-resisting frame with welded connections. The plan dimensions of the model were 0.91 m x 1.22 m with a storey height of 0.61 m, and the total weight was 18.9 kN, equally distributed between the floors. The damping of the bare frame was 0.5% and the three translational natural frequencies in the direction of testing were 2.6 Hz, 10.9 Hz, and 24.5 Hz.

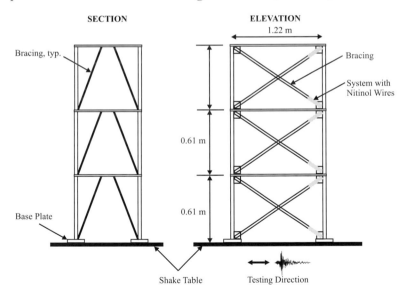

Figure 7.31 Three-Storey Test Frame Used for Shake Table Studies of Nitinol SMA (after Aiken et al. 1992)

Nitinol wires were incorporated at each end of the cross bracing system in the model. In this configuration, the Nitinol was loaded in tension only. This allowed the full volume of Nitinol to dissipate energy.

Figure 7.32 presents the stress-strain hysteretic behaviour that was recorded with no preload in the Nitinol wire. The self-centering (superelastic) characteristics of Nitinol can be observed from the graph. This means that if the design earthquake were exceeded, the structure would stiffen rather than soften. Note that because permanent deformation of the wire occurred during the larger strain cycles, the wire was loose at the end of the test.

With a small preload, the authors reported that it was difficult to achieve uniform behaviour in all six braces. To resolve this problem, a large preload was applied to the Nitinol wires. With this preload, the axial strain in the wires cycled between 2.5% and 6.0% throughout the tests. Thus the Nitinol was continuously cycled in the region of martensite phase, causing a steel-like hysteresis behaviour with maximum energy dissipation. The self-centering capabilities of the Nitinol were lost, however, at those strain levels. This behaviour is illustrated in Figure 7.33 that shows the stress-strain hysteretic behaviour of all braces in a typical shake table test. The loops are similar for all braces and exhibit significant energy dissipation capability.

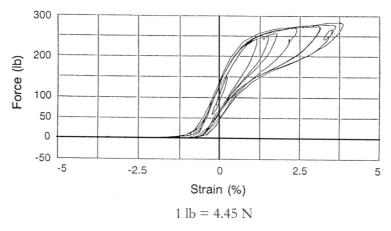

1 lb = 4.45 N

Figure 7.32 Hysteretic Behaviour of Nitinol Wires Recorded During Shake Table Tests (from Aiken et al. 1992, reproduced with the permission of the New Zealand Society for Earthquake Engineering)

Figure 7.34 presents a comparison, for the Zacatula ground motion (1985 Mexico City earthquake), of the floor envelopes of maximum horizontal acceleration (Accel.), interstorey drifts (ISD) and relative displacements (Rel. Displ.) for the bare frame (Dot-Dash), the braced frame incorporating Nitinol wires without preload (Solid), and the braced frame incorporating Nitinol wires with preload (Dotted). The addition of the Nitinol braces caused a significant reduction in all three response parameters.

Witting and Cozzarelli (1992) carried out another experimental study involving SMAs. Shake table tests were carried out on a 2/5-scale steel frame structure incorporating Cu-Zn-Al SMA dampers installed as diagonal braces. As shown in Figure 7.35, the overall dimensions of the test structure were 1.32 m x 1.32 m in plan and 5.69 m in height (Chang et al. 1993a). The weight at each floor (provided by lumped steel plates) was 5.65 kN for the first four floors and 5.83 kN for the top floor. All girder-to-column joints were fully welded. The natural frequency of the bare frame was 3.2 Hz with a first-mode damping

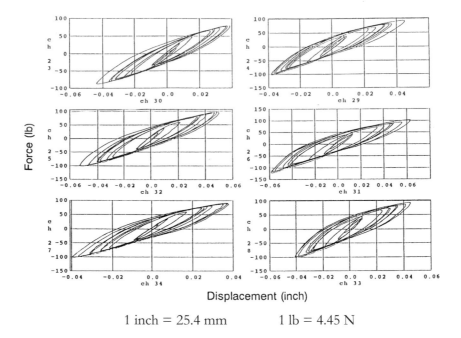

1 inch = 25.4 mm   1 lb = 4.45 N

Figure 7.33 Hysteresis Loops for All Nitinol Braces (from Aiken et al. 1992, reproduced with the permission of the New Zealand Society for Earthquake Engineering)

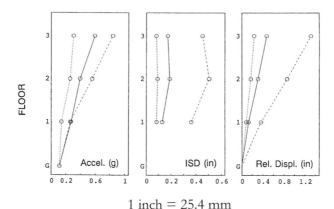

1 inch = 25.4 mm

Figure 7.34 Effect of Nitinol Braces on the Seismic Response of Test Frame – Zacatula Ground Motion, Solid: Nitinol Without Preload, Dotted: Nitinol With Preload, Dot-Dash: Bare Frame (from Aiken et al. 1992, reproduced with the permission of the New Zealand Society for Earthquake Engineering)

ratio of about 1% of critical. As shown in Figure 7.36, the SMA dampers were configured as a torsion bar system. The axial load in a diagonal bracing induced primarily a torsional couple in the SMA cylindrical bar.

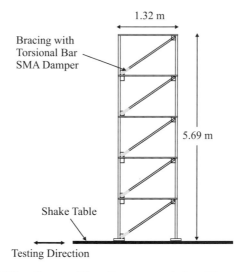

Figure 7.35 Five-Storey Test Structure (after Chang et al. 1993)

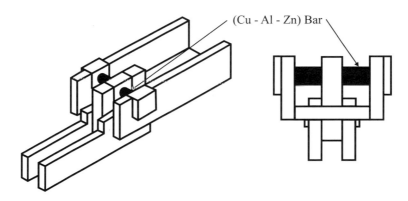

Figure 7.36 Torsional Bar Configuration for SMA Damper (after Witting and Cozzarelli 1992)

Figures 7.37 and 7.38 show the envelopes of maximum floor displacements and accelerations under the 1940 El Centro record and the 1988 Quebec recording of the Saguenay earthquake. Both records were scaled to a peak ground acceleration of 0.06g. The response reduction is considerable for the El Centro record, but is marginal for the higher frequency Quebec record. This record caused only small deformations of the SMA dampers. At these levels of deformations, the stiffness of SMAs is higher than under large deformations. Therefore, the efficiency of SMAs will be higher for low frequency records.

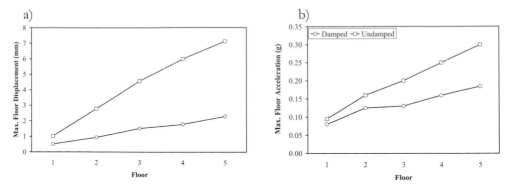

Figure 7.37 Response of Structures for 0.06g El Centro Record: a) Maximum Displacements and b) Maximum Accelerations (after Witting and Cozzarelli 1992)

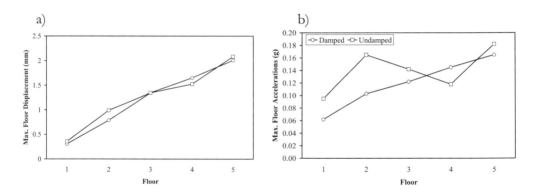

Figure 7.38 Response of Structures for 0.06g Quebec Record: a) Maximum Displacements and b) Maximum Accelerations (after Witting and Cozzarelli 1992)

Desroches et al. (2004) evaluated the properties of Nitinol bars and wires under cyclic loading to assess their potential for seismic applications. The results of the experimental study show that nearly ideal superelastic properties can be obtained in both wire and bar forms of Nitinol. The wire form exhibited higher strength and damping properties than those of the bar form. It was also found that for increased loading rates the damping properties of Nitinol decreased but the re-centering properties remained unaffected.

The cyclic behaviour of steel beam-column connections incorporating rods made of Nitinol in its martensitic phase was investigated by Ocel et al. (2004). Four Nitinol rods, 35 mm in diameter and 381 mm in length were incorporated as axial elements in the connection to act as the main energy dissipation mechanism. The beam-column connection was tested under quasi-static and dynamic cyclic loading. The hysteretic response of the connection was stable with good energy dissipation characteristics up to a drift of 4% as shown in Figure 7.39. After the first test, the Nitinol rods were re-heated above their alloying temperature in order to re-generate an austenitic microstructure, and recovered their initial shape. The rods were heated for approximately 8 minutes at 300°C and about ¾ of their permanent deformations were recovered. Subsequent testing exhibited similar hysteretic response as that observed in the initial test.

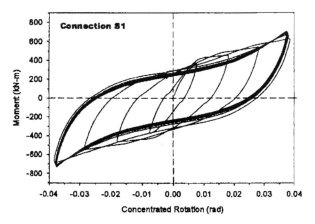

Figure 7.39 Hysteretic Response of a Steel Beam-Column Connection Incorporating Nitinol Bars (from Ocel et al. 2004, reproduced with the permission of the American Society of Civil Engineers)

So far, no large-scale testing of civil engineering structures incorporating SMAs has been carried out. The major problem with the practical implementation of SMAs is their cost. Nitinol, for example, can be priced as high as $70 USD/kg, which would be prohibitive for most structural applications.

7.8.3 Structural Implementations of Shape Memory Alloys

Only a few structural implementations of SMA devices have occurred to date. One application is for the seismic retrofit of the historical San Giorgio bell tower in Italy that was damaged after the 1996 Modena and Reggio earthquake in Emilia (Indirli et al. 2001). For this application, Nitinol wires were introduced and prestressed through the masonry walls of the bell tower to prevent tensile stresses from occurring during a seismic event.

SMAs have also been used in the form of post-tensioning rods for the seismic rehabilitation of monuments and historical buildings as in the cases of the Basilica di San Francesco in Assisi (Croci et al. 2000). This structure was damaged after two consecutive earthquake shocks in the 1997 Umbria-Marche earthquake.

7.9 THE ENERGY DISSIPATING RESTRAINT (EDR)

7.9.1 Hysteretic Behaviour of EDR

Simpler and less expensive mechanical devices can also exhibit flag-shaped hysteretic response. One such device is the Energy Dissipating Restrain (EDR) manufactured by Fluor Daniel, Inc. The EDR was originally developed as a seismic restraint device for the support of piping systems in nuclear power plants.

Figure 7.40 presents details of the EDR, which incorporates a sliding friction mechanism with an internal end stop, limiting the range of motion. The principal components in the device are the internal spring, the steel compression wedges, the bronze friction wedges, stops at both ends of the internal spring and the external cylinder. In operation, the compressive force in the spring acting on the compression and friction wedges causes a normal force on the cylinder wall. This normal force is proportional to the force in the spring. The normal force and the coefficient of friction between the bronze friction wedges and the steel cylinder wall determine the slip force in the device.

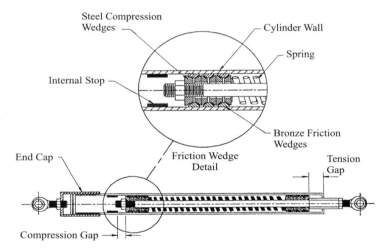

Figure 7.40 Energy Dissipating Restraint (from Nims et al. 1993, reproduced with the permission of the Earthquake Engineering Research Institute)

Unlike the Sumitomo friction device described in Chapter 5, the length of the internal spring in the EDR can be changed to provide a desirable friction slip force. Also, adjusting the lengths of the gaps between the spring ends and the internal stops, as well as the preload in the internal spring, allows for a wide variety of hysteretic behaviours to be achieved. The hysteresis loops for two different configurations of the EDR are shown in Figure 7.41. Figure 7.41a shows the triangular hysteresis loops obtained with zero gaps and zero spring preload. In this case, the slip force is proportional to the device displacement. With non-zero spring preload and very large gaps, the device acts as a standard Coulomb friction damper. With non-zero preload, but no initial gaps, the flag-shaped hysteresis loops of Figure 7.41b are obtained.

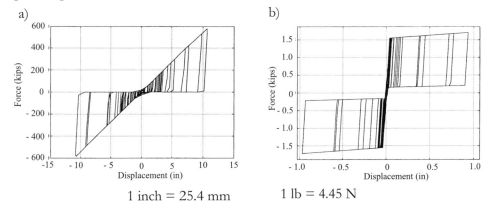

1 inch = 25.4 mm   1 lb = 4.45 N

Figure 7.41 Hysteresis Loops for Various Configurations of EDR (from Nims et al. 1993, reproduced with the permission of the Earthquake Engineering Research Institute)

7.9.2 Experimental Studies with EDR

Aiken et al. (1993) used the same small-scale three storey steel frame described earlier for the SMA damper tests (Figure 7.31) to evaluate the seismic performance of the EDR. The same ground motion records (El Centro and Zacatula) were used again to allow a direct comparison between EDRs and SMAs. Two EDRs were mounted in each of the three stories of the model. Figure 7.42 shows a photograph of the model equipped with the EDRs. The principal variable changed during the testing was the initial slip load and, for the majority of the tests performed, the slip load distribution was uniform throughout the model. In addition to the tests with the device in the self-centering configuration, a series of tests with the EDRs configured to act as a simple Coulomb device was also performed.

Figure 7.43 presents the envelopes of peak accelerations, interstorey drifts and relative displacements for the El Centro (PGA = 0.33 g) and the Zacatula (PGA = 0.36 g) ground motions. On each graph, the response of the bare frame and the EDR with slip loads of 0.33 kN (EDS.75), 0.56 kN (EDS.125), 0.89 kN (EDS.200) and 1.33 kN (EDS.300) are compared. The overall effect of the EDR was to substantially reduce the model deformations and interstorey drifts. Interstorey drifts and displacements consistently decreased with increasing slip load. Acceleration trends were not as well defined. Part of the change in structural response was due to the change in the stiffness of the structure with the EDRs in place, and part was due to the additional damping the EDRs provided to the structure. The change in stiffness was substantial, with the fundamental frequency being 3.9 Hz for the EDR frame compared to 2.6 Hz for the bare frame.

Figure 7.42 Test Frame with EDR (from Aiken et al. 1993, reproduced with the permission of the Earthquake Engineering Research Institute)

7.10 SELF-CENTERING DAMPERS USING RING SPRINGS

7.10.1 Description of Ring-Spring Systems

Another mechanical device that exhibits strong self-centering capabilities uses a ring spring - also known as a friction spring - as the key component. An example of self-centering ring-spring system is the SHAPIA damper manufactured by Spectrum Engineering in Canada (Kar and Rainer 1996, Kar et al. 1996). A section through a typical ring-spring assembly is illustrated in Figure 7.44. The assembly consists of outer and inner rings that have tapered mating surfaces. As the spring column is loaded in compression, the axial displacement is accompanied by sliding of the rings on the conical friction surfaces. The outer rings are subjected to circumferential tension (hoop stress) while the inner rings experience compression. At the time of assembly and fabrication of a damper, special lubricant is applied to the tapered surfaces. In order to align the rings axially as a column stack, a small amount of pre-compression is applied during assembly. When the damper unit is subjected to either tension or compression, the fabrication and assembly details are designed to ensure that the friction springs act always in compression, as shown in Figure 7.45. The ring springs are designed to remain damage-free (elastic) during a seismic event so that no repair or replacement should be required after an earthquake. The friction-based SHAPIA damper is designed to display a symmetrical flag-shaped hysteresis diagram that is stable and repeatable.

7.10.2 Experimental Studies with Ring-Spring Dampers

Filiatrault et al. (2000) performed performance evaluation tests of a 200-kN capacity prototype of the SHAPIA damping system under simulated earthquake ground motions. For this purpose, a two-phase testing program was carried out. In the first phase,

a) El Centro

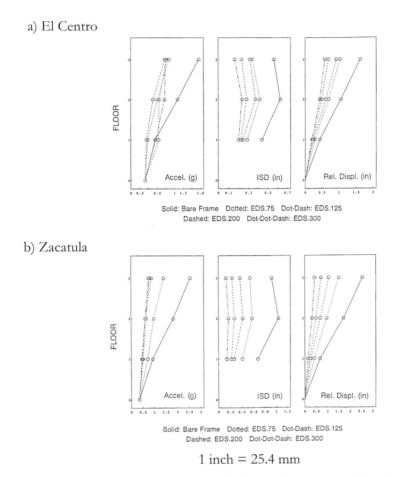

Solid: Bare Frame   Dotted: EDS.75   Dot-Dash: EDS.125
Dashed: EDS.200   Dot-Dot-Dash: EDS.300

b) Zacatula

Solid: Bare Frame   Dotted: EDS.75   Dot-Dash: EDS.125
Dashed: EDS.200   Dot-Dot-Dash: EDS.300

1 inch = 25.4 mm

Figure 7.43 Effects of EDRs on the Seismic Response of Test Frame (from Aiken et al. 1993, reproduced with the permission of the Earthquake Engineering Research Institute)

characterization tests were performed on the damper to provide information on the self-centering capabilities, stability, repeatability and consistency of performance. In the second phase, earthquake simulator tests were carried out on a half scale moment-resisting steel frame (MRF) with and without a damper-bracing assembly.

Figure 7.45 shows a diagrammatic view of the prototype unit tested, which had an outer diameter of 165 mm, a c/c length between the rod end bearings of 710 mm, a force capacity of ±200 kN and a maximum displacement capacity of ±50mm. The friction springs were pre-compressed to a small percentage of the maximum force capacity by means of a centrally located tie-bar. The friction spring stack is restrained at its ends by the flanges of a pair of left cup and right cup, identified with hatch marks in Figure 7.45. As displayed, the unit carries no external load. Under applied external compression force on the left rod end, the left cup compresses the rings in the axial direction while the tie-bar

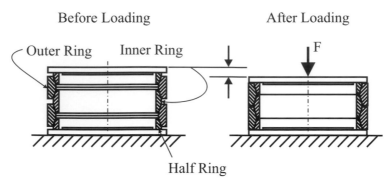

Figure 7.44 Ring-Spring Details (after Filiatrault et al. 2000)

head slides in the slot toward the right. When the external force reverses direction and acts in tension, the right cup is pulled by the tie-bar head toward the left and, again, the friction springs are compressed. Note that the ring-springs have no contact with the inner surface of the housing cylinder at any stage.

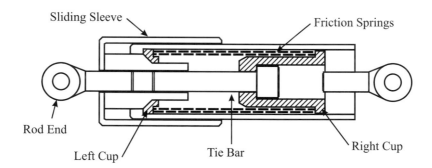

Figure 7.45 200-kN SHAPIA Damper Prototype (after Filiatrault et al. 2000)

(a) Characterization Tests

The measured force-displacement hysteresis loops under quasi-static cyclic loading are reproduced in Figure 7.46. The behaviour is repeatable, stable and identical in tension-compression over 10 loading cycles. The energy dissipating and the re-centering characteristics of the SHAPIA seismic damper are clearly shown in the figure.

As also illustrated in Figure 7.46, the hysteretic behaviour of the SHAPIA damping devices can be characterized by five different physical parameters: an elastic stiffness K_0, a loading slip stiffness $r_L K_0$, an unloading slip stiffness $r_u K_0$, a slip force F_s, and a residual re-centering force F_c. The maximum forces reached upon loading F_{maxL} and unloading, F_{maxU}, are also shown in Figure 7.46. The numerical values of these physical parameters

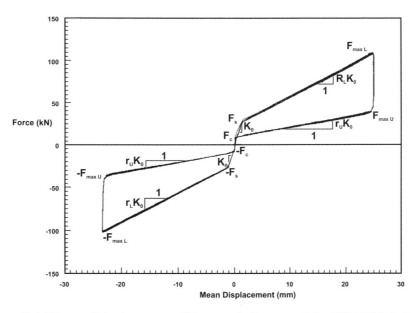

Figure 7.46 Force-Displacement Hysteresis Loops of the SHAPIA Seismic Damper, Sinusoidal Displacement, ±25 mm, 0.5 Hz (after Filiatrault et al. 2000)

for the prototype specimen, as estimated from the force-displacement hysteresis loops of Figure 7.46, are given in Table 7-10.

Figure 7.47 shows the variation of the five physical parameters defining the hysteretic behaviour of the SHAPIA seismic damper with the excitation frequency. The results are presented in terms of the ratio of the parameters obtained at various frequencies to the initial parameters presented in Table 7-10.

Table 7-10: Maximum Values of Response Indices for 10-Storey Frames

Parameter	Numerical values
Elastic stiffness, K_0	23.2 kN/mm
Loading slip stiffness, $r_L K_0$	3.48 kN/mm
Unloading slip stiffness, $r_u K_0$	1.39 kN/mm
Slip force, F_s	28 kN
Residual re-centering force, F_c	9 kN

All the parameters, except the elastic loading stiffness K_0, are practically unaffected by the excitation frequency, as the ratios are practically equal to unity. The large variations observed in the elastic stiffness K_0 can be explained by the fact that the calculation of this stiffness involves very small displacements, occurring during short periods of time. These conditions were close to the limits of accuracy of the position transducers and of the data acquisition system used. Therefore, the variation of K_0 shown in Figure 7.47 may not be representative of the actual behaviour of the damper. The other results indicate that the performance of the damper is nearly independent of the excitation frequency within the range typically expected from seismic input.

(b) Shake Table Tests

Following the characterization tests, the SHAPIA seismic damper was tested in a tension-compression bracing configuration using an existing multi-purpose steel frame installed on the earthquake simulator. Figure 7.48 shows a view of the test structure incorporating the SHAPIA damper.

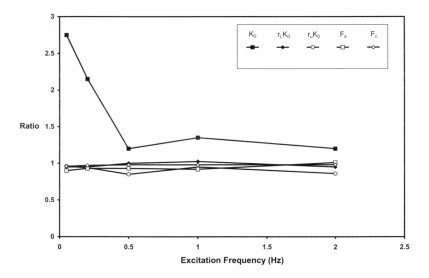

Figure 7.47 Frequency Dependency of SHAPIA Damper Properties (after Filiatrault et al. 2000)

The test specimen is a single-storey moment-resisting plane frame with a height of 1.8 m and a bay width of 2.9 m. The columns of this moment-resisting frame are made of W250x58 steel sections. Each column base was linked to a true pin mechanism which, in turn, was attached to a foundation beam on the shake table. The weight of the model was simulated by four concrete blocks (30 kN each) linked horizontally to the upper beam. These concrete blocks were supported vertically by a peripheral frame so that the test frame would carry only the lateral inertia forces. This peripheral frame was completely pinned in the direction of the shake table motion and braced in the perpendicular direction to ensure no motion of the test plane frame in that direction.

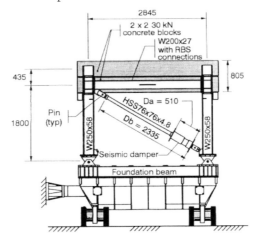

Figure 7.48 Test Structure with SHAPIA Seismic Damper (Filiatrault et al. 2000, reproduced with the permission of the American Society of Civil Engineers)

The lateral load resistance of the structure was, therefore, provided only by the rigid connections between the upper beam and the columns as well as the bracing member. A W200x27 wide flange shape, made of G40.21-300W steel (F_y = 300 MPa, F_u = 450 MPa), was selected for the upper beam. This beam incorporated Reduced Beam Section (RBS) connections at its ends to ensure ductile flexural plastic hinging in the beam away from the column faces. The SHAPIA damper was installed in the bottom corner of the test frame along with a diagonal HSS76x76x4.8 bracing member made of G40.21-350W steel (F_y = 350 MPa, F_u = 480 MPa). This section was selected such that its buckling strength was higher than the design maximum slip load of the damper (150 kN). The end connections of the brace-damper assembly were true pin mechanisms. The connection between the damper and the bracing member was achieved by a threaded rod inserted in the damper and in a threaded end plate welded to the HSS section.

Table 7-11 presents the results of preliminary low level system identification tests performed on the unbraced moment-resisting test frame and on the braced moment-resisting test frame equipped with the SHAPIA seismic damper. The presence of the damper causes a reduction of the fundamental period of the structure and a significant increase of the apparent viscous damping ratio (although the SHAPIA damper was not activated).

Four different seismic tests were conducted in the sequence indicated in Table 7-12. These tests allowed the direct comparison between the seismic behaviour of the unbraced moment-resisting frame and the same structure retrofitted with the bracing element incorporating the SHAPIA seismic damper.

Table 7-11: Results of System Identification Tests (from Filiatrault et al. 2000)

Structural configuration	Natural period (s)	Damping ratio (%)
Unbraced moment-resisting frame	0.350 ± 0.003	3.5
Braced moment-resisting frame with SHAPIA seismic damper	0.207 ± 0.001	10.6

The S00W component of the well-known 1940 El Centro earthquake was used in all tests. Two intensity levels were considered: 100% El Centro at a peak horizontal ground acceleration (PGA) of 0.33 g, and 200% El Centro at a PGA of 0.66 g.

The first intensity may be taken as representative of the conditions in which the SHAPIA damper would operate under a code-design situation, where the moment-resisting frame would remain in the elastic range. The second intensity may be representative of maximum credible earthquake conditions, where the moment-resisting frame would exhibit inelastic deformations.

Table 7-12: Description of Seismic Shake Tests (Filiatrault et al. 2000)

Test No.	Structural configuration	Seismic input
3-1	Braced moment-resisting frame with SHAPIA seismic damper	100% El Centro[*]
3-2	Braced moment-resisting frame with SHAPIA seismic damper	200% El Centro[**]
3-3	Unbraced moment-resisting frame	100% El Centro
3-4	Unbraced moment-resisting frame	200% El Centro[a]

[a] * PGA = 0.33 g, ** PGA = 0.66 g

Figure 7.49a shows the first 20 seconds of the relative displacement time-histories between the floor level and the shake table as recorded during the four seismic tests. The SHAPIA seismic damper was effective in reducing the lateral displacements of the test structure. Under 100% El Centro, the peak relative displacement of the unbraced test structure is reduced by 50% (12 mm vs. 24 mm) when the damper is introduced; the corresponding reduction under 200% El Centro is 38% (26 mm vs. 42 mm). Based on a theoretical yield displacement of 18 mm for the unbraced structure, the displacement ductility demand in the unbraced frame was 1.33 and 2.33 under 100% and 200% El Centro, respectively. The corresponding ductility levels for the structure incorporating the damper were 0.67 and 1.44.

The first 20 seconds of the absolute acceleration time-histories at the floor level recorded during the four seismic tests are shown in Figure 7.49b. Under 100% El Centro, representing design-operating conditions for the damper, the peak acceleration experienced by the test structure is reduced by 30% (0.56 g vs. 0.80 g) when the SHAPIA seismic damper is introduced. Under 200% El Centro, representing maximum credible extreme conditions for the damper, the peak acceleration of the braced frame incorporating the SHAPIA seismic damper is slightly higher than the peak acceleration recorded on the unbraced frame (1.20 g vs. 0.90 g). This can be attributed to the inertia forces in the unbraced structure being limited by the yield capacity of the moment-resisting frames, whereas in the braced structure under maximum credible ground motion input, the restoring force generated by the damper, while slipping, was additive to the yield capacity of the moment-resisting frame. Furthermore, the braced frame incorporating the SHAPIA damper, having a shorter natural period than the unbraced frame, will most likely attract greater energy input from the ground motion than the longer period unbraced frame.

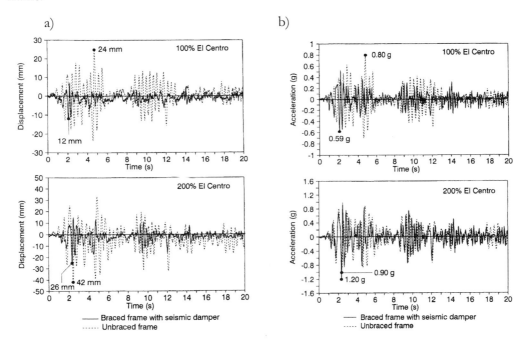

Figure 7.49 Time-History Responses of Frame with SHAPIA Device: a) Relative Displacement and b) Absolute Acceleration (from Filiatrault et al. 2000, reproduced with the permission of the American Society of Civil Engineers)

7.11 POST-TENSIONED FRAME AND WALL SYSTEMS

7.11.1 Self-Centering Systems for Concrete Frames and Walls

The first major modern self-centering systems, conceptually similar to the ancient applications of rocking systems discussed in the previous paragraph, were developed under the U.S. PRESSS (PREcast Seismic Structural Systems) program carried out for a decade in the 1990s and coordinated at the University of California, San Diego (Priestley 1991, Nakaki et al. 1999, Priestley et al. 1999). The primary objective of the program was to develop innovative seismic resistant solutions for precast concrete buildings to replace the emulation of cast-in-place concrete that was used at the time. These innovative solutions used unbonded post-tensioning elements. The inelastic demands on the systems are accommodated by allowing structural elements to separate relative to each other through a rocking motion. This can be achieved with a number of structural configurations such as beams rocking on columns, segmental columns rocking on each other and on their foundations, and walls rocking on their foundations. This is achieved through the opening and closing of an existing gap (rocking motion), while structural elements are basically designed to remain elastic. Rocking systems, with the help of the unbonded pre-tensioning elements, tend to re-center to their original undeformed position at every cycle and therefore display a self-centering response.

Based on this concept, new structural systems that are capable of undergoing inelastic displacements similar to their traditional counterparts, while limiting the damage to the structural system and assuring full re-centering capability without residual displacements, were developed.

The feasibility and efficiency of unbonded post-tensioned solutions were investigated numerically by Priestley and Tao (1993) and experimentally validated through quasi-static loading of interior beam-column joint subassemblies (MacRae and Priestley 1994). These first systems relied only on unbonded post-tensioning to provide moment capacity and self-centering properties and therefore did not dissipate substantial amounts of energy at each loading cycle. As illustrated in Figure 7.50, a *hybrid* system was then suggested where self-centering and energy dissipating properties were combined through the use of unbonded post-tensioning tendons/bars and longitudinal non-prestressed (mild) steel or additional external dissipation devices designed to yield and to provide supplemental damping to the rocking systems.

Similar concepts were also applied to rocking precast concrete shear walls (Priestley 1996, Stanton et al. 1993). In this system, wall panels are split to allow rocking of the individual panels about their respective bases, as illustrated in Figure 7.51. The weight of the panels provides re-centering forces. If the weight is not sufficient to completely re-center the wall panels, unbonded post-tensioning tendons connecting the wall to its foundation can be installed. Energy dissipation can be introduced by grouting reinforcing bars into vertical ducts at the edges of the wall, so that they yield cyclically in tension and compression during an earthquake. An alternative is to place ductile shear connectors

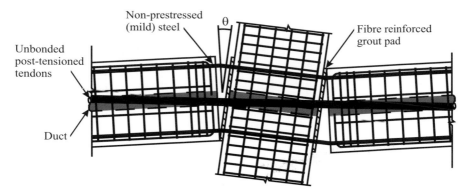

Figure 7.50 Hybrid Frame System (after Stanton and Nakaki 2002)

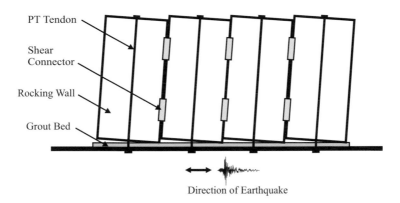

Figure 7.51 Post-Tensioned Rocking Wall System (after Stanton and Nakaki 2002)

between the wall panels, which deform cyclically in shear as the walls rock back and forth. U-shaped rolling stainless steel plates, as shown in Figure 7.52, were designed for energy dissipation and used to couple the walls.

The PRESSS program concluded, after 10 years of research, with the pseudo-dynamic test of a 5-storey building (60% scale) comprised of lateral frame systems in one direction (including four different types of jointed rocking ductile connections) and shear wall panels (coupled via dissipation devices and post-tensioned to the foundation) in the perpendicular direction. Under the largest motion utilized (1.5 times UBC Zone 4 loading), the wall direction experienced a peak drift of 2.9%, yet returned to only 0.055% drift at the end of the motion. Damage during testing in the wall direction was limited to the loss of two concrete cover pieces, one at each end of the wall, approximately the size of a human hand. The structure would have been ready for immediate occupancy after the earthquake.

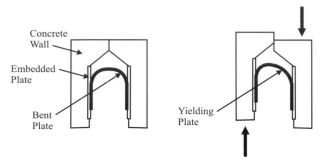

Figure 7.52 Yielding U-Shaped Rolling Steel Plates for Coupled Reinforced Concrete Walls (after Stanton 2003)

In the frame direction, the design drift of 2% under the design earthquake was achieved with no visible damage. The frame was then displaced to a 4% roof drift to investigate its deformation capacity under extreme overload conditions. The hybrid frame performed very well, as shown in Figure 7.53a, suffering only from the initiation of minor spalling of the top and bottom beam cover at the beam-column interface. All the other hairline cracks that formed closed when the load was removed. As shown in Figure 7.53b, the hysteretic response of the system with only the post-tensioning elements included (no energy dissipation) is bilinear elastic. When energy dissipation is added to the system, the response is still self-centering with minimal residual deformations after the loading is removed.

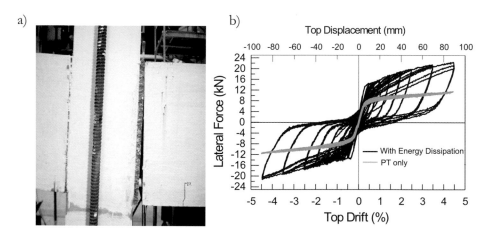

Figure 7.53 Hybrid Connection of Five-Storey PRESSS Building: a) Photo at 4% Drift Ratio and b) Force-Deflection Response (courtesy of S. Pampanin)

7.11.2 Hysteretic Characteristics of Post-Tensioned Connections

A generic post-tensioned energy dissipating (PTED) connection with post-tensioning PT and energy dissipating ED elements is shown in Figure 7.54a. Under cyclic loading, the resulting moment-rotation hysteretic response developed at the rocking interface by the post-tensioning (PT) elements (M_{PT}-θ), the energy dissipating (ED) elements (M_{ED}-θ), and by the combination of PT and ED elements (M_{PTED}-θ) is shown in Figure 7.54b. The total moment in the connection M_{PTED} can be obtained by summing the moment contributed by the PT elements M_{PT} and the moment developed by the ED elements M_{ED}:

$$M_{PTED} = M_{PT} + M_{ED} \tag{7.61}$$

The combination of the bilinear elastic moment-rotation relation characterizing the contribution of the PT elements and the bilinear elastoplastic relation characterizing the contribution of the ED elements results in a flag-shaped hysteresis, in which some energy is dissipated while the system retains its self-centering capabilities. When a negative

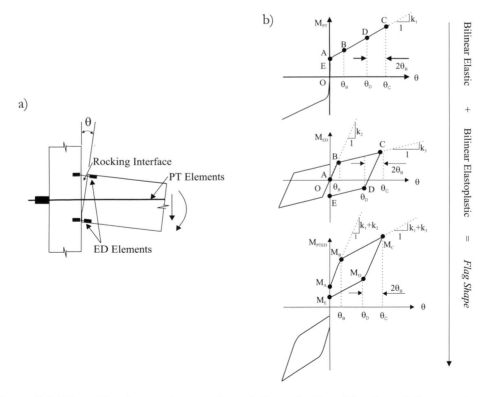

Figure 7.54 Post-Tensioned Connection: a) Generic Post-Tensioned Connection and b) Hysteresis of Post-Tensioned Connection

bending moment occurs at the beam-to-column interface, the connection behaves elastically as long as full contact is maintained between the beam and the column. To this point, the pre-compression provided by the PT force is sufficient to maintain contact between the beam and column over the full depth of the beam. Therefore, no gap opening takes place between point O and point A in Figure 7.54b.

The PT force controls the magnitude of the bending moment M_A beyond which a gap opening exists between the beam and the column. When M_A is reached, a gap opens and the rotational stiffness of the PTED connection is provided by the elastic stiffness of both top ED elements and the PT elements (point A to point B in Figure 7.54b). Note that the behaviour of the connection now becomes nonlinear elastic due to the opening of the gap. This nonlinear elastic behaviour continues until a bending moment M_B is reached. This moment is associated with the tensile yield capacity of the top ED bars and is given by:

$$M_B = M_A + (k_1 + k_2)\theta_B \tag{7.62}$$

where k_1 is the elastic rotational stiffness provided by the PT elements, k_2 is the elastic rotational stiffness provided by the top ED elements, and θ_B is the rotation at which tensile yielding of the top ED elements is initiated.

Under continued loading, the rotational stiffness of the PTED connection is provided by the elastic stiffness of the PT elements and by the post-yield stiffness of the ED elements (point B to point C in Figure 7.54b). Again, the behaviour of the connection is nonlinear elastic due to the continued opening of the gap. This behaviour is maintained until the maximum rotation in the cycle is achieved. The corresponding moment developed in the connection M_C is given by:

$$M_C = M_B + (k_1 + k_3)(\theta_C - \theta_B) \tag{7.63}$$

where k_3 is the post-yield rotational stiffness provided by the top ED bars.

Upon reversing the bending direction, the PTED connection exhibits a nonlinear elastic stiffness until the compression yield capacity of the top ED elements is reached (point C to point D in Figure 7.54b). At that point, the rotation of the connection θ_D is given by:

$$\theta_D = \theta_C - 2\theta_B \tag{7.64}$$

The bending moment at that new yield point is given by:

$$M_D = M_C - (k_1 + k_2)(2\theta_B) \tag{7.65}$$

Note that this nonlinear elastic behaviour is possible only if the top ED elements are prevented from buckling in compression.

During the compression yielding of the top ED elements, the PTED connection exhibits a nonlinear elastic stiffness until full contact is re-established between the beam and the column (point D to point E in Figure 7.54b). The corresponding bending moment is given by:

$$M_E = M_D - (k_1 + k_3)\theta_D = M_D - (k_1 + k_3)(\theta_C - 2\theta_B) \tag{7.66}$$

The behaviour of the PTED connection is symmetric in the opposite positive half cycle of loading, in which tensile and compression yielding of the bottom ED elements are mobilized. At the end of the cycle, when full contact is re-established between the beam and the column ($\theta = 0$), both ED elements develop their yield capacity in compression.

Note that full self-centering of the PTED connection occurs provided that M_E is positive at the end of the first half cycle. Substituting Equations (7.62), (7.63) and (7.65) into Equation (7.66) results in the following condition to ensure full self-centering of the connection:

$$M_A \geq (k_2 - k_3)\theta_B \qquad (7.67)$$

Considering that the moment M_A is controlled by the magnitude of the PT force and that k_2, k_3 and θ_B are controlled by the properties of the ED elements, Equation (7.67) can be used as a necessary condition in the design of the PT and ED elements.

With a properly proportioned PT force, no physical shear connection is required between the beam and the column. Shear transfer can be adequately provided through Coulomb-type friction at the beam-to-column interface. Slotted shear tabs or shear keys can also provide an additional path to carry shear. However, they must be designed as to not impede the gap opening of the connection.

7.11.3 Monotonic Moment-Rotation Characterization of Self-Centering Post-Tensioned Connections

An analytical procedure to predict the complete monotonic moment-rotation relationship of a PTED connection is described in this section. Although the procedure was developed to predict the response of post-tensioned steel frames (Christopoulos 2002a) that are discussed in the next paragraph, the same approach can be used to describe the response of any post-tensioned rocking system.

As long as the moment at the face of the column is below M_A (see Figure 7.54b), the PTED connection behaves as a fully restrained moment connection. Up to this level of loading, the PT force ensures full contact between the beam and the column. When the moment M_A is exceeded, a gap begins to form between the beam and the column. Tensile strains are thus induced in the ED elements crossing the gap. Additional tensile strains are also superimposed on the initial post-tensioning strains in the PT elements. As illustrated in Figure 7.55, the tip of the gap opening, located at a distance c from the bottom of the compression flange of the beam, can be considered as the equivalent neutral axis of the connection interface. After a gap opens, strain compatibility is lost between the end of the beam and the flange of the column. For a given gap opening angle θ and neutral axis position c, the strains developed in the PT elements ε_{PT} and in the ED elements ε_{ED} are given by:

$$\varepsilon_{PT} = \varepsilon_{in} + \left(\frac{(d_b/2 - c)\theta}{L_{PT}}\right)\left(1 - \frac{A_{PT}}{A_b}\right) \qquad (7.68)$$

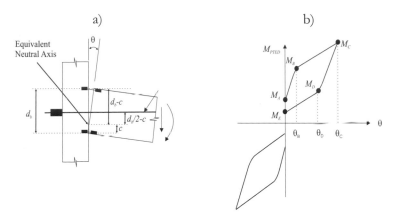

Figure 7.55 Exterior PTED Connection: a) Gap Opening and b) Moment-Gap Opening Angle Relationship

$$\varepsilon_{ED} = \frac{\theta(d_b - c)}{L_{ED}} \qquad (7.69)$$

where d_b is the depth of the beam, ε_{in} is the initial strain in the PT elements, L_{PT} is the length of the PT elements, L_{ED} is the length of the ED elements and A_{PT} and A_b are the cross-sectional areas of the PT elements and beam, respectively. The ratio A_{PT}/A_b in Equation (7.68) accounts for the fact that when the PT force is increased as a result of the gap opening, the beam is subjected to additional axial compression and shortens further. This additional shortening of the beam reduces the PT force. Furthermore, it is assumed that the normal compressive strains over the contact region between the beam and the column vary linearly from zero at the equivalent neutral axis to ε_{max} at the extreme fiber. The relationship between ε_{max} and the position of the neutral axis c is obtained through a member compatibility equation by using an analogy with a classical welded connection and is assumed to be:

$$\varepsilon_{max} = c\left(\frac{\theta}{d_b} + \alpha\phi_y\right) \qquad (7.70)$$

where ϕ_y is the yield curvature of the beam and α is a calibration factor obtained numerically by requiring that the neutral axis be located at the top of the beam ($c = d$) for a very small gap opening angle. Further details on this formulation can be found in Pampanin et al. (2000). This analytical procedure can be implemented in a computer code to construct the complete moment-rotation relationship of a PTED connection. The steps required to compute the moment M_{PTED} corresponding to a given gap opening angle θ are:

a)   assume a position of the neutral axis c ;

b)   compute the axial strain ε_{PT} in the PT elements using Equation (7.68), the axial strain ε_{ED} in the ED bars using Equation (7.69), and the linear normal strain profile in the compression zone characterized by the maximum normal strain ε_{max} by Equation (7.70) at the compression flange of the beam and zero at the neutral axis;

c)   compute the resulting normal stresses using the individual stress-strain relationships for each of the components;

d)   integrate the normal stresses over the respective areas to obtain the corresponding normal force in each component;

e)   sum the normal forces and check for horizontal equilibrium;

f)   iterate over the position of the neutral axis c by returning to step a) until horizontal equilibrium is satisfied;

g)   compute the moment M_{PTED} associated with the corresponding gap opening angle θ once equilibrium is satisfied.

The strains and stresses in the compression zone represent a distribution from the extreme fiber in the compression zone to the last contact point between the beam and the column. Although the strain distribution is assumed linear and is defined by the value ε_{max}, the stress distribution in the compression zone is captured by dividing the compression zone in discrete fibers and determining, based on the strain distribution and the constitutive relationship of the steel in the compression zone, the stress value of each fiber. The procedure is repeated for increasing values of the gap opening angle θ until the complete monotonic moment-rotation relationship is determined. For design purposes, the procedure can be carried out only for the target value of gap opening angle.

Figure 7.56 shows the moment-rotation response of a PTED exterior steel connection (Christopoulos 2002) when only the PT elements are present. Also shown is the response of the connection predicted by the proposed analytical model described above. The predictions of the analytical model are in good agreement with the experimental results. As shown in Figure 7.57, a good agreement also exists between the numerical envelope and the experimental response of the complete PTED connection. Note that in Figures 7.56 and 7.57, the gap opening angle is obtained by subtracting the elastic contributions to the total interstorey drift.

7.11.4 Cyclic Modelling with Equivalent Nonlinear Rotational Springs

The analytical procedure described in the previous section can be further extended to define a cyclic model of the PTED steel connection. For each value of gap opening angle, the moment contributions of the PT elements M_{PT} and of the ED elements M_{ED} are computed. Separating the total moment M_{PTED} into these two contributions allows for the definition of two equivalent rotational springs at the connection level. As illustrated in Figure 7.58, the rotational spring modelling the effect of the PT elements is assigned a

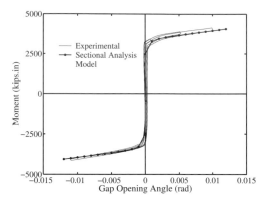

Figure 7.56 Experimental Results and Analytical Prediction of Moment-Gap Opening Angle Relationship for PTED Exterior Steel Connection with Only PT Elements (from Christopoulos 2002)

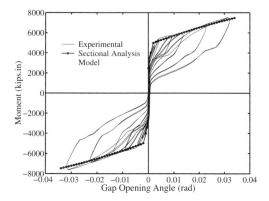

Figure 7.57 Experimental Results and Analytical Prediction of Moment-Gap Opening Angle Relationship for PTED Exterior Steel Connection (from Christopoulos 2002)

bilinear elastic behaviour, while the rotational spring modelling the ED elements is assigned a bilinear elastoplastic hysteretic behaviour. Rather than fitting the entire moment-rotation characteristic to a single hysteretic rotational spring element, this approach allows for a more realistic modelling of the cyclic behaviour since the PT elements are not expected to undergo any inelastic action while the ED bars undergo significant cyclic inelastic deformations. As shown in Figure 7.59, the numerical cyclic model of the PTED connection, based on two parallel rotational springs as discussed above, closely predicts the results of a test conducted on a large-scale PTED exterior steel connection (Christopoulos 2002). This prediction of the rotational spring model was obtained by combining available hysteretic models within the general inelastic dynamic analysis program RUAUMOKO (Carr 2004).

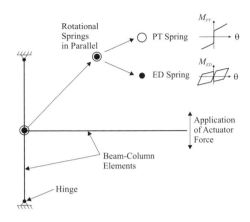

Figure 7.58 Rotational Spring Model for PTED Connections

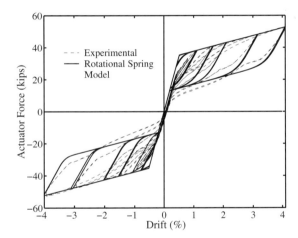

Figure 7.59 Experimental Results and Numerical Cyclic Prediction of Actuator Force versus Interstorey Drift for PTED Exterior Connection (from Christopoulos 2002a)

7.11.5 Extension of Model to Constrained Beams

The analytical procedure presented in the previous paragraphs can be extended to framed systems where columns restrain the gap opening of the beams. Deformation compatibility requires the columns to bend out to accommodate the elongation caused by the opening gaps in framed systems. This longitudinal bending of the columns in turn induces additional compression in the beams. Since the behaviour of PTED connections depends greatly on the axial force present at the beam-to-column interface, this phenomenon has a significant effect. To account for this effect, once the stiffness of the restraining columns is determined, the procedure presented in the previous paragraphs is modified to account for this axial force increase. Note that for modelling purposes, it is quite convenient to assume that this increase in axial load, caused by the restraining columns, is directly a function of the gap opening angle θ and the position of the equivalent neutral axis c, since the definition of these variables is the starting point of the sectional analysis procedure. Such a procedure is explained in more detail in Christopoulos (2002).

7.11.6 Model of PTED Connections Accounting for Beam Depth

To fully capture the effect of the gaps opening at each beam-to-column connection, a simple model accounting for the beam depth can be developed. This model allows for the effect of the column restraint to be captured and be directly included in the modelling of frames incorporating PTED connections. As shown in Figure 7.60, the connection between the beams and the columns is modelled using three nodes spanning the depth of the beam. Within the beam, the top and bottom nodes are slaved in the y direction and in rotation to the central node. The beam central node is slaved in the y direction to the column central node, while the contact between the beam and the column in the beam longitudinal direction is provided by two parallel axial springs located at the top and at the bottom of the section and attached to the corresponding column nodes. The first of these two axial springs represents the ED elements and is assigned a bilinear elastoplastic hysteretic rule with strain hardening. The ED springs are defined by the initial stiffness k_{ED}, the yield force F_{yED} as well as the post-yielding stiffness coefficient α_{ED}. The second spring, acting like a contact (CT) element is assigned a high initial compression stiffness k_{CT} with zero strength in tension to model the contact in one direction and the gap opening in the other. The compression force F_{yCT} defines the force at which the contact spring yields under compressive bearing stresses. These springs are taken as zero length elements. In the hysteresis plots defining the ED and CT springs in Figure 7.60, δ_{ED} and δ_{CT} are the axial deformations of the ED and CT springs respectively. The hysteresis plots indicate that δ_{ED} and δ_{CT} can take negative values. This represents the cases when the contact springs have locally yielded. It must be noted that, if a proper design is carried out, the localized yielding should be very limited. In the former case, where localized yielding does take place, the proposed model is able to capture the softening caused by this yielding. The PT elements are modeled with a prestressed truss element attached to the central node of each exterior column and spanning the entire length of the frame. The truss element is not connected to any other point within the frame. In the case where a single contact element is used for each the top and the bottom contact zones, the model does not allow for a gradual gap opening. The gradual gap opening does not significantly affect the initial and post-gap opening stiffness but allows for a more precise description of the initial stages of the gap opening. Figure 7.61 compares the experimental results of a cyclic test conducted on a PTED exterior steel connection (Christopoulos 2002) with the numerically predicted response using a single contact element spring. The prediction is in good agreement with the experimentally

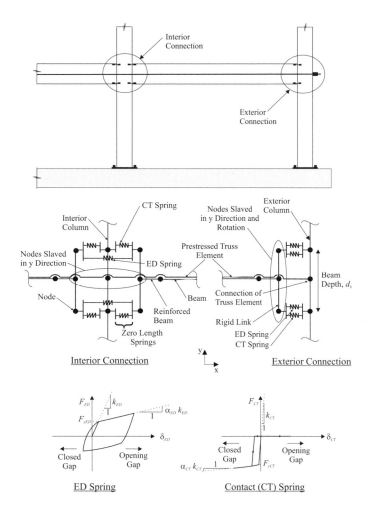

Figure 7.60 Axial Spring Model Accounting for Beam Depth

measured response. A small difference in the unloading stiffness close to the zero displacement position is observed. This is primarily due to the onset of yielding of the contact area. For connections where this yielding is not excessive, the proposed single CT spring beam depth model captures very well the global behaviour. For larger drifts, in order to capture the softening effect of the localized compression yielding in the contact zone, a model with a larger number of contact elements was developed (Christopoulos 2002). These CT elements are assigned a compression yield force corresponding to the tributary area they represent on the beam contact surface.

More refined finite elements as well as fiber elements with an adequate strain distribution along the opening of the gap can also be used to further refine the modelling

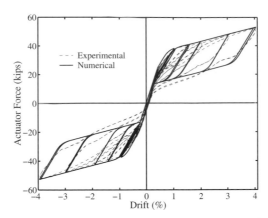

Figure 7.61 Comparison Between Experimental and Numerical Response (Beam Depth Model) of PTED External Connection Test

of PTED connections. Nonetheless, considering that in well designed PTED connections limited yielding of the contact areas is expected, the beam depth model based on axial nonlinear springs offers the best and simplest alternative to develop representative models for the analysis of buildings incorporating PTED connections.

7.11.7 Further Refinements in Self-Centering Systems for Reinforced Concrete Frames and Walls

The concept of post-tensioned reinforced concrete frame systems has been further refined in recent years to improve the constructability of such systems and to further enhance their performance (Pampanin et al. 2004, Pampanin 2005). Proposed refinements include the use of cable-stayed and suspended solutions, that further simplify and expedite the construction sequence. Other improvements include the use of draped tendons or cables to optimize the system's response to combined gravity and lateral loads effects, the use of external supplemental damping devices including hysteretic systems or systems making use of advanced materials such as shape memory alloys or visco-elastic dampers and finally improvements on the shear transfer mechanism through the development of special shear keys or steel corbels.

Restrepo et al. (2002) further extended the self-centering concept proposed by Stanton to reinforced concrete cantilever walls by using a wall system prestressed with unbonded tendons and conventional reinforcement for energy dissipation, as shown in Figure 7.62. The main advantages of this hybrid jointed wall systems are the large lateral displacement capacity, the lack of structural damage associated with large displacements and the ability to return to the original position upon unloading.

Results from nonlinear time-history dynamic analyses indicate that the dynamic response of hybrid wall systems, as reflected by the bending moment and shear force envelopes, is similar to that of conventional monolithic wall systems. Quasi-static and shake table experimental work demonstrated the benefits of these jointed systems (Restrepo et al. 2002, Holden et al. 2003).

Figure 7.63 shows the hysteretic response obtained from a hybrid wall unit. The hysteretic energy dissipation provided by the axial energy dissipators is evident in the lateral force - lateral drift response. No strength degradation occurred below 3% drift. In addition to the gravity load, the prestressing strands provided an additonal restoring force which assured that the wall always returned to its original position upon unloading. After the tendons exceeded the yield limit, some residual drift was observed. The apparent loss of stiffness that was observed at large drift levels was mainly due to irrecoverable compressive strains developed in the confined concrete at the wall toes.

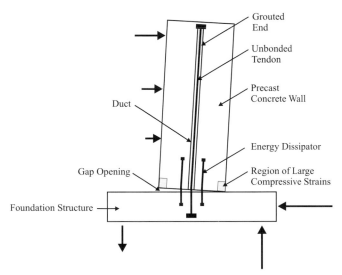

Figure 7.62 Hybrid Reinforced Concrete Cantilever Wall System (after Restrepo 2002, with permission from the Japan Concrete Institute)

Cosmetic spalling of the concrete took place vertically and horizontally. A network of very small width cracks developed on both faces of the wall along the anchorage length of the bars used for energy dissipation.

The self-centering concept has also been extended to other types of reinforced concrete structures, including concrete coupled walls (Shen and Kurama 2000) and cantilever walls with vertical joints (Perez et al. 2004). Kurama and Shen (2004) proposed a new type of hybrid coupled wall system in which coupling of concrete walls is achieved by post-tensioning steel beams to the walls using unbonded post-tensioning tendons. Results of analytical and experimental studies indicated that post-tensioned hybrid coupled walls with initial stiffness similar to walls with embedded steel coupling beams can be designed to provide stable lateral strength levels at large cyclic inelastic deformations. Furthermore, the post-tensioned steel beams provide a significant restoring force to the walls, thereby reducing residual lateral displacements.

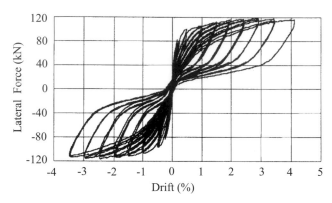

Figure 7.63 Hybrid Reinforced Concrete Cantilever Wall System (after Restrepo 2002, with permission from the Japan Concrete Institute)

7.11.8 Self-Centering Systems for Confined Masonry Walls

Torenzo et al. (2004) proposed the use of self-centering systems for use in conjunction with traditional methods of construction in developing nations. It was suggested to use rocking confined-masonry systems incorporating low-cost external hysteretic energy dissipation devices. Proof-of-concept shake table testing was conducted on a 40% scale three-storey hybrid wall unit. The columns were designed for strain control to ensure that small shear distortions would occur in the wall panel, while the wall rocked at the foundation. Energy dissipation devices, in the way of tapered levers designed to yield in bending with constant curvature, were installed at the wall toes.

This test unit was subjected to 60 dynamic tests on the 200 KN capacity shake table at the University of Canterbury, New Zealand. The seismic response of this unit was excellent. The masonry in-fill maintained its integrity throughout the testing program. No cracking was observed in the in-fill. The maximum residual drift of 0.13% was observed after an excursion to 1.8% drift. The residual drifts were due to the spreading of yield lines in the slabs.

7.11.9 Self-Centering Systems for Steel Structures

Recently, self-centering systems for steel framed structures have been proposed by Ricles et al. (2001) and Christopoulos et al. (2002a, 2002b). Figure 7.65 illustrates the hybrid post-tensioned connection developed by Ricles et al. (2001) for steel moment-resisting frames (MRF). This connection consists of high strength steel strands that run along side the web of the beam and are anchored to the exterior column flange at the end of the frame. In addition, seat and top angles are bolted to both column and beam. Shear resistance is provided by a combination of friction at the beam-column interface and also

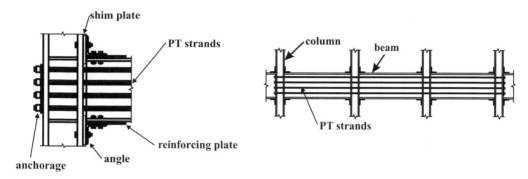

Figure 7.65 Hybrid Post-Tensioned Connection for Steel Frames (after Ricles et al. 2001)

by the steel angles. The system is designed so that the steel angles are the only yielding elements. Therefore, only the steel angles would need to be replaced after a major earthquake. Additional benefits of this connection include i) no field welding required, ii) use of conventional materials and skills, and iii) similar initial stiffness to conventional welded connections.

Figure 7.66 illustrates the Post-Tensioned Energy Dissipating (PTED) steel frame concept proposed by Christopoulos et al. (2002a, 2002b). The post-tensioning (PT) force is provided at each floor by high strength bars or tendons located at mid-depth of the beam. Four symmetrically placed energy-dissipating (ED) bars are also included at each connection to provide energy dissipation under cyclic loading. These ED bars are threaded into couplers which are welded to the inside face of the beam flanges and of the continuity plates in the column for exterior connections, and to the inside face of adjacent beam flanges for interior connections. Holes are introduced in the column flanges to accommodate the PT and ED bars. To prevent the ED bars from buckling in compression under cyclic inelastic loading, they are inserted into confining steel sleeves that are welded to the beam flanges for exterior connections, and to the column continuity plates for interior connections. The ED bars are initially stress-free since they are introduced into the connection after the application of the PT force.

The PTED connection relies on the PT force to maintain contact between the beams and columns. Horizontally slotted shear tabs are welded to the column flanges and bolted to the beam web to provide stability during construction and to ensure an alternative vertical shear transfer mechanism from the beam to the column. The slots in the tabs allow the free opening and closing of the gap at the beam-to-column interface. Nonlinear elastic action is introduced by gap openings at each beam-to-column interface. Inelastic action takes place through yielding of the ED bars once the gap is opened. Quasi-static testing was conducted on a large-scale exterior beam-to-column PTED steel connection by Christopoulos et al. (2002a). The results of the tests show that the PTED test specimen was able to undergo large inelastic deformations without any damage in the beam or column and without residual drift. Figure 7.67 shows an exterior PTED connection at a storey drift of 3%.

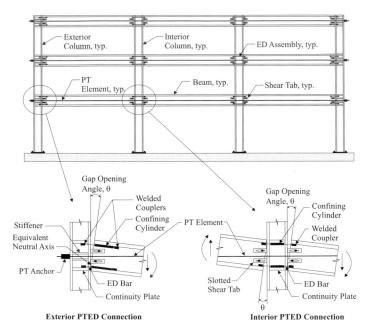

Figure 7.66 PTED Connection for Steel Frames (from Christopoulos et al. 2002)

An experimental study was also conducted on a half-scale steel moment-resisting frame assembly incorporating two exterior and one interior PTED connections (Christopoulos et al. 2002). As illustrated in Figure 7.68, the PTED test frame was able to deform up to 3% interstorey drift without major damage occurring to the primary steel members, while retaining its self-centering capabilities. The presence of a floor slab and gravity loads did not inhibit the performance of the PTED test frame (Collins and Filiatrault 2003). Cracking patterns in the floor slab were uniform and consistent for a 3-column and 2-beam assembly. While the presence of the floor slab produced larger values of initial stiffness, its influence diminished as the interstorey drift increased.

7.11.10 Self-Centering Systems for Bridge Structures

Since the early applications of the self-centering concept to the Rangitikei river bridge in New Zealand, a number of self-centering systems have been suggested for bridges. Following Housner's work on the theory of rigid block rocking motion (Housner 1963), preliminary investigations on pure rocking motion of a single bridge pier on its foundation were proposed by McManus (1980) based on shake table tests. Mander and Cheng (1997)

Figure 7.67 Exterior PTED Connection at 3% Storey Drift (from Christopoulos et al. 2002)

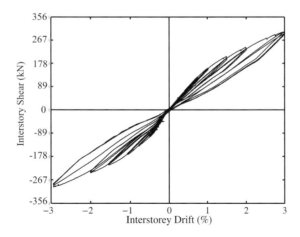

Figure 7.68 Interstorey Shear-Drift Response of PTED Test Frame (from Christopoulos et al. 2002)

carried out shake table tests at the University of Buffalo on coupled bridge piers with unbonded post-tensioned cables combined with viscous dissipation devices at the top and bottom section of the pier.

Analytical and experimental investigations on precast segmented circular piers with centrally located unbonded post-tensioned cables were performed at the University of California at San Diego (Hewes and Priestley 2001). The piers that were tested did not incorporate any supplemental damping or energy dissipation devices. Additional numerical and experimental work on similar systems was also carried out by Kwan and Billington (2003). The concept of hybrid systems was also extended to bridge piers by Palermo et al. (2005) as illustrated in Figure 7.69. Alternative solutions for internal or external (replaceable) devices have also been proposed and validated through quasi-static and pseudo dynamic testing under both uni- and bi-directional loading regimes by Marriott et al. (2006).

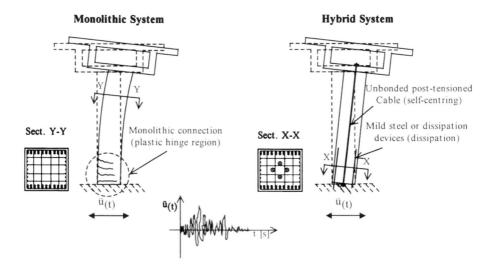

Figure 7.69 Concept of Hybrid System Applied to Bridge Piers (after Palermo et al. 2005)

Xu and Tsopelas (2003) proposed a self-centering base isolation system for bridge structures that consists of flat sliding bearings and precise positioning fluid dampers. The liquid-spring damper consists of a single column of pressurized compressive fluid. The orificing of the fluid body through the piston rod provides the damping characteristics of the system. The precise positioning mechanism uses a neutral position that is rigid before and after a shock. The piston rod is displaced at its limit position because of the pre-compression of the fluid column. A mechanical configuration that compresses the fluid body, whichever the direction of movement of the piston rod is, ensures the repositioning of the rod to its neutral position after a shock has been damped. Precise positioning fluid dampers could be designed to eliminate any permanent displacement especially for isolation systems that lack adequate post-yielding stiffness characteristics.

7.12 CONSIDERATIONS FOR THE SEISMIC DESIGN OF SELF-CENTERING SYSTEMS

Force-based or direct displacement-based design procedures can be used for the design of precast concrete systems by redefining key design parameters, such as the reduction factor R (or behaviour factor q in Eurocode 8) for a force-based approach and the equivalent viscous damping/drift relations for a direct displacement-based design procedure (Priestley 2004). To date, only Appendix B of the NZS3101:2006 Guidelines (NZS 2006) outlines a procedure for the design of post-tensioned reinforced concrete frames and walls.

However, as discussed in previous paragraphs on the dynamics of self-centering systems, if an adequate amount of energy dissipation capacity is provided to self-centering systems (β = 0.75 to 0.90), the maximum displacement response of such systems is usually similar to that of yielding (elastoplastic) traditional systems of similar initial stiffness and strength despite a marked difference between the energy dissipation capacity of these systems.

A general design approach for self-centering systems can therefore be based on first deriving lateral design forces for an equivalent traditional system and then transforming this traditional system into a self-centering system that would achieve similar maximum displacements (within code prescribed maxima) but with no residual deformations. As illustrated in Figure 7.70, this can usually be achieved by assigning a strength to the self-centering system equal to the strength of a traditional yielding system at the target design drift, and designing the self-centering system to have similar initial stiffness (although not necessarily identical) to that of the yielding system and to achieve sufficient energy dissipation (β = 0.75 to 0.90). The systems' strengths are matched at the target drift because self-centering systems usually display greater post-yield stiffness than that of their traditional yielding counterparts.

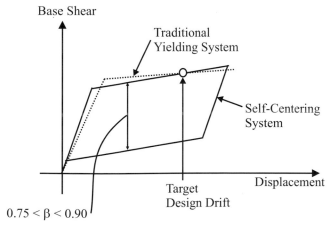

Figure 7.70 General Design Approach for Self-Centering Systems

With some experience on the characteristics of each self-centering system, sizing of these systems to achieve the desired strength levels at the target drift as well as the targeted energy dissipation capacity is possible with little iteration.

7.13 PROBLEMS

Problem 7.1

You are asked to perform an equivalent linear dynamic analysis of a structure equipped with a self-centering damping system exhibiting the flag-shaped hysteresis loop shown in Figure 7.71. This hysteresis loop is characterized by an initial stiffness k_0, a yield force F_y, and a residual re-centering force, F_c, while the displacement amplitude is represented by x_0.

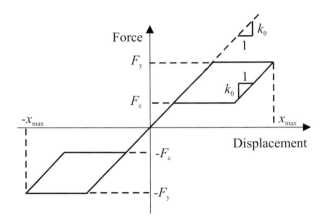

Figure 7.71 Flag-Shaped Hysteresis Loop of Self-Centering System

a)   Determine the effective stiffness of the device k_e to be used in the linear model, as a function of k_0, F_y, F_c and x_{max}.

b)   Determine the equivalent viscous damping ratio ξ_e of the device as a function of k_0, F_y, F_c and x_{max}.

c)   If the damper is initially rigid ($k_0 = \infty$), does the equivalent viscous damping ratio increase or decrease with displacement amplitude?

d)   Comment on the practice of analyzing a nonlinear structure equipped with such re-centering devices using a linear system with equivalent viscous damping.

Problem 7.2

You are asked to perform an equivalent linear dynamic analysis of a structure equipped with an Energy Dissipating Restrain (EDR) device exhibiting the hysteresis loop shown in Figure 7.72. This hysteresis loop is characterized by a slip load F_s, a gap displacement x_g and a loading stiffness k. The displacement amplitude is represented by x_{max}.

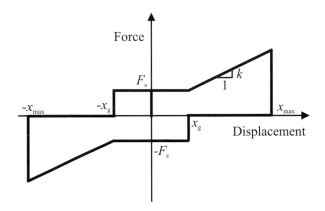

Figure 7.72 Hysteresis Loop for an Energy Dissipating Restrain (EDR)

a) Determine the effective stiffness of the device to be used in the linear model.

b) Determine the equivalent viscous damping ratio of the device to be used in the linear model.

c) What is the value of the equivalent viscous damping ratio if $x_g = 0$ and $F_s = 0$?

d) What is the value of the equivalent viscous damping ratio if $x_g \approx \infty$ (very large)?

CHAPTER 8: TUNED-MASS DAMPERS

8.1 INTRODUCTION

Tuned-mass dampers (TMDs) or vibration absorbers are relatively small mass-spring-dashpot systems that are calibrated to be in resonance with a particular mode of the structure on which they are installed. These systems, usually installed on the roofs of buildings, have been proven effective in reducing wind-induced vibrations in high-rise buildings and floor vibrations induced by occupant activity. More recently, they have been considered for the seismic protection of buildings.

Tuned-mass dampers, first suggested by Frahm (1909), represent an attractive alternative to protect civil engineering structures against external dynamic disturbances. These systems are capable of significantly reducing the dynamic response of a structure, yet their construction is simple. In its simplest form, a tuned-mass damper only requires the assembly of a mass, a spring, and a viscous damper at a given point of the structure, with no need for an external power source or sophisticated hardware.

These systems also have disadvantages. First, they require a relatively large mass, although it usually represents only a small fraction of the total mass of the structure, and, hence, a large space for their installation. Second, since by design they are in resonance with their supporting structures, they usually undergo large displacements relative to the points of the structure to which they are connected. As a result, large clearances are required to accommodate these displacements. Finally, they need to be mounted on a smooth surface to minimize friction and facilitate their free motion.

In this Chapter, the basic theory of TMDs is presented. The potential applications of TMDs for reducing the seismic response of structures are also explored.

8.2 THEORY OF UNDAMPED TUNED-MASS DAMPERS UNDER HARMONIC LOADING

As shown in Figure 8.1, a primary structure to be damped is modeled as an undamped single-degree-of-freedom system, with mass M and elastic stiffness K, subjected to an external sinusoidal dynamic force $P(t)$ of amplitude P_0 and of circular frequency $\overline{\omega}$:

$$P(t) = P_0 \sin \overline{\omega} t \tag{8.1}$$

The TMD consists of a comparatively small vibratory system, of stiffness k and mass m, attached to the main mass M, as illustrated in Figure 8.1. The relative displacement of the primary system and the TMD are denoted $x_1(t)$ and $x_2(t)$, respectively.

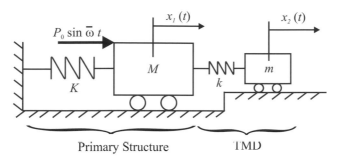

Figure 8.1 Main Structure and TMD

Applying Newton's second law on each mass yields the two equations of motion for this two-degree-of-freedom-system:

$$M\ddot{x}_1 + (K + k)x_1 - kx_2 = P_0\sin\overline{\omega}t$$
$$m\ddot{x}_2 + k(x_2 - x_1) = 0$$

(8.2)

Since the system is undamped, the forced vibration response takes a simple form:

$$x_1(t) = a_1\sin\overline{\omega}t$$
$$x_2(t) = a_2\sin\overline{\omega}t$$

(8.3)

where a_1 and a_2 are constants representing the amplitude of vibration of the main and the secondary mass respectively. Substituting Equation (8.3) into Equation (8.2) yields:

$$(-Ma_1\overline{\omega}^2 + (K + k)a_1 - ka_2)\sin\overline{\omega}t = P_0\sin\overline{\omega}t$$
$$(-ma_2\overline{\omega}^2 + k(a_2 - a_1))\sin\overline{\omega}t = 0$$

(8.4)

Since Equation (8.4) must be satisfied at all times:

$$a_1(-M\overline{\omega}^2 + K + k) - ka_2 = P_0$$
$$-ka_1 + a_2(-m\overline{\omega}^2 + k) = 0$$

(8.5)

For simplification, we introduce the following variables:

$$x_{st} = \frac{P_0}{K} : \text{static displacement of the primary structure}$$

$$\Omega_n^2 = \frac{K}{M} : \text{natural frequency of the primary structure}$$

(8.6)

$$\omega_a^2 = \frac{k}{m} : \text{natural frequency of the TMD}$$

Dividing by K, the first expression of Equation (8.5) yields:

$$a_1\left(1 + \frac{k}{K} - \frac{\bar{\omega}^2}{\Omega_n^2}\right) - a_2\frac{k}{K} = x_{st}$$

$$a_1 = a_2\left(1 - \frac{\bar{\omega}^2}{\omega_a^2}\right)$$

(8.7)

Solving for the amplitudes a_1 and a_2 we get:

$$\frac{a_1}{x_{st}} = \frac{\left(1 - \frac{\bar{\omega}^2}{\omega_a^2}\right)}{\left(1 - \frac{\bar{\omega}^2}{\omega_a^2}\right)\left(1 + \frac{k}{K} - \frac{\bar{\omega}^2}{\Omega_n^2}\right) - \frac{k}{K}}$$

$$\frac{a_2}{x_{st}} = \frac{1}{\left(1 - \frac{\bar{\omega}^2}{\omega_a^2}\right)\left(1 + \frac{k}{K} - \frac{\bar{\omega}^2}{\Omega_n^2}\right) - \frac{k}{K}}$$

(8.8)

From the first of these expressions, it becomes clear that when the natural frequency $\omega_a = \sqrt{k/m}$ of the attached TMD is chosen to be equal to the frequency $\bar{\omega}$ of the disturbing force, the main mass M does not vibrate at all ($a_1 = 0$).

Examine now the second equality of Equation (8.8) when $\omega_a = \bar{\omega}$. The first term of the denominator is then zero, and this equation reduces to:

$$a_2 = -\frac{K}{k}x_{st} = -\frac{P_0}{k}$$

(8.9)

With the main mass standing still and the TMD having a motion $-(P_0/k)\sin\bar{\omega}t$, the force in the TMD varies as $-P_0\sin\bar{\omega}t$, which is actually equal and opposite to the external force, as illustrated in Figure 8.2.

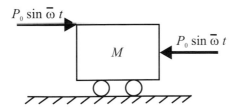

Figure 8.2 Free Body Diagram of Main Mass for Optimum Tuning Conditions of TMD

Now consider the case in which the TMD is in resonance with the primary structure, with $\omega_a = \Omega_n$, which can also be expressed as:

$$\frac{k}{m} = \frac{K}{M}$$

$$\text{or } \frac{k}{K} = \frac{m}{M} = \mu$$

(8.10)

where μ is defined as the ratio of the mass of the TMD to the mass of the primary structure. For this special case, Equation (8.8) becomes:

$$\frac{x_1(t)}{x_{st}} = \frac{\left(1 - \frac{\overline{\omega}^2}{\omega_a^2}\right)}{\left(1 - \frac{\overline{\omega}^2}{\omega_a^2}\right)\left(1 + \mu - \frac{\overline{\omega}^2}{\omega_a^2}\right) - \mu} \sin \overline{\omega} t$$

(8.11)

$$\frac{x_2(t)}{x_{st}} = \frac{1}{\left(1 - \frac{\overline{\omega}^2}{\omega_a^2}\right)\left(1 + \mu - \frac{\overline{\omega}^2}{\omega_a^2}\right) - \mu} \sin \overline{\omega} t$$

The two denominators of Equation (8.11) are identical and are quadratic, with two roots in $(\overline{\omega}^2 / \omega_a^2)$. Thus, for two values of the excitation frequency $\overline{\omega}$, both denominators become zero, and consequently x_1 and x_2 become infinitely large. Obviously, these two frequencies are the natural frequencies of the two-degrees-of-freedom system. These natural frequencies are determined by setting the denominators equal to zero:

$$\left(\frac{\overline{\omega}}{\omega_a}\right)^4 - \left(\frac{\overline{\omega}}{\omega_a}\right)^2 (2 + \mu) + 1 = 0$$

(8.12)

with the solutions:

$$\left(\frac{\overline{\omega}}{\omega_a}\right)^2 = \left(1 + \frac{\mu}{2}\right) \pm \sqrt{\mu + \frac{\mu^2}{4}}$$

(8.13)

This relation is shown graphically in Figure 8.3, from which we find, for example, that a TMD of one-fifth the mass of the main system ($\mu = 0.2$) sets the natural frequencies of the combined system at 1.25 and 0.8 of that of the primary structure. For this same case of $\mu = 0.2$, the spectral amplitudes of both masses (Equation (8.11)) are shown in Figure 8.4.

From Figure 8.4, it can be seen that $x_1/x_{st} = 1$ for $\overline{\omega} = 0$. At the first resonance ($\overline{\omega}/\omega_a = \omega/\Omega_n = 0.8$), x_1/x_{st} passes through zero from positive infinite to negative infinite. When the excitation frequency is in resonance with the primary structure and with the TMD ($\overline{\omega} = \Omega_n = \omega_a$), x_1/x_{st} passes through zero and, for increasing excitation frequencies, x_1/x_{st} becomes positive again. At the second resonance

$(\overline{\omega}/\omega_a = \overline{\omega}/\Omega_n = 1.25)$, x_1/x_{st} becomes negative. The x_2/x_{st} diagram displays similar changes, while changes in signs occur at the resonant points only. These changes in signs, defining the phase between motions of the primary structure and the TMD, are not particularly important. We can then define only amplitude plots by mirror dotted lines in positive amplitudes, as shown in Figure 8.4.

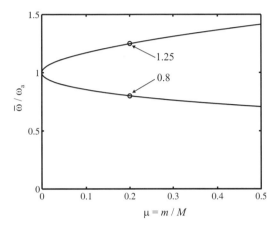

Figure 8.3 Combined Natural Frequencies for TMDs Tuned to the Main Structure: $\omega_a = \Omega_n$, $\mu = 0.2$ (after Den Hartog 1985)

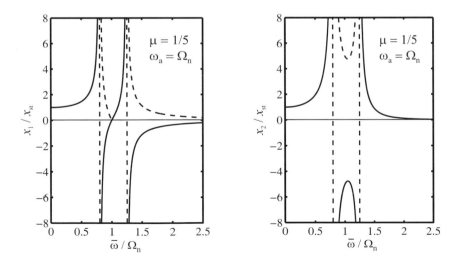

Figure 8.4 Amplitude Spectrum for TMDs Tuned to the Primary Structure: $\omega_a = \Omega_n$, $\mu = 0.2$ (after Den Hartog 1985)

8.3 THEORY OF UNDAMPED TUNED-MASS DAMPERS UNDER HARMONIC BASE MOTION

Since this Chapter focuses on seismic applications of TMDs, let's consider now an undamped primary structure incorporating an undamped TMD that is subjected to a base excitation as illustrated in Figure 8.5.

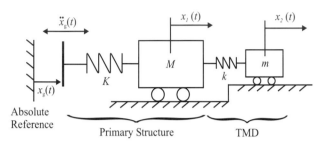

Figure 8.5 Primary Structure with TMD Subjected to a Base Excitation

The ground excitation is defined as a sinusoidal displacement history $x_g(t)$ of amplitude x_0 and constant frequency $\bar{\omega}$:

$$x_g(t) = x_0 \sin \bar{\omega} t \tag{8.14}$$

Applying Newton's second law on each mass now yields the two equations of motion for this two-degrees-of-freedom-system:

$$M\ddot{x}_1 + (K + k)x_1 - kx_2 = M\bar{\omega}^2 x_0 \sin \bar{\omega} t$$
$$m\ddot{x}_2 + k(x_2 - x_1) = m\bar{\omega}^2 x_0 \sin \bar{\omega} t \tag{8.15}$$

Recalling the form of the solution given in Equation (8.3), we get:

$$(-Ma_1\bar{\omega}^2 + (K + k)a_1 - ka_2)\sin \bar{\omega} t = M\bar{\omega}^2 x_0 \sin \bar{\omega} t$$
$$(-ma_2\bar{\omega}^2 + k(a_2 - a_1))\sin \bar{\omega} t = m\bar{\omega}^2 x_0 \sin \bar{\omega} t \tag{8.16}$$

Since Equation (8.16) must be satisfied at all times:

$$a_1(-M\bar{\omega}^2 + K + k) - ka_2 = M\bar{\omega}^2 x_0$$
$$-ka_1 + a_2(-m\bar{\omega}^2 + k) = m\bar{\omega}^2 x_0 \tag{8.17}$$

Using the same variables defined in Equation (8.6), Equation (8.17) becomes:

$$a_1\left(1 + \frac{k}{K} - \frac{\bar{\omega}^2}{\Omega_n^2}\right) - a_2\frac{k}{K} = \frac{\bar{\omega}^2}{\Omega_n^2}x_0$$
$$-a_1 + a_2\left(1 - \frac{\bar{\omega}^2}{\omega_a^2}\right) = \frac{\bar{\omega}^2}{\omega_a^2}x_0 \tag{8.18}$$

Solving for the amplitudes a_1 and a_2:

$$\frac{a_1}{x_0} = \frac{\overline{\omega}^2\left(\frac{1}{\Omega_n^2}\left(1-\frac{\overline{\omega}^2}{\omega_a^2}\right) + \frac{1}{\omega_a^2}\left(\frac{k}{K}\right)\right)}{\left(1-\frac{\overline{\omega}^2}{\omega_a^2}\right)\left(1+\frac{k}{K}-\frac{\overline{\omega}^2}{\Omega_n^2}\right) - \frac{k}{K}}$$

$$\frac{a_2}{x_0} = \frac{\frac{\overline{\omega}^2}{\Omega_n^2} + \frac{\overline{\omega}^2}{\omega_a^2}\left(1+\frac{k}{K}-\frac{\overline{\omega}^2}{\Omega_n^2}\right)}{\left(1-\frac{\overline{\omega}^2}{\omega_a^2}\right)\left(1+\frac{k}{K}-\frac{\overline{\omega}^2}{\Omega_n^2}\right) - \frac{k}{K}}$$

(8.19)

From Equation (8.19), two tuning conditions can be obtained. The first tuning condition is obtained when the displacement of the main mass M relative to the base is equal to zero. For this condition, the main mass moves rigidly with the base, experiencing an absolute acceleration equal to $\ddot{x}_g(t)$, but with no force induced in the main spring K. This tuning condition exists when a_1 is equal to zero, which from Equation (8.19) corresponds to:

$$\frac{1}{\Omega_n^2}\left(1-\frac{\overline{\omega}^2}{\omega_a^2}\right) + \frac{1}{\omega_a^2}\left(\frac{k}{K}\right) = 0$$

(8.20)

Equation (8.20) can be simplified to reveal the following tuning condition on the natural frequency of the TMD:

$$\omega_a = \frac{\overline{\omega}}{\sqrt{1+\mu}}$$

(8.21)

For very small TMDs ($\mu \approx 0$), the optimum tuning is obtained when the natural frequency of the TMD is chosen to be equal to the frequency of the disturbing force, which is the same result obtained for the case of a sinusoidal force excitation presented in the previous section.

The second tuning condition is obtained when the absolute displacement of the main mass M is equal to zero. For this condition, the main mass remains immobile, experiencing an absolute acceleration equal to zero during the movement of the base, but a force $-Kx_g(t)$ is induced in the main spring. This tuning condition exists when a_1 is equal to $-x_0$, which, from Equation (8.19), corresponds to:

$$\frac{\overline{\omega}^2}{\Omega_n^2}\left(1-\frac{\overline{\omega}^2}{\omega_a^2}\right) + \frac{\overline{\omega}^2}{\omega_a^2}\left(\frac{k}{K}\right) = -\left(\left(1-\frac{\overline{\omega}^2}{\omega_a^2}\right)\left(1+\frac{k}{K}-\frac{\overline{\omega}^2}{\Omega_n^2}\right) - \frac{k}{K}\right)$$

(8.22)

Equation (8.22) can be simplified to reveal the following tuning condition on the natural frequency of the TMD:

$$\omega_a = \overline{\omega} \tag{8.23}$$

which is again the same tuning condition obtained for the case of a sinusoidal force excitation presented in the previous section.

8.4 THEORY OF DAMPED TUNED-MASS DAMPERS UNDER HARMONIC LOADING

Consider now a primary structure modeled again as an undamped single-degree-of-freedom system connected to a TMD in which a dashpot of constant c is arranged parallel to the damper k, between the masses M and m, as shown in Figure 8.6.

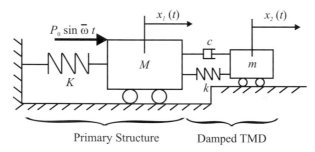

Figure 8.6 Primary Structure and Damped TMD

Applying Newton's second law to the main mass M gives:

$$M\ddot{x}_1 + Kx_1 + k(x_1 - x_2) + c(\dot{x}_1 - \dot{x}_2) = P_0 \sin \overline{\omega} t \tag{8.24}$$

and to the secondary mass m yields:

$$m\ddot{x}_2 + k(x_2 - x_1) + c(\dot{x}_2 - \dot{x}_1) = 0 \tag{8.25}$$

Again, we are interested in a solution of the forced vibrations only and do not consider the transient free vibration. Both x_1 and x_2 are harmonic motions at a frequency $\overline{\omega}$ and can be represented by complex numbers:

$$x_1(t) = C_1 e^{i\overline{\omega}t}$$
$$x_2(t) = C_2 e^{i\overline{\omega}t} \tag{8.26}$$

where C_1 and C_2 are now unknown complex numbers with each an amplitude and a phase and $i = \sqrt{-1}$. We are now interested in finding the amplitude of the main mass a_1. Substituting Equation (8.26) into Equations (8.24) and (8.25) yields:

$$-M\overline{\omega}^2 + KC_1 + k(C_1 - C_2) + i\overline{\omega}c(C_1 - C_2) = P_0$$
$$-m\overline{\omega}^2 C_2 + k(C_2 - C_1) + i\overline{\omega}c(C_2 - C_1) = 0 \tag{8.27}$$

Rearranging Equation (8.27):

$$(-M\overline{\omega}^2 + K + k + i\overline{\omega}c)C_1 - (k + i\overline{\omega}c)C_2 = P_0$$

$$-(k + i\overline{\omega}c)C_1 + (-m\overline{\omega}^2 + k + i\overline{\omega}c)C_2 = 0$$

(8.28)

Solving these two equations for C_1:

$$C_1 = P_0 \frac{(k - m\overline{\omega}^2) + i\overline{\omega}c}{[(-M\overline{\omega}^2 + K)(-m\overline{\omega}^2 + k) - m\overline{\omega}^2 k] + i\overline{\omega}c[-M\overline{\omega}^2 + K - m\overline{\omega}^2]}$$

(8.29)

Since C_1 is complex, it can also be written as:

$$C_1 = P_0(A_1 + iB_1)$$

(8.30)

where A_1 and B_1 are real. The amplitude of C_1 can then be written as:

$$C_1 = P_0 \sqrt{A_1^2 + B_1^2}$$

(8.31)

But Equation (8.29) is not in the form of Equation (8.30) but rather in the form:

$$C_1 = P_0 \frac{A + iB}{C + iD}$$

(8.32)

with:

$$A = k - m\overline{\omega}^2$$

$$B = \overline{\omega}c$$

$$C = (-M\overline{\omega}^2 + K)(-m\overline{\omega}^2 + k) - m\overline{\omega}^2 k$$

$$D = \overline{\omega}c(-M\overline{\omega}^2 + K - m\overline{\omega}^2)$$

(8.33)

Now Equation (8.32) can be rewritten in the form of Equation (8.30):

$$C_1 = P_0 \frac{(A + iB)(C - iD)}{(C + iD)(C - iD)} = P_0 \frac{(AC + BD) + i(BC - AD)}{C^2 + D^2}$$

(8.34)

The amplitude of a_1 can then be evaluated:

$$\frac{a_1}{P_0} = \sqrt{\left(\frac{(AC + BD)}{C^2 + D^2}\right)^2 + \left(\frac{BC - AD}{C^2 + D^2}\right)^2}$$

$$= \sqrt{\frac{A^2C^2 + B^2D^2 + B^2C^2 + A^2D^2}{(C^2 + D^2)}}$$

$$= \sqrt{\frac{(A^2 + B^2)(C^2 + D^2)}{(C^2 + D^2)^2}}$$

$$= \sqrt{\frac{(A^2 + B^2)}{(C^2 + D^2)}}$$

(8.35)

Substituting the values of the constants expressed in Equation (8.33) into Equation (8.35) yields an expression for the amplitude of the response of the main mass M:

$$\frac{a_1}{P_0} = \sqrt{\frac{(k - m\bar{\omega}^2)^2 + \bar{\omega}^2 c^2}{[(-M\bar{\omega}^2 + K)(-m\bar{\omega}^2 + k) - m\bar{\omega}^2 k]^2 + \bar{\omega}^2 c^2 (-M\bar{\omega}^2 + K - m\bar{\omega}^2)^2}} \qquad (8.36)$$

We can rewrite Equation (8.36) by defining the following variables:

$$\mu = \frac{m}{M} = \frac{\text{TMD Mass}}{\text{main mass}} = \text{mass ratio}$$

$$\omega_a^2 = \frac{k}{m} = \text{natural frequency of TMD}$$

$$\Omega_n^2 = \frac{K}{M} = \text{natural frequency of primary structure}$$

$$f = \frac{\omega_a}{\Omega_n} = \text{natural frequency ratio} \qquad (8.37)$$

$$g = \frac{\bar{\omega}}{\Omega_n} = \text{forcing frequency ratio}$$

$$c_c = 2\omega_a m = \text{critical viscous damping constant of TMD}$$

After some further algebraic manipulations, Equation (8.36) can be rewritten as:

$$\frac{a_1}{x_{st}} = \sqrt{\frac{\left(2\frac{c}{c_c}g\right)^2 + (g^2 - f^2)^2}{\left(2\frac{c}{c_c}g\right)^2 (g^2 - 1 + \mu g^2)^2 + [\mu f^2 g^2 - (g^2 - 1)(g^2 - f^2)]^2}} \qquad (8.38)$$

It can be seen that the vibration amplitude of the main mass is function of four variables: μ, c/c_c, f and g. Figure 8.7 shows the variation of the amplitude ratio a_1/x_{st} as a function of the forcing frequency ratio g for a TMD tuned to the primary structure, ($f = 1$), having a mass ratio $\mu = 0.05$ and for several values of damping ratio c/c_c. It is interesting to follow what happens for increasing values of damping. For $c = 0$, we have the same case as Figure 8.4. When the damping becomes infinite, the two masses are virtually clamped together and we have an undamped single-degree-of-freedom system with a mass of $(21/20)M$. Two other curves are drawn for $c/c_c = 0.10$ and 0.32.

The only purpose of adding a TMD is to bring the resonant peak of the amplitude down to its lowest possible value. With $c = 0$, the peak response is infinite; with $c = \infty$, it is also infinite. Somewhere in between there exists an optimum value of c for which the peak becomes a minimum.

Before proceeding to the calculation of this "optimum damping", we observe in Figure 8.7 that all four curves intersect at two points, P and Q, independent of the

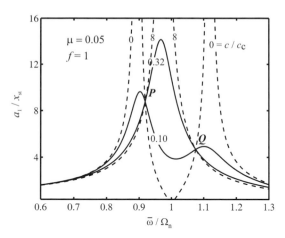

Figure 8.7 Amplitudes of the Main Mass for Various Values of TMD Damping, $\mu = 0.05$, $f = 1$ (after Den Hartog 1985)

damping value of the system. If their locations can be defined, the most favorable response curve is the one which passes with a horizontal tangent through the higher of the two fixed points P or Q.

Tuning of the TMD can be further improved by changing the natural frequency ratio f so that the two fixed points P and Q can be shifted as low as possible. By changing f, one point goes up and the other down. Therefore, the most favorable case is the one where first, by a proper choice of f, the two fixed points are adjusted to equal heights, and second, by a proper choice of c / c_c, the curve is adjusted to pass with a horizontal tangent through one of them. In practice, it makes no difference which one of the two points, P or Q, is chosen.

First the locations of the two points P and Q are found. We can rewrite Equation (8.38) as:

$$\frac{a_1}{x_{st}} = \sqrt{\frac{A\left(\frac{c}{c_c}\right)^2 + B}{C\left(\frac{c}{c_c}\right)^2 + D}} \tag{8.39}$$

with:

$$
\begin{aligned}
A &= (2g)^2 \\
B &= (g^2 - f^2)^2 \\
C &= (2g^2)(g^2 - 1 + \mu g^2)^2 \\
D &= (\mu f^2 g^2 - (g^2 - 1)(g^2 - f^2))^2
\end{aligned}
\tag{8.40}
$$

If $A/C = B/D$, Equation (8.39) becomes independent of damping. This condition is given by:

$$\left(\frac{1}{g^2 - 1 + \mu g^2}\right)^2 = \left(\frac{g^2 - f^2}{\mu f^2 g^2 - (g^2 - 1)(g^2 - f^2)}\right)^2 \tag{8.41}$$

To remove the square sign on each side of Equation (8.41), a $\pm$ must be introduced in front of one side of the equation. With the minus sign, the solution becomes trivial since we find $g^2 = 0$, meaning that the static response is independent of damping.

The other alternative is the plus sign which leads to:

$$g^4 - 2g^2\frac{1 + f^2 + \mu f^2}{2 + \mu} + \frac{2f^2}{2 + \mu} = 0 \tag{8.42}$$

Equation (8.42) is a quadratic function in g^2, giving two roots (g_1 and g_2) which represent the coordinates of the fixed points P and Q. These roots are still function of μ and f.

To adjust the frequency tuning such that the amplitudes of points P and Q are equal, the roots of Equation (8.42) are found and substituted into Equation (8.38). When the expressions for P and Q are equated, a simple relation between μ and f is obtained:

$$f = \frac{1}{1 + \mu} \tag{8.43}$$

Note that c/c_c cancels out since the amplitudes of points P and Q are independent of damping.

Now to find the optimum damping $(c/c_c)_{opt}$, Equation (8.43) is substituted into Equation (8.38). The resulting equation is differentiated with respect to g and set equal to zero while one of the two roots obtained in Equation (8.42) is also replaced in Equation (8.38). From this calculation, we obtain for an optimum at point P:

$$\left(\frac{c}{c_c}\right)^2_{opt-P} = \frac{\mu\left(3 - \sqrt{\dfrac{\mu}{\mu + 2}}\right)}{8(1 + \mu)^3} \tag{8.44}$$

Alternatively, if the derivative is set to zero at point Q, we also get:

$$\left(\frac{c}{c_c}\right)^2_{opt-Q} = \frac{\mu\left(3 + \sqrt{\dfrac{\mu}{\mu + 2}}\right)}{8(1 + \mu)^3} \tag{8.45}$$

Figure 8.8 shows a case of optimum tuning for $\mu = 0.25$ ($f = 0.8$). Two curves are drawn, one using the optimum damping given by Equation (8.44) that passes horizontally through point P and is not horizontal at point Q; the other, using Equation (8.45), that is horizontal at Q and not at point P. Both curves include optimum frequency tuning given by Equation (8.43). It can be seen that for practical applications, the two curves are almost identical. In practice, for optimum tuning, the mean value of Equations (8.44) and (8.45) is used:

$$\left(\frac{c}{c_c}\right)_{opt} = \sqrt{\frac{(3\mu)}{8(1+\mu)^3}} \tag{8.46}$$

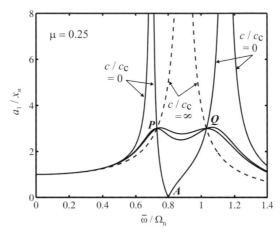

Figure 8.8 Resonance Curves for Optimum Frequency and Damping Tuning, μ = 0.25, f = 0.8 (after Den Hartog 1985)

8.5 APPLICATION OF TUNED-MASS DAMPERS IN EARTHQUAKE ENGINEERING

The optimization technique described by Equations (8.43) and (8.46) was developed by minimizing the displacement of an undamped linear single-degree-of-freedom structure subjected to a sinusoidal dynamic force. This approach, although a useful guideline in a general sense, can possibly be improved further in seismic application since:

- Civil engineering structures can rarely be considered as single-degree-of-freedom systems.

- Civil engineering structures may experience nonlinear behaviour, even when equipped with a tuned-mass damper.

- Earthquake excitations are random in nature.

- Other optimization criteria should be considered (e.g. accelerations).

In fact, different researchers have considered many other criteria. Some of these are listed in Soong and Dargush (1997) and given below:

- Minimum displacement of the main structure (Den Hartog 1985, Thompson 1981, Jacquot and Hoppe 1973, Fujino and Abe 1993).

- Maximum dynamic stiffness of the main structure (Falcon et al. 1967).

- Maximum effective damping of combined structure/TMD system (Luft 1979).

- A mixed criterion involving frequency tuning using minimum displacement criterion and TMD damping determination using maximum effective damping criterion (Luft 1979).

- Minimum travel of damper mass relative to the main structure (Luft 1979).

- Minimum velocity of the main structure (Warburton 1982).

- Minimum acceleration of the main structure (Ioi and Ikeda 1978, Warburton 1982).

- Minimum force in the main structure (Warburton 1982).

Table 8-1 lists optimum tuning conditions (frequency and damping), based on various optimization criteria for damped TMDs attached to undamped primary structures. Note that for all cases, the optimum frequency tuning reduces to $f = 1$ for very small TMDs ($\mu \approx 0$).

Table 8-1: Optimum Tuning Conditions for Damped TMDs Attached to Undamped Primary Structure (after Constantinou et al. 1998)

Loading Case	Optimization Criteria	Optimum Tuning Conditions	
		f	c/c_c
1) Harmonic Load Applied to Primary Structure	Minimum Relative Displacement Amplitude of Primary Structure	$\dfrac{1}{1+\mu}$ [Equation (8.43)]	$\sqrt{\dfrac{3\mu}{8(1+\mu)^3}}$ [Equation (8.46)]
2) Harmonic Load Applied to Primary Structure	Minimum Relative Acceleration Amplitude of Primary Structure	$\dfrac{1}{\sqrt{1+\mu}}$	$\sqrt{\dfrac{3\mu}{8\left(1+\dfrac{\mu}{2}\right)}}$
3) Harmonic Base Acceleration	Minimum Relative Displacement Amplitude of Primary Structure	$\dfrac{\sqrt{1-\dfrac{\mu}{2}}}{1+\mu}$	$\sqrt{\dfrac{3\mu}{8(1+\mu)\left(1-\dfrac{\mu}{2}\right)}}$
4) Harmonic Base Acceleration	Minimum Absolute Acceleration Amplitude of Primary Structure	$\dfrac{1}{1+\mu}$	$\sqrt{\dfrac{3\mu}{8(1+\mu)}}$

Table 8-1: Optimum Tuning Conditions for Damped TMDs Attached to Undamped Primary Structure (after Constantinou et al. 1998)

5) Random Load Applied to Primary Structure	Minimum Root Mean Square Value of Relative Displacement of Primary Structure	$\dfrac{\sqrt{1-\dfrac{\mu}{2}}}{1+\mu}$	$\sqrt{\dfrac{\mu\left(1+\dfrac{3\mu}{4}\right)}{\sqrt{4(1+\mu)\left(1-\dfrac{\mu}{2}\right)}}}$
6) Random Base Acceleration	Minimum Root Mean Square Value of Relative Displacement of Primary Structure	$\dfrac{\sqrt{1-\dfrac{\mu}{2}}}{1+\mu}$	$\sqrt{\dfrac{\mu\left(1-\dfrac{\mu}{4}\right)}{\sqrt{4(1+\mu)\left(1-\dfrac{\mu}{2}\right)}}}$

As an example, the optimum TMD frequency and damping tuning for an undamped structure are presented as a function of the mass ratio in Figure 8.9 and Figure 8.10, respectively. Included in these figures are the six cases listed in Table 8-1. It can be seen that although the tuning conditions are different, the differences are relatively small for small mass ratios.

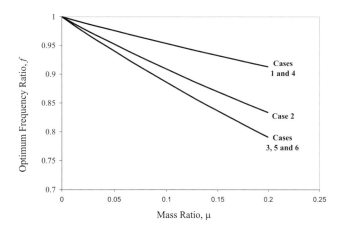

Figure 8.9 Optimum Frequency Tuning for Cases Listed in Table 8-1

8.6 ANALYSIS OF STRUCTURES WITH TUNED-MASS DAMPERS

The tuning of a Tuned-Mass Damper (TMD) described above is valid, of course, only for single-degree-of-freedom structural systems. Therefore, a TMD can only be tuned to a single structural frequency. Since most buildings are multi-degree-of-freedom structural systems, it is thus expected that the effectiveness of a TMD is the greatest when the structure vibrates mainly in a predominant mode.

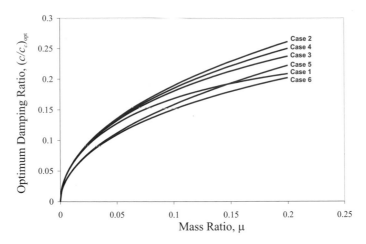

Figure 8.10 Optimum Damping Tuning for Cases Listed in Table 8-1

For seismic applications, TMDs are usually tuned to the fundamental mode of vibration of the structure, and are often installed on the roof of the building, as illustrated in Figure 8.11.

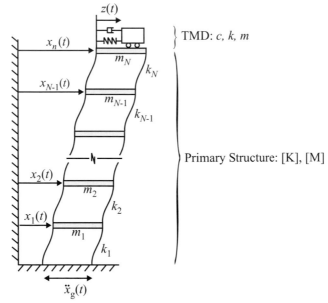

Figure 8.11 Model of Multi-Degree-of-Freedom Structure with TMD on Roof (after Soong and Dargush 1997)

Neglecting the damping in the primary structure, the equations of motions for this coupled system are given by:

$$[M]\{\ddot{x}(t)\} + [K]\{x(t)\} = -[M]\{r\}\ddot{x}_g(t) + \{P(t)\}$$
$$m\ddot{z} + c\dot{z} + kz = -m\ddot{x}_N - m\ddot{x}_g$$
(8.47)

where N is the number of degrees-of-freedom (considering one degree-of-freedom per floor of the building) of the primary structure and represents the Nth level degree-of-freedom, $[M]$ and $[K]$ are the global mass and stiffness matrices of the main structure; $\{x\}$ and $(\ddot{x})$ are the displacements and accelerations of the structure relative to the ground; $\{r\}$ is the dynamic coupling vector; m, c, and k are the mass, damping constant and stiffness of the TMD; $z(t)$ is the displacement of the TMD relative to the roof; and $\{P(t)\} = \{0, ..., 0, c\dot{z} + kz\}^T$. From Equation (8.47), it is clear that the structural analysis needs to be carried in the $(N + 1)$ - dimensional space under general conditions.

Now consider the case where, under a ground motion, the structure responds primarily in its first mode of vibration and where the response vector $\{x(t)\}$ can be approximated by:

$$\{x(t)\} = \{A^{(1)}\}x_N(t)$$
(8.48)

where $\{A^{(1)}\}$ is the first mode shape and $x_N(t)$ is the displacement of the roof relative to the ground.

Substituting Equation (8.48) into the first expression of Equation (8.47), pre-multiplying it by $\{A^{(1)}\}^T$, and using the orthogonality conditions of the mode shapes yields:

$$M_1\ddot{x}_N(t) + K_1 x_N(t) = c\dot{z}(t) + kz(t) - \alpha_1 M_1 \ddot{x}_g$$
(8.49)

where:

$$M_1 = \{A^{(1)}\}^T[m]\{A^{(1)}\} = \text{generalized mass in first mode}$$

$$K_1 = \{A^{(1)}\}^T[k]\{A^{(1)}\} = \text{generalized stiffness coefficient in first mode}$$
(8.50)

$$\alpha_1 = \frac{\{A^{(1)}\}^T[m]\{r\}}{M_1} = \text{modal participation factor in first mode}$$

By comparing the second expression of Equation (8.47) and Equation (8.49) with Equations (8.24) and (8.25), one can conclude that the first modal representation of a multi-degree-of-freedom structure is exactly the same as that of a single-degree-of-freedom structure, except that the modal mass and the modal stiffness are employed instead of the physical parameters in the SDOF case. Therefore, the tuning of a TMD for the fundamental mode of a multi-degree-of-freedom structural system can be performed by using Equations (8.43) and (8.46) or Figures 8.9 and 8.10 or Table 8-1 with:

$$\mu = \frac{m}{M_1} = \text{mass ratio}$$
(8.51)

$$\Omega_N = \omega_1 = \text{fundamental frequency of main structure}$$

Note that this approach can also be used to mitigate the vibrations of any other mode of the structure. Finally, a structure equipped with a TMD may, nevertheless, experience inelastic deformations during a strong earthquake. When inelastic deformations occur, the fundamental frequency of the main structure decreases and consequently the TMD may lose part of its effectiveness due to a de-tuning effect. This phenomenon is discussed in the next section.

8.7 SEISMIC RESPONSE OF INELASTIC BUILDINGS WITH TMDs

Carr (2005) investigated the seismic response of shear wall reinforced concrete buildings equipped with TMDs. The main objective of this study was to investigate the seismic fragility of elastic and inelastic reinforced concrete buildings equipped with TMDs of various sizes under ensembles of ground motions representing various seismic hazard levels.

8.7.1 Building Models

Three reinforced concrete shear wall-type buildings, having 3, 10 and 25 stories were considered for the study. The buildings were designed according to the 1995 edition of the National Building of Canada (NRC 1995) and detailed according to the Canadian concrete code (CSA-A23.3 1994) for a site having design ground motion parameters equivalent to Southern California (Filiatrault et al. 1994b).

Figure 8.12 and Table 8-2 show the configuration along with the dimensions and reinforcing details of the shear walls for the 10-storey building. The computed fundamental period for this building based on gross section properties is 1.64s.

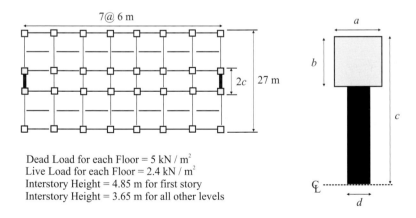

Dead Load for each Floor = 5 kN / m²
Live Load for each Floor = 2.4 kN / m²
Interstory Height = 4.85 m for first story
Interstory Height = 3.65 m for all other levels

Figure 8.12 Layout and Design Loads for 10-Storey Building Model

Table 8-2: Properties of 10-Storey Building

Levels	a (mm)	b (mm)	c (mm)	d (mm)	Concentrated Steel (end columns)	Distributed Steel (wall)
1-2	400	1300	3300	400	36-25M	2 rows of 15M @ 300 mm
3-4	400	1300	3300	400	36-25M	2 rows of 15M @ 400 mm
5-6	400	1000	3300	400	28-25M	2 rows of 15M @ 400 mm
7-8	400	700	3300	400	20-25M	2 rows of 15M @ 400 mm
9-10	400	400	3300	400	4-20M 8-15M	2 rows of 15M @ 400 mm

8.7.2 Analysis Procedure

A two-dimensional lumped-mass model was used to calculate the seismic response of the building models with and without TMDs. Only half of each building was modeled, as all structures are symmetrical, and torsional effects from the rigid diaphragm actions could be considered to be secondary in this study. Each model included only one wall, together with one gravity column that represents all the interior frame columns. The total gravity dead loads acting on the interior columns were applied to the gravity column in the model, and both the gravity column and the shear wall were constrained to experience the same lateral deformation at each floor (Carr 2005).

Each TMD was modeled as a SDOF system on the roof of its corresponding building and was tuned according to Equations (8.43) and (8.46). Three different sizes of TMDs were considered for each building corresponding to a mass ratio $\mu = 0.05, 0.10$ and 0.20, respectively. Table 8-3 shows the properties of the TMDs considered for the 10-storey building.

Table 8-3: Properties of TMDs for 10-Storey Building

Mass Ratio	TMD Natural Period (s)	TMD Damping Ratio
0.05	1.72	0.13
0.10	1.80	0.17
0.20	1.97	0.21

The computer program RUAUMOKO (Carr 2004) was used to perform the nonlinear time-history dynamic analyses. Since the shear wall is a cantilever designed and detailed as a ductile reinforced concrete shear wall, only the base of each wall model was assumed to yield during an earthquake and thus was assigned a degrading bi-linear moment-curvature hysteresis rule (Carr 2005).

8.7.3 Ground Motions

Ensembles of synthetic strong ground motions were generated for a hypothetical Southern California site where the buildings considered were assumed to be located. These synthetic ground motions were generated based on four different seismic hazard levels at the site: 2%, 5%, 10%, and 20% probabilities of exceedence in 50 years (or hazard return periods of 2475, 975, 475, and 224 years, respectively). Each ensemble was comprised of 25 earthquake records for a total of 100 strong ground motions considered in this study. These strong motions were simulated using the Specific Barrier Model (SBM) proposed and developed by Papageorgiou and Aki (1983a, 1983b). This model is based on a stochastic approach for which each earthquake motion is modeled as a spectrum compatible Gaussian noise. The most recent calibration parameters obtained by Halldorsson (2004) were implemented in the SBM. Details on the ground motions used in this study can be found in Wanitkorkul and Filiatrault (2005).

8.7.4 Selected Analysis Results

Figure 8.13 shows the mean peak absolute floor accelerations experienced by the 10-storey building for the four different hazard levels considered in the analyses. The results for the original building without TMD are compared against the results obtained for the same building incorporating three different TMD sizes listed in Table 8-3. The results are also presented assuming that the structural system remains elastic (Figure 8.13a) or can undergo inelastic deformations (Figure 8.13b).

Because yielding of the building limits the seismic forces, the amplitudes of the floor accelerations are much lower for the inelastic case than for the case where the structure is assumed to remain elastic. For this elastic case, the incorporation of a TMD system reduces the peak floor acceleration. As expected, the reduction in peak floor accelerations is proportional to the size (mass ratio) of the TMD. For the inelastic case, however, the effectiveness of the TMD in reducing the peak floor acceleration is limited. For some cases (return periods of 975 and 2475 years in Figure 8.13b), the incorporation of a TMD causes slight increase in peak floor accelerations. These results illustrate the fact that when a building equipped with a TMD undergoes inelastic deformations, its fundamental period is altered, which causes a detuning effect of the TMD and a loss of efficiency of the system. A complete discussion of the results obtained for various building structures can be found in Carr (2005).

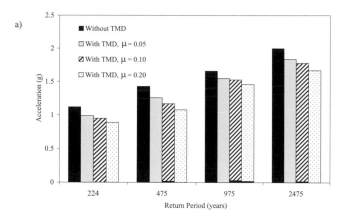

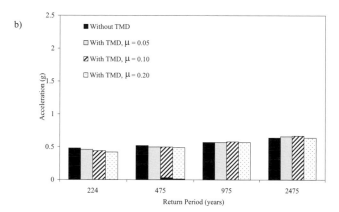

Figure 8.13 Mean Peak Absolute Floor Acceleration, 10-Storey Building with and without TMD: a) Elastic Response, b) Inelastic Response

8.8 DESIGN CONSIDERATIONS

The design procedure of a TMD for a building structure oscillating mainly in its fundamental frequency and mode can be carried out with the following steps.

a) **Step 1: Evaluation of Mass Ratio**: First, the equivalent viscous damping ratio of the structure-TMD assembly needs to be identified. A procedure proposed by Luft (1979) can be used for this purpose. This involves looking at design acceleration and displacement response spectra, S_A and S_D, and selecting an appropriate damping value ξ_{eq} that satisfies:

$$\alpha_1 S_D(\omega_1, \xi_{eq}) \leq x_{N(max)}$$
$$\alpha_1 S_A(\omega_1, \xi_{eq}) \leq \ddot{x}_{n(max)}$$

(8.52)

where $x_{N(max)}$ and $\ddot{x}_{N(max)}$ are the target maximum relative displacement and maximum absolute acceleration at the roof level of the building.

The required mass ratio μ can then be estimated by the following equation (Luft 1979):

$$\mu = 16(\xi_{eq} - 0.8\xi_1)^2 = \frac{m}{M_1} \qquad (8.53)$$

where ξ_1 is the first modal damping ratio of the main structure. Note that, in most practical applications, the selection of μ is limited by physical considerations.

b)   **Step 2: Tuning of TMD Properties**: Figures 8.9 and 8.10 or Table 8-1 can be used to estimate the optimum frequency ratio and damping of the TMD.

c)   **Step 3: Structural Dynamic Analysis Check**: The final step in designing the TMD is to check that the selected TMD parameters result in a building response that is in the range of the predetermined response threshold. Otherwise, the preliminary design has to be refined by trial-and-error.

8.9 PROBLEMS

Problem 8.1

Using the general solution for damped TMDs under harmonic loading (Equation (8.36)), determine the amplitude of the motion of the main mass for the following cases:

a) $k = \infty$

b) $k = 0$, $c = 0$

c) $c = \infty$

d) $c = 0$, $\overline{\omega} = \sqrt{\dfrac{k}{m}} = \Omega_n$

e) $m = 0$

f)   Discuss the physical significance of each result.

Problem 8.2

The transverse vibrations in the first mode of the tower of a cable-stayed bridge are to be controlled by a pendulum tuned-mass damper suspended inside the tower, as illustrated in Figure 8.14. The tuned-mass damper is composed of a mass m suspended from a cable of length l and connected to the tower by a linear viscous damper of constant c. The generalized mass in the first mode of the tower is $M_1 = 4720$ metric tones. The first mode frequency of the tower is $f_1 = 0.18$ Hz.

a)   If the mass of the tuned-mass damper m is limited to 20 metric tones, determine the length of the cable l and the damping constant c of the viscous damper for optimum tuning of the tuned-mass damper.

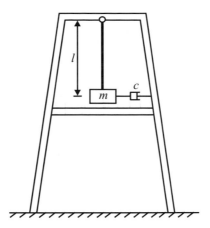

Figure 8.14 Bridge Tower with Pendulum Tuned-Mass Damper

CHAPTER 9: BASIC ANALYSIS AND DESIGN CONCEPTS FOR SEISMICALLY ISOLATED STRUCTURES

9.1 INTRODUCTION

A seismic isolation system involves the installation of isolators beneath key supporting points of the structure. The isolators, having much lower lateral stiffness than the lateral stiffness of the structure, separate it from the ground motion. From an energy point of view, the seismic isolation system limits the seismic energy transfer to the structure. In principle, if the seismic input energy is zero, it is not necessary to design the structure to sustain lateral loads. Although there are many different systems available, the principle of all seismic isolation systems remains the same. Seismic isolation systems combine two main components:

- An isolator, such as sliding surfaces or rubber pads, placed between selected supporting points of the structure (Kelly 1979). Because it has a lateral stiffness much lower than the lateral stiffness of the structure, the isolator shifts the natural period of the structure beyond the most predominant periods of typical earthquakes.

- An energy-dissipation mechanism (damper) that dissipates the residual input energy and limits the forces transmitted to the structure by increased damping.

For elastic structures, the largest spectral accelerations (that are related to the maximum forces that must be resisted by the structure) are usually observed for predominant periods of 0.1 to 1 s with maximum severity often in the range of 0.2 to 0.6 s for typical seismic ground motions. Therefore, structures with natural periods in these ranges are usually more vulnerable to earthquakes. The most important characteristic of seismic isolation is the period shift associated with the increased flexibility of the isolation system. This period shift is illustrated in Figure 9.1a). Figure 9.1b) illustrates how excessive displacements are controlled by the increased damping of the energy-dissipation mechanism of the isolation system. These displacements occur at the base-isolator level and must be accommodated by a "seismic gap". Figure 9.2 shows a reinforced concrete frame that is non-isolated (N-IS), the same frame on an isolation system with no damping (IS) and the same frame on a damped isolation system (IS-D). The fixed (N-IS) frame has a natural period $T_1 = 0.55$ s, while the isolated frames have an elongated natural period of $T_1 = 2.00$ s. The fixed frame and the undamped isolated frame have 5% viscous damping while the damped isolated structure has 20% viscous damping in the first mode. The response of these three structures can be visualized on the acceleration and displacement response spectra for the S00E component of the 1940 Imperial Valley, El Centro, California earthquake in Figure 9.3. It can be seen that large seismic forces act on the conventional structure (N-IS), which can cause permanent deformations and cracking in the structural elements. The forces are much reduced in the isolated frames (IS and IS-D), and most of the displacement occurs across the isolation system, while the structure deforms practically as a rigid body. The IS-D system has an additional advantage over the IS system, since, because of the supplemental damping, the maximum displacement that the isolator must accommodate is smaller $(\Delta_{max}(\text{IS-D}) < \Delta_{max}(\text{IS}))$.

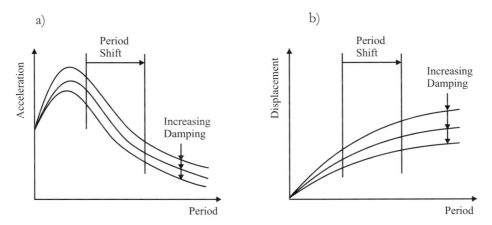

Figure 9.1 Period Shift and Increased Damping Effects of Isolation System: a) Spectral Accelerations, b) Spectral Displacements (after Skinner et al. 1993)

It must be noted, however, that practical implementation of a seismic isolation system represents a trade off between force reduction and increased displacement across the isolation system. As the flexibility of the isolation system increases, movements of the structure relative to its supporting points may become a problem under non-seismic loading, such as wind loads.

9.2 THEORY OF LINEAR SEISMICALLY ISOLATED SYSTEMS

In this section, the simple one-storey building of mass m, stiffness k_s and viscous damping c_s, isolated with a "linear" seismic isolation system made of a linear spring k_b and a linear viscous dashpot c_b, shown in Figure 9.4, is analyzed. The theoretical analysis of linear seismically isolated systems presented in this paragraph was originally developed by Kelly (1990). The mass of the base slab is equal to m_b. The combined structure-isolation system is represented by a 2-DOF system with absolute lateral displacements at

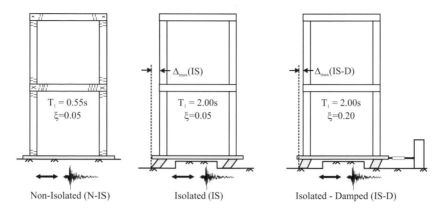

Figure 9.2 Non-Isolated, Isolated and Isolated-Damped Reinforced Concrete Frames

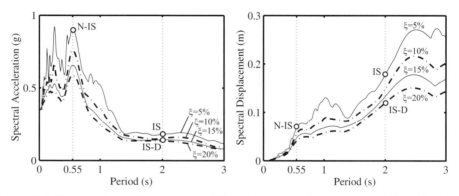

Figure 9.3 Spectral Acceleration and Displacement Response of Non-Isolated (N-IS), Isolated (IS) and Isolated Damped (IS-D) Structures, 1940 Imperial Valley (S00E), El Centro, California Earthquake

the girder and slab level equal to u_s and u_b respectively. The ground displacement is defined as u_g.

Applying Newton's second law to both masses yields the equations of motion:

$$m\ddot{u}_s = -c_s(\dot{u}_s - \dot{u}_b) - k_s(u_s - u_b) \qquad (9.1)$$

and

$$m\ddot{u}_s + m_b\ddot{u}_b = -c_b(\dot{u}_b - \dot{u}_g) - k_b(u_b - u_g) \qquad (9.2)$$

where $\dot{u}_b$ and $\dot{u}_s$ are the absolute velocities at the base slab and at the top of the structure respectively, and $\ddot{u}_b$ and $\ddot{u}_s$ are the absolute accelerations at these same levels.

It is convenient to re-write Equations (9.1) and (9.2) in terms of relative displacements v_s and v_b:

$$v_s = u_s - u_b$$
$$v_b = u_b - u_g$$
(9.3)

Substituting Equation (9.3) into Equations (9.1) and (9.2) yields:

$$m\ddot{v}_b + m\ddot{v}_s + c_s\dot{v}_s + k_s v_s = -m\ddot{u}_g$$
(9.4)

and

$$(m + m_b)\ddot{v}_b + m\ddot{v}_s + c_b\dot{v}_b + k_b v_b = -(m + m_b)\ddot{u}_g$$
(9.5)

If the relative motion between the structure and the base slab is suppressed ($v_s = 0$), Equation (9.5) becomes:

$$M\ddot{v}_b + c_b\dot{v}_b + k_b v_b = -M\ddot{u}_g$$
(9.6)

which is the standard equation of motion for a SDOF system of total mass M ($M = m + m_b$) supported on the isolation system.

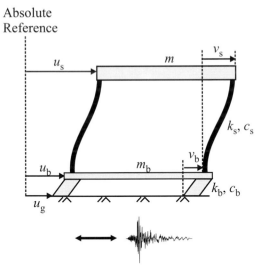

Figure 9.4 Single-Storey Structure with Linear Isolation System

Similarly, if the relative motion between the base and the ground is suppressed ($v_b = 0$), Equation (9.4) becomes the usual equation for a fixed-base SDOF system:

$$m\ddot{v}_s + c_s\dot{v}_s + k_s v_s = -m\ddot{u}_g$$
(9.7)

The equations of motion of the 2-DOF system can be written in matrix form:

$$[M]\{\ddot{v}\} + [C]\{\dot{v}\} + [K]\{v\} = -[M]\{r\}\ddot{u}_g$$
(9.8)

$$[M] = \begin{bmatrix} M & m \\ m & m \end{bmatrix} \qquad \{v\} = \begin{Bmatrix} v_b \\ v_s \end{Bmatrix}$$

$$[K] = \begin{bmatrix} k_b & 0 \\ 0 & k_s \end{bmatrix} \qquad \{r\} = \begin{Bmatrix} 1 \\ 0 \end{Bmatrix} \tag{9.9}$$

$$[C] = \begin{bmatrix} c_b & 0 \\ 0 & c_s \end{bmatrix}$$

Considering the properties of the isolation system and of the structure, we can make the following order of magnitude estimates:

- $m_b < m$, but of the same order of magnitude;
- $\omega_s = \sqrt{k_s / m} \gg \omega_b = \sqrt{k_b / M}$ and we define $\varepsilon = \left(\dfrac{\omega_b}{\omega_s}\right)^2$ which is assumed to be of the order of 10^{-2}; and
- the viscous damping ratio for the structure, $\xi_s = c_s / (2 m \omega_s)$, and for the isolation system, $\xi_b = c_b / (2 M \omega_b)$, are both of the same order of magnitude as ε.

The natural frequencies of the system can be found by solving the eigenvalue problem:

$$\left| [K] - \omega^2 [M] \right| = 0 \tag{9.10}$$

or

$$\begin{vmatrix} k_b - \omega^2 M & (-\omega^2 m) \\ -\omega^2 m & k_s - \omega^2 m \end{vmatrix} = 0 \tag{9.11}$$

Expanding the determinant of Equation (9.11) yields the frequency equation:

$$(1 - \gamma)\omega^4 - (\omega_b^2 + \omega_s^2)\omega^2 + \omega_b^2 \omega_s^2 = 0 \tag{9.12}$$

where $\gamma = \dfrac{m}{M}$.

The solution of Equation (9.12) yields two roots (ω_1, ω_2). These roots are given by:

$$\omega_1, \omega_2 = \frac{1}{2(1-\gamma)}\left\{ (\omega_s^2 + \omega_b^2) \pm \sqrt{(\omega_s^2 + \omega_b^2)^2 - 4(1-\gamma)(\omega_s^2 \omega_b^2)} \right\} \tag{9.13}$$

The term under the square root can be re-written as:

$$\sqrt{(\omega_s^2 + \omega_b^2)^2 - 4(1-\gamma)(\omega_s^2 \omega_b^2)} = (\omega_s^2 - \omega_b^2)\sqrt{1 + 4\gamma\frac{\omega_b^2 \omega_s^2}{(\omega_s^2 - \omega_b^2)^2}} \tag{9.14}$$

Expanding the second right-hand side term of Equation (9.14) into a binomial series yields:

$$\sqrt{(\omega_s^2 + \omega_b^2)^2 - 4(1-\gamma)(\omega_s^2\omega_b^2)} \approx (\omega_s^2 - \omega_b^2)^2 \left(1 + \frac{2\gamma\omega_b^2\omega_s^2}{(\omega_s^2 - \omega_b^2)^2} \right) \qquad (9.15)$$

Substituting Equation (9.15) into (9.13) leads to an expression for the two natural frequencies of the system:

$$\omega_1^2 = \frac{\omega_b^2}{(1-\gamma)} \left[1 - \frac{\gamma\omega_s^2}{(\omega_s^2 - \omega_b^2)} \right]$$

$$\omega_2^2 = \frac{\omega_s^2}{(1-\gamma)} \left[1 + \frac{\gamma\omega_b^2}{(\omega_s^2 - \omega_b^2)} \right] \qquad (9.16)$$

But since $\omega_s \gg \omega_b$, we can re-write Equation (9.16) as:

$$\omega_1 = \omega_b\sqrt{1 - \gamma\varepsilon} \approx \omega_b$$

$$\omega_2 = \frac{\omega_s}{\sqrt{1-\gamma}}\sqrt{1 + \frac{\gamma\omega_b^2}{\omega_s^2}} \approx \frac{\omega_s}{\sqrt{1-\gamma}} \qquad (9.17)$$

The first natural frequency is the isolation frequency that is essentially not affected by the flexibility of the structures (the change is of the order of ε). The second natural frequency is the structural frequency that is significantly increased by the presence of the mass of the base. Combining these two factors further increases the separation between the isolation frequency and the fixed-base structural frequency.

The first mode shape $\{A^{(1)}\}$ is given by:

$$\begin{bmatrix} k_b - \omega_b^2 M & (-\omega_b^2 m) \\ -\omega_b^2 m & k_s - \omega_b^2 m \end{bmatrix} \begin{Bmatrix} A_1^{(1)} \\ A_2^{(1)} \end{Bmatrix} = \begin{Bmatrix} 0 \\ 0 \end{Bmatrix} \qquad (9.18)$$

From the second equation in (9.18):

$$(-\omega_b^2 m A_1^{(1)} + (k_s - \omega_b^2 m))A_2^{(1)} = 0 \qquad (9.19)$$

Setting $A_1^{(1)} = 1$:

$$A_2^{(1)} = \frac{\omega_b^2 m}{k_s - \omega_b^2 m} = \frac{\omega_b^2}{\omega_s^2 - \omega_b^2} = \frac{1}{(1/\varepsilon) - 1} = \frac{\varepsilon}{1-\varepsilon} \approx \varepsilon \qquad (9.20)$$

Therefore, the first mode shape can be written as:

$$\{A^{(1)}\} = \begin{Bmatrix} 1 \\ \varepsilon \end{Bmatrix} \tag{9.21}$$

Similarly, the second mode shape, $\{A^{(2)}\}$, is given by:

$$\begin{bmatrix} k_b - \dfrac{\omega_s^2}{1-\gamma}M & -\dfrac{\omega_s^2}{1-\gamma}m \\ -\dfrac{\omega_s^2}{1-\gamma}m & k_s - \dfrac{\omega_s^2}{1-\gamma}m \end{bmatrix} \begin{Bmatrix} A_1^{(2)} \\ A_2^{(2)} \end{Bmatrix} = \begin{Bmatrix} 0 \\ 0 \end{Bmatrix} \tag{9.22}$$

From the first equation in (9.22):

$$\left(k_b - \dfrac{\omega_s^2}{1-\gamma}M\right)A_1^{(2)} - \dfrac{\omega_s^2}{1-\gamma}mA_2^{(2)} = 0 \tag{9.23}$$

Setting $A_1^{(2)} = 1$:

$$A_2^{(2)} = \dfrac{k_b - \dfrac{\omega_s^2}{1-\gamma}M}{\dfrac{\omega_s^2}{1-\gamma}m} = \dfrac{(1-\gamma)\varepsilon - 1}{\gamma} \tag{9.24}$$

Therefore, the second mode shape can be written as:

$$\{A^{(2)}\} = \begin{Bmatrix} 1 \\ -\left(\dfrac{1-(1-\gamma)\varepsilon}{\gamma}\right) \end{Bmatrix} \tag{9.25}$$

The two mode shapes for the isolated structure are illustrated in Figure 9.5. We can see that the first mode shape represents practically a rigid structure on a flexible base isolation system. In the second mode, the displacement at the top of the structure is out of phase and of the same order of magnitude as the isolation displacement. The second mode is very close to a motion where the two masses are vibrating completely free in space about the center of mass of the combined system. The practical significance of this result is that high accelerations in the second mode of an isolated structure do not generate a large base shear.

Using the modal superposition method, the relative displacements, $v_b(t)$ and $v_s(t)$, can be written as:

$$v_b(t) = u_1(t)A_1^{(1)} + u_2(t)A_1^{(2)} \tag{9.26}$$

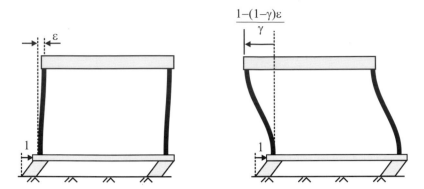

Figure 9.5 Mode Shapes for a Base Isolated Single-Storey Structure

and

$$v_s(t) = u_1(t)A_2^{(1)} + u_2(t)A_2^{(2)} \tag{9.27}$$

Assuming that the damping is low enough to maintain the orthogonality properties of the mode shapes, the modal responses, $u_1(t)$ and $u_2(t)$, satisfy the following modal equations of motion:

$$M_1\ddot{u}_1 + C_1\dot{u}_2 + K_1u_1 = P_1(t) \tag{9.28}$$

and:

$$M_2\ddot{u}_2 + C_2\dot{u}_2 + K_2u_2 = P_2(t) \tag{9.29}$$

where:

$$
\begin{aligned}
M_1 &= \{A^{(1)}\}^T[M]\{A^{(1)}\} & M_2 &= \{A^{(2)}\}^T[M]\{A^{(2)}\} \\
C_1 &= \{A^{(1)}\}^T[C]\{A^{(1)}\} & C_2 &= \{A^{(2)}\}^T[C]\{A^{(2)}\} \\
K_1 &= \{A^{(1)}\}^T[K]\{A^{(1)}\} & K_2 &= \{A^{(2)}\}^T[K]\{A^{(2)}\} \\
P_1 &= -\{A^{(1)}\}^T[M]\{r\}\ddot{u}_g & P_2 &= -\{A^{(2)}\}^T[M]\{r\}\ddot{u}_g
\end{aligned}
\tag{9.30}
$$

We can re-write Equations (9.28) and (9.29) as:

$$\ddot{u}_1 + 2\xi_1\omega_1\dot{u}_1 + \omega_1^2 u_1 = -\alpha_1\ddot{u}_g \tag{9.31}$$

and:

$$\ddot{u}_2 + 2\xi_2\omega_2\dot{u}_2 + \omega_2^2 u_2 = -\alpha_2\ddot{u}_g \tag{9.32}$$

where ξ_1 and ξ_2 are the modal damping ratios and α_1 and α_2 are the modal participation factors given by:

$$\xi_1 = \frac{C_1}{2\omega_1 M_1} \qquad\qquad \xi_2 = \frac{C_2}{2\omega_2 M_2}$$

$$\alpha_1 = \frac{-\{A^{(1)}\}^T[M]\{r\}}{M_1} \qquad \alpha_2 = \frac{-\{A^{(2)}\}^T[M]\{r\}}{M_2} \qquad (9.33)$$

The computation of α_1 involves the following matrix operations:

$$\alpha_1 = \frac{\begin{Bmatrix} 1 \\ \varepsilon \end{Bmatrix}^T \begin{bmatrix} M & m \\ m & m \end{bmatrix} \begin{Bmatrix} 1 \\ 0 \end{Bmatrix}}{\begin{Bmatrix} 1 \\ \varepsilon \end{Bmatrix}^T \begin{bmatrix} M & m \\ m & m \end{bmatrix} \begin{Bmatrix} 1 \\ \varepsilon \end{Bmatrix}} = \frac{M + m\varepsilon}{M + 2m\varepsilon + m\varepsilon^2} \qquad (9.34)$$

Neglecting the term in ε^2, we get:

$$\alpha_1 = 1 - \frac{m\varepsilon}{M + 2m\varepsilon} = 1 - \frac{\varepsilon}{(1/\gamma) + 2\varepsilon} = 1 - \frac{\gamma\varepsilon}{1 + 2\gamma\varepsilon} \approx 1 - \gamma\varepsilon \qquad (9.35)$$

The modal mass in the first mode M_1^* is given by:

$$M_1^* = \alpha_1^2 M_1 = (1 - \gamma\varepsilon)^2 (M + 2m\varepsilon + m\varepsilon^2) \approx M(1 - \gamma\varepsilon^2(1 - 3\gamma)) \approx M \qquad (9.36)$$

Performing the same computation for the second mode, we find:

$$\alpha_2 = \gamma\varepsilon \qquad (9.37)$$

and:

$$M_2^* = M\frac{(1 - \gamma)[1 - 2\varepsilon(1 - \gamma)]}{\gamma} \qquad (9.38)$$

From these results, it can be seen why the seismic isolation system is effective. The participation factor for the second mode α_2, which is the mode involving structural deformation, is of the order of ε and very small if the original natural frequencies, ω_b and ω_s, are well separated. Furthermore, since the natural frequency of the second mode shifts to a higher value than the original fixed-base frequency (see Equation (9.17)), the isolated structure will be out of range of strong earthquake motions with large spectral accelerations at the original structural frequency.

Moreover, since the participation factor for the second mode is very small, this second mode is almost orthogonal to the earthquake input. From Equation (9.30), the generalized loading in the second mode is given by:

$$P_2(t) = -\{A^{(2)}\}^T[m]\{r\}\ddot{u}_g(t) \qquad (9.39)$$

where $\{r\}^T = \{1\ \ 0\}$. Recalling Equation (9.21) we observe that:

$$\{r\} \approx \{A^{(1)}\} \qquad (9.40)$$

and recalling the mass-orthogonality properties of mode shapes, we have:

$$\{A^{(2)}\}^T[M]\{A^{(1)}\} = 0 \approx \{A^{(2)}\}^T[M]\{r\} \tag{9.41}$$

Therefore:

$$P_2(t) \approx 0 \tag{9.42}$$

The result expressed by Equation (9.42) infers that even if the ground motion contains energy at the second mode frequency, it will not be transmitted into the structure ($P_2(t) \approx 0$). A seismic isolation system is effective not by absorbing the seismic energy, but rather by deflecting it through this orthogonality property.

Energy absorption is, however, an important component of the behaviour of an isolation system. In this simple isolation model, energy dissipation is described by linear viscous damping. The question now arises as to how to select the modal damping ratios, ξ_1 and ξ_2. In this case, we are in the unusual situation of being able to make very good estimates of the damping by treating the structure and the base isolation system as separate elements.

A natural rubber isolation system typically provides a degree of damping that is in the range of 10-20% of critical with the structure having significantly less, e.g. of the order of 2% of critical damping. Generally, for conventional structural analysis, a value of damping in the structure of about 5% of critical is assumed. This value presupposes that some degree of structural and nonstructural damage will occur when a conventional structure experiences a strong earthquake. The base isolated structure, however, should experience a much-reduced seismic force level such that no damage will occur to the structure or to the nonstructural elements. Therefore, a lower damping value for the structure is justified.

From Equation (9.33) we can write:

$$\xi_1 = \frac{\{A^{(1)}\}^T[c]\{A^{(1)}\}}{2\omega_1 M_1} = \frac{\begin{Bmatrix} 1 \\ \varepsilon \end{Bmatrix}^T \begin{bmatrix} c_b & 0 \\ 0 & c_s \end{bmatrix} \begin{Bmatrix} 1 \\ \varepsilon \end{Bmatrix}}{2\omega_1(M + 2m\varepsilon + m\varepsilon^2)} = \frac{c_b + c_s\varepsilon^2}{2\omega_b\sqrt{1 - \gamma\varepsilon}(M + 2m\varepsilon + m\varepsilon^2)} \tag{9.43}$$

Neglecting the term in ε^2, we get:

$$\xi_1 \approx \frac{\xi_b(1 - 2\gamma\varepsilon)}{\sqrt{1 - \gamma\varepsilon}} \approx \xi_b\left(1 - \frac{3}{2}\gamma\varepsilon\right) \tag{9.44}$$

Similarly, from Equation (9.33), we can write:

$$\xi_2 = \frac{\{A^{(2)}\}^T [c]\{A^{(2)}\}}{2\omega_2 M_2} = \frac{\left\{\begin{array}{c} 1 \\ \frac{(1-\gamma)\varepsilon - 1}{\gamma} \end{array}\right\}^T \begin{bmatrix} c_b & 0 \\ 0 & c_s \end{bmatrix} \left\{\begin{array}{c} 1 \\ \frac{(1-\gamma)\varepsilon - 1}{\gamma} \end{array}\right\}}{2\omega_s \frac{\sqrt{1+\gamma\varepsilon}}{\sqrt{1-\gamma}} M \frac{(1-\gamma)[1-2\varepsilon(1-\gamma)]}{\gamma}} \tag{9.45}$$

Simplifying, we get:

$$\xi_2 \approx \frac{\xi_s}{\sqrt{1-\gamma}} + \frac{\gamma \xi_b \sqrt{\varepsilon}}{\sqrt{1-\gamma}} \tag{9.46}$$

We can see from Equation (9.44) that the first modal damping ratio corresponding to the deformation of the isolation system is practically equal to the high damping ratio of the isolator itself. Equation (9.46) shows, however, that the second modal damping ratio (which is the structural damping) is increased by the damping in the isolation system to the order of $\sqrt{\varepsilon}$. The product $\xi_b \sqrt{\varepsilon}$ may be a significant addition to the structural damping if ξ_s is very small. This result demonstrates that high damping in the isolation system can contribute significant damping to the structural mode.

Knowing α_1, α_2, ξ_1 and ξ_2, the response of the base isolated structure under a ground acceleration time-history $\ddot{u}_g$ can then be calculated. First, the modal responses, u_1 and u_2, can be obtained from Duhamel's integral:

$$u_1(t) = -\frac{\alpha_1}{\omega_1} \int_0^t \ddot{u}_g(t-\tau) e^{-\xi_1 \omega_1 \tau} \sin \omega_1 (t-\tau) d\tau \tag{9.47}$$

and:

$$u_2(t) = -\frac{\alpha_2}{\omega_2} \int_0^t \ddot{u}_g(t-\tau) e^{-\xi_2 \omega_2 \tau} \sin \omega_2 (t-\tau) d\tau \tag{9.48}$$

Then, the maximum values of u_1 and u_2 are given by:

$$|u_1(t)|_{max} = \alpha_1 S_D(\omega_1, \xi_1) \tag{9.49}$$

and:

$$|u_2(t)|_{max} = \alpha_2 S_D(\omega_2, \xi_2) \tag{9.50}$$

where $S_D(\omega_i, \xi_i)$ is the relative displacement response spectrum for the ground motion $\ddot{u}_g(t)$ at frequency ω_i and damping ratio ξ_i.

In order to estimate the maximum values of the relative displacements, v_b and v_s, the SRSS combination can be used since the natural frequencies are well separated.

$$|v_s(t)|_{max} = \sqrt{\left(A_2^{(1)} |u_1(t)|_{max}\right)^2 + \left((A_2^{(2)}) |u_2(t)|_{max}\right)^2} \tag{9.51}$$

and:

$$|v_b(t)|_{max} = \sqrt{(A_1^{(1)}|u_1(t)|_{max})^2 + ((A_1^{(2)})|u_2(t)|_{max})^2} \qquad (9.52)$$

Substituting the results obtained from Equations (9.21) (9.25), (9.35), (9.37), (9.49) and (9.50), and setting:

$$A_1^{(1)} = 1 , A_2^{(1)} = \varepsilon ,$$
$$A_1^{(2)} = 1 , A_2^{(2)} = ((1-\gamma)\varepsilon - 1)/\gamma ,$$
$$\alpha_1 = 1 - \gamma\varepsilon \text{ and } \alpha_2 = \gamma\varepsilon$$

we get:

$$|v_b(t)|_{max} = \sqrt{(1-\gamma\varepsilon)^2[S_D(\omega_1, \xi_1)]^2 + \gamma^2\varepsilon^2[S_D(\omega_2, \xi_2)]^2} \qquad (9.53)$$

and:

$$|v_s(t)|_{max} = \sqrt{\varepsilon^2(1-\gamma\varepsilon)^2[S_D(\omega_1, \xi_1)]^2 + \gamma^2\varepsilon^2\frac{1}{\gamma^2}[(1-\gamma)\varepsilon - 1]^2[S_D(\omega_2, \xi_2)]^2}$$
$$\qquad (9.54)$$
$$= \varepsilon\sqrt{(1-\gamma\varepsilon)^2[S_D(\omega_1, \xi_1)]^2 + [(1-\gamma)\varepsilon - 1]^2[S_D(\omega_2, \xi_2)]^2}$$

Generally, the second term in Equation (9.53) can be neglected for earthquake spectra where the displacement at high frequencies (corresponding to ω_2) is much smaller than at lower frequencies (corresponding to ω_1). Equation (9.53) can therefore be further simplified to:

$$|v_b(t)|_{max} \approx (1 - \gamma\varepsilon)S_D(\omega_1, \xi_1) \qquad (9.55)$$

Similarly, Equation (9.54) can be estimated as:

$$|v_s(t)|_{max} \approx \varepsilon\sqrt{[S_D(\omega_1, \xi_1)]^2 + [S_D(\omega_2, \xi_2)]^2} \qquad (9.56)$$

9.3 DESIGN CONSIDERATIONS FOR SEISMICALLY ISOLATED BUILDINGS

9.3.1 Design Methods

Early versions of seismic provisions for seismically isolated structures emphasized a simple, statically equivalent method of design that took advantage of the fact that for an isolated structure, the displacements are concentrated at the isolation level, and, therefore, the superstructure moves almost as a rigid body. The design was based on a single mode of vibration, and the design forces for the superstructure were computed from the forces in the isolators at the design displacement. This resulted in a very simple design process. As the seismic provisions have evolved, however, the situations where dynamic analysis must be used have increased, and incentives have been inserted in the provisions to encourage the use of dynamic analysis where it may be required.

Although specific design provisions for seismically isolated buildings have been introduced in many countries, only the seismic design provisions for seismically isolated structures of the 2003 version of the International Building Code (ICC 2003) and of the 2003 NEHRP provisions (BSSC 2003) in the United States are described in this section.

For all seismic isolation designs, it is necessary to first perform a static analysis. This establishes a minimum level for the design displacements and forces. The static analysis is also useful for preliminary design of the isolation system and the structure when dynamic analysis is required. The static analysis (or equivalent lateral force procedure) can be used as the only design method for a seismically isolated structure if all the following conditions are met:

- The design spectral acceleration at a period of 1 second is less than or equal to 0.6 g for the site.

- The structure is located on a soil type A, B, C or D.

- The structure above the isolation interface is not more than four stories or 20 m in height.

- The isolated period of the structure at the design displacement is less than or equal to 3 seconds.

- The isolated period of the structure at the design displacement is greater than three times the elastic fixed-based period of the structure (i.e $\varepsilon \leq 1/9$).

- The structure is regular.

- The effective stiffness of the isolation system at the design displacement is greater than 1/3 of the effective stiffness at 20% of the design displacement.

- The isolation system is independent of the rate of loading.

In all other cases, a dynamic analysis is required. A response spectrum analysis can be used in the following cases:

- The structure is located on a soil type A, B, C or D.

- The effective stiffness of the isolation system at the design displacement is greater than 1/3 of the effective stiffness at 20% of the design displacement.

- The isolation system is independent of the rate of loading.

Furthermore, a site-specific response spectrum must be used when the structure is located on a soil type E or F or when the design spectral acceleration at a period of 1.0 s is greater than 0.6 g for the site.

For all other cases, a time-history dynamic analysis is required.

9.3.2 Design Based on Static Analysis

The static analysis formulas providing displacements and forces are based on a constant velocity response spectrum over the period range 1.0 to 3.0 s. The value of the constant velocity spectrum S_V can be written as:

$$S_V = \frac{gS_{D1}}{2\pi} \qquad (9.57)$$

where S_{D1} is the design 5% damped spectral acceleration (as a ratio of g) at a 1.0 s period and g is the acceleration of gravity in proper units. The displacement spectrum value S_D at the isolated period T_D is then given by:

$$S_D = \frac{gS_{D1}T_D}{4\pi^2} = \left(\frac{g}{4\pi^2}\right)S_{D1}T_D \qquad (9.58)$$

where g is in mm/s^2 when S_D is in mm, and in inches/s^2 when S_D is in inches.

The spectrum is then modified by a damping reduction factor B_D to take into account the effective damping of the isolation system at the design displacement. Therefore, the design displacement D_D at the center of rigidity of the isolation system under the Design-Basis Earthquake (DBE), is the starting point of the design process:

$$D_D = \left(\frac{g}{4\pi^2}\right)\frac{S_{D1}T_D}{B_D} \qquad (9.59)$$

Note that the DBE is associated with a probability of exceedence of 10% in 50 years. The effective damping ratio ξ in the isolation system is obtained from:

$$\xi = \left(\frac{1}{2\pi}\right)\frac{\text{Total area in hysteresis loop}}{k_{D\max}D_D^2} \qquad (9.60)$$

where $k_{D\max}$ is the maximum value of the effective secant stiffness $k_{D\text{eff}}$ at a displacement D_D, as determined by testing.

The damping reduction factor B_D is given in terms of ξ in Table 9-1, with a linear interpolation suggested for intermediate values. A very close approximation to the tabulated values can be obtained from:

$$B_D = \left(\frac{4}{1-\ln\xi}\right) \qquad (9.61)$$

The isolated period at the design displacement T_D to be used in Equation (9.59) is computed from:

$$T_D = 2\pi\sqrt{\frac{W}{k_{D\min}\,g}} \qquad (9.62)$$

where:

- W is the seismic weight of the building.

- $k_{D\text{eff}} = (F_D^+ - F_D^-)/(D_D^+ - D_D^-)$ is the effective secant stiffness of the isolation system at a displacement D_D as determined by testing.

- $k_{D\min}$ is the minimum value of $k_{D\text{eff}}$ at a displacement D_D.

Figure 9.6 illustrates the upper bound and lower bound cycles of response of an isolator under cyclic testing that are used to obtain the values of $k_{D\min}$ and $k_{D\max}$. The terms F_D^+, F_D^-, D_D^+ and D_D^- are the maximum and minimum forces and displacements on the prototype bearings used to determine the mechanical characteristics of the isolation system. Usually, the designer does not know these values during the preliminary design phase. The design procedure will begin with an assumed value of $k_{D\text{eff}}$, which is obtained from previous tests on similar components or by use of material characteristics, and a schematic of the proposed isolator.

Table 9-1 : Damping Reduction Factors, B_D

ξ	B_D	$\dfrac{4}{(1 - \ln\xi)}$
< 0.02	0.8	0.81
0.05	1.0	1.00
0.10	1.2	1.21
0.20	1.5	1.53
0.30	1.7	1.81
0.40	1.9	2.09
≥ 0.50	2.0	2.40

After the preliminary design is completed, prototype isolators will be constructed and tested, and the values of $k_{D\min}$ and $k_{D\max}$ will be obtained from the results of the prescribed program. The results of the prototype tests are then used to refine the preliminary design and, when dynamic analysis is used, they are needed to establish bounds on the various design quantities.

Note that because the effective stiffness and the effective damping are usually dependent on the displacement, the process of computing T_D and B_D is an iterative one.

The IBC and NEHRP Guidelines also require the designer to compute the total design displacement D_{TD} equal to the displacement of a bearing at a corner location of the structure, including the effects of torsion.

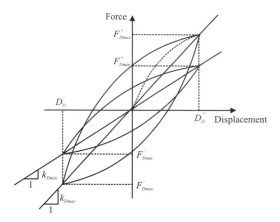

Figure 9.6 Determination of $k_{D\min}$ and $k_{D\max}$ from Testing

This total design displacement, which is obtained by amplifying the displacement at the center of stiffness D_D of the building, cannot be less than:

$$D_{TD} = D_D\left[1 + y\left(\frac{12e}{b^2 + d^2}\right)\right] \tag{9.63}$$

where e is the actual eccentricity plus 5% accidental eccentricity and y is the distance to a corner measured perpendicular to the direction of seismic loading. Equation (9.63) is based on the assumption that the seismic load $k_{Deff} D_D$ is applied through the center of mass, which is located at a distance e from the center of stiffness, as shown in Figure 9.7.

If rectangular plan dimensions b x d and a uniform distribution of isolators are assumed, the global torsional stiffness of the isolation system is $k_{Deff} (b^2 + d^2)/12$, and the torsional rotation θ is therefore given by:

$$\theta = \frac{k_{Deff} D_D e}{k_{Deff} (b^2 + d^2)/12} = \frac{12 D_D e}{b^2 + d^2} \tag{9.64}$$

The additional displacement due to the torsional rotation is obtained by multiplying θ by y. If the actual torsional stiffness of the system is computed and the additional displacement due to the force $k_{Deff} D_D$ through e turns out to be less than the value given by Equation (9.63), then this value can be used but it must be at least $1.1 D_D$.

The IBC and NEHRP Guidelines also require the calculation of the maximum displacement D_M at the center of stiffness of the isolation system under the Maximum Credible Earthquake (MCE). The MCE is associated with a lower probability of exceedence than the DBE, such as 2% in 50 years. The maximum displacement D_M is obtained by using the expression given in Equation (9.59) adapted to the seismic hazard associated with the MCE:

$$D_M = \left(\frac{g}{4\pi^2}\right)\frac{S_{M1} T_M}{B_D} \tag{9.65}$$

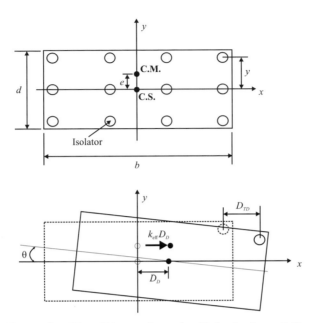

Figure 9.7 Plan Dimensions for Calculation of D_{TD}

where S_{M1} is the 5% damped spectral acceleration at a 1-second period for the MCE. The isolated period at the maximum displacement T_M to be used in Equation (9.65) is computed from:

$$T_M = 2\pi \sqrt{\frac{W}{k_{Mmin}\, g}} \qquad (9.66)$$

where k_{Mmin} is the minimum value of the isolation system stiffness k_{Meff} at a displacement D_M (see Figure 9.6).

Additionally, the total maximum displacement D_{TM} is required for verification of the stability of the isolation system and is obtained using the expression presented in Equation (9.63) but for the seismic hazard corresponding to the MCE. This total maximum displacement cannot be taken as less than:

$$D_{IM} = D_M\left[1 + y\left(\frac{12e}{b^2 + d^2}\right)\right] \qquad (9.67)$$

The design force for which the isolation system and the elements below the isolation system must be designed for V_b is given by:

$$V_b = k_{D\max}D_D \qquad (9.68)$$

The superstructure and structural elements above the isolation system must be designed for the following base shear force V_s given by:

$$V_s = \frac{k_{D\max}D_D}{R_I} \qquad (9.69)$$

The design force reduction factor R_I ranges from 1.0 to 2.0 and shall be taken as 3/8 of the force reduction factor R which would have been used if the structure were founded on a fixed base.

In all cases, the values of V_s should not be less than:

- The seismic force required by the IBC provisions for a fixed-base structure of the same weight W but with a period T_D.

- The base shear corresponding to the factored design wind load.

- The lateral seismic force required to activate the isolation system (e.g. the yield level of a softening system, the ultimate capacity of a sacrificial wind-restraint system, or the break-away friction level of a sliding system factored by 1.5).

The R_I factor for a base isolated structure is much lower than the R factor for the equivalent fixed base structure for a number of reasons. In fixed-base design, several factors lead to the values of R. One major element is the period shift. As the structure yields, the period lengthens and the force demand is reduced. Simultaneously, the damping in the structure is increased because of hysteretic action due to yielding of other elements. In the case of an isolated structure, only overstrength and redundancy are applicable. Period shift in the superstructure counters the effectiveness of the isolation system because it decreases the separation between the fixed base period and the isolated period and could attract larger forces to the structure and more participation from higher modes. In addition, as a consequence of this, the damping in the isolated structure will not be as high as in the fixed base structure.

In early seismic design provisions for base isolated buildings, the vertical distribution of the inertial forces on the structural system was based on the assumption that the participation of the higher modes was negligible and that the accelerations were roughly the same at all levels of the structure. There were some concerns, however, that this might not be sufficiently conservative, and the vertical distribution was changed to one where the lateral force at level i denoted by F_i, is computed from the base shear V_s by:

$$F_i = V_s \frac{h_i w_i}{\sum_{i=1}^{N} w_j h_j} \qquad (9.70)$$

where w_i and w_j are the weights at level i or j and h_i and h_j are the respective heights of the structure above the isolation level.

Equation (9.70) leads to a triangular distribution of force. While the basic theory would indicate that the distribution should be close to a uniform one, a triangular distribution is specified to account for higher mode contributions generated by nonlinearities in the isolation system due, for example, to lead plugs in elastomeric bearings or the effects of friction in sliding bearings.

The maximum interstorey drift limits for isolated buildings are also more severe that the limits for fixed base buildings and should not exceed 1.5% of the storey height.

9.3.3 Design Based on Dynamic Analysis

When a dynamic analysis (spectrum or time-history) is performed, it is possible to obtain design displacements and forces that are less than those given by the equivalent static analysis procedure. As summarized in Table 9-2, these values cannot be lower than a fraction of the values obtained by the equivalent static analysis procedure. If the dynamic analysis yields results that are lower than the values presented in Table 9-2, results from the dynamic analysis must be scaled up to these values.

Furthermore, when a dynamic analysis is performed, D_{TD} and D_{TM} can be calculated by Equations (9.63) and (9.67). The values of D_D and D_M in these equations can be replaced by D'_D and D'_M respectively and given by:

$$D'_D = \frac{D_D}{\sqrt{1 + \left(\dfrac{T}{T_D}\right)^2}} \qquad D'_M = \frac{D_M}{\sqrt{1 + \left(\dfrac{T}{T_M}\right)^2}} \qquad (9.71)$$

where T is the elastic period of the fixed base superstructure computed using the empirical formulas suggested by the code.

Table 9-2 : Design Displacements and Forces when Dynamic Analysis is Used

Value	Response Spectrum Analysis	Time-History Analysis
D_{TD}	$\geq 0.90 D_{DT\text{Static}}$	$\geq 0.90 D_{DT\text{Static}}$
D_{TM}	$\geq 0.80 D_{DT\text{Static}}$	$\geq 0.80 D_{DT\text{Static}}$
V_b	$\geq 0.90 V_{b\text{Static}}$	$\geq 0.90 V_{b\text{Static}}$
V_s	$\geq 0.80 V_{b\text{Static}}$	$\geq 0.80 V_{b\text{Static}}$
Interstorey Drift	1.5% of storey height	2.0% of storey height

This further reduction in displacements is to allow for the flexibility of the superstructure. The static formulas (Equations (9.63) and (9.67)) assume that the superstructure is rigid. If some deformation takes place in the superstructure, the displacement in the isolation system is reduced.

Pairs of horizontal components from at least three recorded seismic events are necessary for a time-history analysis. The events must be representative of the site, soil, and source characteristics and have durations consistent with the DBE or MCE. Time histories developed for a site within 15 km from a major active fault are required to incorporate near-fault characteristics (although the code does not provide additional information as to what this means).

For each ground motion pair, the SRSS of the 5% damped spectrum are computed. The motions are then scaled so that the average SRSS spectrum does not fall below 1.3 times the target spectrum for the DBE or MCE by more than 10% over $T_D - 1\,\text{s}$ and $T_D + 1\,\text{s}$.

When dynamic analysis is used, the design values are calculated in the following way:

- If three time-histories are used, the design must be based on the maximum response quantities determined from the analyses.

- If seven time-histories are used, the design can be based on the mean response quantities determined from the analyses.

9.3.4 Design Review and Testing

Because the design of seismic isolation systems is evolving rapidly and the consequences of failure of a base isolated structure can be catastrophic, the IBC and NEHRP provisions require that a design review of the isolation system and related testing program be conducted by an independent team of design professionals familiar with base isolation technology.

The testing program required by the IBC and NEHRP provisions aims to verify the deformation and damping characteristics of the base isolation used in the design. The testing program is conducted on two full-size specimens of each type of isolator used in the structure, including the wind restraint system. The prototype specimens tested are not used in the actual design. Readers are referred to Chapter 13 of the NEHRP provisions (BSSC 2003) for details of the testing program and acceptance criteria (see also section 4.53 of this book).

9.4 DESIGN CONSIDERATIONS FOR SEISMICALLY ISOLATED BRIDGES

As discussed previously for seismically isolated buildings, base isolation in bridges consists of separating the deck, which accounts for the largest portion of the mass, from the piers that must transmit lateral loads induced by seismic loads to the foundations. Isolators are usually positioned at the top of the piers or bents with the deck supported directly above. This configuration reduces the overturning moment that would be applied to the isolation devices if they were positioned at the base of the piers, and reduces the flexibility of the superstructure that is isolated, making the isolation more effective. Furthermore, the separation of the superstructure from the supporting structural elements below can be very beneficial, since it eliminates large moments that would otherwise be transmitted to the superstructure if it was rigidly connected or if transverse motion is restrained by shear keys. This also simplifies the design of the superstructure that can be designed as a simply supported (or continuous over simple supports) beam or slab-on-beam.

However, the flexibility of the substructure must be taken into account in the design and analysis of an isolated bridge. The design goal in an isolated bridge is to limit or eliminate inelastic action in main structural elements and to concentrate the system's lateral displacements under seismic loads at the isolator level. Concentrating most of the seismic displacement demand at this level presents significant advantages over traditional construction, as it reduces or eliminates ductility demand in the superstructure and substructure, but also allows for rapid inspection and repair following an earthquake, since the isolated portion of a bridge is usually well accessible. If the isolation system is not adequately designed however, the substructure can be subjected to excessive inelastic action during an earthquake, despite the presence of the isolation bearings. It may be desirable to design the isolated bridge structure to completely protect the substructure from inelastic action under a design level earthquake but to allow for controlled inelastic action under a maximum credible seismic event. This implies proper detailing for ductile response in critical regions that are expected to form plastic hinges (Priestley et al. 1996). Figure 9.8 illustrates the typical location of isolation bearings in bridges as well as the deformed shape at peak seismic response. The deformation of the substructure as well as the base rocking motion that may be significant during seismic response must also be considered.

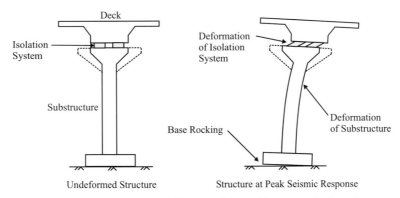

Undeformed Structure   Structure at Peak Seismic Response

Figure 9.8 Effective Lateral Stiffness of Combined Isolation System and Substructure

Considering the level of uncertainty associated with the definition of seismic hazard and, consequently, that the bridge may experience a much larger event than the one considered in design in its life span, design details to provide a collapse prevention safeguard can also be incorporated. As illustrated in Figure 9.8 with a dashed line, one such measure consists of designing for a much larger pier head. In the event of an extreme seismic event, where the isolators would exceed their deformation capacity and fail, the increased area of the top of the pier would allow the deck to be supported and to avoid a catastrophic failure. Another option consists of adding stoppers, such as shear keys that prevent the deck from moving beyond the displacement capacity of the isolators. These shear keys can be constructed on the pier or added to the deck.

9.4.1 Codified Design Methods

Several hundreds of bridges in New Zealand, Japan, Italy, Greece and the United States have been designed using seismic isolation principles and technology (see Appendix D). In this section, the main features of the design provisions for seismically isolated bridges contained in the MCEER/ATC-49 Recommended LRFD Guidelines for the Seismic Design of Highway Bridges (ATC/MCEER 2003a, 2003b) are reviewed. These design provisions are supplemental to the recommendations published by the American Association of State Highway and Transportation Officials (AASHTO 1998).

The design procedures contained in the MCEER/ATC-49 Guidelines are based on the equivalent linearization procedure described in Section 2.5. For this purpose, the energy dissipation of the isolation system is described in terms of equivalent viscous damping, and the stiffness of the isolation system is described as an effective linear stiffness at the design displacement.

For all seismic isolation designs, it is first necessary to determine an equivalent static design force for the superstructure above the isolation system. The statically equivalent seismic design force V is given by:

$$V = C_d W \tag{9.72}$$

where W is the total vertical load for design of the isolation system (dead and live loads) and C_d is a seismic response demand coefficient given by:

$$C_d = \frac{k_{eff} \, \Delta}{W} = \frac{F_v \, S_1}{T_{eff} \, B_D} \tag{9.73}$$

where k_{eff} is the effective linear stiffness of the base isolation system and substructure supporting the superstructure at the total deck design displacement Δ at the center of rigidity of the isolation system, F_v is the site soil coefficient given in Article 3.4.2 of the MCEER/ATC-49 Guidelines, S_1 is the one-second period spectral acceleration given in Article 3.10.2.1 of the MCEER/ATC-49 Guidelines, T_{eff} is the effective period of the isolation system at the design displacement Δ, and B_D is the same damping reduction factor given by Equation (9.61) and Table 9-1.

The effective period of the isolation system in Equation (9.73) is given by:

$$T_{eff} = 2\pi \sqrt{\frac{W}{k_{eff} \, g}} \tag{9.74}$$

Substituting Equation (9.74) into Equation (9.73) yields an expression for the total deck displacement Δ (in meters):

$$\Delta = \frac{0.25 F_v S_1}{T_{eff} \, B_D} \tag{9.75}$$

Note that in calculating the effective stiffness k_{eff}, both the effective stiffness of the isolation system and of the substructure supporting the isolators must be considered.

$$k_{eff} = \frac{k_{sub}\, k_{iso}}{k_{sub} + k_{iso}} \qquad (9.76)$$

where k_{iso} is the effective lateral stiffness of the isolation system at the design isolation displacement Δ_i (as illustrated in Figure 9.9) and k_{sub} is the effective lateral stiffness of the substructure at the corresponding substructure displacement Δ_{sub}.

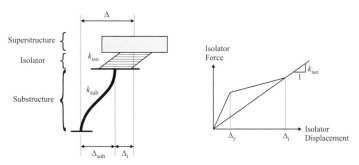

Figure 9.9 Effective Lateral Stiffness of Combined Isolation System and Substructure

Depending on the complexity of the bridge, the design lateral force given by Equation (9.72) is distributed in each orthogonal direction as either a uniform load (single mode) or according to a spectral analysis (multi-mode) using a response spectrum scaled by the damping coefficient B_D. Alternatively, a nonlinear time-history dynamic analysis can be performed according to the same recommendations given in Section 9.3.3.

The design force V_A for the connections between the superstructure and substructure at each isolator i is given by:

$$V_A = k_{iso}^i\, \Delta_t^i \qquad (9.77)$$

where k_{iso}^i is the effective stiffness of the isolator at a displacement of Δ_t^i and Δ_t^i is the total design displacement of the isolation bearing only, including torsional effects (see Section 9.3.2).

9.4.2 Design Properties of Seismic Isolation Systems

The MCER/ATC-49 Guidelines require that bounding analyses be performed to determine the variations in design forces resulting from the minimum and maximum effective stiffness values and damping of the isolation system. For this purpose, the guidelines define a number of property modification factors λ that are established from characterization tests on prototype isolation bearings. These system property modification factors consider the variations in effective stiffness properties and damping of the isolation system from the following effects: temperature, aging (including corrosion), velocity, wear, contamination (sliding systems only) and scragging (elastomeric systems). A brief explanation of the concepts behind these property modification factors is given below. A more detailed presentation can be found in Constantinou et al. (1999).

(a) Concept of Property Modification Factor

Once a nominal value of a property P_n of a seismic isolation system has been established for the reference conditions (e.g. ambient temperature, fresh bearing conditions, reference normal loading, etc.), the maximum and minimum values of this property, P_{max} and P_{min}, can be established by multiplying the nominal value by a series of property modification factors, λ_{max} and λ_{min}, as follows:

$$P_{max} = \lambda_{max} P_n \text{ and } P_{min} = \lambda_{min} P_n \qquad (9.78)$$

where:

$$\lambda_{max} = \prod_i \lambda_{max\ i} \geq 1.0 \text{ and } \lambda_{min} = \prod_i \lambda_{min\ i} \leq 1.0 \qquad (9.79)$$

Constantinou et al. (1999) recognized that the values of P_{max} and P_{min} given by Equation (9.78) could be conservative because of the low probability that all extreme values of property modification factors occur simultaneously in a real earthquake situation. For this purpose, they recommended the use of adjusted property modification factors, $\lambda_{max\ adjusted}$ and $\lambda_{min\ adjusted}$, given by:

$$\lambda_{max\ adjusted} = 1 + (\lambda_{max} - 1)a \text{ and } \lambda_{min\ adjusted} = 1 + (1 - \lambda_{min})a \qquad (9.80)$$

where a is an adjustment factor that depends on the importance of the bridge under consideration. Constantinou et al. (1999) recommended values of $a = 1$ for critical bridges, $a = 0.75$ for essential bridges and 0.66 for all other bridges.

(b) Property Modification Factors for Coefficient of Friction of Sliding Bearings

The maximum and minimum values of the coefficient of friction of sliding bearings, μ_{max} and μ_{min}, can be established from the nominal value of the coefficient of friction, μ_n, as follows:

$$\mu_{max} = \lambda_{max\ a} \lambda_{max\ c} \lambda_{max\ w} \lambda_{max\ t} \mu_n$$
$$\mu_{min} = \mu_n \qquad (9.81)$$

where $\lambda_{max\ a}$, $\lambda_{max\ c}$, $\lambda_{max\ w}$ and $\lambda_{max\ t}$ are the property modification factors for aging, contamination, wear, and temperature, respectively. Values of these property modification factors, as recommended by Constantinou et al. (1999), are given in Tables 9-3 to 9-6, respectively.

Table 9-3 : Property Modification Factors for Effects of Aging on the Coefficient of Friction of Sliding Bearings (after Constantinou et al. 1999)

	$\lambda_{max\,a}$					
	Unlubricated PTFE-Stainless Steel		Lubricated PTFE-Stainless Steel		Bimetallic Interfaces	
Environmental Conditions	Sealed	Unsealed	Sealed	Unsealed	Sealed	Unsealed
Normal	1.1	1.2	1.3	1.4	2.0	2.2
Severe	1.2	1.5	1.4	1.8	2.2	2.5

Table 9-4 : Property Modification Factors for Effects of Contamination on the Coefficient of Friction of Sliding Bearings (after Constantinou et al. 1999)

	$\lambda_{max\,c}$		
Installation Procedure	Unlubricated PTFE-Stainless Steel	Lubricated PTFE-Stainless Steel	Bimetallic Interfaces
Sealed with Stainless Steel Surface Facing Down	1.0	1.0	1.0
Sealed with Stainless Steel Surface Facing Up, Bearing Galvanized of Painting for 30 Years	1.0	1.0	1.0
Sealed with Stainless Steel Surface Facing Up	1.1	1.1	1.1
Sealed with Stainless Steel Surface Facing Down	1.1	3.0	1.1

Table 9-5 : Property Modification Factors for Effects of Wear on the Coefficient of Friction of Sliding Bearings (after Constantinou et al. 1999)

	$\lambda_{max\,w}$		
Cumulative Sliding (m)	Unlubricated PTFE-Stainless Steel	Lubricated PTFE-Stainless Steel	Bimetallic Interfaces
0 - 1000	1.0	1.0	Unknown
1000 - 2000	1.2	1.0	Unknown

Table 9-6 : Property Modification Factors for Effects of Temperature on the Coefficient of Friction of Sliding Bearings (after Constantinou et al. 1999)

| Temperature (°C) | $\lambda_{max\,t}$ | | |
	Unlubricated PTFE-Stainless Steel	Lubricated PTFE-Stainless Steel	Bimetallic Interfaces
20	1.0	1.0	
0	1.1	1.3	
-10	1.2	1.5	Unknown
-30	1.5	3.0	
-40	1.7	Unknown	
-50	2.0	Unknown	

(c) Property Modification Factors for Elastomeric Bearings

The maximum and minimum values of the properties of elastomeric bearings can be established from the nominal values of the properties as follows:

$$P_{max} = \lambda_{max\,a}\,\lambda_{max\,s}\,\lambda_{max\,t}\,P_n$$
$$P_{min} = P_n$$

(9.82)

where $\lambda_{max\,a}$ $\lambda_{max\,s}$ and $\lambda_{max\,t}$ are the property modification factors for aging, scragging, and temperature, respectively. Values of these property modification factors, as recommended by Constantinou et al. (1999), are given in Tables 9-7 to 9-9, respectively.

Table 9-7 : Property Modification Factors for Effects of Aging on the Properties of Elastomeric Bearings (after Constantinou et al. 1999)

| Rubber Type | $\lambda_{max\,a}$ | |
	Factor for Post-Yield Stiffness	Factor for Strength
Low Damping	1.1	1.0
High Damping with Small Differences between Unscragged and Scragged Properties	1.2	1.2
High Damping with Large Differences between Unscragged and Scragged Properties	1.3	1.3

Table 9-8 : Property Modification Factors for Effects of Scragging on the Properties of Elastomeric Bearings (after Constantinou et al. 1999)

Rubber Type	$\lambda_{max\ s}$	
	Factor for Post-Yield Stiffness	Factor for Strength
Low Damping	1.0	1.0
High Damping ($\xi \leq 0.15$)	1.2	1.2
High Damping ($\xi > 0.15$)	1.8	1.5

Table 9-9 : Property Modification Factors for Effects of Temperature on the Properties of Elastomeric Bearings (after Constantinou et al. 1999)

Temperature (^{o}C)	$\lambda_{max\ t}$			
	Factor for Post-Yield Stiffness		Lubricated PTFE-Stainless Steel	
	Lead-Rubber Bearings	High Damping Rubber Bearings	Lead-Rubber Bearings	High Damping Rubber Bearings
20	1.0	1.0	1.0	1.0
0	1.1	1.2	1.2	1.2
-10	1.1	1.4	1.4	1.4
-30	1.3	2.0	1.8	2.3

9.4.3 Minimum Clearances

The clearances between the base isolated deck of a bridge and the surrounding substructure in each orthogonal direction should be at least equal to the maximum total displacement of the deck obtained from analysis. However, to guard against analysis procedures that could produce very small clearances, the MCEER/ATC-49 Guidelines provide the following minimum clearances in each orthogonal direction Δ_{cmin} in units of meter:

$$\Delta_{cmin} = \frac{0.20F_v S_1 T_{eff}}{B_D} \tag{9.83}$$

where all the variables in the equation have been previously defined.

9.4.4 Required Testing Program for Isolation Bearings

The MCEER/ATC-49 Guidelines require that all isolation systems have their design properties and seismic performance verified by testing. Three different types of tests are required: i) system characterization tests, ii) prototype tests and iii) quality control tests. Note that particular seismic isolation systems that have previously undergone a similar testing program do not need to be re-tested. In this case, design properties of the isolation system must be based on pre-approved certified test data from the manufacturer of the isolation system.

The objective of the system characterization tests is to determine the fundamental properties of a new isolation system. These tests are usually not project-specific. The system characterization tests include, as a minimum, cyclic tests on individual isolator units and large-scale shake table tests. The objective of the prototype tests is to validate the design properties of the isolation system used in a particular project. These tests shall be performed on at least two full-size isolator units that can be used in construction. The details of the prototype test programs can be found in the MCEER/ATC-49 Guidelines (ATC/MCEER 2003a, 2003b). Finally, short compression and cyclic shear quality control tests shall be conducted on all isolation units to be used for construction (ATC/MCEER 2003a, 2003b).

9.5 PROBLEMS

Problem 9.1

The relative displacement response spectra computed for one ground motion recorded during the 1995 Kobe, Japan Earthquake are shown in Figure 9.10 for different viscous damping ratios.

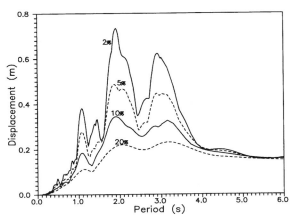

Figure 9.10 Relative Displacement Response Spectra, 1995 Kobe Earthquake

The portal frame shown in Figure 9.11a supports an expensive satellite transmission unit. This unit is extremely sensitive to accelerations. System identification tests on the frame indicate a viscous damping ratio of 2% of critical.

a) If this structure was subjected to the Kobe earthquake and remained in the elastic range, what would be the maximum base shear V_b and the maximum moment in each of the columns M_c?

b) What is the maximum acceleration felt by the satellite transmitter?

To protect the transmitter, a base isolation system made of circular laminated rubber bearings is considered. Figure 9.11b illustrates the base isolated structure. The global lateral stiffness provided by all the base isolators is $GA = 5$ kN, where G is the shear modulus of the laminated rubber and A is the area of the bearings.

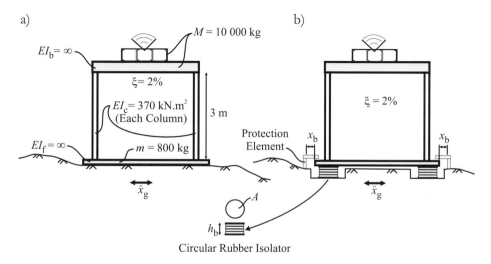

Figure 9.11 Portal Frame Supporting a Satellite Transmission Unit

c) Assuming that the damping in the first mode of the isolated structure increases to 5% of critical, determine the required height of rubber h_b of each bearing to ensure that the maximum acceleration felt by the transmitter is equal to 0.05g under the Kobe earthquake. Base your calculations on the assumption that the base isolated portal frame behaves as a single degree-of-freedom system.

d) Estimate the maximum base shear V_b felt by each column of the isolated portal frame.

e) Estimate the distance x_b at which the protection elements limiting the displacement across the bearings should be positioned. Why are these protection elements important?

f) One engineer on the team suggests to further protect the transmitter by increasing the damping of the base isolated frame to 10% of critical. What is your opinion about this suggestion?

CHAPTER 10: SEISMIC ISOLATION SYSTEMS

10.1 INTRODUCTION

This chapter presents an overview of various isolator components that have been developed, successfully tested in the laboratory and implemented in actual buildings and/ or bridges. This chapter emphasizes two main types of systems that have been widely used in the last fifteen years, namely the laminated-rubber bearing systems and the friction pendulum system. An overview of other systems as well as of recent developments in isolation hardware is also presented.

10.2 LAMINATED-RUBBER BEARINGS

Laminated-rubber bearings (elastomeric bearings) have been used extensively for bridge superstructures to accommodate temperature-induced movements and deformations. In the last fifteen years, the use of these bearings has been extended to the seismic isolation of buildings and other structures. One of the base isolation systems that is the most highly developed is the lead-rubber (lead-plug) bearing. This system, discussed in the next section, is composed of an elastomeric bearing incorporating a central lead plug designed to yield under lateral deformation and to dissipate supplemental energy.

Laminated-rubber bearings can withstand large gravity loads, while providing only a fraction of the lateral stiffness of the superstructure they support. As shown in Figure 10.1, a typical laminated-rubber bearing is composed of elastomeric rubber layers alternating with steel plates solidly joined together under high pressure and temperature through a process called vulcanization.

By alternating steel and rubber layers, the gravity load resisting capacity of laminated-rubber bearings is increased by reducing the thickness of individual rubber layers. Although the lateral stiffness of the laminated-rubber bearing is solely linked to the height and the area of the rubber in the unit, the vertical stiffness of the bearing is greatly enhanced by the presence of the steel plates. The steel plates provide confinement and impede the bulging deformation of the rubber as it is compressed. The layers of steel plates improve the stability of taller bearings under lateral loads.

The key parameters in the design of laminated-rubber bearings are the gravity load carrying capacity, the lateral stiffness and the maximum achievable relative displacement between the top and the base of the bearing. The gravity load carrying capacity must be designed such that the bearings are not overloaded under gravity loads and vertical loads

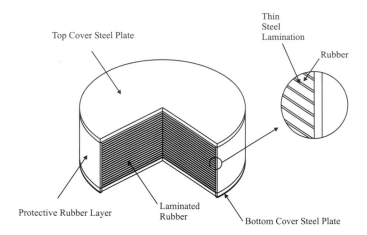

Figure 10.1 Schematic of Laminated-Rubber Bearing

induced by the lateral response of the superstructure. The lateral stiffness of the bearings directly influences the natural period of the isolated structure. The maximum acceptable relative displacement is limited by the allowable strain in the rubber or the overall stability of the bearing.

A disadvantage of laminated-rubber bearings is the relatively low damping provided by the rubber. More recently, high damping rubbers have been suggested for laminated rubber bearings and have been used in Japan (Pan et al. 2004). Laminated bearings made from high damping rubber have been shown to display significantly more energy dissipation than those fabricated with low damping rubbers, reaching values of equivalent viscous damping of approximately 20% at shear strains of 300%. However, high damping rubber is more susceptible to heat-related property changes during cyclic loading and to aging effects influencing stiffness and energy dissipation capacity (Pan et al. 2004). This increases the complexity related to predicting short and long term properties and to defining appropriate bounds on bearing properties for bounded analyses. A recent study by Grant et al. (2005) has proposed a strain-rate independent phenomenological model to capture the bidirectional response of laminated bearings made of high damping rubber.

Isolator damping can also be increased by external components such as lead plugs inserted in the center of the bearing. Lead-rubber bearings will be discussed in the next section. Furthermore, supplemental damping can be provided to a system isolated with laminated-rubber bearings through external supplemental damping devices such as hysteretic or viscous dampers that were discussed in earlier chapters.

10.2.1 Gravity Load Carrying Capacity of Laminated-Rubber Bearings

Consider a laminated-rubber bearing consisting of n equal rubber layers of any compact shape. If the top of the bearing is displaced an amount x_b relative to its base, as shown in Figure 10.2. The deformed shape of the bearing produces an "overlap area" A' between the top and the bottom of the bearing.

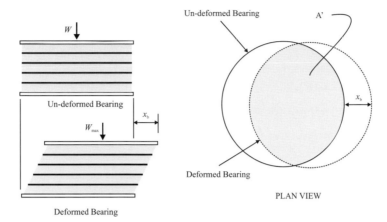

Figure 10.2 Circular Laminated-Rubber Bearing Under Gravity and Lateral Loads

The maximum allowable vertical load that can be carried by a bearing W_{max} can be approximated by the following semi-empirical equation:

$$W_{max} = A'G_rS\gamma_w \tag{10.1}$$

where:

- A' is the overlap area between the displaced top and bottom faces of the bearing (see Figure 10.2);

- G_r is the shear modulus of rubber $\approx$ 0.5 to 1 MPa;

- S is the shape factor of each rubber layer, equal to the loaded area of the bearing divided by the load-free area of the bearing;

- γ_w is the allowable shear strain under gravity load.

Equation (10.1) is obtained from the theory of elasticity by considering a single layer of rubber sandwiched between two steel plates. It is assumed that the rubber is fully constrained laterally at its interfaces with the steel plates. The shear stress developed at the interface of the steel and the rubber τ_s is given by:

$$\tau_s = \frac{W}{6A'S} \tag{10.2}$$

The shape factor for a cylindrical bearing of diameter D and made of rubber layers of thickness t_r is given by:

$$S = \frac{\text{loaded area}}{\text{load free area}} = \frac{(\pi D^2)/4}{\pi D t_r} = \frac{D}{4t_r} \tag{10.3}$$

The shape factor for a rectangular bearing of sides b x d and made of rubber layers of thickness t_r is given by:

$$S = \frac{\text{loaded area}}{\text{load free area}} = \frac{bd}{2t_r(b+d)} \qquad (10.4)$$

The allowable shear strain to be used in Equation (10.1) can be estimated as a ratio of the short-term failure strain of the rubber in pure tension ε_v such as:

$$\gamma_w \approx 0.2\varepsilon_v$$

$$\gamma_w \approx 0.4\varepsilon_v \text{ for design base earthquakes} \qquad (10.5)$$

$$\gamma_w \approx 0.7\varepsilon_v \text{ for maximum credible earthquakes}$$

10.2.2 Lateral Stiffness of Laminated-Rubber Bearings

The steel plates vulcanized to the rubber layers limit severely the flexural deformations of a laminated-rubber bearing. Therefore, it can be assumed that pure shear deformations occur in the rubber only. The lateral stiffness of a laminated-rubber bearing k_b can be approximated as:

$$k_b = \frac{G_r A_r}{h_r} \qquad (10.6)$$

where G_r is the shear modulus of rubber, A_r is the rubber layer area and h_r is the total rubber height.

Note that Equation (10.6) neglects the reduction in lateral stiffness at large displacements. For shape factors S in the order of 10 to 20, this reduction is small and can be neglected.

10.2.3 Natural Period of Vibration of Laminated-Rubber Bearings Supporting a Rigid Structure

Assuming that the superstructure supported by laminated-rubber bearings is rigid, the period of vibration of the bearings T_b is given by:

$$T_b = 2\pi \sqrt{\frac{W_{tot}}{g k_{b\,tot}}} \qquad (10.7)$$

where W_{tot} is the total weight of the superstructure and $k_{b\,tot}$ is the total lateral stiffness of all bearings obtained by summing the individual lateral stiffness of each bearing.

Equation (10.7) can also be written for each bearing of lateral stiffness k_b supporting a portion of the superstructure's weight W_b:

$$T_b = 2\pi \sqrt{\frac{W_b}{g k_b}} \qquad (10.8)$$

10.2.4 Damping Provided by Laminated-Rubber Bearings

Experiments have shown that the energy dissipation through shear deformations in rubber layers of laminated-rubber bearings is proportional to velocity. Therefore, damping in laminated-rubber bearings can be modeled by equivalent viscous damping. Typical bearings used in bridges provide equivalent viscous damping of the order of 5% to 10% of critical. High damping rubbers are now available for bearing applications that can produce viscous damping up to 25% of critical.

10.2.5 Vertical Stiffness of Laminated-Rubber Bearings

The vertical stiffness of a laminated-rubber bearing is much larger than its lateral stiffness. In some applications, however, the vertical deflection of laminated rubber bearings may be important, and the associated vertical stiffness must be known.

The total vertical stiffness of a laminated-rubber bearing k_v is the sum in series of the vertical stiffness due to the rubber shear strain without volume change $k_{v\gamma}$ and the vertical stiffness caused by the volume change of the rubber without shear k_{vV}.

$$k_v = \frac{k_{v\gamma}\, k_{vV}}{k_{v\gamma} + k_{vV}} \tag{10.9}$$

It can be shown (Skinner et al. 1993) that the condition of no volume change yields the following expression for $k_{v\gamma}$:

$$k_{v\gamma} = \frac{6 G_r S^2 A_r}{h_r} \tag{10.10}$$

while k_{vV} is given by:

$$k_{vV} = \frac{\kappa_r A_r}{h_r} \tag{10.11}$$

where κ_r is the compression modulus of the rubber ($\kappa_r \approx 2000$ MPa for typical rubber).

10.2.6 Allowable Lateral Displacement of Laminated-Rubber Bearings

The allowable lateral displacement of a laminated-rubber bearing $x_{b\ all}$ is directly related to the allowable seismic shear strain γ_s:

$$x_{b\ all} = h_r \gamma_s \tag{10.12}$$

In turn, the allowable seismic shear strain γ_s depends on how much shear strain is mobilized by the vertical load (see Equation (10.1)).

Another limit for the allowable seismic displacement $x_{b\ all}$ is the limit of the overlap factor A'/A_r. A lower limit for A'/A_r of about 0.6 is typically used for design basis earthquakes (DBE). The relationship between A'/A_r and $x_{b\ all}$ depends on the shape of the bearing. For a cylindrical bearing of area A_r and diameter D, we have:

$$\frac{A_r}{A'} = 1 - \frac{2}{\pi}(\theta + \sin\theta\cos\theta) \qquad (10.13)$$

where $\sin\theta = x_{b\;all}/D$. For moderate values of $x_{b\;all}/D$, Equation (10.13) can be rewritten as:

$$x_{b\;all} \approx 0.8D\left(1 - \frac{A'}{A_r}\right) \qquad (10.14)$$

Similarly, for a rectangular bearing of dimensions b x d:

$$\frac{A_r}{A'} \approx 1 - \frac{x_{bb}}{b} - \frac{x_{bd}}{d} \qquad (10.15)$$

where x_{bb} is the displacement parallel to the side of dimension b, and x_{bd} is the displacement parallel to the side of dimension d.

When the displacement may be in both directions, a conservative estimate of the displacement limit is obtained by:

$$x_{b\;all} \approx 0.8b\left(1 - \frac{A'}{A}\right) \qquad (10.16)$$

where b is the shorter side of the bearing.

From Equations (10.14) and (10.16), it can be seen that for an overlap factor $A'/A_r = 0.6$, the allowable seismic displacement of the bearing $x_{b\;all}$ is equal to $D/3$ and $b/3$ respectively.

10.3 LEAD-RUBBER BEARINGS

A lead-rubber bearing is composed of a laminated-rubber bearing with a cylindrical lead plug inserted in its center as shown in Figure 10.3. The lead plug is introduced to increase the damping by hysteretic shear deformations of the lead. The main reason why lead is chosen as the material for the central plug is that, at room temperature, lead behaves approximately as an elastic-plastic solid and yields in shear at relatively low stress of about 10 MPa (Skinner et al. 1993). Also, lead is hot-worked at room temperature. This means that the properties of lead are continuously restored when cycled in the inelastic range. Therefore, lead has very good fatigue resistance properties. Finally, another advantage of lead is that it is commonly available since it is used in batteries at a purity level of more than 99.9%.

10.3.1 Properties of Lead-Rubber Bearings

Figure 10.4 compares the force-displacement hysteresis loop of a 695-mm diameter laminated-rubber bearing with the one obtained with the same bearing incorporating a 170-mm lead plug inserted down its center. It can be seen that, before yielding of the lead

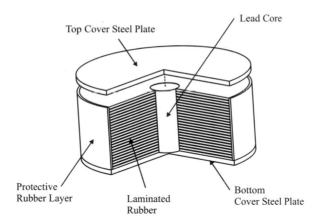

Figure 10.3 Schematic of a Lead-Rubber Bearing

plug, the lateral stiffness of the lead-rubber bearing is much larger than the lateral stiffness of the laminated-rubber bearing since both the lead and the rubber deform elastically. After yielding of the lead plug, however, the lateral stiffness of both bearings is equal to the elastic shear stiffness of the rubber alone.

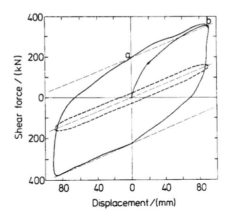

Figure 10.4 Force-Displacement Hysteresis Loops of a (dashed) Laminated-Rubber Bearing and a (solid) Lead-Rubber Bearing (from Robinson 1982, Copyright John Wiley & Sons Ltd., reproduced with permission)

10.3.2 Modelling of Lead-Rubber Bearings

A reasonable model of the hysteretic behaviour of a lead-rubber bearing is a bilinear solid with elastic stiffness k_1, a post-yield stiffness k_2 and a yield force F_y. The elastic stiffness k_1 can be obtained by:

$$k_1 \approx \frac{1}{h_r}(G_p A_p + G_r A_r) \tag{10.17}$$

where:

- h_r is the total rubber height

- A_p is the area of the lead plug

- A_r is the area of the rubber

- G_p is the shear modulus of lead $\approx$ 150 MPa at room temperature

- G_r is the shear modulus of rubber $\approx$ 0.5 to 1 MPa

The post-yield stiffness k_2 is equal to the lateral shear stiffness of the rubber k_b (see Equation (10.6)).

$$k_2 = k_b = \frac{G_r A_r}{h_r} \tag{10.18}$$

For practical size bearings, the lateral stiffness can be estimated as:

$$k_1 \approx 10 k_b \quad \text{and} \quad k_2 = k_b \tag{10.19}$$

The yield force F_y can be estimated by the shear force required to yield the lead plug plus the elastic force carried by the rubber at the corresponding yield displacement.

$$F_y = \tau_{py} A_p \left(1 + \frac{G_r A_r}{G_p A_p} \right) \tag{10.20}$$

where $\tau_{py} \approx 10$ MPa is the shear yield strength of the lead. For practical size bearings, Equation (10.20) can be simplified as:

$$F_y \approx \tau_{py} A_p \tag{10.21}$$

Figure 10.5 schematically illustrates the modelling of a lead-rubber bearing at the base of a superstructure.

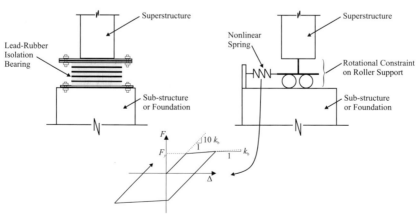

Figure 10.5 Modelling of a Lead-Rubber Bearing

10.4 FRICTION PENDULUM SYSTEM

10.4.1 General Description

The Friction Pendulum System (FPS), manufactured by Earthquake Protection Systems in Richmond California, is a friction-type sliding bearing that uses gravity as the restoring force. Figure 10.6 shows a sectional view of a FPS bearing and a photograph of a large spherical concave sliding surface. The system consists of an articulated friction slider that travels on a spherical concave lining surface.

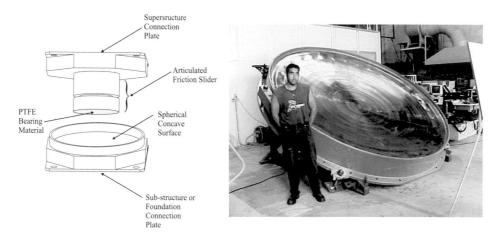

Figure 10.6 Friction Pendulum System

10.4.2 Properties of Frictionless Pendulum System

Consider a rigid structure of weight W supported by an FPS bearing being displaced horizontally by an amount Δ on the spherical concave surface of radius R, as illustrated in Figure 10.7. The horizontal force required to displace the bearing is F and the normal force at the interface is N. Note that it is assumed here that no friction resistance develops at the slider interface. In a real friction pendulum system where friction resistance does develop at the slider interface, F corresponds to the force in excess of the friction force required to initiate the movement.

By horizontal equilibrium, we have:
$$F = N\sin\theta \qquad (10.22)$$

By vertical equilibrium, we have:
$$W = N\cos\theta \qquad (10.23)$$

Substituting Equation (10.23) into Equation (10.22) yields:
$$F = W\tan\theta \qquad (10.24)$$

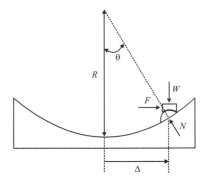

Figure 10.7 Principle of Operation of the Friction Pendulum System

By geometry:

$$\tan\theta = \frac{\Delta}{R} \tag{10.25}$$

Substituting Equation (10.25) into Equation (10.24) leads to a lateral force-displacement relationship for a sliding pendulum system:

$$F = \frac{W}{R}\Delta \tag{10.26}$$

Therefore the lateral stiffness of the Friction-Pendulum base-isolator $k = W/R$. The natural period T is therefore given by:

$$T = 2\pi\sqrt{\frac{W}{gk}} = 2\pi\sqrt{\frac{R}{g}} \tag{10.27}$$

where g is the acceleration of gravity.

Equation (10.27) indicates that the natural frequency of a rigid structure isolated with a frictionless pendulum system depends only on the radius of the bearings. This property presents a significant advantage of the FPS system since a target isolated period can be achieved independent of the mass of the superstructure.

10.4.3 Properties of Pendulum System Including Friction

In reality, friction forces are present at the sliding interface and must be overcome before the bearing can slide. Figure 10.8 shows a typical hysteresis response of a FPS bearing where a certain amount of friction is present at the sliding interface. The system is near rigid until this friction force is overcome. Then the force increase is proportional to the lateral stiffness of the FPS (see Equation (10.26)). The force required to overcome the initial friction is equal to μW where μ is the coefficient of friction of the sliding interface. Because of this initial breakaway friction, the effective stiffness of the isolator is dependent on the friction coefficient of the system μ and the maximum displacement of the isolator

D_{max}. This effective stiffness k_{eff}, which is larger than the one described in Equation (10.26), is given by:

$$k_{eff} = W\left(\frac{1}{R} + \frac{\mu}{D_{max}}\right) \qquad (10.28)$$

In Figure 10.9, an experimentally obtained hysteretic response of an FPS system is shown (Zayas et al. 1991).

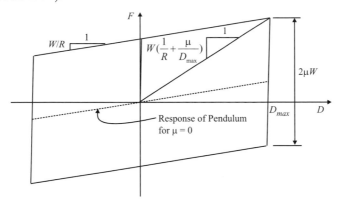

Figure 10.8 Hysteresis Loops of FPS System

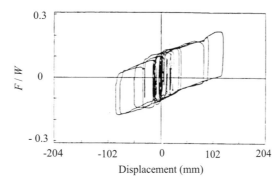

Figure 10.9 Experimental Response of FPS System (after Zayas et al. 1990)

10.4.4 Double Curvature Friction Pendulum Systems

The cost of isolation bearings increases substantially when larger displacement demands are needed. To address this issue as well as to reduce the dimensions of isolator bearings, the double concave friction pendulum has recently been proposed and validated (Constantinou 2004). The double concave friction pendulum system consists of a combination of two single friction pendulum systems. As illustrated in Figure 10.10, both the top and bottom plates are comprised of spherical concave sliding interfaces and joined by an articulated double friction slider.

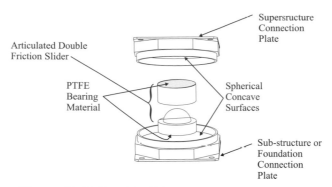

Figure 10.10 Double Friction Pendulum System

As illustrated in Figure 10.11 (Constantinou et al. 2004), sliding is possible on both the top and bottom plates. When the friction resistance is exceeded on the bottom surface, sliding is initiated there with the top surface remaining fixed and moving with the slider. Once the friction resistance of the top surface is reached, sliding is initiated on the top surface and the isolator can displace a total distance of $2d$. If both surfaces are designed

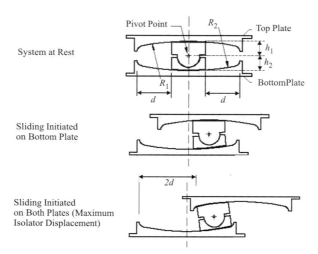

Figure 10.11 Mechanics of Double Friction Pendulum System (after Constantinou et al. 2004)

to display the same friction coefficient μ, and therefore slip simultaneously, the lateral force generated when the isolator is displaced by D (excluding the friction force) is given by:

$$F = \frac{W}{R_1 + R_2 - h_1 - h_2}D \tag{10.29}$$

and the friction force is given by:

$$F_f = \frac{\mu(R_1 - h_1)W + \mu(R_2 - h_2)W}{R_1 + R_2 - h_1 - h_2}$$

(10.30)

where the dimensions R_1, R_2, h_1 and h_2 are defined in Figure 10.11.

If all properties and dimensions of the top and bottom plates are equal, i.e. $R_1 = R_2$, $h_1 = h_2$, and the friction coefficient μ is the same on both surfaces, the double friction pendulum behaves exactly like a single friction pendulum. However, the double friction pendulum can displace an amount equal to $2d$ whereas the single friction pendulum could only accommodate a displacement of d. Figure 10.12 illustrates a double friction pendulum system at its maximum displaced configuration.

Figure 10.12 Double Friction Pendulum System at Maximum Sliding Displacement of Both Surfaces (courtesy of M. Constantinou)

When the two friction coefficients are chosen to be different, the hysteretic response of the double friction pendulum system is multi-linear with sliding occurring first on the surface with the lowest friction coefficient and then on the other surface (for more details see Constantinou 2004).

10.5 OTHER SEISMIC ISOLATION SYSTEMS

This section presents an overview of various isolator components (other than elastomeric bearings and Friction Pendulum Systems) that have been successfully implemented in buildings and bridges. Two types of components are discussed, namely metallic and lead-extrusion dampers. Note that these systems have been discussed previously within the context of hysteretic dissipation devices (See Chapter 5).

10.5.1 Seismic Isolation Systems Incorporating Metallic Dampers

Metallic dampers were already discussed in Chapter 5. Similar type dampers have been used as energy dissipating components for seismic isolation systems. The design procedures presented in Chapter 5 for structures equipped with hysteretic dampers can also be applied to structures isolated with metallic or friction dampers. Considering that structures with effective base isolation respond primarily as SDOF systems with the superstructure sitting atop the isolation as a rigid mass, the design procedures of Chapter 5 can be used to obtain optimal designs of the isolation system.

The development of steel-beam dampers for seismic isolation applications has taken place mainly in New Zealand in the 1970s (Kelly et al. 1972, Skinner et al. 1975, Tyler 1977, Cousins et al. 1991). Three types of steel hysteretic dampers have been developed and used in seismic isolation systems: the uniform-moment bending-beam damper, the tapered-cantilever bending-beam damper and the torsional-beam damper.

(a) The Uniform Moment Bending-Beam Damper

As shown in Figure 10.13, the steel-beam damper (also called Type-U damper) consists of two inclined transverse loading arms that apply pure bending to a solid circular steel beam. To avoid brittle fracture, the circular beam is welded to the transverse loading arms in low-stress regions.

Figure 10.13 Type-U Bending-Beam Steel Damper (from Skinner et al. 1993, Copyright John Wiley & Sons Ltd., reproduced with permission)

(b) The Tapered-Cantilever Bending-Beam Damper

As shown in Figure 10.14, this steel-beam damper (also called Type-T damper) involves a circular tapered cantilever column with its apex at the loading level. The column may be loaded in any horizontal direction. Figure 10.15 shows typical load-displacement hysteresis loops obtained with a 10-kN prototype of this damper.

The steel-cantilever damper was used in 1988 to retrofit the capacitor banks at Haywards Power Station in New Zealand. The retrofit consisted of a combination of rubber bearings and steel-cantilever hysteretic dampers (Skinner et al. 1993). As shown in Figure 10.16, each capacitor bank had two circular tapered-steel dampers with a base diameter of 45 mm, a height of 500 mm and a yield force of 10.6 kN.

Similar steel-cantilever dampers were also used for the seismic isolation of the Mortaiolo bridge in Italy. This 9.6 km long bridge (Figure 10.17) was constructed in 1992 in a seismic region of Italy. Each pier was equipped with sliding bearings and steel-cantilever shaft elements as shown in Figure 10.18 (Parducci and Mezzi 1991).

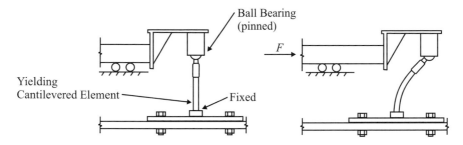

Figure 10.14 Steel Cantilever Type-T Damper (after Cousins et al. 1991)

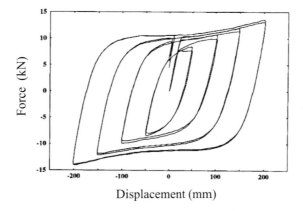

Figure 10.15 Load-Displacement Hysteresis Loops for a 10-kN Steel-Cantilever Damper Prototype (from Skinner et al. 1993, Copyright John Wiley & Sons Ltd., reproduced with permission)

Figure 10.16 Seismic Isolation Retrofit for Capacitor Banks at Haywards, New Zealand (from Skinner et al. 1993, Copyright John Wiley & Sons Ltd., reproduced with permission)

Figure 10.17 Mortailo Bridge in Italy Near Completion (from Skinner et al. 1993, Copyright John Wiley & Sons Ltd., reproduced with permission)

Figure 10.18 Testing of Isolation Devices for Mortaiolo Bridge (from Skinner et al. 1993, Copyright John Wiley & Sons Ltd., reproduced with permission)

Another example of a base-isolated structure incorporating steel-cantilever damper is the High-Tech R&D Center of Obayashi Corporation in Japan (Teramura et al. 1988). As shown in Figure 10.19, this five-storey reinforced concrete building was constructed in 1986 and is equipped with a seismic isolation system consisting of 14 laminated-rubber bearings and 16 steel-bar dampers with a diameter of 32 mm.

(c) The Torsional-Beam Damper

This type of steel damper (also called Type-E damper) involves the uniform inelastic torsion of a prismatic beam as shown in Figure 10.20. Again some care must be given in positioning the welds in low-stress regions.

Steel torsional-beam dampers were used in 1981 for the isolation of the South Rangitikei Viaduct in New Zealand, as discussed in Chapter 7.

a)   b)

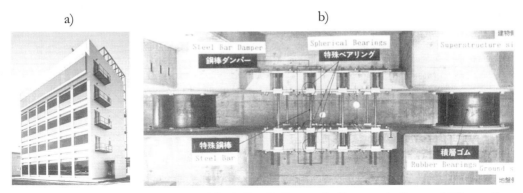

Figure 10.19 Obayashi High-Tech R&D Center in Japan: a) General View of Isolated Building, b) Isolation System Detail (from Skinner et al. 1993, Copyright John Wiley & Sons Ltd., reproduced with permission)

Figure 10.20 Steel Torsional-Beam Damper (from Skinner et al. 1993, Copyright John Wiley & Sons Ltd., reproduced with permission)

(d) Lead-Extrusion Bearings

Lead-extrusion dampers, in which mechanical energy is converted to heat by the extrusion of lead within a tube, have already been discussed in Chapter 5. The properties of lead-extrusion dampers are summarized again here:

- The hysteretic behaviour of lead-extrusion dampers is almost a pure "Coulomb" type. In other words, the force-displacement relationship is nearly rectangular and is practically rate-independent for typical earthquake-like frequencies.

- Because lead is hot-worked at room temperature, work hardening or fatigue does not affect lead-extrusion dampers. Therefore lead-extrusion dampers have a very long life and do not need to be replaced after an earthquake.

So far, lead-extrusion dampers have been used in three bridges and one building in New Zealand and two more buildings in Japan. One of these buildings is the Central

Police Station in Wellington, New Zealand (Charleston et al. 1987) completed in 1991. This 10-storey building is supported on long piles founded on rock, 15 m below ground. The piles are enclosed in oversized casings, with clearance, which allow considerable displacements relative to the ground and, hence, act as a base isolation system. As shown in Figure 10.21, lead-extrusion dampers, connected between the top of the piles and a structurally separate basement, provide energy dissipation for the base isolation system.

Figure 10.21 Lead-Extrusion Damper in Basement of Central Police Station in Wellington, New Zealand (from Skinner et al. 1993, Copyright John Wiley & Sons Ltd., reproduced with permission)

10.6 EFFECT OF AXIAL LOAD VARIATION ON THE RESPONSE OF LAMINATED AND LEAD-RUBBER BEARINGS

As discussed in the previous paragraphs, the response of both laminated-rubber and sliding friction bearings is affected by the axial load that is carried by the bearings. This axial load produced by the self-weight of the superstructure that is sitting on the isolation bearings can fluctuate during a seismic event due to fluctuations in axial loads induced by lateral loading of the superstructure (i.e frame action in the superstructure) and to vertical vibrations of the superstructure and isolation system caused by lateral motion and by vertical ground accelerations. Modal spectral analysis of the isolation system using only horizontal ground accelerations can be used to determine the fluctuations of axial loading on the bearing due to horizontal loading of the superstructure and to extract the peak values of the axial load that should be used in the design. These values can be amplified to account for vertical seismic accelerations by using simple rules that are suggested in building codes to quickly define vertical accelerations. For far-field cases for example, the peak vertical ground acceleration can be taken as 2/3 of the horizontal peak acceleration. Since these peak accelerations do not occur at the same time, it is expected that only 30% of this peak vertical acceleration is applied at the moment where the peak response of the structure (primarily caused by horizontal ground motions) is occurring. For rigid structures, the variation of axial load on the bearings can be estimated then by multiplying the vertical weight of the structure by 30% of the estimated peak vertical acceleration. If the structure has a longer vertical vibration period, vertical acceleration response spectra can be used to capture the dynamic amplification in the vertical direction.

For near-field motion, peak vertical accelerations can be higher than the peak horizontal accelerations and therefore a more conservative estimate should be used. In addition to the higher peak vertical accelerations, the times of occurrence of peak horizontal and vertical accelerations are closer to each other and therefore it should be assumed that a larger fraction of the peak vertical acceleration is occurring during the peak response of the structure (primarily caused by horizontal ground motion).

Once the design is complete, verifications can be made through nonlinear time-history dynamic analyses, including vertical ground accelerations, to check that the maximum vertical load on the bearings is similar to what was assumed in the design.

Since these fluctuations occur both downward and upward, both the effect of an increase in the compressive load and of a reduction in the compressive load on the bearings must be considered. In some cases, this reduction is larger than the initial static axial load carried by the bearings and results in tensile stresses in laminated-rubber bearings and in uplift in sliding friction bearings. Special hold down systems have been suggested to limit vertical movement of isolation bearings.

10.7 PROBLEMS

Problem 10.1

The one-storey steel portal frame shown in Figure 10.22a has the following properties:
m = mass at the roof = 1 kN s^2/mm
k = lateral stiffness of frame = 39.5 kN/mm
ξ = critical damping ratio = 0.05

The base of each column is fixed to the foundation. The frame is to be designed for a ground motion having the elastic response spectra shown in Figure 10.23. It can be assumed that the structure remains elastic during the earthquake.

a) Compute the maximum lateral displacement at the roof of the structure under the design earthquake.

b) Compute the maximum shear force developed at the base of the structure under the design earthquake.

A seismic isolation system is being considered for the seismic retrofit of the structure as shown in Figure 10.22b. The isolation system consists of two "partial" cylindrical lead-rubber bearings in which a lead plug is inserted only in the bottom half of each isolator.

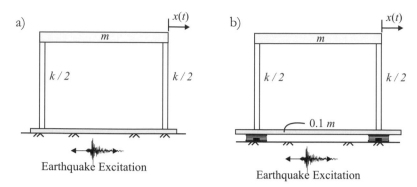

Figure 10.22 One-Storey Portal Frame: a) Fixed to the Ground, b) Isolated Frame

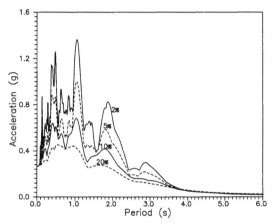

Figure 10.23 Elastic Response Spectra of Design Earthquake

At room temperature, the shear modulus of the rubber G_r = 1MPa, the shear modulus of the lead G_p = 150 MPa, and the shear yield stress of the lead τ_{yp} = 10 MPa.

The mass of the rigid foundation mat required to link the columns of the frame is assumed to be equal to 10% of the mass at the roof of the structure.

c) Plot the shear load-deformation diagram for the seismic isolation system (i.e. for both lead-rubber bearings).

d) Determine the isolated period of the structure (after yielding of the lead plug).

e) Assuming that the seismic isolation system provides an equivalent viscous damping ratio of 10% of critical, estimate (through equivalent linearization) the maximum lateral displacement across the isolation bearings under the design earthquake.

f) For the same damping ratio, estimate (through equivalent linearization) the maximum shear force developed at the base of the structure under the design earthquake.

g) Discuss the performance of the proposed seismic isolation system for this structure.

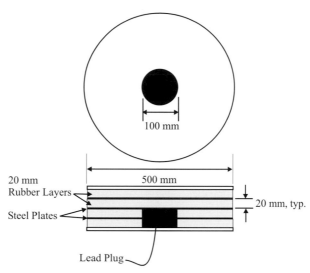

Figure 10.24 Partial Cylindrical Lead-Rubber Base Isolation System

Problem 10.2

A different seismic isolation system is being considered for the one-storey steel portal frame of Problem 10.1. The isolation system consists of two Friction Pendulum System (FPS) bearings, as shown in Figure 10.25. The radius of each bearing R is 1 m and the average coefficient of friction at the sliding interface $\mu = 0.05$.

The mass of the rigid foundation mat required to link the columns of the frame is assumed to be equal to 10% of the mass at the roof of the structure.

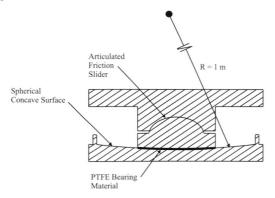

Figure 10.25 Friction Pendulum System (FPS) Bearing

a) Plot the shear load-deformation diagram for the seismic isolation system (i.e. for both FPS bearings). Plot the diagram for a displacement range of ±50 mm.

b) Determine the isolated period of the structure (after sliding has been initiated).

c) Assuming that the seismic isolation system provides an equivalent viscous damping ratio of 10% of critical, estimate (through equivalent linearization) the maximum lateral displacement across the FPS isolation bearings under the design earthquake.

d) For the same damping ratio, estimate (through equivalent linearization) the maximum shear force developed at the base of the structure under the design earthquake.

e) A double friction pendulum system (DFPS) is now considered for the isolation of this structure. If the properties of the top and bottom plates are identical, i.e. $R_1 = R_2$, $h_1 = h_2$ and the friction coefficient $\mu = 0.05$ is the same on both surfaces, design the DFPS bearings to achieve the exact same response as the single FPS bearings considered in a). What advantages does a designer have in using the double friction pendulum system instead of the single friction pendulum system?

f) In general, discuss the performance of the proposed base isolation systems for this structure.

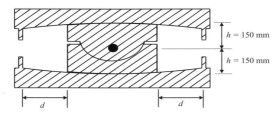

Figure 10.26 Double Friction Pendulum System (FPS) Bearing

Problem 10.3

A one-storey steel portal frame is to be retrofitted with two circular laminated elastomeric bearings, as shown in Figure 10.27. The mass of the rigid foundation mat required to link the columns of the frame is assumed to be equal to 10% of the mass at the roof of the structure. The degrees-of-freedom shown are defined as $x_1(t)$: the relative displacement of the foundation mat with respect to the ground and $x_2(t)$: the relative displacement of the roof with respect to the ground.

The frame has the following properties:
m = mass at the roof = 1.5 kN s^2/mm
k = lateral stiffness of frame = 240 kN/mm
ξ = critical damping ratio = 0.05

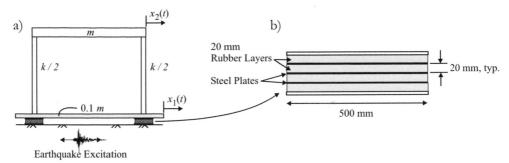

Figure 10.27 One-Storey Portal Frame: a) Isolated Frame, b) Laminated-Rubber Bearing

It can be assumed that the hysteretic behaviour of the rubber in shear can be treated as a Kelvin solid viscoelastic element with a shear storage modulus, $G_E = 1$ MPa, and a loss factor $\eta = 0.40$.

a) Determine the two natural frequencies of the system.

b) Determine and sketch the two mode shapes of the system in terms of the degrees-of-freedom $x_1(t)$ and $x_2(t)$.

c) Determine the modal participation factors in each mode of vibration.

d) Determine the modal damping ratios in each mode of vibration.

e) Based on the results obtained in c) and d), what can be concluded on the effect of the second mode on the seismic response? Construct a simplified dynamic model of the base isolated frame.

The frame is to be designed for a ground motion having the elastic response spectrum shown in Figure 10.23. Assuming that the structure remains elastic during the earthquake:

f) Compute the maximum lateral displacement at the roof of the base isolated frame under the design earthquake.

g) Compute the maximum shear force developed at the base of the frame under the design earthquake.

h) Assuming that the frame has a fixed base, repeat the calculations in f) and g).

i) Discuss the performance of the proposed seismic isolation system for the retrofit of this frame.

CHAPTER 11: SAMPLE SEISMIC RETROFIT PROJECTS

11.1 INTRODUCTION

Hands-on applications are essential in order to gain experience and skills in the seismic design and/or retrofit of structures incorporating supplemental damping or base isolation systems. With this in mind, this chapter describes two sample retrofit projects that can be utilized for term projects in a classroom environment. The goal of the first sample project is the seismic retrofit of a moment-resisting steel framed building, while the seismic retrofit of a bridge structure is considered in the second sample project.

The objective of each sample project is to evaluate the effect of supplemental damping or base isolation systems for the seismic retrofit of a particular structure (a building or a bridge). For this purpose, a student version of the general-purpose nonlinear time-history dynamic analysis computer program RUAUMOKO (Carr 2004) along with its user's manual is supplied in the CD-ROM accompanying this book. Also, a model of the structure considered in each sample project in the form of an input file to the RUAUMOKO program (Building.txt and Bridge.txt) is also supplied on the same CD-ROM. This allows the students to get familiar with the features of the RUAUMOKO program and to assess the seismic performance of the original structural models without having to build the data input files on their own.

Students should be divided into teams of three or four members to perform one of the two sample projects. Each team would be working on the same structure but would have to consider different specified earthquake design ground motions. Each assignment represents a phase of the project, and is related to a particular supplemental damping or seismic isolation system discussed in class based on the material covered in this book. For each system, an optimum retrofit strategy is sought. Each team should hand in only one project report at the end of the course. The project report should reflect the various phases of the project and must include the optimum solution for each supplemental damping or base isolation system considered. A final recommendation among the various systems studied should be given at the end of the report. At the end of the project, each team should make an oral presentation to the class on the main findings of their project. This session should be open to the public.

11.2 PERFORMANCE INDICES

Performance-based seismic design procedures require a quantification of performance, based on one or multiple structural response indices. Traditionally, ductility demand, energy dissipation, or a combination of both have been identified as the parameters that best evaluate the performance level of structural elements. A number of response/damage indices (Park and Ang 1985, Fajfar 1992, Cosenza and Manfredi 1993) have been proposed to carry through such an evaluation by one of these parameters, or weighted sums of both. These parameters are usually calibrated against experimental data to result in a value of 1 corresponding to failure of the structural system (e.g. Fardis 1995). The basic idea behind these approaches is a low-cycle fatigue type failure of the structural system, where the number of available cycles before failure reduces as the amplitude increases.

Although the performance of structures retrofitted by various supplemental damping and seismic isolation systems would be established through engineering response indices obtained from the results of nonlinear time-history dynamic analyses, it is highly recommended that the students make an attempt to translate these response indices into performance indices that can be understood by non-engineers, such as building owners and architects. It is recommended that the instructor encourage the students to refer to published materials containing a description of seismic performance levels in terms of engineering response indices

At the time of writing this book, the Vision 2000 document by the Structural Engineering Association of California (SEAOC 1996) and the FEMA-356 pre-standard document (ASCE 2000) defined anticipated seismic performance levels of building structures in terms of engineering response indices. Table 11-1 presents an excerpt from the FEMA-356 document applicable to moment-resisting steel framed buildings. Students are encouraged to make use of these tables while assessing the seismic performance of the building structure considered in the first sample project.

Table 11-2 presents performance criteria for bridge structures according to the MCEER/ATC-49 Recommended LRFD Guidelines for the seismic design of highway bridges (ATC/MCEER 2003a, 2003b) based on permanent deformations of the bridge.

Considering the importance of damage to nonstructural elements in the full assessment of the seismic performance of a structure, other criteria such as peak accelerations and velocities or floor accelerations and velocity spectra also represent important information in the characterization of the effectiveness of a retrofit strategy.

11.3 SEISMIC HAZARD

(a) Design Basis Ground Motion

A suite of 20 historical ground motions ranging from M6 – M7.3 in magnitude, which were scaled to match the 10% probability of exceedence in 50 years uniform hazard spectrum for Los Angeles (SAC Joint Venture 1997), have been selected and are included in the CD-ROM accompanying this book. In addition, the S00E component of the May

18, 1940 Imperial Valley Earthquake recorded at El Centro, is also included. The El Centro record has been used extensively in the past 50 years for research in earthquake engineering.

Table 11-1 : Anticipated Seismic Performance of Moment-Resisting Steel Framed Buildings in Terms of Engineering Response Indices (after ASCE 2000)

		Engineering Response Index		
		Description of Structural Damage	Maximum Drift	Residual Drift
Performance Level	Collapse Prevention [a]	Extensive distortion of beams and column panels; many fractures at moment connections, but shear connections remain intact.	5%	5%
	Life Safety [b]	Plastic hinges form; local buckling of some beam elements; severe joint distortion; isolated connection and element fractures, but shear connections remain intact.	2.5%	1%
	Immediate Occupancy [c]	Minor local yielding at a few locations; no fractures; minor buckling or observable permanent distortion of members.	0.7%	-

[a] Collapse Prevention: Structure supports gravity loads but has no margin against collapse.

[b] Life Safety: Damaged structure supports gravity loads with margin against collapse.

[c] Immediate Occupancy: Structure can be reoccupied immediately after the earthquake.

Table 11-2 : Anticipated Performance of Bridges in Terms of Permanent Deformations (after ATC/MCEER 2003b)

Type of Permanent Deformation	Immediate Service Level[a]	Significant Disruption Service Level[b]
Vertical Offset	$\Delta \leq 0.03$ m	$\Delta \leq 0.20$ m
Horizontal Offset	$\Delta \leq 0.10$ m	$\Delta \leq$ Shoulder width to avoid vehicle impact
Tilting of Cross Section	$\Delta\theta \leq 0.001$ rad	-

[a] Immediate Service Level: Full access to normal traffic is possible following inspection.

[b] Significant Disruption Service Level: Limited access (reduced lanes, light emergency traffic) may be possible after shoring. However the bridge may need to be replaced.

(b) Near-Fault Ground Motion

In addition, a particular near-fault ground motion, called NF13, and available in the CD-ROM as well, has been derived from one horizontal component of the ground motion recorded at the Rinaldi station (distance = 7.5 km) during the 1994 Northridge earthquake (Moment Magnitude = 6.7). The near-fault record represents an unusually severe ground motion and is included to illustrate that careful attention should be given to the full definition of the seismicity of an area and the possibility of near-fault ground motion when considering the retrofit of a structure equipped with supplemental damping or seismic isolation devices.

(c) Definition of Ground Motion Records for Use in Project

It is suggested that the instructor define a suite of three records from the ensemble of design-basis ground motions for each team. In addition, the well known El Centro record should be assigned to all teams. Based on the seismic hazard defined by these four ground motions (e.g. by developing the average spectrum of the four records), the design of the retrofit strategies using supplemental damping devices and base isolation is carried out. Once the retrofit strategies have been finalized, nonlinear time-history dynamic analyses are carried out to fully assess the seismic performance of the retrofitted structure. For this purpose, three sets of records can be considered:

- The four records considered in the design.

- The four records considered in the design scaled by a factor of 1.5 to approximately represent a seismic hazard of 2% in 50 years (MCE).

- The near-fault record.

While the first set of records allows for an assessment of the effectiveness of the retrofit strategy to raise the performance level of the structure under the design level earthquake, the second and third sets are necessary to check the collapse prevention performance level under significantly higher intensity ground motions.

The ground motions suggested above can also be replaced by other ground motion records at the discretion of the instructor.

11.4 SAMPLE PROJECT 1:
RETROFIT OF A MOMENT-RESISTING STEEL FRAMED BUILDING

In this section, the various phases associated with the first sample project, dealing with the seismic retrofit of a moment-resisting steel framed building, are described. The first three phases of the sample project are preliminary phases that relate to the original building structure. Phases four to seven deal with the retrofit of the building structure with various supplemental damping or seismic isolation systems covered in this book. The objective of the last phase of the sample project is to evaluate the collapse prevention performance of the optimally retrofitted building under more severe ground motions and under an impulsive near-fault ground excitation. In the context of a class room environment, not all phases from four to eight need to be assigned. Also, each phase of the sample project should be assigned when the pertinent material is covered in class.

11.4.1 PHASE 1: Building Identification

The objective of this first phase of the project is to familiarize students with the building structure to be retrofitted with various supplemental damping and seismic isolation systems. The same six-storey building structure used as example in sections 5.7.4 and 6.8.3 is considered for this first sample project. This structure was first studied by Tsai and Popov (1988) and was modified by Hall (1995). As shown in Figure 11.1, the building is rectangular in shape and is braced in the North-South direction by two exterior moment-resisting frames. The design complies with the 1994 UBC code requirements (ICBO 1994) for a building located in Zone 4 on soil type S2. Design gravity loads include the roof dead load of 3.8 kPa, the floor dead load of 4.5 kPa, the roof live load of 1.0 kPa, the floor live load of 3.8 kPa, and the weight of the exterior cladding of 1.7 kPa. Wind loads are derived assuming a basic wind speed of 113 km/h and an exposure type B. The steel grade is assumed to be A36 (nominal F_y = 290 MPa) for all members.

(a) Modelling Assumptions

All seismic/dynamic analyses are performed using the nonlinear dynamic analysis computer program RUAUMOKO (Carr 2004). A data input file, representing a two-dimensional model of the building in the North-South direction (building.txt), is available in the CD-ROM accompanying this book.

Only half of the building is modelled, as the structure is symmetrical. As shown in Figure 11.1, the model then includes only one exterior frame, together with a gravity column that represents all interior frame columns. The total gravity loads acting on the interior columns are applied to the gravity column in the model and both the gravity column and the exterior frame are constrained to experience the same lateral deformation at each floor.

Only the bare steel frame is included in the analyses, i.e., the slab participation as a composite beam is not included. The inelastic response is concentrated in plastic hinges that could form at both ends of the frame members. These plastic hinges are assigned a bi-linear hysteretic behaviour with a curvature strain-hardening ratio of 0.02 (see Figure 11.2), and their length is set equal to 90% of the associated member depth. The plastic resistance at the hinges is based on expected yield strength of 290 MPa.

An axial load-moment interaction, as per LRFD 1993 (AISC 1993), is considered for the columns of the structure. Rigid-end offsets are specified at the end of the frame members to account for the actual size of the members at the joints. The panel zones of the beam-column connections are assumed to be stiff and strong enough to avoid any panel shear deformation and yielding under strong earthquakes. This assumption represents the most critical condition for the inelastic curvature demand on the welded

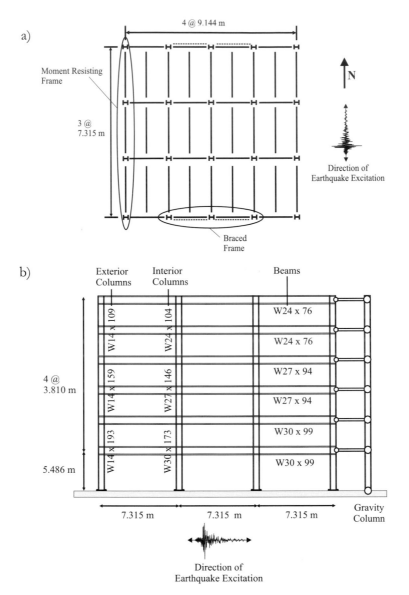

Figure 11.1 Building Structure Considered for Retrofit Sample Project: a) Plan View and b) Elevation

beam-to-column joints, as all the hysteretic energy must be dissipated only through plastic hinging in the beams and the columns. The columns are fixed at the ground level, except the gravity column that is assumed pinned at the base and at each level.

Gravity loads acting on the frame during the earthquake are assumed equal to the roof and floor dead loads, the weight of the exterior walls, and a portion of the floor live load

(0.7 kPa). P-Δ effects are accounted for in the analyses, including P-delta forces generated in the interior frames. Half the weight of the building, along with a 0.5 kPa live load, is included in the reactive weights at each level. Rayleigh damping of 5% based on the first two elastic modes of vibration of the structure is assigned. The specified time-step increment for the time-history dynamic analysis is 0.002 s.

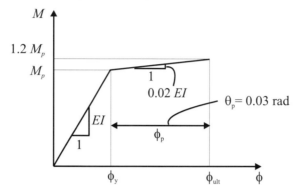

Figure 11.2 Bi-Linear Moment-Curvature Model

Task 1.1: Geometry and Members' Properties

- Draw an elevation view of the analyzed frame indicating the positions of all nodes and members.

- Create a table indicating the following properties for each member: member's depth, cross-sectional area, moment of inertia around the appropriate bending axis, yield bending moment, and yield axial force.

- For each column member, draw a graph of the axial load-moment interaction diagram.

Task 1.2: Curvature Ductility Capacity Evaluation

For this project, the failure criterion assumed for all steel beam and column elements is based on a plastic hinge rotation limit of 0.03 radian. This limit was adopted by the AISC design provisions following the 1994 Northridge earthquake (AISC 1997) for ductile steel moment resisting frames. Consequently, the bi-linear moment-curvature relationship shown in Figure 11.2 is adopted for all beam and column ends. In this figure, $0.2\ M_p$ represents the increase in moment due to strain hardening whereas ϕ_p is the plastic curvature corresponding to failure of the section.

- For each member, verify that the plastic curvature ϕ_p indicated in Figure 11.2 corresponds to the plastic rotation limit $\theta_p = 0.03$ radian.

- For each member, determine the curvature ductility capacity at failure ($\theta_p = 0.03$ rad).

Task 1.3: Dynamic Characteristics of Structure

- Draw a table showing the first five periods of vibration of the building structure.

- For each of these five periods of vibration, draw the corresponding mode shape. Indicate the numerical values corresponding to the lateral modal displacement of each floor level.

Task 1.4: Pushover Analysis

In a pushover analysis, as described in section 2.4.3, a lateral monotonic load is applied to a structure until the ultimate load is approached. This static analysis, much easier to perform than a dynamic analysis, allows for a first nonlinear evaluation of the response of the structure under lateral loads. The results of a pushover analysis depend on the lateral load distribution considered.

- Using the procedure described in page 15 of the RUAUMOKO examples manual contained in the CD-ROM accompanying this book, perform a pushover analysis on the structure. A proper seismic loading distribution must be selected and justified.

- Present the results of the pushover analysis in graphical form, similar to that of page 17 of the RUAUMOKO examples manual, indicating the variation of the base shear with the top floor lateral displacement.

- On this graph, clearly indicate i) the formation of the first plastic hinge in the beams and its location in the structure, ii) the formation of the first plastic hinge in the columns and its location in the structure, iii) the first expected failure of a beam or a column and its location in the sructure.

11.4.2 PHASE 2: Characterization of Design Ground Motions

The objective of this second phase of the project is to retrieve and determine the characteristics of the ground motions considered for the retrofit of the building structure. The instructor should choose the type of ground motions that should be considered among the suites of records presented in section 11.3.

Task 2.1: Characteristics of Time-Histories

- For each earthquake ground motion assigned, plot the acceleration time-history indicating clearly the Peak Ground Acceleration (PGA). Use the same scale for all time-histories.

Task 2.2: Characteristics of Response Spectra

- For each earthquake ground motion, compute and plot the absolute acceleration and relative displacement response spectra for 5% damping on a period range of 0.01 s to 4 s, by increment of 0.01 s. The computer program RESAS, available in the CD-ROM accompanying this book, can be used to compute the response spectra.

- For each suite of records, compute and plot the mean spectrum and the mean + 1 standard deviation spectrum.

Task 2.3: Discussion on Damage Potential of Ground Motions

- Compare, in terms of amplitude, frequency content, duration and spectral responses, the characteristics of the design ground motions assigned, and discuss their potential to cause damage to the original building.

11.4.3 PHASE 3: Performance Evaluation of Original Building Structure

The objective of this third phase of the project is to evaluate the seismic response of the original building structure (before retrofit) under each of the design ground motions considered in the previous section. The computer program RUAUMOKO and its post-processor DYNAPLOT contained in the CD-ROM accompanying this book are used to analyze the original building structure under each of the ground motions considered in this study. The ground motions are used as recorded without time or amplitude scaling.

Task 3.1: Energy Balance

- For each of the analyses, plot time-histories of various energy components and verify that energy balance is achieved following the discussion presented in Chapter 3 of this book.

- For each analysis, determine the maximum difference in percentage between the seismic input energy and the sum of the internal energy components following the discussion of section 3.3.4.

Task 3.2: Plastic Hinging Distribution

Draw an elevation view of the building and indicate the occurrence of a plastic hinge at the end of a member using the symbols shown in Figure 11.3

- For each yielded member, indicate also the maximum curvature ductility demand, the maximum plastic rotation demand and indicate if failure of some members have occurred according to the failure criterion defined in the previous section (i.e. $\theta_p \geq 0.03$ rad).

- Discuss the results obtained in light of the performance indices discussed in section 11.2.

  ● Bi-directional hinging in beams and columns

  ◐ Uni-directional hinging in columns

  ◖ Uni-directional hinging in beams

Figure 11.3 Sign Convention for Element Hinging

Task 3.3: Envelopes of Peak and Residual Interstorey Drifts

Interstorey drift is an indicator of both structural and nonstructural damage. For instance, the Vision 2000 document (SEAOC 1996) suggests that a steel building is operational with light damage if the interstorey drift is less than 0.5% and that structural damage is expected to develop at an interstorey drift of 1.5%.

- Draw graphs comparing the variations of the peak and residual interstorey drifts along the building height for the three ground motions considered.

- Discuss the results obtained in light of the performance indices given in section 11.2.

Task 3.4: Envelopes of Peak Absolute Floor Accelerations

Horizontal inertia forces that develop at each level of a building are proportional to the absolute horizontal accelerations experienced by the building, and this parameter is therefore important to assess the performance of nonstructural elements such as ceilings, attachments for mechanical equipment, shelves, office furniture, etc.

- Draw a graph comparing the variations of the peak absolute horizontal acceleration along the building height for the three ground motions considered.

- Discuss the results obtained in light of the performance indices given in section 11.2.

11.4.4 PHASE 4: Retrofit of Building Structure with Hysteretic Dampers

The objective of the fourth phase of the project is to retrofit the original building structure with hysteretic dampers of the type discussed in Chapter 5 of this book for the different design ground motions considered. The retrofit strategy for the structure consists of introducing a chevron braced frame in the middle bay of each moment resisting frame and installing hysteretic dampers at one end of the bracing members, as shown in Figure 11.4. The bracing members must be designed to sustain the activation load assigned to the hysteretic dampers. Brace forces induced by gravity loads can be ignored in the design of the bracing and hysteretic energy dissipating systems, as the braces would be installed to the existing building and that live loads will have a negligible effect on the bracing members. The retrofit system considered incorporates at one end of the bracing members hysteretic dampers of the type discussed in Chapter 5, that are activated at a predetermined load. Once connected to a bracing member, this system exhibits the well-known elasto-plastic hysteretic behaviour discussed in Chapter 5.

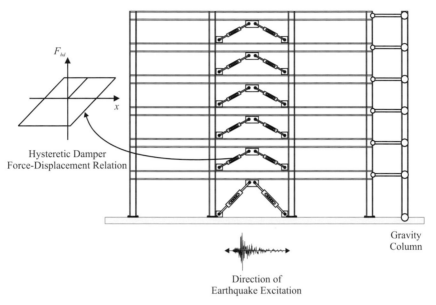

Figure 11.4 Locations of Added Bracing and Hysteretic Dampers

Task 4.1: Design of Hysteretic Dampers

The two parameters to be determined for the retrofit of the building structure are:

- The activation load F_a of each damper along the building height.

- The section of each diagonal cross-brace along the building height.

Based on the various design procedures for hysteretic dampers discussed in Chapter 5 of this book, the procedure adopted for determining the optimum activation load and cross-bracing distributions must be clearly presented, and all the methods and assumptions used must be substantiated and referenced. For the retrofit, it is specified that hollow steel sections (HSS) must be used for the cross-braces.

All intermediate analyses leading to the final design must be documented and the key results presented in appendices along with design calculations. The final choice of the optimum activation load and cross-bracing distributions must be clearly presented, and the reason why this optimum solution was retained must be clearly argued.

Task 4.2: Performance Evaluation of Building Structure Retrofitted with Hysteretic Dampers

- The computer program RUAUMOKO and its post-processor DYNAPLOT must be used to analyze the building retrofitted with the final hysteretic damping solution under each of the design ground motions considered. The following analysis results must be compared with the ones obtained for the original building in Phase 3 of the project: energy balance, plastic hinge distribution, envelopes of peak and residual interstorey drifts, envelopes of peak absolute floor accelerations.

- Discuss the merits of the optimum solution in improving the seismic response of the original building in light of the performance indices discussed in section 11.2.

11.4.5 PHASE 5: Retrofit of Building Structure with Viscous Dampers

The objective of the fifth phase of the project is to retrofit the original building structure with linear viscous dampers of the type discussed in Chapter 6 of this book for the ground motions considered in this study. The retrofit strategy for the structure consists of introducing a chevron braced frame in the middle bay of each moment resisting frame and installing linear viscous dampers at one end of the bracing members, as shown in Figure 11.5. The bracing members must be designed to sustain the maximum load developed by the viscous dampers. Brace forces induced by gravity loads can be ignored in the design of the bracing and viscous energy dissipating systems, as the braces would be installed to the existing building and live loads would have a negligible effect on the bracing members.

Task 5.1: Design of Retrofit

The two parameters to be determined for the retrofit of the building structure are:

- The damping constant C_L for each damper along the building height.
- The section of each diagonal cross-brace along the building height.

Based on the various design procedures for viscous dampers discussed in Section 6.4, the procedure adopted to determine the optimum viscous damping constant and cross-bracing distributions must be clearly presented and all the methods and assumptions used must be substantiated and referenced. For the retrofit, it is specified that Hollow Steel Sections (HSS) must be used for the cross-braces.

All intermediate analyses leading to the final design must be documented and the key results presented in appendices along with design calculations. Validation of the dashpot element in the computer program RUAUMOKO on a single-degree-of-freedom system could be considered. The final choice of the optimum viscous damping and cross-bracing

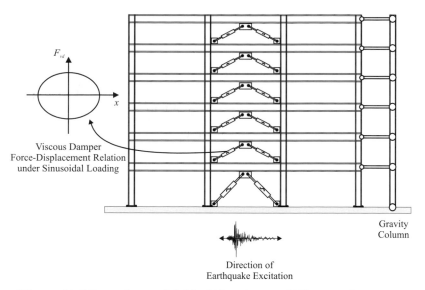

Figure 11.5 Locations of Added Bracing and Viscous Dampers

distributions must be clearly presented and the reason why this optimum solution was retained must be clearly argued.

Task 5.2 Performance Evaluation of Building Structure Retrofitted with Viscous Dampers

- The computer program RUAUMOKO and its post-processor DYNAPLOT must be used to analyze the building retrofitted with the final viscous cross-braced solution under each of the design ground motions considered. The following analysis results must be compared with the ones obtained for the original building in Phase 3 of the Project: energy balance, plastic hinge distribution, envelopes of peak and residual interstorey drifts, envelopes of peak absolute floor accelerations.

- Discuss the merits of the optimum solution in improving the seismic response of the original building in light of the performance indices discussed in section 11.2.

- For this optimum solution, determine the maximum axial force for which each viscous damper must be manufactured.

11.4.6 PHASE 6: Retrofit of Building Structure with a Tuned-Mass Damper

The objective of the sixth phase of the project is to retrofit the original building structure with a tuned-mass damper of the type discussed in Chapter 8 of this book for the design ground motions considered in this study.

The retrofit strategy for the structure consists of introducing a tuned-mass damper on the roof of the building, as shown in Figure 11.6. The tuned-mass damper consists of a mass m attached to the roof of the building by a linear spring of stiffness k, and a linear viscous damper with constant c. It can be assumed that the mass can slide on a special low-friction horizontal surface installed on the roof of the building.

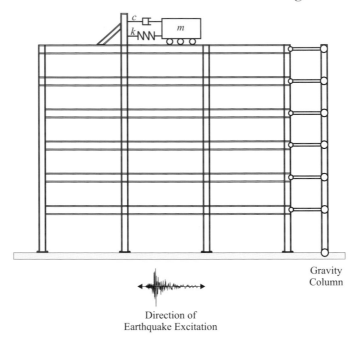

Gravity
Column

Direction of
Earthquake Excitation

Figure 11.6 Building Structure with Tuned-Mass Damper on Roof

Task 6.1: Design of the Tuned-Mass Damper

The three parameters to be determined for the retrofit of the building with a tuned-mass damper are:

- The optimum mass m of the tuned-mass damper.

- The optimum linear stiffness k of the tuned-mass damper.

- The optimum viscous damping constant c of the tuned-mass damper.

Based on the design considerations for tuned-mass dampers discussed in Section 8.6, the procedure adopted to determine the optimum mass m, stiffness k and damping constant c for the tuned-mass damper must be clearly presented and all the methods and assumptions used must be substantiated and referenced. All intermediate analyses leading to the final design of the tuned-mass damper must be documented and the key results presented in appendices along with design calculations.

The final choice of the optimum mass m, stiffness k and damping constant c for the tuned-mass damper must be clearly presented and the reason why this optimum solution was retained must be clearly argued.

Task 6.2: Performance Evaluation of Building Structure Retrofitted with Tuned-Mass Damper

- The computer program RUAUMOKO and its post-processor DYNAPLOT must be used to analyze the building retrofitted with the final tuned-mass damping solution under each of the design ground motions considered. The following analysis results must be compared with the ones obtained for the original building in Phase 3 of the Project: energy balance, plastic hinge distribution, envelopes of peak and residual interstorey drifts, envelopes of peak absolute floor accelerations.

- Discuss the merits of the optimum solution in improving the seismic response of the original building in light of the performance indices discussed in section 11.2.

- Specify the required length for the sliding surface to be installed on the roof of the building.

- Present a preliminary design of the tuned-mass damper including the material and dimensions of the rigid mass, the dimensions and shape of the spring element, and the connection between the tuned-mass damper and the structure.

11.4.7 PHASE 7: Retrofit of Building Structure with a Lead-Rubber Seismic Isolation System

The objective of the seventh phase of the project is to retrofit the original building structure with a lead-rubber base isolation system of the type described in Chapter 10 of this book for the ground motions considered in this study.

The retrofit strategy for the structure consists of introducing lead-rubber bearings at the base of the structure. For this purpose, it can be assumed that a large foundation mat supports the building and that retrofit work will be required to introduce a link-frame between the columns and this mat. The isolators will be installed between this link-frame and the top surface of the mat. The weight of the link-frame for the entire building can be estimated at 2000 kN. For modelling purposes, it can be assumed that all bearings operate in parallel and therefore the complete base isolation system can be modeled as a single horizontal bilinear spring at the base of the structure as shown in Figure 11.7. The material properties at room temperature for the lead and rubber to be used in retrofit are shown in Table 11-3.

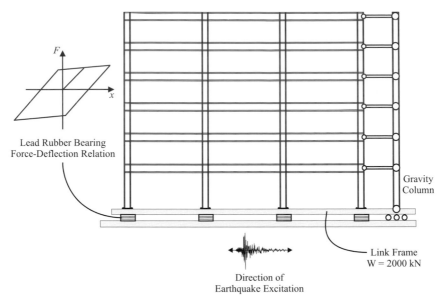

Figure 11.7 Building Structure with Lead-Rubber Bearings at the Base

Table 11-3 : Material Properties for Lead-Rubber Isolation Bearings

Material	Shear Modulus (MPa)	Compression Modulus (MPa)	Shear Yield Strength (MPa)
Rubber	0.75	2000	-
Lead	150.0	-	10

The three parameters to be determined for the retrofit of the building with a lead-rubber isolation system are:

- The optimum initial elastic stiffness k_1 of the seismic isolation system.
- The optimum post-yield stiffness k_2 of the seismic isolation system.
- The optimum shear yield load F_y of the seismic isolation system.

Furthermore, the seismic isolation system needs to meet the following design requirements:

- Maximum seismic displacement of lead-rubber bearings, $x_b = \pm 300 \text{ mm}$,
- Minimum overlap factor for individual bearings $A'/A_r = 0.6$,
- Shape factor for individual bearings $10 \le S \le 20$.

Task 7.1: Design of Seismic Isolation System

Based on the design considerations for base isolation systems discussed in section 9.3 of this book, the procedure adopted to determine the optimum initial elastic stiffness k_1, post-yield stiffness k_2 and shear yield load F_y of the entire seismic isolation system must be clearly presented and all the methods and assumptions used must be substantiated and referenced. All intermediate analyses leading to the final design of the lead-rubber seismic isolation system must be documented and the key results presented in appendices along with design calculations.

The final choice of the optimum initial elastic stiffness k_1, post-yield stiffness k_2 and shear yield load F_y of the base isolation system must be clearly presented and the reason why this optimum solution was retained must be clearly argued.

Task 7.2: Performance Evaluation of Building Structure Retrofitted with Lead-Rubber Seismic Isolation System

- The computer program RUAUMOKO and its post-processor DYNAPLOT must be used to analyze the building retrofitted with the final lead-rubber seismic isolation solution under each of the design ground motions considered in this study. The following analysis results must be compared with the ones obtained for the original building in phase 3 of the Project: energy balance, plastic hinge distribution, envelopes of peak and residual interstorey drifts, envelopes of peak absolute floor accelerations. The response of the isolation system must also be presented in terms of maximum isolator displacements and variation in axial loads.

- Discuss the merits of the optimum solution in improving the seismic response of the original building in light of the performance indices discussed in section 11.2.

- Present a preliminary design for the individual lead-rubber bearings including the number of bearings to be used, the shape and dimensions of each bearing and the diameter of each lead plug.

11.4.8 PHASE 8: Performance Assessment of Optimum Retrofit Strategies Under the 2% in 50 Years Ground Motions and Near-Field Ground Motions

As discussed in section 11.3, the retrofitted structures are subjected to a second series of earthquakes to investigate the collapse prevention performance of the optimally retrofitted structure under a greater seismic hazard, as well as the expected performance in the case that the construction site would be located at proximity (less than 10 km) from an active fault.

TASK 8.1: Analysis of Retrofitted Building Structure under 2% in 50 Years Probability of Exceedence Records

- The computer program RUAUMOKO and its post-processor DYNAPLOT must be used to analyze the original and optimally retrofitted buildings. The following analysis results must be compared: energy balance, plastic hinge distribution, envelopes of peak and residual interstorey drifts, envelopes of peak absolute floor accelerations.

- Discuss the performance of the optimally retrofitted building and the resulting design implications in light of the performance indices discussed in section 11.2.

TASK 8.2: Analysis of Retrofitted Building Structure under Near-Field Records

- The computer program RUAUMOKO and its post-processor DYNAPLOT must be used to analyze the original and optimally retrofitted buildings. The following analysis results must be compared: energy balance, plastic hinge distribution, envelopes of peak and residual interstorey drifts, envelopes of peak absolute floor accelerations.

- Discuss the performance of the optimally retrofitted building and the resulting design implications in light of the performance indices discussed in section 11.2.

11.4.9 PHASE 9: Summary of Results and Comparison of Retrofit Strategies

In this last Phase of the project, a general summary of each of the retrofit techniques is to be presented and an overall comparison of all strategies is to be carried out.

Issues related to the practical implementation and cost as well as the expected performance levels should be considered before recommending a final retrofit strategy. The definition of the seismic hazard considered in the study must also be discussed.

This final phase of the project can also be associated with an oral presentation to invited practicing engineers.

11.5 SAMPLE PROJECT 2: RETROFIT OF A CABLE-STAYED BRIDGE

In this section, the various phases associated with the second sample project, dealing with the seismic retrofit of a cable-stayed steel bridge, are described. The first three phases of the sample project are preliminary phases that relate to the original bridge structure. Phases four to seven deal with the retrofit of the bridge structure with various supplemental damping or seismic isolation systems covered in this book. The objective of the last phase of the sample project is to evaluate the collapse prevention performance of the optimally retrofitted bridge under more severe ground motions and an impulsive near-fault ground excitation. In the context of a class room environment, not all phases from four to eight need to be assigned. Also, each phase of the sample project should be provided to the students at a rate that is consistent with the material covered in class.

11.5.1 PHASE 1: Identification of Bridge Structure

The objective of this first phase of the project is to familiarize students with the bridge structure to be retrofitted with various supplemental damping and seismic isolation systems. As shown in Figure 11.8, the bridge structure consists of a twin leg steel tower, double-plane fan-type cables, and two longitudinal steel box girders supporting a composite concrete steel bridge deck. The total length of the bridge is 183 m, and is made up of four equal spans between cable anchorages and supports as shown in Figure 11.9.

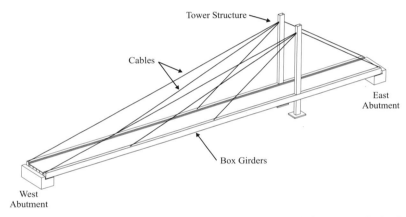

Figure 11.8 Cable-Stayed Bridge Structure Considered for Retrofit in Second Sample Project

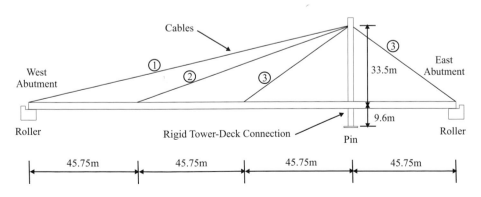

Figure 11.9 Elevation of Cable-Stayed Bridge Structure (4% upward slope from west abutment to east abutment not shown in the Figure)

(a) Bridge Deck

A typical cross section of the bridge deck is shown in Figure 11.10. The road deck is a 165 mm concrete slab, 11.0 m wide, with two nonstructural precast parapets. Five longitudinal steel stringers are spaced at equal transverse intervals of 2.4 m. Floor beams, transverse to the main girders and spaced at 7 m intervals, transfer stringer loads to the main box girders at the outer edges of the deck. The 1.5 m x 3 m box girders are made of welded flanges, webs, stiffeners, and diaphragms along the longitudinal direction. The thickness of the flanges and webs of the box girders is 50 mm. The cables are connected to the deck at the top flange of the main box girders, which are stiffened to allow proper load transfer. There is a 4% upward slope from the west abutment to the east abutment along the deck.

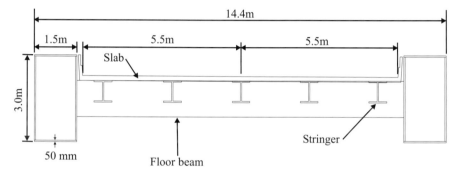

Figure 11.10 Typical Cross Section of Bridge Deck

(b) Tower

The tower illustrated in Figure 11.11 consists of two 1.5 m x 2.4 m rectangular box steel legs and a cross-beam supporting the deck. The top of the tower is 43 m tall. The thickness of the flanges and webs of the box steel legs is 50 mm. Each leg of the tower is rigidly connected to the intersecting box girder at the deck level.

(c) Bearing Supports

The support system of the bridge is assumed to be founded on hard rock. At each of the abutments there are roller supports resisting uplift generated by the cables. These supports act like horizontal low friction sliding bearings, which are designed to allow for sliding in the longitudinal direction of the bridge. The bearings under each leg of the tower prevent horizontal and vertical movements and are designed to allow rotation around the transversal axis of the bridge only.

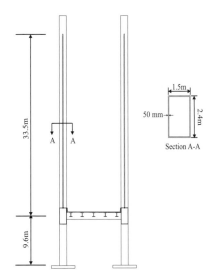

Figure 11.11 Elevation of Bridge Tower

(d) Cables

The bridge incorporates 4 cables per tower, each composed of 18 strands. Each strand has a cross-sectional area of 65.1 mm^2, as shown in Figure 11.8. The cables are constructed from standard galvanized bridge strands with a Young's modulus of 175,000 MPa, yield strength of 1500 MPa, and ultimate strength of 1725 MPa.

(e) Modelling Assumptions

All seismic/dynamic analyses are performed using the nonlinear dynamic analysis computer program RUAUMOKO (Carr 2004). A data input file, representing a two-dimensional model of the bridge in the longitudinal (East-West) direction (file bridge.txt), is available in the CD-ROM accompanying this book.

Only half of the bridge width is modeled, as the structure is symmetrical. As shown in Figure 11.12, the model then includes one main box girder (18 frame elements), one tower (12 frame elements), 4 sets of cables (modeled as tension-only truss elements) and three supports. The nodal coordinates used in the model are based on the assumed locations of field connections of the box girder and the tower. The concrete deck, steel stringers and floor beams were considered rigid and their dead load (assumed to be 25 kN/m for half of the bridge) was applied to the model.

The inelastic flexural response of the box girder and tower is concentrated in plastic hinges that could form at both ends of the frame members. These plastic hinges are assigned a bi-linear hysteretic behaviour with a curvature strain-hardening ratio of 0.02 (see Figure 11.13), and their length is set equal to 90% of the associated member depth. The plastic resistance at the hinges is based on expected yield strength of 290 MPa. An axial

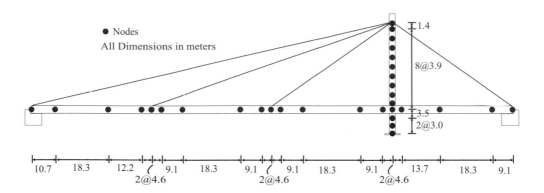

Figure 11.12 Nodal Coordinates for Bridge Structure Model (4% upward slope
from west abutment to east abutment not shown in the Figure)

load-moment interaction, as per LRFD 1993 (AISC 1993), is considered for the tower of
the structure. Rayleigh damping of 1% based on the first two elastic modes of vibration of
the structure is assigned. The specified time-step increment for the time-history dynamic
analysis is 0.002 s. The inelastic tensile response of the cables is modeled with a tension-
only bi-linear hysteretic behaviour with a tensile yield force T_y, a tensile ultimate strength
T_u that were obtained based on the cable properties. The tensile strain-hardening ratio is
set at 0.10 (see Figure 11.14).

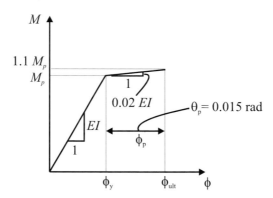

Figure 11.13 Bi-Linear Moment-Curvature Model for Box-Girder and Tower

Task 1.1: Geometry and Members' Schedule

- Draw an elevation view of the bridge structure model indicating the positions
  of all nodes and members.

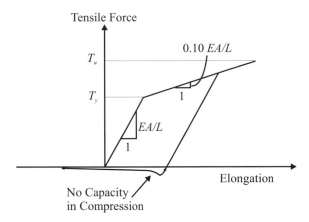

Figure 11.14 Bi-Linear Tensile Force-Elongation Model for Cables

- Create a table indicating the following properties for each member (if applicable): member's depth, cross-sectional area, moment of inertia around the bending axis, yield bending moment, and yield axial force.

- For each tower member, draw a graph of the axial load-moment interaction diagram.

Task 1.2: Evaluation of Curvature Ductility Capacity of Structural Members

For this project, the failure criterion assumed for all box girder and tower elements is based on a plastic end rotation limit of 0.015 radian, which is lower than the plastic rotation capacity of a class 1 section. Consequently, the bi-linear moment-curvature relationship shown in Figure 11.13 is adopted for all box girder and tower element ends. In this figure, $0.1\ M_p$ represents the moment increase due to strain hardening whereas ϕ_p is the plastic curvature corresponding to failure of the section. Similarly, the failure criterion for the cables is based on the tensile strength of the cables.

- For each box girder and tower member, verify that the plastic curvature ϕ_p indicated in Figure 11.13, corresponds to the plastic rotation limit $\theta_p = 0.015$ radian.

- Determine the curvature capacity at failure corresponding to an ultimate plastic rotation of $\theta_p = 0.015$ rad for each box girder and tower member.

- For each cable set, determine the axial tensile ductility capacity at failure.

Task 1.3: Dynamic Characteristics

- Draw a table showing the first 5 periods of vibration of the bridge structure.

- For each of these 5 periods of vibration, draw the corresponding mode shape. Indicate the numerical values corresponding to the lateral displacement of each tower node and the vertical displacement of each box girder node.

Task 1.4: Pushover Analysis

In a pushover analysis, as described in section 2.4.3, a lateral monotonic load is applied to a structure until the ultimate load is approached. This static analysis, much easier to perform than a dynamic analysis, allows the evaluation of the elastic and inelastic responses of the structure under lateral loads. The results of a pushover analysis depend on the lateral load distribution considered. A possible distribution of lateral load for the pushover analysis of the bridge structure considered can be defined as proportional to the mass distribution of the deck and the tower.

- Using the procedure described on page 15 of the RUAUMOKO examples manual contained in the CD-ROM accompanying this book, perform a pushover analysis in the longitudinal direction of the bridge structure. A proper seismic loading distribution must be selected and justified.

- Present the results of the pushover analysis in graphical form, similar to that of page 17 of the RUAUMOKO examples manual, indicating the variation of the longitudinal base shear with the top of the tower lateral displacement.

- Clearly indicate on this graph i) the formation of the first plastic hinge in the box girder; identify also its location, ii) the formation of the first plastic hinge in the tower, and its location, iii) the first yielding of a cable set, and identify which cable set is yielding, and iv) the first failure of a box girder element or a tower element or a cable element, and the location of this failure.

11.5.2 PHASE 2: Characterization of Design Ground Motions

The objective of this second phase of the project is to retrieve and determine the characteristics of the ground motions considered for the retrofit of the building structure. The instructor should choose the type of ground motions that should be considered among the suites of records presented in section 11.3.

Task 2.1: Characteristics of Time-Histories

- For each earthquake ground motion assigned, plot the acceleration time-history indicating clearly the Peak Ground Acceleration (PGA). Use the same scales for all three time-histories.

Task 2.2: Characteristics of Response Spectra

- For each earthquake ground motion, compute and plot the absolute acceleration and relative displacement response spectra for 5% damping on a period range of 0.01 s to 4 s, by increment of 0.01 s. The computer program RESAS, available in the CD-ROM accompanying this book, can be used to compute the response spectra.

- For each suite of records, compute and plot the mean spectrum and the mean + 1 standard deviation spectrum and compare it with code prescribed spectra.

Task 2.3: Discussion on Damage Potential of Ground Motions

- Comment on and compare, in terms of amplitudes, frequency content, duration and spectral responses, the characteristics of the design ground motions assigned, and discuss their potential to cause damage to the moment resisting frame that is studied.

11.5.3 PHASE 3: Performance Evaluation of Original Bridge Structure

The objective of this third phase of the project is to evaluate the seismic response of the original bridge structure (before retrofit) under each of the different design ground motions considered in the previous section. The computer program RUAUMOKO and its post-processor DYNAPLOT contained in the CD-ROM accompanying this book are used to analyze the original bridge structure under each of the design ground motions considered. The ground motions are used at their actual scale without time or amplitude distortions.

Task 3.1: Energy Balance

- For each of the analyses, plot time-histories of various energy components and verify that energy balance is achieved following the discussion of section 3.3.3.

- For each analysis, determine the maximum difference in percentage between the seismic input energy and the sum of the internal energy components following the discussion of section 3.3.4.

Task 3.2: Plastic Hinging in Tower and Cable Yielding Distribution

- Draw an elevation view of the bridge structure and indicate the occurrence of a plastic hinge at the end of a member or the yielding of a cable using the symbols defined in Figure 11.15.

● Bi-directional hinging in box girder and tower members

◑ Uni-directional hinging in box girder members

◒ Uni-directional hinging in tower members

⊗ Yielding of cables

Figure 11.15 Sign Convention for Element Hinging

- For each yielded member, indicate also the maximum curvature ductility demand, the maximum plastic rotation and indicate if failure of some members have occurred according to the failure criterion defined in the previous section (i.e. $\theta_p \geq 0.015$ rad).

- On the same figure, indicate the maximum tensile ductility of each cable set and indicate if some cables have failed according to the failure criterion defined in the previous section.

- Discuss the results obtained in light of the performance indices presented in section 11.2.

Task 3.3: Envelopes of Peak and Residual Displacements

- Draw graphs comparing the variations of the peak and residual horizontal displacements along the height of the tower for the design ground motions considered.

- Draw graphs comparing the variations of the peak and residual vertical displacements along the length of the box girder for the design ground motions considered.

- Discuss the results obtained in light of the performance indices presented in section 11.2.

11.5.4 PHASE 4: Retrofit of Bridge Structure with Hysteretic Dampers

The objective of the fourth phase of the project is to retrofit the original bridge structure with hysteretic dampers of the type discussed in Chapter 5 of this book for the different design ground motions considered.

The retrofit strategy for the bridge structure consists of introducing hysteretic dampers between the box girder and both abutments, as shown in Figure 11.16. Once connected to the abutment and box girder, each damper exhibits the elasto-plastic hysteretic behaviour shown in Figure 5.1.

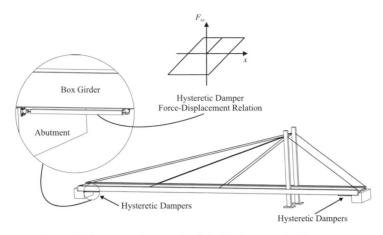

Figure 11.16 Locations of Added Hysteretic Dampers

Task 4.1: Design of Hysteretic Dampers

The two parameters to be determined for the retrofit of the building structure are:

- the activation load F_a of each hysteretic damper.

- the dimensions of the brace element connected to the abutment.

Based on the various design procedures for hysteretic dampers discussed in Chapter 5 of this book, the procedure adopted to estimate the optimum activation load of each hysteretic damper and the size of bracing member connecting it to the abutment must be clearly presented, and all the methods and assumptions used must be substantiated and referenced. All intermediate analyses leading to the final design must be documented and the key results presented in appendices along with design calculations.

The final choice of the optimum activation load of each hysteretic damper and the size of the bracing member connecting it to the abutment must be clearly presented and the reason why this optimum solution was retained must be clearly argued. Provide a preliminary design of the hysteretic dampers including the geometry and connection details for each damper.

Task 4.2: Performance Evaluation of Bridge Structure Retrofitted with Hysteretic Dampers

- The computer program RUAUMOKO and its post-processor DYNAPLOT must be used to analyze the bridge retrofitted with the final hysteretic damping solution under each of the design ground motions considered. The following analysis results must be compared with the ones obtained for the original bridge in Phase 3 of the Project: energy balance, plastic hinge and cable yield distribution, and envelopes of peak and residual deformations.

- Discuss the merits of the optimum solution in improving the seismic response of the original bridge in light of the performance indices presented in section 11.2.

11.5.5 PHASE 5: Retrofit of Bridge Structure with Viscous Dampers

The objective of the fifth phase of the project is to retrofit the original bridge structure with linear viscous dampers of the type discussed in Chapter 6 of this book for the different design ground motions considered.

The retrofit strategy for the bridge structure consists of introducing linear viscous damping devices between the box girder and both abutments, as shown in Figure 11.17.

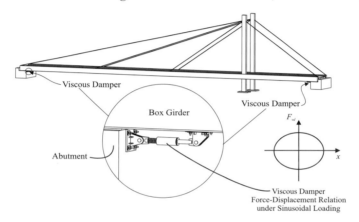

Figure 11.17 Locations of Added Bracing and Viscous Dampers

Task 5.1: Design of Viscous Dampers

The parameter to be determined for the retrofit of the bridge structure is the damping constant C_L for each linear viscous damper. It is assumed that the dampers will be connected directly to the abutment and to the deck without supplemental bracing elements. Based on the various design procedures for viscous dampers discussed in Chapter 6 of this book, the procedure adopted to determine the optimum viscous damping constant for each damper must be clearly presented and all the methods and assumptions used must be substantiated and referenced. All intermediate analyses leading to the final design must be documented and the key results presented in appendices along with design calculations. Validation of the dashpot element on a single-degree-of-freedom system could be considered.

The final choice of the optimum viscous damping constant for each damper must be clearly presented and the reason why this optimum solution was retained must be clearly argued.

Task 5.2: Performance Evaluation of Bridge Structure Retrofitted with Viscous Dampers

- The computer program RUAUMOKO and its post-processor DYNAPLOT must be used to analyze the bridge retrofitted with the final viscously damped solution under each of the design ground motions considered. The following analysis results must be compared with the ones obtained for the original bridge in Phase 3 of the Project: energy balance, plastic hinge and cable yield distribution, and envelopes of peak and residual deformations.

- Discuss the merits of the optimum solution in improving the seismic response of the original bridge in light of the performance indices presented in section 11.2.

- For this optimum solution, determine the maximum axial force for which each viscous damper must be manufactured.

11.5.6 PHASE 6: Retrofit of Bridge Structure with Tuned-Mass Dampers

The objective of the sixth phase of the project is to retrofit the original bridge structure with tuned-mass dampers of the type discussed in Chapter 8 of this book for the different design ground motions considered. The retrofit strategy for the bridge structure consists of introducing two sets of tuned-mass dampers, as shown in Figure 11.18. The first set of tuned-mass dampers of mass m_1, stiffness k_1 and damping constant c_1 is attached to each box girder in order to reduce the vertical vibrations of the deck. The second set of tuned-mass dampers of mass m_2, stiffness k_2 and damping constant c_2 is attached to the top of each tower leg in order to reduce the horizontal vibrations of the tower.

Task 6.1: Design of Tuned-Mass Dampers

The four parameters to be determined for the retrofit of the building with a tuned-mass damper are:

- The optimum mass, m_1 and m_2, of each tuned-mass damper.

- The optimum linear stiffness, k_1 and k_2, of each tuned-mass damper.

- The optimum viscous damping constant, c_1 and c_2, of each tuned-mass damper.

- The optimum location on the box girder of the first tuned-mass damper.

Based on the design considerations for tuned-mass dampers discussed in Chapter 8 of this book, the procedure adopted to determine the optimum mass, stiffness, and damping constant for each tuned-mass damper must be clearly presented and all the methods and assumptions used must be substantiated and referenced. All intermediate analyses leading

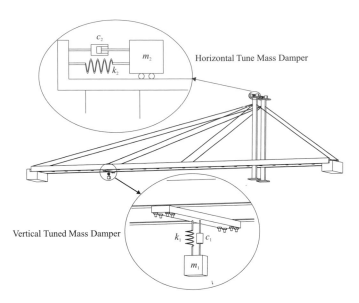

Figure 11.18 Bridge Structure with Tuned-Mass Dampers

to the final design of the tuned-mass dampers must be documented and the key results presented in appendices along with design calculations.

The final choice of the optimum mass, stiffness, and damping constant, for each tuned-mass damper must be clearly presented and the reason why this optimum solution was retained must be clearly argued.

Task 6.2: Performance of Bridge Structure Retrofitted with Tuned-Mass Dampers

- The computer program RUAUMOKO and its post-processor DYNAPLOT must be used to analyze the bridge retrofitted with the final tuned-mass damping solution under each of the design ground motions considered. The following analysis results must be compared with the ones obtained for the original building in Phase 3 of the Project: energy balance, plastic hinge and cable yield distribution, envelopes of peak and residual deformations, envelopes of peak absolute accelerations.

- Discuss the merits of the optimum solution in improving the seismic response of the original bridge in light of the performance indices presented in section 11.2.

- Present a preliminary design for each tuned-mass damper including the material and dimensions of the rigid mass, the dimensions and shape of the spring element, and the connection between the tuned-mass damper and the bridge structure.

11.5.7 PHASE 7: Design of Bridge Structure with Friction Pendulum Seismic Isolators

The objective of the seventh phase of the project is to evaluate an alternative solution for a similar bridge with a friction pendulum seismic isolation system of the type described in Chapter 10 of this book along with linear viscous dampers. As shown in Figure 11.19, the alternative solution consists of building two additional concrete piers at the location where the cables were connected to the deck, removing the top part of the tower and the cables and isolating the entire deck with friction pendulum isolators. The concrete piers could be designed based on gravity loads only since the bridge will be isolated. Two friction pendulum isolators are introduced at each of the piers. At the abutments, frictionless bearings allowing for free movement of the deck are installed. The isolators can be designed as either single or double friction pendulum systems. The maximum seismic displacement of the friction pendulum isolators must be limited to ± 300mm in order to avoid pounding between the deck and the abutment.

The seismic isolation system can be modeled as a rigid friction spring as discussed in Chapter 10 of this book. To increase damping, linear viscous dampers could also be inserted next to the friction pendulum bearings at the piers. Four viscous dampers, two on each side of each pier, could be installed between the beams supporting the deck and the piers.

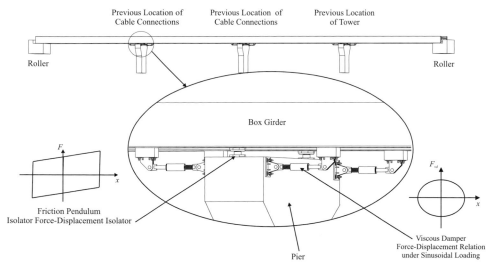

Figure 11.19 Bridge Structure with Friction Pendulum Seismic Isolation System

Task 7.1: Design of Isolated Bridge

The coefficient of friction for the friction pendulum bearings is set at 0.05. The parameters to be determined are the size and properties of the friction pendulum isolators as well as the size and properties of the viscous dampers. Based on the design considerations for seismic isolation systems discussed in Chapter 9 and the modelling of the friction pendulum bearings presented in Chapter 10, the procedure adopted to determine the properties of each isolator and the optimum damping constant c of each viscous damper must be clearly presented and all the methods and assumptions used must be substantiated and referenced. All intermediate analyses leading to the final design of the base isolation system must be documented and the key results presented in appendices along with design calculations. The lateral flexibility of the concrete piers should be considered in the design of the seismic isolation system.

The final choice of the optimum properties of each friction pendulum bearing and the optimum damping constant c of each viscous damper must be clearly presented and the reason why this optimum solution was retained must be clearly argued.

Task 7.2: Performance of Bridge Structure Retrofitted with Friction Pendulum Seismic Isolators

- The computer program RUAUMOKO and its post-processor DYNAPLOT must be used to analyze the bridge structure with the final friction pendulum isolation solution under each of the design ground motions considered. The following analysis results must be compared with the ones obtained for the original bridge in phase 3 of the Project: energy balance, plastic hinge and cable yielding distribution, envelopes of peak and residual deformations, envelopes of peak absolute accelerations.

- Discuss the merits of the optimum solution in improving the seismic response of the original bridge in light of the performance indices listed in Table 11-2.

- Present a preliminary design for each friction pendulum bearing and each viscous damper.

11.5.8 PHASE 8: Performance Assessment of Optimum Retrofit Strategies Under the 2% in 50 Years Ground Motions and Near-Field Ground Motions

As discussed in section 11.3, the retrofitted bridge structure is subjected to a second series of earthquakes to investigate the collapse prevention performance of the optimally retrofitted structure under a greater seismic hazard, as well as the expected performance in the case that the construction site would be located at proximity (less than 10 km) of an active fault.

TASK 8.1: Analysis of Retrofitted Bridge Structure under 2% in 50 Years Probability of Exceedence Records

- The computer program RUAUMOKO and its post-processor DYNAPLOT must be used to analyze the original and optimally retrofitted buildings. The following analysis results must be compared: energy balance, plastic hinge distribution, envelopes of peak and residual deformations, envelopes of peak absolute accelerations.

- Discuss the performance of the isolated bridge and the resulting design implications in light of the performance indices presented in section 11.2.

TASK 8.2: Analysis of Retrofitted Bridge Structure under Near-Field Records

- The computer program RUAUMOKO and its post-processor DYNAPLOT must be used to analyze the original and optimally retrofitted structures. The following analysis results must be compared: energy balance, plastic hinge distribution, and envelopes of peak and residual deformations.

- Discuss the performance of the isolated bridge and the resulting design implications in light of the performance indices presented in section 11.2.

11.5.9 PHASE 9: Summary of Results and Comparison of Retrofit Strategies

In this last phase of the project, a general summary of each of the retrofit techniques is to be presented and an overall comparison of all strategies is to be carried out.

Issues of practical implementation and cost as well as expected performance levels should be carried out to finally recommend a retrofit strategy. The definition of the seismic hazard considered in the study must also be discussed.

This final phase of the project can also be associated with an oral presentation with invited practicing engineers.

REFERENCES

AASHTO, 1998. "LRFD Bridge Design Specifications, 2nd Edition", American Association of State Highway and Transportation Officials, Washington, D.C.

Aiken, I.D. and Kelly, J.M., 1990. "Earthquake Simulator Testing and Analytical Studies of Two Energy-Absorbing Systems for Multistorey Structures", Report No. UCB/EERC-90/03, EERC, University of California, Berkeley, CA.

Aiken, I.D., Nims, D.K. and Kelly, J.M., 1992. "Comparative Study of Four Passive Energy Dissipation Systems", Bulletin of the New Zealand National Society for Earthquake Engineering, 25 (3), 175-192.

Aiken, I.D., Nims, D.K., Whittaker, A.S. and Kelly, J.M., 1993. "Testing of Passive Energy Dissipation Systems", Earthquake Spectra, 9 (3), 335-370.

Aiken, I.D., 1997. "Dampers for Seismic Protection - 1) Friction and Viscous Dampers, 2) Viscoelastic and Metallic Dampers", Technical Seminar on Seismic Isolation and Energy Dissipation Technology, Vancouver, B.C., Canada.

AISC, 1993. "Load and Resistance Factor Design Specification for Structural Buildings", American Institute of Steel Construction, Inc., Chicago, IL.

AISC, 1997. "Seismic Provisions for Structural Steel Buildings", American Institute of Steel Construction, Inc., Chicago, IL.

AISC, 2005. "Seismic Provisions for Structural Steel Buildings," American Institute of Steel Construction, Inc., Chicago, IL.

AISC/SEAOC. 2001. "Recommended Provisions For Buckling-Restrained Braced Frames", American Institute of Steel Construction, Chicago, Il., Structural Engineers Association of California, Sacramento, CA.

Antoniou, S., Rovithakis, A. and Pinho, R., 2002. "Development and Verification of a Fully Adaptive Pushover Procedure", Proceedings, 12th European Conference on Earthquake Engineering, London (available on CD-ROM).

Arima, F., Miyazaka, M., Tanaka, H. and Yamazaki, Y., 1988. "A Study on Buildings with Large Damping Using Viscous Damping Walls", Proceedings, 9th World Conference on Earthquake Engineering, Tokyo/Kyoto, Japan.

ASCE, 2000. "Prestandard and Commentary for the Seismic Rehabilitation of Buildings", FEMA-356, American Society of Civil Engineers, Reston, Virginia.

Asher, J.W. et al., 1990. "Seismic Isolation Design of the USC University Hospital", Proceedings, 4th U.S. National Conference on Earthquake Engineering, Palm Springs, CA.

Ashour, SA. and Hanson, R.D., 1987. "Elastic Seismic Response of Buildings with Supplemental Damping", Report No. UMCE 87-01, University of Michigan, Ann Arbor, MI.

ATC/MCEER, 2003a. "MCEER/ATC-49 Recommended LRFD Guidelines for the Seismic Design of Highway Bridges Part I: Specifications", Report MCEER-03-P03, Multidisciplinary Center for Earthquake Engineering Research, University at Buffalo, Buffalo, NY.

ATC/MCEER, 2003b. "MCEER/ATC-49 Recommended LRFD Guidelines for the Seismic Design of Highway Bridges Part I: Commentary and Appendices", Report MCEER-03-P03, Multidisciplinary Center for Earthquake Engineering Research, University at Buffalo, Buffalo, NY.

Badrakhan, F., 1988. "Dynamic Analysis of Yielding and Hysteretic Systems by Polynomial Approximation", Journal of Sound and Vibration, 125 (1), 23-42.

Baktash, P. and Marsh, C., 1986. "Seismic Behaviour of Friction Damped Braced Frames", Proceedings, 3rd U.S. National Conference on Earthquake Engineering, Charleston, SC, Vol. II, 1099-1105.

Baktash, P. and Marsh, C., 1987. "Damped Moment-Resistant Braced Frames: A Comparative Study", Canadian Journal of Civil Engineering, 14, 342-346.

Bannantine, J.A., Comer, J.J. and Handrock, J.L., 1990. "Fundamental of Metal Fatigue Analysis", Prentice-Hall, Upper Saddle River, New Jersey.

Belytschoko, T., Chiapetta, R.L. and Bartel, H.D., 1976. "Efficient Large Scale Nonlinear Transient Analysis by Finite Elements", International Journal of Numerical Method in Engineering, 10, 579-596.

Bergman, D. M. and Goel, S. C., 1987. "Evaluation of Cyclic Testing of Steel-Plate Devices for Added Damping and Stiffness", Report UMCE 87-10, Civil Engineering Department, University of Michigan, Ann Arbor, MI.

Bergman, D.M. and Hanson, R.D., 1993. "Viscoelastic Mechanical Damping Devices Tested at Real Earthquake Displacements", Earthquake Spectra, 9 (3), 389-418.

Bertero, V. V., 1995. "Tri-Service Manual Methods", Vision 2000, Part 2, Appendix J, Structural Engineers Association of California, Sacramento.

Beshara, F.B.A. and Virdi, K.S., 1991. "Nonlinear Finite Element Dynamic Analysis of Two-Dimensional Concrete Structures", Computers and Structures, 41, 1281-1294.

Black, C.J., Makris, N. and Aiken, I.D., 2004. "Component Testing, Seismic Evaluation and Characterization of Buckling-Restrained Braces", ASCE Journal of Structural Engineering, 130(6), 880-894.

Bolt, B.A., 1988. "Earthquakes", W.H. Freeman and Company, New York.

Bommer, J.J., Elnashai, A.S. and Weir, A.G., 2000. "Compatible Acceleration and Displacement Spectra for Seismic Design Codes", 12th World Conference on Earthquake Engineering, Auckland, New Zealand, Paper No. 207.

Bondonet, G. and Filiatrault, A., 1997. "Frictional Response of PTFE Sliding Bearings at High Frequencies", Journal of Bridge Engineering, ASCE, 2 (4), 139-148.

Bouc, R., 1971. "Modèle mathématique d'hystérésis", Acustica, 24 (1), 16-25 (in French).

Bowden, F. P. and Tabor, D., 1973. "Friction: An Introduction to Tribology", Anchor Press, Garden city, New York, U. S. A.

Brewer, L., 1993. "Analysis of the Effect of Hysteretic Relationships in Beam-Column Connections on the Earthquake Response of Precast Concrete Frame Systems", M.S. Thesis, University of Texas at Austin.

Briscoe, B. J., Ramiez, I. and Tweedale, P.J., 1988. "Disc Brakes for Commercial Vehicles - Friction of Aramid Fibre Composites", Proceedings, International Conference of the Institution of Mechanical Engineers, Birdcage Walk, London, U.K.

Brown, A.P., Aiken, I.D. and Jafarzadeh, F., 2003. "Buckling Restrained Braces Provide the Key to the Seismic Retrofit of the Wallace F. Bennett Federal Building" (available on line at www.reaveley.com/pdffiles/BennettBldg.pdf).

BSSC, 1997. "NEHRP Guidelines for the Seismic Rehabilitation of Buildings", FEMA-273, Building Seismic Safety Council, Washington, D.C.

BSSC, 2003. "NEHRP Recommended Provisions for Seismic Regulations for New Buildings and Other Structures: Parts 1 and 2", FEMA-450, Building Seismic Safety Council, Washington, D.C.

Capecchi, D. and Vestroni, F., 1985. "Steady-State Dynamic Analysis of Hysteretic Systems", Journal of Engineering Mechanics, American Society of Civil Engineers, 111 (12), 1515-1531.

Carr, A.J., 1998. "RUAUMOKO - Inelastic Dynamic Analysis Program", Department of Civil Engineering, University of Canterbury, Christchurch, New Zealand.

Carr, A.J., 2002. "RUAUMOKO - Inelastic Dynamic Analysis Program", Department of Civil Engineering, University of Canterbury, Christchurch, New Zealand.

Carr, A.J., 2004. "RUAUMOKO Volume 2: User Manual for the 2-Dimensional Version, RUAUMOKO2D", Department of Civil Engineering, University of Canterbury, Christchurch, New Zealand.

Carr, J., 2005. "Seismic Response of Buildings Equipped with Tuned-Mass Dampers", Master of Science Project, Department of Civil, Structural and Environmental Engineering, University at Buffalo, State University of New York, Buffalo, NY.

Caughey, T.K., 1960. "Sinusoidal Excitation of a System with Bilinear Hysteresis", Journal of Applied Mechanics, American Society of Mechanical Engineers, 27 (4), 640-643.

CEN, 2004. "Eurocode 8 - Design Provisions for Earthquake Resistance of Structures", ENV 1998-2, Comité Européen de Normaliation, Brussels, Belgium.

Chang, K.C., Soong, T.T., Lai, M.L. and Nielsen, E.J., 1993a. "Development of a Design Procedure for Structures with Added Viscoelastic Dampers", ATC17-1 on Seismic Isolation, Passive Energy Dissipation and Active Control, 2, 473-484.

Chang, K.C., Lai, M.L., Soong, T.T., Hao, D.S. and Yeh, Y.C., 1993b. "Seismic Behaviour and Design Guidelines for Steel Frame Structures with Added Viscoelastic Dampers", Report No. NCEER 93-0009, National Center for Earthquake Engineering Research, Buffalo, NY.

Chang, K.C., Shen, K.L., Soong, T.T. and Lai, M.L., 1994. "Seismic Retrofit of a Concrete Frame with Added Viscoelastic Dampers", 5th National Conference on Earthquake Engineering, Chicago, IL.

Chang, K.C., Soong, T.T., Oh, S-T. and Lai, M.L., 1995. "Seismic Behaviour of Steel Frame With Added Viscoelastic Dampers", ASCE Journal of Structural Engineering, 121(10), 1418-1426.

Charleson, A.W., Wright, P.D. and Skinner, R.I., 1987. "Wellington Central Police Station: Base Isolation of an Essential Facility", Pacific Conference on Earthquake Engineering, Auckland, New Zealand, (2) 377-388.

Chopra, A.K., 2001. "Dynamics of Structures - Theory and Applications to Earthquake Engineering", Prentice Hall, New Jersey.

Chopra, A.K. and Goel, R., 2002. "A Modal Pushover Analysis Procedure for Estimating Seismic Demands for Buildings", Earthquake Engineering and Structural Dynamics, 31, 561-582.

Chou, C.C. and Uang, C.-M., 2000. "Establishing Absorbed Energy Spectra - an Attenuation Approach", Earthquake Engineering and Structural Dynamics, 29, 1441-1455.

Chou, C.C. and Uang, C.-M., 2003. "A Procedure for Evaluating Seismic Energy Demand of Framed Structures", Earthquake Engineering and Structural Dynamics, 32, 229-244.

Christopoulos, C., 2002. "Self-Centering Post-Tensioned Energy Dissipating (PTED) Steel Frames for Seismic Regions", Ph.D. Thesis, Department of Structural Engineering, University of California, San Diego, CA.

Christopoulos, C., Filiatrault, A., Folz, B. and Uang, C-M., 2002a. "Post-Tensioned Energy Dissipating Connections for Moment-Resisting Steel Frames", ASCE Journal of Structural Engineering, 128 (9), 1111-1120.

Christopoulos, C., Filiatrault, A. and Folz, B., 2002b. "Seismic Response of Self-Centering Hysteretic SDOF Systems", Earthquake Engineering and Structural Dynamics, 31 (5), 1131-1150.

Christopoulos, C., Pampanin, S. and Priestley, M.J.N., 2003. "New Damage Index for Framed Systems Based on Residual Deformations: Part I", Journal of Earthquake Engineering, 7(1), 97-118.

Christopoulos, C., 2004, "Frequency-Response of Flag-Shaped SDOF Hysteretic Systems", Journal of Engineering Mechanics, American Society of Civil Engineers, 130 (8), 894-903.

Christopoulos, C. and Pampanin, S., 2004. "Towards Performance-Based Design of MDOF Structures with Explicit Consideration of Residual Deformations", Invited Paper, ISET Journal of Earthquake Technology, Special Issue on Performance-Based Design.

Ciampi, V. and Samuelli Ferretti, A., 1990. "Energy Dissipation in Buildings Using Special Bracing Systems", Proceedings, 9th European Conference on Earthquake Engineering, Moscow, 3, 9-18.

Ciampi, V., Arcangeli, M. and Ferlito, R., 1991. "Dissipative Bracings for Seismic Protection of Buildings", International Meeting on Earthquake Protection of Buildings, Ancona, Italy, 87/D-100/D.

Ciampi, V., Paolone, A. and De Angelis, M., 1992. "On the Seismic Design of Dissipative Bracings", Proceedings, 10th World Conference on Earthquake Engineering, Madrid, 7, 4133-4138.

Ciampi, V., 1993. "Development of Passive Energy Dissipation Techniques for Buildings", International Post-SmiRT Conference Seminar on Isolation, Energy Dissipation, and Control of Vibrations of Structures, Capri, Italy.

Ciampi, V., De Angelis, M. and Paolacci, F., 1995. "Design of Yielding or Friction-Based Dissipative Bracing for Seismic Protection of Buildings", Engineering Structures, 17, 381-391.

Clark, P.W., Aiken, I.D., Nakashima, M., Meyzaki, M. and Midorikawa, M., 2000. "The 1995 Kobe (Hyogo-Ken Nanbu) Earthquake as a Trigger for Implementing New Seismic Design Technologies in Japan", Lessons Learned Over Time, Learning from Earthquake Series, Earthquake Engineering Research Institute, 3, 79-109.

Clark, P.W., Aiken, I.D., Ko, E., Kasai, K. and Kimura, I., 2003. "Design Procedures for Buildings Incorporating Hysteretic Damping Devices" (available online at http://www.siecorp.com/braces/).

Collins, J.H. and Filiatrault, A., 2003. "Application of Post-Tensioned Energy Dissipating (PTED) Connections in Steel Moment-Resisting Frames", Report No. SSRP-2003/05, Department of Structural Engineering, University of California, San Diego.

Connor, J.J., 2003. "Introduction to Structural Motion Control", Prentice Hall, New Jersey.

Constantinou, M.C., Caccese, J. and Harris, H.G., 1987. "Frictional Characteristics of Teflon-Steel Interfaces Under Dynamic Conditions", Earthquake Engineering and Structural Dynamics, 15(6), 751-759.

Constantinou, M.C. and Symans, M.D., 1992. "Experimental and Analytical Investigation of Seismic Response of Structures with Supplemental Fluid Viscous Dampers", Technical Report NCEER-92-0032, National Center for Earthquake Research, Buffalo, New York.

Constantinou, M.C., Symans, M.D. and Tsopelas, P., 1993. "Fluid Viscous Dampers in Applications of Seismic Energy Dissipation and Seismic Isolation", ATC17-1 on Seismic Isolation, Passive Energy Dissipation and Active Control, 2, 581-591.

Constantinou, M.C., Soong, T.T. and Dargush, G.F., 1998. "Passive Energy Dissipation Systems for Structural Design and Retrofit", MCEER Monograph No. 1, Multidisciplinary Center for Earthquake Engineering Research, University at Buffalo, Buffalo, New York.

Constantinou, M.C., Tsopelas, P., Kasalanati, A. and Wolff, E.D., 1999. "Property Modification Factors for Seismic Isolation Bearings", Technical Report MCEER-99-0012, Multidisciplinary Center for Earthquake Engineering Research, Buffalo, NY.

Constantinou, M.C., Tsopelas, P., Hammel, W. and Sigaher, A.N., 2001. "Toggle-Brace-Damper Seismic Energy Dissipation Systems," ASCE Journal of Structural Engineering, 127(2), 105-112.

Constantinou, M.C., 2004. "Friction Pendulum Double Concave Bearing", Technical Report, University at Buffalo, State University of New York, Buffalo, NY.

Cormack, L.G., 1988. "The Design and Construction of the Major Bridges on the Mangaweka Rail Deviation", Transaction of the Institute of Professional Engineers of New Zealand, 15, 16-23.

Cosenza, E., Manfredi, G. and Ramasco, R., 1993. "The Use of Damage Functionals in Earthquake Engineering: A Comparison Between Different Methods", Earthquake Engineering and Structural Dynamics, 22, 855-868.

Cousins, W.J., Robinson, W.H. and McVerry, G.H., 1991. "Recent Developments in Devices for Seismic Isolation", Pacific Conference on Earthquake Engineering, Auckland, New Zealand, (2) 221-232.

Croci, G., Bonci, A. and Viscovic, A., 2000. "Use of Shape Memory Alloy Devices in the Basilica of St. Francis of Assisi", Final Workshop on Shape Memory Alloy Devices for Seismic Protection of Cultural Heritage Structures", ISTECH.

Crosby, P., Kelly, J.M. and Singh, J., 1994. "Utilizing Viscoelastic Dampers in the Seismic Retrofit of a Thirteen Storey Steel Frame Building", ASCE Structures Congress XII, Atlanta, GA, 1286-1291.

CSA, 1994. "Design of Concrete Structures", Canadian Standard Association, A23.3, Rexdale, Ontario, Canada.

DebChaudhury, A., 1985. "Periodic Response of Yielding Oscillators", Journal of Engineering Mechanics, American Society of Civil Engineering, 111 (8), 977-994.

De la Llera, J.C., Almazan, J.L. and Vial, I.J., 2005."Torsional Balance of Plan-Asymmetric Structures with Frictional Dampers: Analytical Results", Earthquake Engineering and Structural Dynamics, 34, 1089-1108.

Den Hartog, J.P., 1985. "Mechanical Vibrations, 4th Edition", McGraw-Hill, New York, Mechanical Vibrations, 4th Edition.

DesRoches, R., McCormick, J. and Delemont, M. 2004. "Cyclic Properties of Superelastic Shape Memory Alloy Wires and Bars", ASCE Journal of Structural Engineering, 130 (1), 38-46.

DesRoches, R. and Smith, B., 2004. "Shape Memory Alloys in Seismic Resistant Design and Retrofit: a Critical Review of their Potential and Limitations", Journal of Earthquake Engineering, 8 (3), 415-429.

De Silva C.W., 1981. "An Algorithm for the Optimal Design of Passive Vibration Controllers for Flexible Systems", Journal of Sound and Vibration, 74 (4), 495-502.

Dobry, R., Idriss, I.M. and Ng, E., 1978. "Duration Characteristics of Horizontal Components of Strong Motion Earthquake Records", Bulletin of the Seismological Society of America, 68 (5), 1487-1520.

Dowdell, D.J. and Cherry, S., 1996. "On Passive and Semi-Active Friction Damping for Seismic Response Control of Structures", Proceedings, 11th World Conference on Earthquake Engineering, Acapulco, Mexico, Paper No. 957.

Elliot, J., McCaffrey, G., Guruswami, G., Pall, R. and Pall, A., 1998. "High-Tech Seismic Rehabilitation of Justice Headquarters Building, Ottawa", Proceedings, Structural Engineers World Congress, San Francisco, Paper No. T189-3.

Eurocode 8, 2003. "Design of Structures for Earthquake Resistance, Part I: General Rules, Seismic Actions and Rules for Buildings", pre-ENV 1998-1, CEN, Brussels.

Fajfar, P., 1992. "Equivalent Ductility Factors: Taking into Account Low-cycle Fatigue", Earthquake Engineering and Structural Dynamics, 21, 837-848.

Fajfar, P., 1999. "Capacity Spectrum Method Based on Inelastic Demand Spectra", Earthquake Engineering and Structural Dynamics, 28, 979-993.

Falcon, K.C., Stone, B.J., Simcock, W.D. and Andrew, C., 1967. "Optimization of Vibration Absorbers: A Graphical Method for Use on Idealized Systems with Restricted Damping", Journal of Mechanical Engineering Science, 9, 374-381.

Fardis, M.N., 1995. "Damage Measures and Failure Criteria for Reinforced Concrete Members", Proceedings, 10th European Conference on Earthquake Engineering, Vienna.

Filiatrault, A. and Cherry, S., 1987. "Performance Evaluation of Friction Damped Braced Steel Frames Under Simulated Earthquake Loads", Earthquake Spectra, 3 (1), 57-78.

Filiatrault, A. and Cherry, S., 1988. "Seismic Design of Friction Damped Braced Steel Plane Frames by Energy Methods", Earthquake Engineering Research Laboratory Report UBC-EERL-88-01, Department of Civil Engineering, University of British Columbia, Vancouver, Canada.

Filiatrault, A. and Cherry, S., 1990. "Seismic Design Spectra for Friction Damped Structures", ASCE Journal of Structural Engineering, 116 (5), 1334-1355.

Filiatrault, A., Leger, P. and Tinawi, R., 1994a. "On the Computation of Seismic Energy in Inelastic Structures", Engineering Structures, 16 (6), 425-436.

Filiatrault, A., D'Arronco, D. and Tinawi, R., 1994b."Seismic Shear Demands for Ductile Cantilever Walls: A Canadian Code Perspective", Canadian Journal of Civil Engineering, 21(3), 363-376.

Filiatrault, A., Tremblay, R. and Karr, R., 2000. "Performance Evaluation of Friction Spring Seismic Damper", ASCE Journal of Structural Engineering, 126 (4), 491-499.

Filiatrault, A., Tremblay, R. and Wanitkorkul, A., 2001. "Performance Evaluation of Passive Damping Systems for the Seismic Retrofit of Steel Moment Resisting Frames Subjected to Near Field Ground Motions", Earthquake Spectra, 17 (3), 427-456.

Filiatrault, A., 2002. "Elements of Earthquake Engineering and Structural Dynamics - Second Edition", Polytechnical International Press, Montreal, QC, Canada.

Filiatrault, A. and Folz, B., 2002. "Performance-Based Seismic Design of Wood Framed Buildings", ASCE Journal of Structural Engineering, 128 (1), 39-47.

Filiatrault, A., Isoda, H. and Folz, B., 2003. "Hysteretic Damping of Wood Framed Buildings", Engineering Structures, 25 (4), 461-471.

Foutch, D.A., Wood, S.L. and Brady, P.A., 1993. "Seismic Retrofit of Nonductile Reinforced Concrete Frames Using Viscoelastic Dampers", ATC17-1 on Seismic Isolation, Passive Energy Dissipation and Active Control, 2, 605-616.

Frahm, H., 1909. "Device for Damping Vibrations of Bodies", US Patent No. 989958, Oct. 30, 1909.

Freeman, S.A., Nicoletti, J.P. and Tyrell, J.V., 1975. "Evaluations of Existing Buildings for Seismic Risk - A Case Study of Puget Sound Naval Shipyard, Bremerton, Washington", Proceedings, 1st National Conference in Earthquake Engineering, 113-122.

Freeman, S.A., 1998. "Development and Use of Capacity Spectrum Method", Proceedings, 6th U.S. National Conference on Earthquake Engineering, Seattle (on CD-ROM).

Fu, Y. and Cherry, S., 1999. "Simplified Seismic Code Design Procedure for Friction Damped Steel Frames", Canadian Journal of Civil Engineering, 26, 55-71.

Fu, Y. and Cherry, S., 2000. "Design of Friction Damped Structures Using Lateral Force Procedure", Earthquake Engineering and Structural Dynamics, 29, 989-1010.

Fujino, Y. and Abe, M., 1993. "Design Formulas for Tuned Mass Dampers Based on a Perturbation Technique", Earthquake Engineering and Structural Dynamics, 22, 833-854.

Fujita, S., Fujita, T., Furuya, O., Morikawa, S., Suizu, Y., Teramoto, T. and Kitamura, T., 1992. "Development of High Damping Rubber Damper for Vibration Attenuation of High-Rise Buildings", Proceedings, 10th World Conference on Earthquake Engineering, Madrid, Spain, 2097-2101.

Funakubo, H., 1984. "Shape Memory Alloys", Gordon and Breach Science Publications.

Gluck, N., Reinhorn, A.M., Gluck, J. and Levy, R., 1996. "Design of Supplemental Dampers for Control of Structures," ASCE Journal of Structural Engineering, 122 (12), 1394-1399.

Godin, D., Poirier, R., Pall, R. and Pall, A., 1995. "Renforcement Sismique du Nouveau Campus de l'Ecole de Technologie Supérieure de Montréal", 7th Canadian Conference on Earthquake Engineering, Montreal, Canada, 967-974.

Goel, R.K., 2001. "Simplified Analysis of Asymmetric Structures with Supplemental Damping", Earthquake Engineering and Structural Dynamics, 30 (9), 1399-1416.

Graesser, E.J. and Cozzarelli, F.A., 1991. "Shape-Memory Alloys as New Materials for Aseismic Isolation", Journal of Engineering Mechanics, ASCE, 117 (11), 2590-2608.

Grant, D.N., Fenves, G.L. and Auricchio, F., 2005. "Modelling and Analysis of High-Damping Rubber Bearings for the Seismic Protection of Bridges", IUSS Report 88-7358-028-9, IUSS Press, Milan, Italy.

Graves, R. and Saikia, C., 1995. "Characterization of Ground Motions During the Northridge Earthquake of January 17, 1994", Technical Report SAC95-03, SAC Joint Venture, Sacramento, CA.

Grigorian, C.E., Yang, T.S. and Popov, E.P., 1993. "Slotted Bolted Connection Energy Dissipators", Earthquake Spectra, 9 (3), 491-504.

Grigorian, C.E. and Popov, E.P., 1994. "Energy Dissipation with Slotted Bolted Connections", Report No. UCB/EERC-94/02, EERC, University of California, Berkeley, CA.

Gross, J.L, Engelhardt, M.D., Uang, C.-M., Kasai, K. and Iwankiw, N.R., 1999. "Modification of Existing Welded Steel Moment Frame Connections for Seismic Resistance", Design Guide No. 12, American Institute of Steel Construction, Chicago, IL.

Gupta, B. and Kunnath, S. K., 2000. "Adaptive Spectra-Based Pushover Procedure for Seismic Evaluation of Structures", Earthquake Spectra, 16 (2), 367-392.

Gurgoze, M. and Muller, O.C., 1992. "Optimal Positioning of Dampers in Multi-Body Systems", Journal of Sound and Vibration, 158 (3), 517-530.

Halldorsson, B., 2004."Calibration of the Specific Barrier Model to Earthquakes of Different Tectonic Regions and the Synthesis of Ground Motions for Earthquake Engineering Applications", Ph.D. Dissertation, Department of Civil, Structural and Environmental Engineering, University at Buffalo, State University of New York, Buffalo, N.Y.

Hale, T., Tokas, C. and Pall, A., 1995. "Seismic Retrofit of Elevated Water Tanks at the University of California at Davis", 7th Canadian Conference on Earthquake Engineering, Montreal, Canada, 959-966.

Hall, J. F., 1995. "Parameter Study of the Response of Moment-Resisting Steel Frame Buildings to Near-Source Ground Motions", Technical Report SAC95-05: Parametric Analytical Investigation of Ground Motion and Structural Response, Northridge Earthquake of January 17, 1994. Sacramento, CA, 1.1-1.83.

Hewes, J. and Priestley, M.J.N., 2001. "Experimental Testing of Unbonded Post-Tensioned Precast Concrete Segmental Bridge Columns", The 6th Caltrans Seismic Research Workshop Program, Radisson Hotel, Sacramento, California, Division of Engineering Services, California Dept. of Transportation, Sacramento, 8 pages.

Holden, T., Restrepo, J.I. and Mander, J.B., 2003. "Seismic Response of Precast Reinforced and Prestressed Concrete Walls", ASCE Journal of Structural Engineering, 129 (3), 286-296.

Housner, G.W., 1956. "Limit Design of Structures to Resist Earthquakes", 1st World Conference on Earthquake Engineering, Berkeley, CA, 5.1-5.13.

Housner, G.W., 1963. "The Behaviour of Inverted Pendulum Structures During Earthquakes", Bulletin of the Seismological Society of America, 53, 404-417.

Housner, G.W., 1984. "Historical View of Earthquake Engineering", Proceedings, 8th World Conference on Earthquake Engineering, San Francisco, CA, July 21-28, Englewood Cliffs, NJ: Prentice-Hall, 764-777.

ICBO, 1994. "Uniform Building Code", International Conference of Building Officials, Whittier, CA.

ICBO, 1997. "Uniform Building Code", International Conference of Building Officials, Whittier, CA.

ICC, 2003. "International Building Code", International Code Council, Building Officials and Code Administrators International Inc., Country Club Hills, IL., International Conference of Building Officials, Whittier, CA, Southern Building Code Congress International, Inc., Birmingham, Alabama.

Indirli, M., Castellano, M.G., Clemente, P. and Martinelli, A., 2001. "Demo-Application of Shape Memory Alloy Devices: the Rehabilitation of the S. Giorgio Church Bell Tower ", Proceedings, SPIE - The International Society for Optical Engineering, SMART Systems for Bridges, Structures and Highways - SMART Structures and Materials, Newport Beach, CA, 4330, 262-272.

Ioi, T. and Ikeda, K., 1978. "On the Dynamic Vibration Damped Absorbed of the Vibration System", Bulletin of Japanese Society of Mechanical Engineering, 21 (151), 64-71.

Iwan, W.D., 1965. "The Steady-State Response of the Double Bilinear Hysteretic Model", Journal of Applied Mechanics, American Society of Mechanical Engineering, 32, 921-925.

Iwan, W.D. and Gates, N.C., 1979. "Estimating Earthquake Response of Simple Hysteretic Structures", Journal of the Engineering Mechanics Division, American Society of Civil Engineering, 105, EM3, June, 391-405.

Iwan, W. D., 1999. "Implications of Near-Fault Ground Motion for Structural Design", U.S.-Japan Workshop on Performance-Based Earthquake Engineering Methodology for RC Building Structures, Maui, Hawaii (available from PEER, UC Berkeley).

Jacquot, R.G. and Hoppe, D.L., 1973. "Optimal Random Vibration Absorbers", Journal of Engineering Mechanics, ASCE, 99, 612-616.

Jennings, P.G., 1964. "Periodic Response of a General Yielding Structure", Journal of the Engineering Mechanics Division, American Society of Civil Engineers, (EM2), 131-166.

Jennings, P.G., 1968. "Equivalent Viscous Damping for Yielding Structures", Journal of the Engineering Mechanics Division, American Society of Civil Engineers, 94 (1), 131-166.

Kajima Corporation, 1991. "Honeycomb Damper Systems", Tokyo, Japan.

Kar, R. and Rainer, J.H., 1996. "New Damper for Seismic Control of Structures", Proceedings, 1st Structural Specialty Conference, Edmonton, AL., 835-842.

Kar, R., Rainer, J.H. and Lefrancois, A.C., 1996. "Dynamic Properties of a Circuit Breaker with Friction-Based Seismic Dampers", Earthquake Spectra, 12 (2), 297-314.

Kelly, J.M., 1979. "Aseismic Base Isolation: A Review", Proceedings, 2nd U.S. National Conference on Earthquake Engineering, Stanford, CA, 823-837.

Kelly, J.M., Skinner, R.I. and Heine, A.J., 1972. "Mechanisms of Energy Absorption in Special Devices for Use in Earthquake Resistant Structures", Bulletin of the New Zealand Society for Earthquake Engineering, 5 (3), 63-88.

Kelly, J.M., 1990. "Base Isolation: Linear Theory and Design", Earthquake Spectra, 6 (2), 223-244.

Kim, H.-J., Christopoulos, C. and Tremblay, R., 2004. "Experimental Characterization of Bolt-stressed Non-Asbestos Organic (NOA) Material-to-Steel Interfaces", Report No. UT2004-3, Department of Civil Engineering, University of Toronto, Canada.

Kirekawa, A., Ito, Y. and Aano, K., 1992. "A Study of Structural Control Using Viscoelastic Material", 10th World Conference on Earthquake Engineering, Madrid, Spain, 2047-2054.

Kobori, T., Yamada, T., Takenaka, Y., Maeda, Y. and Nishimura, I., 1988. "Effect of Dynamic Tuned Connector on Reduction of Seismic Response - Application to Adjacent Office Buildings", 9th World Conference on Earthquake Engineering, Vol. 5, Tokyo/Kyoto, Japan.

Krawinkler, H. and Seneviratna, G.D.P.K., 1998. "Pros and Cons of a Pushover Analysis for Seismic Performance Evaluation", Engineering Structures, 20 (4-6), 452-464.

Krawinkler H., Parisi F., Ibarra L., Ayoub, A. and Medina, A.R., 2000. "Development of a Testing Protocol for Wood Frame Structures", CUREE Report No.W-02, Richmond, CA.

Kulak, G. L., Fisher, J. W. and Struik, J. H. A., 2001. "Guide to Design Criteria for Bolted and Riveted Joints", 2nd edition, AISC, Chicago, IL.

Kulak, G. L. and Grondin, G. Y., 2002. "Limit states design in structural steel", 2nd edition, Canadian Institute of Steel Construction, Toronto.

Kunnath, S.K. and Gupta, S.K., 2000. "Validity of Deformation Demand Estimates Using Nonlinear Static Procedures", U.S.-Japan Workshop on Performance-Based Earthquake Engineering Methodology for RC Building Structures, Sapporo, Japan.

Kurama, Y.C. and Shen, Q., 2004. "Post-Tensioned Hybrid Coupled Walls Under Lateral Loads", ASCE Journal of Structural Engineering, 130 (2), 297-309.

Kwan, W.-P. and Billington, S.L., 2003. "Unbonded Post-Tensioned Concrete Bridge Piers. I: Monotonic and Cyclic Analyses", ASCE Journal of Bridge Engineering, 8 (2), 92-101.

Lai, M.L., Chang, K.C., Soong, T.T., Hao, D.S. and Yeh, Y.C., 1995. "Full-Scale Viscoelastically Damped Steel Frame", ASCE Journal of Structural Engineering, 121(10), 1443-1447.

Lavan, O. and Levy, R., 2004. "Optimal Design of Supplemental Viscous Damping for Linear Structures", 13th World Conference on Earthquake Engineering, Vancouver, Canada, Paper No. 42.

Lee, D., 2003. "Taylor Devices Inc., Building Today for Tomorrow Since 1955" (personal communication).

Levy, R., Marianchik, E., Rutenberg, A. and Segal, F., 2000. "Seismic Design Methodology for Friction Damped Braced Frames", Earthquake Engineering and Structural Dynamics, 29, 1569-1585.

Levy, R., Marianchik, E., Rutenberg, A. and Segal, F., 2001. "A Simple Approach to the Seismic Design of Friction Damped Braced Medium-Rise Frames", Engineering Structures, 23, 250-259.

Li, Z.X., He, Y.A. and Franciosi, C., 1996. "Optimal Damper Control of 3-Dimensional Tall Buildings Under Earthquake Excitations", 10th World Conference on Earthquake Engineering, Balkema, Rotterdam, 4159-4164.

Lin, R.C., Liang, Z., Soong, T.T. and Zhang, R.H., 1991. "An Experimental Study on Seismic Structural Response with Added Viscoelastic Dampers", Engineering Structures, 13, 75-84.

Lin, W.H. and Chopra, A.K., 2001. "Understanding and Predicting Effects of Supplemental Viscous Damping on Seismic Response of Asymmetric One-Storey Systems", Earthquake Engineering and Structural Dynamics, 30 (9), 1475-1494.

Lobo, R.F., Bracci, J.M., Shen, K.L., Reinhorn, A.M. and Soong, T.T., 1993. "Inelastic Response of R/C Structures with Viscoelastic Braces", Earthquake Spectra, 9 (3), 419-446.

Lopez-Garcia, D., 2001. "A Simple Method for the Design of Optimal Damper Configurations in MDOF Structures," Earthquake Spectra, 17(3), 387-398.

Lopez Garcia, D., 2003. EUGENIA Program User's Manual (personal communication).

Luft, R.W., 1979. "Optimal Tuned Mass Dampers for Buildings", Journal of Structural Division, ASCE, 105 (12), 2766-2772.

Marriott, D., Palermo, A. and Pampanin, S., 2006. "Quasi-Static and Pseudo-Dynamic Testing of Damage-Resistant Bridge Piers with Hybrid Connections", Proceedings of the 1st ECEES, Geneva, Switzerland.

McManus K.J., 1980. "The Seismic Response of Bridge Structures Free to Rock on Their Foundations", Masters Thesis, Civil Engineering Department, University of Canterbury, Christchurch, New Zealand.

MacRae, G.A. and Priestley, M.J.N., 1994. "Precast Post-Tensioned Ungrouted Concrete Beam-Column Subassemblage Tests", Report No. SSRP-94/10, Department of Applied Mechanics and Engineering Sciences, University of California, San Diego.

Mahmoodi, P., Robertson, L.E., Yontar, M., Moy, C. and Feld, I., 1987. "Performance of Viscoelastic Dampers in World Trade Center Towers", Dynamic of Structures, ASCE Structures Congress, Orlando Florida.

Mander, J.B. and Cheng, C-T., 1997. "Seismic Resistance of Bridge Piers Based on Damage Avoidance Design", Technical Report NCEER-97-0014, NCEER, Department of Civil and Environmental Engineering, University at Buffalo, Buffalo, New York.

Mansour, N. and Christopoulos, C., 2005. "Explicit Performance-Based Seismic Design of Structures Equipped with Hysteretic Dampers", Report No. UT2004-4, Department of Civil Engineering, University of Toronto, Canada.

Martinez-Romero, E., 1993. "Experiences on the Use of Supplemental Energy Dissipators on Building Structures", Earthquake Spectra, 9 (3), 581-625.

Masri, S.F., 1975. "Forced Vibration of the Damped Bilinear Hysteretic Oscillator", Journal of the Acoustic Society of America, 57 (1), 106-112.

Matthewson, C.D. and Davey, R.D., 1979. "Design of an Earthquake Resisting Building Using Precast Concrete Cross-Braced Panels and Incorporating Energy-Absorbing Devices", South Pacific Regional Conference on Earthquake Engineering, Vol. 1, Wellington, New Zealand.

Minorski, N., 1947. "Nonlinear Mechanics", J.W. Edwards, Ann Arbor, Michigan.

Miyazaki, M. and Mitsusaka, L., 1992. "Design of a Building with 20% or Greater Damping", 11th World Conference on Earthquake Engineering, Acapulco, Mexico.

Monjoine, M.J., 1944. "Influence of Rate of Strain and Temperature on Yield Stress of Mild Steel", Journal of Applied Mechanics, 11, 211-218.

Muto, K., 1969. "Earthquake Resistant Design of 36-Storied Kasumigaseki Building", 4th World Conference on Earthquake Engineering, 3, J-4, 16-33.

Naeim, F. and Kelly, J.M., 1999. "Design of Seismic Isolated Structures" John Wiley & Sons, New York.

Nagarajaiah, S., Reinhorn, A., Cli, A. M. and Constantinou, M.C., 1993. "3D-Basis-Tabs, Computer Program for Nonlinear Dynamic Analysis of 3-Dimensional Base Isolated Structures", Report NCEER-93-0011, National Center for Earthquake Engineering Research, University at Buffalo, Buffalo, New York.

Nakaki, S.D., Stanton, J.F. and Sritharan, S., 1999. "An Overview of the PRESSS Five-Storey Precast Test Building", PCI Journal, 44 (2), 26-39.

Nayfeh, A.H. and Mook, P.T., 1979. "Nonlinear Oscillations", John Wiley, New York.

Nims, D.K., Richter, P.J. and Bachman, R.E., 1993."The Use of Energy Dissipating Restraint for Seismic Hazard Mitigation", Earthquake Spectra, 9 (3), 467-489.

NRC, 1995. "National Building Code of Canada", National Research Council, Ottawa, Ontario, Canada.

NRC, 2005. "National Building Code of Canada", National Research Council, Ottawa, Ontario, Canada.

NZS, 2006. New Zealand Standards. Concrete Structures Standard. NZS 3101:2006 Appendix B: "Special Provisions for the Seismic Design of Ductile Jointed Precast Concrete Structural Systems".

Ocel, J., DesRoches, R., Leon, R.T., Hess, W.G., Krume, R., Hayes, J.R. and Sweeney, S., 2004. "Steel Beam-Column Connections Using Shape Memory Alloys", ASCE Journal of Structural Engineering, 130 (5), 732-740.

Ozdemir, H., 1976. "Nonlinear Transient Dynamic Analysis of Yielding Structures", Ph.D. Thesis, University of California, Berkeley, CA.

Pall, A.S., Marsh, C. and Fazio, P., 1980. "Friction Joints for Seismic Control of Large Panel Structures", Journal of Prestressed Concrete Institute, 25 (6), 38-61.

Pall, A.S. and Marsh, C., 1981. "Response of Friction Damped Braced Frames", Journal of the Structural Division, ASCE, 108(ST6), 1313-1323.

Pall, A.S., Verganelakis, V. and Marsh, C., 1987. "Friction Dampers for Seismic Control of Concordia Library Building", 5th Canadian Conference on Earthquake Engineering, Ottawa, Canada.

Pall, A.S. and Pall, R., 1993. "Friction-Dampers Used for Seismic Control of New and Existing Buildings in Canada", Seminar on Seismic Isolation, Passive Energy Dissipation and Active Control, (ATC 17.1), Applied Technology Council, San Francisco, 2: 675-686.

Pall, A.S. and Pall, R., 1996. "Friction Dampers for Seismic Control of Buildings: A Canadian Experience", 11th World Conference on Earthquake Engineering, Acapulco, Mexico.

Palermo A., Pampanin S. and Calvi, G.M., 2005. "Concept and Development of Hybrid Solutions for Seismic Resistant Bridge Systems", Journal of Earthquake Engineering, Imperial College Press, 9 (6), 899-921.

Pampanin, S., Priestley, M.J.N. and Sritharan, S., 2000. "Frame Direction Modelling of Five-Storey PRESSS Precast Test Building", Report No. SSRP 99/20, University of California, San Diego.

Pampanin, S., Christopoulos, C. and Priestley, M.J.N., 2003. "New Damage Index for Framed Systems Based on Residual Deformations: Part II", Journal of Earthquake Engineering, 7 (1), 119-140.

Pampanin, S., Pagani, C. and Zambelli, S., 2004. "Cable-Stayed and Suspended Post-Tensioned Solutions for Precast Concrete Frames: The Brooklyn System", Proceedings of the New Zealand Concrete Society Conference, Queenstown, NZ.

Pampanin, S., 2005. "Emerging Solutions for High Seismic Performance of Precast/Prestressed Concrete Buildings", Journal of Advanced Concrete Technology (ACT), Special Issue on "High performance systems", 2005:202-23.

Pampanin, S., 2006. "Controversial Aspects in Seismic Assessment and Retrofit of Structures in Modern Times: Understanding and Implementing Lessons from Ancient Heritage", Bulletin of the New Zealand Society of Earthquake Engineering, 39 (2), 120-133.

Pan, P., Zamfiresku, D., Nakashima, M., Nakayaso, N. and Kashiwa, N., 2004. "Base-Isolation Design Practice in Japan: Introduction to the Post-Kobe Approach", Journal of Earthquake Engineering, 9 (1), 1-25.

Papageorgiou, A.S. and Aki, K., 1983a. "A specific Barrier Model for the Quantitative Description of Inhomogenous Faulting and the Prediction of Strong Ground Motion, Part I: Description of the Model", Bulletin of the American Seismological Society of America, 73, 693-722.

Papageorgiou, A.S. and Aki, K., 1983b. "A specific Barrier Model for the Quantitative Description of Inhomogenous Faulting and the Prediction of Strong Ground Motion, Part II: Applications of the Model", Bulletin of the American Seismological Society of America, 73, 953-978.

Parducci, A. and Mezzi, M. 1991. "Seismic Isolation of Bridges in Italy," Pacific Conference on Earthquake Engineering, Auckland, New Zealand, (3), 45-56.

Park, Y.J. and Ang, A.H.S., 1985. "Seismic Damage Analysis of Reinforced Concrete Buildings", ASCE Journal of Structural Engineering, 111, 4, 740-757.

Pasquin, C., Pall, A. and Pall, R., 1994. "High-Tech Seismic Rehabilitation of Casino de Montreal", Structures Congress, ASCE Structures Congress, Atlanta, GA.

Pasquin, C., Leboeuf, N. and Pall, R., 2002. "Friction Dampers for Seismic Rehabilitation of Eaton Building, Montreal", Proceedings, Canadian Society of Civil Engineers Conference, Montreal.

Patoor, E. and Beveiller, M., 1990. "Les alliages à mémoire de formes", Technologies de Pointes, Hermes (in French).

PEER, 2003. "Pacific Earthquake Engineering Research Center", University of California, Berkeley, CA (available on line at: http://peer.berkeley.edu).

Perez, F.J., Pessiki, S. and Sause, R., 2004. "Lateral Load Behaviour of Unbonded Post-Tensioned Precast Walls with Vertical Joints, PCI Journal, 49 (2), 48-63.

Popov, E.P. and Tsai, K.C., 1989. "Performance of Large Seismic Steel Moment Connections Under Cyclic Loading", Engineering Journal, American Institute of Steel Construction, 26 (2), 51-60.

Priestley, M.J.N., 1991. "Overview of the PRESSS Research Programme" PCI Journal, 36 (4), 50-57.

Priestley, M.J.N. and Tao, J.R.T., 1993. "Seismic Response of Precast Prestressed Concrete Frames with Partially Debonded Tendons", PCI Journal, 38 (1), 58-69.

Priestley, M.J.N., 1993. "Myths and Fallacies in Earthquake Engineering - Conflicts Between Design and Reality", Bulletin of the New Zealand National Society for Earthquake, 26 (3), 329-341.

Priestley, M.J.N, Seible, F. and Calvi, G.M., 1996. "Seismic Design and Retrofit of Bridges", John Wiley and Sons, New York, NY.

Priestley, M.J.N., 1998. "Displacement-Based Approaches to Rational Limit States Design of New Structures", Keynote Address, Proceedings, 11th European Conference on Earthquake Engineering, Paris, France.

Priestley, M.J.N., Sritharan, S., Conley, J.R. and Pampanin, S., 1999. "Preliminary Results and Conclusions from the PRESSS Five-Storey Precast Concrete Test Building", PCI Journal, 44 (6), 42-67.

Priestley, M.J.N., 2000. "Performance Based Seismic Design", Keynote Address, Proceedings, 12th World Conference on Earthquake Engineering, Auckland, New Zealand (22 pages on CD-ROM).

Priestley, M.J.N., 2004. "Displacement-based Design of Precast Jointed Ductile Systems", PCI Journal, 47 (6), 66-79.

Priestley, M.J.N. and Grant, D.N., 2005. "Viscous Damping in Seismic Design and Analysis", Journal of Earthquake Engineering, (9), 229-255.

Rabinowicz, E., 1966. "Friction and Wear of Materials", John Wiley & Sons, Inc., New York, U. S. A.

Ramirez, O.M., Constantinou, M.C., Kircher, C.A., Whittaker, A., Johnson, M., Gomez, J.D. and Chrysostomou, C.Z., 2001. "Development and Evaluation of Simplified Procedures of Analysis and Design for Structures with Passive Energy Dissipation Systems", Technical Report MCEER-00-0010, Revision 1, Multidisciplinary Center for Earthquake Engineering Research, University at Buffalo, Buffalo, New York.

Ramirez, O.M., Constantinou, M.C., Gomez, J.D., Whittaker, A., Johnson, M. and Chrysostomou, C.Z., 2002a. "Evaluation of Simplified Methods of Analysis of Yielding Structures with Damping Systems", Earthquake Spectra, 18 (3), 501-530.

Ramirez, O.M., Constantinou, M.C., Gomez, J.D., Whittaker, A., Johnson, M. and Chrysostomou, C.Z., 2002b. "Elastic and Inelastic Seismic Response of Buildings with Damping Systems", Earthquake Spectra, 18 (3), 531-547.

Reinhorn, A. M., 1997. "Inelastic Analysis Techniques in Seismic Evaluations", Seismic Design Methodologies for the Next Generation of Codes, Fajfar, P. and Krawinkler H., Balkema, Rotterdam.

Restrepo, J.I., 2002. "New Generation of Earthquake Resisting Systems", First *fib* Congress, Federation Internationale du Beton, Paper E-208, Osaka, Japan.

Restrepo-Posada, J.I., 1993. "Seismic Behaviour of Connections Between Precast Concrete Elements", Research Report No. 93-3, Department of Civil Engineering, University of Canterbury, New Zealand.

Restrepo-Posada, J.I., Dodd, L.L., Park, R. and Cooke, N., 1994. "Variables Affecting Cyclic Behaviour of Reinforcing Steel", ASCE Journal of Structural Engineering, 120 (11), 3178-3196.

Ribakov, Y. and Gluck, J., 1999. "Optimal Design of ADAS Damped MDOF Structures", Earthquake Spectra, 15 (2) 317-330.

Ricles, J.M., Sause, R., Garlock, M. and Zhao, C., 2001. "Post-Tensioned Seismic-Resistant Connections for Steel Frames", ASCE Journal of Structural Engineering, 127(2), 113-121.

Robinson, W.H. and Greenbank, L.R., 1976. "An Extrusion Absorber Suitable for the Protection of Structures During an Earthquake", Earthquake Engineering and Structural Dynamics, 4, 251-259.

Robinson, W.H., 1982. "Lead-Rubber Hysteretic Bearings Suitable for Protecting Structures During Earthquakes", Earthquake Engineering and Structural Dynamics, 10, 593-600.

Robinson, W.H. and Cousins, W.J., 1987. "Recent Developments in Lead Dampers for Base Isolation", Proceedings, Pacific Conference on Earthquake Engineering, 2, 279-283.

Sabelli, R., 2001."Research on Improving the Design and Analysis of Earthquake-Resistant Steel Braced Frames", EERI/FEMA NEHRP Fellowship Report, Earthquake Engineering Research Institute, Oakland, CA.

SAC Joint Venture, 1994. Proceedings of the Invitational Workshop on Steel Seismic Issues, Report No. SAC-94-01, Sacramento, CA.

SAC Joint Venture, 1997. "Develop Suites of Time Histories", Project Task: 5.4.1, Draft Report, March 21, 1997, Sacramento, CA.

Sakurai, T., Shibata, K., Watanabe, S., Endoh, A., Yamada, K., Tanaka, N. and Kobayashi, H., 1992. "Application of Joint Damper to Thermal Power Plant Buildings", Proceedings, 10th World Conference on Earthquake Engineering, 7, 4149-4154, Madrid Spain.

Sasaki, K. K., Freeman, S. A. and Paret, T. F., 1998. "Multimode Pushover Procedure (mmP) - A Method to Identify the Effects of Higher Modes in a Pushover Analysis", Proceedings, 6th U.S. National Conference on Earthquake Engineering, Seattle (on CD-ROM).

Savard, G., Lalancette, J.R., Pall, R. and Pall, A., 1995. "High Tech Seismic Design of Maison 1 McGill, Montreal", 7th Canadian Conference on Earthquake Engineering, Montreal, Canada, 935-942.

SEAOC, 1995. "Vision 2000 - Performance-Based Seismic Engineering of Buildings", Structural Engineering Association of California, Sacramento, CA.

SEAOC, 1996. "Recommended Lateral Force Requirements and Commentary, Appendix B - Vision 2000, Conceptual Framework for Performance-Based Seismic Design", Seismology Committee, Structural Engineers Association of California.

Shen, J. and Akbas, B., 1999. "Seismic Demand in Steel Moment Frames", Journal of Earthquake Engineering, 3 (4), 519-559.

Shen, K.L., Soong, T.T., Chang, K.C. and Lai, M.L., 1995. "Seismic Behaviour of Reinforced Concrete Frame with Added Viscoelastic Dampers", Engineering Structures, 17 (5), 372-380.

Shen, Q. and Kurama, Y.C., 2000. "Lateral Load Behaviour of Unbonded Post-Tensioned Hybrid Coupled Walls", Proceedings, 6th International Conference on Steel-Concrete Composite Structures, Los Angeles, CA.

Shuhaibar, C., Lopez, W. and Sabelli, R., 2002. "Buckling-Restrained Braced Frames", ATC-17-2 Seminar on Response Modification Technologies for Performance-Based Seismic Design, Applied Technology Council, Redwood City, CA., 321-328.

Shukla, A.K. and Datta, T.K., 1999. "Optimal Use of Viscoelastic Dampers in Building Frames for Seismic Force," ASCE Journal of Structural Engineering, 125 (4), 1394-1399.

Sigaher, A.N. and Constantinou, M.C., 2003." Scissor-Jack-Damper Energy Dissipation System," Earthquake Spectra, 19 (1), 133-158.

Singh, M.P. and Moreschi, L.M. 2001. "Optimal Seismic Response Control with Dampers", Earthquake Engineering & Structural Dynamics, 30 (4), 553-572.

Skinner, R.I., Kelly, K.M. and Heine, A.J., 1975. "Hysteresis Dampers for Earthquake-Resistant Structures", Earthquake Engineering and Structural Dynamics, 3, 287-296.

Skinner, R.I., Tyler, R., Heine, A. and Robinson, W.H., 1980. "Hysteretic Dampers for the Protection of Structures from Earthquakes", Bulletin of the New Zealand Society for Earthquake Engineering, 13, 22-36.

Skinner, R.I., Robinson, W.H. and McVerry, G.H., 1993. "An Introduction to Seismic Isolation", John Wiley & Sons, New York.

Soong, T.T. and Dargush, G.F., 1997. "Passive Dissipation Systems in Structural Engineering", John Wiley & Sons, New York.

Spencer, B.F., Suhardjo. J. and Sain, M.K., 1994. "Frequency Domain Optimal Control Strategies for Aseismic Protection", ASCE Journal of Engineering Mechanics, 120(1), 135-157.

Stanton, J., Stone, W. and Cheok, G.S., 1993. "A Hybrid Reinforced Precast Frame for Seismic Regions", PCI Journal, 42 (2), 20-32.

Stanton, J.F. and Nakaki, S.D., 2002. "Design Guidelines for Precast Concrete Structural Systems", PRESSS Report No. 01/03-09 (Available from PCI).

Stanton, J., 2003. "Self-Centering Structures for Use in Seismic Regions", Proceedings, ASCE Structures Congress, Seattle, WA, Paper No. 622, 8 p. on CD-ROM.

Staudacher, E., Habacher, C. and Siegenthaler, R., 1970. "Erdebensicherung in Baum", Neue Zurcher Zeitung, Technikbeilage, Zurich, Switzerland (in German).

Stiemer, S.F., Godden, W.G. and Kelly, J.M., 1981. "Experimental Behaviour of a Spatial Piping System with Steel Energy Absorbers Subjected to a Simulated Differential Seismic Input", Report No. UCB/EERC-81/09. EERC, University of California, Berkeley, CA.

Su, Y-F. and Hanson, R.D., 1990. "Seismic Response of Building Structures with Mechanical Damping Devices" Report No. UMCE 90-02, University of Michigan, Ann Arbor, MI.

Takewaki, I., 1997. "Optimal Damper Placement for Minimum Transfer Functions," Earthquake Engineering and Structural Dynamics, 26 (11), 1113-1124.

Takewaki, I., Yoshitomi, S., Vetani, K. and Tsuji, M., 1999. "Non-Monotonic Optimal Damper Placement Via Steepest Direction Search", Earthquake Engineering and Structural Dynamics, 28 (6), 655-670.

Teramura, A. Takeda, T., Tsunoda, T., Seki, M., Kageyama, M. and Nohata, A., 1988. "Study on Earthquake Response Characteristics of Base-Isolated Full Scale Building", 9th World Conference on Earthquake Engineering, Tokyo, Japan, V-693-698.

Thompson, A.G., 1981. "Optimum Tuning and Damping of a Dynamic Vibration Absorber Applied to a Force Excited and Damped Primary System", Journal of Sound and Vibration, 77, 403-415.

Tolis, S.V. and Faccioli, E., 1999. "Displacement Design Spectra", Journal of Earthquake Engineering, 3 (1), 107-125.

Toranzo, L., Restrepo, J.I., Mander, J.B. and Carr, A.J., 2004. "Seismic Design of Rocking Confined Masonry Walls with Hysteretic Energy Dissipators and Shake Table Validation", Proceedings, 13th World Conference for Earthquake Engineering, Paper No. 248, Vancouver, Canada.

Tremblay, R. and Stiemer, S.F., 1993. "Energy Dissipation Through Friction Bolted Connections in Concentrically Braced Steel Frames", ATC 17-1 Seminar on Seismic Isolation, Passive Energy Dissipation, and Active Control, 2, 557-568.

Trifunac, M.D. and Brady, A.G., 1975. "A Study of the Duration of Strong Earthquake Ground Motion", Bulletin of the Seismological Society of America, 65, 581-626.

Tsai, K.-C. and Popov, E.P., 1988. "Steel Beam-Column Joints in Seismic Moment Resisting Frames", Report No. UCB/EERC-88/19, Earthquake Engineering Research Center, University of California, Berkeley, CA.

Tsai, K.C., Chen, H.W., Hong, C.P. and Su, Y.F., 1993. "Design of Steel Triangular Plate Energy Absorbers for Seismic-resistant Construction", Earthquake Spectra, 9 (3), 505-528.

Tsai, K.C., 1995. "Design of Steel Plate Devices for Seismic Energy Dissipation, European Seismic Design Practice: Research and Application", Proceedings, 5th SECED Conference, 445-453.

Tsuji, M. and Nakamura, T., 1996. "Optimal Viscous Dampers for Stiffness Design of Shear Buildings," The Structural Design of Tall Buildings, 5 (3), 217-234.

Tyler, R.G., 1977. "Damping in Building Structures by Means of PTFE Sliding Joints", Bulletin of the New Zealand Society for Earthquake Engineering, 10 (3), 139-142.

Uang, C.-M. and Bertero, V.V., 1990. "Evaluation of Seismic Energy in Structures", Earthquake Engineering and Structural Dynamics, 19, 77-90.

Ugural, A. C. and Fenster, S. K., 1995. "Advanced Strength and Applied Elasticity", 3rd Edition, Prentice-Hall, Inc. Upper Saddle River, New Jersey 07458, U. S. A.

Vail, C. and Hubbell, J., 2002. "Structural Upgrade of Boeing Commercial Airplane Factory at Everett, WA", Proceedings, Applied Technology Council (ATC 17-2), Seminar on Response Modification Technologies for Performance-Based Seismic Design, Los Angeles, CA.

Veletsos, A.S. and Newmark, N.M., 1960. "Effect of Yielding on the Behaviour of Simple Systems Subjected to Earthquake Motions", Proceedings, 2nd World Conference on Earthquake Engineering, Tokyo, Japan, 895-912.

Vamvatsikos, D. and Cornell, C.A., 2002. "Incremental dynamic analysis", Earthquake Engineering and Structural Dynamics, 31(3), 491–514.

Vezina, S., Proulx, P., Pall, R. and Pall, A., 1992. "Friction Dampers for Aseismic Design of Canadian Space Agency", Proceedings, 10th World Conference of Earthquake Engineering, Madrid, Spain, 4123-4128.

Vezina, S., Assaad, L. and Pall, R., 2002. "Seismic Retrofit of MUCTC Building, Palais des Congres, Montreal", Proceedings, CSCE Conference, Montreal.

Vulcano, A. and Mazza, F., 2000. "Comparative Study of the Seismic Performance of Frames Using Different Dissipative Braces", Proceedings, 12th World Conference on Earthquake Engineering, Auckland, New Zealand, Paper No. 1982.

Wagner, P., Vavak, L., Pall, R. and Pall, A., 1995. "Seismic Rehabilitation of the New Hamilton Courthouse", Proceedings, 7th Canadian Conference on Earthquake Engineering, Montreal, Canada, 951-958.

Wakabayashi, M., Nakamura, T., Iwai, S. and Hayashi, Y., 1984. "Effects of Strain Rate on the Behaviour of Structural Members", Proceedings, 8th World Conference on Earthquake Engineering, San Francisco, CA, IV, 491-498.

Wanitorkul, A. and Filiatrault, A., 2005. "Simulation of Strong Ground Motions for Seismic Fragility Evaluation of Nonstructural Components in Hospitals", Technical Report MCEER-05-0005, Multidisciplinary Center for Earthquake Engineering Research, University at Buffalo, State University of New York, Buffalo, NY.

Warburton, G.B., 1982. "Optimal Absorber Parameters for Various Combinations of Response and Excitation Parameters", Earthquake Engineering and Structural Dynamics, 10, 381-401.

Wen, Y.K., 1976. "Method of Random Vibration of Hysteretic Systems", Journal of Engineering Mechanics, ASCE, 102 (2), 249-263.

Whittaker, A.S., Bertero, V.V., Thompson, C.L. and Alonso, L.J., 1991. "Seismic Testing of Steel Plate Energy Dissipation Devices", Earthquake Spectra, 7 (4), 563-604.

Whittaker, A.S., Constantinou, M.C., Ramirez, O.M., Johnson, M.W. and Chrysostomou, C.Z., 2003. "Equivalent Lateral Force and Modal Analysis Procedures of the 2000 NEHRP Provisions for Buildings with Damping Systems", Earthquake Spectra, 19 (4), 959-980.

Wilson, J.C. and Wesolowsky, M.J., 2005. "Shape Memory Alloys for Seismic Response Modification: a State of the Art Review", Earthquake Spectra, 21 (2), 569-601.

Witting, P.R. and Cozzarelli, F.A., 1992. "Shape Memory Structural Dampers: Material Properties, Design and Seismic Testing", Report NCEER-92-0013, National Center for Earthquake Engineering Research, University at Buffalo, Buffalo, New York.

Wolff, E.D., 1999. "Frictional Heating in Sliding Bearings and an Experimental Study of High Friction Materials", Thesis for the degree of Master of Science, University at Buffalo, Buffalo, New York.

Wu, B., Ou, J.P. and Soong, T.T., 1997. "Optimal Placement of Energy Dissipation Devices for Three-Dimensional Structures", Engineering Structures, 19 (2), 113-125.

Xu, D. and Tsopelas, P., 2003. "Application of Precise Positioning Fluid Damper on Seismic Isolation Systems for Bridges", Proceedings, ASCE Structures Congress, Seattle, WA, Paper No. 478 (8 pages on CD-ROM).

Yokota, H., Saruta, M., Nakamura, Y., Satake, N. and Okada, K., 1992. "Structural Control for Seismic Load Using Viscoelastic Dampers", Proceedings, 10th World Conference on Earthquake Engineering, Madrid, Spain.

Zahrai, S.M. and Bruneau, M., 1998. "Seismic Retrofit of Slab-on-Girder Steel Bridges Using Ductile-end Diaphragms", Report No. OCEERC 98-20, University of Ottawa.

Zang, R.H. and Soong, T.T., 1992. "Seismic Design of Viscoelastic Dampers for Structural Applications", ASCE Journal of Structural Engineering, 118 (5), 1375-1392.

Zayas, V.A., Low, S. and Mahin, S., 1990. "Simple Pendulum Technique for Achieving Seismic Isolation", Earthquake Spectra, 6 (2), 317-333.

APPENDIX A: Implementation of Metallic Dampers in Structures. [N]: New Construction, [R]: Retrofit

Structure	Location	Year	Damper Type	Number of Dampers	Reference
Government Building [R]	Wanganui, New Zealand	1978	Steel Tube	---	Matthewson and Davey 1979
Rangitikei Bridge [N]	New Zealand	1980	Torsional Beam	10	Skinner et al. 1980
Chimney [R]	Christchurch, New Zealand	---	Tapered Plate	---	---
Motorway Overbridge [N]	Dunedin, New Zealand	---	Tapered Plate	---	---
Cronwell Bridge [N]	New Zealand	---	Flexural Beam	6	---
Slopping Highways [N]	Wellington, New Zealand	---	Lead Extrusion	---	---
15-Storey Building [N]	Tokyo Japan	1985	Honeycomb	---	Kobori et al. 1988
5/9 Storey Buildings (connected) [N]	Japan	1987	Bell Damper	3	Kobori et al. 1988
29-Storey Building [N]	Tokyo Japan	1990	Honeycomb	---	Kajima Corporation 1991
Steel Suspension Building [N]	Naples Italy	1990	Tapered Plate	---	Ciampi 1993
Izazaga #38-40 Building [R]	Mexico City Mexico	1990	ADAS	250	Martinez-Romero 1993
Cardiology Hospital [R]	Mexico City Mexico	1990	ADAS	90	Martinez-Romero 1993
Reforma #476 Building [R]	Mexico City Mexico	1992	ADAS	400	Martinez-Romero 1993
Wells Fargo Bank Building [R]	San Francisco California	1992	ADAS	7	Martinez-Romero 1993

Structure	Location	Year	Damper Type	Number of Dampers	Reference
Osaka Int. Conf. Centre [N]	Osaka, Japan	2000	Unbonded Braces	---	---
UC-San Francisco IBBQB Center [N]	San Francisco California	2000	Unbonded Braces	---	---
UC-Davis, Env. Sciences Bldg. [N]	Berkeley California	2000	Unbonded Braces	---	Clark et al. 2003
W. F. Bennett Fed. Building [R]	Salt Lake City,Utah	2002	Unbonded Braces	344	Brown et al. 2003
UC-Berkeley Stanley Hall [N]	Berkeley California	2003	Unbonded Braces	---	Black et al. 2002
San Bernardino Library [N]	San Bernardino California	2003	Unbonded Braces	---	---
Taipei County Building [N]	Taipei, Taiwan	2003	Unbonded Braces	---	---
Matsushita YRP Research Lab. [N]	Yokosuka City Japan	2003	Unbonded braces	---	---

APPENDIX B: Implementation of Friction Dampers in Structures. [N]: New Construction, [R]: Retrofit

Structure	Location	Year	Damper Type	Number of Dampers	Reference
McConnel Library Concordia Univ. [N	Montreal, Canada	1991	Pall	143	Pall et al. 1987.
Sonic Office Building [N]	Omiyama City, Japan	1988	Somitomo	8	Aiken and Kelly 1990
Asahi Beer Building [N]	Tokyo, Japan	1989	Somitomo	4	Aiken and Kelly 1990
Ecole Polyvalente Sorel [R]	Sorel, Canada	1990	Pall	64	Pall and Pall 1996
Canadian Space Agency [N]	St-Hubert, Canada	1992	Pall + Panel dampers	58	Vezina et al. 1992
CCRIT Building [N]	Laval, Canada	1992	Pall	---	---
Montreal, Casino [R]	Montreal, Canada	1993	Pall	32	Pasquin et al. 1994
Canadian Dept. of Nat. Defence [N]	Ottawa, Canada	1992	Pall	---	---
L. H. Hoover Bldg. Stanford [R]	Palo Alto, California	1994	Slotted Bolted Connections	8	---
Bldg. 610 Stanford [R]	Palo Alto, California	1994	Slotted Bolted Connections	80	---
Maison 1, McGill [N]	Montreal, Canada	1995	Pall	65	Savard et al. 1995
Hamilton Courthouse [R]	Hamilton, Canada	1995	Pall	74	Wagner et al. 1995
Ecole Technologie Superieure [R]	Montreal, Canada	1995	Pall	74	Godin et al. 1995
Federal Building [R]	Sherbrooke, Canada	1995	Pall	30	---
Desjardins Life Insurance Bldg [N]	Levis, Canada	1995	Pall	30	---

Structure	Location	Year	Damper Type	Number of Dampers	Reference
Overhead Water Tank [R]	Beaux Arts Washington	1995	Pall	16	---
St. Luc Hospital [R]	Montreal, Canada	1995	Pall	34	---
Residence Maisonneuve	Montreal, Canada	1996	Pall	42	---
Harry Stevens Building [R]	Vancouver, Canada	1996	Pall	38	---
Justice Headquarters [R]	Ottawa, Canada	1996	Pall	84	Elliott et al. 1998
UC Davis Water Tanks [R]	Davis California	1996	Pall	48	Hale et al. 1995
BCBC Selkirk Office Building [N]	Victoria, Canada	1997	Pall	74	---
Maisons de Beaucours [R]	Quebec City, Canada	1997	Pall	42	---
Maison Sherwin Williams [R]	Montreal, Canada	1997	Pall	64	---
251 South Lake Av. Building [R]	Pasadena, California	1998	Pall	---	---
Quebec Provincial Police Hdq. [R	Montreal, Canada	1999	Pall	---	---
Freeport Water Tower [R]	Sacramento, California	1999	Pall	---	---
Boeing Airplane Factory [R]	Everrett, Washington	2001	Pall	---	Vail and Hubbell 2002
Moscone West Conv. Center [N]	San Francisco, California	2001	Pall	---	---
1000 Lenora Squ. Arts Building [R]	Seattle, Washington	2001	Pall	---	---
Boeing Cafeteria and Auditorium [R]	Seattle, Washington	2001	Pall	56	---
ACC Sharp Mem. Hospital [N]	San Diego, California	2001	Pall	---	---
La Gardenia Towers [N]	Gurgaon, India	2001	Pall	---	---

Structure	Location	Year	Damper Type	Number of Dampers	Reference
Eaton's Building [R]	Montreal, Canada	2002	Pall	161	Pasquin et al. 2002
MUCTC Building [R]	Montreal, Canada	2002	Pall	88	Vezina et al. 2002
Water Towers [R]	Renton, Washington	2003	Pall	---	---

APPENDIX C: Implementation of Viscoelastic and Viscous Dampers in Structures. [N]: New Construction, [R]: Retrofit

Structure	Location	Year	Damper Type	Number of Dampers	Reference
4-storey RC building [N]	Tsukuba Japan	1987	Viscous Damped Walls (Oiles and Sumitomo Corp.)	Unknown	Arima et al., 1988
15-storey building [N]	Shizuoka City Japan	1991	Viscous Damped Walls (Oiles and Sumitomo Corp.)	Unknown	Miyazaki and Mitsusaka, 1992
24-storey steel building [N]	Japan	1991	Viscoelastic Dampers (Shimuzu Corp.)	Unknown	Yokota et al., 1992
School Building 2-stories [N]	Phoenix Arizona	1992	Viscoelastic beam-column connectors	Unknown	Aiken, 1997
Santa Clara County Civic Center, east Wing Building 13-storey steel frame, 51 m x 51 m plan, constructed in 1976 [R]	San Jose California	1993	Viscoelastic Dampers (3M)	96	Crosby et al., 1994
Pacific Bell North Area Operation Center 3-storey steel braced frame [N]	Sacramento California	1995	Fluid Viscous Dampers (Taylor)	62	Aiken, 1997
Science Building II, California State University, Sacramento 6-storey steel frame [N]	Sacramento California	1996	Fluid Viscous Dampers (Taylor)	40	Aiken, 1997

Structure	Location	Year	Damper Type	Number of Dampers	Reference
Woodland Hotel 4-storey non-ductile RC frame/shear wall constructed in 1927 [R]	Woodland California	1996	Fluid Viscous Dampers (Taylor)	16	Aiken, 1997
San Francisco Opera House [R]	San Francisco California	1996	Fluid Viscous Dampers (Enidine)	16	Aiken, 1997
Building 116, Naval Supply Facility 3-storey non-ductile RC wall flat-slab Structure 121 ft x 365ft plan. [R]	San Diego California	1996	Viscoelastic Dampers (3M)	64	Soong and Dargush, 1997
Rockwell Building 505 [R]	Newport Beach California	1997	Viscous Dampers (Taylor)	Unknown	Aiken, 1997
San Francisco Civic Center Building 15-storey steel frame [N]	San Francisco California	1997	Viscous Dampers (Taylor)	292	Aiken, 1997
The Money Store 11-storey steel frame [N]	Sacramento California	1997	Viscous Dampers (Taylor)	120	Aiken, 1997
Los Angeles Police Department Recruit Training Center 4-storey steel frame constructed in 1988 [R]	Los Angeles California	1997	Viscoelastic Dampers (3M)	Unknown	Aiken, 1997
San Mateo County Hall of Justice 8-storey steel frame with precast cladding, constructed mid-1960s [R]	Redwood City California	1997	Viscoelastic Dampers (3M)	Unknown	Aiken, 1997
Arrowhead Medical Center [N]	Colton California		Fluid Viscous for Base Isolation (Taylor)	186	Lee, 2003
Los Angeles City Hall [R]	Los Angeles California		Fluid Viscous for Base Isolation (Taylor)	52	Lee, 2003

Structure	Location	Year	Damper Type	Number of Dampers	Reference
Hayward City Halls	Hayward California		Fluid Viscous (Taylor)	15	Lee, 2003
Tokyo-Rinkai Hospital	Japan		Fluid Viscous (Taylor)	45	Lee, 2003
Jimbo-Cho Office Building	Tokyo Japan		Fluid Viscous (Taylor)		Lee, 2003
San Francisco Oakland Bay Bridge [R]	San Francisco California		Fluid Viscous (Taylor)		Lee, 2003
Millennium Bridge [R]	U.K.		Fluid Viscous (Taylor)		Lee, 2003
Petronas Twin Towers	Malaysia		Fluid Viscous (Taylor)		Lee, 2003
28 State Street Office Building [N]	Boston Massachusetts		Fluid Viscous (Taylor)	40	Lee, 2003
Torre Mayor Office Building 57-storey steel frame [N]	Mexico City Mexico		Fluid Viscous (Taylor)	98	Lee, 2003
999 Sepulveda Building [N]	Los Angeles California		Fluid Viscous (Taylor)		Lee, 2003
Enron Field Stadium [N]	Houston Texas		Fluid Viscous (Taylor)	16	Lee, 2003
California State University – Administration Building [N]	Los Angeles California		Fluid Viscous (Taylor)	14	Lee, 2003
Computer Data Storage Center [N]	Northern California		Fluid Viscous (Taylor)	32	Lee, 2003
Kaiser Corona Data Center [N]	Corona California		Fluid Viscous (Taylor)	16	Lee, 2003
Money Store National Headquarters [N]	Sacramento California		Fluid Viscous (Taylor)	120	Lee, 2003
Novelty Bridge [N]	Seattle Washington	2000	Fluid Viscous (Taylor)	8	Lee, 2003
Bill Emerson Memorial Bridge [N]	Cape Girardeau Missouri		Fluid Viscous (Taylor)	16	Lee, 2003

Structure	Location	Year	Damper Type	Number of Dampers	Reference
SAFECO Field Stadium [N]	Seattle Washington		Fluid Viscous (Taylor)	44	Lee, 2003
Beijing Railway Station [N]	Beijing China		Fluid Viscous (Taylor)	32	Lee, 2003
Park Hyatt Hotel [N]	Chicago Illinois		Fluid Viscous part of Tuned Mass Damper (Taylor)		Lee, 2003
Yerba Buena Tower / Four Seasons Hotel [N]	San Francisco California		Fluid Viscous (Taylor)	20	
British Columbia Electric Company Building [R]	Vancouver Canada		Fluid Viscous (Taylor)		Lee, 2003

APPENDIX D: Implementation of Base Isolation Systems in Buildings and Bridges. [N]: New Construction, [R]: Retrofit

Implementations in Buildings

(Over 500 isolated buildings in Japan not included in this list)

Building	Location	Year	Isolation Type	Reference
Elementary School [N]	Skopje, Yugoslavia	1969	Neoprene Bearings	Staudacher et al. 1970
House [N]	Huaping, Yunnan, China	1975	Sand Layer	http://nisee.berkeley.edu/prosys/chinabldgs.html
House [N]	Xichang, Sichuan, China	1975	Sand Layer	http://nisee.berkeley.edu/prosys/chinabldgs.html
Weigh Bridge Building [N]	Anyang, Henan, China	1980	Sand Layer	http://nisee.berkeley.edu/prosys/chinabldgs.html
New Fire Station Headquarters [N]	Naples, Italy	1981	Mechanical Dissipators and Isolators	http://nisee.berkeley.edu/prosys/italybldgs.html
William Clayton Building [N]	Wellington, New Zealand	1981	Lead-Rubber Bearings	http://nisee.berkeley.edu/prosys/nzbldgs.html
Apartments and Earthquake Observation Center [N]	Beijing, China	1981	Sand Layer	http://nisee.berkeley.edu/prosys/chinabldgs.html
Union House [N]	Auckland, New Zealand	1983	Sleeved Piles with Steel Triangular Plate Dampers	http://nisee.berkeley.edu/prosys/nzbldgs.html
Equipment Building [N]	Hashi, Xinjiang, China	1983	Sand Layer	http://nisee.berkeley.edu/prosys/chinabldgs.html
Foothill Communities Law & Justice Center [N]	Rancho Cucamonga, CA	1985	High Damping Rubber Bearings (LTV)	http://nisee.berkeley.edu/prosys/usbldgs.html

Building	Location	Year	Isolation Type	Reference
2nd Fire Station Building [N]	Naples, Italy	1985	Neoprene Bearings and Oleodynamic Restraints	http://nisee.berkeley.edu/ prosys/italybldgs.html
Apartment Building [N]	Xichang, Sichuan, China	1985	Graphite and Lime Mortar	http://nisee.berkeley.edu/ prosys/italybldgs.html
Salt Lake City and County Building [R]	Salt Lake City, Utah	1987	Lead-Rubber and Rubber Bearings (Dynamic Isolation Systems)	http://www.dis-inc.com/
Stanford Linear Accelerator Center Mark II Detector [N]	Menlo Park, California	1987	Lead-Rubber Bearings (Dynamic Isolation Systems)	http://www.dis-inc.com/
Evans & Sutherland Building 600 University of Utah Research Park [N]	Salt Lake City, Utah	1988	Lead-Rubber and Rubber Bearings (Dynamic Isolation Systems)	http://www.dis-inc.com/
USC University Hospital [N]	Los Angeles, California	1989	Lead-Rubber and Rubber Bearings (Dynamic Isolation Systems)	Asher et al., 1990; http:// www.dis-inc.com/
Civic Center at Monte d'Ago [N]	Ancona, Italy	1989	Neoprene Bearings	http://nisee.berkeley.edu/ prosys/italybldgs.html
Telecom Administration Center - Buildings A1, A2, B & C [N]	Ancona, Italy	1989	High Damping Rubber Bearings	http://nisee.berkeley.edu/ prosys/italybldgs.html
Marina Apartments [R]	San Francisco, California	1990	Friction Pendulum Bearings (Earthquake Protection Systems)	http:// www.earthquakeprotection.co m/marina_apts.html
Fire Command and Control Center [N]	Los Angeles, California	1990	High Damping Rubber Bearings (Fyfe)	http://nisee.berkeley.edu/ prosys/usbldgs.html
Wellington Central Police Station [N]	Wellington, New Zealand	1990	Sleeved piles with Lead Extrusion Dampers	http://nisee.berkeley.edu/ prosys/nzbldgs.html

Building	Location	Year	Isolation Type	Reference
Press Hall, Press House [N]	Petone, New Zealand	1991	Lead-Rubber Bearings	http://nisee.berkeley.edu/ prosys/nzbldgs.html
Kaiser Permanente Facility [N]	Southern California	1992	Lead-Rubber and Rubber Bearings (Dynamic Isolation Systems)	http://www.dis-inc.com/
Rockwell International Corporate Headquarters (Building 80) [R]	Seal Beach, CA	1992	Lead-Rubber and Rubber Bearings (Dynamic Isolation Systems)	http://www.dis-inc.com/
Oakland City Hall [R]	Oakland, California	1992	Lead-Rubber and Rubber Bearings (Dynamic Isolation Systems)	http://www.dis-inc.com/
Two Residences [N]	Los Angeles, California	1992	Spring Isolation System (GERB)	http://nisee.berkeley.edu/ prosys/usbldgs.html
Titan Solid Rocket Motor Storage [N]	Vandenburg Air force Base, CA	1992	High Damping Rubber Bearings (LTV)	http://nisee.berkeley.edu/ prosys/usbldgs.html
SIP Center of Marche Province [N]	Ancona, Italy	1992	High Damping Rubber Bearings	http://nisee.berkeley.edu/ prosys/italybldgs.html
Apartment Building [N]	Squillace Marina (Catanzaro), Italy	1992	Rubber and High Damping Rubber Bearings	http://nisee.berkeley.edu/ prosys/italybldgs.html
Apartment Building [N]	Darli, Yunnan, China	1992	Slide Steel Piece	http://nisee.berkeley.edu/ prosys/chinabldgs.html
Navy Building [N]	Ancona, Italy	1992	High Damping Rubber Bearings	http://nisee.berkeley.edu/ prosys/italybldgs.html
Navy Medical Center [N]	Augusta (Sicily), Italy	1993	High Damping Rubber Bearings	http://nisee.berkeley.edu/ prosys/italybldgs.html
Apartment Houses, Italian Navy [N]	Campo Palma (Augusta, Siciliy), Italy	1993	High Damping Rubber Bearings	http://nisee.berkeley.edu/ prosys/italybldgs.html
Apartment Building and Shops [N]	Xian, Xanshi, China	1993	Slide Steel Piece	http://nisee.berkeley.edu/ prosys/chinabldgs.html

Building	Location	Year	Isolation Type	Reference
Apartment Building and Shops [N]	Shantou, Guangdong, China	1993	High Damping Rubber Bearings	http://nisee.berkeley.edu/ prosys/chinabldgs.html
Long Beach V.A. Hospital [R]	Long Beach, California	1993	Lead-Rubber, Rubber and sliding Bearings (Dynamic Isolation Systems)	http://www.dis-inc.com/
Campbell Hall Western Oregon State College [R]	Monmouth, OR	1993	Lead-Rubber and Rubber Bearings (Dynamic Isolation Systems)	http://www.dis-inc.com/
Portland Water Bureau Water Control Center [N]	Portland, Oregon	1993	Lead-Rubber and Rubber Bearings (Dynamic Isolation Systems)	http://nisee.berkeley.edu/ prosys/usbldgs.html
Mackay School of Mines [R]	Reno, Nevada	1993	High Damping Rubber and Sliding Bearings (Furon)	http://nisee.berkeley.edu/ prosys/usbldgs.html
New Zealand Parliament [R]	Wellington, New Zealand	1994	Lead-Rubber, Rubber and sliding Bearings (Dynamic Isolation Systems)	http://www.dis-inc.com/
U.S. Court of Appeals [R]	San Francisco, California	1994	Friction Pendulum Bearings (Earthquake Protection Systems)	http:// www.earthquakeprotection.co m/US_Court_Appeals.html
Emergency Operations Center [N]	Los Angeles, California	1994	High Damping Rubber and Sliding Bearings (Furon)	http://nisee.berkeley.edu/ prosys/usbldgs.html
Traffic Management Center [N]	San Diego, California	1994	High Damping Rubber Bearings (Bridgestone)	http://nisee.berkeley.edu/ prosys/usbldgs.html
Hughes Building S-12 [R]	El Segundo, CA	1994	Lead-Rubber and Rubber Bearings (Dynamic Isolation Systems)	http://nisee.berkeley.edu/ prosys/usbldgs.html

Building	Location	Year	Isolation Type	Reference
San Pietro Church [R]	Frigento (Avellino)	1994	High Damping Rubber Bearings	http://nisee.berkeley.edu/ prosys/italybldgs.html
AutoZone Corporation [N]	Memphis, Tennessee	1995	Lead-Rubber and Rubber Bearings (Dynamic Isolation Systems)	http://www.dis-inc.com/
San Francisco Main Library [N]	San Francisco, California	1995	Lead-Rubber and Rubber Bearings (Dynamic Isolation Systems)	http://www.dis-inc.com/
Martin Luther King Drew Medical Center [N]	Los Angeles, CA	1995	High Damping Rubber bearings (Dynamic Isolation Systems)	http://www.dis-inc.com/
National Museum of New Zealand [N]	Wellington, New Zealand	1995	Lead-Rubber and Rubber Bearings with Sliding Bearings	http://nisee.berkeley.edu/ prosys/nzbldgs.html
Apartment Building and Restaurants [N]	Anyang, Henan, China	1995	High Damping Rubber Bearings	http://nisee.berkeley.edu/ prosys/chinabldgs.html
Industrial, Apartment and Store Buildings [N]	Xichang, Sichuan, China	1995	High Damping Rubber Bearings	http://nisee.berkeley.edu/ prosys/chinabldgs.html
Student Housing Building [N]	Guangzhou, Guangdong, China	1995	High Damping Rubber Bearings	http://nisee.berkeley.edu/ prosys/chinabldgs.html
Apartment and Office Building [N]	Darli, Yunnan, China	1995	High Damping Rubber Bearings	http://nisee.berkeley.edu/ prosys/chinabldgs.html
San Bernardino County Medical Center [N]	Colton, California	1996	High Damping Rubber Bearings (Dynamic Isolations Systems) with Fluid Viscous Dampers (Taylor)	http://nisee.berkeley.edu/ prosys/nastrspd.html
Langenbach House [N]	Oakland, California	1996	Fluid Viscous (Taylor)	http://nisee.berkeley.edu/ prosys/nastrspd.html

Building	Location	Year	Isolation Type	Reference
Quebec Iron and Titanium Smelter [N]	Tracy, Canada	1996	Spring Isolataors with Fluid Viscous Dampers (Taylor)	
Kaiser Data Center [N]	Corona, California	1996	Rubber Bearings with Fluid Viscous Dampers (Taylor)	http://nisee.berkeley.edu/ prosys/nastrspd.html
Kerckhoff Hall UCLA Campus [R]	Westwood Village, CA	1996	Lead-Rubber and Rubber Bearings (Dynamic Isolation Systems)	http://www.dis-inc.com/
Liquefied Natural Gas Tanks [N]	Revithoussa, Greece	1996	Friction Pendulum Bearings (Earthquake Protection Systems)	http:// www.earthquakeprotection.co m/LNG_tanks.html
Missouri Botanical Garden Research Center [N]	St.-Louis, Missouri	1996	High Damping Rubber Bearings (Skellerup)	http://nisee.berkeley.edu/ prosys/usbldgs.html
Hayward City Hall [N]	Hayward California	1997	Friction Pendulum Bearings (Earthquake Protection Systems) with Fluid Viscous Dampers (Taylor)	Lee, 2003; http:// www.earthquakeprotection.co m/Hayward_City_Hall.html
Arrowhead Medical Center [N]	Colton California	1997	High Damping Rubber Bearings (Dynamic Isolation Systems) with Fluid Viscous for Base Isolation (Taylor)	http://nisee.berkeley.edu/ prosys/nastrspd.html; http://www.dis-inc.com/

Building	Location	Year	Isolation Type	Reference
San Francisco Airport International Terminal [N]	San Francisco, California	1998	Friction Pendulum Bearings (Earthquake Protection Systems)	http://nisee.berkeley.edu/ prosys/usbldgs.html
San Francisco 911 [N]	San Francisco, California	1998	High Damping Rubber Bearings (BTR/Andre)	http://nisee.berkeley.edu/ prosys/usbldgs.html
Washington State Emergency Operations Center [N]	Camp Murray, Washington	1998	Friction Pendulum Bearings (Earthquake Protection Systems)	http:// www.earthquakeprotection.co m/WSEOC.html
San Francisco City Hall [R]	San Francisco, California	1998	Lead-Rubber Bearings (Dynamic Isolation Systems)	http://nisee.berkeley.edu/ prosys/usbldgs.html
Atatürk International Airport Terminal [N]	Istanbul, Turkey	1999	Friction Pendulum Bearings (Earthquake Protection Systems)	http:// www.earthquakeprotection.co m/Ataturk_Int.html
LAC + USC Medical Center [N]	Los Angeles California	2000	High Damping Rubber Bearings (BTR/Andre)	http://nisee.berkeley.edu/ prosys/usbldgs.html
Los Angeles City Hall [R]	Los Angeles California	2001	High Damping Rubber Bearings (Bridgestone) with Fluid Viscous Dampers (Taylor)	Lee, 2003, http:// nisee.berkeley.edu/prosys/ nastrspd.html
AboveNet Building [N]	San Francisco, California	2001	Friction Pendulum Bearings (Earthquake Protection Systems)	http:// www.earthquakeprotection.co m/abovenet.html

Building	Location	Year	Isolation Type	Reference
Seahawks Football Stadium [N]	Seattle, Washington	2002	Friction Pendulum Bearings (Earthquake Protection Systems)	http:// www.earthquakeprotection.com/seahawks_stadium.html
San Francisco International Airport Terminal [N]	San Francisco, California	2003	Friction Pendulum Bearings (Earthquake Protection Systems)	http:// www.earthquakeprotection.com/sfo_airport.html

Implementation in Bridges

(Over 300 isolated Bridges in Japan not included in this list)

Bridge	Location	Year	Isolation Type	Reference
Motu [N]	New Zealand	1973	Steel U-Beams in Flexure	http://nisee.berkeley.edu/ prosys/nzbridges.html
Bolton Street [N]	New Zealand	1974	Rubber Bearings with Lead-Extrusion Dampers	http://nisee.berkeley.edu/ prosys/nzbridges.html
Aurora Terrace [N]	New Zealand	1974	Rubber Bearings with Lead-Extrusion Dampers	http://nisee.berkeley.edu/ prosys/nzbridges.html
Toetoe [N]	New Zealand	1978	Lead-Rubber Bearings	http://nisee.berkeley.edu/ prosys/nzbridges.html
King Edward Street [N]	New Zealand	1979	Rubber Bearings with Steel Cantilevers	http://nisee.berkeley.edu/ prosys/nzbridges.html
Cromwell [N]	New Zealand	1979	Rubber Bearings with Steel Flexural Beams	http://nisee.berkeley.edu/ prosys/nzbridges.html
Rangitikei Railway Bridge [N]	New Zealand	1981	Rocking Piers with Steel Torsional-Beam Dampers	Cormack, 1988
Clyde [N]	New Zealand	1981	Lead-Rubber Bearings	http://nisee.berkeley.edu/ prosys/nzbridges.html
Waiotukupuna [N]	New Zealand	1981	Lead-Rubber Bearings	http://nisee.berkeley.edu/ prosys/nzbridges.html
Ohaaki [N]	New Zealand	1981	Lead-Rubber Bearings	http://nisee.berkeley.edu/ prosys/nzbridges.html
Maungatapu [N]	New Zealand	1981	Lead-Rubber Bearings	http://nisee.berkeley.edu/ prosys/nzbridges.html
Scamperdown [N]	New Zealand	1982	Lead-Rubber Bearings	http://nisee.berkeley.edu/ prosys/nzbridges.html
Gulliver [N]	New Zealand	1983	Lead-Rubber Bearings	http://nisee.berkeley.edu/ prosys/nzbridges.html
Donne [N]	New Zealand	1983	Lead-Rubber Bearings	http://nisee.berkeley.edu/ prosys/nzbridges.html

Bridge	Location	Year	Isolation Type	Reference
Whangaparoa [N]	New Zealand	1983	Lead-Rubber Bearings	http://nisee.berkeley.edu/ prosys/nzbridges.html
Karakatuwhero [N]	New Zealand	1983	Lead-Rubber Bearings	http://nisee.berkeley.edu/ prosys/nzbridges.html
Devils Creek [N]	New Zealand	1983	Lead-Rubber Bearings	http://nisee.berkeley.edu/ prosys/nzbridges.html
Upper Aorere [N]	New Zealand	1983	Lead-Rubber Bearings	http://nisee.berkeley.edu/ prosys/nzbridges.html
Rangitaiki (Te Teko) [N]	New Zealand	1983	Lead-Rubber Bearings	http://nisee.berkeley.edu/ prosys/nzbridges.html
Ngaparika [N]	New Zealand	1983	Lead-Rubber Bearings	http://nisee.berkeley.edu/ prosys/nzbridges.html
Hikuwai Nos. 1 – 4 [R]	New Zealand	1984	Lead-Rubber Bearings	http://nisee.berkeley.edu/ prosys/nzbridges.html
Oreti [N]	New Zealand	1984	Lead-Rubber Bearings	http://nisee.berkeley.edu/ prosys/nzbridges.html
Rapids [N]	New Zealand	1984	Lead-Rubber Bearings	http://nisee.berkeley.edu/ prosys/nzbridges.html
Tamaki [N]	New Zealand	1984	Lead-Rubber Bearings	http://nisee.berkeley.edu/ prosys/nzbridges.html
Deep Gorge [N]	New Zealand	1984	Lead-Rubber Bearings	http://nisee.berkeley.edu/ prosys/nzbridges.html
Twin Tunnels [N]	New Zealand	1985	Lead-Rubber Bearings	http://nisee.berkeley.edu/ prosys/nzbridges.html
Tarawera [N]	New Zealand	1985	Lead-Rubber Bearings	http://nisee.berkeley.edu/ prosys/nzbridges.html
Moonshine [N]	New Zealand	1985	Lead-Rubber Bearings	http://nisee.berkeley.edu/ prosys/nzbridges.html
Makarika No. 2 [R]	New Zealand	1985	Lead-Rubber Bearings	http://nisee.berkeley.edu/ prosys/nzbridges.html
Sierra Pt. Overhead [R]	San Francisco, California	1985	Lead-Rubber Bearings (Dynamic Isolation Systems/ Furon)	http://nisee.berkeley.edu/ prosys/usbridges.html
Makatote [R]	New Zealand	1986	Lead-Rubber Bearings	http://nisee.berkeley.edu/ prosys/nzbridges.html

Bridge	Location	Year	Isolation Type	Reference
Santa Ana River Bridge [R]	Riverside, California	1986	Lead-Rubber Bearings (Dynamic Isolation Systems/ Furon)	http://nisee.berkeley.edu/ prosys/usbridges.html
Eel River Bridge [R]	Rio Dell, California	1987	Lead-Rubber Bearings (Dynamic Isolation Systems/ Furon)	http://nisee.berkeley.edu/ prosys/usbridges.html
Main Yard Vehicle Access Bridge [R]	Long Beach, California	1987	Lead-Rubber Bearings (Dynamic Isolation Systems/ Furon)	http://nisee.berkeley.edu/ prosys/usbridges.html
Kopuaroa Nos. 1 & 4 [R]	New Zealand	1987	Rubber Bearings with Steel Cantilevers	http://nisee.berkeley.edu/ prosys/nzbridges.html
Glen Motorway and Railway [N]	New Zealand	1987	Lead-Rubber Bearings	http://nisee.berkeley.edu/ prosys/nzbridges.html
Grafton Nos. 4 & 5 [N]	New Zealand	1987	Lead-Rubber Bearings	http://nisee.berkeley.edu/ prosys/nzbridges.html
Northern Wairoa [N]	New Zealand	1987	Lead-Rubber Bearings	http://nisee.berkeley.edu/ prosys/nzbridges.html
Ruamahanga at Te Ore Ore [N]	New Zealand	1987	Lead-Rubber Bearings	http://nisee.berkeley.edu/ prosys/nzbridges.html
Maitai [N]	Nelson, New Zealand	1987	Lead-Rubber Bearings	http://nisee.berkeley.edu/ prosys/nzbridges.html
Bannockburn [N]	New Zealand	1988	Lead-Rubber Bearings with Lead Extrusion Dampers	http://nisee.berkeley.edu/ prosys/nzbridges.html
All-American Canal Bridge [R]	Winterhaven, Imperial Co., California	1988	Lead-Rubber Bearings (Dynamic Isolation Systems/ Furon)	http://nisee.berkeley.edu/ prosys/usbridges.html
Hairini [N]	New Zealand	1988	Lead-Rubber Bearings	http://nisee.berkeley.edu/ prosys/nzbridges.html

Bridge	Location	Year	Isolation Type	Reference
Viana do Castelo [N]	Portugal	1989	Hydraulic Shock Transmitters with Hydraulic Dissipators (FIP Industriale)	http://nisee.berkeley.edu/prosys/worldbridges.html
Limeworks [N]	New Zealand	1989	Lead-Rubber Bearings	http://nisee.berkeley.edu/prosys/nzbridges.html
Waingawa [N]	New Zealand	1990	Lead-Rubber Bearings	http://nisee.berkeley.edu/prosys/nzbridges.html
Mangaone [N]	New Zealand	1990	Lead-Rubber Bearings	http://nisee.berkeley.edu/prosys/nzbridges.html
Portimao [N]	Portugal	1990	Hydraulic Dissipators (FIP Industriale)	http://nisee.berkeley.edu/prosys/worldbridges.html
Deas Slough Bridge [R]	Richmond (BC), Canada	1990	Lead-Rubber Bearings (Dynamic Isolation Systems/ Furon)	http://nisee.berkeley.edu/prosys/usbridges.html
Sexton Creek Bridge [N]	Alexander Co., Illinois	1990	Lead-Rubber Bearings (Dynamic Isolation Systems/ Furon)	http://nisee.berkeley.edu/prosys/usbridges.html
Toll Plaza Road Bridge [N]	Montgomery Co., Pennsylvania	1990	Lead-Rubber Bearings (Dynamic Isolation Systems/ Furon)	http://nisee.berkeley.edu/prosys/usbridges.html
Rio Guadiana [N]	Portugal	1991	Elastomeric Bearings (FIP Industriale)	http://nisee.berkeley.edu/prosys/worldbridges.html
Cache River Bridge [R]	Alexander Co., Illinois	1991	Lead-Rubber Bearings (Dynamic Isolation Systems/ Furon)	http://nisee.berkeley.edu/prosys/usbridges.html

Bridge	Location	Year	Isolation Type	Reference
Route 161 Bridge [N]	St. Clair Co., Illinois	1991	Lead-Rubber Bearings (Dynamic Isolation Systems/ Furon)	http://nisee.berkeley.edu/ prosys/usbridges.html
Wabash River Bridge [N]	Terra Haute, Vigo Co., Indiana	1991	Lead-Rubber Bearings (Dynamic Isolation Systems/ Furon)	http://nisee.berkeley.edu/ prosys/usbridges.html
Miyagawa Bridge [N]	Shizuoka, Japan	1991	Lead-Rubber Bearings	http://nisee.berkeley.edu/ prosys/japanbridges.html
Uehara Bridge [N]	Nagoya, Japan	1991	Lead-Rubber Bearings	http://nisee.berkeley.edu/ prosys/japanbridges.html
Route #12 Interchange Bridge [N]	Tokyo, Japan	1991	Lead-Rubber Bearings	http://nisee.berkeley.edu/ prosys/japanbridges.html
Karasaki Bridge [N]	Fukushima, Japan	1991	High Damping Rubber Bearings	http://nisee.berkeley.edu/ prosys/japanbridges.html
Moriguchi Route [N]	Osaka, Japan	1991	Lead-Rubber Bearings	http://nisee.berkeley.edu/ prosys/japanbridges.html
Moriguchi Route [N]	Osaka, Japan	1991	Lead-Rubber Bearings	http://nisee.berkeley.edu/ prosys/japanbridges.html
NB I-170 Bridge [N]	St. Louis, Missouri	1991	Lead-Rubber Bearings (Dynamic Isolation Systems/ Furon)	http://nisee.berkeley.edu/ prosys/usbridges.html
Ramp 26 Bridge [N]	St. Louis, Missouri	1991	Lead-Rubber Bearings (Dynamic Isolation Systems/ Furon)	http://nisee.berkeley.edu/ prosys/usbridges.html
Springdale Bridge [N]	St. Louis, Missouri	1991	Lead-Rubber Bearings (Dynamic Isolation Systems/ Furon)	http://nisee.berkeley.edu/ prosys/usbridges.html

Bridge	Location	Year	Isolation Type	Reference
SB I-170/EB I-70 Bridge [N]	St. Louis, Missouri	1991	Lead-Rubber Bearings (Dynamic Isolation Systems/ Furon)	http://nisee.berkeley.edu/ prosys/usbridges.html
UMSL Garage Bridge [N]	St. Louis, Missouri	1991	Lead-Rubber Bearings (Dynamic Isolation Systems/ Furon)	http://nisee.berkeley.edu/ prosys/usbridges.html
East Campus Drive Bridge [N]	St. Louis, Missouri	1991	Lead-Rubber Bearings (Dynamic Isolation Systems/ Furon)	http://nisee.berkeley.edu/ prosys/usbridges.html
Geiger Road Bridge [N]	St. Louis, Missouri	1991	Lead-Rubber Bearings (Dynamic Isolation Systems/ Furon)	http://nisee.berkeley.edu/ prosys/usbridges.html
Pequannock River Bridge [N]	Morris & Passaic Co., New Jersey	1991	Lead-Rubber Bearings (Dynamic Isolation Systems/ Furon)	http://nisee.berkeley.edu/ prosys/usbridges.html
West Street Overpass [R]	Harrison, Westchester Co., New York	1991	Lead-Rubber Bearings (Dynamic Isolation Systems/ Furon)	http://nisee.berkeley.edu/ prosys/usbridges.html
Moriguchi Route [R]	Osaka, Japan	1991	Lead-Rubber Bearings	http://nisee.berkeley.edu/ prosys/japanbridges.html
Pont de Socorridos [N]	Portugal	1992	Hydraulic Shock Transmitters	http://nisee.berkeley.edu/ prosys/worldbridges.html
Linda Velha, P6 No2/A [N]	Portugal	1992	Hydraulic Shock Transmitters (FIP Industriale)	http://nisee.berkeley.edu/ prosys/worldbridges.html
Dog River Bridge [N]	Mobile, Alabama	1992	Lead-Rubber Bearings (Dynamic Isolation Systems/ Furon)	http://nisee.berkeley.edu/ prosys/usbridges.html

Bridge	Location	Year	Isolation Type	Reference
Carlson Boulevard Bridge [N]	Richmond, California	1992	Lead-Rubber Bearings (Dynamic Isolation Systems/ Furon)	http://nisee.berkeley.edu/ prosys/usbridges.html
US-51 over Minor Slough [N]	Ballard Co., Kentucky	1992	Lead-Rubber Bearings (Dynamic Isolation Systems/ Furon)	http://nisee.berkeley.edu/ prosys/usbridges.html
Relocated NH Route 85 over NH Route 101 [N]	Exeter-Stratham, Rockingham Co., New Hampshire	1992	Lead-Rubber Bearings (Dynamic Isolation Systems/ Furon)	http://nisee.berkeley.edu/ prosys/usbridges.html
Squamscott River Bridge [N]	Exeter, New Hampshire	1992	Lead-Rubber Bearings (Dynamic Isolation Systems/ Furon)	http://nisee.berkeley.edu/ prosys/usbridges.html
I-80 Bridges B764E & W [R]	Verdi, Washoe Co. (Nevada)	1992	Lead-Rubber Bearings (Dynamic Isolation Systems/ Furon)	http://nisee.berkeley.edu/ prosys/usbridges.html
Clackamas Connector [N]	Milwaukie, Oregon	1992	Lead-Rubber Bearings (Dynamic Isolation Systems/ Furon)	http://nisee.berkeley.edu/ prosys/usbridges.html
Blackstone River Bridge [N]	Woonsocket, Rhode Island	1992	Lead-Rubber Bearings (Dynamic Isolation Systems/ Furon)	http://nisee.berkeley.edu/ prosys/usbridges.html
Providence Viaduct [R]	Providence, Rhode Island	1992	Lead-Rubber Bearings (Dynamic Isolation Systems/ Furon)	http://nisee.berkeley.edu/ prosys/usbridges.html

Bridge	Location	Year	Isolation Type	Reference
Ompompanoosuc River Bridge [R]	Rte. 5, Norwich, Vermont	1992	Lead-Rubber Bearings (Dynamic Isolation Systems/ Furon)	http://nisee.berkeley.edu/ prosys/usbridges.html
Cedar River Bridge [N]	Renton, WA	1992	Lead-Rubber Bearings (Dynamic Isolation Systems/ Furon)	http://nisee.berkeley.edu/ prosys/usbridges.html
Lacey V. Murrow Bridge, West Approach [R]	Seattle, Washington	1992	Lead-Rubber Bearings (Dynamic Isolation Systems/ Furon)	http://nisee.berkeley.edu/ prosys/usbridges.html
Main Bridge, Second Severn Crossing [N]	England	1993	Hydraulic Shock Transmitters with Elastomeric Bearings (FIP Industriale)	http://nisee.berkeley.edu/ prosys/worldbridges.html
Nantua, Sapra A40 [N]	France	1993	Hydraulic Shock Transmitters	http://nisee.berkeley.edu/ prosys/worldbridges.html
Nayrolles, Sapra A40 [N]	France	1993	Elasto-Plastic Yielding Steel Devices (FIP Industriale)	http://nisee.berkeley.edu/ prosys/worldbridges.html
Burrard Bridge Main Spans [R]	Vancouver, Canada	1993	Lead-Rubber Bearings (Dynamic Isolation Systems/ Furon)	http://nisee.berkeley.edu/ prosys/usbridges.html
Olympic Boulevard Separation [N]	Walnut Creek, California	1993	Lead-Rubber Bearings (Dynamic Isolation Systems/ Furon)	http://nisee.berkeley.edu/ prosys/usbridges.html
RT 41 over Pigeon Creek [N]	Evanville, Indiana	1993	Eradiquake Sliding Bearings (R.J. Watson)	http://nisee.berkeley.edu/ prosys/usbridges.html

Bridge	Location	Year	Isolation Type	Reference
Main Street Bridge [R]	Saugus, Massachussets	1993	Lead-Rubber Bearings (Dynamic Isolation Systems/ Furon)	http://nisee.berkeley.edu/ prosys/usbridges.html
Foundry Street Overpass 106.68 [R]	Newark, New Jersey	1993	Lead-Rubber Bearings (Dynamic Isolation Systems/ Furon)	http://nisee.berkeley.edu/ prosys/usbridges.html
Aurora Expressway Bridge [R]	Erie Co., New York	1993	Lead-Rubber Bearings (Dynamic Isolation Systems/ Furon)	http://nisee.berkeley.edu/ prosys/usbridges.html
Bridge over County Road 3 [N]	Near Shinnston, West Virginia	1993	Lead-Rubber Bearings (Dynamic Isolation Systems/ Furon)	http://nisee.berkeley.edu/ prosys/usbridges.html
Onnetoh Bridge [N]	Hokkaido, Japan	1993	Lead-Rubber Bearings	http://nisee.berkeley.edu/ prosys/japanbridges.html
Nagakigawa Bridge [N]	Akita, Japan	1993	Lead-Rubber Bearings	http://nisee.berkeley.edu/ prosys/japanbridges.html
Yama-age Bridge [N]	Tochigi, Japan	1993	High Damping Rubber Bearings	http://nisee.berkeley.edu/ prosys/japanbridges.html
Sakai Route [N] and [R]	Osaka, Japan	1993	Lead-Rubber Bearings	http://nisee.berkeley.edu/ prosys/japanbridges.html
Chuo Expressway (Senkawa) [N]	Tokyo, Japan	1993	High Damping Rubber Bearings	http://nisee.berkeley.edu/ prosys/japanbridges.html
Porirua Ramp Overbridge [N]	New Zealand	1993	Lead-Rubber Bearings	http://nisee.berkeley.edu/ prosys/nzbridges.html
Porirua Ramp Stream Overbridge [N]	New Zealand	1993	Lead-Rubber Bearings	http://nisee.berkeley.edu/ prosys/nzbridges.html
Knot of Odivelas, IC22 [N]	Portugal	1994	Hydraulic Shock Transmitters (FIP Industriale)	http://nisee.berkeley.edu/ prosys/worldbridges.html

Bridge	Location	Year	Isolation Type	Reference
Riberia da Seica [N]	Portugal	1994	Hydraulic Shock Transmitters with Elastomeric Bearings (FIP Industriale)	http://nisee.berkeley.edu/ prosys/worldbridges.html
Queensborough Bridge [R]	New Westminster (BC), Canada	1994	Lead-Rubber Bearings (Dynamic Isolation Systems/ Furon)	http://nisee.berkeley.edu/ prosys/usbridges.html
Alemany Interchange [R]	San Francisco, California	1994	Lead-Rubber Bearings (Dynamic Isolation Systems/ Furon)	http://nisee.berkeley.edu/ prosys/usbridges.html
Route 242/I-680 Separation [R]	Concord, California	1994	Lead-Rubber Bearings (Dynamic Isolation Systems/ Furon)	http://nisee.berkeley.edu/ prosys/usbridges.html
Bayshore Boulevard Overcrossing [R]	San Francisco, California	1994	Lead-Rubber Bearings (Dynamic Isolation Systems/ Furon)	http://nisee.berkeley.edu/ prosys/usbridges.html
Bayshore Boulevard Overcrossing [R]	San Francisco, California	1994	Lead-Rubber Bearings (Dynamic Isolation Systems/ Furon)	http://nisee.berkeley.edu/ prosys/usbridges.html
Saugatuck River Bridge [R]	Westport, Connecticut	1994	Lead-Rubber Bearings (Dynamic Isolation Systems/ Furon)	http://nisee.berkeley.edu/ prosys/usbridges.html
Chain-of-Rocks Road over FAP 310 [N]	Madison Co., Illinois	1994	Lead-Rubber Bearings (Dynamic Isolation Systems/ Furon)	http://nisee.berkeley.edu/ prosys/usbridges.html

Bridge	Location	Year	Isolation Type	Reference
Poplar Street East Approach, Roadway B [N]	E. St. Louis, Illinois	1994	Lead-Rubber Bearings (Dynamic Isolation Systems/Furon)	http://nisee.berkeley.edu/ prosys/usbridges.html
Neponset River Bridge [N]	Boston, Massachussetts	1994	Lead-Rubber Bearings (Dynamic Isolation Systems/Furon)	http://nisee.berkeley.edu/ prosys/usbridges.html
South Boston Bypass Viaduct [N]	South Boston, Massachussett	1994	Lead-Rubber Bearings (Dynamic Isolation Systems/Furon)	http://nisee.berkeley.edu/ prosys/usbridges.html
South Station Connector [N]	Boston, Massachussett	1994	Lead-Rubber Bearings (Dynamic Isolation Systems)	http://nisee.berkeley.edu/ prosys/usbridges.html
Everett Turnpike over Nashua River & Canal [N]	Nashua, New Hemsphire	1994	Eradiquake Sliding Bearings (R.J. Watson)	http://nisee.berkeley.edu/ prosys/usbridges.html
Pine Hill Road over Everett Turnpike [N]	Nashua, New Hemsphire	1994	Lead-Rubber Bearings (Dynamic Isolation Systems/Furon)	http://nisee.berkeley.edu/ prosys/usbridges.html
Wilson Avenue Overpass W105.79SO [R]	Newark, New Jersey	1994	Lead-Rubber Bearings (Dynamic Isolation Systems/Furon)	http://nisee.berkeley.edu/ prosys/usbridges.html
Conrail Newark Branch Overpass E106.57 [R]	Newark, New Jersey	1994	Lead-Rubber Bearings (Dynamic Isolation Systems/Furon)	http://nisee.berkeley.edu/ prosys/usbridges.html
Wilson Avenue Overpass E105.79SO [R]	Newark, New Jersey	1994	Lead-Rubber Bearings (Dynamic Isolation Systems/Furon)	http://nisee.berkeley.edu/ prosys/usbridges.html

Bridge	Location	Year	Isolation Type	Reference
Relocated E-NSO Overpass W106.26A [N]	Newark, New Jersey	1994	Lead-Rubber Bearings (Dynamic Isolation Systems/ Furon)	http://nisee.berkeley.edu/ prosys/usbridges.html
Mohawk River Bridge [N]	Herkimer, New York	1994	Lead-Rubber Bearings (Dynamic Isolation Systems/ Furon)	http://nisee.berkeley.edu/ prosys/usbridges.html
Moodna Creek Bridge [R]	Orange County, New York	1994	Lead-Rubber Bearings (Dynamic Isolation Systems/ Furon)	http://nisee.berkeley.edu/ prosys/usbridges.html
Conrail Bridge [N]	Herkimer, New York	1994	Lead-Rubber Bearings (Dynamic Isolation Systems/ Furon)	http://nisee.berkeley.edu/ prosys/usbridges.html
Coldwater Creek Bridge No. 11 [N]	Washington State	1994	Lead-Rubber Bearings (Dynamic Isolation Systems/ Furon)	http://nisee.berkeley.edu/ prosys/usbridges.html
East Creek Bridge No. 14 [N]	Washington State	1994	Lead-Rubber Bearings (Dynamic Isolation Systems	http://nisee.berkeley.edu/ prosys/usbridges.html
Home Bridge [N]	Home, Washington	1994	Lead-Rubber Bearings (Dynamic Isolation Systems	http://nisee.berkeley.edu/ prosys/usbridges.html
West Fork River Bridge [N]	Shinnston, West Virginia	1994	Lead-Rubber Bearings (Dynamic Isolation Systems	http://nisee.berkeley.edu/ prosys/usbridges.html
Knot of Odivelas, IC22 [N]	Portugal	1995	Hydraulic Shock Transmitters (FIP Industriale)	http://nisee.berkeley.edu/ prosys/worldbridges.html

Bridge	Location	Year	Isolation Type	Reference
Amoreira, Via rapida Camara-lobos [N]	Portugal	1995	Hydraulic Shock Transmitters (FIP Industriale)	http://nisee.berkeley.edu/ prosys/worldbridges.html
Main Bridge, East Link across Storebaelt [N]	Danemark	1995	Hydraulic Shock Transmitters (FIP Industriale)	http://nisee.berkeley.edu/ prosys/worldbridges.html
1st Street over Figuero [R]	Los Angeles, California	1995	Lead-Rubber Bearings	http://nisee.berkeley.edu/ prosys/usbridges.html
Colfax Avenue over L.A. River [R]	Los Angeles, California	1995	Lead-Rubber Bearings (Dynamic Isolation Systems) and Eradiquake Sliding Bearings (R.J. Watson)	http://nisee.berkeley.edu/ prosys/usbridges.html
Lake Saltonstall Bridge [N]	E. Haven & Branford, Connecticut	1995	Lead-Rubber Bearings (Dynamic Isolation Systems/ Furon)	http://nisee.berkeley.edu/ prosys/usbridges.html
Poplar Street East Approach, Roadway C [N]	E. St. Louis, Illinois	1995	Lead-Rubber Bearings (Dynamic Isolation Systems/ Furon)	http://nisee.berkeley.edu/ prosys/usbridges.html
North Street Bridge No. K-26 [R]	Grafton, Massachussett	1995	Lead-Rubber Bearings (Dynamic Isolation Systems)	http://nisee.berkeley.edu/ prosys/usbridges.html
Poplar Street Bridge [R]	E. St. Louis, Illinois	1995	Elasto-Plastic Isolators with Hydraulic Dampers	http://nisee.berkeley.edu/ prosys/usbridges.html
Old Westborough Road Bridge No. K-27 [R]	Grafton, Massachussetts	1995	Lead-Rubber Bearings (Dynamic Isolation Systems)	http://nisee.berkeley.edu/ prosys/usbridges.html

Bridge	Location	Year	Isolation Type	Reference
Summer Street Bridge [R]	Boston, Massachussetts	1995	Lead-Rubber Bearings (Dynamic Isolation Systems)	http://nisee.berkeley.edu/ prosys/usbridges.html
Park Hill over Mass. Pike (I-90) [N]	Millbury, Massachussetts	1995	Eradiquake Sliding Bearings (R.J. Watson)	http://nisee.berkeley.edu/ prosys/usbridges.html
Hidalgo-San Rafael Distributor [N]	Mexico City, Mexico	1995	Lead-Rubber Bearings (Dynamic Isolation Systems/ Furon)	http://nisee.berkeley.edu/ prosys/usbridges.html
Berry's Creek Bridge [R]	E. Rutherford, New Jersey	1995	Lead-Rubber Bearings (Furon)	http://nisee.berkeley.edu/ prosys/usbridges.html
Conrail Newark Branch Overpass W106.57 [R]	Newark, New Jersey	1995	Lead-Rubber Bearings (Dynamic Isolation Systems)	http://nisee.berkeley.edu/ prosys/usbridges.html
Maxwell Ave. over I-95 [N]	Rye, New York	1995	Eradiquake Sliding Bearings (R.J. Watson)	http://nisee.berkeley.edu/ prosys/usbridges.html
Hood River Bridges [N]	Hood River, Oregon	1995	Rubber Bearings (Furon)	http://nisee.berkeley.edu/ prosys/usbridges.html
Marquam Bridge [R]	Oregon	1995	Elasto-plastic Isolators with Hydraulic Shock Rransmitters (FIP Industriale)	http://nisee.berkeley.edu/ prosys/usbridges.html
Seekonk River Bridge [R]	Pawtuckett, Rhode Island	1995	Lead-Rubber Bearings (Dynamic Isolation Systems)	http://nisee.berkeley.edu/ prosys/usbridges.html
Duwamish River Bridge [R]	Seattle, Washington	1995	Lead-Rubber Bearings (Dynamic Isolation Systems)	http://nisee.berkeley.edu/ prosys/usbridges.html
Tagus, 2nd Crossing of the Tagus River [N]	Portugal	1996	Hydraulic Shock Transmitters with Elasto-Plastic Isolators (FIP Industriale)	http://nisee.berkeley.edu/ prosys/worldbridges.html

Bridge	Location	Year	Isolation Type	Reference
Jamuna Multipurpose Bridge, Jamura [N]	Bangladesh	1996	Elasto-Plastic Yielding Steel Devices (FIP Industriale)	http://nisee.berkeley.edu/ prosys/worldbridges.html
Gerald Desmond Bridge [R]	Long Beach, California	1996	Rubber Bearings with Fluid Viscous Dampers (Enidine)	http://nisee.berkeley.edu/ prosys/nastrspd.html
Roberts Park Overhead [N]	Vancouver, Canada	1996	Lead-Rubber Bearings	http://nisee.berkeley.edu/ prosys/usbridges.html
Granville Bridge [R]	Vancouver, Canada	1996	Crescent Moon and Spindle Steel Elasto-Plastic Devices (FIP Industriale)	http://nisee.berkeley.edu/ prosys/usbridges.html
RT 15 Viaduct [N]	Hamden, Connecticut	1996	EradiQuake Sliding Bearings (RJ Watson)	http://nisee.berkeley.edu/ prosys/usbridges.html
RT 13 Bridge [N]	Near Freeburg, Illinois	1996	EradiQuake Sliding Bearings (RJ Watson)	http://nisee.berkeley.edu/ prosys/usbridges.html
Mass Pike (I-90) over Fuller & North Sts. [N]	Ludlow, Massachussett	1996	EradiQuake Sliding Bearings (RJ Watson)	http://nisee.berkeley.edu/ prosys/usbridges.html
Endicott Street over RT 128 (I-95) [N]	Danvers, Massachussett	1996	EradiQuake Sliding Bearings (RJ Watson)	http://nisee.berkeley.edu/ prosys/usbridges.html
I-93 Mass Ave. Interchange [N]	S. Boston, Massachussett	1996	High Damping Rubber Bearings (Seismic Energy Products)	http://nisee.berkeley.edu/ prosys/usbridges.html
Holyoke/South Hadley Bridge [N]	South Hadley, Massachussett	1996	Rubber and Lead-Rubber Bearings (Seismic Energy Products)	http://nisee.berkeley.edu/ prosys/usbridges.html
Norton House Bridge [R]	Pompton Lakes Borough and Wayne Township, New Jersey	1996	Lead-Rubber Bearings (Dynamic Isolation Systems)	http://nisee.berkeley.edu/ prosys/usbridges.html

Bridge	Location	Year	Isolation Type	Reference
Tacony-Palmyra Approaches [N]	Palmyra, New Jersey	1996	Lead-Rubber Bearings (Seismic Energy Products)	http://nisee.berkeley.edu/ prosys/usbridges.html
Rt. 4 over Kinderkamack Rd. [N]	Hackensack, New Jersey	1996	Rubber and Lead-Rubber Bearings (Seismic Energy Products)	http://nisee.berkeley.edu/ prosys/usbridges.html
Baldwin Street/ Highland Avenue [N]	Glen Ridge, New Jersey	1996	Rubber and Lead-Rubber Bearings (Seismic Energy Products)	http://nisee.berkeley.edu/ prosys/usbridges.html
JFK Terminal One Elevated Roadway[N]	NewYorkCity, New York	1996	Lead-Rubber Bearings	http://nisee.berkeley.edu/ prosys/usbridges.html
Buffalo Airport Viaduct [N]	Buffalo, New York	1996	EradiQuake Sliding Bearings (RJ Watson)	http://nisee.berkeley.edu/ prosys/usbridges.html
Hood River Bridge [R]	Hood River, Oregon	1996	Crescent Moon and Spindle Steel Elasto-Plastic Devices (FIP Industriale)	http://nisee.berkeley.edu/ prosys/usbridges.html
Montebella Bridge Relocation [N]	Puerto Rico	1996	Rubber and Lead-Rubber Bearings (Seismic Energy Products)	http://nisee.berkeley.edu/ prosys/usbridges.html
I-295 to Rt. 10 [N]	Warwick/ Cranston, Rhode Island	1996	Lead-Rubber Bearings (Seismic Energy Products)	http://nisee.berkeley.edu/ prosys/usbridges.html
Chickahominy River Bridge [N]	Hanover-Hennico County, Virgina	1996	Lead-Rubber Bearings (Dynamic Isolation Systems)	http://nisee.berkeley.edu/ prosys/usbridges.html
Stossel Bridge [R]	Carnation, Washington	1996	Lead-Rubber Bearings (Dynamic Isolation Systems)	http://nisee.berkeley.edu/ prosys/usbridges.html
West Kenmore Bridge [R]	Kenmore, Washington	1996	Lead-Rubber Bearings (Dynamic Isolation Systems)	http://nisee.berkeley.edu/ prosys/usbridges.html

Bridge	Location	Year	Isolation Type	Reference
Cape Girardeau Bridge [N]	Cape Girardeau Missouri	1997	Rubber Bearings with Fluid Viscous Dampers (Taylor)	http://nisee.berkeley.edu/ prosys/nastrspd.html
Santiago Creek Bridge [N]	California	1997	Rubber Bearings with Fluid Viscous Dampers (Enidine)	http://nisee.berkeley.edu/ prosys/nastrspd.html
Sacramento River Bridge at Rio Vista [R]	Rio Vista, California	1997	Fluid Viscous Dampers (Enidine) to Control Uplift of Towers	http://nisee.berkeley.edu/ prosys/nastrspd.html
White River Bridge [N]	Yukon, Canada	1997	Friction Pendulum Bearings (Earthquake Protection Systems)	http:// www.earthquakeprotection.co m/white_river_bridge.html
3-Mile Slough [R]	California	1997	Lead-Rubber Bearings (Skellerup)	http://nisee.berkeley.edu/ prosys/usbridges.html
Rio Vista [R]	Rio Vista, California	1997	Friction Pendulum Bearings (Earthquake Protection Systems)	http://nisee.berkeley.edu/ prosys/usbridges.html
Rio Mondo Bridge [R]	California	1997	Friction Pendulum Bearings (Earthquake Protection Systems)	http://nisee.berkeley.edu/ prosys/usbridges.html
American River Bridge City of Folsom [N]	Folsom, California	1997	Friction Pendulum Bearings (Earthquake Protection Systems)	http://nisee.berkeley.edu/ prosys/usbridges.html
I-93 over Fordway Ext.[N]	Derry, New Hampshire	1997	EradiQuake Sliding Bearings (RJ Watson)	http://nisee.berkeley.edu/ prosys/usbridges.html
Yonkers Avenue Bridge [N]	Yonkers, New York	1997	EradiQuake Sliding Bearings (RJ Watson)	http://nisee.berkeley.edu/ prosys/usbridges.html

Bridge	Location	Year	Isolation Type	Reference
GGB North Viaduct [R]	San Francisco, California	1998	Lead-Rubber Bearings	http://nisee.berkeley.edu/prosys/usbridges.html
The Golden Gate Bridge [R]	San Francisco, California	1999	Rubber Bearings with Fluid Viscous Dampers (Taylor)	http://nisee.berkeley.edu/prosys/nastrspd.html
Rio Hondo Busway Bridge [R]	El Monte, California	1999	Friction Pendulum Bearings (Earthquake Protection Systems)	http://www.earthquakeprotection.com/rio_honda_bus_bridge.html
Vincent Thomas Bridge [R]	Long Beach, California	2002	Rubber Bearings with Fluid Viscous Dampers (Enidine)	http://nisee.berkeley.edu/prosys/nastrspd.html
Benicia-Martinez Bridge [R]	Benicia, California	2002	Friction Pendulum Bearings (Earthquake Protection Systems)	http://www.earthquakeprotection.com/benicia_martinez_bridge.html
American River Bridge [N]	Folsom, California	2003	Friction Pendulum Bearings (Earthquake Protection Systems)	http://www.earthquakeprotection.com/american_river_bridge.html
Coronado Bridge [R]	San Diego, CA	2004	Rubber Bearings (Dynamic Isolation Systems) with Fluid Viscous Dampers (Enidine)	---
Kodiak-Near Island Bridge [R]	Kodiak Island, Alaska	2004	Friction Pendulum Bearings (Earthquake Protection Systems)	http://www.earthquakeprotection.com/kodiak_bridge.html

LIST OF SYMBOLS

a	Geometrical constant defining position of damper in reverse toggle-brace damping system / Adjustment factor for property modification factors for seismic isolation systems
a_1	Vibration amplitude of primary structure
a_2	Vibration amplitude of secondary structure
a_g	Peak ground acceleration
a_{max}	Normalized maximum absolute acceleration
$\bar{a}_{max}$	Mean value of a_{max}
a_{opt}	Optimum peak acceleration
A	Steady-state amplitude of response / Parameter in solution of damped TMD under harmonic loads
A'	Overlap area of laminated rubber bearing
$\bar{A}$	Normalized steady-state amplitude
A^*	Minimum resonant amplitude
$\bar{A}^*$	Normalized steady-state amplitude at resonance for self-centering SDOF system
$A(\tau)$	Time-varying amplitude of response
A_0	Parameter in solution of damped TMD under harmonic loads
A_1, A_2	Real constants
A_b	Area of cross-brace / Beam cross-sectional area
A_{exc}	Normalized excitation amplitude
$\{A^{(i)}\}$	Mode of vibration i
A_i^j	Component i of mode shape j
A_i^R	Component i of residual mode
A_{max}	Maximum absolute acceleration
$A_{max\,i}$	Maximum absolute acceleration at floor i
A_{PT}	Cross-sectional area of PT element in PTED connection
A_r	True contact area / Rubber layer area of laminated rubber bearing
A_s	Shear Area
A_r^1	Roof component of fundamental mode shape

A_p	Area of lead plug in lead-rubber bearing
$ADAS$	Added damping added stiffness system
b	Short dimension of rectangular rubber bearing
$b(x)$	Variable width of steel plate damper along dimension x
b_o	Constant width of steel plate damper
b_{xd}	Plan dimensions of base isolated foundation
B	Damping reduction factor / Parameter in solution of damped TMD under harmonic loads
B_1	Real constant
B_{1D}	Total effective first mode damping reduction factor
B_{1E}	Elastic first mode effective damping reduction factor
B_D	Damping reduction factor at design isolated period
B_R	Total effective residual mode damping reduction factor
B_{v+I}	Damping reduction factor for viscous and inherent damping in SFRS
BIF	Base isolated frame
$BMRF$	Braced moment resisting frame
BRB	Buckling-restrained brace
BSE	Basic safety earthquake
BSO	Basic safety objective
c	Viscous damping constant / Distance of tip of gap opening from compression flange in PTED connection
$\bar{c}$	Viscous damping constant of viscoelastic damper
$[\bar{c}]$	Viscous damping matrix attributed to viscous or viscoelastic dampers
c_b	Damping constant of base isolation system
c_c	Critical damping constant of TMD
c_{jk}	Element of $[\bar{c}]$ matrix
c_s	Damping constant of superstructure
C	Parameter in solution of damped TMD under harmonic loads
$C(A)$	Integral of hysteresis loop of analogous nonlinear oscillator
$\bar{C}(A)$	Normalized integral of hysteresis loop of analogous nonlinear oscillator
$[C]$	Global damping matrix
C_1, C_2	Complex numbers
C_a	Acceleration design coefficient
C_d	Deflection amplification factor / Seismic response demand coefficient for base isolated bridges
C_h	Interstorey damping constant at each floor

C_i	Generalized damping coefficient in mode i
$\bar{C}_i$	Generalized damping coefficient in mode i for structure equipped with viscous dampers
$\tilde{C}_i$	Generalized damping coefficient in mode i for structure equipped with viscoelastic dampers
C_L	Linear viscous damper constant
C_L^n	Damping constant of added linear viscous damper at floor n
$[C_L]$	Global damping matrix generated by linear viscous dampers
C_{NL}	Damping constant of a nonlinear viscous damper
C_S	Seismic coefficient
C_{S1}	First mode seismic coefficient
C_{SR}	Residual mode seismic coefficient
C_t	Empirical coefficient to estimate fundamental period
C_T	Contact element in PTED connection model
C_v	Velocity design coefficient
d	Long dimension of rectangular rubber bearing / Side dimension of double friction pendulum system / Width of steel plate damper
$d(x)$	Variable width of steel damper
d_0	Width at the end of steel plate damper
d_b	Beam depth
dt	Incremental time
dx_g	Incremental ground displacement
$d\dot{x}_g$	Incremental ground velocity
$\{dx\}$	Vector of incremental relative displacements
$\{d\dot{x}\}$	Vector of incremental relative velocities
$\{d\ddot{x}\}$	Vector of incremental relative accelerations
D	Design displacement / Parameter in solution of damped TMD under harmonic loads / Diameter of cylindrical bearing
D_{1D}	First mode roof design displacement
D_D	Design displacement at center of rigidity of base isolation system under design-basis earthquake
D'_D	Reduced value of D_D to account for superstructure flexibility
D_D^+, D_D^-	Maximum and minimum displacements for prototype base isolation bearings
$D_i(t)$	Displacement of storey i relative to the ground at time t
D_M	Maximum displacement at center of rigidity of base isolation system under maximum credible earthquake

D'_M	Reduced value of D_M to account for superstructure flexibility
D_{max}	Maximum displacement of base isolator
D_{TD}	Total design displacement for corner base isolation bearings under design-basis earthquake
D_{TM}	Total design displacement for corner base isolation bearings under maximum credible earthquake
D_y	Yield first mode roof displacement
DBE	Design-basis earthquake
DMRSF	Ductile moment resisting space frame
DOF	Degree of freedom
e	Eccentricity
E	Elastic modulus
$E_a(t)$	Absorbed energy at time t
$E_a^i(t)$	Absorbed energy in element i at time t
E_{abs}	Normalized maximum absorbed energy
$\bar{E}_{abs}$	Mean value of E_{abs}
$E_{D\Delta_t}$	Energy dissipated per cycle at the target displacement Δ_t
$E_{es}(t)$	Recoverable elastic strain energy
$E_{es}^i(t)$	Recoverable elastic strain energy in element i
E_f	Energy dissipated by friction
$E_h(t)$	Energy dissipated through hysteretic damping
$E_h^i(t)$	Energy dissipated through hysteretic damping in element i
E_{in}	Seismic input energy
$E_{in}^a(t)$	Absolute seismic input energy at time t
$E_{in}^r(t)$	Relative seismic input energy at time t
$E_k(t)$	Kinetic energy at time t
$E_k^a(t)$	Absolute kinetic energy at time t
$E_k^r(t)$	Relative kinetic energy at time t
$E_{sd}(t)$	Energy dissipated by supplemental damper at time t
$E_{st}(t)$	Work done by static loads at time t
$E_{vb}(t)$	Vibrational energy at time t
$E_{vd}(t)$	Energy dissipated by equivalent viscous damping or viscous damper at time t
E_{ved}	Energy dissipated per cycle by viscoelastic damper

$EBE(t)$	Energy balance error
$EBE^a(t)$	Energy balance error based on absolute energy formulation
$EBE^r(t)$	Energy balance error based on relative energy formulation
ED	Energy dissipating
EDR	Energy dissipating restraint
f	Geometric amplification factor for supplemental damping system / Ratio of natural frequency of TMD to natural frequency of primary structure
$\tilde{f}(x, u, t)$	Hysteretic restoring force per unit initial stiffness
$\tilde{f}_a$	Load to activate hysteretic damper per unit initial stiffness
f_i	Natural frequency in mode i
$\tilde{f}_y$	Yield load per unit initial stiffness
F	Force
$F(t)$	Axial force induced in damping element at time t
F_a	Hysteretic damper activation load (yield load for metallic dampers or slip load for friction dampers)
F_{ai}	Activation load of hysteretic damper i
F_c	Recentering force of self-centering device
F_D^+, F_D^-	Maximum and minimum forces at displacements D_D^+ and D_D^- for prototype base isolation bearings
$\{F_d(t)\}$	Vector of global forces generated by supplemental damping system at time t
F_f	Friction force
F_{fa}	Friction force due to adhesion
$F_h(t)$	Nonlinear force provided by hysteretic damper time t
$F_{hd}(t)$	Force in hysteretic damper at time t
F_i	Lateral force at floor level i
F_{i1}	First mode design lateral force at level i
F_{iR}	Residual mode design lateral force at level i
F_{lat}	Lateral force required to activate hysteretic damper
F_{lat}^*	Lateral activation force of hysteretic damper minimizing resonant amplitude
F_{lat}^{opt}	Optimum value of lateral activation force of hysteretic damper
F_{maxL}	Maximum force reached during loading of SHAPIA device
F_{maxU}	Maximum force reached during unloading of SHAPIA device
$F_r(t)$	Nonlinear restoring force at time t
$F_r^i(t)$	Nonlinear restoring force of element i at time t

$\{F_r(t)\}$	Vector of global nonlinear forces at time t
F_s	Slip force of self-centering device
$\{F_s\}$	Vector of global static loads
F_{si}	Slip load for friction damper i
F_t	Top level static lateral force for higher mode effects
F_u	Ultimate strength of steel
F_v	Soil site coefficient
F_{vd}	Force in viscous damper
F_{ved}	Force in visco-elastic damper / lateral force provided by added visco-elastic damper
F_y	Yield strength of steel / Yield force / Elastic limit of device
F_{yct}	Yield force of contact element in PTED connection model
F_{yed}	Yield force of ED spring in PTED connection model
$FDBF$	Friction damped braced frame
FPS	Friction pendulum system
g	Acceleration of gravity / Ratio of frequency of excitation to natural frequency of TMD
g_1, g_2	Roots giving coordinates of intersecting points of damped TMD frequency curve
G	Single valued function
G_c	Shear damping modulus of viscoelastic material
$G_c\bar{\omega}$	Shear loss modulus of viscoelastic material
G_E	Shear storage modulus of viscoelastic material
G_p	Shear modulus of lead plug
G_r	Shear modulus of rubber
h	Height
h_1	Height of top portion of double friction pendulum system
h_2	Height of bottom portion of double friction pendulum system
h_f	Final reading of manometer in rain flow analogy
h_i	Height of floor level i above the base
h_r	Height of roof relative to base / Total rubber height of laminated rubber bearing
h_s	Thickness of viscoelastic material
H	Single valued function
H_{ci}	Height of storey i
I	Importance factor / Moment of inertia

I_f	Impulse factor in viscoplastic friction model
I_{fi}	Initial impulse factor in viscoplastic friction model
ID	Interstorey drift
ID_i	Maximum interstorey drift at storey i
IS	Isolated system
$IS-D$	Damped isolated system
k	Elastic lateral stiffness / Stiffness of TMD
$\bar{k}$	Lateral stiffness of supplemental damping system / Elastic stiffness of the viscoelastic damper
$[\bar{k}]$	Global stiffness matrix attributed to viscoelastic dampers
$[\hat{k}]$	Global stiffness matrix corresponding only to fictitious springs
k_0	Initial stiffness / Initial stiffness of device
$\hat{k}_0$	Fictitious spring constant replacing viscous damper
$\hat{k}_0^n$	n^{th} fictitious spring constant
$\hat{k}_{0tr}^n$	Trial value of nth fictitious spring
k_1	Elastic stiffness of lead-rubber bearing / Elastic rotational stiffness provided by the PT elements
k_2	Post-elastic stiffness of lead-rubber bearing / Elastic rotational stiffness provided by the ED elements
k_3	Post-yield rotational stiffness of PTED connection
k_b	Lateral stiffness of fully braced structure (before activation of hysteretic dampers) / Lateral stiffness of laminated rubber bearing / Lateral stiffness of base isolation system
k_{btot}	Total lateral stiffness of all laminated rubber bearings
k_{CT}	Initial stiffness of contact element in PTED connection model
k_d	Lateral stiffness provided by diagonal bracing members connected to hysteretic damper
k_e	Effective stiffness of damper
k_{Dmin}	Minimum value of effective secant stiffness of base isolation system at design displacement
k_{Dmax}	Maximum value of effective secant stiffness of base isolation system at design displacement
k_{Deff}	Maximum value of effective secant stiffness of base isolation system at design displacement
k_{ED}	Stiffness of ED spring in model of PTED connection
k_{eff}	Secant lateral stiffness at the target displacement / Effective stiffness of friction pendulum system
k_i	Lateral stiffness of storey i

$\bar{k}_i$	Added elastic stiffness due to viscoelastic dampers at a storey i
$\hat{k}_i$	Generalized stiffness coefficient in mode i for a structure composed only of fictitious springs.
k_{iso}	Effective lateral stiffness of isolation system at design displacement Δ_i
$\bar{k}_{jk}$	Element of $[\bar{k}]$ matrix
k_{Mmin}	Minimum value of effective secant stiffness of base isolation system at maximum displacement
k_{Mmax}	Maximum value of effective secant stiffness of base isolation system at maximum displacement
k_{Meff}	Maximum value of effective secant stiffness of base isolation system at maximum displacement
k_s	Lateral stiffness of superstructure
k_{sub}	Effective lateral stiffness of substructure at design displacement Δ_{sub}
k_u	Lateral stiffness of structure without hysteretic dampers or after activation of dampers
k_v	Total vertical stiffness of a laminated rubber bearing
$k_{v\gamma}$	Vertical stiffness of laminated rubber bearing due to rubber shear strain without volume change
k_{vV}	Vertical stiffness of laminated rubber bearing caused by volume change of rubber without shear
K	Elastic lateral stiffness of primary structure
$[K]$	Global stiffness matrix
$[\hat{K}]$	Global stiffness matrix of fictitiously braced structure
K_0	Elastic stiffness of SHAPIA device
K_1, K_2, K_3	Constants in frequency response of flag-shaped system
K_i	Generalized stiffness coefficient in mode i of original structure without damper
$\bar{K}_i$	Generalized stiffness coefficient attributed only to viscoelastic dampers in i [th] mode of vibration
$\tilde{K}_i$	Generalized stiffness coefficient in mode i for structure with viscous or viscoelastic dampers
$\hat{K}_i$	General stiffness coefficient of fictitiously braced structure in i [th] mode of vibration
l	Length of cable
L	Distance, length
L_{ED}	Length of ED element in PTED connection
L_P	Total plate thickness of a bolted connection
L_{PT}	Length of PT element in PTED connection
LED	Lead extrusion device
m	Mass / Mass of TMD
$[\bar{m}]$	Global mass matrix associated with added dampers

m_b	Mass of base slab
M	Mass of primary structure / Mass of superstructure and base slab
$M(x)$	Bending moment at section x
$[M]$	Global mass matrix
M_A	Moment in post-tensioned connection beyond which a gap opens between the beam and column
M_B	Moment in PTED connection when tensile yield capacity of ED elements is reached
M_C	Moment in PTED connection corresponding to maximum rotation
M_D	Moment in PTED connection when compression yield capacity of ED elements is reached
M_E	Moment at re-contact in PTED connection
M_{ED}	Moment in PTED connection caused by energy dissipating elements
M_i	Generalized mass in ith mode of vibration
M_i^*	Modal mass in ith mode of vibration
$\tilde{M}_i$	Generalized mass in ith mode of vibration for structure with added viscoelastic damper
M_p	Plastic moment
M_{po}	Plastic moment at ends of metallic damper
M_{PT}	Moment in PTED connection caused by post-tensioning element
M_{PTED}	Moment generated by PTED element
MCE	Maximum credible earthquake
MDOF	Multi-degree-of freedom system
MRF	Moment resisting frame
n	Power factor for transformation of hazard level / Number of rubber layers in laminated rubber bearing
N	Normal force / Total number of degrees of freedom
N_d	Number of dampers in multi-storey structures
N_f	Number of floor levels above base
N–IS	Non-isolated system
NSP	Nonlinear static procedure
O_1, O_2	Ordinates to construct optimum hysteretic design spectrum
p_0	Equivalent lateral static load / Amplitude of external sinusoidal dynamic force
P	Axial load in a bolt / Intersection point of damped TMD frequency response curve
$P(t)$	External sinusoidal dynamic force
$\{P(t)\}$	Load vector applied on roof of main structure by TMD

P_i	Generalized load in i^{th} mode of vibration
$\tilde{P}_i$	Generalized load in mode i for structure with viscoelastic dampers
$P_{min,\,max}$	Minimum and maximum values of of isolation system property
P_n	Nominal value of isolation system property
P_u	Ultimate axial load in a bolt
P_w, P_{wt}	Decreased values of bolt preload after sliding
PGA	Peak ground acceleration
PL_i	Performance level i
PT	Post-tensioning
$PTED$	Post-tensioning and energy dissipating element
q	Behaviour factor in Eurocode 8
Q	Single valued function / Intersection point of damped TMD frequency response curve
$\{r\}$	Vector coupling the direction of ground motion with direction of DOFs of the structure
r_L	Loading slip stiffness ratio of SHAPIA device
r_u	Unloading slip stiffness ratio of SHAPIA device
R	Force reduction factor / Radius of friction pendulum bearing
R_1	Top radius of double friction pendulum system
R_2	Bottom radius of double friction pendulum system
R_I	Force reduction factor for base isolated structure
RBS	Reduced beam section
RD	Residual drift
$RDDI$	Residual deformation damage index
RID_i	Residual interstorey drift at storey i
RMS	Root mean square
RPI	Relative performance index
s	Shear strength of junctions
S	Sliding displacement / Shape factor of rubber layer
$\dot{S}$	Sliding velocity
$\ddot{S}$	Sliding acceleration
$S(A)$	Integral of hysteresis loop of analogous nonlinear oscillator
$\bar{S}(A)$	Normalized form of $S(A)$
$S(T)$	Seismic response factor, function of fundamental period T
S_1	One second spectral acceleration

S_A	Spectral acceleration
S_{ACode}	Code design spectral acceleration
$\dot{S}_{crit}$	Critical sliding velocity
S_D	Spectral displacement
$S_{D0.05}$	Spectral displacements at 5% equivalent viscous damping
S_{D1}	One second period design spectral acceleration
S_{DCode}	Code design spectral displacement
S_{DS}	Short period design spectral acceleration
S_{DT_r}	Design spectral displacements corresponding to a return period T_r
$S_{D\xi_{eq}}$	Spectral displacements at equivalent viscous damping ξ_{eq}
S_{M1}	One second period spectral acceleration under maximum credible earthquake
$\dot{S}_{max}$	Maximum sliding velocity
S_V	Velocity response spectrum
$SDOF$	Single-degree-of-freedom system
SEA	Strain energy area, the area under the strain energy time-history for all structural members of an hysteretically damped structure
SEA_0	Strain energy area for a zero activation load
$SFRS$	Seismic force resisting system
SL	Activation load of hysteretic damper load expressed as a fraction of the structural weight
SL_e	Maximum elastic load developed in bracing system containing hysteretic damper is activation of the damper is impeded
SMA	Shaped memory alloy
$SMRF$	Special moment-resisting frame
$SRSS$	Square root of the sum of the squares
SSF	Soft storey frame
t	Time
t_1	Duration of short pulse
t_d	Total duration of seismic input
t_f	Beam flange thickness
t_r	Thickness of rubber
T	Fundamental period of vibration / Fundamental period of rigid structure supported on laminated rubber bearings
T_0	Fundamental / Initial period of vibration
T_{1D}	Effective fundamental period at design displacement

T_b	Fundamental period of braced structure / Period of vibration of laminated rubber bearing
T_D	Design isolated period
T_{eff}	Effective elastic secant period of vibration / Effective period of isolation system
T_g	Predominant period of ground motion
T_i	Fundamental period of vibration in mode i
$\hat{T}_i$	Fundamental period of vibration in mode i of structure braced with fictitious springs
$\hat{T}_{itr}$	Trial value of $\hat{T}_i$
T_M	Isolated period at maximum displacement
T_r	Return period of ground motion in years
T_R	Period of residual mode
T_S	S_{D1}/S_{DS}
T_u	Fundamental period of unbraced structure / Ultimate tensile yield strength
T_y	Tensile yield strength
$TADAS$	Triangular added damping and added stiffness system
TMD	Tuned mass damper
u	Secondary stiffness parameter of hysteretic damper
u_b	Absolute lateral displacement at base slab level
$\dot{u}_b$	Absolute lateral velocity at base slab level
$\ddot{u}_b$	Absolute lateral acceleration at base slab level
u_g	Ground displacement
$\ddot{u}_g$	Ground acceleration
u_i	Displacement response of generalized coordinate i
$\dot{u}_i$	Velocity response of generalized coordinate i
$\ddot{u}_i$	Acceleration response of generalized coordinate i
$u^i(t)$	Deformation in element i at time t
u_s	Absolute lateral displacement at top of superstructure
$\dot{u}_s$	Absolute lateral velocity at top of superstructure
$\ddot{u}_s$	Absolute lateral acceleration at top of superstructure
U_{max}	Maximum value of the strain energy stored in all structural members of an hysteretically damped structure
U_{max0}	Maximum strain energy for a zero slip load
$\{v\}$	Relative displacement vector for base isolated structure
$\{\dot{v}\}$	Relative velocity vector for base isolated structure

$\{\ddot{v}\}$	Relative acceleration vector for base isolated structure
v_{1D}	First mode interstorey velocity
v_b	Absolute lateral displacement at base slab level
$\dot{v}_b$	Absolute lateral velocity at base slab level
$\ddot{v}_b$	Absolute lateral acceleration at base slab level
v_D	Design interstorey velocity
v_{RD}	Residual mode interstorey velocity
v_s	Absolute lateral displacement at top of superstructure
$\dot{v}_s$	Absolute lateral velocity at top of superstructure
$\ddot{v}_s$	Absolute lateral acceleration at top of superstructure
V	Design base shear / shear force
V_0	Total shear force required to activate all hysteretic dampers in a structure
V_1	First mode design base shear
V_{1D}	First mode interstorey velocity
V_a	Shear force required to activate hysteretic damper
V_A	Design force for connections between superstructure and base isolated substructure
V_{ai}	Shear force required to activate hysteretic dampers at storey i
V_b	Design base shear at target displacement
V_{br}	Lateral force resisted by bracing system
V_d	Volume of rainwater collected by equivalent viscous damping pail in rain flow analogy
V_D	Design interstorey velocity
V_E	Elastic base shear, capacity required for elastic structure
V_h	Volume of rainwater collected by the hysteretic energy pail in rain flow analogy
V_{in}	Volume of rainwater recorded by flow gauge in rain flow analogy
V_{min}	Minimum design base shear
V_R	Residual mode design base shear
V_{RD}	Residual mode interstorey displacement
V_s	Design base shear for superstructure
V_S	Lateral force causing friction damper to slip
V_{Si}	Slip shear at level i
V_t	Total lateral force
V_{uy}	Yield strength of unbraced frame

V_y	Yield base shear
$VDBF$	Viscously damped braced frame
W	Seismic weight / Vertical load carried by laminated rubber bearing
W_1	First modal weight
W_b	Portion of superstructure's weight supported by a single laminated rubber bearing
W_{eff}	Effective seismic weight
W_i	Seismic weight at floor level i
W_{max}	Maximum allowable vertical load that can be carried by a laminated rubber bearing
$\overline{W}_R$	Residual modal weight
W_{tot}	Total weight of superstructure
$WMRF$	Welded moment-resisting frame
x	Distance
$x(t)$	Relative displacement at time t
$\dot{x}(t)$	Relative velocity at time t
$\ddot{x}(t)$	Relative acceleration at time t
$\{x(t)\}$	Vector of relative displacements at time t
$\{\dot{x}(t)\}$	Vector of relative velocities at time t
$\{\ddot{x}(t)\}$	Vector of relative accelerations at time t
$\{\dot{x}_a(t)\}$	Vector of absolute velocities at time t
$\{\ddot{x}_a(t)\}$	Vector of absolute accelerations at time t
x_0	Lateral displacement required to activate hysteretic damper / Amplitude of ground displacement
$x_1(t)$	Relative displacement of primary structure at time t
$x_2(t)$	Relative displacement of TMD at time t
x_b	Displacement of top of laminated rubber bearing
x_{bb}	Displacement of top of laminated rubber bearing parallel to its side of dimension b
x_{bd}	Displacement of top of laminated rubber bearing parallel to its side of dimension d
x_{ball}	Allowable lateral displacement of laminated rubber bearing
x_g	Gap displacement
$x_g(t)$	Ground displacement at time t
$\dot{x}_g(t)$	Ground velocity at time t
$\ddot{x}_g(t)$	Ground acceleration at time t
x_{max}	Maximum displacement

$x_N(t)$	Roof relative displacement
$x_{N(max)}$	Target maximum relative displacement at roof level
$\ddot{x}_{N(max)}$	Target maximum absolute acceleration at roof level
x_{res}	Normalized residual displacement
$\bar{x}_{res}$	Mean value of x_{res}
x_{st}	Equivalent static lateral displacement / Static displacement of primary structure
x_y	Yield displacement
X_0	Displacement amplitude between the two ends of damping element
y	Distance from center to a corner isolator measured perpendicular to the direction of seismic loading
Y	Equivalent yield displacement in viscoplastic friction model
$z(t)$	Displacement of TMD relative to roof level at time t
$\dot{z}(t)$	Velocity of TMD relative to roof level at time t
Z	Hysteretic parameter in viscoplastic friction model / Seismic zone factor
α	Ratio of lateral stiffness after activation of the damper to the initial stiffness / Post-elastic stiffness expressed as a fraction of initial stiffness / Calibration factor for maximum compressive strain in PTED connection
α_0	Stiffness proportional constant in Rayleigh damping model
α_{ED}	Post-yielding stiffness coefficient of ED spring in PTED connection model
α_i	Modal participation factor in mode i
α_L	Geometrical angle on left side of a bolt
α_R	Residual mode participation factor / Geometrical angle on right side of a bolt
α_{vd}	Velocity coefficient of nonlinear viscous damper
β	Dimensionless constant in viscoplastic friction model / Energy dissipation coefficient for self-centering systems
β_{eff}	Effective damping ratio of SFRS
β_H	Damping ratio of hysteretic dampers and SFRS
β_I	Inherent damping ratio of SFRS
β_L, β_R	Geometrical angles on left and right side of a bolt
β_v	Viscous damping ratio of viscous dampers
β_{vy}	Damping ratio provided by viscous dampers at or just below yield of the SFRS
β_{v+I}	$\beta_v + \beta_I$
β_δ	Displacement ratio causing yielding
γ	Angle of inclination of cross braces with horizontal / Ratio of mass of superstructure to total mass of superstructure and base slab
γ_c	Shear strain through viscous component of viscoelastic material

γ_E	Shear strain through elastic component of viscoelastic material
γ_i	Angle of inclination of cross braces with horizontal in storey i
γ_s	Shear strain / Allowable seismic shear strain of laminated rubber bearing
γ_w	Allowable shear strain of laminated rubber bearing under gravity load
Γ	Gamma function
δ	Lateral displacement
δ_{by}	Yielding displacement of braced frame
δ_{CT}	Axial deformation of contact element in PTED connection model
δ_{ED}	Axial deformation of ED element in PTED connection model
δ_i	Interstorey drift at storey where i^{th} damper is located
δ_{max}	Maximum inelastic lateral displacement
δ_{uy}	Yielding displacement of unbraced frame
δ_y	Lateral displacement at first yield
Δ	Displacement between two ends, in direction parallel to bracing member / Total deck displacement / Displacement
Δ_{1D}	First mode interstorey drift
Δ_{act}	Activation displacement of structure equipped with hysteretic damper
Δ_b	Elongation of a bolt
Δ_{bi}	Initial elongation of a bolt
Δ_{bt}	Elongation of a bolt after increase in temperature
Δ_{btd}	Elongation of a bolt after increase in temperature and accumulation of debris
Δ_{bw}	Elongation of a bolt after wearing effect
Δ_{bwt}	Elongation of a bolt after wearing effect larger than temperature rise
Δ_{by}	Elongation of a bolt at first yield
Δ_{Cmin}	Minimum clearance for each orthogonal direction of a base isolated bridge
Δ_D	Design interstorey drift
Δ_i	Design displacement of isolation system
Δ_{max}	Maximum relative displacement
$\Delta_{max}(IS)$	Maximum displacement of isolated system
$\Delta_{max}(IS-D)$	Maximum displacement of damped isolated system
Δ_{opt}	Optimum maximum displacement
Δ_r	Maximum roof lateral displacement
Δ_{RD}	Residual mode interstorey drift

Δ_{res}	Residual displacement
Δ_s	Shear storey deflection
Δ_{sub}	Design displacement of substructure
Δ_t	Target displacement / Total base isolator displacement including torsion
Δ_{wt}	Elongation of a bolt after wearing effect and increase in temperature
Δt	Time increment
ε	Constant / Ratio of the squares of base isolation natural frequency to fixed base superstructure natural frequency
ε_{in}	Initial strain in PT element of PTED connection
ε_{max}	Maximum compressive strain between beam and column of a PTED connection
ε_{pt}	Strain in PT element of PTED connection
ε_v	Short term failure strain of rubber in pure tension
ζ	Small perturbation to the phase angle
$\bar{\zeta}$	Constant portion of small perturbation to the phase angle
η	Loss factor of viscoelastic material / Strength ratio for self-centering SDOF system
η_i	Loss factor of viscoelastic material in frequency ω_i
η_u	Yield strength ratio of unbraced frame
θ	Angular response parameter / Torsional rotation / Gap opening angle in PTED connection
θ^*	Angular response parameter
θ_1, θ_2	Angles defining geometrical configuration of toggle-brace damping system / Parametric angles in frequency response solution of self-centering SDOF system
θ_3	Parametric angle in frequency response solution of self-centering SDOF system
θ_B	Rotation at which tensile yielding of ED elements is reached in a PTED connection
θ_D	Rotation at which compression yielding of ED elements is reached in a PTED connection
θ_p	Plastic hinge rotation
κ_r	Compression modulus of rubber
λ	Braced to unbraced frame stiffness ratio / Property modification factor for isolation system
$\lambda_{min, max}$	Minimum and maximum values of property modification factors for seismic isolation systems
$\lambda_{min \text{ adjusted}}$, $\lambda_{max \text{ adjusted}}$	Minimum and maximum adjusted values of property modification factors for seismic isolation systems
$\lambda_{max \text{ a}}$	Maximum value of property modification factor for effects of aging on seismic isolators

$\lambda_{max\,c}$	Maximum value of property modification factor for effects of contamination on seismic isolators
$\lambda_{max\,s}$	Maximum value of property modification factor for effects of scragging on seismic isolators
$\lambda_{max\,t}$	Maximum value of property modification factor for effects of temperature on seismic isolators
$\lambda_{max\,w}$	Maximum value of property modification factor for effects of wear on seismic isolators
Λ	Parameter of frequency response solution of self-centering SDOF system
Λ_{hd}	Hysteretically damped system parameter
μ	Friction coefficient / Ratio of the mass of TMD to the mass of primary structure
μ_B	Static coefficient of friction when sliding starts
μ_D	Effective ductility demand of SFRS at design displacement
μ_{Hu}	Cumulative ductility of unbraced frame
μ_i	Initial coefficient of friction
μ_k	Kinematic coefficient of friction
μ_{min}	Minimum coefficient of friction
μ_{max}	Maximum coefficient of friction
μ_{mss}	Modified steady-state coefficient of friction
μ_n	Nominal value of coefficient of friction
μ_s	Static or initial coefficient of friction
μ_{ss}	Steady-state coefficient of friction
μ_u	Displacement ductility ratio of unbraced frame
μ_Δ	Displacement ductility ratio
$\bar{\mu}_\Delta$	Mean value of μ_Δ
ξ	Viscous damping ratio
$\bar{\xi}$	Equivalent damping ratio of viscoelastic damper
ξ_0	Initial viscous damping ratio
ξ_b	Damping ratio of rigid superstructure on base isolation system
ξ_{eq}	Equivalent viscous damping ratio
ξ'_{eq}	Corrected equivalent viscous damping ratio
ξ_i	Modal damping ratio in mode i
$\tilde{\xi}_i$	Damping ratio in mode i due to added viscoelastic damper
ξ_s	Damping ratio of fixed-base superstructure
ξ_s	Total viscous damoing of structure

ρ	Power of the exponential of perturbations to the amplitude and phase
σ	Excitation frequency ratio
σ_r	Resonant frequency ratio
σ_r^*	Optimal resonant frequency ratio
σ_{Rmin}, σ_{Rmax}, σ_{Lmin}, σ_{Lmax}	Minimum, maximum normal pressure on right and left side of a bolt
σ_v	Excitation frequency ratio corresponding to vertical tangency
σ_{v1}, σ_{v2}	Roots of σ_v
σ_x	Normal pressure on sliding interfaces
σ_y	Elastic limit, yield stress
τ	Non-dimensional time variable
τ_E	Shear stress carried by elastic component of viscoelastic material
τ_C	Shear stress carried by viscous component of viscoelastic material
τ_{py}	Shear yield strength of lead
τ_s	Shear stress
φ	Average value of time-varying phase of response
$\varphi(\tau)$	Time-varying phase of response
φ_0	Steady-state phase of response
φ_p	Plastic curvature
φ_y	Yield curvature
Φ	Constant in frequency response of flag-shaped system
χ	Small perturbation to the amplitude
$\bar{\chi}$	Constant portion of small perturbation to the amplitude
ψ	Angle of inclination with horizontal of scissor-jack damping system / Constant in frequency response of flag-shaped system
ω	Circular forcing frequency
$\bar{\omega}$	Oscillating circular frequency of viscoelastic damper / Circular frequency of external sinusoidal dynamic force
ω_0	Circular natural frequency
ω_a	Circular natural frequency of TMD
ω_b	Circular natural frequency of braced structure / Circular natural frequency of rigid superstructure on base isolation system
ω_{di}	Damped circular frequency in mode i
$\tilde{\omega}_{di}$	Damped circular frequency in mode i of structure with added viscoelastic damper
ω_g	Circular frequency of ground excitation

ω_i	Circular natural frequency in mode i
$\tilde{\omega}_i$	Undamped circular frequency in mode i of structure with added viscoelastic damper
ω_s	Circular natural frequency of fixed-base superstructure
ω_u	Circular natural frequency of unbraced structure
Ω_0	Overstrength factor
Ω_1, Ω_2, Ω_3, Ω_4	Parameters of frequency response of self-centering SDOF system
Ω_n	Circular natural frequency of primary structure

ANSWERS TO PROBLEMS

Chapter 3:
Problem 3.1

a) $E_k^r(t) = 2.93[kN \cdot mm] \cdot \cos^2(6.04(t - 0.01[s]))$; $E_{es}(t) = 2.93[kN \cdot mm] \cdot \sin^2(6.04(t - 0.01[s]))$; $E_{in}^r(t) = 0$

b) $E_k^r(t) = 0.03[kN \cdot mm] \cdot e^{-0.604(t - 0.01[s])} \cdot (9.79 \cdot \cos(6.04(t - 0.01[s])) - 0.49 \cdot \sin(6.0415(t - 0.01[s])))^2$

$E_{es}(t) = 2.93[kN \cdot mm] \cdot e^{-0.604(t - 0.01[s])} \cdot \sin^2(6.04(t - 0.01[s]))$

$E_{vd}(t) = 2.93[kN \cdot mm] - (E_k^r(t) + E_{es}(t))$

Problem 3.2

a) Elastic-perfectly plastic with a yield force of 80 kN.

b) Elliptical response with peak damping force of 17.7 kN.

Chapter 5:
Problem 5.1

a) $A_b = 11060[mm^2]$

b) $P_o = 1640[kN]$

c) Initial stiffness = 247 [kN/mm]; Post-slip stiffness = 39.5 [kN/mm]; Slip Shear = 1418 [kN]; Displacement at slipping = 5.8 [mm].

d) $\Delta_{max} = 128[mm]$ without damper.

e) $\Delta_{max} = 42[mm]$ with damper.

Problem 5.2

a) $k_{eff} = \dfrac{F_y}{x_o}$

b) $\xi_{eq} = \dfrac{2}{\pi}$

c) The response of the structure with yielding devices may be larger than the response of the original structure. The response with equivalent viscous damping will always be lower than the original structure.

Chapter 6:

Problem 6.1

   a) $\bar{c} = 1[kN \cdot s/mm]$

   b) $\bar{k} = 4[kN/mm]$

   c) $G_E = 0.0024[kN/mm^2]$

       $\eta = 1.57$

Problem 6.2

   a) $\bar{\bar{T}} = 0.71[s]$

   b) $\bar{k} = 39.5[kN/mm]$

   c) $\bar{c} = 5.33[kN \cdot s/mm]$

Problem 6.3

   a) $C_{L1} = 0.34[kN \cdot s/mm]$; $C_{L2} = 0.68[kN \cdot s/mm]$

   b) $\xi_2 = 0.94$

Problem 6.4

First storey retrofit: $\xi_{1eq} = 0.24$, Second story retrofit: $\xi_{1eq} = 0.004$
First storey retrofit is obviously more efficient.

Chapter 7:

Problem 7.1

   a) $if \ x_o \leq \dfrac{F_y}{k_o} \Rightarrow k_e = k_o$

       $if \ x_o > \dfrac{F_y}{k_o} \Rightarrow k_e = \dfrac{F_y}{x_o}$

   b) $if \ x_o \leq \dfrac{F_y}{k_o} \Rightarrow \xi_e = 0$

$$if \ x_o > \frac{F_y}{k_o} \Rightarrow \xi_e = \frac{1}{\pi}\left(1 - \frac{F_c}{F_y}\right)\left(1 - \frac{F_y}{k_o x_o}\right) + \frac{(F_y - F_c)^2}{2\pi k_o x_o F_y}$$

   c) $if \ k_0 \rightarrow \infty, \ \xi_e = \frac{1}{\pi}\left(1 - \frac{F_c}{F_y}\right) \rightarrow$ Independent of x_o!

   d)   Linear analysis should be used only for preliminary analysis since it can yield non-conservative results.

   e)   Analysis does not capture re-centering capabilities.

Problem 7.2

a) $\quad if\ x_o \le x_g \Rightarrow k_e = F_s/x_0\,,$ $\qquad\qquad if\ x_o > x_g \Rightarrow k_e = \dfrac{F_s + k(x_0 - x_g)}{x_0}$

b) $\quad if\ x_o \le x_g \Rightarrow \xi_e = 2/\pi\,,\ if\ x_o > x_g \Rightarrow \xi_e = \dfrac{4F_s\,x_g + (x_0 - x_g)(2F_s + k(x_0 - x_g))}{2\pi(F_s + k(x_0 - x_g))x_0}$

c) $\quad \xi_e = 1/(2\pi)$

d) $\quad \xi_e = 2/\pi$

Chapter 8:

Problem 8.1

a) $\quad x_1 = \dfrac{P_o}{K - (M+m)\omega^2}$; Response of an undamped SDOF system with mass M+m (masses clamped).

b) $\quad x_1 = \dfrac{P_o}{K - M\omega^2}$; Response of an undamped SDOF system with mass M (mass m not connected M).

c) $\quad x_1 = \dfrac{P_o}{K - (M+m)\omega^2}$; Response of an undamped SDOF system with mass M+m (masses clamped).

d) $\quad x_1 = 0$; Tuned-mass damper and exciting force tuned to the natural frequency of the main system.

e) $\quad x_1 = \dfrac{P_o}{K - M\omega^2}$; Response of an undamped SDOF system with mass M (mass m is zero).

Problem 8.2

$l = 8.2[m];\ \ c = 1.7$ [metric tons s/ m]

Chapter 9:

Problem 9.1

a) $\quad V_b = 62.5[kN]$

b) $\quad a_{max} = 1.26[g]$

c) $\quad h_r = 0.19[m]$

d) $\quad V_b = 2.47[kN]$

e) $\quad x_b = 0.20[m]$

f) $\quad$ No difference, S_D is the same for $T = 4$ s.

Chapter 10:

Problem 10.1

a) $\quad$ 114.3 [mm]

b) $\quad$ 4515 [kN]

    c)   Initial stiffness = 8.28 [kN/mm]; Post-yield stiffness = 4.71 [kN/mm]; Yield force = 1822 [kN]
            Yield displacement = 22 [mm].

    d)   3.04 [s]

    e)   228.6 [mm]

    f)   1155 [kN]

    g)   Maximum shear strain in rubber = 300%, unlikely the rubber will resist. Better to include lead plug
            over the entire height of the isolator.

Problem 10.2

    a) $V = \pm810[kN]$ at zero displacement; $V = \pm1620[kN]$ at a displacement of 50 mm.

    b) $T_1 = 2.0[s]$

    c)   114 [mm]

    d)   1.94 [MN]

Problem 10.3

    a) $f_1 = 0.27[Hz]$, $f_2 = 6.73[Hz]$

    b) $\{A^{(1)}\}^T = \{1.00, \ 1.02\}$, $\{A^{(2)}\}^T = \{1.00, \ -0.098\}$

    c) $\alpha_1 = 1.008$; $\alpha_2 = 0.018$

    d) $\xi_1 = 0.2$; $\xi_2 = 0.25$

    e)   Simplified Model: mass = $1.1m$; stiffness = k_b; $\xi = 0.2$

    f) $x_{max} = 203[mm]$ at isolator level.

    g) $V = 997[kN]$

    h) $x_{max} = 64[mm]$ at roof level; $V = 15.2[MN]$

    i)   Base isolation system reduces the base shear by a factor of 15
            but the displacement increases by a factor of 3.

INDEX

R

S